797,885 Books
are available to read at

www.ForgottenBooks.com

Forgotten Books' App
Available for mobile, tablet & eReader

ISBN 978-1-333-51977-3
PIBN 10514681

This book is a reproduction of an important historical work. Forgotten Books uses state-of-the-art technology to digitally reconstruct the work, preserving the original format whilst repairing imperfections present in the aged copy. In rare cases, an imperfection in the original, such as a blemish or missing page, may be replicated in our edition. We do, however, repair the vast majority of imperfections successfully; any imperfections that remain are intentionally left to preserve the state of such historical works.

Forgotten Books is a registered trademark of FB &c Ltd.
Copyright © 2017 FB &c Ltd.
FB &c Ltd, Dalton House, 60 Windsor Avenue, London, SW19 2RR.
Company number 08720141. Registered in England and Wales.

For support please visit www.forgottenbooks.com

1 MONTH OF FREE READING

at

www.ForgottenBooks.com

By purchasing this book you are eligible for one month membership to ForgottenBooks.com, giving you unlimited access to our entire collection of over 700,000 titles via our web site and mobile apps.

To claim your free month visit:

www.forgottenbooks.com/free514681

* Offer is valid for 45 days from date of purchase. Terms and conditions apply.

English
Français
Deutsche
Italiano
Español
Português

www.forgottenbooks.com

Mythology Photography **Fiction**
Fishing Christianity **Art** Cooking
Essays **Buddhism** Freemasonry
Medicine **Biology** Music **Ancient Egypt** Evolution Carpentry Physics
Dance Geology **Mathematics** Fitness
Shakespeare **Folklore** Yoga Marketing
Confidence Immortality Biographies
Poetry **Psychology** Witchcraft
Electronics Chemistry History **Law**
Accounting **Philosophy** Anthropology
Alchemy Drama Quantum Mechanics
Atheism Sexual Health **Ancient History**
Entrepreneurship Languages Sport
Paleontology Needlework Islam
Metaphysics Investment Archaeology
Parenting Statistics Criminology
Motivational

This work is limited to 250 copies, each copy being numbered.

No. 24

AN ACCOUNT

OF THE

FAMILIES OF LENNARD AND BARRETT

From the Author.

ascribed to Holbein   Emery Walker Ph. sc.

Thomas Fynes, Lord Dacre.

AN ACCOUNT OF THE FAMILIES OF LENNARD AND BARRETT.

COMPILED LARGELY FROM ORIGINAL DOCUMENTS

BY

THOMAS BARRETT-LENNARD

WITH PORTRAITS

Printed for Private Circulation
1908

AN ACCOUNT OF THE FAMILIES OF LENNARD AND BARRETT.

COMPILED LARGELY FROM ORIGINAL DOCUMENTS

BY

THOMAS BARRETT-LENNARD

WITH PORTRAITS

Printed for Private Circulation

1908

PREFACE

MY great-great-grandfather, Thomas Barrett Lennard, 29th Baron Dacre,[1] was very greatly interested in all matters connected with the history of his family. He arranged, more or less in order, a great mass of family deeds, letters, and other documents. He compiled a manuscript account of the families of Lennard and Barrett, and also a second manuscript volume, a miscellaneous collection of pedigrees, copies of wills, records of arms, &c., &c., relating to those families. These manuscript volumes were copied out for him in a beautiful handwriting by the Rev. G. Pattrick, Vicar of Aveley from 1777. In 1855 my cousin, the late Henry Barrett Lennard, for many years of 29 Great Cumberland Place, London, arranged a great quantity of the original letters and miscellaneous documents in four large folio volumes, which he called 'The Lennard Papers,' and to these letters he added very copious notes.

Some years ago it seemed desirable to move the whole collection of documents from Belhus to Horsford, where for a considerable period I did nothing with them beyond giving them house-room, and sending many of them to the Record Office for inspection by the Historical Manuscripts Commission. The Commission have reported on them twice—viz. *XIII.*[h] *Report, Appendix* 4, and *Report on Various Collections*, Vol. III. One day I called the attention of my friend Mr. Walter Rye,

---

[1] Debrett, by leaving out several generations, reckons him as 25th Baron.

the well-known antiquary, to them. He expressed himself greatly interested in the collection, and his enthusiasm at last made me feel ashamed of letting them remain so long neglected. Accordingly I set to work to get them into some sort of order, and this was a work that took me more than a year, as there were many thousand documents to deal with of almost every imaginable description. Receipts and letters not fifty years old were mixed up with marriage settlements, leases, and other legal documents of over three hundred years old; with letters and accounts of the time of Elizabeth which had escaped the notice of my cousin Henry; and many deeds of the fourteenth century, and some even earlier. I gradually reduced this very large mass of documents into some sort of order. I then thought of having Lord Dacre's history printed, lest fire or some other misfortune should cause the loss of the only authentic account of our family. But Lord Dacre had excluded from his history all letters and almost everything calculated to give the reader any insight into the individuality, the passions, or troubles of his ancestors, and had contented himself with recording the mere facts of their existences, marriages, and above all the arms borne by their respective wives. A more dull record of facts could hardly have been put together; moreover, as a mere record it was greatly lacking, as Lord Dacre did not, as a rule, give the dates of the marriages, births, or deaths of the persons whose existence he chronicled. I have endeavoured to give as many dates as I could ascertain, in many instances from searches of parish registers, and at the same time to include as many letters as the limits of one volume would permit.

The Earl of Sussex seems to have destroyed many documents of the seventeenth century, which is very unfortunate; and I have found no letters of his, nor of his wife, nor of his father, which is much to be regretted, as they might have been

PREFACE

of considerable interest, considering the period at which they were written and the position in life occupied by their writers.

At the risk of being tedious I have given very ample references for my statements; not one person in a hundred will care for these references, which add considerably to the cost and trouble of the book, but possibly some day a reader may be interested to see how far he considers my statements accurate, and with these references he will be able to find the sources of my information, and consult them himself.

I have had help from many kind friends on different points, and to all of them I am most grateful for their assistance; but, above all, my thanks are chiefly due to Mr. Walter Rye, without whose help and encouragement I should never have started on this work, which, by fits and starts, has lasted me now more years than I care to confess.

I cannot hope that a book of this class, mentioning so great a number of dates and dealing with so long a period of time, is free from errors, but I sincerely trust that such will not be found to be many in number.

For the benefit of anyone interested in our family history, I may refer them to the following papers I have written on special departments of this subject:—'An Account of the Manor of Horsford,' *XV. Norfolk and Norwich Arch. Society*; 'Household Account-book of Herstmonceux Castle,' *XLVIII. Sussex Arch. Society*; 'Some Essex Manors, &c.,' *XV. Essex Review*; 'Family Pictures at Belhus,' *V. The Ancestor*; 'Sir F. Barnham,' *IX. The Ancestor.*

T. B.-L.

HORSFORD MANOR:
    NORWICH, 1908.

CONTENTS

CHAPTER		PAGES
	PREFACE	v–vii
I.	JOHN LENNARD	1–150
II.	HISTORY OF THE FYNESES	153–212
III.	⎧ SAMSON LENNARD ⎫ ⎨ HENRY LENNARD, LORD DACRE ⎬ . . . ⎩ RICHARD LENNARD, LORD DACRE ⎭	215–266
IV.	⎧ FRANCIS LENNARD, LORD DACRE ⎫ ⎨ THOMAS LENNARD, EARL OF SUSSEX ⎬ . .	267–339
V.	HISTORY OF THE BARRETTS	341–391
VI.	RICHARD BARRETT, DOWN TO 1687 . . .	392–483
VII.	⎧ RICHARD BARRETT ⎫ ⎨ DACRE BARRETT ⎬	484–578
VIII.	⎧ THOMAS BARRETT LENNARD, LORD DACRE ⎫ ⎨ AND HIS DESCENDANTS ⎬ .	579–639
	ADDENDA	641
	INDEX	653

LIST OF GENEALOGICAL TABLES

	PAGE
EARLY PEDIGREE OF THE LENNARDS	xviii
DESCENT OF MARGARET FYNES.	152
DESCENT OF MAUD DE MONCEUX	163
DESCENT OF JOAN DACRE	175
DESCENDANTS OF SAMSON AND MARGARET LENNARD . .	214
TABLE TO SHOW RELATIONSHIP IN BLOOD BETWEEN THE EARL OF SUSSEX AND HIS WIFE	306
MALE DESCENDANTS OF ROBERT BARRETT	340

LIST OF PORTRAITS

THOMAS FYNES, LORD DACRE	*Frontispiece*	
From a painting ascribed to Holbein	*see p.* 192	
SAMSON LENNARD	*To face p.* 68	
MARGARET FYNES, BARONESS DACRE	,,	78
HENRY LENNARD, LORD DACRE	,,	214
CHRYSOGONA LADY DACRE	,,	242
From a painting by C. de Vos		
RICHARD LENNARD, LORD DACRE	,,	252
From a painting ascribed to Van Dyck		
DOROTHY LADY DACRE	,,	256
From a painting ascribed to Van Dyck		
FRANCIS LENNARD, LORD DACRE AND LADY DACRE .	,,	276
From a painting by Sir Peter Lely		
THOMAS LENNARD, LORD DACRE AND EARL OF SUSSEX .	,,	304
From a painting ascribed to Willem Wissing		
ANNE FITZROY, COUNTESS OF SUSSEX . . .	,,	308
From a painting by Michael Dahl		
SIR EDWARD BARRETT, LORD NEWBURGH . . .	,,	364
From a painting by Cornelius Janssen		
RICHARD BARRETT	,,	392
From a painting by John Riley		
ANNE LENNARD	,,	410
From a copy by Cosway of a miniature painting by Cooper		

DACRE BARRETT . . . . *To face p.* 436
    From a painting by Jonathan Richardson

LADY JANE BARRETT . . . . ,, 454

LADY ANNE LENNARD . . . . ,, 550

THOMAS BARRETT-LENNARD, LORD DACRE, HIS WIFE,
    AND THEIR ONLY CHILD . . . . . . ,, 600
    From a painting by Pompeo Battoni

SIR THOMAS BARRETT-LENNARD, 1ST BARONET . . ,, 624
    From a painting by John Opie

BELHUS IN THE TIME OF DACRE BARRETT . . ,, 586

BELHUS AT THE PRESENT TIME 588

LIST OF SUCH FACSIMILE AUTOGRAPHS GIVEN IN THIS WORK AS DO NOT APPEAR UNDER THE PORTRAITS

	PAGE
JOHN (IV) LENNARD.	66
SAMUEL LENNARD.	67
GREGORY FYNES, LORD DACRE	79
RICHARD LENNARD	217
GREGORY LENNARDE.	240
JOHN (VI) LENNARD	240
ELIZABETH THROCKMORTON	254
FRANCIS LENNARD, LORD DACRE.	284
HENRY (III) LENNARD	303
LADY BARBARA (II) LENNARD	329
KATHARINE, LADY NEWBURGH.	384
RICHARD (II) BARRETT	394
DOROTHY (I) BARRETT (WHO USED THE NAME OF LENNARD)	433
A. MILDMAY	490
RICHARD LENNARD BARRETT	555
DOROTHY (II) BARRETT	567
JANE BARRETT	574
THOMAS LENNARD BARRETT	579

LIST OF ABBREVIATIONS

Add. . . .	Additional MSS., B. Mus.
Analyt. . .	Analytical Index to the 'Remembrancia.'
Anc. . . .	'The Ancestor' (a quarterly publication), 1902-5.
Ann. . . .	'Annals of George I.'
Arch. C. .	'Archæologia Cantiana.'
Archd. . .	Archdale's 'Monasticum Hibernicum.'
Ashm. . .	Ashmolean MSS.
B. A. L. .	Bohn's Antiquarian Library.
B. & B. . .	Brayley and Britton's 'Essex.'
B. Mus. . .	British Museum.
Bad. R. . .	Badminton Library, 'Racing.'
Bar. . . .	'British Family Names,' H. Barber.
Beauties . .	'Some Beauties of the Seventeenth Century,' Allan Fea.
Blaauw . .	Blaauw's 'Barons' Wars,' ed. 1871.
Blom. . .	Blomfield's 'Norfolk,' fol. ed.
Bod. . . .	Bodleian, Oxford.
C. B. . . .	'The Complete Baronetage,' by G. E. C.
C. D. . . .	'The Century Dictionary.'
C. H. . . .	Calendar of Wills, Court of Hustings.
C. P. . . .	'The Complete Peerage,' by G. E. C.
C. R. . . .	'Rotuli Litterarum Clausarum'; 2 vols.
C. S. P. . .	Camden Society's Publications.
,, *Ch. of C.* .	,, ,, ,, 'Chronicles of Calais.'
,, *Three* .	,, ,, .. 'Three Fifteenth-Century Chronicles.'
,, *Wrio. Ch.*	,, ,, ,, 'Wriothesley's Chronicles.'
Cal. Inq. . .	'Calendar Inquisitions Post Mortem temp. Henry VII.' (only 1 vol. published).
Cal. Rot. Chart.	'Calendarium Rotulorum Chartarum etc.'
Cam. . . .	Camden's 'Elizabeth.'
Cam. Brit. .	Camden's 'Britannia,' by Gough; ed. 1759.
Camp. . .	Campbell's 'Lives of the Chancellors.'
Ch. Reg. . .	Chevening Parish Register.
Cla. . . .	Clarendon's 'History of the Rebellion.'
Coll. Let. . .	'Letters and Memorials of State,' by Collins.
Coll. P. . .	Collins's 'Proceedings, &c.'
Coll. Peer. .	Collins's 'Peerage' (revised by Sir E. Brydges).
Collinson .	Collinson's 'Somerset.'
Commune .	'Commune of London,' by J. H. Round.
Cot. . . .	Cotton MSS. in B. Mus.
Cox . . .	'Royal Forests of England,' by J. C. Cox.

LIST OF ABBREVIATIONS

D. Arch.	'Derbyshire Arch. and Nat. Hist. Society's Journal,' 1905.
D. N. B.	'Dictionary National Biography.'
Diehl	'The True Story of My Life,' by A. M. Diehl.
Duch.	Duchesne, 'Histoire de la Maison de Chastillon sur Marne.'
Dug. Bar.	Dugdale's 'Baronage.'
Dug. Fens	Dugdale's 'History of Embanking Fens and Marsh.'
Dug. Mon.	Dugdale's 'Monasticon.'
E. Arch. N. S.	'Transactions Essex Archæological Society' (New Series).
E. C. P.	'Early Chancery Proceedings.'
E. E. T. S.	Early English Text Society.
E. R.	'The Essex Review' (a quarterly publication).
Eger.	Egerton MSS., B. Mus.
Eve.	Evelyn's 'Memoirs.'
Excerp.	'Excerpta e Rotulis Finium.'
Excerpta	'Excerpta Historica.'
F. Aids.	Inquisitions and Assessments relating to Feudal Aids.
F. A. O.	Foster's 'Alumni Oxonienses.'
F. P.	Family Papers: a large, miscellaneous collection of deeds and other documents relating to families of Barrett and Lennard, which have been twice reported upon by the Historical MSS. Commissioners.
Faul.	Faulkener's 'Chelsea' (ed. 1829).
Full.	Fuller's 'Worthies.'
G. I. R.	'Gray's Inn Register,' by Foster.
Geneal.	'The Genealogist' (New Series).
God.	Godwin's 'Annales.'
Green.	Greenwood's MS. Account Book, F. P.
Gros.	Groses' 'Antiquities.'
H. A. B.	Herstmonceux Account Book, 1643-9, F. P.
H. K.	Harris's 'Kent.'
H. L.	'Journal of the House of Lords.'
H. R.	'Historical Register.'
Hal. D.	'Halliwell's Dictionary.'
Har.	Harleian MSS., B. Mus.
Har. So.	Harleian Society's Publications.
,, *R.*	,, ,, ,, Registers.
Has.	Hasted's 'Kent.'
Hay. Dig.	Haydon's 'Book of Dignities.'
Herst. Reg.	Herstmonceux Parish Register.
Hist. Com.	Historical MSS. Commissioners' Reports.
,, *in V. C.*	,, ,, ,, ,, on MSS. in Various Collections.
Hol.	Holinshed's 'Chronicles.'
Hors.	Horsfield's 'Sussex.'
I. K.	Ireland's 'Kent.'
I. P. M.	'Calendar of Inquisitions Post Mortem' (4 vols., H. 3 to Ri. 3).
,,	Or MSS. ,, ,, ,, F.P.
J. R. H. A. I.	'Journal of Royal Historical and Archæological Association of Ireland.'

Jeakes	. . .	Jeakes's 'Cinque Ports.'
Jess.	. . .	Jessopp's 'Lives of the Norths.'
Kil.	. . .	Kilburne's 'Survey of Kent,' 1659.
Knole	. . .	'Knole House,' by L. Sackville-West, 1906.
L. I. R.	. .	'Lincoln's Inn Register.'
L. P.	. . .	Lennard Papers: a collection in 4 vols. of some of the letters and papers relating to the Barretts and Lennards, arranged by the late Henry Barrett Lennard, 1855.
L. and P.	. .	'Letters and Papers of the Reign of Henry VIII.,' the first 4 vols. edited by Brewer, the rest by Gairdner.
Lansd.	. .	Lansdown MSS., B. Mus.
Ld. D. His.	. .	MSS. History of Families of Barrett and Lennard, *circa* 1770, by Thomas Lord Dacre.
Ld. D. Mis.	. .	MS. Miscellaneous Pedigrees, Extracts from Deeds, &c., relating to said families by said author.
Le. Coll.	. .	J. Leland's 'Collectanea' (edition of 1770).
Le. His.	. .	Thos. Leland's 'History of Ireland,' 3rd ed.
Le. N. M. A.	.	Le Neve, 'Monumenta Anglicana.'
Lip.	. . .	Lipscombe's 'Bucks.'
Low.	. . .	Lower's 'Chronicle of Battle Abbey.'
Lutt.	. . .	Luttrell's 'State Affairs.'
M. & B.	. .	Manning and Bray's 'Surrey.'
M. & B. v. B.	.	MS. Pleadings in Mildmay and Barrett *v.* Barrett. F. P.
Mac.	. . .	Macaulay's 'History.'
Mad. Ex.	. .	Maddock's 'History of Exchequer.'
Mag. Rot.	. .	'Magnum Rotulum Scaccarii.'
Mis. Gen.	. .	'Miscellanea Genealogica et Heraldica.'
Mis. G. H.	. .	'Miscellaneous Works of George Hardinge' (pub. 1818).
Mo.	. . .	Morant's 'Essex.'
N. & B.	. .	Nicholson and Burns' 'History of Westmoreland and Cumberland.'
N. Lit. An.	. .	J. Nichols's 'Literary Anecdotes.'
N. Lit. Ill.	. .	,, 'Literary Illustrations.'
N. Pro.	. .	,, 'Progresses of Queen Elizabeth.'
P. C.	. . .	'Calendar of Proceedings in Chancery in reign of Elizabeth.'
P. C. C.	. .	Prerogative Court of Canterbury.
P. D.	. . .	Pepys's 'Diary' (ed. 1899).
P. S. A.	. .	'Proceedings of Society of Antiquaries.'
P. S. G. B.	. .	'Political State of Great Britain.'
P. S. P.	. .	Parker Society Publications.
Pal.	. . .	Palin's 'Stifford and its Neighbourhood.'
Pal. M. St.	. .	,, 'More about Stifford and its Neighbourhood.'
Par. His.	. .	'Parliamentary History of England.'
Par. R.	. .	Parliament Rolls.
Parl. Rep. C.	.	'Parliamentary Representation of Cornwall,' Courtney.
Pat. R.	. .	Calendar of Patent Rolls.
Phil.	. . .	Phillpott's 'Kent.'
Pla.	. . .	Placita de quo Warranto.
Play.	. . .	Playfair's 'British Family Antiquity.'

LIST OF ABBREVIATIONS

Poems	'Poems on Affairs of State' (published in 1697).
Q. E.	'Queen Elizabeth,' by Creighton.
Rap.	Rapin's 'History.'
Rawl.	Rawlinson, MSS. Bod., Oxford.
Rog.	Roger's 'Protests of the Lords.'
Rot. Chart.	'Rotuli Chartarum.'
Rot. de Ob.	'Rotuli de Oblatis et Finibus,' by Hardy.
Rot. Orig. Ab.	'Rotulorum Originalium in Curia Scaccarii Abbreviatio.'
Rot. Se.	'Rotuli Selecti ad Res Anglicas, &c.'
Rush.	Rushworth's 'Historical Collections.'
Rym.	Rymer's 'Foedera' (ed. 1710).
S. Arch.	'Sussex Archæological Collections.'
Sev. Reg.	Sevenoaks Parish Register.
S. L.	Strype's 'Life of Parker.'
S. P. Dom.	'Calendar State Papers, Domestic Series.'
S. P. I.	,, ,, ,, Irish (Mahaffy).
S. T.	'State Trials.'
Shir.	Shirley's 'Monaghan.'
Star C. P.	Star Chambers Proceedings.
Stein.	Steinman's 'Duchess of Cleveland' (privately printed, 1871).
Stow	Stow's 'Annales.'
Straf. L. & D.	Strafford's 'Letters and Dispatches.'
Strick.	Strickland's 'Queens of England.'
T. & G.	'Topographer and Genealogist,' by J. G. Nichols.
T. de N.	Testa de Nevill.
T. S. E.	Traill's 'Social England' (ed. 1903).
Tan.	Tanner, MSS. Bod., Oxford.
Test. Vet.	Sir N. H. Nicolas's 'Testamenta Vetusta.'
Thur.	Thurloe's 'State Papers.'
Tryal	'The Tryal of the E. of Strafford,' by Rushworth (published 1680).
Ven.	Venables's 'History of the Castle of Herstmonceux.'
Vis. S.	'Visitations of Suffolk,' by W. C. Metcalf.
W. A. F. M.	Weever's 'Ancient Funeral Monuments.'
W. His. P.	H. Walpole's 'History of Painting.'
W. I.	Sir J. Ware's 'Ireland,' translated from Latin by W. Harris (ed. 1764).
Wake	E. Wakefield's 'An Account of Ireland.
Wat.	Watson's 'Earls of Warren.'

ABBREVIATIONS USED IN THE GENEALOGICAL TABLES IN THIS BOOK

b.	Born.
d.	Died.
dau.	Daughter.
d.s.p.	Died without issue.
d.s.p.m.	Died without male issue.
d.s.p.s.	Died without issue surviving.
人	Died leaving issue.

EARLY PEDIGREE OF THE LENNARDS

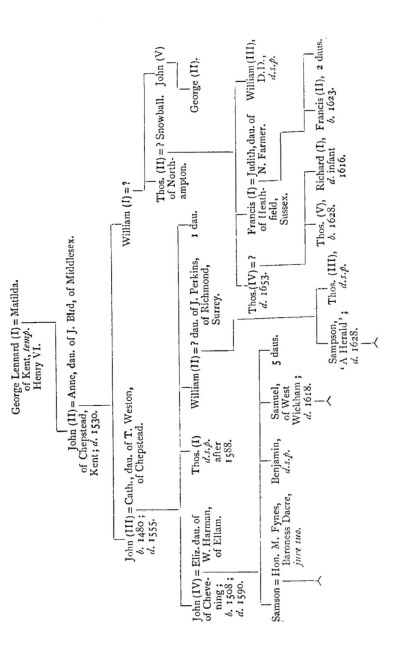

HISTORY OF THE LENNARDS

CHAPTER I

JOHN LENNARD

LORD DACRE begins his account of the Lennards thus:—
'This family which for a long time held rank amongst those of the first note in Kent, was, as appears by the books in the Herald's office, and other authentick evidences, settled in Chevening in that county as early as King Henry the Sixth's time, when George Lennard was then living there.' In support of this statement· he cites several authorities, none of whom, however, mention at what period this George lived.

A Mr. Ebenezer Leonard (died 1894) of Boston, U.S.A., a very diligent antiquary, said he had discovered a John Lennard of Chepsted in 1440 who was the father of this George, and was probably born in the end of the fourteenth century, but he gives no reference to where he found him mentioned.

While on the subject of this Mr. Ebenezer Leonard I may mention that he was a member of a family in America, who for more than 200 years have maintained a tradition that they are descended from the Lennards of Chevening. At the time of the War of Independence they remained loyal to England, and one of them is said to have fitted out a small 'fleet' at his own expense to fight for the Crown. In 1770 George Leonard, a colonel in the Royal American Guards, visited England and had several interviews with Thomas Lord

Dacre, both at Belhus and Bruton Street. The latter placed his family muniments at his guest's disposal with every wish that he would be able to prove his relationship with him, as he would have greatly preferred that his title should descend to one of his own name than to one of his mother's descendants by her second marriage. These American Leonards believe that they are descended from Samson Lennard of Chevening, or from his cousin Sampson Lennard the herald.

Mr. J. H. Round and other modern antiquaries have poured much well-deserved scorn upon those writers of family histories who, in a most unblushing manner, lay claim to fictitious progenitors of high degree, frequently said to have come over with the Conqueror, or even to have been at home to receive him upon his arrival. Assertions that might have passed unquestioned years ago, are nowadays apt to be considered critically by at least some of one's readers, and it behoves any person writing a family history at the present time to be very careful before he places implicit confidence in pedigrees made out by the older school of genealogists, and especially in those manufactured by the Elizabethan heralds. He ought, moreover, to mention any facts he may have discovered in the course of his researches which bear on his subject, whether such facts tend to exhibit the person of whom he is writing in an exalted or a humble sphere of life. This being so, I think I ought to draw attention to the following entry among the archives of the city of Canterbury:

'1480, 1481, *Nomina Carnificum forinsecorum qui tenent shamella cooperta*;' here follows a list of twelve names of persons each apparently paying a rent of 'xii^s,' and among these names is 'Joh. Lenard.'[1] I have no evidence to show that this 'Joh. Lenard' the butcher was any relation to George Lennard the squire, and indeed I have no reason to think that he was, but it is proper to mention the occurrence of the name in this list. The name of 'Lennard' is not a very common one in England, and the conjunction with it of the Christian name John, which about

[1] *Hist. Com.* ix. Part i. p. 132.

this period was a very favourite one in our family, is somewhat suggestive: moreover, Canterbury and Chepsted are both in the same county, and I feel it is not impossible that this John was some relation to George Lennard.

This George married some one whose Christian name was Matilda, but I have not been able to discover whose daughter she was.[1] He was succeeded by his son John, who was the first of three John Lennards in succession, and married Ann (or Alisea), daughter and heiress of John Bird of Middlesex, who was an armigerous person;[2] her mother was heiress of the Bickworth family. John and Ann had two sons, John and William. By a deed of 15th August, 22 Henry VIII. (1530), reciting a deed of the previous year whereby land in Chepsted was settled on John, the father, for life, remainder to his eldest son John, remainder to William, the trustees enfeoffe John the son, his father having died since the execution of the deed therein recited;[3] so that the latter must have died in 1529 or 1530.

Before following the line of this John it will be well to dispose of the descendants of the second son William. William had two sons, Thomas and John; the former appears to have settled in the county of Northampton and to have married a lady of the name of Snowball. John had a son George, but of neither of these do I know anything. I have a little more information about the issue of Thomas and the lady whose maiden name was Snowball; there is an inscription on a tombstone in Heathfield Church, Sussex,[4] and also entries in the register there, which enable one, to some extent, to construct their pedigree. They appear to have had three sons, Thomas, Francis, and William. Thomas died 1653, and had two sons, viz. Thomas, born 1628, and Richard, who died an infant 1616; Francis married Judith, daughter of a Sussex squire named Nicholas Farmer, and had a son Francis, born 1623, and two

---

[1] *L. P.* iv. Pedigree, *circa* 1600, in the handwriting of Samson Lennard.
[2] His arms were Quarterly arg. and sa. in the 1st a spread eagle of the 2nd.
[3] *Ld. D. Mis.*
[4] I am told this tombstone is no longer there.

daughters—Philadelphia, born 1619, and Catherine, who died an infant in 1623. William seems to have been a Doctor of Divinity and not to have married. It is remarkable that Lord Dacre, when he corrected the proofs of Collins' 'Peerage,' made no mention of this branch of his family. These Lennards of Heathfield are referred to[1] when staying at Herstmonceux, as 'Lennard of Bailey,' which was the name of a park in Heathfield parish, but I have no means of knowing what brought Thomas Lennard or his sons there from Northamptonshire, nor whether Thomas, born 1628, or Francis, born 1623, left any issue.

To go back to the John Lennard who was the eldest son of John and Ann his wife, he married Catherine, the daughter of Thomas Weston of Chepstead, in Kent, and in 1555 or 1556 was buried in Chevening Church under a black marble tomb, which bears the following inscription:—'Hic reponitur Johannes Lennard Generosus qui obijit mense Julij Annis Regnorum Regis et Reginae Philippi et Mariae secundo et tertio aetatis 76,'[2] and this shows him to have been born in 1479 or 1480.

John and Catherine had three sons, John, Thomas, and William,[3] and a daughter Maria. We will consider first the younger children. Thomas was admitted a member of Lincoln's Inn by special admission[4] November 22nd, 1542,[5] and died without issue,[6] at some date later than June 1547, as we have a Fine dated 'Holy Trinity 1st E^d VI' (1547), in which John Lennard,

---

[1] *Post*, pp. 285-7.

[2] The inscription does not give the day of July on which John died; this being so it is not possible to fix within a year the date of his death, as 2nd and 3rd Ph. and Mary begins on July 25th, 1555, and ends on July 24th, 1556.

[3] *Ld. D. Mis.*

[4] I am informed by a Bencher of Lincoln's Inn that 'Special admission' means an admission granted with certain privileges, such as exoneration from keeping vacations or serving offices, the right of sitting at the Benchers' Commons instead of the Fellows' Commons until Call, &c., and that such admissions were granted not very infrequently to men of good family or friends of a Bencher.

[5] *L. I. R.* A 'Thomas Lennard' was admitted to Gray's Inn in 1573, but he may have been a cousin, being possibly Thomas, son of William, son of John Lennard and his wife Ann.

[6] *Ld. D. Mis.*

'gent,' and Thos. Lennard, 'generosus,' were querents. I think it is likely that he did not die for another forty years or more, although Thomas is not mentioned by name as one to whom 'black' was to be given at Mrs. John Lennard's funeral; we shall see there is this entry:—'My oncle a gowne'[1] which almost certainly referred to him. Then again we shall see later that Samson Lennard's son Henry was admitted a member of Lincoln's Inn at request of his *uncle* Thomas Lennard, October 15th, 1588.[2] Henry had no such uncle; but it may well have been this Thomas, his great-uncle.

William, the third son, was buried at Chevening on July 30th, 1588.[3] He married a daughter of J. Perkins of Richmond, Surrey, and had two sons: Sampson, a somewhat distinguished member of the College of Heralds, who attained the rank of 'Bluemantle.' Many of his visitations and other heraldic writings remain; he died 1628. The other son of William was Thomas, who died unmarried. Maria married John Talbot, who held some post at the Court of Henry VIII.[4]

The eldest son of John and Catherine being, as we have seen, also named John, and the third John in succession, is the first Lennard of whom we know any particulars beyond those of their descents, marriages, pedigrees or settlements of estates. He may be regarded as the founder of the Lennard family, one which for the next 200 years was to hold a somewhat prominent position from its alliances and possessions, and also from the fact that it represented the ancient barony of Dacre, which was held by Lennards from 1612 until 1786.

John was no doubt ambitious, and not content to remain inactive until such time as he should inherit his father's property, and to spend his life in the obscure position of a country squire. He possessed great shrewdness and tact; and these qualities, combined with perseverance, caused him not merely to attain

---

[1] *Post*, p. 48. [2] *Post*, p. 242.
[3] *Ch. Reg.* This William may have been the author of William Lennard's Law Reports, *temp.* Eliz.; there was also a William Lennard who was Mayor of Dover and member of Parliament in 1597.
[4] *Har. So.* Visitation of Kent, 1619, *vide* pedigree of Chowne.

distinction in his profession and considerable riches, but also to put him on terms of friendship with some of the leading men of the day. He was no doubt not infrequently present at the Queen's Court, as during one of her journeys through Kent she recognised him at Dartford, and addressed him by name.

I have a MS. account of the life of this John in the handwriting of his son Samson, which is as follows :—[1]

The Life of John Lennard Esq.
Borne 1508.
Died 1590.

He was borne att Cheuening in Kent where hee enioyed by discent from his father both house and lands, part whereof hee sold, & left the rest to his heirs. His father brought him vp in good letters, & after hee had attayned the latine tongue placed him wth his Vncle Mr Weston a Protonotarie in the Common Pleas vnder whom he so profited that about the 25th yeare of his age, in the 27th of K. Henry the eight, hee was thought fitt by the King and Coūcell & the whole Parliament to bee made the Protonotarie of the 9 shires in Wales and the Clerk of the Crowne there, and so was appointed to bee in the Act of Parliament for the division of Wales into Shires, & had Letters Patents of the same from the King, the Lord Audley then Lord Chauncellour being his honourable good freind.

About the same time hee was admitted a gentleman of Lincolnes Inne, where hee was afterwards called to the Barre, & grew to bee ye aunciontest of ye Bench.[2]

In the 33 yeare of K. Henry 8 hee married ye daughter of William Harman Esqe., a gentleman of good reputation in Kent his owne Country & nere in blood to the Butlers of Hertfordshire, by whom hee had all his children.

In the 34th yeare of K. Henry 8 hee obteyned the office of the second Protonotarie of ye Common Pleas. Hee was also about that time put into the Commission of Peace, wherein hee continued about the space of fifty yeares vntil his death.

King Edward the sixt graunted him a standing fee for the

---

[1] *L. P.* iv.

[2] He was admitted on December 26th, 1533, by 'Special admission' *L. I. R.*, and he was a Bencher as early as 1569, as his son Benjamin was admitted to that Inn on February 2nd, 15$\frac{69}{70}$, and is described as 'Second son of John,' a 'Bencher.'

JOHN LENNARD

execution of his offices in Wales & enlarged his letters pattents of the same in diuers points.

Queene Mary rewarded his faithful seruice with a Lordship worth 1000th.[1]

In the 4th yeare of Queene Elizabeth's raigne (1561-2) hee obtayned the office of Custos Breuium of ye Common Pleas to which office before him diuers Knights and others of greate reputation had been advanced.

It pleased her M^{atie} in ye 13th yeare of her raigne[2] to make him High Sheriffe of her County of Kent.

Hee married all his children in houses either Honble or Worth.

In the execution of his offices being of greate confidence and labour he carried himself with such integrity that neuer any suspition of corruption was once concieued against him, which this faithful industry of God so blessed that hee left to his eldest sonne 2 thousand marks Land & to his younger 500 marks by ye yeare and so deceased the 12th day of March 1590 in the 82 yeare of his age.

All ages and states well ordered haue euer had in greate regard those men who by their painfull and vertuous courses haue beene the Authours of their owne advancement. Wherefore his wealth & reputation obtayned not by base & manual trade but by seruice of witt and learning, will be adiudged by ye equall minded as proper rewards of his vertue, & memorialls of his wisdome : howsoeuer the Envious, whose only graice consisteth in disgracing others, may labour to detract him.

As has been stated in this account of his life, John was born just before King Henry VIII. came to the throne, and he married in 1542, when he would have been about thirty-three years of age. His wife was Elizabeth, daughter of William Harman of Ellam, Crayford, Kent, whose will was proved in

---

[1] *Vide* as to this *post*, p. 11.

[2] This would be 1571; a letter dated 1579, written to him by Sir W. C., addresses him as High Sheriff. Harris, in his history of Kent, gives him as High Sheriff in 12th of Elizabeth (1569-70). We have a document which is headed 'Computus Johannis Lennard Armigeri de Anno xiij° E. Reginæ dum fuit Vice comes com. Kant.,' and this settles the point and shows that his son Samson was correct in his date, as it might have been expected he would be.

1547, by his wife Margaret, daughter of Sir John Butler. William Harman was son to Henry, also of Ellam, clerk to the Crown to Henry VII.; his will was proved 1502.

John Lennard had three sons, Samson, Benjamin, and Samuel, and five daughters, Mary, Timothea, Rachael, Elizabeth, and Anne. Lord Dacre only mentions two sons, viz. Samson and Samuel, so probably Benjamin died unmarried while still young. Unfortunately neither the registers of Chevening nor of Sevenoaks record the birth of any of John's children except that of Anne, whose name appears as being baptized on June 13th, 1563,[1] and who, born some twenty-one years after his marriage, was no doubt his youngest child. Samson must have been born about 1545, as the inscription on his tomb records his death in 1615, in the seventy-first year of his age.

We know that in 1569-70 Benjamin was old enough to be admitted to Lincoln's Inn,[2] but that does not help us much to his probable age at that period, as in those days young men were often admitted when still in their teens. I think it probable that he lived later than 1579, because he is referred to by Sir William Cordell in some notes he made on John Lennard's will, and though these notes are not dated, a letter from Sir William, written in December 1579 seems to refer to them as if then recently made. If the inscription on the tomb of Samuel is correct he must have been born in 1553, as he is there said to have been sixty-five at the time of his death. He was admitted a member of Lincoln's Inn on February 1st, 1576-7,[3] and was ancestor of the Lennards of West Wickham, Kent.[4]

Samuel is always spoken of as 'Sir Samuel,' so he was

---

[1] *Ch. Reg.*   [2] *Ante*, p. 6, *n.* 2.
[3] *L. I. R.*
[4] We have a deed dated May 20th, 29th of Eliz. (1587), by which he grants a rent-charge to his brother Samson. This deed, in which he is described as the 'Younger Sonne of John Lennarde of Knolle,' recites that this rent-charge was created by John Lennard in the 12th of Eliz., and that it was assigned to him by the original grantee on October 12th, in 14th Eliz. (1572). No consideration is mentioned, so that it may have been in the nature of some family settlement, and therefore nothing as to his age can be deduced from dates in this document.

JOHN LENNARD'S CHILDREN

presumably knighted, and 'he died on the 1st April, 1618, at the house of (his mother in law,) Lady Slaney, in the parish of St. Swithen in the City of London, and was buried in the country but the register says not where.'[1]

The marriages which John Lennard's daughters contracted are as follows:

Mary married, firstly, Guildford Walsingham in 1579,[2] and secondly, on August 23rd, 1587, Sir Thomas Gresham of Titsey, Surrey; she died at Titsey, December 7th, 1620.

Timothea, or Timothe, married, as his first wife, Sir Walter Covert of Slaugham, Sussex;[3] she had no children, and there is the following entry in the register at Slaugham, '1610 10th June The Ryght vertious Ladey Timothey Covert was buried.'[4]

Rachael married Edward Nevill, afterwards Lord Abergavenny, and was buried at Birling, Kent, on October 15th, 1616.[5]

Elizabeth married, on September 30th, 1589,[6] Sir Francis Eure, Chief Justice of North Wales, and second son of William Lord Eure.[7]

Anne must have been nearly twenty-nine when she married, on May 24th, 1592,[8] Sir Marmaduke Darrell of Fulmer, Bucks, cofferer[9] to James I., by whom she had two sons and one daughter. She was buried at Fulmer, which church her husband built at his own charges, and where there is an elaborate monument to his and her memory.[10]

---

[1] *Ld. D. Mis.*

[2] As to negotiations for this marriage *vide post*, p. 105, *et seq.*

[3] This family, now extinct, was once of great wealth and importance.—*Hors.*

[4] *S. Arch.* xlvii. p. 142.

[5] The brass plate in this church which records Rachael's interment does not mention what age she was when she died, nor the date of her marriage. The *C. P.* says that Rachael was John's third daughter. As to her marriage settlements *vide post*, p. 110, *et seq.*

[6] As to negotiations for this marriage *vide post*, p. 111, *et seq.*

[7] Title extinct 1707. In the *Sev. Reg.* the name 'Eure' is in error written 'Everest.' [8] *Sev. Reg.*

[9] A cofferer was one of the principal officers of the royal household; his duties are now performed by the lord steward and paymaster of the household.—*C. D.*

[10] *Ld. D. Mis.*

John Lennard early in life gave promise of the successful career which awaited him, for, as has been said, he was made prothonotary of Wales within two years of his being admitted to Lincoln's Inn, and in 1542 his name appears among those of persons in Kent who were wealthy enough to be obliged to contribute to a forced loan to the King. Among the list of names with their contributions is that of 'Joh'n Leonard of Chevenyng prenotary of N. Walles XX marc.'[1]

John was made second prothonotary of the Court of Common Pleas in 1543, the year after he was married, and about the same time he was put into the Commission of the Peace for the county of Kent. This is a further indication that he had by this date become possessed of some considerable property and influence in his native county.

It was also in this same year that he obtained from John Mills[2] a lease for fourteen years of his manor of Chevening, and all his lands, messuages, &c., in the parishes of Chevening, Sandwich, Nockholt and Halstead in Kent, at a rent of 12*l*. for the first ten years and other rents for residue of the term.

There were special stipulations as to what we should now think rather unimportant details, namely, that the old swans were to continue on the manor, and that John Mills was to have one-third part of the fish in the moat and ponds, and a fourth part of the fruit that should grow on the premises. How it was to be arrived at what, in any one year, was John Mills' proper share of fish and fruit is not clear, and such a stipulation looks likely to provide grounds for plenty of litigation later on. This lease contained a covenant that if Mills should sell these premises, then John Lennard should have the option of buying them for twenty years' purchase.

In 1551, in pursuance of this agreement, John did buy the property, and Lord Dacre says[3] that in the reign of Queen Mary he obtained from her a grant of the neighbouring manor of Chepsted which had escheated to the Crown. This is no

[1] *Arch.* C. xi. p. 401.   [2] *Ld. D. Mis.*
[3] *Ibid.*

doubt what Samson referred to when he said that Sovereign had rewarded his father's 'faithful seruice with a Lordship worth £1000.'[1] I think that anyone reading these statements would be inclined to imagine that the Queen had made a free gift to John of the manor of Chepsted, but this was far from the case, the facts according to Hasted being as follows :—

This Manor had belonged to Sir Henry Isley (or Islay) who soon after 1st Edward VI (1547–8) conveyed it to Robert Cranwell[2] by way of mortgage with a power of redemption on payment of £100 at any time before Michaelmas. Cranwell by deed dated Feb. 14, 1st. Mary (1554), sold all his interest in this property to John Lennard. Sir Henry Isley having been executed and his estates forfeited to the Crown on account of taking part in Sir Thomas Wyatt's rebellion, the Queen, by letters patent, dated 16th. June 1 Mary, after reciting the attainder of Sir Henry Isley and that Cranwell had sold his interest in Chepsted to John Lennard, released to the latter and his heirs all the claim of the Crown to that estate.[3]

It might be thought that John had obtained by this grant an absolute title to Chepsted, but it would seem that Sir Henry's son and heir, William, had still some sort of claim on it, as among our papers I have a deed of Fine, dated 'Easter week 1st & 2d Phil & Mary' (1555), whereby William Isley conveys the manor of Chepsted and 650 acres of land to John Lennard in consideration of 400*l*. Subsequently John had to bring a bill in Chancery against Isley in order to recover the title deeds of these premises.[4]

We have a very long letter from John Lennard to the Chancellor, Sir Thomas Bromley, dated from Knole, May 1st, 1584, which is too technical to print. In it he explains that the reason he wrote this letter was because 'Mr. Studley [the Chancellor's chaplain] told me yn the country that Mr Isley had put a supplycacyon to my lord of Leycester agaynst me

---

[1] *Ante*, p. 7.
[2] No doubt a near relation of the Edward Cranewell mentioned *post*, p. 136, *et seq.*
[3] *Has.* i. 364.   [4] *P. C.* ii. p. 162.

for those lands, which supplycacyon his Lordship had with hys letter sent to your Lordship prayyng you to deale with me in the cause.'

Proceedings had been taken in the Court of Exchequer as early as 21st Eliz. (1578–9) to upset John's title to certain lands which had once belonged to Mr. Isley, but without success.[1] This second attempt to accomplish, by the intervention of the Earl of Leicester, in a Court of Equity that which had already failed in a Court of Law, looks as if we have here an example of how accessible that favourite of the Queen was to the influence of bribes, and we shall find another instance of this later on.[2] The estates of Sir Henry Isley, which, as we have seen, were forfeited to the Crown, were restored to his son William on March 8th, 1555, on condition of his paying a fine of 1,000*l.* and making certain annual payments. In those days, when money was scarce, it would probably be a very difficult matter for a man in William Isley's position to pay so large a sum as 1,000*l.*, and the need of raising it may well have been the beginning of his pecuniary embarrassments. These ultimately became so acute that when he owed to the Crown and others nearly 4,000*l.*, which was the case in 19 Eliz. (1576–7), a body of commissioners, among whom were included Lord Burghley and Sir Thomas Bromley, were appointed to sell sufficient of his lands to satisfy his debts.

Hasted says, in his 'History of Kent,'[3] that these commissioners, in pursuance of their parliamentary powers, on May 12th, 19 Eliz. (1577), conveyed the manor of Brasted and certain other lands which belonged to William Isley, to Samson and Samuel Lennard and their heirs in consideration of 2,000*l.*

John's version of the transaction, as set out in the abovementioned letter, does not differ very materially from this statement. He says that Mr. Isley owed 2,020*l.* to one Alderman Calthorp, who accepted these lands from the commissioners

---

[1] *Has.* i. p. 377.   [2] *Post*, pp. 96–7, 99.
[3] i. p. 377.

in satisfaction of his debt; and then in consideration of 2,100*l*. passed them on to his (John's) sons Samson and Samuel, to the use of their father, or, as we should say now, as trustees for him.

In the course of his letter to the Chancellor, John, evidently smarting under an accusation made against him by Isley, says :—'and so ys there nether Conyng practise nor malyce on my part, as the bylle supposeth, but playne honest and charytable dealyng on my behalf hereyn, but on the other syde, verie strange and malycyous dealyng.' If this attempt to oust John Lennard from Brasted was persisted in, which I think is not probable, it was certainly no more successful than the proceedings in the Court of Exchequer had been, as he was the owner of the manor in question at the time of his death.

We have many deeds relating to many purchasers of different parcels of land by John at various times which are not of sufficient interest to enumerate individually. Among other of his acquisitions was that of the manor of Cudham in 1562, and the advowson of Hever, which he is said to have obtained from C. Waldegrave in 12 Eliz. (1569–70).[1] It is more probable that he purchased it at an earlier date from Sir Edward Walgrave, as we know it was from that person that John obtained a long lease of the manor and park of Hever.

Among our papers is a lease dated October 10th, 2nd Eliz. (1560), between John Lennard of Chevening, Esquire, and Reginald Woodgate of Hever, yeoman. After reciting that John held the manor and park for an unexpired term of years from 'Sir E. Walgrave Knyght and Dame Fraunceyse his wife,' it goes on to lease to Woodgate and his wife the lodge within the park, and 83 acres of ground parcel of the Park, for twelve years, at a rent of 6*l*. 13*s*. 4*d*. per annum. Some of the lessee's covenants are worthy of note. He covenants to store with black conies that part of the park heretofore stored, and the 'berys[2] boroughes & holds' so stocked, to 'keep and maintain

---

[1] *I. K.* iii. p. 397.   [2] Rabbits' burrows.—*C. D.*

with plashers hedgings,[1] as shall be best for the increase' of these conies. He also covenanted to take with nets and deliver to John at his request such numbers of them as can 'Wekely' be spared, 'kepyng the ground fayre & suffycyently replenyshed with game & conies for the next brede.'

Woodgate further covenanted that he would 'keep & se to the ponds within the said park, & the banks of them shall help to save from rage of water by openyng of the slusys as nede shall require; and the fysshes there and the encrease of them '. he was to preserve for John's use.

John Lennard no doubt lived at Chevening until about 1570, when he obtained the residue of a lease for ninety-nine years of Knole,[2] where he died, and where he probably lived most of the last twenty years of his life. It is clear from these purchases that he must have done very well at the Bar and in his legal appointments. In this connection I have found a small scrap of paper on which the following is written in John's handwriting :—'The profits of the Session in Wales October xviij Eliz. (1576) Sum total of this amount besides all charges £57 .. 6 .. 8.' In further proof of John's increasing prosperity it may be mentioned that among our papers we find him buying a quantity of hangings from Archbishop Parker's executor at Lambeth. A careful person, such as he evidently was, would not have spent money in mere ornaments and luxuries unless possessed of an easy income. The document from which I get this information as to his purchases is endorsed :—'The contents and pryce of the hangyngs yt I bought of the exec of Mr Parker late Archbysshop of Canterbury,'[3] and goes on :—

The admesurements of the hangyngs you bought at lambeth.

---

[1] Hedge trimmings, heaps of which thrown near and over rabbits' burrows would be calculated to afford them harbour, and so encourage their presence.

[2] Knole at Sevenoaks is well known as one of the most beautiful old country houses in England. As to John's negotiations about obtaining this lease, *vide post*, p. 116, *et seq.*

[3] Archbishop Parker died 1575.

JOHN LENNARD

The feiste pece conteyneth ells [1]				xxx
„ seconse ells				xxv
„ thirde „				xxv
„ fourthe „				xxv
„ fyfthe „				xxxv
„ syxte „				xxv
„ seventhe „				xx
„ eyghte „				xxx
„ nynthe „				xxv
„ tenth „				xxv
„ eleventh „				xl
„ twelvethe „				xxx

   sma (summa) [2] of elles . cccxxxv

alowynge for euye (every) elle . . . . ijs. viijd.
wch comes in the whole the some of . xliiij^{li} xiijs. iiijd.
Item one Turkye carpyt at . . . . xiijs. iiijd.
Item one longe wyndow clothe conteynynge elles ix . . . . xs.
Three pecs of hangyngs that hunge in ye halle at lambeth.

The fyrste conteyneth ells	.	.	.	xxx
„ seconde ells	.	.	.	xxxv
„ third „	.	.	.	xxv

   sma . lxxxx

allowynge for euye elle . . . . . xxd.
w^{eu} comes in ye whole the some of . . . vij^{li} xs.

So we see here that John spent the sums of 44*l*. 13*s*. 4*d*., 13*s*. 4*d*., 10*s*., and 7*l*. 10*s*., or 53*l*. 6*s*. 8*d*. in all, in buying these hangings.

That he did not obtain his post of Custos Brevium from merit only, but by virtue of an agreement between himself and Sir William Cecil, the previous holder of that office, is shown by a deed among the Lennard papers, bearing date the sixth year of Elizabeth (1562), made between Sir William Cecil, Knt., of

---

[1] An ell = 1¼ yards.   [2] Sum total.

the one part and John Lennard, therein described as Custos Brevium, of the other part, whereby John grants to Sir William an annuity of 240*l.* charged upon his estates in Kent which seems to show that John practically bought the post. The deed in question contains several covenants by John to ensure to Sir William the punctual payment of this annuity, and also one to the effect that if it be not paid punctually, John would surrender his office of Custos Brevium to Sir William's eldest son. John also agreed that Sir William was to have the nomination and appointment of the Clerk of the Juries in the Common Pleas, and covenanted that he would do all he lawfully could to cause Sir William's nominee to be appointed.

An extract quoted by Lord Dacre [1] from Peck's 'Desiderata Curiosa' [2] says that 'Lord Burleigh, then Mr. William Cecil, was made Custos Brevium of the Common Pleas in 1547 as appears from his own MS. diary.'

'Anno 1547 (1 Edw. 6) Collatum est mihi officium custodis Brevium in Communi Banco cum feodo annuo . . . . . li xiii iiii
Proficua hujus officii Communibus Annis (ultra stipendium deputati) Terminis Michaelis et Hilarii . . cxxxi o o
Ter. Paschae et Trinitatis . . . cii o o

ccxxxix xiij iiij ' [3]

and continues: 'He had a grant of the Reversion of this place in King Henry the 8th's time, he kept this place as long as the year 1556 [4] when John Lennard succeeded him in this office.'

This shows, with fees, an income from the office of Custos Brevium of only 284*l.* 13*s.* 4*d.*, and from this must be deducted the annuity of 240*l.* before mentioned as being granted by John to Sir William. Unless John saw his way to obtain an increase

[1] *Ld. D. Mis.* [2] p. 6, footnote.
[3] I make this addition—284*l.* 13*s.* 4*d.*
[4] Peck was not correct here, as this date does not agree with the one mentioned in the life of John by his son (*ante*, p. 6), which is also the date of the before-mentioned deed between Lennard and Cecil.

of the emoluments of this office, the result of this bargain with Sir William would have been that he would have taken over all the duties and responsibilities of the office for a net profit to himself of only 44*l.* 13*s.* 4*d.* However, the whole of John's career shows him to have been a good man of business, and, no doubt, he saw that some further advantages, pecuniary or otherwise, which we have now no means of estimating, would accrue to him from this arrangement with Sir William.[1]

The Custos Brevium of the Court of Common Pleas was, after the four judges, the principal officer of that court : it was his duty to receive and keep all writs returnable therein and also all records of Nisi Prius, which were delivered to him by the clerks of the Assizes of each circuit. The rolls were filed together by him and carried into the Treasury of the Records, and he also had to make the copies and exemplifications of all records and writs, &c. After having held this office for many years, John Lennard, in 1576, wrote[2] to his patron Cecil, who by this time had become Lord Burghley, to complain that the Lord Chief Justice of the Common Pleas,[3] who he said 'hath yn the right of that offyce the bestowyng of aboute xxiiij offycis yn y^t Court,' had very considerably raised the fees payable to the offices in his appointment—in many cases he had doubled the fees, and in some instances quadrupled them.; while he had not raised the fees payable to the Custos Brevium, nor to the Clerk of the Juries, the appointment to which office was a perquisite of the Custos Brevium. John considered that this action was very prejudicial to his own interests, and accordingly he begs the Lord Treasurer to cause the fees payable to himself and to the Clerk of the Juries to be raised also to a reasonable

---

[1] As to the value of this post some light is thrown on it in a note in the *C. P.* under the title 'Teynham.' The first peer of this name succeeded John as Custos Brevium, and the note '(f)' runs thus: 'The grantee held the valuable office of Custos Brevium, for the reversion of which, for two lives, 3,500*l.* was offered and refused in 1604. From the secret history of Court Intrigues it seems the peerage was given him as a compensation for some place (qy. if not the one above named) which Villiers the favourite wrested from him.'

[2] Lansd. 23. 70.   [3] Sir Jas. Dyer, *Hay. Dig.*

extent, but less than the 'Chyef Justyce raysenges,' which he says 'is to mych'; and by way of inducing Lord Burghley to listen to his petition he adopted what was no doubt the regular system in those times, and said that : ' I for my offyce, & the Clerk of the Juries for hys offyce, wyll eyther gyf [give] you xx marc by yere, or c marc yn money, for eyther of them, which for both ys eyther xl marc by yere or cc marc yn money.' I regret I have not been able to discover whether the Lord Treasurer considered the proffered bribe sufficiently tempting to make him accede to this petition.

As John held the office of Custos Brevium for the rest of his life, he may be assumed to have performed his duties satisfactorily. As we have seen, Samson, in finishing the account of his father's life, refers to 'the Envious whose only graice consistheth in disgracing others,' and says that they 'may labour to detract him.'

In the year 1587 the Earl of Oxford, or as he was frequently called 'Oxenford,'[1] appears to have 'laboured to detract him.' We have a letter from John Lennard to Lord Burghley about 'a very hard bylle of complaynt' put into the 'Starre Chamber' against him by the Earl. The original documents connected with this 'bylle of complaynt' are now in the Record Office,[2] and it is a somewhat curious coincidence that the cause of the trouble arose out of a question relating to the title of lands in Aveley, the parish in which is situated Belhus, now the seat of John Lennard's direct male representative. Lord Oxford had purchased the remainder of a long lease of certain lands in Alvethley, or as it is now called Aveley; one Richard Payne was disputing Lord Oxford's title to these lands, and a certain writ, called an exigent,[3] which had issued against one of his lordship's predecessors in title, was an important part of Payne's evidence. This writ was dated 'xxi November 9

[1] Oxenforda was the name used for Oxford in Latin deeds.
[2] *Star* C. P. 35 Eliz. O. iij. 35.
[3] This form of writ, now obsolete, lay where a defendant could not be found, or after a return of *non est inventum* on former writs.—C. D.

Eliz.,' and Lord Oxford alleged that John Lennard allowed Payne to have possession of it, 'to be carried from hand to hand to Seargeants Inn in Chancery Lane, the Inner Temple and elsewhere contrary to his duty, to whom it appertaineth to keep and preserve the writs & records . . . by this means the writ became so torn that j of the date of the day xxi on the back of the same was lost making the day xx.'

John replied that the writ was not delivered into his custody until twenty years after it had been issued, and if any injury was done to it, it might have received such injury before it came to his hands. He said that he caused the bundle containing the writ to be taken to the Court of Common Pleas, when requested, as was his duty, for a fee of 2s. 4d., and he sent it by his deputy into the King's Bench, upon being ordered to do so by the Justices; and at the request of Lord Burghley, the High Treasurer, he also sent the writ to him, but never sent the writ to any other place or person.

He further said: 'The writ never was at Sergeants Inn or the Inner Temple, otherwise in a chest in the Chapel of the Temple Church where thousands of records and writs remain; and where they have, time out of mind, been kept for a certain time, and as they accumulate the older ones have been removed to S. Stephens at Westminster and the new records placed in the said Chapel.'[1]

John writes a letter on this subject from 'Lyncolnes Yn this third of December 1587,' which he addresses:—' To the right Honorable my very good Lord the Lord Burghley Highe Threazourer of England.' The following is the first part of this letter, the latter half of which is of too technical a nature to be of general interest:—

My duty humbly remembered vnto yo^{ur} hono^{ur}, I have sent you by thys brynger[2] such duty as I am to pay you at Crystmas

---

[1] This system of the custody of documents, many of great importance to antiquaries, suggests a shocking amount of carelessness.

[2] Messenger.

next;[1] further more yt may please you to be advertysed that there ys truely a very hard bylle of complaynt put ynto the Starre Chamber by the Right Honorable The Earle of Oxenford agaynst me & my deputy & another of my clerks & Mr Payne & others concerning an exigent affyled in my office as thoughe I had very myche mysbehaved myself yn the usyng of my offyce of Custos Brevium yn carryeng & crossyng ye wryt to & fro at Mr. Payne's wylle; the lyke complaynt hath not been seen agaynst any other the lyke offycer. Thank god I am ynnocent of all the facts [?] therein objected agaynst me, and as I have sayd yn my answere yt ys well knowen y^t exigents, whereyn the defendants ar [are] outlawed, commonly come to ye clerk of the outlawryes, ye Quene's Attorney's clerks, before they come to ye Custos Brevium's offyce & lye there a long tyme, & such merchandyse have been made of many of them yn tymes past yt they never came to Custos Brevium.

John's letter explaining the facts of the case appears to have satisfied the 'Highe Threazourer' that he had been guilty of no negligence in the discharge of his duties, for, as we have seen, he continued to hold his office of Custos Brevium in spite of the Earl's complaint.

History is often said to repeat itself; many country gentlemen are now anxious to avoid the considerable cost to which they are put by serving the office of High Sheriff, and in Elizabeth's reign, as at present, it was not everyone who coveted that dignity. There is the following letter in the Record Office, dated November 6th, 1568, from John Lennard to Sir William Cecil,[2] asking him to 'provyde that he be not Sheryf of Kent'; as he did not serve as High Sheriff until three years later, it may be presumed that it was owing to Sir William's influence that John obtained these three years' respite from the honour he was so unwilling to accept [3]:—

My duety most humbly remembred unto yo^{ur} honour the money that I am to pay you at Crystmas next I wylle pay you

---

[1] This possibly refers to the annuity granted by John to Sir William Cecil in consideration of his obtaining the post of Custos. *Ante*, p. 16.

[2] At this period the Earl appears to have been in bad odour at the Court, so it is not to be wondered at if a complaint preferred by him should carry but little weight. —*S. P. Dom. Eliz.* cli. No. 57.   [3] *Ibid.* xlviii. No. 38.

wythyn thyes foure dayes fully trustyng that as my sute was to you yesterday you wylbe so good m^r [master] to me as to p̃vyde [provide] aswell beyng p̃rsent [present] at the co^{rt} [court] as by yor frends yn yor absence that I be not sheryf of Kent you ar my patrone yn thoffyce of Custos brium [Brevium], none knoweth better then you that aswell a grete nomber of records, beyng the Quenes ma^{ties} [majesty's] evydence for a good porcyon of her graces revenue as the substaunce of the records for thenherytaunce of the subiects of this realme ar yn my custody, & that I do dayly attend; thyes records ar threasure not valuable, & money not told, compared wyth them: if then such as haue had the custody of money, & but of smalle sōmes yn comparyson of thyes records, haue therefore been forborne, as Sr Wyllm Dansell & other hath been, I truste also by yor mastership's good helpe to be spared for the c̀auses aforesaid. I am named but thys yere, besyde all this I p̃fesse [profess] learnyng yn the lawe, for I was utter-barrester though I p̃ceded [proceded] not to reade yn Court; an evyll p̃sydent [precedent] therefore ys yt to nomynate any suche, thoughe Mr Justyce Southcots pleasure was to do yt, notwythstondyng my sute to hym, & Mr Wrayes[1] mynd to the contrary, Justyce of assyse wyth hym. And so stayeng hereyn upon none but yor mastership I wysshe you encrease of honor. At lyncolns yñ thys saterday mornyng the vith of November 1568.

     Yo^r s̃runt to cõmaund,   J. LENNARD.

Addressed:—To the right honorable & hys veray good master Sr Wyllm̃ Cecyll knyght chyef Secretary to the Quenes ma^{tie}.

It is probable that Sir William acceded to this request, and by his powerful influence obtained for John a little respite from serving as sheriff; but it was only putting off the evil day for a short time, as two years later he was obliged to fill that post. Accordingly in 157$\frac{0}{1}$ he attended the assizes at Dartford held on 'Munday the 2nd week in Lent' in the capacity of High Sheriff, and also those at Maidstone on July 16th following.[2] Mr. Justice Southcote was the senior judge of those assizes, and it is

---

[1] The Justices of the Assize, held in Kent in 1568, were Mr. Justice Southcote and the Queen's Sergeant Wray.

[2] *Kil.*

to be hoped that he did not make it too uncomfortable for John because he had for a time evaded serving. The system of selecting judges for circuit was very different in those days from what it is now, as then the same judge appears to have gone the same circuit year after year; for instance, Mr. Justice Southcote went circuit in Kent at every assize from 1563 to 1582.[1]

The following interesting memoranda relate to preparations for the assizes to be held in Kent in 1567, but what, if any, connection they had with John is not clear. It may be that he borrowed these papers the year he was sheriff in order to obtain hints as to what it was usual to provide, and that he neglected to return them. One of them is described in Lord Dacre's catalogue as 'Note of goods lent to Mr. Cromer[2] for his shrievalty.' If this description is accurate, people would appear in those days to have lent goods to, and helped each other, in the same free and easy way that still obtains in parts of India and other portions of the empire. In out-of-the-way stations in India it would still be no unusual thing for anyone giving a party to borrow all the necessary things, beyond what he himself had, from his few neighbours and friends, and in 1567 this friendly, unostentatious system probably obtained in England also.

Some of the following memoranda do not seem to relate to things borrowed, as much as to things provided for the dinners, which no doubt then, as now, formed a not unimportant part of the routine of the assizes.

The xiiijth of ffebruarie Anno 1567 victualles & other things to be boughte againste the lent assises nexte ensuynge vizt [note the abundant provision of fish and absence of meat, probably on account of Lent] :—

    Inprimis large lynge . . . xvj
    Itm. Salte Salmondes . . viij

[1] *Kil.*
[2] The family of Cromer, or Crowmer, of Tunstall, near Sittingbourne, sprung from Sir William Cromer, Lord Mayor of London *temp.* Henry IV,. furnished a High Sheriff of Kent on several occasions; among other members of the family who filled that office was William Cromer, sheriff in both 9th and 27th Elizabeth.

PROVISIONS FOR ASSIZES

	Itm. Grenefisshes [1]	. . .	xx
	„ Salt Eles .	. . .	xxx
	„ white herrings .	. .	di barrell [½ barrell]
	„ redde herrings .	. .	by yn the Towne
	„ ffresshe Salmonds	. .	ij
⎧ Salte ffysshe	„ Smelts .	. . .	j hundred l^{tie} [150]
⎨ & ffresshe	„ rosting lampreys	. .	ij hundred
⎩ ffysshe	„ middling lampreys	.	iiij hundred
	„ Shrympes .	. . .	j panyer [pannier]
	„ Trouts	. . .	l^{tie} [50]
	„ Crefisses	. . .	iiij hundred
	„ Turbotts	. . . .	—
	„ Pykes	. . . .	l^{tie}
	„ Carpes	. . . .	iiii^{xx} [fourscore]
	„ fresshe eles	. .	xl^{tie} [40]
	„ Tenches	. . . .	l^{tie}
	„ Breames	. . . .	xxx
	„ Pearches	. . .	v^c [500]
	„ Mulletts	. . . .	—
	„ Sea ffisshe	. .	iij Seames [an obsolete measure]
	„ Oysters	. . .	xij bz. [bushels]
	„ Musculles .	. .	vj bz.
	„ as much Tunney as will coste		iiij^s
	Inprimis pepper	. . .	j pound
	Itm. Cloves and macs [sic]	.	di „ [½ lb.]
	„ whole mace	. .	di
	„ whole cloves	. .	j quarter of a pound
	„ nutmyggs	. . .	iij quarters of a pound
	„ Cynamon .	. .	i pound
Spycs.	„ gynger	. . .	i „
	„ Saunders [2]	. .	j quarter of a pound
	„ Safron	. . .	di ounce
	„ fyne Suger	. .	xxv pounds
	„ course [sic] Suger	.	xxxv pounds
	„ coriander & comfitts .		ij „
	„ bisketts & carrowayes	.	iiij „
	„ Suger plate [sweetmeats]	.	ij

[1] Green fish: fresh or undried fish of any kind before being cured for market. —C. D.

[2] Alexander seed, *post*, p. 25, note 2.

	Itm. suger comfitts	ij pounds
	,, orenge cumfitts	ij ,,
	,, cynomon cumfitts	ij ,,
	,, almonde cumfitts	ij ,,
	,, muske cumfitts	ij ,,
	,, Biskett Bread	ij ,,
	,, boxes of wafers	ij ,,
	,, Coriander sede	ij ounces
	,, Gallingale [1]	ij ,,
	,, Turnsole [2]	j ,,
	,, Isnglasse	j pound
	,, Rice	x pounds
	Inprimis prunes	xx pounds
	Itm. currants	xvj ,,
	,, dates	viij pounds
	,, ffiggs	j Tapnett [3]
	,, almonds	xxx pounds
	,, raisons of the Sonne	xvj pounds
ffruits	,, Orengs	ij° [200]
	,, lemans	j hundreth
	,, Chessenutts	v hundreth
	,, Quinces	xl
	,, Wardens [pears]	ij bz.
	,, Peares	
	,, Pippins and other apples	vj bz.
	Inprimis drie Suckett [4]	iiij pounds
	Itm. marmalade	vj pounds
	,, marche panes [5]	vj
	,, rose water	j gallon
Conserves	,, Barbaries	j ,,
	,, Picktothes	
	,, Damaske water	
	,, perfumes	
	Inprimis salte Butter	j firkyn
Butter &	Itm. swete butter	l^tie pounds
oyle	,, swete sallett oyle	iiij galls.

[1] Or 'Galangal,' an aromatic stimulant of the nature of ginger, formerly used as a seasoning.—*C. D.*
[2] Chrozophora, formerly used to colour red wine.—*Ibid.*
[3] Tapnett: a basket made of rushes in which figs were imported.—*Ibid.*
[4] Drie Suckett: dried sweetmeats.—*Ibid.*
[5] Marzipan: a confection made of pistachio nuts, sugar, white of egg, &c.—*Ibid.*

PROVISIONS FOR ASSIZES

Sawce	Itm. Creame	xij galls.
	” eggs	xij^c [1,200]
	Inprimis vergis [1]	iiij galls.
	Itm. vinegar	iiij galls.
	” mustarde	ij galls.
	” yeste	j kylderkyn
	” whyte salte	j bz.di [1½ bushels]
Herbes	Inprimis Spynage as muche as will coste	xx^d
	Itm. white suckerye & white endiffe	xij^d
	” parselie, Tyme, & Rosemarye	ij^s vj^d
	” Carriotts redde & white	viij bunches
	” Capers	iiij pounds
	” Onyons	j bz
	” fflowers	
	” alixander Budds [2]	
	” Scarrett roots [3]	
Wynes	Inprimis muscaden [4] a runlett [5] of	iiij galls.
	Itm. Secke a runlett of	vij galls.
	” rackte [6] reynysshe wine a runlett of	vj galls.
	” a hogeshed of gasconie clarrett wyne j hogeshed of white wine	
Flower & Bread	Inprimis fyne white fflower	vj bz.
	Itm. Bread	
Torches & Candells	Inprimis quarriers or Waxe Tapers	xij pounds
	Itm. Staffe Torches	xij ”
	” of Cotton Candells	vj dozen
Rushes	Inprimis Rushes [7]	x dozen
	Inprimis Coles	

[1] Verjuice: an acid liquor expressed from crab-apples.—*C. D.*

[2] Smyrnium olusatrum: a plant of the parsley family, formerly greatly cultivated as a vegetable.—*Ibid.*

[3] Scaret root: the herb skirwort.—*Hal. D.*; *cf.* skirret, middle English skyrwyt, a species of water parsnip long cultivated in Europe, but now fallen into disuse.—*Ibid.*

[4] Muscadel? made from muscat grapes.

[5] Rundlet, a barrel of 18½ galls.—*Ibid.*

[6] Strained.

[7] To strew floors with.

HISTORY OF THE LENNARDS

ffuell	Itm. Tallwood	
	„ Ostree ffaggotts [1]	
	Inprimis haye	
Horsemeate	Itm. lyttor	
	„ Otes	ij quarters
	„ horsebreade [2]	
	Inprimis small racks	j payer
	Itm. small Broches [3]	iiij
	„ greate pannes	iij
	„ midle pannes	iij
	„ a smale panne to frye yn	j
Implements	„ Brasse potts	iij
of howsehold	„ woodden ladles	iiij
wch the cooke	„ Brasen ladles	ij
must bring	„ Scommers [scummers or	
wth hym	skimmers]	iiij
	„ Gredirons	iij
	„ a grater	j
	„ a stone morter & a pestle	j
	„ a brazen morter & a pestle	j
	„ Trevetts	iiij
	„ greate ffier Shovells	ij
	„ a settyng peele [4]	j
	„ hand peeles	iiij
	„ fflasketts [5]	viij
	„ greate Trayes	vj
	„ Collanders	ij
	„ pailes	ij
	„ dripping pannes	
	„ a gellie Bagge	j
	Inprimis earthen pipkyns of a gallon di [1½ gall.] apeece	iiij
	Itm. earthen pipkyns of dyvers bygness betwene a potle & a gallon	viij
	„ earthen pypkyns	vj

---

[1] Ostric, or hostry: middle English for an inn.
[2] A coarse form of bread was then in this country (as nowadays in Switzerland), commonly given to horses.
[3] Broach: a spit.—*C. D.*
[4] A baker's long-handled shovel.
[5] A vessel in which viands were served.—*Ibid.*

PLATE FOR ASSIZES

{ Implements Itm. perfumyng pannes of earthe iiij
{ of household „ greate Stone Juggs . . ij
{ to be boughte„ lytle stone Juggs . . xij
      „ Black Jacks . . . iiij
      „ Boxes of fruite Trenchers
        round & square . . iiij dozen
      „ other square white Trenchers vj dozen
      „ Square course Trenchers . ij dozen
      „ Tubbs of di Hogeshedds
        a peece . . . . vj
      „ of Strayners . . . vj yeards
      „ lockerem [1] for dresser clothes vj elles
      „ of Soultw^{ch} [2] for dishe clothes x elles
      „ of course canvas napkyns
        to wype the plate &
        trenchers . . . I dozen

  A note made the of Februarye 1567 of suche plate lynnen & other houshould stoof as Mr Walsingham lendeth vnto my brother cromer [3] for the furnishinge of his house agaynst the assises.

Plate all this
{ Inprimis ij basens & earons [4] [ewers?] p[ar]cell gilte wth there covers
{ Item iiij wyne pootes wth there covers ij gilte
{ It: iiij white candlestyckes
{ It: ij dossin of trenchers on di p[ar]cell gylte [5]
{ It: iiij gilte booles wth ij covers
{ It: ij gilte saltes wth ij covers
{ It: j standinge cupp wth a covere [cover]
{ It: xij spoones vj gylte wth bulles heddes & vj wheite wth longe gylte knobes
{ It: ij casting boottelles [6]
{ It: a spice boxe wch you haue

---

[1] A cheap coarse linen.—*C. D.*

[2] Possibly intended for 'Soutage,' a coarse sort of cloth.—*Ibid.*

[3] I am not aware of any relationship in blood between John Lennard and Mr. Cromer. The expression 'brother' may refer to their both being in different years High Sheriffs of Kent.

[4] This word, which occurs three times in this list, is certainly so spelled; I am unable to find it in any dictionary. Before the introduction of forks, and they were by no means in common use at this period, ewers filled with scented water were handed to the guests at dinner between the courses for them to rinse their fingers.

[5] One half partly gilt.—*C. D.* [6] A vial for sprinkling perfumes.

All this
- It: vj damaske & dyeper boord clothes
- It: iij damaske & dieper cupper clothes [1]
- It: viij dossyn of damaske & dieper napkins lackinge ij
- It: vj longe damaske & dieper towells
- It: iiij levery diep[er] towells [2]
- It: ij damaske napkins for wafers
- It: iiij diep[er] armynge towells [3]

y^{is} you will
- Item iiij payre of fyne shetes
- It: iiij payer of fyne pillobirs [4]
- It: vij playne boord [5] clothes [6]

- It: ix beddes
- It: ix boolsters
- It: iiij matrecies
- It: viij payre of pillos
- It: vj coverlettes iij redd rogge & iij tapestrye
- It: v payer of fustians
- It: iiij payer of wollen blanketes all marked wth T. W.
- It: on tester wth the vallons & v curtens to it
- It: valons to a bede wth v curtens to yt
- It: iij long cusshins
- It: x square cusshins
- It: ij carpetes for cupperd [1] of turkeye worke
- It: on grene carpett for a boorde
- It: on grene carpett for a cupperd
- It: a close chayer [7]
- It: ij payre off andiers [8]
- It: iij feyre shovells
- It: v old coverletes } to truste [9] the stoof in
- It: v old blanketes
- It: iiij garnishe [10] of fyne vessell to every garnishe xij platers xij dyshes & xij sawsers, on graven garnishe marked wth T. W. D. the rest wth T. W.

---

[1] Cupboard, or cuppebord, originally a table upon which cups of gold or silver were displayed.—*C. D.*

[2] Cloths used in serving meals.

[3] I can find no such combination of words, but this is certainly how it is written.

[4] Pillow-cases.—*C. D.* [5] Table.—*Ibid.* [6] This word is written 'chothes.'

[7] A night-chair. [8] Old French for andirons.—*Ibid.*

[9] To truss it in: do it up in. [10] Garnish: a set of pewter.

HOUSEHOLD STOOF' FOR ASSIZES

It : xv sallet dishes
It : ij basons & carons
It : viij candlestickes
It : ïj dossyn of trenchers
It : ij great byre [beer?] pootes
It : iij saltes
It : v pye plates
It : vj water pootes

From my cossin Walsingham.
Inprimis vj white booles wthout covers
Plate   It : ij gilte saltes wth covers, thone [the one] a trencher salte w^t a peperboxe
It : v wheite byre pootes wth covers fastened to them
It : xij spoones wth great knobes

From my mother.
Plate   { It : on bason and earon p[ar]cell gylte
       { It : v gylte spoones & vij wheite ons wth knobes
It : a diep[er] table clothe
It : a dieper towell
It : a payre of shetes
It : ij payre of pillobirs
It : xij peyter[1] trenchers vj p[ar]cell gylte
It : iiij peyter candlesticks

I think I have given sufficient, and possibly too many, of these lists, but they by no means end here; on the contrary there are several others enumerating various articles of a nature similar to those already mentioned which were lent by various other persons.

Lord Dacre says that John was an 'active magistrate' for the county of Kent.[2] He, no doubt, came to that conclusion by the perusal of several documents of John's relating to magisterial work; they are of some interest now as throwing light on the state of crime then existing, and on the powers exercised by magistrates. One of these documents, written on quite a small sheet of paper, was, no doubt, brought to him by

[1] Pewter.   [2] *Ld. D. His.*

one Horsolder, probably the parish constable for Chepsted, in order to obtain instructions how he was to act. John wrote certain notes or comments on this paper, and in order to show which are in his handwriting, I have put them within brackets :—

The names of all suche persons as followethe are these whiche comytted faultes & offences at Cheapstead upon Soundaye the xxv daye of Apryell, 1586.
Robert Robynson alehousekeper (without lycence lay hym by
    ye heles)
Rycharde Permynger the elder   } (bound yn x^{li} apece to seke
Olberde Robert Stubberfeld's man }   out ye Griff Howell.)
Gryffen Howell.
Arnold's soune   Shorryes man.

(Horsolder of Chepsted I charge you yn the Quenes name that you bryng before me all the persons beforenamed to answere certayne offences done & comytted by them, bryng them spedely   John Lennard.)

There were a good many turbulent, lawless characters in the neighbourhood of Chepsted in the sixteenth century, as we have several papers relating to highway robberies committed there. There was from very early times a fish market at Chepsted where fish brought from the Sussex coasts was sold to be taken on to London, and it has been said that the men who carried the fish from Sussex to Chepsted were called 'Rypers,' 'Ripers,' or 'Ripiers,'[1] from the town of Rye, whence much of this fish came. It appears that a certain R. Baker, a 'Riper' by trade, was robbed at Chepsted by a gang of men, one of whom, named Robson, confessed his share in the crime. We have a letter from a Mr. Frankeleyn, telling John Lennard of this confession ; it is addressed 'To the Worshipfull and his lovyng Freinde M. Lennard be this delyvered w̄t grett speede,' and runs thus :—

Sr. Robson hath confessyth all the Robbery and that one Hall Mr. Nevell man was one of them and the ꝑcurer [procurer] of all the robbery and ther where ij men more about Chepsted whych he knoweth nott and for Mr. Heron matter I wyll deale no further theryn.

[1] *H. K.* p. 74 ; also *Phil.*

And thus I take my leave from Rochester this p̃sent [present] Saturday, Yr Worship to use, John Frankeleyn.[1]

In the following letter, which from the handwriting is evidently written by some professional scribe, Robson alludes to his confession, and expresses regret that he did not 'manyfest the whole truthe' unto John at the time of his apprehension :—

To the right Worshipfull Mr. Lennard Esquier, one of her Maties Justices of Peace in the County of Kent :—
As god of his mercies hath moued yor hart to pitie my miserie, and accordinglie to doe very much for mee as I am credibilie enfourmed. So now I doe most humblie beseeche yor wo^rship for gods cawse, and y^r own vertues sake to goe through with that, wherin yo^u haue alreadie vowchsaued so greate paines : Trulie wo^rshipfull S^r it hath repented mee manie atyme that I did not manyfest vnto yor goodnes (upon yor faithfull p̃messe [promesse] of frendship geuen vnto mee at myne apprehension) the whole truthe, wch since I haue signified vnto yor wo^rship, and others, wherunto I will stand till the Death. Thus referringe my wretched estate and unfained repentance vnto gods manifold mercies and yor reuerende wysdom I take my leaue with my dailie and dutifull prayers for the encrease of y^r wo^rship in all felicytie.

The wretched and penytent prisoner most bounden at y^r wo^rships com̃aundem^t for ever :

EDWARD ROBSON.

(In another hand.)

Script iiij Julij 1576.
Thomas Alfey a m^r [master] of fence of Maydestone kepyng a vytelyng house at the sygne of the thre maryners by the waters syde there, dyd fetch halle out of the gayle to a gentleman of Sussex aboute a fortnyght synce.

The following document, which refers to this robbery, appears to be a sort of petition, and has no proper ending, or indeed beginning :—

---

[1] A 'John Franklyn' is referred to later, in a letter from Sir William Cordell, as being a trustee for John Lennard, *post*, p. 122.

These be the names of the townes wher all these good-felowes[1] be bowlesterd[2] and hidden :—

Westram [Westerham].
Sondridge.
Brasted.
Hawsted.
Chepsted and the hundred of Ratan.

My humble request is to my good Lords that these men whose names be vnderwrytten may be the examinars of the prsons suspected for the robbreys as well nowe as in tymes past as also for serttayne lrs [letters] and rymes set up in Churches and cast abrod.

Sir Christopher Aleyn Knight.
John Lennard Esquier.
Raufe Bosewell[3] Esquier.
Thomas Willowbie Esquier.
Robt. Binge Esquier.

Also ther is one Hall whiche was one of them that robbed Richard baker the Rypper who will confesse nothinge. But Robson his partener hath confessed yt. And therefore my humble request is that he and suche others as wee shall thinke to be suspected may be removed from the comen Gayle vuto the Tower or some other place where yor honores shall thinke mete.

I have also an anonymous letter (or probably a copy of it) addressed to R. Baker, the prosecutor, from a man who confesses that he is the robber, and that Baker is wrongly accusing some one, presumably Hall. It is addressed thus :—

These be delivered to the Ryper which was robbed on Christmas Eve at night at Chepstead.

Ahe thow false and piured [perjured] villayne w[ch] goeth abowt to hange him who is Ignorante, of thys cawse, althowgh his hap was suche to be in places w[ch] is not for him to confesse, yet God I take him to wytnes, he is Ignorante of the faete, for

---
[1] Thieves.—*C. D.*   [2] Supported or maintained.—*Ibid.*
[3] A Mr. Bossevyle and a Christopher Willoughbye are referred to in a letter from Sir N. Bacon (*post*, p. 40) ; and in 1594, Mary Lennard (who was born in 1574), a daughter of Samson and therefore granddaughter of John, married a Ralph Boswell, of Sevenoaks. *Post*, p. 216.

that hand whiche wrate this lrē [letter] pulled awaye thy purse, But thow false lynge varlet, yf others will cause him to haue troble, I knowe y^u wilt not let; ffor wch fault I am to be revenged at thy hands, vnles thou make an open confessyon. ffor whereas y^u swearestes thou lost xvj^{li}, thou lyeste falselye in thye throte, neither didest thou loose xvj nobles. Perchance thou wilt thinke how he caused this lre to be writen for his owne excuse wch I protest, he is not onely ignorant of the wrytynge of yt but also vnknowne to the wryter, who dothe yt for a remorse of conscience, for because he beinge Ignorant of the dede, ys in hassarde to abyde the ponyshm^t. Wherefore I wold wishe yow to leave of from doinge execusyon on his innocensye, leste yt encrease yor myserey. ffor pswade wth yo^{r}self that thow canst not offer him that ponyshement whereof thow shalt not feele the torment, for if thow make him to be Imprisoned I will cause the to be bethered [*sic*]: And if throughe thy false othes thou shouldeste hange him, By the deathe of Christ I wold hange the [thee] vpp in the high way wythe the halter of thyne owne horse, nether shalt thow, nor no man vnder the [thee], travayle on the way vnrevenged, no not so muche as thy horses, but insted of ther haytes shall haue pyke staves in ther bellyes. Thus advysinge you to loke before you leape, takinge my leave from the towne of Collewesson, who lyvethe not but to worke the spite aboue aney enemye thow hast in the wórlde, yf thow doe any ponyshm^t to that goodfellowe who deserves yt not.

Yor mortall frende and a spryte of Ryver hille.[1] This bee deliverd to the Rypeer wch was robbed one Christmas Eve at night at Chepsted.

It would be interesting to know if this vicious letter of threats did prevent Richard Baker, the 'Ryper,' from prosecuting Hall, and what was the upshot of the affair. The only other reference that I can find to it is another letter from John Frankelin[2] to John Lennard, written on the back of the previous anonymous one, in which he urges the latter to have quite a gang of 'lewde felowes' apprehended. He seems to accuse one Henry Isley[3] of being the 'chife doer in the

---

[1] Riverhead is a parish near Chepsted.

[2] In the previous letter he spells his name 'Frankeleyn.'

[3] Probably a relation, perhaps a son, of the Sir Henry Isley before referred to, and who had gone down in the world.

robberye,' and a widow named Williams of telling Isley 'what gestes be in the howse that bathe anye money.' The letter is as follows :—

Sr, I hertelye comend me vuto y^u certifyinge yo^u that I have caused Dawkes to be deliuered, yor fees be to the Clerke of the Assyses and to me & the ij marshalls iij^s, and the keeper claimeth vij^s viij^d. Also I haue talked withe Robson this presente morninge by the comaundmete of the Justyce of the Assyses & he bathe appeached diuerse lewde psons [persons] in yor quarters abowte yo^u. As Mr. Henry Isleye to be the chife doer in the robberye, and one Cherles a Tanner & dwellinge w^{t}he one Cakett's wedowe that was withe them at the Robberye.

Henrye Isleye lyethe allwayes .... when he is about yow, at the seide Catketts widows howse, she hathe ij or iij fayre dawghters as it is reported. And one Williams wedow of Chepsted, a lewd howse for gevinge of knowledge what gests be in the howse that hathe anye money, as Robson bathe declared to me that Henry Isley dothe knowe allways what gests be there, and who bathe money, and who hathe none. Yo^r wo^{r}ship shalle do a godlye dede to apprehende these lewde felowes, for theye remaine abowte yo^u stille. I wille certifye Mr. Justice Southcote[1] of the case, and that I have writen to yo^u in the matter, for Robson is greately affrayde to be destroyed bye them, for confessinge of ye company, and so theye haue tolde him if it please yor worship to deale in the cause you shalle [?beate] owte a greate cōpany [company] of eville men, abowte yo^u. And thus beinge bolde to tro^{u}ble yor wo^{r}shipe in the certyfyinge of Robson's confession I take my leave, from Maydestone this p̄sent (present) Thursdaye being the xxj daye of Marche.

Yor Worships to vse
JOHN fFRANKELIN.

Charles that worketh with Catkets widowe bathe a wiffe and a howse abowte Detforde as Robson telleth me.

The following correspondence is about a man named John Edling in the service of a Mr. Peckham, that John Lennard appears to have committed to prison upon a charge of murder preferred against him by this Peckham, to whose ears a report

---

[1] *Ante*, p. 21 note.

had come that Edling, when in the employment of a Mr. Wendy, had been guilty of this crime.

Edling found some means to write from prison to Mr. Wendy and ask him to speak for him to John Lennard, and this Wendy accordingly did. Lennard then sends a copy of Wendy's letter to Peckham, with a note suggesting that Peckham should procure the release of Edling. Peckham replies that the gaoler at Maidstone refuses to deliver him unless Lennard sends a warrant for his release, and asks him to do so by the bearer of his letter.

We are so far removed from the days when Justices of the Peace could, merely upon the request of a friend, order the delivery of a prisoner from gaol, that it is difficult for us to realise the amount of arbitrary power that they enjoyed in those times.

The letters are as follows:—Mr. Wendy's letter is addressed :—

To the Right Worshippfull Mr. Leonerd Esquier these be d. d. [delivered].

S^r At the request of a poore prisoner named John Edling, some tyme my s[er]vaunt and (as I am enfourmed) comitted by you vpon the Accusacōn of one Mr. Peckham for the killing of a man of myne when he was in my service : I am for the zeale I beare to the advauncement of Justice, wch consisteth as well in acquitting of the Innocent as in Condemning of the guyltie, to advertise you of the truth of the matter wthout affection or p[ar]cialitie, and that vpon the p[er]ill of my poore creditt. About twoo yeeres sithence he, being in my service, by mishapp killed a horse of a neighbo^r of myne and fearing some trouble to growe vnto him (as I suppose) for the said horse, and being vnable to satisfie the partie that susteyned the losse he slipt soodenlie wthout making me privie to his gooing. His behavio^r otherwise was suche as, if this had not happened, I thinke he had continwed with me to this day. As for killing any man of myne, or any other to my knowledge, he is as Innocent as any man lyving, nay, I never knewe or heard that ev^r [ever] he strake any man wth weapon. Thus having advertised you of the truth of my knowledge of his behavio^r I leave him and his cause to yor wise consideracōn, And so ceasing from further troubling you, I end in hast And comend you to the p[ro]teccion of thallmightye.   At Haslingfield [1] the last of May 1589.   Yo^r frend unknowne.   THO: WENDY.

John Lennard endorsed the following note to Peckham on the back of this letter:—

Sr After my right harty comendacyons Whereas vpon yor Accusacyon of one John Edlyn for kyllyng of a man in Cambrydge shire, Whylest the seyd Edlyn was yn servyce ther wyth one Mr. Wendy, I the last weke comytted the seyd Edlyn to the gayle for that facte: thyes ar toadvertyse you that thys sonday mornyng the fyrst of June, I receyved a lre [letter] from Mr. Wendy by thys brynger that Edlyn ys not gylty of any suche acte, as you may p[er]ceyve by Mr. Wendyes lre [letter], the copy Wherof I send you hereynclosed. Wherefore, except ye knowe otherwyse, ye shall do welle to deale wyth the gayler for the delyvery of the seyd John Edlyn; Whereunto I assent as I may, seyng he was not arested vpon any felony, but stayed vpon some suspycyon. And so God keep you. Lyncolns yn the fyrst of June 1589.
                  Yo^r assured frend.   JOHN LENNARD.

The following letter is Peckham's reply to this one, and is addressed:—

To the right worshipfull my very good freind Mr. Lennarde esquiere geue this at Lincolnes Inne.

S^r accordinge to your appointment I sent your lre [letter] to the gaoler of Maidstone, for the deliverye of my late servante, his answere was, that as he receaued him by warrante he must deliuer him by the like, wch I beseche you to send me by this bearer, yt apperethe by his old m^r [Master] his lre, that he ys not to be touched wth murder, yet I assure you he confessed to his bedfelowe that he had done a murder and was fled for the same, wch was justified to his face; also he metinge wth one of his felowes, Mr. Wendyes man, at the campe in Essex, asked him how he scaped, he answered he had a good mr. [master] otherwise he had hanged for their offence, but said he, thou didst well to ron awaye for so thou hast escaped, but I aduise the come no more there. All this was auouched to his face,

---
[1] Haslingfield is five miles from Cambridge.

wherefore I doe assure my selfe he hathe comitted some felonye, and ys come awaye for yt.

   Your freind to my pover. JAMES PECKHAM.

It would seem that John Lennard made an unsuccessful attempt to obtain the freedom of the City of London, as I think there can be little doubt that the following letter quoted from referred to him. I have, however, seen at the London Guildhall a copy of this letter, and as it gives no address after the name of 'John Leonard,' nor makes any reference to his profession, one cannot be certain that it does not refer to some other person of that name.

Among the Archives of the City there is a letter dated November 24th, 1579, from the Lord Mayor to the Earl of Warwick, in which he acknowledges the receipt of the Earl's several letters requesting the grant of the freedom of the City to Henry Rodes and John 'Leonard.' They had agreed to admit the former, but on account of many grants of a like nature, both to his lordship and his friends, to the great dissatisfaction of the poor and the artificers of the City, they requested him to forbear pressing them any further in the matter.[1]

If anyone is anxious to have a fine tomb erected to his memory, or to be buried in any special building, he shows his knowledge of human nature if he provides for such memorial of himself while he yet lives. The ancient Egyptians acted upon this principle, and the fact that their tombs were often so splendid is largely explained by the fact that they usually erected them during their own lives. Sometimes in Egypt you see a fine tomb unfinished, and upon inquiry it generally turns out that, although its inhabitant had begun it, he had died before the last touches were put to it; and that his successor was too busy looking after what he had inherited, to occupy himself or his fortune in building or finishing a tomb to the memory of his predecessor.

This seems to have been John's idea, as a few years before

---

[1] *Analyt.*

his death, namely, in 1584, we find him entering into the following contract for building a chapel to Chevening Church, and it is in this chapel that he and his wife now repose.

A byll of Covenaunts made the xxiiijth. of Februarye 1584 betwene John Lennard of Knowll Esquyer one [on] thone partye & William Chapman of Rothered, Carpenter one [on] thother partye for the Settynge up of the Ruffe of the Chappell at Chevenyng Churche & the makyng of three partitiones in the same Chappell vizt.

Itm. the sayd William Chapman covenaunteth wth the sayd John Lennard to buyld the Sayde Ruffe of the same Chappell in manner & forme followinge :—

Itm the sayd Ruffe to be made Rownd within and one currante [1] to be layd betwen the Chappel & the Chansell for a gutter of Lead.

Itm the sayd Chapman to make thre particiones in ye said Chappell, that is to Saye, one of them betwyxte the Churche & the Chappell, & the other ij perticiones betwyxte the Chansell & the Chappell that is on eyther syde the hole pyller one, & one payer of Chansell dores towards the Churche, & one other payer of Chansell Doores towards the Chansell.

Itm all the Rough tymber to be provided at the costs & charges of the sayd John Lennard & all other caryages also.

Itm all hewynge, squaryng & Sawynge to be done at the charges of the sayd William Chapman.

Itm all Eyerne [iron] worke, naylles, Lead or other necessaryes not before expressed to be provided at the Charges of the sayd John Lennard.

Itm the Sayd John Lennard promysethe to paye the sayd Willm Chapman for the workmanshipe of the sayd Chappell & for the Hewynge Squarynge & Sawinge of the tymber for the same, the Some of xvj^{li}.

In 1581 John appears to have tried his hand at law reform, and to have drafted the following bill for shortening the Michaelmas Law term :—

WHEREAS Michaelmas term is usually held in the season of the year when infection of the plague & other sicknesses is

---

[1] Currante for current: the amount of depression given to a roof to cause the water which falls upon it to flow in a given direction.—C. D.

most rife, after the heat of summer (especially the three first returns, viz. the Octave, Quindene, & 3 weeks of Michaelmas) so that the Queen has often had to adjourn them ; it were well to remove those 3 returns to a later date, placing them at the end of Michaelmas term. The term being long is one in which causes can best be heard, & the adjournments so often practised cause great loss to the Queen's revenue, as the justices have to be paid. The Queen therefore enacts that the said 3 returns be discontinued, & the term commence a month after Michaelmas, the 2^d return being the Morrow of All Souls, the 3rd the Morrow of St. Martin, &c.

(There are 5 days between term end & Christmas Day for termers[1] to repair home, & if they live very far they can take a little longer before Christmas.)

All writs to be issued in conformity with such arrangement, but in such cases as have special days assigned to them, the justices shall appoint special days as heretofore.

(Endorsed) 14 Martij 1580.

Mr. Leonard Bil for ye cutting off of Michās Terme.'[2]

Law reform is, like all things legal, extremely slow to move. I have not been able to discover whether John was successful in his attempted reform. The preamble of his bill, however, shows some indication of how insanitary was the state of the public health in the time of Elizabeth.

John Lennard seems to have been on friendly, and even intimate, terms with the leading judges of the day. We have seen that his son Samson says that the 'Lord Chauncellour' Audley was his 'honourable good friend.' If Lord Campbell's account of Audley is at all accurate, I am not sure how much having such a man for his 'honourable good friend' redounds to John's credit. That author says of Audley :—'Such a sordid slave does not deserve that we should say more of his vices and demerits ;' and 'no eunuch in a seraglio was ever a more submissive tool of the caprice and vengeance of a passionate and remorseless master than was Lord Chancellor Audley.'[3]

---

[1] Those attending the 'terms' in the Law Courts.
[2] *S. P. Dom. Eliz.* cxlviii. No. 25.
[3] *Camp.* i. p. 633.

Lord Campbell, however, praises greatly Sir Nicholas Bacon, who, as Lord Keeper, was one of Lord Audley's successors, and Sir Nicholas appears also to have been on friendly terms with John, for we have the following letter from the Lord Keeper to him and a Sir C. Allen :—

I com̃end me hartely unto you ; & understanding by the complaynte of Mr Bossevyle of the Court of Wards as well on hys owne behalfe, as one [on] the behalfe of one Xr̄ofer [Christopher] Willoughbye, that the same Willoughbye, beyng owner of the Manor of Boswell yn the Countye of Kente, hath by hys Indenture solde to hym the woods growyng there for cīīīj^{li} [180*l.*] which he hathe fullye satysfied to the said Mr Willoughbye, as he saythe, & informeth further that you by a s^{ur}mysed [surmysed [1]] bargayn by worde tenn yeres paste, clayme the same for the some of cc [200] mks [marks [2]] whereof you have payed, as he sayethe, as yet nothing at all duryng the seid tyme : And that yor seid bargayne ys utterlye denyed you by the seid Mr Willoughbye vnles ye had paide the seid cc mks to hym at the days thon^o [thereunto] appointed, and nowe ye knowyng of that bargayne by Indenture have taken vppon you to fell the same woods wythout anye other tytle or considerāc̄on [consideration] as he seythe. Therfore he suethe to me to haue Injunction to staye the falle of the same woods vntyll there may be tryall by ac^{t}ion [action] or otherwyse. And surely yf ye had any such bargayne so long sence & shulde then have fallen the same, and all that tyme hath not payed any money & meane to wynne tene yeres more groethe and no encrease of pryce, & thys gentleman ys thereby dryven to breake up hys howse & to make harde bargaynes to hys greate losse, otherwyse to s^{r}ue [serve] his turne for wante of that money ; thees thyngs beyng true it seemethe he ys hardely delt wthall, and althoughe thys case requyreth helpe, yet vnderstandyng how nere neighbo^{u}rs ye all bene & yo^{ur} callyng there, wyshe rather amongeste yourselves quyetnes than sute & therefore I haue spared otherwyse to deale then by thys means ; advysyng you, as I haue done hym, rather that frends may ende the same than sute. And nevertheles yn the meane tyme youe to doo as he bathe p̱mysed [promysed], that ys, not to felle or carye awaye anye of the same woods vntyll it may take ende one waye or other, or els that you

---

[1] Alleged.—*C. D.*   [2] A mark = 13*s.* 4*d.*

advertyse me of some good cawse whye you should not so doe. And so I byd youe farewell thys xxvi^{th} of Marche 1569.

      Yo^{ur} lovyng frynd   N. BACON.

Addressed:—To hys lovyng frynds Sir C. Allen Knyghte and John Lennerd Esquyer geve thies.

Although Sir Nicholas evidently considered that Mr. 'Bossevyle,'[1] who complains to him, 'ys hardely delt withall' by Sir C. Allen and John in the transaction about the purchase of timber, yet he writes to them in this friendly manner. Some six years later John endorsed the letter in question with an explanation of the whole transaction, saying that the Lord Keeper, after hearing all the facts of the case, had entirely taken his (John's) view of the matter, and had 'dysmyssed hys hands of yt,' and that he (John) still enjoys the wood. This endorsement, if an accurate statement of facts, entirely clears John's character from the charge of dealing unfairly with Mr. Boswell. The endorsement runs thus:—

My lo Kepers lre [letter] touchyng Sr C. Alyn myself and Mr. Boswell.

yt ys vj yeres at Marche last sythens thys lre came as apereth by yt. The fallyng oute for thys wood betweene Sr C. Aleyn, me, & Mr Boswell began a yere before that Sr Cryse [Chrystopher] had a leas of ground yet contynueng, & bought the wood on yt fyrst, & sold me the wood, & then Mr B. toke a leas of the ground yn reucyon [reversion] over Sr Crise hed, & bought the wood of the forseid lesso^r that he knewe had sold yt alredy. And S^r cryse & I, vpon the comyng of my l. Kepers [Lord Keeper's] lre, by our seueral [several] lres to my l. Kepr [Lord Keeper] dysclosed our tytles, and acqueynted my l. [Lord] wyth hys coarse dealyngs besydes: Whereon my l. Kepr dysmyssed hys hands of yt, & I enjoye the wood, & yet do, for the tyme of fellyng yt yet contynueth. And therefore hys sayeng that I bere hym malyce, because he was my l. Bukh [Lord Buckhurst's] frend for Knolle,[2] ys false & saith yt to colour hys fond dealyngs & to sharpen my l. B, as he hath doon others, ageynst me; but my l. Buckhurst knoweth howe vyperous he ys, as he found hym, & so I hope he wille telle hym, & howe he fyndeth.

[1] Also spelt indifferently 'Bosewell' and 'BoSwell.'
[2] As to this, *vide post*, p. 121, *et seq.*

Another very eminent judge with whom John Lennard appears to have been upon most friendly and intimate terms is Sir William Cordell, Master of the Rolls. He sent his will to Sir William asking him his advice as a friend upon it, and Sir William evidently took a good deal of trouble in the matter, as we have quite a long document from him with suggestions on different points arising therein. For a member of the Bar to ask a Master of the Rolls to do what practically amounts to 'settling' his will shows that a very considerable friendship must have existed between them.

In the following letter, I believe, that 'the booke yow left with me to be considered' relates to John's draft will.[1] Besides thanking John and his wife for a present of 'phesants and p[ar]triches,' he also thanks Mrs. Samson for 'the fattest couple of coneys I did see this yere.' Rabbits must have been scarcer then than now, as they would nowadays be a curious present to make to so important a person as the Master of the Rolls, were they ever so fat.

Sir William Cordell, like many famous judges since, wrote an atrocious hand, and one, which written in a character, and with many abbreviations, and curious modes of spelling now unfamiliar, is exceedingly difficult to decipher. He seems himself to have been painfully conscious of how difficult this letter was to make out, as in the course of it he prays God that John can 'well rede yt.'

Wth my very harty comendacons vnto you & to Mrs Lennard, and my like thanks unto you bothe for the phesants & p[ar]triches, which yow sent by this berer. Accordyng to y^{or} desyre I haue sent unto yow herclosed [herein enclosed] the booke yow left wth me to be considered. My oppynyon, & advice therein, I have brefely towched in a shete of paper, which I haue wrytten wth my owne hand, & therfore I p[ra]ye god yow can well rede yt, or picke owte my meanyng therin. Yf you like of my device I p[ra]ye yow, after you haue wrytten yt owt fayre, to bryng yt with yow on y^{or} next comyng

---

[1] The original meaning of book was a written document, especially a deed.— C. D. See also *post*, p. 85, when 'booke' is used to mean a deed.

to London, which I wilnt [will not] looke for before the begynyng of the next terme, & then upon conferens togythr yow
& I will reforme yt, accordyng to y^or mynde, & in the meane
tyme I p[ra]ye yow accept my good will.

I send yow herclosed in the paquet my lre [letter] to the
three kepers of Eltham Parkes, I thynk ther be so many, when
I doute not but yow shall receyve of ether of them a good doe.
I have lefte ther lres vnsealed, & not dated, or dyrected to them
by ther p[ro]per names, bycause I haue forgotten ther names,
& likewyse for that I wold haue yow to date them a lyttle
before the tyme yow will send for them, & then you may seale
the lres accordyngly. And in anywyse let me vnderstand how
yow spede. I trust on Cristemas to send yow a hynde yf ther
be ony good in Ashedown,[1] or yf yow will have ony good does
ther, such as they be I trust to get yow a brace or ij. Or yf
my l of Norff [Lord of Norfolk] hath ony nye vnto yow send
me word where the groundes be, and I will send yow a warr[a]nt
for a brace or two. I will soner p[er]forme thys p[rom]ysse
then helpe yow to xl^li more of Mr Dudly the next terme, but I
will do what I can to satisfye y^or desyre thein [therein].

Yow do very wisely in my oppynyon, & like one that fereth
god, to haue a remembrans of your generall account, & to
thynk this late patent yow haue, wherby yow shalbe made an
acconīn [accountant] in the [Ex]chequer, will not dyscharge
the greater. I p[ra]ye yow cm̄ed [commend] me to y^or son,
& to hys very good & modeste wiff, except I be myche
deceyved, as I am suer I am not, & thank her for the fattest
cople of conyes I did see this yere. Fare ye hartely well &
god contynew you in helthe & send yow & me abundans of his
grace. 1 of Dec. 1579.

Yours as yow know assured duryng lyf,
WILLM CORDELLS. [*sic*]

To my verie lovinge frend John Lennard Esquyer Highe
Sherife of Kent [2] this lre be dd [delivered].

About a year later John sends Sir William a more valuable
present than game, viz., 'two potts of sylver,' and this causes
him to write the following letter of thanks, in which he says he
sends John ' a warrant for 2 does at Knolle Park nye unto you

---

[1] Ashdown Forest, Sussex?
[2] John was High Sheriff in 1571; *ante*, pp. 7, 20-1.

and bycause you shall not surfitt of the fleshe I send ... a oxhead of very good claret wine.'

After my very herte commendacons vnto to yow gentle Mr Lennard, & to good M^{res} Lennard yor wiffe, wth my like thankes vnto yow for the two potts of sylũ [sylver] yow sent me by my seunt [servant] for a newe yers gyfte as he sayd. Albeyt I haue juste cawse to geve yow herte thankes for yor good will thein, yet I was not contented wth hime for the bryngyng of them, for that the gyfte do the farre surmount ony plesur that ether I haue, or can mynyster vuto yow, & between vs beyng ancyent frendes, & as made by mutual amyte, thyngs of smaller valew myght serve to recognyse that love and frendshippe that one of vs bereth to another, I can saye no more. Whereas yow had before of me one that for frendshippe sake was y^{or} own, now by this mean tyme besides the same yow have me y^{or} bonde frend; and god wyllynge yf we doth lyve I will by godds grace recompense fully y^{or} charge & good will. Yet to be pleyn wth yow I did & doo p[ro]fesse as myche frendshippe towards yow wtoute [without] this great plere [pleasure] as one frend maye owe vnto other. And somewhat to answer y^{or} greatuyte & to observe the custom of o^r [our] countrey, that ys at the begynyng of the newe yere one frende to vysitt another wth some plere [pleasure], I do send vnto yow her enclosed one warrant for 2 does in Knoll Parke nye vnto yow.[1] And bycause you shall not sfitt [surfitt] of the flesshe, I send unto yow & to Mrs Lennard a oxhed of very good claret wyne, except I be deceyved of my frendes. Accept yt as a remembrance sent from y^{or} assured frend in token of this newe yere the which I wysshe as prperos [prosperous] vnto yow as I wold haue myselff.[2] From St. Ives this last of December 1580.
Your very ass[u]red frende & olde acqueyntans
WM. CORDLLE. [sic]

There is endorsed on this letter, in the handwriting of Samson Lennard, 'Sir W. Cordels curteous letter to John

---

[1] As John was, at the date of this letter, living at Knole, I am unable to understand this passage.

[2] This shows how much more it was the custom in those days to give presents on New Year's Day than is now the case in England. Another instance of this is the entry in some accounts rendered to John Lennard by a steward or bailiff of 'Item Geven amongst them y^t broughte presents to my master on newe yeres daye iij^s iiij^d.' See also *post*, p. 210.

Lennard.' Sir William died in the following year, and in him John must have lost a very good and influential friend. Another friend of John's was Sir Henry Cobham,[1] who writes thus to him :—

Mr. Lennard I do hartely thanke yow for yo^{ur} cleare dealenge. I am to pleasure yow or yo^{urs} in any thynge I maye & thereof assure yo^{ur} selfe ; thus wyth my most harty comendacyons, I bid yow farewelle.
From Sutton the xviij of Aprylle
                Yo^{ur} assured frend.   HENRY COBHAM.
To my woorshipfull good frend Mr. John Leonard esquier at Knowle.

There arose, however, a coolness between John and Sir Henry, for one of our papers is described in Lord Dacre's catalogue as 'Notes of a difference between John Lennard and Sir Henry Cobham,' and is in John's own handwriting. Sir Henry appears to have asked John, being a magistrate in Kent, to undertake a somewhat delicate inquiry for him in the village of Otford, which is only about five miles from Knole where John was then living. From these notes John appears to be quite ignorant of any cause of dispute between them ; and the above letter which John quotes, seems to have been sent by way of thanking him for holding this inquiry for Sir Henry. The 'notes' are as follows :—

Abowte Ester last past Sr Henry Cobham sent to me his lre [letter] by Mr. Sheres, beyng vycary[2] of Sutton, therby earnestly requestyng me, as I wold do hym any pleasure, to examyn a mayden dwellyng att Ottford, late hys s[er]vant, vpon certeyne ynterrogataries whych he sent me enclosed yn the lre.

'The ynterrogataryes, wyth the maydes answere to euỹe [every] of them, I sent to hym agayne enclosed yn a lre wythyn a fewe dayes by my s[er]vant. Yt semed by the ynterrogataryes, & by talke that I had wyth the foreseyd

[1] Sir Henry Cobham (1538 to 1605) was a celebrated diplomatist, and was entrusted with many important missions to foreign Powers.
[2] Vicar.—*C. D.*

M{r} Sheres, who was pryvy to the secrecy of the matter (as he sayd), that S{r} Henry was had yn gelowsy [jealousy] by my lady hys wyf for vnmete famylyaryty wyth the mayde.

The maydes aunswere to the ynterrogataryes declared S{r} Henry, & her self, to be ynnocent, & to be suspected wythout any cause at all gyven on àny of theyr behalf, wherof I was ryght gladde, (and so as I thynke) I wrate to S{r} Henry.

I can not yet fynde hys seyd lre sent to me, nor any copy of my lre sent to hym, I hope that I shall; but as I remember I was so bolde by my lre sent to S{r} Henry wyth the ynterrogataryes to put hym yn mynde that God had sent hym & my ladye hys wyf goodly chyldren betwene them, & the rather he beyng the stronger vesselle was to beare paciently that wronge accusacyon (as I thougth yt to be).

Whereapon I receyved from S{r} Henry another lre the copy of yt ensueth.

John then quotes the preceding letter from Sir Henry, and continues:—

Yn Ester t{r}me [term], or Trynyty t{r}me next followyng, S{r} Henry and I mette yn the Sterre Chamber, & there for my doyng yn that matter he gave me dowble thankes, & desyred me to gyve hym some carpe frye, which I promysed hym & sent hym thys last sommer, I thynke fyve hundreth.

Worse than thys have not I doon to S{r} Henry Cobham, yf for thys he nowe beare me dysplesure he offereth me wronge, and God forgyve vs both.

John Lennard's wife died on October 26th, 1585,[1] and appears to have been buried the following day at Chevening.[2] There remains the following memoranda of the expenses connected with her funeral, but it is difficult to see how all the necessary arrangements could have been made out in the short space of twenty-four hours.[3] The first memorandum seems to be a rough estimate of the persons for whom it was necessary to provide funeral garments, and the second one a more detailed estimate of what they would actually cost.

[1] See inscription on tomb.   [2] *Ch. Reg.*
[3] As to date of her death and funeral, *vide* also *post*, p. 49, *n*. 3.

'BLACKS' FOR FUNERAL

The total cost of providing mourning clothes for the near relations of the deceased and for her husband's relations, servants, and retainers amounted to 76*l.* 18*s.* 8*d.* Until quite recent years there remained a trace of this custom of providing the mourners with mourning, as all persons attending funerals were given black gloves and long black silk scarves to wear over the shoulder, and it was then the habit of such clergymen as were careful to take care of these scarves and give them to their wives to make into silk dresses. The memoranda as to the cost of Mrs. Lennard's funeral only show us the cost of the mourning, but if the other expenses connected therewith were in proportion, the total cost must have been very considerable, allowing for the difference in the purchasing power of money now and in those days.

It is clear, whoever it may have been who wrote the memoranda,[1] that he was determined not to waste money in giving mourning where it was not necessary to do so. This can be seen on the first memorandum by observing that some names are crossed out, as if, on second thoughts, the person who drew this paper up had been careful to eliminate from the list the names of as many as he could of those he had at first put down.

A note of such blacke as are convenyent [proper] for ye funeralle. One Harald yf it be used at women's funerals.

Black to hang ye Church	gowns iij	x Scholemaster
[2]Mistress Lennard and her mayde	yards at	x Maykins
Mistress Nevell and her mayde	xiij[s] iiij[d]	x Roger
Mistress Covert and her mayde	ye yard	x Harrys
[3] Mistress Walsingham & her mayde		x Smallwood
Mistress Elizabeth	for ye	x Edmond
Mistress Anne	children	x Jakson ·
Mr Lennard & Mr Nevells daughters	ij yard &	x Blanks
[4] My Aunt Lennard	a quarter	x Parseley
	ye yard x[s]	x Wyllm Stere
		x Walkelyn
		x Coper

[1] Probably Samson, John Lennard's eldest son.
[2] Daughter-in-law.   [3] Daughters.   [4] William Lennard's wife?

HISTORY OF THE LENNARDS

1 {
My father
Mr Covert iij or iiij servants
Mr Nevell ij servants
Mr Lennard ij servants
} clokes iiij yards at xvj^s ye yard

2 Samuel one servant
Henry Nevelle
Edward Nevelle
3 {
Henrye Lennard
Gregorye Lennard
Thomas Lennard
Christopher Nevelle a cote
}
4 My oncle a gowne
Her mayd servants
Wakers wyf
Cannoes wydowe

Clokes for children ij yards & a quarter ye yard xiiij^s

x ~~Coper~~
x Burton
x Phyllup
~~Th. Coke~~
. . . . . .

Sybelle
Anne Blank
Dorothye Lambert
} gowns ij yards iij quarters ye yard at viij^s

For xx s[er]vyng men cotes a yard di [& a half] ye yard viij^s
For xij pore women gownes ij yards di [& a half] at ye yard vij^s

x Rafe
x Tapsell
x Ch. Cater
~~Old Thomas~~
x ~~Mylles~~
x ~~Jack Waller~~
(~~Mr Nevelle man~~)
Neylborod hys man

One harrold yf any be vsed for a maryed wyf
Black to hang the Church & [cover?] ye women
Black for gentlewomen

Mrs Lennard & her mayde vj yards at xiij^s iiij^d ye yard . . . . . iiij^{li}
Mrs Nevyle & her mayde lykewyse . . iiij^{li}
Mrs Covert & her mayde lykewyse . . iiij^{li}
Mrs Walsingham & her mayde lykewyse . iiij^{li}
Mrs Elizabeth . . . . . . xl^s
Mrs Anne . . . . xl^s
Mrs Lennard of Chevening . . . xl^s
Mr Nevyls daughters . ij
Mr Lennards daughters iiij
Mr Walsinghams daughter
} xiiij yards at viij^s ye yard

} xxvij^{li} xij^s

---
[1] Sons-in-law. [2] Son. [3] GrandSons.
[4] Possibly Thomas, John Lennard's brother?

'BLACKS' FOR FUNERAL

Mr Covert hymself a cloke iiij yards
   at xiij^s iiij^d ye yard . . . iiij marc
His iiij men vj yards at viij^s ye yard xlviij^s
   (If he mean to were his mornyng
     cloke longer than the funeral
     day, or els ij servants as the
     other have)
Mr Nevyle for his cloke . . . iiij marc
Hys ij men . . . . . xxiv^s
Mr Sampson for his cloke . . iiij marc
Hys ij men . . . . . xxiiij^s
Samuels cloke . . . . iiij marc
Hys man . . . . . xij^s
[1] Mr W. Lennard a gowne . . iiij marc

                                 xviij^{li} xiiij^s viij^d

vj men chyldren xij yards att viij^s ye yard vj^{li}
xxx yards for xx s[er]vyngmen att viij^s ye
   yard . . . . xij^{li}
iiij maydes xj yards & a quarter at viij^s ye
   yd. . . . . iiij^{li} vj^s
xij poore women ij yards di [& a half]
   apeece att vj^s ye yard . . . . x^{li} x^s

                                 xxx^{li} xij^s [2]

I haue a . . . cape
another cape for myself if that fasshyon be not vsed.

We have also the following bill of the 'blacks' sold for this funeral:—

Black sowld for the funerall of Mrs Leonrd this xxix day of october A° 1584.[3]

Item. xxv yerds of fyne black at xviij^s xxij^{li} x^s
  „   xvij yerds fyne black at xiiij^s . xj^{li} xviij^s
  „   xix yerds d. [*i.e.* a half] black
      at xij^s iiij^d . . . . xij^{li} vj^d

---

[1] No doubt John Lennard's brother.
[2] This total does not appear to be correct.
[3] I am unable to reconcile this date with that ascribed to the death of Mrs. Lennard in the Chevening Register—namely, October 27th, 1585, or with that on her tomb, which is 'Octo. 26, 1585.' The writing on this account is quite clear, and leaves no room for doubt as to the figures on it.

Item. xxv yerds iij q^{rs} black at x^s	.	xij^{li}	xvij^s vj^d
„ 38 yerds of black at viij^s	.	xv^{li}	vj^s
„ xliij yerds d : black at ix^s	.	xix^{li}	xj^s vj^d.

While on the subject of accounts, the following items taken from an account may be inserted, as, though of no special interest in themselves, they throw light on the prices which obtained in those days. They are accounts delivered by a servant named Johnson to John Lennard, and although the wages and charges of this servant are to our present ideas very low, we may infer that he was a head servant or steward, as it is not probable that any other than a head man could at that period have made out accounts. The accounts are headed :—

A note of suche Reckenyngs as ys betwyxte my maister & me for my waygs [wages] & expencs in his affayres as followeth :

Item. for my waygs for the laste yere the some   xl^s [1]
„ for my waygs this yere from the xvjth daye of Aprill vnto the xvjth daye of October beyinge di [half] yere . . l^s
„ more for my boord waygs all mydsomer terme laste . . . . . . xiiij^s
„ Receved of my maister the xxviijth daye of October in the eyghtenthe [1576] yere of the Raigne of our Sovereign ladie Quene Elizabeth uppon all accompts waygs and laying out . . v^{li} v^s vj^d
ye tythe of Erythe dyscharged fullye the some of . . . . xxxiiij^s
Item. for my expenses Thursdaye Frydaye & Satterdaye when you were at my Lady Dacres funerall [2] . . . . . ij^s vj^d

---

[1] Another account mentioned his wages as being 40s. a year, so I cannot follow the reason for the next item, which makes these wages come to 50s. for half a year.

[2] This is an interesting entry; it refers, no doubt, to the funeral of the Dowager Lady Dacre, widow of the Lord Dacre who was hanged. It is true that this sheet of accounts bears no date, but it appears to form part of the previous accounts, dated 1576.

Item. for my horse mete then and for one showe [shoe]	xv^d
Item. for my expenses Thursdaye & Frydaye & Satterdaye nexte after the Funerall when you sent me to my lo. [Lord] Thresorers [Treasurer's]. . . .	ij^s vj^d
Item for my dynner supper on Wednesdaye & my dynner & supper on Thursdaye & my breakfast on Frydaye when you sent me to my lorde Threasorers before Mydlent the sum	ij^s iiij
Item for bothyres [1] [boat hires] at seuall [several] tymes & for my lodgynge at Westminster	xviij^d
Item for my horsemeat then & for my bothyre	xx^d
Item for Tomsouns drynkyng & myne at Eryth	vj^d
Item for my dynners & horsebayt at twyce sendynge me to my lord Treasurers when the court laye at Grenwyche . . .	xxj^d
Item for a book of Statutes in easter terme last	xvj^d
Item for my boardwages from Mondaye till Satterday when you left me to p[ro]vyde yor wyne at 6^d a mele	vj^s

One of Johnson's statements of accounts is made out on the back of a grocer's bill, which is too long to give in full. It is headed: 'Bought of Jasper Watson grocer the xxj day of December 1573.' The bill gives items supplied each month until November 4th, 1574, when a receipt is given for the total sum due, which amounted only to 11*l*. 10*s*. Many of the items of this bill are charged at prices absolutely higher than they would cost now, without making any allowance for the great difference in the purchasing power of money which now exists. It will be noticed that very large quantities of pepper and various spices were consumed, but neither tea, coffee, nor cocoa, which go far to swell the modern grocer's bill, had come into European use at the period that John Lennard was running up

---

[1] Bot. : a middle English form of boat.—*C. D.* As to importance of the Thames as a waterway see also *post*, p. 233.

an account with Mr. Jasper Watson. The following is the bill for December 1573:—

Resons vj^{li}	xxj^d
Proynes iiij^{li}	xiiij^d
Corrants ij^{li}	xx^d
Peper I^{li}	iij^s iiij^d
Clovis ij^{oz}	xiiij^d
L Mase j^{oz}	xij^d
M Mase j^{oz}	x^d
Nutmegs ij^{oz}	x^d
Ginger ij^{oz}	viij^d
Sinamond ij^{oz}	xij^d
Suger vj^{li}	vj^s vj^d
	19^s 11^d

When one once begins to give items of accounts it is very difficult to know where to stop, and I have had very great doubt whether to give here any more examples; at last, having reflected that such persons as are not interested in them can skip over these lists, I have decided to give the further following examples of John Lennard's household payments, dated 1583:—

Payd to Romney ye xiijth of ffebruare for ye cariadge of halfe a tonne of Wyne & a rundlet of maulmesy of 10 hondredweight	viij^s iiij^d
to him for a barrel of herryng of iij hondred	ij^s vj^d
to him for a basket of fishe of ij hondred	xx^d
to him for a quarter of salt of v hondred	iiij^s ij^d
to him for a hondred of hoppes	x^d
for a crocke [earthen pot] for ye butler to put salt yn	j^d
for whyttynge to scoure vessells wth	j^d
delyued to Davy Howells boy to fetch russhes [1]	iij^s iiij^d
for ij pounds of sope	vj^d
to ye cooke who hadd boughte somych potato roots as cost [2]	xij^d

[1] Rushes for strewing the floors were still, in the time of Elizabeth, part of the ordinary provision of all households.

[2] This is a very early notice of potatoes, which some books say were not introduced into England until a few years later.

ACCOUNTS

for provyson agaynst my Lord Montagues [1] comynge as appereth by a byll therof . .	vj^{li} xvij^s
Payd to Rychard Whyte for takynge of iij dozen and x moules at xij^d ye dozen [2] . .	iij^s x^d
payd to Richard Martyn ye iiijth of Apryll 1584 for ye sawynge of viij^c [800] of boords at xx^d the C.	xiiij^s iiij^d
Rec. for v kettles beynge ould brasse y^t wayed xlij pounds at iiij^d ye pound . . .	xiiij^s
Rec. of ye bell founder for vij^c [700] of Bryckes	vij^s
payd to Clement Denys of Shoram [3] for two quarters and two bushells of wheate at xx^s the quarter [4].	xlv^s
payd to Humffrey the Drugger for two shovells	x^d
payd for four halters	viij^d
The vijth of Decemb^r for iij bellowes & one Launterne at eyght pence ye peece . .	ij^s viij^d
payd for foure plates to hould Candle y^n ye stalle	viij^d
payd for two syves to goe to Chevenynge .	xij^d
p^d for a shawld to dresse corne wthall . .	xij^d
for v newe kettelles y^t wayd xl pounds & a haulf at xj^d ye pound	xxxvij^s ij^d
for iij dozen of woode spones at iij^d ye dozen .	ix^d
for ij elles of canvas to mende bedds at x^d ye elle	xx^d
for an hundreth of thre penye nayelles . .	iij^d
To a wench that brought sprotts [5] . . .	ij^d
for three pounds of Candle weeke [6] . . .	xij^d
for flaunders tyle [7] to ye scoolyon . . .	iiij^d
for C. [100] of iiij^d nayle, and C. of iij^d nayle & an C. of ij^d nayle	ix^d
payd ye sayd day for two yards of Bunter [bunting ?] at viij^d the yarde . . .	xvj^d

[1] Probably A. Browne, 1st Viscount Montague; one of the judges of Mary Queen of Scots.

[2] Moles cost about 1s. to 2s. a dozen to catch at the present time.

[3] Shoreham, near Sevenoaks.

[4] A great price, considering the then value of money. Wheat has been sold as low as this within the last ten years, and in 1894-5 the average price was only 21s. 5d.

[5] Rushes.—C. D.

[6] Showing that it was then customary for households to make their own candles.

[7] Flanders brick : Bath brick.

For three yards of Baveller at iiij^d ye yarde .	xij^d
for a mynsynge [mincing] knyfe & a Choppinge knyfe	ij^s vj^d
For a Dozen of bromes	iij^d
for half an hundreth of iiij^d nayles to sett upp ye seat yn ye parke	ij^d
for a rowlynge pynne for ye Cooke . . .	ij^d
for a quyer of paper	iiij^d
Payd ye xxiiijth day of Decemb^r 1583 unto Henrye Blaucke for hys haulfe yeres wages due at Alhaloutyde [Nov. 1st] ye sayd yere .	xx^s [1]
for rozen	ij^d
to Pyrretts boy y^t broughte a capon to my Master	ij^d
To mother [used in the sense of Mrs.] Wood ye bruers wyfe for ye makynge of iiij quarters of mawlt at xij^d ye quarter I paid ye xth of Januar 1583	iiij^s
It. to Davy Howell the xvij day of January for haulf a bushell of Oysters & hys chardges yn fetching them from London . . .	iij^s iiij^d
For a yard & a halfe of Buckram . . .	xviij^d
Payd ye same day for mendyng of ye musterd quarne[2]	ij^d
Payd to Crouke ye Spuyngler[3] ye xxvth of January	xx^s
for a stone pot to put yest yn	j^d
Payd to Basset ye viij of Februarye for fower yron hookes for ye Cooke to take up meate wth	ij^s
Item geven amongst them y^t broughte presents to my master on newe yeres daye . .	iij^s iiij^d

While on the subject of prices paid for things in those days it is worth mentioning that I have a contract between John Lennard and a 'mylwryght' named Cobbe to build a mill for him, and to receive for his pay 1s. 2d. a day and 'also meate & drinke.'

[1] I have no clue as to what position Blaucke filled, but 20s. for half a year's service seems very small wages for any person.

[2] Quern : a stone hand-mill.

[3] Springler : one who makes springles, *i.e.* rods about four feet long for thatching.

The following letter shows that in one of his disputes John had recourse to the process of the Ecclesiastical Courts against an adversary named Boswell. In those times the Ecclesiastical Courts had still jurisdiction over laymen, and they enforced obedience to their decrees by the power they then possessed of excommunicating those who showed themselves recalcitrant. At one period excommunication was a very terrible disability to be under, as anyone daring to trade with, or even speak to, a person under that ban ran the risk of being subjected to the same punishment himself. There is nothing to show whether this Mr. Boswell was the same person with whom we have seen he had a dispute some twenty years before about the purchase of timber,[1] nor have I found any clue to the cause of his proceeding against him in these Courts, but it was probably to enforce payment of tithes. From the contents of this letter, John appears as usual to have carried his point, and to have got the better of his opponent.

My Worshipfull & good Master this ys to testifie youe that the next spũall [spiritual] cõ̀te [court] day shalbe kept on Mondaye next. And the p[roc]esse y^t I tooke oute last ageynst [against] Mr Boswell was an excommnycacon geñally [generally] directed, omibiz [omnibus] et singlis [singulis] clicis [clericis] et trate [litteratis] quibuscnque [quibuscunque] either in citie or contrye. The w^{cu} excommunycacon I delivered to the mynister of St Clements who hath it, as he telleth me, at this p̃sent [present] in his own custodie. But he sayeth that he hath not as yet denounced the same exc. [excommunication] accordyng to the tenor thereof, because he was wylled to stay it for that yor W. [worship] and Mr Boswell were in talke upon an agreem̃^{t} between yor selfes, and as he thought youe were agreed before this tyme. Neyther yntendeth he to doe anye thynge therein untylle he heare farther from us. The bylle of charges of the last tm̃e [term] cometh to xix^s viij^d; the whiche Mr Boswell p[ro]mysed to paye me this next tm̃e. The other byll of the tm̃e before I delyvered to yor W. the wch as I remember cometh to xxj^s or xxij^s. The doctors[2] fees of this last tm̃e

[1] *Ante*, p. 40 *et seq.*
[2] Formerly, those who practised before the Ecclesiastical Courts were Doctors of Law, not Barristers.

were not putt in the bylle of costs neyther of the tm̄e before, so farre as I can remember. And thus most humblie acknowledgynge my dutie to yor Wo. I com̄ytt youe to the p[ro]teccyon of Almightie god wth most hartie prayer fo^r yor long lyfe & welfare. London this xxiijth of May 1589 yor wo. s[er]uant at com̄and.

ANTHONY GREGORY.

This hath been a troblesome and a heavie whitsontyde unto me by reason of my brother Edward Clarks death.

The following unsigned and undated document is endorsed 'Brydgers accusacyon by Roucet,' and is curious as showing how suspicious a circumstance non-attendance at church was looked upon in those days :—

This shalbe to setefy your worshipe that I haue to declare vnto you of olde bredgers mysorder towards your Worshipe ; firste takynge up of a house of of [off] your grounde and settynge of it one [on] his owne, and all so [also] of your stalles, the rakes and mangers are myssinge and gone, one racke he bathe conveide away to a barne of his, and all so he hathe Inclosed to the valew of anaker [an acre] or more of howre brooke to his own yuse, and all so for the myseorder of his house ; firste that he hathe kepte a copper [cooper] at worke in his house working with your palles [pales], and all so the ashe that growethe uppon the grounde ; likewise a furder [further] mysorder that he kepethe shuche persons in his house that hathe not com at the Churche, but lyethe lurkynge at home watchinge for theire pray [prey] when honeste men are at the Churche to heare gods word ; and allso he hath sett a poor womin in one of youre houses whiche I am muche troubled withe all, and bathe not come at the Churche in x weekes together, but lies at home to watche for her praye, so that amonge them I can keepe nothynge in quiett ; more over he kepethe v dogges in his house that my wife cannot keppe anegge [an egg] for them, my wife sett a hen of xiiij egges and he cam and spoilde them all, and I am In doupte that they will do the like by your swann & your turtle.[1] More over his sonn, Harvey Bredger, hathe taken a gate from the new parke, and hathe sett it vppon his grounde, and allso he bathe a greate Ireon harrowe of youres for two horse to drawe, longe agoo they did name it to be youre harrowe, now since they said you had none theire, and all so a greate

[1] Turtle dove?

SYSTEM OF ARRANGING MARRIAGES 57

many of thinge more may be founde if they be prively searched for.

The following note on this document is in John Lennard's handwriting :—

A house taken down from the place & set on hys ground—Racks & mangers taken away, one rack taken away & set in a barne of his—wrongfully enclosing of an acre of ground at Hoores brooke ; he keepeth a cupper that felleth ashes & spoileth pales to make his gayne ; he kepeth divers lewd persons that do spoil about the house & grounds—his son hath p[ur]loined a gate from the new park, & he hath p[ur]loined a harrow.

In the days when John Lennard lived and for many years later marriages were usually arranged by the father of the lady to be married. He arranged with the parents of the proposed husband if they were living, or otherwise with the suitor himself, how much he would give his daughter, and how much her intended husband would settle on her, and on the children of the marriage. It frequently happened that the sum of money which a father agreed to pay over as his daughter's dowry was either received by the father of her intended husband for his own use, or else in order to provide portions for his younger children ; while he on his part settled the landed estate upon his son and upon the issue of the intended marriage. After these details had been arranged the young people were allowed to meet with the object of their agreeing to the proposed match ; and one can imagine that, when parental authority was so much stronger than it is now, the position of a girl who refused to fulfil an engagement to marry which her father had arranged for her would have been far from a pleasant one.

In this connection I may mention two very interesting deeds of the time of Henry VI. among our family papers concerning the marriage of Joan, daughter of Sir Thomas Dacre. The first of these deeds is dated November 1445, and was made between Sir Thomas Dacre of the one part and John Filoll of the other part. In it it was agreed that 'John should have to wyfe Jobane doughter to the seid sire Thomas yf upon sight and spech badde bytwene [t]hem they can therto agree to, the which sight and speche withyn reasonable tyme to be hadde in London,' and part of the bargain was that John was to give Sir Thomas 200*l.*, half to be paid at the date of the marriage. Some six months later, in June 1446, we find Sir Thomas Dacre entering into a fresh agreement about his daughter's 'mariage.' This time it concerns not only 'Johane' but also her sister Philippa, whom he proposes to marry, the one to Richard and the other to Robert, two sons of Sir Roger Fynes. I have no means of knowing Philippa's age at this period, but Joan was then about thirteen years old.[1] Sir Thomas was to receive 200 marks for the marriage of Johane and 250 marks for that of Philippa. The intended father-in-law, Sir Roger, was to 'doo his parte to fecche the seyde dowghters to London atte his own costes.' That John Fyloll had not given up all pretension to the hand of Joan[2] when this deed was executed is shown by the following clause therein contained, namely:—'that there [London] John Fyloll be not lett to see the seide Johane & there with here to speke.'

At this distance of time I have no hope of discovering why John Fyloll was to be thus jilted, and not apparently by Joan, but by her father, as the agreement to prevent the young folks meeting in London obviously must have originated with him. As we shall see[3] the marriage contemplated by the second agreement duly took place, and Sir Thomas Dacre's two daughters, Joan and Philippa, married respectively Sir Roger Fynes' two sons, Richard and Robert.

The deeds in question are interesting and not very long: in early times deeds were not long, and, as a rule, the older the deed the shorter it is. They gradually became spun out to a terrible length, and got to their greatest length in the century lately completed, when at last an Act, passed in 1881, had the effect of greatly curtailing the length of ordinary conveyances. When

---

[1] The C. P. says that she was twenty-five in 1458.
[2] The name is spelt differently in each deed.
[3] *Post*, p. 170.

SIR THOMAS DACRE

deeds were at their longest, instead of dating the deed, say '15 July 1799,' it would run thus: 'the 15th day of July in the 39th year of the reign of our Sovereign Lord George the 3d by the Grace of God of Great Britain, France and Ireland, King Defender of the Faith &c., and in the year of our Lord 1799;' and in a like verbose manner, instead of simply naming the amount of the consideration money, say '£500,' the conveyancers of those times would say, 'the sum of £500 sterling of good and lawful money of Great Britain and Ireland well and truly paid;' and the whole of the document would be conceived and drawn in this spirit. Fortunately for the patience of anyone who may care to read these two deeds, Henry VI.'s reign was anterior to the period when lawyers used in their documents as many words as they could possibly manage to employ. The date of the first of these deeds is November 23rd, 1445.

For the information of any reader who is not conversant with antiquarian matters I may mention here that at one period the date of all legal documents was reckoned by the year of the reign of the particular sovereign in whose reign it was executed. In order, therefore, to arrive at the exact date, it is necessary to know in what month the reign of that sovereign commenced; and also to remember that until 1752 the new year began on March 25th.

The first deed is endorsed contemporaneously: 'Covenauntes for the mariadge of the dowghter of Sir Thomas Dacre knyght to Jhon Filol esqiryer,' and goes on:—

This endenture made at london the xxiijth day of Nouember the xxiiijth yeer of King Henry the sixt after the conquest, [1445] bytwyxt sire Thomas Dacre knyght on yat [that] one part, and John Filoll Esquier on that other part; Witnesseth that the seid parties been accorded in the fourme ensuyng That is to sey, that the seid John shall haue to wyfe Jabane doughter to the seid sire Thomas, yf upon sight and speche hadde bytwene hem they can therto agree: To the which sight and speche withyn resonable tyme to be badde at london, as for the part of the seid Jabane, the seid sire Thomas shall do effectuelly and resonably his part at ye comon costes of ye seid sire

Thomas and John, in cas the seid John and Jahane after the seid sight and speche so badde to ye seid mariage agree. And in cas the seid John therto agree, and ye seid Jabane not, then the seid costes shull be born onely by the seid sire Thomas: And yn cas the seid Jabane to ye seid mariage agree and the seid John not, than [then] the said costes shull be born onely by the seid John: And the seid sire Thomas shall yeve[1] to the seid John and Jahane, time of ther lyves, lawfull estate of londes and tenements in the shire of Sussex, to the yeerly value of x^{li} ouer all charges: And in cas Thomas lord Dacre dye lyvyng Elizabeth wyfe to the seid sire Thomas, that then he shall yeve to the seid John and Jabane, time of her [their] lyves, lawfull estate of other ten pounds worth londes and tenements yerely, ouer all charges of such londs and tenements, as by ye deth of ye seid lord, to the seid sire Thomas shall come: And that as good suertee [surety] as kan be deuised by ye counseilles of both ye seid parties shall be hadde, so that no (? discontynuance) shall be made of the inheritance of ye seid Elizabeth, but that hir issue may as seurely [surely] rejoise[2] the seid enheritance as though by the deth of the seid Elizabeth it shold descend, And for this the seid John shall do, make, lawfull joynture to ye seid Jahane, time of here lyve, of xl mark worth londes and tenements yeerly aboue all charges in the shire of Sussex, and yeve to the seid Sire Thomas cc^{li} of money, the half therof to be paide at the tyme of ye seid mariage, And that other half yōf [thereof] to be payde withyn half a yeer then next folowyng, yf suche seurtee of thenheritance of the seid Elizabeth be badde by that tyme as is aboue reherced, or elles yf withyn ye seid tyme the seid Jahane be enherited in xx^{li} worth lond: Also, by thauyse [the advice] of the seid counseilles, resonable seurtee shall be badde that ye issue male comyng betwene the seid John and Jahane, shall enherite or haue by the ordinaunce of the seid John, c^{li} worth lond of estate of fee after the deth of the seid John, at suche tyme as the seid issue shall come to full age.

To the which couenaunts to be holde[n], and performed on either partie, eche of the seid parties byndeth hym to other in [? c^{li} defaced] to paie.

In witnesse wherof the parties abouseid to this writyng enterchangeably haue putte her [their] seales, writen at the place, day, and yeer aboue reherced.

[1] 'Give.' Middle English.—*C. D.*
[2] To enjoy, or have the fruition of. Obsolete.—*Ibid.*

SIR THOMAS DACRE 61

The second one is endorsed : ' A graunt from Sir Thomas Daker knyght to Sir Roger fines knyght, of the ij daughters & heyres of the seyd Sir Thomas, to be maryed to ij sonnes of the sayed Sir Roger.'

This endenture maad betwyne Sir Thomas Dacre knyght on that oon parte, and Sir Roger Fenys knyght on the othere parte, Wytnessyth that the sayde Sir Thomas bathe graunted the seyde Sir Roger the mariagys of Johane & Philippa, the dowghters & beires of the seyde Sir Thomas, to be maryed to Richard & Robart, sones of the seide Sir Roger, paying to the seyde Sir Thomas for the mariage of that dowghter, of the said dowghters, that shall be maried to the seyde Richard, atte day of that mariage, cc marks of lawful mone of Englond,[1] and for that dowghter, of the seyde dowghters, that shall be maried to the seyde Robart, atte the day of that mariage, ccl marks of lawful mone of Englond : Purueyed all way that yff so be that the seyde Johane agre to be weddyd to John Fyloll, that thanne this graunte & couuenaunt as for the mariage of the seide Jobane, be voyde & of no strength : And that the seyde Sir Roger shall doo his parte to fecche the seyde dowghters to London, atte his own costes & expenses, withynn resonable tyme, and that there the sayde John Fyloll be not lett to see the seide Johane, & there with here to speke ; And that the seyde Sir Thomas shall lawfully assent, agre, & avowe the seyde fecchying of the seyde dowghters, and all othere thyngs that ys expedyent, & nedefull to the seyde mariages, atte costis of the seide Sir Roger; And that the seyde mariages shall be doo atte the costes & expencis of the seyde Roger, And that the seyde Sir Thomas shall not aleyn, ne yeve, no londes, ne tenementys in to disheiritaunce of the seyde dowghters, that he or hys wyffe holdyth, or byth sesid[2] in demene, or in revercionn, or eny man to theyr use ; And that the seyd Sir Thomas, nothyng shall doo, whereby the seyde dowghters, of the seyde londes & tenymentys myght be disheirityd,[3] to the which couuenauntis & grauntis to be

[1] The payment made to Sir Thomas is stated, in a petition to the Lord Chancellor made by ' Richard Fenys ' and ' Jobane ' after Sir Thomas's death, to be ' xviij^c m̃c.'

[2] Be Seized : ' bith,' early form of ' be.'—*C. D.*

[3] After the decease of Sir Thomas Dacre his widow Elizabeth unsuccessfully attempted to defeat the settlement as far as it related to property in Norfolk, but Joan and her husband Richard Fynes obtained a decision in their favour.—*E. C. P.* Bundle 27, No. 501.

holde & performed on ethere party, eche of the seyde partis byndyth hem, eche to others in c^{li} to be payd. In witnesse wherof the partys aforsayde to the present writyng enterchaungably have put to here seallis, yeve & writen the first day of June in the xxiiij^{ti} yere of Kyng Henri the sixt, aftere the conquest of Englond [1446].

We have seen that John Lennard's eldest daughter, Mary, married Guildford Walsingham, and in the negotiations for that marriage John arranged the whole business with Guildford's parents, and there is no evidence of the young people's inclinations in the matter being even consulted by their elders. Also in the case of the marriage of his eldest son, Samson, to Margaret Fynes the match seems to have been arranged entirely by the elders, but in respect to this marriage we have unfortunately no correspondence.

Collins's 'Peerage,' referring to the marriage of Samson Lennard and Margaret Fynes, says that 'the first overture for this alliance came from the lady's relations, though it was so desirable a one not only from her noble birth and great expectations, but also from her singular worthiness;' and as an authority for this statement it gives the following note: 'This circumstance appears from a passage in a paper written by John Lennard *penes* Lord Dacre.' Collins is not quite accurate as to this 'passage,' which runs thus: 'Ould Mr. Lennard being solycyted by dyverse of my Lord Dacres hys nere kyndred to marry his eldest sonne unto thys gentlewoman, when he demanded what porcyon of money should be geven wyth her yt was styll told hym that thys possibilytye [1] was a porcyon great enoughe. . . . Hereupon Mr. Lennard proceded to thys match takyng no further but a bare promysse of fyve hundred markes in money.' [2]

That even as late as the eighteenth century the first steps in arranging marriages frequently appear to have been taken

---

[1] 'Thys possibilytye' refers to Margaret's reversion to the title and estates of the Dacres, should she survive her brother Gregory, Lord Dacre, and he leave no issue.

[2] 'The Greyfes of M^{rls} Margaret Lennard.' *Post*, p. 80.

by the parents is shown by the following letter, which was written by Mr. Walter Dawson, who had at one time been his agent, to Dacre Barrett.

Ardmagh ye 24th of Decemr 1714

Sr.

I have been of Late very Infirm. I have onely two Sons, ye youngest is not healthy, but I thank God my eldest is, and is now goeing in the 24th yeare of his age, whom I should be very Glad to see setled in my time; he has been six years at the university in Dublin, and has had all other advantages of Education that this Kingdom could aford. I have a Reall Esstate being 40 tates[1] in right of my wife and my father, yt is worth 600li or more P. ann : it is in the county of Monaghan, and three thousand pounds worth of wood on it, part of it Joynes yr Esstate at Cumber Bridge and the greatest part Joynes that Esstate which you have in right of yr Second Lady. I presume the young Lady that you had by her is Marriageable, and if I might obtaine the young Lady's, and your permission, that my eldest Son might make his addresses to her, I should think my Son and my fortune happily disposed of to her; if the aforesaid fortune may be acceptable, I belive his person and his education may be agreable, and if it should please god, that my youngest Son die without Issue, I shall add to my eldest sons fortune 200li P. añn : wh I have in the County of ardmagh : half of my monaghan Esstate I will settle for present maintenance on him, and the other half at my Death and wifes, if you designe to match ye Lady in this Kingdom I am sure no familly in it could have a greater respect for her and yr familly yn mine, I shall take it as a perticuler favoure to hoñnr me with yr answere and be pleased to direct to me to Ardmagh, where I now Live since my fathers decease, my most humble service to yr Lady, and all the young Ladys . . . to ye Lady above mentioned and to yr Son I am

. . . . .

I wish you & yrs a merry Christmas.

This marriage, however, did not take place, for, as we shall see, the young lady in question married in 1719 a Mr. Sloane. Captain Dawson's son married a Miss Dawson from Roscommon

---

[1] A 'tath' is a local measure of land formerly in use in the county of Monaghan, usually taken to mean sixty acres.—*W. I.* ii. p. 227.

with a fortune of 2,000*l.*; but the following extract from a letter of our Irish agent shows that this marriage was not a fortunate one.

Endorsed: E. Kain to Dacre Barrett.

June 9, 1718. Clownis.

Capt. Walter Dawson that writ to y^r Hon.^{r} about his son dyed suddenly last week without any manner of sickness, but he maryed his son to one Dawson as I gave yor. Hon^r. acc^t. and she prooves the worst woman that ever was known she will be drunk allways, and smoke tobaco, and if her husband come in her way when she is soe drunk she will throw every thing at him that comes in her way this it his thought broke Capt. Dawsons hart, and I believe will do the same with the yong man who is a very good man and worth now nine hundred a year.

The negotiations for these different marriages bear out my contention, that formerly the parties who contracted the marriages had frequently only a very small voice in the matter. When one considers how badly many love matches turn out, there is a good deal to be said in favour of the old system. If parents instead of leaving the question of their children's marriages to chance, as is now frequently the case, or if instead of considering that they have arranged a satisfactory marriage provided they have induced their child to marry a person who is rich, would carefully consider who from social position, health, character, and fortune would be likely to prove good alliances for them, and would give them opportunities of meeting together, and generally do all they could to bring about such marriages as they from their experience consider advantageous for both parties—I believe marriages so arranged would on the whole have a far happier average of results than those which take place from two persons merely 'falling in love,' and getting married without considering whether the married career upon which they are embarking has any reasonable chance of being a success.

It is usually admitted that the first year or two of married life is the most trying time, as each of the persons married is, more or less, slowly finding out that the other one is not absolute perfection, but an ordinary mortal, with lots of faults as well as perhaps several good qualities. Then a feeling of disappointment arises from having expected too much, and from having put the person you are in love with on too high a moral pedestal; while if people marry with mutual esteem for each other, but without this ideal and romance of love, they expect only what is reasonable in human beings—namely, both good and bad qualities. If too much is not expected at first, and if the parties to the marriage are fairly well suited, they are not so likely to be disappointed when they realise that neither is perfect. Instead of the glamour of love wearing off in the every-day trials of life, and leaving exposed such future rocks ahead to happiness as constitutional bad health, want of sympathy, being of a different social position, or having means too small for absolute requirements, the young people will find that, thanks to the wisdom and forethought of their elders, they have at hand all the chief attributes which make for a happy union. However, whichever system is best, whether to leave it all to chance or to attempt to arrange your children's marriages for them, we may conclude that in 'the days of good Queen Bess,' and much later, the latter was the plan usually adopted.

But there is no rule without an exception, and we find an instance of just such a one in the wooing of Mary Darrell by John Lennard's eldest son Samson. Not that Samson was undutiful enough to wish to marry anyone without his father's consent, but the lady to whom he was paying his addresses, in defiance of her parents' express wishes, exhibiting a determination and independence more characteristic of the twentieth than of the sixteenth century, declared she would have none of him, and in order to avoid being obliged to marry Samson, engaged herself to another man. In view of the brilliant alliance that Samson afterwards made, both he and his descendants had reason to be extremely grateful to Mary Darrell for what in those times must have been considered her very

66   HISTORY OF THE LENNARDS

unusual and undutiful conduct. The story is told at some length by Strype in his Life of Archbishop Parker,[1] and some original letters concerning this matter are in the British Museum, and some in the Record Office.[2]

I have had considerable doubts whether it were better to print the letters as they stand and let them tell their own story, or to give an abridged abstract of them in modern English, which, though less vivid, would be shorter and simpler for many persons to read; I have come to the conclusion that on the whole the former is the better plan to adopt, and for those whose eyes are not accustomed to reading English of this period I give the following hints. Let the reader say aloud the words which at first sight may seem unfamiliar, and he will find no difficulty in recognising, for example, 'laffe' as 'laugh' or 'in dede' as 'indeed,' 'here' as 'hear,' and so on. There seems to have been no definite system of spelling in those days, and men spelled 'as seemeth right in their own eyes,' and not unfrequently the same word differently in the same letter. Among the most common difference between spelling then and now is that i, u, and y were often used where we should use j, v, and i respectively; 'on' was often written for 'one' and 'off' for 'of,' and the genitive case was formed by an addition of 'es' instead of our apostrophe ''s'.

While on the subject of spelling it may be remarked that at this period we are at the parting of the ways as it were, both in spelling and in handwriting, and so we find the older men, such as John Lennard, using the older spelling and the character called modern Gothic.

---

[1] *S. L.*, Book ii. chap. xvii.
[2] They are all printed in *English Reprints: Barnabe Googe.*

His son Samson not only spelled much more in the way we do now, but he wrote a hand almost quite like a modern one, except in that it was easier to read than most modern hands are, as the letters were all carefully formed.

The curious sort of hieroglyphic flourish after John Lennard's signature occurs in all those signatures of his that I have seen. The facsimile of Samson's writing[1] is taken from a signature when he was quite young, and at that period his brother Samuel wrote much the same hand as he did. The following signature of the latter is taken from a letter written when he was over sixty years of age, and, as might be expected in so old a man, it shows a handwriting much more formed than the specimen given of his eldest brother's writing.

But to return to the love affairs of the attractive Mary Darrell; in 1563, when about nineteen years of age, Samson, apparently with his father's consent, if not indeed at his instigation, was paying court to a Miss Mary Darrell, daughter of Mr. Thomas Darrell, of Scotney Manor House, in the parish of Lamberhurst, which is on the borders of Kent and Sussex. Mr. and Mrs. Darrell were anxious for the match, as well they might be, for his portrait shows Samson to have been a handsome young man, while his father had the reputation of being unusually wealthy. Strype speaks of John Lennard as being 'proud and hasty' by reason of his riches; and he says 'Lennard's riches I suppose might accrue to him by a wealthy office held by him and his father. For in King Edward's Book of Warrants for the seal under the year 1550 there is specified the grant of the office of Pronotary or Clerk of the Crown to John Lennard and Thomas Lennard[2] for life, of the counties of Glamorgan, Monmouth, Brecon, Radnor, in all Courts.'

[1] Vide Facsimile facing p. 68.   [2] Probably John's brother.

However, in spite of all his good looks and his good expectations from his father, Strype says that in the eyes of the wayward Mary Darrell Samson was a 'person belike whom she could not affect; Being not so much moved with the Consideration of his money as her Parents were.' In order to avoid the attentions of Samson, and the better to resist the pressure to marry him which was put upon her by her parents, Mary engaged herself to a young man named Barnaby Googe, who had then recently been appointed one of the Queen's gentlemen pensioners, and who was a kinsman and in the employment of that powerful minister Sir William Cecil.

This step on Mary's part reduced Samson to despair, as we have Strype's authority for the statement that he 'had a great amour for her,' while John was much offended at the slight she put upon his son; and both he and her parents did all they could to break off her engagement to Barnaby. In order to counteract these efforts the favoured suitor enlisted the help of his kinsman Sir William Cecil, who in turn wrote to Archbishop Parker on the subject.

It must be a very unusual experience for a girl to find that the management of her love affairs has passed into the hands of persons as influential as the Prime Minister and the Archbishop of Canterbury, and in Tudor days with such partisans anyone might feel confident of success.

Sir William Cecil warmly espoused the part of Barnaby, and wrote very strongly on the matter to Mary's father, and also to John Lennard. All-powerful as Cecil was, and important to John as was the continuance of their friendship, the latter was a man too pertinacious in carrying through his designs to submit tamely to any rebuff, even from his powerful patron, without putting before him in a dignified manner his own version of the matter. The following correspondence consists of Sir William Cecil's two letters, the one to John Lennard, and the other to Mr. Darrell; John's letter in reply (containing three enclosures) to Sir William, and the reply of the Archbishop to the same.

Samson Lennard

However, in spite of all his good looks and his good expectations from his father, Strype says that in the eyes of the wayward Mary Darrell Samson was a 'person belike whom she could not affect; Being not so much moved with the Consideration of his money as her Parents were.' In order to avoid the attentions of Samson, and the better to resist the pressure to marry him which was put upon her by her parents, Mary engaged herself to a young man named Barnaby Googe, who had then recently been appointed one of the Queen's gentlemen pensioners, and who was a kinsman and in the employment of that powerful minister Sir William Cecil.

This step on Mary's part reduced Samson to despair, as we have Strype's authority for the statement that he 'had a great amour for her,' while John was much offended at the slight she put upon his son; and both he and her parents did all they could to break off her engagement to Barnaby. In order to counteract these efforts the favoured suitor enlisted the help of his kinsman Sir William Cecil, who in turn wrote to Archbishop Parker on the subject.

It must be a very unusual experience for a girl to find that the management of her love affairs has passed into the hands of persons as influential as the Prime Minister and the Archbishop of Canterbury, and in Tudor days with such partisans anyone might feel confident of success.

Sir William Cecil warmly espoused the part of Barnaby, and wrote very strongly on the matter to Mary's father, and also to John Lennard. All-powerful as Cecil was, and important to John as was the continuance of their friendship, the latter was a man too pertinacious in carrying through his designs to submit tamely to any rebuff, even from his powerful patron, without putting before him in a dignified manner his own version of the matter. The following correspondence consists of Sir William Cecil's two letters, the one to John Lennard, and the other to Mr. Darrell; John's letter in reply (containing three enclosures) to Sir William, and the reply of the Archbishop to the same.

The letter sent by Cecil to the father of this Kentish 'Helen' was as follows:—

After my very hearty commendations. Where as I understand that Googe my servant hath been a sutor to your daughter, moved chiefly as I take it by the virtuous report of her & the friendly entertainment that he found at your hands, as both by his information & certain your letters written to him, I understand since he hath so far provided that there hath assurance passed between them evidently to be proved by his allegation & her own letters. These shall be to require you not to go about to break the bond so perfectly knit between them, whereof you have been so long a favorer. Considering that you knew as well his estate for living at the first, as at any time since, and allthough his living be not great, ye shall not need to fear that he lacketh friends and wellwishers being both my Kinsman and my servant. Thus I require you to show him such friendship as you have done before, as you would require any friendship at my hands. I haue thought to haue written to my Lord of Canterbury to have made anend of the matter but I trust my letters to you in this case shall be sufficient.

Sir William also sent the following letter to John[1]:—

Mr. Lenard I have ben Certiffyed ~~by my man~~ by who being my is also my kinsma ~~an~~ Googe a servant[2] ~~of myne~~ that wheras ther hath off late passed a ~~full~~ agrement betwen hym and the dawghter off m̄r Thomas Darell in Kent as Concernyng maryage havyng her Freuds Consent theryn as I vnderstãd by her Fathers Letters wc I have redd wrytten vnto hym and beyng thorowly att a poynt. For all ben hindred thyngs betwen them he hath off Late bye your means ~~Intercepted~~

---

[1] *S. P. Dom. Eliz.* xxxi. No. 1. The draft original letter is in the Record Office, and the corrections are in the handwriting of Sir William.

[2] Formerly the word servant implied protection on the part of the sovereign, lord, or master, and the notion of clientage, the relation involved being one in no sense degrading to the inferior; only in modern use it denotes specifically a domestic, or helper.—*C. D.*

to his greate ~~hindrans~~ & greyff, as also agaynste all dewe order off well vysng, whereby he hathe declard vnto me that myndyng to do vnto hym so great an Iniury your ~~vtter~~ opynyon is that he is vtterlye destytute off Frends, & thatt I make no other acownte off hym butt as off on off [of one of] my men, whearas I esteame hym as my near kynsman, & so he shalbe sure to reasonable cause,
Fynde me in any ~~such necessytye~~ wherffor I praye you heryn to vse hym no otherwyse then ~~sun~~ on [one] whom I well esteame. I have seene the Letters that have passed between hir Father & hym, & also her own letters, wherby the matter is made playne vnto me that she hath Fully assured her selff vuto him.

(Endorsed) p⁰ 8 bris. 1653.
M. of my m̅rs. ir̅es to m̅r. Lenard.
for Ba. Googe.

Strype says that John was much put out at the receipt of this letter, which was probably the common talk for the moment in Court and legal circles; and that this statement of the biographer was accurate is borne out by the tone of the following extremely long letter which John sent to Sir William in justification of his conduct in the matter :—

My Duety done vnto your honor. Youre lettre directed to me touching master Googe was delyvered a moneth after the date thereof to a boye of my howse by a ploughe boye. The cause [is] not yours but master Googes. I hasted the lesse to sende the answer for lacke of his messenger: The matter not worth my sending saving to satisfie you. The effect of your lettre is that master Googe hath enformed you he is hindred by my meanes concerning his mariage with master Darrell his daughter; and that my opinion is that he is destitute of frendes and that you accompt not of him but as one of your men. Ye write further that the matter is made plaine to you by the maides lettres and her fathers, which you haue sene and redde, that she hath assured herselfe to master Googe: and in asmuche as it hath pleased you so to put the one side, it occasioneth me to offer to you th[e] other, to that ende which els I woulde not, for the tedyousnes thereof which may not be shortened.

I praie you doubte not that I haue good will to pleasure
any man of yours much more your honest Kyndesman. There
is cause why I shoulde, you being my good Master. But for
this marrage I myght and must haue done, with honesty as I
did, with reuerence I speake it, though it had touched your
sonne or the best subiecte in this Realme. I knowe not master
Googe who as he hath sclaundered me to you for your accompt-
ing of him being hidden to me so vntruely and scornefully he
as one that seemeth to haue a whotte hedde [1] and a sicke
braine, wrote to me this somer past that by the extreme highte
of my promysed mountaines [2] master Darrell had altered his
mynde from him, and for riches sake ment to matche his
daughter with my sonne, and that frendes of the best, which
shoulde be able to beare strooke with the best of his aduersaries,
shoulde do and write in the cause. He hath also mysused me
in an other lettre the copy is here inclosed. They that knowe
him and my sonne, thyncke aswell or better of my sonne as
of him to all respectes. And there were not cause why I
would wyshe my sonne buryed. Mountaynes be lyke I promysed none, for master Darrell will confesse that he and
his wyfe, before master Googes sute, were earnest suters to
me, and that their daughter was as forwarde in desire as
woman bedde, would geue leaue to matche my sonne ; and
that I never commended but still disabled [3] my sonne to them
all thre ; and they all thre as fast habiled [4] and commended my
sonne.

Master Darrell telleth me that, vppon your lettre sent to
him for master Googe, he wrote to you that his promyse, his
wifes, and daughters, were past them to me for my sonne
before master Googes sute, and that the talke which he had
with master Googe thereof happened by his mystaking of a
lettre of myne. He wrote truely to you therein which clereth me.

I had divers talkes with the maide for my sonne in his
absence, and yet no mo [5] than she was glad of, and then delyvered
me by her parents. And hereto I call god to witnesse that not-
withstandyng my obieccions (as of purpose to trye her I moued
many to longe to be recyted here) that myght haue stayed her

---

[1] Hot head.—*C. D.*
[2] Mountain in the plural was sometimes used to express something of extraordinary
magnitude ; in this instance it clearly means a great amount of money.
[3] Disparaged.—*C. D.*   [4] Praised.—*Ibid.*
[5] More.—*Ibid.*

from matching with my sonne; so farre was she from a nay that she neuer offred any delay to be my sonnes wif, but was most desirous of it in worde and gesture: so that at our last talke, hearynge her mylde and loving answers with full consent to haue my sonne who I know loved her entierly, and therefore I hauing good lyking in me that he shoulde be her husband, nature wrought in me for her to lay my ryght hande on her brest, and to speake thus in effecte; 'then I see that with gods helpe the frute that shall come of this body shall possesse all that I haue and therevpon I will kyss you.' And so in dede I kyssed her. I gaue her after this, silke for a gowne (she neuer wore none so good), and she in token of her good will gave my sonne a handkercher, and in affirmance of this her father wrote a letter to me, by her consent he saith, and that he redde the lettre to her, the copy is here inclosed that declareth her full consent to be my sonnes wife.

Master Darrell dwelleth from me nere xx myles; a way that I never vsed but for this purpose, and then in somer, and at my comyng thither at Bartholomewtide last I tolde the parents and maide that I hearde say she shoulde haue a husband, whereat I mervailed considering the talke that has passed betweene vs. They all thre answered me, and others for me, very often that it was not so, and that master Googe was but a suter. To prove that to be true the parents sent me afterward a copy herinclosed of the maides lettre sent to Master Googe of late, wherein she termed him to be but a suter, and prayeth him to leue his suit, and the parents still say that he bathe no holde of her except that by secrete intysement ageinst their wills he hath caught some worde of her, a thynge odyous to god, and not to be favoured by man.

Now if the talke that she had with me had beene to my sonne it had been a full contracte, but my sonne being absent it is not soo. Yet is it suche matter as therevpon he myght the rather be a suter as Master Googe is, for it is no rare thynge for one woman to haue dyuers suters at ones.

Thus haue I made you a true discourse of all my doings, whiche I trust you, in whose iudgement I durst put all my lands, lyving, and lyfe, can not iudge to be ageine any due order of well vsing, thoughe, by master Googes false informaccion, ye write in your lettre to me to be ageinst all due order of well vsing.

I shoulde be no geyner by this my sonnes matching, but should haue forgone a M marks with matching in as good a stocke in the countrey where I dwell, and sithens[1] suche encumbrance is wrought, as I perceyue there ys on the maides part, who as I here wavereth in this case, I, and my sonne, may with honestie geue vp our sute therein for I were too madde to match my eldest sonne where any entangling is and no stedfastnes at all, I pray you thyncke not that I woulde so do, as surely I wold not for any treasure in this worlde. And so I knytte vpp[2] that thoughe she woulde my sonne, surely he will not haue her, and I say he shall not haue her.

Master Googe by fyrst talke with me vppon good cause showed, might haue staied my sonnes sute soner than by sawsy lettres, some sent by ruffians. Yf I sought to marry a beggers daughter I wolde therein offer her father no despite. Master Darrell sayeth that master Googe vsed him so evell, seking aide at his ennemyes hande in the countrey about him, and hath faced[3] him that he wold tell the Quene of him, and that a seriaunt at armes shoulde fetche his daughter from him, and that you shoulde fetche her within a month, with a number of other straunge dealings which haue troubled the gentleman muche.

And so I leave to trouble you, Wishinge you increase of honor; At Chevening the xth of November 1563
                    Your seruant assuredly to command
                                      I. LENNARD.

Addressed:—To the right honourable and his very good Master Sir William Cecil Knyght chefe Secretary to the Quenes maiestie.

The three enclosures referred to in John's letter are as follows:—

A. The effect of one of master darells letters sent to master Lennard which as master Darrell yet sayethe he wrote by his daughters consent And dyd read yt to her and so sent yt to master lennard.

After my ryght harty commendations etc., presumynge of youre good wyll and goodnes towardes my daughter Mary; althoughe that before yat[4] I moued ye mariage betwene youre sonne and her I knewe ryght well yat it was my daughters goodwyll and desire to haue it to come to passe, and so moued it by her consent and desire. Yet according to youre godly admonition in youre letter, I haue agayne fully trauayled with

---

[1] Since.—*C. D.*   [2] I wind up or conclude.—*Ibid.*
[3] To face, to brag, to boast.—*Ibid.*   [4] That.

her therein: and fynde her moste wyllyng and desirouse to matche with youre sonne, so yat she is truly master Sampsonnes: who shalbe sure to haue of her a louynge and obedient wife, and you, and mastres Lennarde, an obedient daughter. And although nature myghte moue my tonge, and penne, to say, and write muche in fauour of my daughter, yet as god shall iudge me in this case, if I knewe any spotte in her I would expresse it to you: she is truly gods seruaunt, and I trust yat he wyll so preserue her, &c., &c.,

your louynge friend, T. DARRELL.

Endorsed :—A copy of ye effect of one of master Darrells letters sent to master Lennard.

B. A copy of Marye Darelles letter sent to master Goge.

After my harty commendations gentle master Googe where you haue binne, and yet do continue a Sutor to me in ye waye of Maryage, whereunto nether presentlye I haue, nor am I well assured shall haue, ye good wyll or consent of father nor mother, to whome I am both by ye lawe of god and nature bound to geue honoure and obedyence, and in no wyse wyllyngly to greue or offend them. And do well consider yat my chefe obedience and dutye towardes them is to be bestowed in maryage by there consentes, and to there good contentation.[1] Assurynge my selfe in meditation and thinkynge hereof, hereof yat beynge there obedient chylde, and to them most bounden in disobayenge them therein, I shall not only be depriued from yat blessinge which god hath promised to suche as truly honor there parentes, but allso shalbe assured to fynde, and haue, ye like disobedience of my chyldren ; yf euer god shall geue me any : which by gods grace I wyll eschue. Wherfor I hartely beseche you ientle master Googe, if euer any true loue or goodwyll you haue borne towarde me, cease, and leave of from all further sute or meanes to me in this matter, lettynge you to wete[2] yat knowynge my parentes myndes to ye contrarye hereof, I wyll in no wyse match with you in any case. And thus wisshinge to you, in other place, to matche accordynge to your own hartes desire, and to youre farre greter aduancemente, I bid you farewell. From my fathers house at Scotney this thursday the xxth of octobre.

MARYE DARELL.

Endorsed :—A copy of marye Darrells but sent to master Goge verye latelye.

[1] Satisfaction.—*C. D.*   [2] To wit, to know.—*Ibid.*

C. Ryght worshipfull and my louynge frindes I haue recaued youre letters wherein you write yat you perfectly understand ye hole state of ye case, yat hath passed betwene master lennard and youre cosinne mary before my acquayntaunce with her, even so I have binne certyfied of a pretye laffynge toye as touchynge a precontracte, declarynge at full ye sharp inuencyon of master lennardes graue bedde, whereat if old Democritus were now alyue, I would thynke yat he should haue iuster cause to laffe then at his countrymens folly. Ye seame to wyll a meatynge to be had betwene vs, whereunto I with all my hart consent, althoughe a number consyderyng my case would not doe, consyderynge the martiall furniture yat hath benne prepared agenyst me, and ye Italyon inuentyons yat haue binne menaced towardes me, which when ye counsell shall vnderstande, I trust they will not altogether commend. For all this takyng you to be my verye fryndes, I reioyse to meate you, neither if my aduersaryes should be in commission would I feare to see them. Of one thyng I must craue pardonne, for not beynge able to meate you on sundaye, because I haue sent my manne to ye courte, who wyll retorne on Munday, as I trust, but whether he do or not, I wyll with godes leaue wayte vppon you at yat daye; in hast from Dongeon[1] the xvi[th] of octobre.

    Youre louynge frynd   BARNABE GOGE.

Endorsed :—A copy of a scornfull letter written by master Goge to master George Darrell and master Edward Darrell.

I have not discovered the letter that Cecil wrote to Parker, but the following reply to him from the Archbishop, dated November 20th, 1563,[2] sufficiently shows what its purport was. After giving thanks for the preferment of a chaplain, he refers to a letter he had received from Sir William :—

Wherein ye wryght for your cousyn, & seruaunt, Barnaby Goge to haue his matter heard according to lawe & equytie, which matter, as yesterdaye, I haue examined advisedly, having not only the yong gentlewoman before me, to vnderstond of herself the state of the cause, who remaineth fyrme & stable to

[1] Or Donegone, a manor-house near Canterbury, the residence of his grandmother, Lady Hales.
[2] Also in *Correspondence of M. Parker.* P. S. P. p. 198.

stand to that contract which she hath made, as also her father & mother, whom I find the most earnest parents against the bargain as I could see. In fyne I haue sequestrated her out of both their hands into the costodye of one Mr. Tufton, a right honest gentleman, vntil the precontract, which is by hir parents alleged for one Leonard's son, a pronotary, be induced;[1] but this maye giue occasion to bryng it into the Arches[2] to spend moneye; how be yt I mean to dull that expectation, & to go *plane et summarie* to worke to spare expences, which mr Leonard & the wilful parents wuld fain enter to. wery the yong gentleman, paraventure not superfluously monyed so to sayle the seas with them.

Barnaby and Mary being successful in gaining their point, were married on February 5th of the following year (1563–4).

Googe who was born in 1540, and died 1594, was a poet and author of no small repute.[3] He had several children by Mary, and two of his sons became somewhat distinguished in their day.

In spite of Googe's success as an author, and of his powerful kinsman, he appears some years after his marriage to have been so much pushed for money as to be obliged to apply to John Lennard for assistance. We have the following letter with an endorsement in John's handwriting, 'Mr. Goches lre to borowe money.' The letter is not dated, but it was probably written about 1576, as John has used the back of it on which to write a draft letter to another person which bears that date. The writer signs himself 'Barnabe Goche,' but as it is written from 'Cecyll howse,' and as spelling, as I have already said, was in those days largely a matter of individual taste, I think we may safely assume that the writer was the same 'Barnaby' who some thirteen years before was able to induce the headstrong Mary to engage herself to him in spite of all opposition from her parents.

---

[1] Obsolete: to bring in; to introduce.—*C. D.*

[2] The ecclesiastical Court of that name.

[3] Besides his poetry he wrote four 'Books of Husbandrie,' published in 1577, in which he mentioned clover as being then known in English farming, and advocated its use as a means of restoring fertility to exhausted soil.—*T. S. E.* iii. p. 488.

Syr I Besecche yowe shewe mee so much ffriendship as to Lend me ffyve pownds ffor eyght or nyne Dayes. Itt may att thys present doo mee greater pleasure then yow wold suppose. Thus am I bold to trouble yow Trustyng to ffynd yow as I have allwayes ffound yow. I have no newes ffor yow Butt that the progresse to buxtons holdethe nott, God have yow in hys keepyng, in hast ffrom Cecyll howse thys present Saterday.

Your allways assured ffrend
BARNABE GOCHE.

From the contents of the following letter which is among our papers, John appears to have acceded to this request to the extent of lending five marks (3*l.* 6*s.* 8*d.*), not 5*l.*, which was what he was requested to advance. It is to be hoped that this loan to his kinsman pleased Cecil, and that so John got some indirect advantage for his assistance, as it appears tolerably certain that he was never repaid this loan :—

Addressed :—To the right worshypefull Mr. John Lennard at Knolle geve thys.

Sure youre whorshepe shall vndere stand that I haue sent mye mane to Mistryse ghoche for the fyfe marke that she othe you, and se hathe sente ansure that she hath yt not, nor cane not paye yt tyll the nyxt teareme for thene she saythe that Mr Ghoche ys to resefe monye, and yf yt come then you shalle be payde, or ellse she knowethe not when she shall be abelle, and thys ys hyre ansur..... and so I lefe to trubelle youre whorsshype anye furder at thyse p[re]sent tyme desyreyinge god to send you longe lyfe and prosepruse to hys wyll and plesure frome peckehame thys xxiij of Desember 1577.

By yourese to commande
EDWARD WOODGATE.

Samson's courtship of Mary Darrell having come to an end in 1565, John Lennard negotiated for the marriage of this son of his, when he was about twenty years of age, with Margaret, sister of Gregory Fynes, Lord Dacre, then in her twenty-third year.[1] Margaret who was, or at any rate became, a Protestant

---

[1] For their ages *cf.* tombstone at Chevening, and remembering that March 10th, 1611, was what we should now reckon as 1612. An Inquisition states in error that she was forty years of age in 1595.

in religion,[1] appears in herself to have been a very desirable person to marry, as it is said 'she abounded as much in worth and virtue as in honour,'[2] and besides her own attractions, she was heir presumptive to her brother, and as such would, in the event of his having no children and her surviving him, be entitled not only to his entailed estates, but also to the Barony of Dacre, which title was one of those capable of being inherited in the female line. Gregory seems to have been pressed by his mother and his uncle, Lord Abergavenny, to give a sum of 700*l.* as a marriage portion to Margaret.

He wrote to his father-in-law, Sir Richard Sackville, Chancellor of the Exchequer, saying that he is too much in debt to give so large a sum, and that indeed even if he were not in debt he would not give her so much, but he offers to pay five hundred marks in five years and to give security for so doing. Gregory says that he considers so large a sum as 700*l.* would be a sufficient portion to give on the marriage of his daughter[3] hereafter, and that he is not bound to give his sister anything, but that he wishes to act to her as a natural brother, and therefore makes this offer provided that Mr. Lennard will settle what he had offered to. Gregory's father-in-law appears to have been a party to these negotiations, as Gregory asked him to make his mother and Mr. Lennard 'previe' to his decision on this subject.

The letter to Sir Richard (which is the earliest of the Lennard correspondence) is as follows:—

My very good father in lawe, I have receaved your letters thone from my Lorde Aburgavenie one other from my Mother and one from you tuchinge the maryage of my syster

---

[1] In *Walter Younge's Diary*, C. S. P. p. 118, there is this reference to Margaret. The writer, wishing to indicate some of those who professed the Protestant religion, has at the end of his diary the following note:—' Observations of inclinations of certain noble personages out of the Dedication of some good books;' then comes a short list of books and those to whom they are dedicated, and among these entries there is this:—' Mr. Topsell dedicated his works on Ruth, published in 1605, to the Lady Dacres Prot.'   [2] *Anc.* ix.

[3] He had issue one daughter, who died during his lifetime while very young.

Margaret Fynes

in religion,[1] appears in herself to have been a very desirable person to marry, as it is said 'she abounded as much in worth and virtue as in honour,'[2] and besides her own attractions, she was heir presumptive to her brother, and as such would, in the event of his having no children and her surviving him, be entitled not only to his entailed estates, but also to the Barony of Daere, which title was one of those capable of being inherited in the female line. Gregory seems to have been pressed by his mother and his uncle, Lord Abergavenny, to give a sum of 700*l.* as a marriage portion to Margaret.

He wrote to his father-in-law, Sir Richard Sackville, Chancellor of the Exchequer, saying that he is too much in debt to give so large a sum, and that indeed even if he were not in debt he would not give her so much, but he offers to pay five hundred marks in five years and to give security for so doing. Gregory says that he considers so large a sum as 700*l.* would be sufficient portion to give on the marriage of his daughter[3] hereafter, and that he is not bound to give his sister anything, but that he wishes to act to her as a natural brother, and therefore makes this offer provided that Mr. Lennard will settle what he had offered to. Gregory's father-in-law appears to have been a party in these negotiations, as Gregory asked him to make his answer and Mr. Lennard 'previe' to his decision on this subject.

The letter to Sir Richard (which is the earliest of the Lennard correspondence) is as follows:—

My very good father in lawe, I have receaved your letters thone from my Lorde Aburgavenie one other from my Mother and one from you tuchinge the maryage of my syster

---

[1] In *Walter Yonge's Diary*, C. S. P. p. 118, there is this reference to Margaret. The writer, wishing to indicate some of those who professed the Protestant religion, has at the end of his diary the following note:—'Observations of inclinations of certain noble personages out of the Dedication of some good books;' then comes a short list of books and those to whom they are dedicated, and among these entries there is this:—'Mr. Topsell dedicated his works on Ruth, published in 1605, to the Lady Dacres Frot.' [2] *Anc.* ix.
[3] He had issue one daughter, who died during his lifetime while very young.

Margaret Fynes

wth my gyfte therto of vij^li [700*l*.]. S^r my state ys well knowen vnto my Mother and you to be such, as yf my daughter were of age to be marryed, I could not make suche p[re]sent payment. And I trust, yf I lyve, wth this some nowe axed by my Mother that I should gyve wth my syster, to marrye my daughter herafter.

Assuringe you I mean not yf I were out of debt to gyve so great a some of money to my systers maryage.

But as a naturall brother not beinge bounde to gyve anythinge I will bestowe a reasonable porcyon to her maryag, and yet far vnder thys request, but this I will doo if Mr Lennarde wilbe bounde to thys he hath offred, and will lykewyse take suche dayes as I may be able to paye. I will gyve fyve hundreth markes and be at no further charge, and for the payment thereof in fyve yere next after her maryage, I will assygn some of my lands, and thys ys that I mynd to doo, and no further, vntil suche tyme as I am out of debte. Whereof I praye you make my mother and Mr Lennard previe ; and thus most hartylie fare you well the xvij of December 1565

Your lovinge sonne in lawe

In spite of his large estates Gregory probably lived in a more or less chronic state of comparative impecuniosity, as several years later we find him writing to 'Walsyngham' in order to certify that he can only bring into the field for the defence of her Majesties person '10 lances, 10 light horse, 10 petronels,[1] 40 corselets,[2] 20 muskets and 20 calivers[3] and is right sorry that his ability to do no more is so weakened by long suits at law.'[4]

---

[1] A hand firearm introduced in the sixteenth century, shorter than the harquebus but longer than the pistol.—*C. D.*   [2] Armour for the body.

[3] In the sixteenth century a hand firearm lighter than the musket.

[4] *S. P. Dom. Eliz.* ccxii. No. 76. In a document dated 1588 Lord Dacre's name appears as offering to furnish, in order to attend her Majesty's person, the

Lord Dacre in his history refers to Camden's statement that Gregory was 'a man of cracked brain,' and says that 'the family have good reason to agree with him [Camden] for [he, Gregory], being entirely governed by Anne his wife, she persuaded him to leave a great many fine manors to her, in prejudice of his sister, who had never offended him, and had it been in his power he would most likely have given his whole estate away from her to his said wife, so great was her influence upon him.'

With all respect to my great-great-grandfather, it seems to me that the mere fact of Gregory preferring his wife to his sister in no way proves him to be of 'cracked braine.' Many persons quite sane and who have life interests in entailed estates, have strong prejudices against those in remainder who must one day succeed them, and would willingly cut them out if they could do so.

In this connection I call to mind the well-known case of a noble lord who, having quarrelled with his heir presumptive, determined to cut him out of the succession. To this end he married a second time at the age of sixty-eight a young lady aged eighteen, and by her he had several sons.

Anyway, whether cracked or sane, Gregory and his wife seem to have had many disputes with his sister Margaret, and with her father-in-law John; and these disputes appear to have ultimately ended in a compromise. A considerable amount of information relating to these disputes and to the negotiations for the marriage of Samson to Margaret is to be found in the interesting document entitled 'The Greyfes of Mr̃is Margaret Lennard, syster & heyre apparent, vnto yᵉ now Lord Dacres of yᵉ Sowthe,' which was probably drafted by John himself; as it is, like most recitals of griefs, rather lengthy, I have attempted to give a shortened account of its contents.

It states that Gregory Lord Dacre held his possessions under an 'entayle' made by his 'greate'-grandfather, Thomas Lord Dacre, and that by the terms of that entail if anyone who

following force: Lances 10, light horse 10, footmen 80. *Hist. Com.* xv. *App.* Part v. (Foljambe), p. 40.

should hold lands by virtue thereof attempted to break this entail, then those lands he might endeavour to dispose of were to be forfeited to Lord 'Norryce'; who was descended from the great-grandfather through a daughter, and was first cousin once removed to Gregory and Margaret.[1] The forfeiture clause shows how very anxious Thomas Lord Dacre was that 'hys possessyons' should 'contynue yn hys bloode,' meaning his male line.

'The Greyfes' then go on to assert that Lord Dacre's 'nere kyndred' proposed the marriage, and had held out as an inducement that in the event of Gregory's death without issue Margaret would inherit all his 'yntayled' estates, and that although 'Lady Dacre her selfe was a furtherer att the begynnynge and yn shew[2] a well wyller also, att the tyme, unto thys maryage, and gave oute kynd words to the same effect,' 'after thys maryadge past, my Ladye Dacre began to deale unkyndly wyth her syster Lennard.' Lady Dacre then bribed Lord 'Norryce,' by giving him land worth 200 marks a year, to allow the entail to be cut off, so that the whole of the rest of the estates would be entirely in the absolute possession of her husband. This caused Margaret and her friends to take such vigorous action that 'after muche longe sute some small releyfe was obtayned,' and it was agreed that one portion of the estates should be settled on Lord Dacre absolutely, a second portion on Lord Norris absolutely, and that a third portion should go to Margaret or her children provided Gregory died without issue. Lady Dacre's jointure, however, was to be charged on that portion of the property which was to be resettled on Margaret, and moreover Lady Dacre was, during her life, to have the power to cut timber 'which she have doon with extremytye yn most of thoese groundes,' and grant long leases over it. In order to obtain even this concession 'ould Mr. Lennard' had to agree to pay all the legal expenses connected not only with this resettlement on Margaret, but also those incurred by the alienation of the rest of the estates to Lord Dacre

---

[1] Genealogical table, *post*, p. 152.   [2] 'Yn Shew': in appearance.—*C D.*

G

and to Lord Norris. All this cost 'hym fyve hundreth marks;' and he had to give Lord Dacre (who had never paid 'anye penye' of his promised 'porcyon' of 500 marks on his sister's 'maryage') 100*l.* 'yn monye.' This, however, was not the end of the liabilities which John Lennard was obliged to undertake in order to arrange this compromise. Both he and his son had to covenant, and enter into recognizances, to pay no less than 2,000*l.* to Gregory's executors for the benefit of his widow if he should die without children.

This agreement was embodied in an indenture dated June 16th, in the 13th of Eliz. (1571), which in many subsequent documents is referred to as the 'quadripartite Indenture'; and the parties to it were Lord Dacre and his wife; Sir Henry, afterwards Lord Norris, and his wife; Samson Lennard and his wife; and three trustees. Although the 'quadripartite Indenture' mentions by name the lands which were the subject of the agreement, there is nothing in it to indicate the extent of these respective estates. In some cases the names mentioned in it are also the names of parishes; in others I cannot trace them, and they are doubtless the names of manors only.

I have put an asterisk against the names of such of the lands as bore the name of a parish, and which would probably represent as a rule larger manors than those which had a name different from the parishes in which they were situated. The following manors were settled on Lord Dacre absolutely:—

Sussex . . .	*Herstperpoint als Herst Dannye [Danny] *Westmeaston Smythwicke *Newycke [Newick] Nooington	*Streete als Southbarwicke als Barricke Knights & Dowlands 100 acres of Marsh called the newe Inned marsh
Southampton .	Compton Mounseux	
Berkshire . .	The Manor of Fynes als Wollefynes The Office of Bailiff of Twychin als Fynes Baylywicke	

DACRE ESTATES

Derby . . .	*Beighton [1]
Wiltshire . .	*Staunton Quinteyne als Staunton St Quynteyne

Yorkshire . .
- Brausburton als Braudesburton
- *Moiety of lands in Sedbarghe [Sedbergh]
- *Moiety of the manor of Bellerby
- Moiety of lands in Ellingstring
- Woodhall
- Edwardby
- *Dent
- *Thirkylby [Thirkleby]
- Ellerbye

Lincolnshire .
- Wintringham
- Fishery in the River Humber

Northamptonshire *Lutton

Nottingham . *Carleton Kingston & Carleton Bacon

Northumberland
- The Mediety of the Manors of
- Bempton
- Halywell
- Ardingmoare
- Langherst
- Raffeley
- Chevington
- Moorewicke
- Havingdon

Middlesex . . Lands & tenements in the City of London

On Lord Norris and his wife absolutely.

Suffolk . . .
- *Northhales [or Covehithe]
- Wymples in Thorrington
- Burghe next Grandesburgh
- *Wrentham Cove
- *South Cove
- Beawflory
- *Benacre
- *Henstead

Berks . . . . The Manor or farm of Bradley

Notts . . . . The Manor & farm of Bothinstall [Bothamsall]

On Mary Lady Dacre, mother of Gregory Lord Dacre, for life: with remainder to Gregory.

Dorset . . .
- *Frome Quyntyne [St. Quintin]
- *Evershott

On Mary Lady Dacre for life, remainder to Gregory Lord Dacre; in default of issue remainder to Margaret Lennard.

Kent . . . . Hundred & Manors of
- *Burham
- *Cudham

---

[1] Lord Dacre lost no time in disposing of this manor, which he sold in the same year as the Quadripartite Indenture was executed, and in this conveyance Samson Lennard and his wife were parties. —*D. Arch.*

Essex . . . . Nashe Hall

On Gregory Lord Dacre and his wife for their lives; remainder in default of heirs to Margaret Lennard.

Sussex . . .	*Horsemounseux [Herstmonceux] Olde Courte [in Wartling?] Gotchmer [Gotham in Pevensey]	Ingrames Buckholte [in Bexhill?] *Ewherst [Ewhurst] *Hayleshmere [Hailsham?]
Norfolk . . .	*Horsforde *Hawtboyes [Hautbois]	

On Gregory for his life; remainder in default of heirs to Margaret Lennard.

Lincoln . . . *Holbeach

Yorks. . . .	*Staveley *Scorton	Thume Mapleton & Nether Calcotts

Among our papers is an ancient document in the handwriting of the sixteenth century, giving particulars of the manor of Wintringham, which we have just seen was one of the estates settled on Lord Dacre. It is of interest as being an early record of letting sporting rights, the tenant hiring a 'fisshing called the Salmon garthe rented yearlie at xl^s [40s.] withe the fowlinge rented yearlie at v^s [5s.].'

I have found a greatly worn and faded deed dated November 20th in 10th of Henry VIII. [1518] between Thomas Lord Dacre[1] and others which is a lease of this fishing in Wintringham Manor, except 'Sturgeon, poppas [porpoise?] & seale,' at the rent of 40s.

While on the subject of sporting rights, I may mention that Francis Lennard Lord Dacre in 1650, when he granted a lease of a farm in Chevening for twenty-one years, reserved the right to fish, hunt, hawk and fowl over the premises; and also specially reserved the right of fishing in the 'mote' and fishponds.

The letting value of land at any period long since past is of such interest that at the risk of somewhat interrupting the

---

[1] The great-grandfather of Gregory.

continuity of my story, I give here some particulars of the acreage of these lands at Wintringham, and the rents Lord Dacre derived from it. The property consisted of a stone thatched house, with stables and dove-house, and twelve 'oxgangs' of arable land, part of the 'Common field.' An 'oxgang' in those parts was said to have consisted of 16 acres, so the arable land was 192 acres; there were also 30 acres of marsh meadow; of other 'medes' 65 acres; pasture ground 90 acres; another pasture of 2 acres; 12 rode (rood) of coarse grass; and a meadow of 168 acres called Ancolme Marsh; in all 550 acres; with a windmill and the above sporting rights, for all of which the tenant paid a rent of 24*l*. 17*s*. 8*d*.; this however is said, in a note written at some subsequent period, to have been increased to 'xlj^{li} xix^s iiij^d' (41*l*. 19*s*. 4*d*.), or less than 1*s*. 6*d*. per acre. The rest of this estate, consisting of 710 acres arable in the 'Common field,' was let to seven tenants at a total rent of 21*l*. 15*s*.; which appears by the same note referred to above to have been increased to 45*l*. 4*s*. 6*d*., or about 1*s*. 3*d*. per acre.

We have a paper endorsed in the handwriting of Samson Lennard, 'How ye lo Dacres lande should have byn conveyed in Quinto of ye Quene.' This document consists of a list of the family estates, which list is practically identical with the one we have just seen, as far as the names of the various estates are concerned, but the number of them settled on Margaret by this earlier arrangement is far larger than those which were to pass to her under the terms of the 'quadripartite agreement.'

The heading of the paper is 'By ye Booke[1] made ye last day of May Anno V. E. Regine [1563] these landes are apoynted to Margaret fines immediatlye if my lord dye w'out issue of his bodye.' Then follows a list of four manors in Sussex, including Herstmonceux, six in Yorkshire, and two in Norfolk; then comes this note:—'thyes ij and the v underwritten she gett not tyll my l. her mother decease who hath them for her lyfe by thorder of ye booke;' then a list of one manor in Dorset, one in

---

[1] The word 'Booke' is used here in the now obsolete sense, meaning a writing or deed.

Essex, four in Suffolk and one in Kent. Then comes the name of one manor in Kent, with this note :—'This Mrs M. Fynes hath not tyll after my l. her mothers & Mr F. Thursbyes deceases who haue them for lyfe by the order of the booke.' Then follows this note. 'And by y^t booke thyes landes ar apoynted to ye younge lady Dacres [1] ioyntour,' and after that come the names of six manors in Sussex :—

One in Southampton.	One in Wilts.
Two in Yorkshire.	Two in Notts.
One in Lincoln.	One in Derbyshire.
One in Northampton.	Two in Berks.

Then the names of two manors in Lincoln and three in York, with this note :—'thyes she hath after my lords mothers decease who hath them for her lyfe by thorder of the booke.'

This is succeeded by the following note :—'and by y^t booke thyes lands are apoynted to the old Lady Dacres [2] for her lyfe tyme.' Then come the names of—

One manor in Dorset.	One in Essex.	Four in Suffolk.
Two in Kent.	One in Lincoln.	Four in York.

The document concludes with this note :—'And by y^t booke thyes landes are appoynted to Mr F. Thursbye [3] for his lyfe tyme ;' and then follows the name of one manor in Kent.

I am sorry that among our large mass of old papers I have not come across this 'booke,' as one would have liked to see who were the parties to it, and what was the consideration for the agreement; but its chief provisions, as far as regards Margaret, appear to be pretty fully set out in the above paper. It will be observed that Lord Norris is not mentioned, and that Margaret was, upon the death of her brother, to become entitled either in possession or reversion to her mother, her step-father and her sister-in-law respectively, to no less than over sixty manors scattered over different counties of England. There were probably not many heiresses of the period who had greater expectations, and that her relations were, as we have seen, not

---
[1] Gregory's wife. [2] His mother. [3] His stepfather.

only willing, but absolutely anxious, she should marry Samson is a very remarkable testimony to the wealth and reputation to which John Lennard had attained, as his son says, by his 'painfull and vertuous courses.'

I have mentioned that Strype speaks of John as being very rich, and it is interesting that we have some of his rent rolls; one of them, which is headed '1586, the whole yerly revenew of certeyne of my manners & lands,' gives their annual value as 2,333*l.* 3*s.* 5*d.* From this deductions amounting to 563*l.* for quit and other rents, and for some annuities which he had to pay, has to be made. This leaves a net total of what was for that period the extremely large income of 1,750*l.* 3*s.* 5*d.*; and besides this there must be added the fees to be derived from his appointments of Custos Brevium and Prothonotary in Wales, and also the rents from some manors which he owned, the names of which do not appear in the above rent roll. I think we may safely put the total of John's income at not less than 2,000*l.*, or equal to about 40,000*l.* at the present day.

As the 'booke' was executed in 1563, and Margaret's marriage not arranged for until 1565, John, of course, considered, when the negotiations for it were in progress, that she would ultimately inherit all the vast family possessions of the Fynes, and the necessity which was forced upon him of agreeing to the compromise effected by the 'quadripartite agreement' in 1571 was no doubt a very bitter pill for him to swallow, as by it she became entitled in reversion to less than one-third of the manors that would have ultimately come to her under the previous settlement. One wonders how it came about that so astute a man as John, and moreover a barrister, should have allowed the marriage to take place without settlements of Margaret's reversions being so drawn up that no question should arise later as to their validity; but it may well be that he was dazzled by the brilliancy of her prospects both as regards estates and title and that he feared lest the match might fall through were he too exigeant. If John was greatly annoyed, as he doubtless was, at having to agree to the compromise effected by the 'quadripartite agreement,' what must have been his disappointment when, having gone to great expense, and having incurred considerable liabilities in order to effect this compromise, he suddenly found that a mine had been sprung upon him. It appears that Lady Dacre had considerable litigation with a Mr. Hurlston, of the Temple, who claimed an 'annuitye which my Lord Dacre had graunted hym for the kepynge of hys Courts.' In the course of this litigation flaws in Gregory's titles under the entail came to light, and a large portion of the estates were in danger of reverting to the Crown owing to the attainder of Thomas Lord Dacre.[1] Lady Dacre, however, being evidently a very resourceful woman, managed to convert what might have been a great misfortune into a considerable advantage to herself She 'havynge greate frends yn Courte,' compounded with the Crown, and obtained a grant to herself, and her husband, of that principal portion of the estates, which under the resettlement were to be theirs absolutely, while as to the portion which was settled in remainder to Margaret and her heirs, she either left 'the remaynder thereof to remayne yn Her Majestie styll, or els hath procured yt to be assygned over unto my Lord Treasorer and my Lord of Leycester to some secret use.'[2] If this were so, John would not only have spent his 500 marks and his 100*l.* in vain, but he and his son would be still liable to pay to Lord Dacre's executors the 2,000*l.* upon his death, while ' Mŕis Lennard, or hyr heyres, shall be put to grete charges of sute, unable to recover theyre ryght yn yt [the estates settled on her], be yt never so good.' And to make matters worse, it is suggested that Lord Norris in spite of what he had gained by these transactions, and of his covenants, had 'layd certeyne secret estates and yncombrances upon all the land' previous to the resettlement.

Some few years later—namely, in 1585—Lord and Lady

[1] *Post*, p. 201.
[2] There is reference to a grant in reversion on July 29th, 1581, to Lords Burghley and Leicester of various manors in Sussex, Norfolk, Lincolnshire, Yorkshire, Kent, and Essex belonging to Gregory Lord Dacre and his wife.—*S. P. Dom. Eliz.* cxlix. No. 76.

Dacre and Lady Norris obtained a private Act of Parliament,[1] which, after reciting the indenture of settlement of 1571, goes on to declare that any charges or incumbrance of any sort made previously to the date of that settlement by Lord Norris upon any lands the subject of that settlement, shall be void, and not have any effect against Lord and Lady Dacre and their heirs, or against Margaret and Samson Lennard or their heirs.

The fact that it was necessary to obtain this Act shows clearly that what Margaret stated as to Lord Norris having encumbered this land was true. This confiscating Act may have worked shameful injustice on some *bonâ fide* incumbrancer who had advanced money to Lord Norris on the security of the property, which security the Act quietly destroys without giving him any sort of compensation. This is a good instance of the great material advantages possessed in those days by people of position and influence, and of the corresponding drawbacks suffered by those less fortunately situated.

If all these allegations of Margaret were true, Lady Dacre had clearly got a good deal the best of the Lennards, and their chance of getting any equivalent for all their expenditure of money was very small. The last paragraph of 'the Greyfes' runs thus:

By these strange dealings Mris Lennard and her chyldren which be manye be lykly to be defeated of all possibilitye of injoyeng anye of the Lord Dacre's lands whereunto they be yet hytherto boeth yn bloode, law, and equytie the rightfull, and next heyres, yn all appearancye; and her father yn lawe, and husband, to lose moreover to the value, verye nere, of thre thousand pounds, whych they have dysbursed, and ar to dysburse for the same, if some conˢcyonable[2] provicyon be not made to the contrary; which they humbly besech your Honours may be doon.

This document is not dated, nor is there in it anything

---

[1] The Act is not printed; I have seen the original in the Tower of the House of Lords; the reference to it is 27 Eliz. No. 44. There are references to the dispute between Gregory Lord Dacre and Lord Norris in *S. P. Dom. Eliz.* clxxvi. Nos. 36, 37, 38.

[2] Conscionable: conformable to conscience, proper, just.—*C. D.*

to show by the expression 'your Honours' for whom it was intended, but most likely Lord Burleigh and the Earl of Leicester, who were Lord Keepers in 1579, were there referred to. The date was probably 1579, as in the following letter to Lord Burleigh, dated June 24th of that year, John speaks of the worries, and says plaintively that 'yt wold dysquyet many men and strike some halfe dede to here a rumour of daunger of losse of thousands as by thys match ys offered to me and myne.' The first part of this letter relates to some other litigation John had then in hand about some purchase of wood, and he offers a hundred marks to compromise the matter :—

My duty humbly remembered to yor hono^{ur} [1] yt may please the same tobe advertysed that I payd Mr Freke before my day, & I haue been wyth my Lord Dyer [2] at hys lodgyng yn the towne, & wyth the rest of the Justyces, & they ar agreed that the defauts yn yor fynes shalbe amended. And concernyng the wood yn stryfe there ar berers [3] ageynst me yn yt, thoughe yt be truly myne by lawe, & conscyence. And yet yor hono^{ur} shall comand me, yf yow so please, so farre furth [4] as C m̃cs [100 marks] cometh to—tobe bestowed at yo^{ur} l [Lordship's] pleasure to advoyde further trouble & to enioye myne owne quyetly, otherwyse I beseche you of a favorable heryng of yt, & yt tobe the fyrst matter on Thursday nexte comeing. According to yor comandnt I have sent yor l [Lordship] hereynclosed a note of suche somes of money as I can yet lerne the Lady Dacres hath raysed by sales & fynes of my lo [Lord's] lands wythyn thyes fewe yeres, but Mr Hurleston talketh of farre greter somes—I have also sent you hereynclosed a note of such lands as were coveyed to my sone's Wif, & how mych therof was the lo FitzHughes lands, as Yo^{ur} l [Lordship's] pleasure was I shuld—wyth some other matter thatt I am bold to acqueynte yo^{ur} l [Lordship] wyth to p[er]use at Yo^{ur} best leysure, because I se that as my memory wylle fayle me bryefely to speke yt, so by reason of the grete nomber of suters to you you have no tyme to here me by word of mouthe—And althoughe ye shall

---

[1] Lord Burleigh was in 1579 one of the two Lord Keepers.—*Hay. Dig.*

[2] Sir E. Dyer, author of well-known law reports, Judge of Queen's Bench, died 1558.   [3] 'Berers': witnesses.

[4] Forth: formerly used intensively to strengthen some adverbs and prepositions: as far forth, beneath forth, within forth, &c.—*C. D.*

DACRE ESTATES

fynd thereyn some superfluous matter, yet I beseche you bere wyth me thereyn, for yt wold dysquyet many men, & stryke sõme halfe dede, to here a rum°r [rumour] of daunger of losse of thousands as by thys match ys offered tome & myne; but I truse [trust] that god, the quene, and good men, wylle helpe vs yn yt: And so I wysshe you encrease of honoʳ

lyncoln's Yn the xxiijᵗʰ of June 1579.

Yoᵘʳ honoᵘʳs of duty to cõmand,

J. LENNARD.

Sales of lands, gyftes of lands, fines for leases, and wood sales as others do report.

Fitzhue	The Lord Norres had lands in Suffolk and other shyres worth.	mmmmˡⁱ
	Beyghton sold for	mˡⁱ
Fitzhue	Staunton Quinton sold for.	mmˡⁱ
	Compton Monceux sold for	mcccˡⁱ
Fitzhue	Lutton sold for.	cclxˡⁱ
	Bellarby sold	
	Sedberghe.	
	The moytyes of iij or iiij manners in Northumberland sold for	
Fitzhue	Fynes for leasses of Horsford in Northfolke	mˡⁱ
	Fines for lands in Dorsetshire.	mˡⁱ
	One chapman for a fine of Wolfines in Barkshire	ccˡⁱ
	Afine for a shepe walk neere Lewas.	lxˡⁱ
	Many mo fines and grete wood sales and other lands sold the certaynty I cannot lerne yet	
	And grete improvements in Kent and other places.	
	Nottinghamshire — Carelton Kyngeston otherwise Carleton Baron	
	Yorkshire—Woodhall, Edwardby, Thyrkelby.	

There is more information about this dispute in the Record Office,[1] as there we have Lady Dacre's counterblast to Margaret's 'Greyfes,' and some further answers of the latter.

Lady Dacre presented a supplication to the Queen, in which she said she would 'with as few wordes as she cann simplie and

---

[1] *S. P. Dom. Eliz. Addenda*, xxvi. No. 37.

plainelie answer everie parte' of the 'Greyfes.' This document is a tremendously long one, and it is dreadful to think how long it might have been had not Lady Dacre made the resolution to be as brief as possible.

The following is a condensed account of the contents of this document, which begins thus :—

To the Quenes most Exelent Matie.

I ame in moste humble manno^r to be a moste earneste suter vnto yor ma^{tie}, wherevnto I ame extremelie vrged by the vniuste and slaunderous Complaints of my lo:[1] sister now the wief of yonge m^r Leonarde, who with her vncourteous Father in lawe, olde m^r Leonarde, Cesseth not dailie to raise by all the meanes she and they can, most vntrewe reports against me, and my doings, and aswell by supplcacon to yor highenes, as other waies, seeketh to be bereafe me of my highest worldlie Comfort, that is of yor M$_a^{ties}$ good opinion of me, the losse whereof I holde more dearer, than the prise of my lief. Therefore most gracious sou^{r}eigne of you^r most accustomed clemencie, graunte me this favo^r as that I maie, with as fewe wordes as I cann, first simplie and plainelie as I will to everie parte answere, and sett fourthe the whole Course of my prosedinge and dealinges towardes my sister, and then in like sorte to discover the vnnaturall and badd dealeings of her and herr Confederatts towardes my lorde her brother and mee.

Lady Dacre then goes on to say that she and her husband married very young, before he was old enough to have charge of his own estates ; that, until Gregory came of full age, her mother-in-law managed his property, and she took 'fower hundred pounde a year of my lordes landes.' But she does not say how this money was expended, whether for the joint maintenance of mother, son, daughter, and daughter-in-law, which was probably the case, or whether for the Dowager Lady Dacre's sole benefit. She, however, admits that during this period she had 'a smale pencion whiche, for my owne findinge, was yearlie paid unto mee by my lo. mother while she had the rule.' After the dowager ceased to manage her son's affairs, they appear for a time to have been in the hands of persons

[1] Lord's.

whom Lady Dacre describes as 'my lord's officiers.'[1] She says that it was not long after she herself 'hadd anie libertie of my lo. lyvinge' (by which she means managed his affairs) before Margaret married; 'and for my parte I did during that smale tyme and before her marridge supplie her wants in suche sorte as a gratefull receavor woulde hauve confessed the same.' This is a very vague statement, but she goes on to say that 'for further proffe of my owne perticuler care and love I bore her I was alwaies readie to further her with all the good I coulde, and for her well bestowing in marriage I procured Sir John Pelham,[2] a nere Kinsman of myne owne a gentleman of good worshipp, and of faire lyvinge in possession to come to see her, & I hadd conference wth her mother, and herself, in that matter, wch was like to have come to good ende if it hadd so pleased her Mother and herself.'

Lady Dacre then says that Gregory was advised by his 'frendes and learned Counsell' that in order better to secure his title, he should levy a fine and suffer a recovery of all his lands; that one Philip[3] Fynes was found to be in remainder after Gregory, and before Margaret, and that Gregory and herself did their uttermost to make Margaret the next in remainder. She says that Gregory covenanted in 10,000*l*. 'bands' (*i.e.* bonds) that he would convey his lands to Margaret and her heirs if he himself had no heirs, that he induced Philip Fynes to be a party to this agreement, and besides 'dyvers sommes of monie gave him fower score pounde a yere during his lieff to release them his titell.' Lady Dacre

then further growing to some more understanding and finding by conferaunce wth my lo. and my best frendes that my lo: and his lyving, by the littell care of those that hadd the chardge aboute him, fell into great wrecke, as himself into iij^{m} v$^{li\,o}$ [3,500*l.*] debte;

[1] The first meaning of the word is 'one to whom has been entrusted the management of some business.'—*C. D.* In this case Lady Dacre may have used the word in the sense of guardians or trustees.

[2] Was this Pelham a descendant of Sir N. Pelham, in whose park the fatal affray took place which cost Thomas Lord Dacre his life?

[3] As to whose son this Philip was, *vide post*, p. 186, *n.*

the greatest p̄te [part] of his lands leased,[1] much of his woodes solde, and himself and his howses vtterlie vnfurnished, both of plate, and all other necessaries, yt was thought good, thoughe some what to late, that my lo: should take vpon him the goumēnte of his owne lvying, and for the better bringing that to good passe, my Father then became a most humbell suter vnto yo{r} ma{tie}, & by yo{r} gracious goodnes, made a good order therein, though somewhate to my lo: mothers misliking, wherevpon she then went to her owne dwelling, & my lo: sister w{th} her, desiring rather to be w{th} her mother, then to tarrie w{th} me in her brothers howse.

It is not odd that Margaret should have preferred living with her mother, to 'tarrying' with her sister-in-law in her brother's 'howse.' This document, when one reads between the lines, affords a painful spectacle of the family disputes; and rather bears out Camden's statement that Gregory was of 'cracked brain' or in any case dreadfully weak, and tossed about in the quarrels between his mother and his wife, both of whom were no doubt much stronger minded than he was. Margaret would certainly have led a wretched life had she chosen to remain with her strong-minded sister-in-law, and would have been probably driven to marry the kinsman Pelham, who, although he may have been of 'good worshipp,' was evidently not to her taste.

Lady Dacre goes on:—

Not long after, either by her self or by the advise of her mother, and other Frends, fell into lykinge to matche w{th} the husbonde she now bathe, and therevpon requested to know what my lo: woulde be Contented to bestowe w{th} her in marriage that waie, and thoughe it woulde much better have pleased my lo: that his sister shoulde haue ben bestowed vpon my Cozen Pelhame, for dyvers verie good respects, Yet for that it seemed vnto him that my Ladie his mother, and his sister, liked better otherwaies, he was Contented to referr yt to his sisters owne Choice, and would also bestowe w{th} her Five hundred pounde,[2] w{ch} offer olde m{r} Leonarde

---

[1] This must mean that the lands were not leased at rack rents, but on some easy terms as to annual rents in consideration of sums of money paid down upon the granting of the leases.

[2] As to this see Gregory's letter offering 500 marks, not 500*l.*, *ante*, p. 78.

vtterlie refused, and so the matter rested for a time, and within a while after one Mr Barrome, at whose howse my lo: mother and his sister then laie, came vnto me and tolde mee, That the yong Coppells[1] meaninge m^r leonarde, and my sister, woulde Marrie and seeke their Frendes good will after; and required of mee monie for her apperell, where vpon I deliued vnto him the same nighte a hundred marke, and within ij daies after they were married openlie at Mr Leonardes howse, my lorde, nor I, nether bidden to yt, nor otherwaies made pryvie.

This being this [thus] done and the marriage betwene my sister and m^r leonarde paste, some vnkindnes remained betwene my lo: and his sister, in that wee were no better delte wthall, yet the matter was not greate, nor continued longe.

She then says that Gregory, being involved in law suits with Lord Norris, found that his best course was to come to some arrangement with him, which he could have done without obtaining the consent of Margaret; 'yet such care he hadd of her and hers, to be next in remainder to him, & his, as he did call her wth her husband & Father [father-in-law] and made them pryvie to the whole matter.' From what one sees of Gregory's weak character, it is impossible to believe that he took any part in these negotiations except acting under the directions of his wife. Lady Dacre goes on to say that a new settlement was made by the consent of all parties, ' by wch assurauance theire was entailed, of my lo: best lande and moste auncunte inheritance and chief howse to my sister wth ij partes of the lande, or verie nere theirunto,' and the remaining third part was to be free for Gregory to sell ' for payments of his debtes and other necessarie chardges W^{ch} were then verie greate, and were grown by disorder, whiles his mother, and other officiers, hadd the rule as ys aforesaid.' She says also that Gregory could have made much better terms with Lord Norris, and so had more land free to sell, had he consented that Lord Norris should be next in remainder

---

[1] The C. P. gives 1564 as date of this marriage; an *I. P. M.* states that when Margaret died in 1611 she was seventy years of age, and that when Samson died in 1615 he was seventy-one years of age, so that she was born in 1541 and he in 1544. This would make them respectively twenty-three and twenty years of age at date assigned for their marriage.

to him, but this 'for the love he bore to his sister woulde not agree vnto, wch manno^r of dealinge towarde his sister my lo: and I assured our selves were sufficient to haue tied both olde Mr Leonarde, his sonne, and his wief, wth their children, at all tymes to be faithfull frinds and earneste lovyers, both of my lo: and me, as wth good reason they oughte: yet all this not w^th-standing they most vnthankfullie, and for my sister pte most vnnaturallye, tourned all this to my lo: extreme troble.'

Lady Dacre then continues that Margaret knowing my brother of Buckhurste to be then verie hardlie dispoced towardes me, and Extreme vnkindness to be betwixte him and mee, my sister leonarde wth the Consente both of her Father, and husbande, seekinge to make my brother of my greate enemye to be their faste frende, did attempte him wth this offer; that he shoulde haue herr eldest sonne, and Mr Nevells eldest sonne[1] for ij of his daughters in marriage, vpon condicōn that the lo: Buckhurst shoulde pcure from Yo^r Matie, a graunte in possession to yong leonarde, and his wief, of all suche my lo: landes as Yo^r Matie anie waye hadd anie tytell vnto and what shoulde be paied for the same olde Mr Leonarde would paie, wch offer wth other perticulerytes was excepted [accepted]. Wherevpon my lo: of Leicester was first treated wth all, to gett this graunte at Yo^r Maties bandes, and was verie lyberallye offred for the same.

This statement of Lady Dacre's about the proposed marriages is further evidence of what little choice was, in those days, left to young people as to whom they should marry.[2] It also seems to show that Gregory, or she herself, had procured some of the lands in settlement to be 'assygned over' to my Lord of Leicester as Margaret in her 'Greyfes' alleges;[3] and that his lordship was considered to be willing to be bribed in order to use his influence with Elizabeth to have these lands conveyed to whoever would offer him an adequate consideration.

The following extract from a letter, dated April 1587, and written to Lord Burghley, by one R. Fynes, a cousin of Gregory,[4] throws some further light on the part taken by Lord

---

[1] Samson's sister Rachael married E. Nevill, afterwards Lord Abergavenny.
[2] See also *ante*, p. 57 *et seq.*   [3] *Ante*, p. 88.
[4] *Hist. Com.* (Salisbury), iii. p. 251.

Leicester in this matter, and bears out my statement that he was willing to be bribed. The writer begins his letter by telling Lord Burghley of an interview he had had with the Earl of Leicester at Wanstead, and after speaking of other matters, goes on :—

Then it pleased him [Leicester] to tell me that he had lately spoken unto her Majesty to confirm her first grant made unto him touching my Lord Dacre's lands, 'the which' saith he 'I will transfer unto you, and we will agree well enough, but as yet I will not tell you in what sort.' 'My Lord' quoth I 'if it might please your Lordship to let me know in what manner your pleasure were to transfer it, and that it might be known unto her Majesty that your lordship's meaning is so to do, I doubt not but that in respect it hath already pleased her Majesty to ask my Lady Dacres, whether I were not of that house saying "Madam, he is an honest man and one that we like well of, and it cannot be better done of my lord than to wish well to his name."' My Lady Dacres replied that I was the kinsman that 'my Lord of all others had best cause to like of.' 'And therefore my Lord, not as one that intendeth to be either in duty or thanksgiving less thankful to your lordship than shall be thought fit by your lordship, but rather hoping that my name being used therein, the enterprise in respect it should appear to all men that your Lordship doeth it for the next heir male, shall be adjudged for your lordship the more honourable, and receive the freer passage. I take boldness thus much humbly to advertise your lordship for my lord, under reformation, although your lordship's own merit deserve much more from her Majesty, yet may it seem happily more pleasing to the world that the next heir male should participate with the sister, and the nearest in blood, rather than a stranger. Although notwithstanding the due thanksgiving that I shall therefore yield your lordship may be such and so great, as my poor ability may to the uttermost yield.' 'It is true,' saith his lordship, 'and indeed at the last time I found my Lord Treasurer[1] somewhat inclined to Mr Leinorde.' 'Truly my lord' quoth I 'I do not think but that my Lord Treasurer doth much more respect your lordship than Mr Leinorde, although the nearness of blood between my Lord

---

[1] Lord Burleigh, to whom this letter was written, was then Lord Treasurer.—*Hay. Dig.*

Dacres and Mr Leinorde might justly move my Lord much; but my Lord when his lordship shall see your lordships honourable disposition in seeking nothing more than to advance and enable thereby a branch of the same tree; such hath been in all other cases his honourable disposition, as that his lordship hath ever had a religious regard of the continuance of ancient houses, insomuch as, although my own desert can challenge nothing from him, yet the great interest your lordship hath in him, as also the respect of the name and house, will move him.'

Lady Dacre suggested that Mr. Hurlston's action against Gregory was instigated by 'olde Mr Leonarde' in order to get a legal decision as to the Queen's title to those lands said to have been conveyed to her[1] which is quite a different suggestion from that made by Margaret Lennard. She further says that the Lennards procured Mr. Thursby to cause Gregory to be sued on his bond to him and others for 10,000*l.*, and that 'my sister to myne owne Face wth vehement wordes did threaten me that the most extremitie that mought bee [might be] should bee soughte against my lo:' the result of this being that Gregory found it difficult to sell those lands which were resettled on him in fee simple 'to his extreme daunger and overthowe' (overthrow), and 'my sister contynewing wth most slaunderous reports affirming to psons of good Creaditt in yor M$_a^{ties}$ Courte, that I hadd spoyled and soughte to overthrowe my lo: Barromye [Lord's barony] And that I hadd Conveyed awaie the greateste pte of his landes to my frendes and that I hadd gone aboute to prove my lo: a Basterde, all wch is vtterlie most vntrewe.'

It is probably 'vntrue' that Margaret ever made any such allegations about the legitimacy of her brother being called in question by his wife, although, as it is clear these ladies were on the worst possible terms, they no doubt each said the most

---

[1] I have an ancient copy of an indenture, dated January 7th, 22nd Eliz. (1579), some eight years later than the date of the quadripartite agreement (*ante*, p. 82), by which Gregory grants to the Queen and her heirs the manors that had belonged to his grandfather in the counties of Berks, Notts, and some of those in Yorkshire. This deed contains no mention of any valuable consideration for the grant, and some of the manors in Berks had been allocated to Lord Norris by the previous deed of 1571.—*Ante*, p. 83.

spiteful things they could think of, one against the other. From what Lady Dacre says herself it seems not improbable that she had made, or any way endeavoured to make, some conveyances of part of the settled estates in order to defeat the resettlement made in 1571.

That the sympathies of herself and her husband, as far as he had any views on the matter, were entirely against the Lennard family in spite of all her protestations of love for Margaret to the contrary, is shown by a letter dated April 9th, 1592, from R. Fiennes to Lord Burghley,[1] where, after referring to Gregory Lord Dacre as being the head of his family, and saying that he was on very good terms with him, the writer goes on to say that he hopes Gregory will have a long line of male descendants, and that he himself will never use any means to obtain any portion of the estates which Gregory has the power to dispose of, although when the resettlement of his estates was made, both Lord and Lady Dacre said unto him, 'Cousin albeit we may not show ourselves contrary to our Covenant to Mr. Lennard, to whom we have transferred our right, yet we would not be sorry if you could procure the title of the rest from Her Majesty.'

At first sight it would seem to be impossible to alienate settled property, but in those days of almost universal corruption it appears to have been done in this ingenious manner. The life tenant conveyed estates to the Queen, whose title could not be called in question, and then by influence, and probably bribes, induced some favourite of Elizabeth, such as Leicester, to obtain a grant back from the Crown of the same estates in fee simple. By this means any settlement could be rendered entirely useless. Lady Dacre says that she did get Leicester to intercede with the Queen to confirm the sale of 'suche lande as my lo: did then entend to sell.' This account of the then system of obtaining the personal intervention of the Sovereign in family legal disputes by means of Court intrigues, brings vividly to the mind the very great difference that exists between

[1] *S. P. Dom. Eliz.* ccxli. No. 120.

the state of things now and in the times when John Lennard lived. Then if you were fortunate enough to be in what we should now call the Court 'Ring,' or if you could bribe those who were in it to act on your behalf, you could no doubt have perpetrated all sorts of dishonest or unjust practices with absolute impunity.

Lady Dacre makes a further complaint in order, as she says, 'to shewe somewhat farder of Mr Leonards hardd dealings wth my lo:' but she only alleges that John bought a manor[1] from Gregory for 'ij thousande pounde, and had iij yeres daie of payement; whereas my lo: mighte have hadd of others xxij^{li} [2,200l.] in shorter daies,' and that John insisted on having an allowance of 'iij^{li}' (60l.) made to him as Gregory had previously disposed of the next presentation to the living. There appears on her own showing to be nothing here to require the Queen's interference; for all she says amounts to this, that if Gregory had not sold the manor to John Lennard he might have sold it on better terms to someone else.[2]

This lengthy document is at last brought to an end, after asserting that for the sake of brevity she has omitted to mention many of her good deeds towards Margaret, and her 'ill Acquittall towardes mee,' by a request for what we should now call an injunction; whereby Margaret 'maie be comaunded either to use good speaches of me wch I feare she lothlie[3] will, or to forbeare vntrewe complaints of me wch in good reason me thinkes she oughte to do.'

The other documents in the Record Office relating to this dispute consist of answers by Margaret to some of the statements contained in this supplication, Lady Anne's replies to these

---

[1] Probably Staunton Quinton, Wilts; it is mentioned in a list of Gregory's possessions as sold by him for 2,000l., *ante*, p. 91, and in 1586 John held the advowson of that place, *post*, p. 142, and he also owned that manor at his death, *post*, p. 150.

[2] Gregory brought a bill in Chancery against John to be relieved of a bond of 1,000l. that he had given him to warrant his title.—*P. C.* i. p. 223.

[3] Unwillingly: old form of loathly.—*C. D.*

answers, and further answers by Margaret to these replies. These documents are all dated 1579, but the matter, however, seems to have dragged on, as legal business usually does, for more than a year after this date we have the following draft letter in John's handwriting. The letter is for Lord Burghley, and it evidently purports to be by Margaret Lennard; it is written in very small handwriting, and contains so many corrections and interlineations that it is most difficult to decipher:—

My duty wyth my humble comendacyons doon unto yor Lordship, yor honor knoweth that aboute thys tyme twelvemoneth I dyd put vp a suplicacyon to the Queenes Mat^{ie} that yt myght plese her Highness of her clemencie to stay her . . . . to a sute that my Lady Dacres was then in hand wyth for the conveyeng from her Mat^{ie} of certeyn of my lord my brothers lands, as lands supposed to be concealed [?], whereof I was yn remaynder, tylle such tyme as the state of thees lands were throughly seen yn to by such of the nobles of her most honourable pryvay counsell, and learned judges in her lawes as to her Mat^{ie} should be thought mete which I stylle desire of her Highness, yf by her gracius faur [favour] I may do so, for els yf her Highness graunted [?] vnder her grete seale . . . . of the seid ladyes sute or any others lyke sute, yt wold be such a countenance to the tytle of such as shuld clayme thereby, were her Highness ynterest yn yt never so weke, and such a dyscredyte to my remayndr yf yt shuld falle to me or myne, thoughe yt be welle assured to us, that hardely and with myche charge & dyffyculty shuld I, or they, enioy the same; and, though I enquyred of some of my frends nere, I could not lerne tylle my husbands father sent me word wythyn thyes fewe dayes that any such sute was folowed by my Lady, but this he advertysed me, that such a sute ys now p[ro]secuted by my Lady, or some other. He also advertysed me that I must answere spedely whether I wille stand to the assurance alredy made of the porcyon of land assigned to me in remayndr, which ynydede was delyerd me for dcclxxxv^{li} xi^s vi^d by yere, or els that I wylle relynquyshe that and take cc^{li} by yere of the old rent by another conveyance. I am by a late chyld byrth[1] such a prysoner as I can not come abrode to do my duty and wayte and answere yn person as els I wold, but yf I must nedes chose thone [the one] or thothr [the other], then fyrst besechyng her Mat^{ie} to be my good and gracyous lady, as hytherto

[1] The first of her two daughters, christened Elizabeth, was born June 5th, 1580.

she hath been, for whom I and myne shall yncessantly pray to god to blysse her wyth all happyness as duty byndeth us, and prayeng you to be my good lord as heretofore ye haue bin, I do signyfye to yor Lo by thys my lr̄e [letter] that I rather chose, wyth her Highnes fau^r [favour], to stand to the porcyon of land & assurance that I haue alredy, trustynge that god wylle rayse up frends to seave me in my . . . . I shuld not els do well, for there ar yn remayndr after me my Lō Norrys and fyve or sixe more whom yt concerneth as well as me, the conveyance was made by grete advyse of many lerned men by fyne and yndenture quadryp[ar]tyte whereof the Lord Norres hath one part, my lo my brother another, I a thyrd, & my lo chyef Baron & other feoffees the iiijth I may not hereyn forget what damage my father [1] & husband ar yn ; for thassurrance stode my father yn dccc mar̄s & he & my husband ar yn grete bands [bonds] to pay mm^{li} to the p[er]formance of my lo my brothers wylle, and so almyghty god p[re]serve you yn myche hono^r Knolle the xvjth of June 1580 your honors most humbly to com̄and
         MARGARET LENNARD.

To the right honorable her especyall good Lord the Lord Burghley Highe Threasourer of England.

We have amongst our family papers the following two letters on this matter from the Queen's celebrated minister Walsingham to John Lennard. The commencement of the first one is in terms unintelligible to persons not conversant with the rudiments of the law relating to real—*i.e.* landed—property. It is only a comparatively small number of lay persons who have such knowledge, and for those of my readers who have not I paraphrase the passage thus: 'Her Majesty having decided to convey to trustees for the benefit of Lord Dacre certain lands to which her Highness is entitled,' &c., &c.

The letter is addressed 'To the right worshipfull my verie loving frend Mr. John Lennard in Kent':—

S^r, hir ma^{tie} [majesty] having been of late moved to passe vnto certaine ffeoffees certaine lands of the L: [Lord] Dacres to his vse wherunto hir highnes is intitled, wherof you are not ignorant; for that this matter doth somewayes towch you in

---
[1] Meaning her father-in-law, John Lennard.

respect of yo[r] soon [son] by his match w[th] the L: Dacres sister; hir mat[ies] [majesty's] pleasure is, before shee passe the said lands, that you bee talked w[th]all; and to that end hath given order that both you and yo[r] soon make yo[r] repaire presentlie[1] hither to the Court where, the L: Thrēr [Treasurer], and I, am appointed to conferre w[th] you of this matter, as you shall more fully understand at yo[r] comyng. And therfore I pray you faile not to bee here as soone as convenientlie you may. So wth my hartie comendations I byd you farewell. From the Court at Otelands the xvij[th] of Julie, 1580.

    Yo[r] verie loving frend, FRA: WALSINGHAM.
 Mr. Leonard.

If this conference took place the matter does not appear to have been then decided by the Queen, as a little more than a month later John had the following letter upon the same subject:—

After my bartie commendacons. Theis are to let you vnderstand that her M[te] [Majesty's] pleasure is, you, and your sonne, should presentlie make your repaire hether for that she meaneth to take some order in the matter of controversie betwin you and the L: Dacres, as at yo[r] comminge you shall more particularlie vnderstand. In the mean while I commit you to God. At the Cōte [Court] the last of August 1580.
    Your verie lovinge frind, FRA: WALSYNGHAM.

Whether Elizabeth did then and there decide in John's favour, or whether he had to resort to further petitions and negotiations before he gained his point, I have no means of knowing:[2] but anyhow in the end Margaret did, upon her brother's death, succeed to those portions of the estates which

---

[1] Presentlie is here used in the old sense, meaning 'at once.' In the French language of to-day we have the same form in 'présentement,' which is the basis of a joke in *Punch* a few years ago. A couple of English tourists are represented as looking at a notice of apartments to let in Paris, where is displayed on a notice board the announcement that the rooms are 'à louer présentement.' The one who considers that he 'understands the foreigners' says to the other, 'How funny these French chaps are; everything is to be let presently!'"

[2] John and his son Samson brought a bill in Chancery to have the settlement carried out; the bill is not dated, but it is addressed to Sir Thos. Bromley, Lord Chancellor. He held that office from April 1579 to April 1587; so the bill must have been filed at some period between those dates.—*P. C.* ii. p. 140.

104 HISTORY OF THE LENNARDS

had been resettled upon her by that conveyance of 1571, for which John had to pay five hundred marks. The following is a list of the lands that she thus obtained; the rents here given are, no doubt, in many cases much less than the rack rents would have been:—

Landes apoynted to Mrs. Lennard, the Lord Dacres sister by the assuerance made in Trynitye terme anno xiij° E. Regine [1571].

Norfolk . .	The Manners of Horsford & Hautboys . . .	l^{li} . . iij^d
Sussex . . .	The Manners of Herstmonseux, olde Corte, & Goteham [Gotham] . . .	ccc^{li}
	The Manners of Buckhold .	xl^{li}
	The Manners of Ewhurst	lxxxx^{li}
	The [Manor ?] of Ingrammes	xxiij^{li} xiij^s iiij^d
	The Manner of Haylsham .	v^{li} xij^s j^d ob.
Yorkshyre .	The Manner of Mapleton .	xix^{li} x^s
	The Manner of Thirne . .	viij^{li} . . iiij^d
	The Manner of Scorton.	xxxvj^{li} xij^s
	The Manner of Staveley	xxxij^{li} ix^s iiij^d
	The Manner of nether Calcats	iij^{li} xvj^s vj^d
Lincolneshere.	The Manner of holebech .	c^{li}
Kent . . .	The Manner of Burham	xxxvj^{li} x^s ij^d
	The Manner of Cowdham	xxxiij^{li} vj^s viij^d
Essex . . .	The Manner of Nashalle .	vj^{li}
	dcclx^{li} xv^{li} viij^s ij^d.[1]	

As has been stated by the terms of the quadripartite indenture, Lady Dacre had power reserved to her of granting long leases over those lands which were settled in remainder on Margaret, and no doubt she availed herself freely of this power.

[1] I cannot explain the form of this total of 775*l*. 8*s*. 2*d*. with two amounts in the £ column, but so it is in the original. The above items when added up come to 785*l*. 10*s*. 8*d*.

We have a lease by Gregory Lord Dacre, of Nashe Hall, Essex, dated 13th of the July following the execution of the 'quadripartite Indenture,' whereby in consideration 'of his painful & diligent service and also for divers good causes &c.,' he granted the said manor to A. Jackson for forty years at a yearly rent of 6*l*., and John Lennard, in a letter to Lord Burghley, speaks of Lord Dacre obtaining 1,000*l*. for leases of Horsford.[1]

John appears to have been within the mark in mentioning 1,000*l*. as the amount received by Lord and Lady Dacre by way of fines for long leases of Horsford, with power to the tenants to cut timber. I have twelve counterpart leases which they granted over that estate, and by virtue of these leases they obtained nearly 1,100*l*. in fines, while they demised the lands for terms of forty years at merely nominal rents; and this accounts for why, in Samson's time, Horsford only produced him about 50*l*. a year, and was nearly entirely devoid of timber.

Between December 1584 and November 1586 John Lennard, rich as he was, appears to have been driven to borrow money; these borrowings may have been effected in order to meet some of the very heavy charges which he was put to in connection with his daughter-in-law Margaret's claims against her brother. We have a bond dated December 2nd, 27th Eliz. (1584), by which John and his sons, Samson and Samuel, are responsible for the payment of 300*l*. by the following April to James Astyn; and an indenture dated November 29th, 29 Eliz. (1586), which recites that John and Samson are bound in 2,000*l*. to William Tyndale by a recognisance made before Edmund Anderson, Knt., C.J. of the Common Bench, but that by this deed Tyndale grants that this recognisance shall be void if he is paid the sum of 1,000*l*. on November 31st in the following year. I think that, certainly as regards the second of these deeds, the money may have been raised for Samson's benefit; but it is not so clear why, if the former borrowing was also for Samson, his brother should have been made a party to it.

We must now consider John Lennard's negotiations for the

[1] *Ante*, p. 91.

marriages of his daughters. His eldest one, Mary, married on December 27th, 1579,[1] Guilford Walsingham, son of Sir Thomas Walsingham of Scadbury, Chislehurst, or as it was formerly written 'Chesilhurst,' in Kent. Sir Thomas died in 1583, and his wife Dorothy in the following year, and both are buried at Chislehurst;[2] he was a cousin of Queen Elizabeth's famous minister of that name.

In reference to the negotiations for this marriage there are some rather interesting letters still existing.[3] John evidently tried to arrange for it, and as the matter hung fire somewhat, he sent his daughter-in-law to see how the land lay; and the result of her visit was that Lady Walsingham wrote to him making an appointment in order to talk the matter over. John's reply to her letter (or rather a rough draft of it) is difficult to read, being written in a small crabbed hand in the style of that period, and full of corrections. It is as follows:—

After my most harty comendacyons unto Sir T. Walsyngham, you, and yr son, my very good lady, yt may please you to be aduertysed, that comyng from mornyng prayer yn lyncolns yn chapelle thys present wensday to my chamber, I rec[eived] by a servant of yours y^{or} lre [letter] to me dyrected. The effect of yt ys that when my sonnes wyf was lately with you of good wylle to se you, she did then put you yn mynd from me of a sute that I made to Sir Th. you, and y^{or} son, for a maryage to be had betwene y^{or} son and my daughter; which by my sonnes wyfs report to me, and as yt semeth by y^{or} letter, Sir Th. and you, take in good part as heretofore ye have, and have appoynted me to come to y^{or} lodgyng to morowe yn the afternone for further conference therof betwene us. I answered y^{or} man by word that I wold attend the tyme & place, which God wyllyng I wold observe, but I shall rather have wrytten so to you sythers[4] you wrate to me. Pardon me good Madame that I did not so, for having in my hed a grete cause of myn own that was to be heryd thys day before my l. Thresorer, for want of tyme to wryte, I answered you by word

---

[1] *Sev. Reg.* [2] *Has.* i. p. 99. [3] *L. P.*
[4] Form of 'sithe' or Since.—*C. D.*

that I wold not fayle to come whereapon ye may surely bynd.

And so I wysshe you y̅r harts desyre.

Lyncolns yn thys xxvij of May 1579.

It will be seen by this letter that John wished to be considered to be mindful of his religious observances, as otherwise he would not have mentioned, what was not at all to the point, the fact that he had been to church that weekday. It may be noted that, although he usually uses 'y' where we now use the letter 'i,' he does not appear to have always done so.

In these days if a father is desirous that a man paying attention to one of his daughters should become engaged to her, and that engagement be brought to a successful issue, he would be likely to show attention to his prospective son-in-law; and what would be more natural, if he had shooting or hunting to offer, than to have among his guests invited for sport his daughter's admirer? As in Queen Elizabeth's days the parents were the chief parties to consult in their children's 'matching,' John probably did not think it worth while troubling himself about Guilford Walsingham, but wrote and asked his father, Sir Thomas, to come and kill some deer, as is shown by the following reply to John from the latter:—

S^r, for that the Queens Maties goinge from Greenewitche is as yet deferd, and therebie the cominge of those that I haue long loukte for yet vncerten by meanes therof, and my other occasions of business to be donne at the Courte, wch lyes so near, I can not as yet, accordinge to my good will, & yor desire, come vnto youe to kill a Bucke as this bearar whom I haue sent to declare it vnto yow. But hereafter when her Matie is removed from Greenewitche, and my lasur better, yow shall hear from me again to come vnto yow at such tyme as yow shall hereafter appointe. So leavinge you in the meantyme wyth my bartie commendacions. Skadburie the 3rd. of August 1579.

Your lovinge friend   THOMAS WALSYNGHAM.

In the following month Sir Thomas again writes to John: this time about the marriage portion.

Mr. Lennard for answer to your lre [letter] wch was as strainge to me as the tow lrs [letters] yow receved in one day, the one besydes myne was vtterlie vnknowne to me. My wiffe maide request to me for the increasinge of his former porcon graunted by me to him, wch I agreed vnto; but for anie of his demands towards yo^u, and your answer to hime touchinge the same as I protest afore God was, and is, unknowne to me, but by your lre [letter]. So that if I may have goode assurance for my demaunds agreed upon betweene yo^u & me, I can not for my pte [part] require no more at your hand, vnlesse yo^u will, vppon yor owne good will, agree to gyve him more vppon the good lykinge of bothe the pties [parties], wch I can not be againste. So the Lord keepe yo^u & yours in helthe. Scadburie the xi of September 1579.

  Your lovying frende   THOMAS WALSYNGHAM.

By this letter it is evident that Guilford had tried to get his future father-in-law to give Mary a larger portion than had been agreed upon; Sir Thomas appears to be quite straightforward in the matter, and to repudiate having any hand in his son's attempt to squeeze more money out of John. There were still, however, difficulties in the way of this proposed marriage, as Lady Walsyngham writes to John :—

Sir I cannot p[er]swade w^t [with] myself that you meane to furnishe y^or da. [daughter] w^t aparell so very meanly as I here you have apynted. I suppose y^or great affares & doinges y^is [this] tarme hathe yet w^t drawne you to cōsyder [consider] therof as is mett (& as I hope you will). The aparell & jewels you have yet apynted for your da. . . . so verry lytell as yf you had mached her to ye very lowest gentlemans son in o^r shere. I am sure you (should?) for y^or owne credit, & worshipe, have gyven your da. tow suits of aparell and lynen . . . I can not se you have apynted to give her . . . yf I dyd thinke you ment no other wyse to bestowe on y^or da. than ys yet set downe I should c[on]serve great vnkyndness in you, but I verely thinke y^or purpose is this meanly to seme to aparell her, because I should intreat you to inlarge it; to the end you may seme somethinge to recompense me for my travell and procuringe (w^t ye helpe of my frendes) Mr Wall. [Walsyngham] to abate hys detarmyned (yea & offered) som of money in maryage w^t his son; & indeed obtained it to y^e

---

[1] 'Lettre' and 'letre': obsolete forms of 'letter.'—*C. D.*

hinderonce of myself, and other my children. Well I will leve farther to wryt what I have in trught more to say in this, and very hartly and arnestly desire you to geve y^{or} da. Mary against her maryage on [one] good sute more of aparell, or a fare pare of borders.[1] Yf you shall refuse at my request y^{is} [this] to do I can not take it well, nether will I willingly be at the maryage (nor indeed will) yf I can be any meanes intreat Mr Wall. to the co[n]trary. But hoping or rather assuring meself that you will willingly and frauncly graunt y^{is} my request I do w^t my very harty commendacyons for y^{is} tyme take my leve of you and wysshe you a very ganefull tarme and many after.

Scadbury the xix of Nove[m]ber 1579.

Y^{or} assured frend   Do. WALSINGHAM.

Addressed 'To the ryght worshipful my very good frend John Lenard Esquyer with sped.'

Although Lady Walsingham was so anxious that John should provide handsomely for his daughter, Guilford's father did not settle much on him, unless indeed there were other settlements than I know of. The one I have found was executed on November 24th, 22 Eliz. (1579), and among the witnesses to it were the bride's two brothers, Samson and Samuel. By this document Sir Thomas, described as of 'Chyelshurst,' settles on his son only a rent-charge of 80*l*. arising out of the manor of Little Peckham in the parishes of Mereworth, Hadlow, and Peckham in Kent.

Of the remaining three letters from Lady Walsingham to John in our collection, two are dated, the one 'Thursday' and the other 'Sunday,' and one is not dated at all, so that then, as now, women were frequently somewhat unbusinesslike in respect of dating their letters. Lady Walsingham was evidently a clearheaded woman, but she of course would never have imagined that more than three hundred years after her letters were written anyone would trouble as to their exact date, nor even if she had thought about it would she perhaps have cared. In writing

---

[1] A piece of ornamental trimming about the edge of a garment; 'borders' were made detachable and were often richly embroidered, and of such value as to be specially mentioned in wills and inventories.—*C. D.*

a book of this nature it often happens that one is enabled to fix a date, perhaps of relative importance, from chance references occurring in letters written upon other subjects if only these letters be dated. The usual habit of men to date their letters fully has frequently proved of very great assistance to me, while the equally usual habit of women, even if methodical in other matters, to content themselves with such a date as 'July 23' has still more often been a cause of great exasperation.

It is clear from the contents of these letters from Lady Walsingham that at least two of them were written after this marriage had taken place, and as they are couched in very friendly terms, we may hope that John did give his daughter 'on good sute more of aparell or a fare pare of borders,' and that her ladyship did grace the ' maryage' by her presence.

The object of these letters was to thank John and 'Mistress Lenerd' for presents of 'fruites and whit wyne,' and in one, speaking with satisfaction of the 'well lykinge and good agreement of our beloved,' which presumably refers to the newly married pair getting on well together, Lady Walsingham speaks of herself being remiss in not having returned 'Mistress Lenerd' her 'bottells' which contained her 'good wyne.' These bottles were therefore apparently of some value, and were probably leather ones. The white wine was presumably some sort of home-made wine, such as cowslip or gooseberry, which is still not unfrequently made by cottagers. In the second of these letters she evidently refers to some joke John had made in a letter to her, as she says she will 'bere in store a merry laffinge' until they next meet.

Guilford Walsingham did not long enjoy the pleasures of matrimony as he died while still young, leaving two daughters: Dorothy, who appears to have died unmarried, and Elizabeth, who married a Mr. John Scrivener. On August 23rd, 1587, Guilford's widow married, as her second husband, Thomas Gresham, of Titsey, Surrey.[1]

In reference to the marriage of John's daughter Rachael, we

[1] *Sev. Reg.*

have a fragment which appears to be part of the pleadings in some lawsuit. From it we learn that John, believing that Edward Nevill was heir to a considerable property, some sixteen years before the date of the document in question, ' by medyacyon of frends entred ynto comunycacyon wyth hym [E. Nevill, the father] for a maryage to be held betwene Edward Nevyle the younger hys son,' and one of his daughters. John paid the elder Nevill upon this marriage taking place 'a grete some of monye,' and for a long time the bridegroom lived with his father-in-law. This unfortunately is all that can be gathered from the fragment, which is not of sufficient length to enable the object of the action at law to be understood.

The only other correspondence which I have found concerning the marriage of any of John's children is an unsigned draft letter in his handwriting, written on the lower part of a letter, dated April 1587, that he had received from a Mr. Cranewell[1] about a business transaction in which they were engaged. This draft letter is dated April 1587, but is not addressed, nor does John refer in it by name to the daughter whom it concerned. As we shall see when he made his will, which he did in the following November, his daughters Elizabeth and Anne were the only ones then left unmarried, and this letter no doubt referred to one of them, probably to the former, as John most likely married them off in order of age as far as he was able to do so.

It has been stated that Elizabeth married Sir Francis Eure, but as she did not do so until 1589, it is quite possible that this letter was not written to Lord Eure, his father, but to some other person to whose son John was trying to marry Elizabeth. It will be observed that in this letter he offers 1,500*l.* as his daughter's portion, while in his will, made some six months later, he leaves only 1,000*l.* as marriage portions for each of his unmarried daughters :—

After my right harte comēndacyons yt may please you to be

[1] As to the correspondence between John Lennard and Edward Cranewell, *vide post*, p. 136 *et seq.*

advertysed that whereas my son Covert, about half a yere syns, had some speche wyth you for a maryage tobe had betwene yor son & my daughter whereof ye knowe upon that hys mocyon to you of that matche my self spake wth you thereof at yor house at the black Fryers, my son Covert as hys beyng wyth me at Knolle aboute fortnyght agoo, told me y^t he had renewed y^t matter to you & found you welle enclyned thereyn, upon the p[ar]tyes lykyng, if we could agre in ye pryce, he sayed further to me y^t he had lerned y^t xv^{li} [1,500*l.*] was offred you by others to wch some you agreed, but you broke of [off] upon the daye of payment, & therfore he offred you for me that sume, referrynge ye dayes of paym^t to me; wherfore for as mych as I heryd by hym that ye ar contented to talk wyth me ageyn of that matche thyes ar to sygnyfye to you y^t I wylle gyve you xv^{li} [1,500*l.*] & to yor sun xl^{li} [40*l.*] tobe payd as you wylle have yt, not doubtyng of yor lyberality to yor son every way, nor of yor alowance of a resonable joynter, yor plesure hereyn I wold be glad to knowe nowe or at yor convenyent leysure, and if your son wyth yor lycense myght & wold come to Knolle thys Ester weke to se whyther that he can lyke of my daughter or nay, he shalbe hartely welcome and so god kepe you Knolle the xiiijth of Apryle 1587.

I have found a fragment of a draft marriage settlement to be made upon a marriage agreed shortly to take place between Francis Eure and Elizabeth Lennard dated August in the 31st Eliz. (1589). The parties to the settlement are Lord Eure and Samson Lennard; there is not enough of this draft remaining to enable us to see what was settled thereby; it contains a recital that Lord Eure was possessed of lands in Yorkshire worth 100*l.* a year, and other lands the value of which is not stated, and here the fragment comes to an end, so we are left without information as to what it was proposed to settle on the marriage, or why Samson was a party to the deed instead of his father; it possibly was on account of the latter's advanced age.

In an account of the manor of Romford, *alias* Mawneys, Morant's 'Essex,'[1] states that John Lennard purchased it in

---

[1] Vol. i. p. 65.

1573, and that his son Samson obtained a license to alienate it in 1599 to Francis Ewre and others. We shall see later that John by his will left 10s. to the poor of Romford as being one of the places whence he received or had received ' rent & revenue,' but that in his devise of manors to his son he does not mention Romford. It may be that upon Elizabeth's marriage John parted with all his beneficial interest in the manor of Romford, and that Samson became a trustee for his sister, and when, ten years after the date of the draft settlement, he obtained the before-mentioned license to alienate Romford, it was merely in order to convey what lawyers call the legal estate.

From the contents of two draft letters which we have from John Lennard, it appears that he had purchased the manor of Sevenoaks, of which he had already a lease, from Lord Hunsdon for 200*l.* at some period previous to August 1573, and that the latter was anxious to have the bargain rescinded. Lord Dacre, who does not seem to have been aware of the existence of more than one of these letters, was evidently under the impression that it was Knole that Lord Hunsdon wanted,[1] but this is, I think, clearly a misapprehension, founded upon the erroneous supposition that Lord Hunsdon had originally granted John the lease of that house.

The draft letter, which seems from its contents to be the former of the two, is not dated, and is as follows:—

My duty humbly remembred vnto yor Honour, I haue rec[eived] yor lres [letters], & Sr George Carye your sones, for the rehavyng of Sevenock. Sir George Carye moved me of yt at Knolle, and I thought yor l. [Lordship] wold have spoken to me of yt there. Yt may please yor Hono^{ur} to be adutysed [advertysed] that, before that I bargayned yor Lordship, I had a leas of yt wythout ympechm^t [impeachment] of Wast,[2] paying no rent for xxi yeres wyth all p[ro]fyts—as well the gyft of the benefyce as others. Which bestowyng of the benefyce, yor l. [Lordship] had by my sufferance, & good wyll,

---
[1] *Ld. D. His.*
[2] Without impeachment of waste means that a tenant is not bound to repair, and may fell trees, dig stone, &c.

at the last advoydance. thys leas cost me dere. I fere that by this p̃chase [purchase] my leas ys yn perylle to be voyde, which I must looke to, & p[ro]vyde for—for beyng so fre to me for so many yeres I esteeme yt better then the ynherytaunce, & that chyefly made me pawse, & not to agre sodenyly tu releas my bargeyn. Yo^r Lordship wryteth honorablye, & Sir George Carye worshipfullie, & yet Sir George offereth me wronge to wryte that I haue from hym an undyrectly stolen ryght. Yo^r Lordship must defend me of that cryme. Yo^r Honour knoweth I sought yt not, but you offered yt me, and I was not hasty of yt, & I may not be shent [1] for takyng of an offred bargeyn. Y^{or} Honour dyd put Sr George Carye yn the bargeyn, as many noble & worshipfull men do their sonnes & heyrs at the p̃chaser [purchaser's] request, both yn sales, and leases, for M [a thousand] tymes more then Sevenock ys worth, and the p̃chaser dealeth ever only wyth the fathers. My l. [Lord] Lomley was in all my l. of Arundell's sales, the old l. La Warre's sonnes were lykewise yn hys sales, I have used my sonne so C. [a hundred] tymes. Sr George wryteth also that if I agre not to leve the bargeyn, he wylle kepe me out of possessyon, which though I wold not leave yt, he may not do, tylle my leas be ended, more then he may kepe me from the possessyon of my house; for, as yor Lordship knoweth, my leas begynneth before your Lordship's p̃chase. Sr George wryteth smartely otherwyse more then he neded [needed]. I marvayle he wold do so fyndyng me as he dyd, not obstynate, but well ynclyned, as yet I am, to plesure yor Lordship and hym. He myght by suche sharpe words have myssed of hys p̃pose [purpose] at some men's hands, thoughe yt be thought good enoughe to wyn yt of me. Yo^r Lordship wryteth that the Quene's Mat^{ie} knoweth of yt, & ys not contente wythall. God forbyd that I shuld be a partener yn any thyng that shuld dyscontent her Hyghnes. I had wyth other gentlemen, my neyghbors, her Mat^{ies} comfortable countenance, & speche at her entre ynto Kent, and at Knolle; & her Highnes bad me good morowe by my name at Otford. God graunt her a long & happy reygn over us! I marvayle how yt shuld come to her Mat^{ies} ere? if yt be a certaine busyheded neyghbour of myne that loveth to meddle yn other folks matters, to whom for that neyther of us ys beholdyng, told yt to some that ys aboute her? If nede so requyre your l. may safely say to her Matie that the mony that I pay for yt wylle, wyth welle bestowyng,

---

[1] Be put to shame.—*C. D.*

p̱)chase to you, & yor heyrs, more then doble the yerely rent that you haue, or shall haue for yt thyes xx yeres.

(Endorsed) My Lord of Hunsdoune for his rehavyng of Sevenock which I had bought of hym.

The letter which I imagine to be the second one is dated 'at C. my house the vjth of August 1573.'[1] In it John says:—

that att yor pleasure yt ys yo^{rs} ageyn, as I told yor lordship I was wythout mony when I bargeyned wyth you, & god ys my wytnesse I toke up cc^{li} for you, & payd xiiij^{li} ynterest, or very nere yt, for every c^{li}. I meane at yor lordships & Sr George Caryes desyre to let you have ageyne the bargeyn I had of you yn thys sorte folowyng better then you require y^t. . . .

John then states his condition, and continues:—

And doyng thus wherefore Sir George Carye offreth me xx^{li} & yor lordship offreth me what I wille reasonablye aske, & therefore lykely that you wold be brought to more, if I wold do as some man wold; I wylle take no peny gayne of you, but you shall pay me at my house by thys day seven nyght the cc^{li} you had of me, & the charges that I payde for the assurance, & vj^s viij^d that the Trumpetours, & vj^s viij^d that the knyght marshall, had of me for their fees, when her ma^{tie} was at Knolle, because yt ys a market towne, and I wylle bere the losse my self of the ynterest that I pay for the cc^{li} you had of me, which ys chargeable to me as I have told you.

Lord Hunsdon was not only a cousin of the Queen's but also one of her favourites, and probably no one knew better than John did how unwise it would be to have any dispute with so influential an adversary. In the course of this letter he says:—

I pray your l. & my l. yor wyf[2] & Sr George, to thynk welle of me, as nowe you se you have, so shall you have, no other cause nor never had, though there were a stormy tyme, to my habylytye[3] & for the smalle rome I have you shalbe as welcome

---

[1] I am not able to reconcile the fact that this letter was written from Chevening with what I have written as to John being by this date in possession of Knole.—*Post*, p. 121.

[2] 'Your lordship and my lady your wife.'

[3] Obsolete form of 'ability.'—*C. D.*

to my house as any mans, & I trust to se you & my l. yor wyf there if yor iourney lye at any tyme that way.

In one edition of Collins' 'Peerage,' that author says that in 3 Eliz. (1561) John purchased from Lord Hunsdon a long lease of Knole which he held under the Crown. This statement is not an accurate one, though Lord Dacre must have considered it to be so, as he corrected the proofs of the edition in question as far as it related to our family. Knole, formerly belonging to the Archbishop of Canterbury, was acquired by the Crown in the reign of Henry VIII. We have an ancient copy of a grant of this manor by Edward VI. 'To the L[ord] Seymore,' dated August 19th, 1547; he was executed on March 20th, 1549, and the manor then reverted to the Crown. We have also an ancient copy of a grant of Knole in the next reign to Cardinal Pole, dated March 13th, 2nd and 3rd Ph. & Mary (155$\frac{5}{6}$).

John Lennard had very great difficulties in obtaining the lease of Knole. There is among our papers quite a long document, much of which is in John's writing, endorsed 'Notes and Letters touching the lease of Knole Park,' and signed by himself; but one or two points in the controversy he unfortunately does not make as clear as one would wish. The 'Notes' contain a sort of abstract of John Lennard's claim, being a recapitulation of the points on which he relied, and copies of letters to him on the subject; and on these 'Notes' is pinned, with a very quaint old pin, an original letter from Sir William Cordell.

A certain Mr. Rolf appears to have been first in the field, and to have obtained a lease of Knole. We have an ancient copy of this lease, which was made on February 1st, 8th Elizabeth, 156$\frac{5}{6}$, between Robert Earl of Leicester and Thomas Rolf By this lease the manor and mansion-house of Knole and the park, with the deer, and also Panthurst Park and other lands, were demised to the latter for the term of ninety-nine years at a rent of 200*l.* The landlord was to do all repairs, and reserved the very remarkable right to himself and his heirs of occupying the mansion-house as often as he or they chose to do so, but this right did not extend to the gate-house, nor to certain other premises. The tenant was given power to alter or rebuild the mansion-house at his pleasure.

John got a Mr. Dudley [1] to try to induce Rolf to give up this lease, but Rolf objected to do so, saying, he 'wolde lever lose his lyfe' than part with it; as it turned out it was not long before he did lose the former. Rolf's letter, in which he alludes to being in bad health, is dated March 3rd, 1565, and the 'Notes' mention that he died in the November following; the date of his will, which, although it is not quite clear, appears to have been made in 1566. Whether Rolf died in 1565 or 1566, it is certain that the poor man did not live long to possess that which he says he did 'most covet to obteyne and enjoy.' The whole tone of his refusal to let John have Knole is of a most friendly nature, and he winds up by saying that 'yf hereafter at any tyme I shall parte from the same, you shall forsake [2] yt or any man lyvinge shall have yt.' The letter is as follows :—

After my hartie comendacōns; beinge right sorye that bothe oʳ desiers is bent to covet one thinge, considering that one of us must want that most ernestlie he desierethe, how willinglie I haue alwayes desiered to enioye Knoll my contynuall travell & paynes thereabowtes may sufficiently declare how lothe I haue ben to forgoe yt ons [once] obteyned; my answer made to my Lord Warden's officers (moving me therevnto in my Lords behalf when an exchange shulde haue passed betwene my Lord of Leycestre and him) may make manifest, wᶜʰ was that I wolde lever lose my lyfe then pte [parte] wᵗʰ my lease, whereuppon (as I suppose) thexchange betwene them tooke no place; And my Lord of Leic[ester], vnderstandinge my desier, was very willinge that I should still enioye that I then so coveted yet notwᵗʰstanding afterwardes, knowing my Lorde to be very desierous (for certen consideracōns his honor then movinge) to haue the same at my hands, And his Lordship moving me therevnto, I didd, as yow have herde, delyver him vp the same

---

[1] Probably a relation of Robert Dudley Lord Leicester, as one of the above 'Notes' runs—'Mr. Dudleys letter to Leonard confirmeth yᵗ for Leonard was then a Suitor to have it at my Lord of Leyc[ester's] hands by Mr Dudleys help.'

[2] Give up, or renounce.—*C. D.*

wth answer that, not onlie that (althoughe yt was a thinge that I moche coveted to possess) but all that I ells had was, and shoulde be at his honors comaundem^t. And my Lorde, vnderstanding howe lothe I was to pte [parte] from the same, sent Mr Dudley and Mr Glasier to me to give me knowledge that his mynde was that I shoulde still enioye Knoll accordinge to my owlde lease, Or ells I should haue a new lease made thereof, wch then I somewhat paussed to agree vnto. But sithence by lres [letters] that hathe passed betwene Mr Dudley & me yt is agreed to goe thoroughe wth the new lease according to certen coveūnts [covenaunts] agreed vppon as by my last lre [letter] sent unto Mr Dudley by his owne man yt appearethe. And accordinglie I am determened to go vpp to London, wth suche spede as my helth will suffer, to finishe the same; Wherefore I most hartelie pray yo^w bere wth me that I graunt not to parte from that to yow that I most covet to obteyne and enioye, he that of allmen I accompt my self most bound unto [viz. Mr Dudley] bathe so ernestlie and frendlie written vnto me in yor behalf that yf I were not fullie determined to stablish my self, and to contynwe in the same, I neither could nor woulde denye but graunt to yor request. But I assuer yo^w I am determened to kepe the same. And because I woulde yow shoulde be satisfied that this my determinacōn is trewe, and not fayned, I do hereby faithefullie p[ro]mise bothe to yow, and Mr Dudley in yor behalf, that yf hereafter at any tyme I shall parte from the same, yow shall forsake yt, or any man lyvinge shall have yt. And thus desiering yow to conceave of this my answer as you would I should in the leeke case do of yo^{rs} I take my leave, from Swingfelde[1] the iij^d of Marche A° 1565.

Yores I assuer yow,   THOMAS ROLF.

The following month Mr. John Dudley, the mutual friend of Rolf and John Lennard, wrote to the latter, evidently not knowing that Rolf had already written to him. He points out that he 'advysed' him to 'travell[2] with Mr. Rolf for his opinion[3] and goodwill therein.' He speaks of Mr. Rolf's 'affection therein,' meaning his 'disposition of mind,' and says that he has received no answer to a letter he had written,

---

[1] Swingfield in Kent, near Folkestone.   [2] Labour, toil.—*C. D.*
[3] Favourable judgment.—*Ibid.*

'wherefore I have some marvell.' The full text of this letter is as follows :—

To the Right Woorshipfull and my very frende Mr. Leonard.

Mr. Leonard I have receaved yor lr̃es [letters] and do p[er]ceave yor desier to talke towching Knoll either by purchase or by lease; yow knowe my mynde in that matter. And what was myne advyse for yow to travell wth Mr Rolf for his opinion and goodwill therein, wch beinge knowne, you know then what I p[rom]ised yow, wch I will p[er]forme, and to that ende yowe might wth the more spede knowe Mr Rolfs affection therein, I dyd ernestly wryte to him my mynde on yor behalfe, wherefore I knowe yow may easelie have answer yf yow will p[ro]cure yt. But trulie as yet I haue receaved no answer, wherefore I haue some marvell, Because the matter standeth now even at the verie pinch to kepe yt, or to departe wth yt, by exchange, or otherwyse by sale. But when yow shall haue answer from Mr Rolf wthout wch I maye not wth myne honestie deale, yow shall fynde me reddy to come to yow where yow will to take wth yow & to growe towarde some conclusion, that my Lords pleasure maye thereuppon be fullie knowne, wch I woulde might be done wth spede for so the case requireth. And for this tyme wth my right hartie Comendacōns I take my leave.

At the Courte in hast this ixth of Aprill 1566.[1]

Yor assuered to vse.   JOHN DUDDELEY.

As soon as Rolf died John Lennard appears to have made another attempt to obtain the lease of Knole. Mr. Dudley and Sergeant Lovelace were executors of Rolf's will, and John paid Dudley 600 marks for the lease and offered a like sum to the Sergeant, which he refused, and he then got a friend, John Frankelyn (from whom there are several letters among the Lennard papers), to go and see the Sergeant. This is the account which Frankelyn gives of his negotiations :—

To the right Woorshipfull Mr. Leonard Esquior at Cheveninge be this delyvered.

S^r after my hartie Comendacōns unto yor worshipp and to good Mysteris Leonarde and to all the rest of the gent & gentlewomen yor sonnes and daughters And as touching answer

---

[1] It is difficult to make out whether Rolf died in November 1565 or 1566; if the former, the ancient copy of this letter must be by mistake dated 1566 instead of 1565.

of yor worshipps lre sent to me, ye shall understand that I was at Canterbury wth Mr Seriant Lovelace wth yor lre sent to him. And I dyd desier of him that you mought[1] come to the howse of Knoll & grounde quyetly, vntill yow twoe did mete together. And then he answered me yow mought goe to the grounde yf yow woulde. Then I answered him 'No Sir yor men kepe the howse wth force,' And then he said, 'No there is no force at all for there is but one pore knave[2] that kepethe the howse.' And then I answered him 'S^r I vnderstand that the gates be kepte fast shett.' Then Mr Lovelace saide 'I thinke so for there is a chayne to the gate wch I dyd comaunde him to kepe chained and to let no man in vntill such tyme as he herde from me, to thintent that I will understand their title that shall other meddle, or make any thinge there, or come in to the howse.' Then I desiered him that yow mought come to the howse and to looke vppon the howse wthin for I did declare to him that the howse did goe in Ruine and great decaye for lacke of rep[ar]acōns And then he said, 'Well the Quenes ma^{tie} must kepe the rep[ar]acōns. And yt will not belong before he & I shall mete at London yf the terme holde, And then wthin thre or fower dayes I will make him answer therein. And wheras yow say he wilbe contented to take one Judge, and I another judge, I will not refuse that offer, so as he do not take Mr Welche,[3] for I will not that he shall meddell wth no matter of myne. As for the rents there, Mr Leonarde may take half them, yf he please, for the lands are all leased for yeares all reddy,' But he would not agree that yow shoulde come in to the howse, before yow and he didd mete together, w^{ch}, yf the terme did not holde, he wolde appoynt a place for to mete wthin x dayes to talke, and conclude wth yow in thoes matters, wch I did desier him might be at my howse yf it did please him. And then he answered me he would devyse some place where yow and he wolde mete, not farr of from that place of Knoll, 'Marry,' said he, 'my Lord of Buckhurst was in talke wth me for the obteyninge of the lease of Knoll And thereuppon bathe made a survey of yt wch bathe coste him great chardge as he hathe written to me about xx markes or xiiij^{li} or thereabouts, wch chardges must be recompensed againe, And for my parte I will paye the one half, yf my p[ar]tener will paye the other halfe, for yt is reason yf he have not the lease that he have his chardges for I p[er]ceave by a lre [letter] sent me by Mr Dudley that he hathe departed wth

---

[1] Obsolete form of 'might.' [2] Servant.—*C. D.* [3] Vide *post*, p. 123, *n.*

his interest to M{r} Leonarde w{th}out warrantie,[1] But I will sell my p[ar]te w{th} warrantie.' And all theis sayengs I trust will not be denyed for I will depose as mych uppon my othe as I have written herein. And thus I take my Leve of yo{r} worshipp; from Charte[2] this p[re]sent xxj{th} daye of october.

Yo{r} Worshipp to comande assuredlie during lyef

JOHN FFRANKELYN.

In spite of what the Sergeant had said to Frankelyn, John Lennard complains that 'he did flee from his promice,' and he said that he would call Frankelyn to prove this. John in his 'Notes' says, 'The Interest that I obtained of Mr Dudley in the lease of Knoll & the rest, I forthw{th} graunted to my sonne & his wyf, and presentlie I have nothing in yt.' I have found a deed dated May 12th, of Eliz. (1570) whereby John let Knole, Panthurst Park and Whitney Wood to his son Samson and his wife Margaret for twenty years at the rent of 40*l*. I suspect that this lease to Samson and his wife was not a *bona fide* one, but was granted by way of strengthening John's title in some way. It would enable Samson to bring actions as lessee, and put his adversary to the expense and difficulty of upsetting his title under the lease. My reasons for suggesting that this lease was granted by John for some such object is, that it is clear John resided at Knole in spite of the lease to his son during the existence of the term which was created by that lease. We have several letters addressed to John at Knole, and letters from Puleston who was his agent, written to him at Lincoln's Inn from Knole between 1570 and 1590, which was the period covered by the lease to Samson. Moreover, the fact that the lease was granted by John to his son and his daughter-in-law suggests to me a doubt as to its *bona fides*. John appears, however, to have been at Chevening at the time of his death.[3]

In the 'Notes' John also complains that 'the possession of Knoll howse is forcibly kept by my Lord's servants, & the bridges

---

[1] Security, or guaranty.
[2] Chart, near Ashford, Kent.
[3] *Inq. P. M.* at Maidstone, September 24th, 14th James I.

broken downe; my sonne & his wyf have attempted no entree there, otherwise than by their quiet cominge thether to wayt on, and to speak wth my Lord, as to require their possession, as ons [once] they did nighe vj weks now past; and ons sithence by their gentell wrytinge, but it was, and ys, denyed them.'

John evidently sent copies of these letters and of all the facts upon which he rested his claim to Knole to Sir William Cordell, in order to induce the latter to help him. The following letter from Sir William to Lord Buckhurst shows that he considered John had made out a good *prima facie* claim to the lease. It is not clear what Lord Buckhurst had to do with the matter, but there is no doubt but that it is he who is referred to as 'my Lord' in John's complaint of his son being kept out of possession. Sir William's letter is addressed:—

To the right Honorable and my sd Lord, the L. Buckhurst at C . . (?) orels wher his L. ys this letter be delyvered.

My very good Lord, I ment not any more to have delt w[th] yo[r] l. [Lordship] towchyng knoll or to have reme[m]bred[1] the name therof vnto yow, but this occasion ys now happened. Yesterdaye after I had dispatched Jones w[th] lres vnto yo[r] l. & other my good ll. [lords] & frends at the Court, I receyved a lre from M[r] Lennard & in the same inclosed a pacquett of wrytyngs p[ar]te wherof conserne suche proofs & allegacions as he hath collected to p[ro]ve his interest & lawfull comyng by the lease of the said howse, and p[ar]t of them are dobles of lres wrytten vnto hym consernyng the said lease, and of M[r] Sergeant lovelace p[ro]ceedyngs w[th] hym for his interest therof: And further wryteth vnto me by thes words, in effect that ys, the seying ys that by my meanes only M[r] Lovelace brake w[th] hym. Thys ys very stronge, but as I am fully p[er]swaded that this report cam not from yo[r] l. [lordship], nor from anie of yo[rs], Soe I have wrytten vnto hym agayne that, yf he do not cause the reporter therof to Justifye yt vnto my face, or to saye he hath done me wrong, I will burden hym therew[th]. I have thought good to send vnto yo[r] l. the said wrytyngs to make consideracon of them accordyng to ther force & valydyte, which I thynk ys great till thei[2] be answered, and savyng yo[r] l.

[1] Meaning to mention; obsolete.—*C. D.*
[2] Middle English form of 'they.'

[lordships] correccyon, I do not thynk yt amysse, but rather convenynt for the avoydyng of troubles & charges, and to enjoye that which yor l. by lawe thynk to be yo^{rs} quyetly, to yeld vnto that Mr Sergeant lovelace was lately contented wth (yf ffranklyn by his letter wrot the trothe [1]) that ys that ij of the Justices, wherof Mr. Welche [2] to be none, to here the matter, & as yt shall by lawe fall out so to be ordered, or as I think thei wille [contend?] that, or any other ij men of vnderstandyng & judgme^t [judgment] wherof yor l. [lordship] to name one & he the other, shall ende the matter. I cannot see what p[re]-judice yor l. can have therby, the Choice beinge wisely made, & the thyng desyred by them. Ne^{r}theless [nevertheless] I do referre yt vnto yor l. [lordship's] wisdom & better consideracōn, & to the good advice & counsell of those that still [shall?] counsell yow to the best. And this wth my holle dewty unto yor good l. I leve to trouble the same.

From my pore howse of Melford Hall this 29 of No. 1569.
Yo^r Lordshipps assuered to comānd
WILLIAM CORDELL.

Besides this letter there is a reference to Lord Buckhurst wanting the lease of Knole in the Notes already referred to that John Lennard made, after he had received the letter previously quoted from Sir N. Bacon in 1569, about the dispute between himself and a Mr. Boswell, and Sir C. Alyn.[3] As usual John's efforts were crowned with success, and he won the day as far as the lease of Knole was concerned, but as late as 1575–6 there were still disputes pending as to what deer Lord Buckhurst had a claim to there under some grant from Sergeant Lovelace. The merits of this dispute are not easy to discover from the following letters; it seems somewhat like Mr. Midshipman Easy's triangular duel, as Lord Buckhurst appears to claim deer in Knole by virtue of a grant from Sergeant Lovelace; and a Sir Henry Sydney also had some claim to deer there, a part of which claim for deer had been satisfied, and the rest he was contented to 'remytt'; besides

---

[1] Obsolete form of 'truth.'—C. D.
[2] Foss's *Judges of England* gives no name of 'Welche,' but Walsh (who he says was sometimes called Welsh), Judge of Common Pleas 1563, died 1572. He lived and died at Fivehead, Somerset. [3] *Ante*, p. 40.

these two claimants for deer a Mr. Lewkenor had also some claims in that respect.

These letters are endorsed: 'M[r] Walkers lre [letter] to S[er]iaunt Lovelace & M[r] Lewkenors lre to my L[ord] Bukherst both touchyng dere y[t] M[r] Lovelace demandeth yn Knolle;' and addressed: 'To the Right Worshippfull my very good frende M[r] S[er]iaunt Lovelace with spede.'

My humble dewty Remembered; as touchynge the dere mencyoned yn yo[r] lre, w[ch] yow are informed that my L[ord] should receive yn Northfryth as parte of the produce yow gaue hym out of Knoll, my L[ord] spake vnto M[r] Lennard for them; & did appointe hys s[er]vaunt for the takynge of them; but M[r] Lennard came to Penshurst, & sayd that he dyd not know yt you had any deere at Knolle, and there vppon he would first talke w[th] my L. Buckherst & then yf yt so fell out that they were yo[rs] of right he wold be contente to satysfye my L[ord] my M[r] [master], & offered to geve hym five yn Northfryth yn part of Satisfaccon of the xv, & M[r] Lewknor confessed v to be dew [due] to M[r] Lennard, but for as much as M[r] Lennard dyd denye any deere to be dew vnto yow yn Knolle, my L[ord] wolde not seeme to make any tryall thereof, but gave yow yo[r] warrant agayne of the whole xv & his L[ordship] toke noe deer yn Northfryth of M[r] Lewknor durynge his lyfe, nor sythence of Master Lewknor, hys exe [executor], neither doth he meane to have any as p[ar]cell of the sayd xv deere. Thus much I thought good to answer vnto yo[r] worshippes lre, I knowe & am p[ri]vye to my L[ords] dealinge hereyn. And so I leave yo[r] worshipp to the tuissyon [tuition [1]] of the Allmighty—from my house at Lighe xvij of June 1575.

Yo[r] worshippes at comandment.   RO. WALKER.

And on the back of the previous letter there is the following:—

My dewtye vnto yo[r] honorable L. humbly remembered yt may please yo[r] good L: to be advertysed, that M[r] Lennard cumynge to my cosyn Richard Lewkenor, late of Northfrythe, deceased, when he dyd lye sick yn his deathe bedd, taulked w[th] my sayd Cosyn for certeyne dere w[ch] Sr. Henry Sydney should have had of hym, for deere w[ch] as I, the sayd Sr. Henry

[1] The keeping, or protection.—C. D.

do remember should have had out of Knolle, my sayd cosyn then confessed yn the p[re]sence of me, & other gentelmen then p[re]sent, that the sayd Sr. Henry Sydney agreed to take syxe deere in Northfrythe, yn recompence of the sayd dere he should have had in Knolle, whereof he had parte allready, and the reste he was contentyd to remytt. And thus much Mr Waker, Sr. Henry Sydneyes hys solycytor, dyd declare vnto me at the buryall of my sayd cosyn. All wch I thought good at the request of the sayd Mr Lennard & for the truthes sake only to advertise yor L : of, and thus much I haue heretofore advertysed M^r S[er]jaunte Lovelace of.

And so I humbly take my leave of yor L : this xvij of July 1576.
    Yo^r L : humble to com̄and. Ry. Lewkenor.

To the Rt. Hon : my especiall good L : the L : Buckhurst & yf yt stands wth hys L : good pleasure, to Mr. S[er]iaunt Lovelace also.

We have the following other letter (a draft letter in John Lennard's writing, but no name on it to show for whom it was intended) about these claims to deer in Knole :—

After my right harty com̄endacyons ; I rec. yor letter of the fyrst of thys present September Whereby you desyred me that Mr Sellynger myght have of yor gyft one of the bucks wythyn Knolle reserved to you upon the conveyance betwene my Lord Buckerst & you, that he myght use hys pleasure yn the kyllenge therof, which I assure you he shuld have doon right wyllyngly but he came not thyther, but heugh [Hugh?] my cosen lovelace old servant, whom I think you knowe, came to have the bucke kylled by my Keper, & that he wold carry hym from thens to Mallyng, & from thens yt shuld to London as heughe sayd I thynk as I [send ?] that that tossyng of yt wold have made yt lytle worth, and yt myght have chaunsed to have been pulled from heuge by the way ; & a buck ys not sune kylled yn Knolle where bucks ar thyn,[1] & you knewe the ground ys strong ; but I apoynted hym that yt shuld be redy wythyn ij dayes for any that shuld come for yt, & as yt [was, or went ?] & Cheseman wrotte for yt yn yor name & had yt ; I

---

[1] 'Thin' is still used in Norfolk to express 'scarce'; so they would say, *e.g.*, if it were a bad season for partridges, that 'They fare to be wonnerful thin t' year.'

thynk there were not many better bucks kylled yn Kent thys season, therefore if they that had yt thank you not, they are evyll worthy to [eate?] good venyson but to spede worse another tyme, I thought yt good tadvertyce you hereof, and so wysshe you encrease of worship at Knolle thys viijth of September 1576.

Besides these claimants for venison, poachers were then, as now, a trouble. The following letter from Roger Pulston, and a second letter neither signed nor addressed, but no doubt written to John Lennard, show that park owners in the days of Elizabeth had as much difficulty in protecting their deer as occupiers of coverts now have in protecting their pheasants :—

To the right Wo^r his very good M^r [master] Mr John Lennard Esquire att Lyncolns yn—yeve these :—

If yt may please you (right Wo^r), so yt ys that one Roots, wth Robert Waler, and one Mederse, were seene on Sevenocks vyne wth a Crosse bowe, sayinge[1] & tryinge yt, howe yt would shoote ; This was on Saterday before Alsaynts day[2] and the Wendesday next after, a male deare was hurte, of the wch I have wrytten to you heretofore att large by Hugh the horsekeeper ; on Alsaynts day two poore men, wch wrought in Godwyne wood, sayd that a lytle before day they sawe iij younge men come oute of the parke wth a deare on their shoulders, the Keeper went to them to knowe the truth of the matter, and (as he sayeth) they deny their former sayings altogether, on the next day after Alsaints day being Saterday the ijth of November, younge moyle came to Knoll, and yn greate ferrett[3] toulde my M^{rs} [mistress] that he wth others woulde hunte in the parke that night, my M^{rs} appoynted some to watch wth the Keeper and his man, but they neither sawe, nor hearde any sturringe att all, the next day being Sonday Moyle came againe to Knoll, & sayd that he, and Robert Waler, wth others, had byn the nyght before in the parke, and that Waler shott twyse att a deare and myssed, and further he sayde that he, and they, would be there also that nyght ; my M^{rs} apoynted some to watch that nyght, and the next nyght after, but they nether sawe any man, nor hard [sic] of any sturring att all. The foresayd Roots, wch is brother yn lawe to

---

[1] To test ; obsolete.—C. D.   [2] November 1st, All Saints' Day.
[3] Ferret : v.t. to worry ; obsolete.—C. D.   So in this case 'in great agitation' or 'worry,' or, as we should say in Norfolk, in a 'puckatary.'

the Hyxes, w^{th}in these two or three days upon a soddayne (or as yt were unawares) did thrust Hayward the brewer of Rethered wth his dagger throwe the armes, & therupon fledd away & hath not byn seene synce; herby may be gathered that these wicked lyvers, unlesse they amende, will all noe doubte, att one tyme or other, come to a shamfull ende.

On Saterday last v quarters of Barly was sent to Maultinge. The fysh wch George Pococks bought ys all spente.

There ys spyce to be bought against the holydayes yf you will have mee come up then I may bye the fysh & the spyce both in one day.

I see the Laborers att worke every day and doe suffer non of them all to be ydle & by Gods grace you shall not heare of my neglygence theryn.

There hath byn a quarrel & much branling[1] betwixt some of ou^r men and Mrs Lauxfords men, Mr Samuell can certyfy you of that matter att large.

God kepe you. Knoll the xiiij^{th} of November 1588.

You^r poore servant in the lord.
ROGER PULESTON.

The second letter is as follows:—

(Endorsed) Suspycyous hunters sene on the backsyde of Knolle parke.

S^r. A monday was iij wekes Roberd Harmans wyffe went down into senockes welld[2] to hur fathers old barre, and as shee went over the hethe, a thissyde pocokes shee did se on archer of Nysells bothe lye in a grete brake bushe wythe ij Redd balde[3] valode[4] doggs, and ij crossbowe arrowes in his hand, and when he sawe hur he went Awaye from hur a grete pace, & under the palle[5] in the dike there stode iij more, and they stode stomping as thowght they had wyped ther fitte uppon the bothe, and then they followed the same archer, and on[6] of

---

[1] Branle, or brandle: to shake, agitate, or confuse; obsolete.—*C. D.*

[2] 'Sevenoaks weald to her father's old [barn?], and as she went over the heath on this side of Pocok's farm.' There were tenants of this name both in Knole and Panthurst, paying rents to John, as appears from his rent rolls.

[3] Bald, *i.e.* swift; balde, *i.e.* bold.—*Hal. D.*

[4] Probably meaning: 'Velters' (valtri or veltri), which were running hounds, like, but not the same as, greyhounds.—*Cox.*

[5] 'Under the pale on the bank of the fence there stood three more, and they stood stamping.'

[6] One.

them a crosbow in his hand, the whiche she saythe she doth not knowe them, but saythe toe of them went in blacke gaskins: her boye sayd to hir yt was master pollie of our towne, & she thinkes y[t] that other was Rychebell; & there was on [one] other in yellow lether both gasgens[1] and doblett, ye whiche she thinke it to be Wylliam Waller—forthermore the same daye I did informe your worshipe of a byll,[2] when I did com home Wylliam Waler had gotte Rycherd Pollie, and Wyllyam Rychebell, to gether at the alle[3] howse, & at Pollies howse, most parte of that daye in grete countring,[4] ye which we do suspecte they had some knowledge what I had sertified your worship; and forther more a saynt Tandrewes Eve[5] that your worshipes parke was hunted, John Wakelin of seale,[6] Rychard Pollie, Wyllyam Rychebell, was in great counter of talke betwen x & xj of the cloke in ye nyght as Thomas Jenyngs sayth; and a boute on[7] of the clok I Wylliam Porter went to calle Jenings to Ryd[8] wth me to Rochester, Wakelin went out of his owne howse, & went downe to Pollies as I did see.

John had other troubles and worries connected with Knole besides those arising from the deer, as in course of time questions arose as to the repairs to the house and premises, and some years after John had taken possession he sent a particularly clear, well-written letter to Lord Burghley. He says that 'the goute ys my gryef yn hande and foote wyth a rupture that I have all on my left syde'; but in spite of these physical troubles, and of the fact that he was seventy-eight years old, the handwriting is perfectly steady, and shows no trace that the writer is advancing in years. The object of this letter is to induce Lord Burghley to take a favourable view of John's claim for an allowance to be made to him for 'reparacyons done at Knole.' He asks for 400*l*. and abatement of 30*l*. a year on his rent for the rest of his term. He declares that he spent 400*l*. in 'reparynge' besides 'stone walynge the house and gardeyne'; and that 'yf yt had not been don yn tyme but lett gow, a thousand pounds wolde not

---

[1] Gaskins. [2] Bill, *i.e.* a writing of any kind.—*C. D.*
[3] Ale. [4] Encountering, disputing.
[5] St. Andrew's Eve. St. Andrew's Day is November 30th.
[6] Seal, a parish near Sevenoaks. [7] One o'clock. [8] Ride.

REPAIRS TO KNOLE

nowe have done yt.' He had applied to 'Mr Chancelour,'[1] who appears to have offered to allow him 200*l*. and 16*l*. off his rent yearly if he would undertake to do the repairs, which the Crown was liable for under the lease. John pleads very hard for better terms, saying that 'my rent ys two hundred pounds by the yeare; Her Majestic hath not any farmor[2] of lands that payeth so greate a rent for so lyttle grounde as I have for yt.' This letter, which is rather a long one, is as follows :—

My duty humbly remembred vnto yor Hono^{ur} yt may please you to be advertysed that I hoped all this terme hytherto to haue been able to haue wayted on you myself to haue finished my sute to yor Honour and Mr. Chancelour, by yor favours, for my allowance of ye reparacyons for Knolle and the members. But I am yet so lame y^t I cannot travayle to attend. Yf I may be so bold to speake yt the goute ys my gryef, yn hande & foote, wyth a rupture that I haue all on my left syde. I never felt ye goute tille the last terme. And as I haue heryed saye yor Honour hath been lately syck, whereby I stayed to send my lre [letter] a weke & more synce I wrote yt, as appeareth by the date, I trust in god ye are amended, which god contynue. And fearynge that I shall not this terme (growynge so fast to an ende) be able to travayle to wayte on you myself to haue an ende of this long sute, mych desyrynge yt nowe yn the xvth yeare of my leas, am so bold yn that behalfe to sende thys brynger,[3] I thynk not unknown to yor Honor, he ys an honest man, my deputy in my offyce, & Justice Stanford's[4] son.

I beseech you allowe of hym to wayte on you to haue an ende yn thys my sute. This brynger broughte you my lre to the Court at Grenewich more than a yeare syns yn thys behalfe; whereupon ye wrate to Mr. Chancellor to deale wth me yn yt. I wayted on hym, & shewed hym the leas, which ys that both ye parke of Knolle & Panthurst to be paled, & both the houses of Knolle & Panthurst, and fyve houses mo[5] & xij shopps, or

---

[1] Sir Christopher Hatton, Lord Chancellor 1587.

[2] 'Farmor': meaning that he had lands leased to him at a rent for which he was responsible to the Crown, but he in turn subleased them. John could not have carried on his office of Custos Brevium in Lincoln's Inn, and at the same time follow the business of a 'farmer' in Kent in the sense that we now use the word.

[3] Messenger.   [4] Justice Stanford, a Judge in Court of Common Pleas, 1554.

[5] Old form of more.—*C. D.*

K

shambels, in Sevenock markett place, p[ar]cells of the leas, w[th] all manner of buyldyng stuffe, workmanshippe, & caryadge ys to be found and doon at her maj[ties] charge. Vpon yo[r] lre I found M[r] Chancellor my good m[r] [master] & frend, but yet lothe to allowe me, withoute yo[ur] prevytye, that w[ch] yn ryght ought to be allowed me: hys allowance he hath sett downe with hys owne hande yn thende of one of y[e] bookes (for there were two books made v[er]batim thys brynger hath them bothe to show you) of the s[ur]vey & vewe of the ruynes & decayes therof, taken upon cõmyssyon dyrected to M[r] Bynge & M[r] Flud s[ur]veyo[urs] vpon my entre yn to y[e] leas, which ruyne & decayes therof ys there sett downe by them to be, att my entre, ccciiij[li] v[s] v[d] [304*l*. 5*s*. 5*d*.]. M[r] Chancellor hath sett downe yn thende of one of thoes books that I should have cc[li] [200*l*.] to be allowed me of [off] my rent y[e] next two halfe yeares, and yearly, duryng my leas, xvj[li] [16*l*.] to be deducted of my rent, yf I wold dyscharge the Quene of y[e] covenante Wysshyng me to consider of yt & so to ympart to yo[ur] Honor, which allowance ys to shorte by halfe, & so I sholde fynde & fele yt, yf I were bound to reparacyons for, yf yt please yo[ur] Honor, I will take my othe before you that I have layd oute yn reparynge yt standynge with the covenante cccc[li] [400*l*.] & more, besydes stone walynge y[e] house, & gardeyne, & other voluntarye actes for the which I ask no thynge.

Yf yt had not been don yn tyme but lett gow, m[li] [1,000*l*.] wolde not nowe have don yt; the late charges of reparyring of Otford house now agayn ynlarged, which Maner bryngeth lytle or nothyng whereonto her maj[ties] purse, affyrmeth thys my sayeng. And seyng that I found that ccciiij[li] v[s] v[d] yn ruyne, & decaye, besydes the said farme houses, & xij shoppes, y[t] were not thoroughly s[ur]veyed; & that yo[ur] Honor & M[r] Chancellor vpon juste cause vnder yo[ur] handes remayneng w[th] M[r] Audytor allowed to my Lord Buckhurst ccxl[li] for iiij yeares vpon the sayd leas; w[ch] is lx[li] for eũry yeare of hys iiij yeares; Lett me have, I humbly beseche you, allowance now eyther cccc[li] w[ch] & more, I have layd owte, or so mych as yt was fownde yn rvyne and decaye att my Comynge to yt; w[ch] is ccciiij[li] v[s] v[d], and so shall I haue lytle aboue xx[li] a yeare for my xv yeares, now nyghe at thend of thoes yeares, dysbursynge and forberynge yt some by all y[t] tyme as I haue, wherevnto the covenant byndeth me not. And seyng that I pay so grete a rent take order, I beseche you, y[t] eyther the covenante from henceforth be p[er]formed at her maj[ties] charge, or els gyve me yn recompense therof yearly thirty pounds, to be abated yn my rent, for wth yo^{ur} Honor's favour, I will not otherwyse release ye covenante, for xxx^{li} pounds yearly wylle not do yt, for when I bought ye leas I was credybly told that y^t xl^{li} to be abated yerely haue been offred to ye farmo^{ur} for to dyscharge y^t covenante, wch covenante drewe me to gyve M marcs more for the leas than els I would haue doon. Good my Lord satysfye my reasonable petycyon : lett me have an end hereyn nowe at good lengthe yf not such alowance as I desyer for reparacyons past, then such as you will alowe savynge the covenante or els xxx^{li} yearly for yt. My rent ys cc^{li} by yeere. her ma^{tie} hath not any farmor of lands y^t payeth so grete a rent for so lyttle grounde as I haue for yt.

I beseche yo^{ur} Honor sett yt down in the one booke or ye other, wch thys brynger bryngeth you, and then of Mr Chancellor's good lykeing favor & consent, upon hys syght of yo^{ur} hand wrytenge I doubte not at all (for I, beyng lame as nowe I am, shall hardly fynde you togeyther) to harken to thys my poor sute when ye mete for greter causes. And so the Lord god p[re]serve you wth thencrease of mych honor.

Lyncolne's Yn thys xvith of November 1587.

Your Honor's most humble of-duty to comand,
JOHN LENNARD.

Postcript.

Herynge y^t yo^{ur} Hono^{ur} was sycke I stayed to send thys lre a week & more, syns I wrate yt, as appareth by the date. I trust in god ye be amended wch god contynue.

Lord Dacre mentions that William Cowdrey sold John Lennard certain lands situated in the parish of Sundridge in 6 of Ed. VI. (1552–3).[1]

The following letter from Mr. W. Cowdrey of Penshurst to John, and the latter's reply to it, contain some rather quaint expressions, and give further evidence of what a good man of business he was.

John had evidently sent Cowdrey some venison before he pressed his demand for manor rents, and it was this present, no doubt, which caused Cowdrey to attempt to soften down the

---

[1] *Ld. D.'s Mis.*

previous part of his letter by the following apology for his haste and irritation in writing as he did, 'But gentle Mr. Lennarde I do write unto yowe tumultuarie and as it were upon a sodayne as unto my deare and speciall friende beinge of long & familiar acquaintance almost from our cradells;' and in the last part of his letter he speaks sadly of his age, and winds up with an apology for 'these my rude and grosse letters.'

John was not taken in by this; he says, 'For answere to that last parte I say your letter ys more cutted than neded betwene yowe and me,' and goes on to prove the justice of his demand, and finishes with a reiterated request for payment, saying, 'Good Mr. Cowdrey let yt be quyetly payd. I have for your sake forborn yt long.'

At this time not only was the tenure of land by copyhold far more common than it is now, but the rents were of much greater relative value; and I expect that country gentlemen more often acted as stewards of their own manors, and were therefore more conversant with all the intricacies of copyhold law than most landowners are in these days.

Cowdrey's letter is as follows:—

After my humble cōmendacyons—Sir, I receaved from yowe two lres bothe tendyng to one effect, saving in the former, ye did more at lardge declare yor interest and clayme, that ye do make unto certayne rent goyng out of certayne of my lands lying at Chevenyng called Porter's, due and paiable vnto yor Manour of Chevening, wch sometyme was one Mr Myll's.[1] And in yor lres ye do write that one John Parmyger, being sometyme occupyer of the said p[ar]cell, did eū [ever] in his lifetyme trulie paie vnto you the rent due for the same untill now, synce his decease for my sake it hath ben of longe tyme forborne; but y^t nowe ye meane to call for the rent, and the arrerages[2] therof of them wch do occupie the lande. I do remember right well that ye haue demāded [demanded] suche a rente of me longe ago, and I haue awnswered yow that my mother in lawe, young Palmer's wife, wold ever tell me that, nether her husband in his

---

[1] We have seen that John Lennard bought Chevening of John Mills, *ante*, p. 11.
[2] Arrerage, *i.e.* arrears.—*C. D.*

lifetyme, nether she after her husband's deathe, did ever paie any suche rent ether to Mr Mylls, or to any other Lorde after hym. I thinke if yor demāde be just ye be able to shewe some Court Rolls that maketh menc̄[y]on of some p[rese]ntment made of the deathe of the said younge Palmer, and that by his death ther grewe vnto the Lorde an heryott, and of relief due vnto the Lorde by reasone of his death according to the custome of y^r Manour. He died seased of the lande, and made his will therof Yf this rent be in suche sorte due as ye do write, these things cannot be omytted, or neglected by the Steward in the Court Rolls. Yf Parmyger did trulie paie the rent, (as ye say), he was a fermor[1] and no owner, nether had he comanden^t, or warrant, ether of me, or of any other by my comanden^t, to do so. But nowe p[er]haps fyndyng some better matter for the meyntenance and defence of yor clayme and tytle that ye could not attayne vnto before this tyme, ye do nowe p[ro]cede fordre [sic][2] to clayme, and demande tharrerages of the rent, being almost behind these xxx or xl yeres—and of hym specyallie that hathe been my fermor not past vj or vij yeres. Quid summum ius postulat nescio, certe meo judicio, non nisi summa iniuria extorquere potes. that the fermor of vj yeres cōtynuaunce [continuance] shuld paye the arreages of a rent so many yeres runne before this tyme, And if ye did knowe the same due, and wold not distreyne for hit[3] accordinge to lawe, yor negligence ought not to be ymputed to the fermor and occupier that nowe is, but rather to yor own folie. Volenti non fit iniuria. But gentle Mr Lennarde I do write vnto yowe tumultuarie, and as it were vpon a sodayne as vnto my deare and spē[ci]all frende, beinge of longe and famyliare acquayntance almost from our cradells. As I wold not gladlie, (God is my judge), defraude, or denye any man his right, so wold I be lothe to paie to any man that wch is not my duetie to pay. And yet of both—malim in hanc peccare partem—I can not hold of twoo Lords one p[ar]cell of lande—I cannot holde of yowe, as of yor Manor of Chevenyng, and of Mr Peckham as of his Manor of Morant's Courte. Mr Austen demandeth rent for the same p[ar]cell of lande, and yowe likewise for the same p[ar]cell. I ought not to paie to bothe, Wherefore I shall desire yowe to graunt me some leasure that I might wright to Mr Austen

---

[1] Middle English form of farmer, used here in sense of steward.—C. D.
[2] 'Fordo': to overpower.—C. D. Meaning here in an overpowering manner.
[3] Original form of 'it.'—C. D.

concernyng this matter, wherbie beyng more p[er]fectlie instructed by hym, I maie the better answere your demaund, and to do to ether of you, that of right I ought to do. I shall desire you to send me ageyn the dede, w[ch] ye did send me at the first tyme by yo[r] servaunt, (yf it belonge vnto yow) I will eftsones [1] remyt the same vnto yowe, if it shall appere vnto me that it doth belong unto yow. Nowe besides all this your Bailie dothe threpen [2] my fermor Gedden to distreyne hym for certyane am[er]cement [3] growen for each of my apparences at your Co̅te [Court] of Knoll Manor. Yf nether attornyship,[4] nether my contynuall maladie, be no reasonable causes for to essoyne [5] me in yo[r] Co̅te,—w[ch] are allowed in weyghty matters in the Lawe, then let yo[r] officer do as he thinketh best to plese yow.

Seldome cometh any venysone to me in these megre old daies; [6] Wherefore I gyve unto yo[r] Worshipp the hartier thanks for your Venysone. Sir I shall desier yowe to take in good p[ar]te these my rude and grosse lres [letters]. I maie forget myself in the Ordre and wrytyng of my letters—that I shall desire yowe to ympute unto my great yeres, and to forgetfulnes and weaknes of my memorie w[ch] followe great yeres. Thus I com̅yt yo[r] Worship vnto Almightie God who preserve yowe bothe in the ynward, and outward, man, to his good will and pleasure.

Penshurst the xiij[th] day of Januarie.

Yours to his power.   WILLIAM COWDREY.

[Addressed] To the right Worshippfull and his singular frende Mr. John Lennarde Esquyer be these d.d. [delivered].

John Lennard's answer to William Cowdrey is as follows :—

---

[1] Old English: meaning 'Soon again.'

[2] Note this old form of 'threaten,' also next page.

[3] Formerly both free and copyhold tenants of a manor had to attend the Courts of the Lord, under pain of being amerced for their neglect to do so.

[4] The first meaning of attorney is a proxy. This sentence may be thus paraphrased : 'If neither the fact that I have appointed someone to act for me, nor that I am a confirmed invalid, is sufficient, as would be the case in a court of law, to excuse my personal attendance at your Manor Court.'

[5] Essoine: an excuse for not appearing in Court.

[6] Mr. Cowdrey died within a couple of years from writing this letter, as we have a copy of a power of attorney granted by his heirs, dated May 1589, which was sent to John Lennard.

Mr. Cowdrey after my harty comendayons—I rec[eived] from you of late a lre whereyn, yn a sorte, ye answere to ij lres y^t I wrate to you lately for a rent servyce, due oute of yo^{ur} land, vnto my Maner of Chevenyng—and yn yo^{ur} lre you wryte y^t my Baylyf doth threpen Godden yo^{ur} fermor to distreyn hym for certen am[er]cyaments [amercements] growen for lack of yo^{ur} apparence at Knolle $Co^{ur}te$ [Courtes], & say y^t, if neyther yo^{ur} attornayshyp, nor malady, be causes to essoyn yo^u yn the $Co^{ur}ts$ [Courtes] ye byd my Offycer do as he thinkethe best to please me. And for answere to that last parte I say yo^{ur} lre ys more cuttyed then neded betwene you & me. Ye ar a good Stuard of $Co^{ur}ts$, & knowe y^t sute of $Co^{ur}ts$ ys an ynherytance, and may be lost if the sute be neyther doon, nor releassed for tyme, nor essoyn cast. I am the Quenes fermor;[1] and yt ys semely for me to p[re]serve her ynherytance y^t I haue yn leas. Yo^{ur} $atto^{ur}nayshyp$, or malady, but chyefly our old acqueyntance, shall be a satysfaccyon to me yn that behalf wythout $paym^t$ [payment] of money. Bayles of $co^{ur}se$ demand such $amcyam^{ts}$ [amercements], as my bayly dyd wi^{th} threpenyng, thoughe yo^{ur} fermor enforme you otherwyse.

And to the matter for rent, I say y^t the last Mr Mylles yn all hys tyme, as I have heryd say, kept fewe or no $Co^{ur}ts$ at Chevenyng. I nevyr had $Co^{ur}t$ Rolles y^t he dyd kepe any. Hys father kept some, wherof I send you one notable one, y^t Palmer came yn to the $Co^{ur}te$ as xv h vij [in the 15th of Hen. VII.], & confessed the tenure of thys pece of lande, & payd hys releyf, & v^s for a heryot (I have set 'nota' & a parchment string at yt) which as you knowe ys stronger then the p[re]sentment of tenants. I send you also a rentalle of Mr. Mylles owne hand y^t y^e rent was payd hym, & I myself haue rec [received] yt. Ye cannot have stronger Evydence against yow. And because ye wrate yt Mr Austyn demanded rent for yt, I sent to Mr Austyn the $Co^{ur}te$ Rolle, & wrate to hym that he wold answere me, as he hath doon yn y^t my lre to hym, and hys answere I send you here ynclosed. He claymeth nothyng yn thys pece of land, neyther pay you to any other any rent for yt. Good Mr Cowdrey let yt be quyetly payd. I haue for yo^{ur} sake forborne yt long. God strengthen & kepe you.

Knolle the xix^{th} of January 1587.

The more one reads of John's correspondence, the easier it is

[1] *Vide ante*, p. 128, *n.* 2.

to understand his success in life. Whilst tactful and courteous, he was so tenacious of his rights, and so persistent in urging his claims, that in the long run his efforts were usually rewarded by the attainment of the objects he had in view.

We have among our papers part of a draft of a letter from him, neither dated nor addressed, which relates to one of his numerous disputes in which there occurs this passage :

As I remember S[i]r Chrystopher Alyn & Mr Multon toke the knowledge of ye fynes of me & my wyfe, & then a peece of sylke for a gowne for my wyfe was p[ro]mysed by them; whyther Mr Rivers, or Mr Fane, or els both of them yndyfferently should be at ye charge of yt, they y^t p[ro]mysed yt know best. And I thynke I baue at tymes used some small speche for yt towards them both for their nerenes, w^{tb}out any grete adoo, because my wyfe had yt not; but at lengthe she had yt. S[i]r J. Rivers hath sayd yt was at his charge.

Knowing as we do the pertinacity of John's character, it is easy to imagine how annoying he may have made himself in this 'small speche,' 'without any grete adoo,' and at last he evidently shamed Sir J. Rivers into giving 'the peece of sylke' which was 'promysed.'

The following correspondence selected from several letters written by Edward Cranewell also illustrates this pertinacity. Edward Cranewell, who lived at 'Dryhill' in Sundridge—a parish lying between Knole and Chevening—entered into some sort of partnership arrangement with John Lennard concerning timber in Whitely Wood. This wood, which in those days belonged to the Crown, still exists, and from the map appears still to cover a considerable tract of land. We have already seen [1] that John in 1569 was partner with a Sir Christopher Allen in the purchase of a portion of this wood, and the result was a threatened litigation with a Mr. Boswell.

At this period when there were comparatively few openings for the investment of money, it was not uncommon for persons to take leases of woods for a term of years, with powers of felling timber during their lease; and, judging from what we know of

[1] *Ante*, p. 40.

John's experience in such matters, these transactions often led to considerable disputes.

John frequently wrote drafts of the letters he intended to send, and we have portions of two such drafts of letters to Mr. Cranewell about Whitely Wood. In the first letter he writes to complain that the latter had objected to a certain William Hayt, employed by him to cart timber, coming into Whitely Wood for that purpose. This produced a very long reply from Cranewell, written on July 12th, 1586, in which he charges John with untruthfulness, and says, 'In one breath you can blow both hot and cold in so much that in good faith I know not what to do upon any of your words except hereafter you will set them down in writing;' and then he goes on,

I said if your own teem [team] had been there [in Whitely Wood] I would have turned it out . . . as you say you looked not for such speeches I say that if I would have broken with you (as you did with me being before fully agreed upon all points) I would rather have had my nose ground upon a grindstone; but who can make a man stand to his word that thinketh all becometh him well that he doth or sayeth, be it never so strange.

Cranewell brings his lengthy letter of complaint to a close in these words:

If any covenant be broken you are the greatest breaker yourself, you will find fault with other men's doings but you will amend nothing yourself. Your letters stand upon so many points that I am weary in answering them (being no good secretary) wherefore I beseech you to leave writing & to send the least boy in your house for me when you would speak with me, and I will attend your pleasure; I could have been at Knoll before I can answer your letter.

The tone and prolixity of Cranewell's letter irritated John, who then wrote another letter in reply, in which he says:

Wryteng ys well alowed of to be betwene resonable men for they speke as if they were present together, & often cometh to better passe than ranglyng, face to face, my letter is aboute xx or

xxx lynes, it myght have been resonably answered yn as fewe or fewer, but yo{r} letter ys thryes [thrice] as many or more; one myghte have ryden further then Knolle, I thynk to London, yn the whyle ye wrate yt, belyke ye delyght yn yo{r} secretary-shyp, whatsoever ye say yo{r} letter ys so long & fryvelous that I have caused yt to be copyed oute, & bryefly set my answer to every other artycle of yt, which I wyll stand to before our betters, & I have sent y{t} you hereynclosed & soe fare ye welle.
Knolle.

The combined effect of John's letters, and of the notes he made on the letter from Cranewell, was to cause the latter to write the following reply of a conciliatory, and indeed of almost an apologetic, nature:

[Addressed] To the Worshipfull and his lovinge frende John Lennard Esquier at his house at Knoll—These—

I besought yo{u} as before is remembred not to write any more to me, and I would wayte vppon yow at any tyme that yow shall sende for mee, W{ch} request I contynewe still vnto yo{u} promysinge yo{u} likewise that if any thinge mislike mee I will tell yo{u} of it w{th}out writinge. Yo{u} comende writinge one to another rather than Jangling face to face. Truth it is, it is most comodious to frendes beinge farre a sunder, but for vs that are neighbo{rs} it is a thinge almost needles, men may talk though they Jangle not, and wordes are but wynde, and yet much writinge may breed offence I feare by my much writinge myngled w{th} my rudenes, I may offende yow, otherwise then[1] my good will is, And therefore surely if yow write any more, except yow urge me greatly, I will not aunswere yow, and so yow shall loose yo{r} labo{r}, fynally I crave at yo{r} handes not to offer me wronge, & I protest unto yow I will be as redy at yo{r} comaundement as any s{er}unt [servant] of yo{r} owne, yf you will still offer mee wronge, p[ar]don me I pray yow if I seeke to defende my self.
Sundrishe this . . . of July 1586.
Yo{r} poore neighbo{r} & lovinge frende
EDWARD CRANEWELL.

On April 8th in the following year Cranewell writes to John and says: 'tomorrowe mornyng dyvers workmen will be w{th} me

---

[1] Obsolete form of 'than.'—C. D.

EDWARD CRANEWELL

for money, I praye yo^u send me by this bearer other iij^{li} & then I have hadd vj^{li} of yo^u towards any layeing out.' In a few days' time John sent the money as requested, but he evidently made some remarks about wanting a proper account, which, judging from the following letter, greatly exasperated Cranewell :—

S^r I knowe not what the matter is that youe desier to knowe howe the recknynge nowe standeth betwene vs, truth it is that I cannott by any meanes sende youe a Just accompt what is laid out, bicause [1] eūy [every] man that hath felled wood hath received mony vppon a recknynge & not in full payment of their worke . . . [long details of wood cut, &c.]

S^r forasmuch as yo^w haue desired for quietnes sake (as youe haue said) either to give or take for o^r p[ar]te refuse not this my reasonable offer, protestinge before god that I would fayne receive the holy comvnyon in love & charity, wch truly I cannott doe consideringe the hard measures youe offer mee to make me wearye. I call to God to witnes that if youe offer mee ne wronge I wilbe as redy at yor Comandem^t either to ryde, or goe as any se͡unte [servant] youe keepe : But if yo^u still live in hope by meanes of sutes & extremities, and bicause I am poore to wrynge me from myne owne, I feare that thereby, and through my rudenes, I shall care les to offend youe then becometh mee, for whosoever offreth mee as I haue offred yo^u, if I doe refuse to take it, lett all the world condempne [2] me for one that hateth quietnes, or meaneth Injurye.

S^r I pray youe let it be agreed betwene us that misrecknynges be no payment.

Receipt (at foot), signed Giles Cranewell for his father, of 3*l.* 6*s.* 8*d.*, from John Lennard, Esq., dated April 13th, 1587.

In some of his other letters Cranewell speaks of thefts of wood from Whitely. In one he says that if the tenants of a certain man in Whitely are searched, 'you shall not fayle to fynd corde wood uppon their fyers & in their houses.' 'Goodman Wall hath rayled his newe tenement in with byrchen poles.' In another, 'It is reported that Benkyn hath used cartynually

---

[1] Middle English form of 'becauSe.'—*C. D.*
[2] 'Condemn.' The epenthetic 'p' in *dam[p]nare* is 'common form' in Mediæval Latin : any 'carta' contains instances *passim.*—*Ibid.*

[continually] to carry corde wood, & other wood, out of Whitley upon horse back wth hookes to hange vppon eche side of the horse for that purpose.'

I have a sort of partnership account as to how matters stood between Cranewell and John respecting their dealings with timber in Whitely, which is too long to be inserted here.

It appears from these letters and accounts, and from the following letter, that one of the uses to which John put all this wood was to heat a glass furnace which he had at Knole, and for this purpose a 'Colyar' was employed to 'cole' or make the wood into charcoal. I have found nothing to show whether he made the glass only for his own use, or for the purpose of sale.

I have three letters, written in November 1587, to John Lennard from Roger Puleston, who was, no doubt, his steward at Knole. These letters were evidently written in reply to letters from John, who, although occupied by his legal work in London, and seventy-eight years of age, appears to have taken the keenest possible interest in all the details of what was going on at his country home during his absence.

I have selected for printing the following letter as being rather more interesting in its diction than the other two are. It is directed :—

To the ryght Worshipfull his very good M^r [master] Mr. John Lennard Esquire at Lyncolns yn geve these.

Yf yt may please you (right worshipfull) soe yt is that there hath byn charged since you^r wo^r [worships] dep[ar]ture, xxiiij Cords of wood to the glasshowse, and I have receaued so much glasse as amounteth to v^{li} & for the other iij cords I shall receave glasse tomorowe. Valyan & Ferris haue p[ro]mised to deliuer me xx^s worth of glasse towards the payment of their debte before Saterday at night. They agree very well, god be praysed for yt : they worke night and day, bout only whyles the founder is tempering his mettell, on the one syde of the furnes Valyan & Ferris doe worke, & on the other side Brussell & the other younge man. Tomorrow, god willinge, Mr Onoby is determined to begyn to worke & Mr Brussell his son shall work wth hym, wch already is come to the Glasshowse : your

Wo[r] [worship] wrate vnto mee that I should not forgett, forslowe [1] nor deceave you in those things you put me in trust. Forgett I might, & forslowe, but God forbid I shoulde live to deceave you, & yet I am sure I have offended in nether of the three, for I goe twyse or thryse euy [every] day to the glasshowse, & the glassmen were never at such unyty and concord amongst themselves as they are at this instant. The outward Courte gate is alwayes locked at supper tyme, and all the night after supper. The towne gate & all the gates abowte the p[ar]ke are kept locked night & day. I tould Cogger in manner & forme as you[r] worshipp wrytt vnto mee. The Cater [carter?] hath filled vpp all the sawpytts in the p[ar]ke. Pocock hath caryed all the rayles & piled them vpp on the backe syde of the kytchin as you[r] worshipp comaunded. I spake w[th] Lawe & he hath taken a vew of the trees w[ch] you appointed Adams to fell, of the w[ch] he will take as much as will suffice his terne [turn]. Adams & George doe worke at the Painted gate, & they doe not sett vpp the cords halfe so fast as they are caryed away, therefore yf you will haue the glassmen to contynew att worke you must ether graunte that more wood cutters may be sett a worke or ells suffer them to carry out of some other place in the p[ar]ke, for all the clefte cords that were in hooke wood are caryed to the glasshowse already. Thus comyttinge you to the tuityon [2] of the Almighty I cease. Knoll the xvijth of November 1587.

You[r] poor servante in the Lord to comande
ROGER PULESTON.

The following letter is a specimen of the endeavours of an energetic wine merchant of the period to push his wares :—

Worshippfull S[r] wth my hartie comendacons vnto yo[u] remembred. Yo[u] shall vnderstand y[t] nowe I haue some Gascon wines come: thearfoer yf it please yo[w] to haue anie I cann serve yo[w] nowe verie good, and better cheap thenn the last, for it was sold for xxiiij[li] the toun [3] & nowe yo[w] shall haue better wines for xxij[li] p [per?] toun. Thearfor yf yo[w] please to sennd me yo[r] letter howe much yo[w] will haue, & howe yo[w] will haue

---

[1] To hinder, or impede.—*C. D.*
[2] Tuition, keeping, or protection.—*Ibid.*
[3] A tun, *i.e.* 252 gallons; so this wine was offered at rather less than 3*s.* 6*d.* a dozen.

them sorted, I will send yo^w accordinglie at yor pleasure, thus desiringe yor answear for y^t I had occasion to sennd the bearer hearof to see a child wch I haue at nurse.¹ I thought good to write vnto yo^w and soe I comitt yor Wo^r to god. from London the 6th of January anno 1588.

Yo^r Wo^rshippes to comande

ROBERT LEE.

It may be noted that in this communication the letter 'i' is used more and the letter 'y' less than in most of the previously printed letters. It is not likely that Mr. Lee was better educated than Sir N. Bacon, Sir W. Cordell, and John Lennard, and I imagine that in 1588 the custom of using 'y' where we now use 'i' was going out of fashion, and that the use of 'y' was confined more especially to the older generation, and was gradually dying out.

A Mrs. Mason, at the request of her son-in-law, Mr. Byng, wrote to John on St. Lawrence's Day, 1588, to give him information as to the age of her late daughter 'frawncys' Byng, and her way of calculating her daughter's age is quaint. She says :—

Althoughe I cannot certaynely declare the veraye tyme of her byrthe yet the best token that I haue to put me in Remembrance therof is that I was young withe chylde withe her at the christenyng of the quenes ma^tie that nowe is quene Elizabeth, and as I thynke went not moche aboue haulfe a yere after before I was delyvered.

In April 1586 John Piers,² Bishop of Salisbury, wrote thus to John, asking him to appoint a Mr. Ecklesfield to a living in Wilts. The letter is beautifully written in the old handwriting of the day, then going out, in which the letter 'h' goes downward more like a modern 'g' and with several abbreviations. The signature is in a different handwriting :—

¹ It has been said that some seventy years later children in their earliest years were as a rule put out to nurse with country women.—*T. S. E.* iv. p. 678.

² Dean of Salisbury, 1571-7; Bishop, 1577-89; Archbishop of York, 1589-95. —*Hay. Dig.*

THE BISHOP OF SALISBURY

Right worshipfull after my heartie comendacons Mr Ecklesfield the bearer herof a godlie learned p[re]acher hath requested my lrs [letters] vnto yo^w in hes behalf that it would please yo^w to bestowe uppon him the Benefice of Staunton Quinton now voyd by the death of the last incūbent. He is a man in euie respect verie sufficient for that place. Yo^w shall doe a great benefite both to that p̄ish [parish] and the country round about it if yt will please yow to furnish them wth so good a pastor. And I shall thinke my selfe verie much beholdinge to yo^w for p[re]ferringe so fitt a man in my diocesse to the settinge forth of the glorie of the ghospell of o^r Sauio^r Christ to whose mercifull tuecon I leave yo^w.

ffrom my house in ffulham p̄ish the xijth of Aprill 1586.
Yo^r assured frend.   JO. SARŪ.

I have inquired of the Rev. F. J. Backly, Rector of Staunton St. Quinton, as to whether there is any record of this Mr. Ecklesfield being appointed, and he tells me that there does not appear to have been any vacancy between 1574 and 1609, and that at the former date the patrons were John Danvers, Esq., and Robert Franklyn.

The following letter is from a Mr. Harryson, who appears to have been surety for some one of the name of Gallant,[1] who owed money to John. John had evidently written to Harryson to press him to pay, and he begs for time, saying that he is utterly 'undone for ever,' that he has 'beryed his good wyfe,' and trusts that John may, as he has already done, 'bare wth me a tyme to gett a wyfe to helpe me out of my troble and to pay my detts.' Obviously Mr. Harryson intended to find out a woman having some money, and then to marry her without telling her of his liabilities, and to take her fortune to put him on his legs again. This barefaced avowal of his intentions makes one realise what dreadful hardships this state of the law must often have given rise to. It seems astonishing that it was not until three hundred years after this letter was written that a wife had any

---

[1] John brought a lawsuit against Gallant relating to the lease of a farm in Weston, co. Cambs. In order to defray the costs of this action Gallant was driven to mortgage lands in that county and borrow the money at 12 per cent. interest.—*P. C.* i. p. 342.

legal rights in property which belonged to her previous to her marriage.

A well-known legal writer has said: 'The very being or legal existence of women is by the Common Law suspended during her marriage; or at least it is incorporated and consolidated into that of her husband, under whose wing, protection and cover she performs everything.' The Courts of Equity have for more than one hundred and fifty years afforded the wife some protection as to property settled upon her, but it was not until 1870 and 1882 that laws were passed giving a wife the same full power over every sort of property possessed by her as she would have had had she remained single.

The letter is thus endorsed :—

Mr. Harrysons letter for Gallants det.

My duete in humble maner remebred to y^r worshipe gevyng you most harty thankes for yor jentill favor shewyt vnto me at all times, I have resavyd yor worships letter wch muche doth greve me, the lorde knoweth I am not able to paye the moñy w^c is as I thinke xl^s for I haue payed as y^r worshyp knoyth xij^{li}; I never gaue my worde for one grott to paye, as Jesus criste knowethe w^c yor bruther can full well tell, but I am contentid to falle w^t my folly: I wolde y^{or} wurshype did knowe the truthe : I desier yor worshyp for Gods saike be not grevid w^t me, nether yor displesur faule vppon me, for then I am vtterly vndone. I haue had so many trubles for that wikid man, god amend him, that I am vtterly vndone for ever, therfor I desyer yow, for Gods cavse, stande my good m^r [master], & do not truble me in thys my ferefull time. I haue solde all my stufe to pay for that wikid man, my house ys at morgage for iij yers, I haue nothyng to lyve on but as my frends gevithe me met & drink, not so muche as a bede to lye on; as yt ys well knowne I haue beryed my good wyfe I truste that yf yor worshyp, as yow haue done, bare w^t me a tyme to gett a wyfe to helpe me out of my troble, and to paye my detts, I desier yor worshyp to lett me haue my wode I haue payed for it, elles let yt be solde & take yow the moñy, yet for Gods sake, let me have one lode for fyeryng for I haue nether fireing nor mony; thus I have openid my holl estatte desyringe yow for god cause to stande my frende, as yow haue hertofore.

Thus wishinge vnto yow increse of worship most humbly I take my leave the iiijth of Desember.
Yo^r worshyps humbly at comanndemet.
PETER HARRYSŌ.

The next letter is of no particular interest, but the language is quaint. It appears to be from a farmer, as the writer speaks of having bestowed two hundred marks in stocking his farm. It must have been rare in those days for a farmer to be able to write even as well as this man does:—

[Addressed] To the ryght whorshipe full and hys verye good frynd Mr. Johne lennard esquyre at knolle geue thys.

Sur wher I requestyd your whorshypes letr in cravynge fryndshype of good man[1] locke to for bere [forbear] me a whyl for the monye awhyche he gaue hys word for and payd yt for me, your whorshype shull vnderstand that, when I telde hym that I had mad you pryeue [privy] what monye he had payd for me and that I had a letr whiche youre whorshype had sent hyme, he sayd he wolld not se yt, but he wolld have hys monye or ellese shurtye, and wolld ellese yn no wyse agre, and yt is so inded that I ame kept frome monye whiche I shulld a had longe a gone, and ame nowe dryuene to ryd doune thre score myllese out of lond, and in to bedforthshere, and carye wyth me to corn sellers to be at a cort [court] ther frydaye before whytson daye: whiche wyll be a gret charge vnto me, and yt ys so in dyd that locke hathe mad a gret complaynte unto mye fryndese for hys monye, and ys lycke [like] to torne me to gret dyscredyt; where fore I shall desyre your whorshype to stand mye frynd, and that you wyll send for hyme, and take some order wythe hyme; and that you wyll paye hym the monye whiche yse xij^{li} x^s, and that you wyll let me haue the reste of mye monye; or ellese yt wyll be to mye gret hyndranc and oondoynge, for I must sell awaye mye catell, or elles mye corene vppone the grounde; whiche wyll be mye undoynge yf youre whorshype do not let me haue yt presentlye; wherefore I be seche you to consyder of me I haue be stode to hundred [bestowed 200] markes yn stockyng mye fareme, and nowe yf youre whorshyppe do not helpe me wythe that monye whiche

[1] Goodman: obsolete, a term of respect, nearly equivalent to Mr. —C. D.

ys betwyxt us, where bye I may lyfe and kepe at an even hand wythe allmen, but to rune in det, yt wyll be to mye gret gryfe and decaye, thus wythe sorofulle hart that I cane not haue to content locke as I wolld a done, I lefe to trobelle youre whorshype anye furder; desyreynge god to preserue you, and send you longe lyfe wythe increse of whorshyppe, and youre heartese desyre from my myud; at the spore yn Sudworke thys xiij of Maye 1578.

bye youresé to command, EDWARD WOODGATE.

John made his will in November 1587, and it was proved at Canterbury on April 27th, 1591. We have seen in his son's biography of him that he died on March 12th, 1590, and the Register gives this as the date of his burial.[1] It is remarkable how close in former times a person's funeral followed on his death. John appears to have been buried the same day on which he died, and his wife the day after her death, and the same course was followed in the case of Samson their son, and Richard their great-grandson, and there are other instances of this in our family. Although long delays in burying a corpse are much to be deprecated, funerals taking place so very close upon the death may not occasionally have resulted in persons being buried before death had actually supervened; and in any case it left a most inconveniently short period in which to make the necessary preparations and summon the mourners. As at that period the New Year began on March 25th, the date that probate was obtained was within a few weeks of John Lennard's death, and not, as it might at first sight appear, over a year after that event had taken place.

In those days a sort of declaration of the testator's belief in the doctrines of the Christian Church, and a bequest to God of his soul, was 'Common form' in all wills; and indeed this continued to be the custom for quite a hundred years later than the date of John Lennard's will. Still as to some this form of will may be unfamiliar, I have thought it well to print the

[1] *Ch. Reg.*

first part of John's will as a specimen of the wills of that day, and it has some peculiarities, such as his charge to his children as to how they are to bring up their children, and also his giving them his blessing.

Considering that John was himself so successful a barrister, and moreover had got the Master of the Rolls, Sir W. Cordell, to advise him upon his will, I do not think that it redounds to his skill as a draughtsman. He does not seem to have followed Sir W. Cordell's advice contained in his letter of 1587, whereby the legacies to his unmarried daughters would have vested in them at the age of twenty-one, if unmarried at his death. In fact all of them but Anne did marry during their father's lifetime, and as she married a person of position, let us hope that her brothers Samson and Samuel did not withhold their consent, as if they did so she would apparently have been quite unprovided for.

The will begins :—

In the name of God the Father, God the Son, and God the Holy Ghost, three persons and one God, I John Lennarde of Knoll, in the Parish of Sevenock, in the County of Kent, Esqre, of the age, by my parents saying, of three score eighteen years at St. Edward's [1] tide last past; before the making and declaring of this my last Will and Testament stedfastly believing in the same my Lord God, and being whole in Body Mind and Memory, I give thanks therefore to my Lord God Almighty, do make ordain and declare this my Present last Will, and Testament, in name and form following the eighteenth day of November in the year of our Lord God, after the computation of the Church of England, 1587, and in the 30th year of the Reign of our Sovereign Lady Queen Elizabeth, By the Grace of God, Queen of England, France and Ireland, Defender of the Faith &c. First I commend my soul to the mercy of God in our Lord and Saviour Jesus Christ in, and by, whose bitter Passion, Death, and Resurrection only, without Meritt or Desert of mine, I verily trust to attain to Salvation, and Joy Everlasting; my body but Earth I committ to the Earth, and I will the same to be buryed,

[1] March 18th.

and bestowed at and in Chevening Church. or Chappell in such sort as the body of a Christian man ought to be, after, and by the discretion of my two sons Sampson, and Samuel; heartily praying them to foresee that in the bestowing thereof nothing be done that may seem offensive to God, but that that be only done which may stand with his Sacred Word. Next to that I will exhort and charge all my children on God's behalf, and on my Blessing, whom in God's Name I do bless, that they read, hear, and remember this Article Vizt that they be Watchfull, and Carefull, with a Vigilent Eye and Mind over their children, and such other as they have, and take the charge and Government of, to keep them from Loose and dissolute Life, and to see that they spend their time in the love and fear of God. Item I will that within convenient time after my Departure out of this Earthly Tabernacle, or rather in my lifetime, when I shall be *in extremis*, there be distributed by mine executor among the Poor Aged, and Impotent people, inhabiting within the parishes herinafter named, such several sums of money herein to each Parish appointed, because presently I have, and by a good time have had and received, Rent, and Revenue, in every, or most of those parishes; that is to say To the Poor of Chevening three pounds, Ottford ten shillings, Shoreham ten shillings, Sevenock forty shillings, Heaver ten shillings, Brasted thirty shillings, Sandrych twenty shillings, Romford in Essex ten shillings, Carlton Cambridgeshire twenty shillings, Weston there forty shillings, Horton in Yorkshire twenty shillings, Stanton Quinton in Wiltshire twenty shillings, Brodmaston in Somersetshire twenty shillings, and although I have little or no lands in the Parishes of Nockholt, and Halsted in Kent, yet because they border upon Chevening Parish, wherein I was borne, I give to the Poor of Nockholt six shillings and eightpence, and to the Poor of Halsted six shillings and eightpence, and my Will and Mind is that Consideration be had upon the Poor of other Parishes by and at the Discretion of mine executor.

He then goes on to leave to his daughters Elizabeth and Ann, towards their marriage, 1,000*l.* each if before his death 'they be not preferred in marriage, nor any bond made by me to any person for payment of any sum of money in consideration of their marriage,' one half to be paid upon their marriage, and one half at 'the years end then next following.' These legacies evidently contemplate marriage as the inevitable lot of his daughters, so probably it was not then so difficult as it is now for young women to find husbands. It was stipulated that these sums of money were only to be paid if his daughters 'bestowe themselves in marriage' by the consent of their brothers Samson and Samuel, or 'the Overlivest of them.'

We have seen that Elizabeth married during her father's lifetime, but if Ann did not get a chance of marrying, which she cared to accept, and which her brothers Samson and Samuel, or the 'overlivest' of them approved of, then she would not appear to have inherited anything from her father except indeed his blessing, which intangible gift is conferred on all his children. The will then goes on, leaving 10*l.* to every son of Samson, and 5*l.* to each of his daughters, and so on to all his grandchildren born or to be born of his married daughters. He leaves 10*l.* to his brother William; to his men-servants 10*s.* each, and to his women-servants 6*s* 8*d.* each; a long lease of some lands called Barton Heath, in Kent, to Samuel, his second son, and an annuity of 50*l.* to his brother William, and all the rest of his real and personal property to his eldest son Samson, and his heirs male. This real estate must have been very considerable, as it consisted of

The Manors, Lands. tenements which belonged to the father of the testator, known as :—

Chevening	Northsted	
Chepsted		In the County of Kent.
Apulfield	Wickhurst	

Also all other his own Manors, Lordships, Lands, &c. in the parishes of :—

Chevening	Heaver	Brasted	
Chepsted	Shoreham	Down	In the County
Sundridge	Ottford	Codham [Cudham]	of Kent.
Sevenoaks	Chelsfield		

All his Manors, Lands, &c. in the parishes of :—

Carlton	Brinckley Borough	
Weston Colville	Baborougham [1]	In the County of
Willingham	Balsham	Cambridgeshire.
Wickham	Pannesworth [2]	

And the Manors of :—

Horton	Yorks.
Broadmarston	Somerset.
Stamton Gumton	Wilts.[3]

[1] Now Babraham.
[2] The nearest name to this I can find is Pampesford, which is near Babraham.
[3] Obviously Staunton Quinton.

THE DESCENT OF MARGARET FYNES

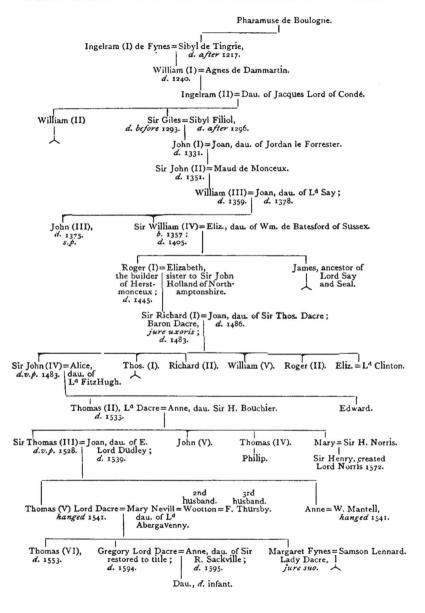

CHAPTER II

AN ACCOUNT OF THE FAMILIES OF FYNES, MONCEUX, VAUX, MOULTON, AND DACRE

BEFORE pursuing further this history of the Lennards, it is necessary to consider at some length the family of which, upon Gregory Lord Dacre's death, his sister, Margaret Lennard, became the representative.

I do not, of course, propose to deal with the various families into which the Lennards married, in this full manner, but this marriage stands on quite a different footing from those contracted by any of Samson's descendants. It was in virtue of this match that the Lennards entered into the ranks of the nobility, as it was through Margaret that the title of Dacre came into this family, and was then borne by different persons of that name for a period of nearly two hundred years.

The early portion of this chapter, dealing as it does with persons living at a period so remote from the present, must of necessity mainly consist of brief references to the public records. This I fear will be found too dry reading for all persons, except perhaps those few who are greatly interested in genealogies; and to those who are disposed to skip the whole of this chapter, as consisting merely of materials wherewith to construct a pedigree, I would suggest that before doing so they look at the War Charter between Henry V. and Roger Fynes (p. 165); the award of Edward IV. (p. 173); and the account of the deer-stealing fray which led to the execution of Thomas Lord Dacre and others (p. 196 *et seq.*).

154   HISTORY OF THE FYNESES

Margaret Fynes[1] was descended from a very ancient family which for many generations was one of the most considerable in the south of England, and derived its origin from Conon de Fiennes,[2] who in 1112 was Earl of Boulogne, taking his name from a village in the Boulonnais territory. John de Fiennes, one of the same family (but, according to Duchesne, of another branch), accompanied the Conqueror, and was, it is said, by him made hereditary Constable of Dover Castle[3] and Warden of the Cinque Ports; and at the same time he received large grants of land in order to enable him to provide for the defence of this important post. These offices were enjoyed by five of his descendants[4] till the time of King John,[5] when William de Fynes was removed on the plea that 'it was not consistent with the security of the country that a foreigner who owed allegiance to another sovereign, should hold the principal castle in the kingdom, which was as it were the lock and key of the whole realm.' The wardenship was then given to Hubert de Burgh,[6] and William de Fynes had an equivalent granted him elsewhere. The statement given by Collins and others is, that he received the manor of Wendover, Bucks, in exchange for the constableship of Dover; but this is probably incorrect as that manor came into the family by the marriage of Ingelram, or Enguerrand[7] de

[1] The name is spelled indifferently Fienes, Fiennes, ffienes, Fenys, Fiesnes, Fynes, and in other ways.
[2] *Duch.* pp. 288, 289.
[3] *Add.* 5679, 699. *Ibid.* 5485, 108 *et seq.* This MS. has in the margin the following note interesting to members of our family:—' Out of the feodary Rools [*sic*] of Kent lent vuto Mr. Lennard.' The hand in which this note is written is said by the authorities at the British Museum to date from about 1650, and if this date is proximately accurate, it could not refer to Samson Lennard, as I first thought it did, unless the marginal note, like the document itself, is a copy of one previously existing. Samson, when proving his wife's pedigree in order to substantiate her claim to the title of Dacre, might well have been glad to borrow the document in question.
[4] *Jeakes*, p. 47. *Has.* i. p. 119 (*m*).
[5] Mr. J. H. Round asserts that the family of Fynes were not hereditary Constables of Dover.—*Commune*, p. 279.
[6] *Add.* 5679, 699.
[7] The former spelling is found in *Add.* 5485, fol. 114, but the latter is used by J. H. Round.—*Geneal.* xii. p. 150.

Fynes, with Sibyl de Tingrie,[1] the daughter and heiress of Pharamuse, or Faramus, of Boulogne, the nephew of Maud, the Queen of Stephen.

Pharamuse was Comptroller of King Stephen's household,[2] and was granted by him the manors of Wendover in Bucks[3] and Clapham and Carshalton in Surrey;[4] the manor of Martok in Somerset he was already possessed of by inheritance from Eustace Earl of Boulogne, to whom it had been given by William the Conqueror.[5] Sibyl inherited the whole of her father's large possessions, which, by her marriage with Ingelram de Fynes, she transferred to that family, who from that time appear to have made England their principal home. Ingelram accompanied Philip Earl of Flanders to the Holy Land, and was slain at the siege of Acre,[6] A.D. 1190. Nine years later the widowed Sibyl purchased, at the price of 200 marks, the confirmation of her manors, and 'licence to marry whomsoever she pleased of the King's faithful subjects.'[7]

Sibyl did not marry again, so presumably her object in giving King John 200 marks was that she should not be forced to marry someone against her will. John derived a considerable portion of his income from payments or bribes of this nature. In those days people made presents to the King of money, or in kind, for a great variety of reasons.

The following are some of the objects for these bribes :—to be allowed to proceed at law; to obtain justice; if a plaintiff, to have your suit expedited; if a defendant, to have a suit brought against you delayed. By men, in order to marry a particular woman; by women, to remain single, or to marry whom they pleased. For leave to trade; for leave to build a windmill; for leave to go abroad; or for leave to stay at home. Indeed bribery seems to have been the recognised system for obtaining your desire in almost every relation of life. And the bribes

---

[1] Tingrie is a small village in the vicinity of Boulogne.
[2] *Dug. Bar.* [3] *Lip.* ii. p. 467. [4] *M. & B.* iii. p. 360; ii. p. 508.
[5] *Collinson*, iii. p. 4. [6] (Haley) *Add.* 6343, 739.
[7] *Rot. de Ob.* p. 2. *M. & B.* iii. p. 360, refer to a similar record relating to the manor of Clapham in the reign of Richard.

were no less varied in their nature; thus the King was tempted by offers of money, palfreys, war-horses, hawks, hounds, jewels, pigs, hens, and cheeses.

Two very remarkable instances of these bribes are recorded.

Robert de Vallibus presented the King with five best palfreys in order that he should hold his peace, or say nothing about (*ut Rex taceret de uxore*) the wife of H. Panel. It may be that Robert had in some way compromised this lady, and that if he were able to purchase the King's silence on this subject he felt that no one else would dare to mention it.

Another still more remarkable instance of a bribe is that of the wife of H. de Nevill, who offered 200 hens for permission to sleep one night with her husband (*eo quod possit jacere una nocte cum domino suo*). One regrets that these records are not fuller; it is not at all clear why this permission to follow the ordinary custom among married persons should have been applied for. Mr. de Nevill may have been in prison; or it may be that he had separated from his wife, and that this application by her to the King was somewhat analogous to a modern suit in the Divorce Court for restitution of conjugal rights.

Sibyl after her husband's death, 'in viduitate et libera potestate mea,' confirmed the grant of a hide of land in Balham, belonging to the manor of Clapham, to the Abbey of Bec, in Normandy.[1] Another gift of hers which is on record might strike those who are not antiquaries as somewhat extraordinary; she granted William Hauwis, a freeman belonging to her manor of Wendover, with all belonging to him, 'and all the progeny he has or ever may have, together with all his goods and chattels,' to Reginald, son of Alexander Lord of Hampden, who was in return to render to her and her heirs two capons yearly at Martinmas.[2] A similar benefaction is recorded on the part of her son William, who gave to the Canons of S. Mary Missenden in frank almoigne[3] all the land which Wimond held of him

---

[1] *Dug. Mon.* vii. p. 1068.   [2] *Add.* 5485, 107 or 174.

[3] Frank almoigne was the tenure by which almost all the monasteries and religious houses held their lands; they were free from all temporal services on condition of praying for the soul of the donor.

in Wendover, and Wimond himself *cum tota sequela et progenie sua*.[1]

Sibyl, who in 1201 gave the King twenty marks for leave to cross the seas,[2] was alive in 1217;[3] her manors seem to have been transferred in her lifetime to her son William,[4] who married Agnes de Dammartin, sister of Renaud Earl of Boulogne, and Simon Count of Ponthieu.

In 1206, April 19th, King John granted William de Fynes 'such plenary seisin of the manor of Martok, Somerset, as his mother Sibyl had';[5] in the following month of March this manor and that of Wendover were still in her hand, and the King issued his warrant from Farnham to the sheriffs of these two counties to give William possession of the lands 'which his mother Sibyl gave up before us in our court,' and to allow her a reasonable provision, 'rationabile estuverium,' from the same land.[6]

From the various entries in the Close Rolls, William would appear, at one time, to have stood high in his sovereign's favour; but both Wendover and Martok, being portions of the royal demesne, were continually taken into the King's hand, and transferred from the Fyneses to other lords,[7] who might happen for the time to stand higher in the favour of the fickle Sovereign, or whose goodwill it was desirable to purchase by some substantial mark of royal approbation, and these frequent changes caused great intricacy in the records of this period.

In 1210-11, the King appears to have taken Wendover from William, and granted it to Hugh de Gournay, who paid a fine of 700 marks for it.[8] In 1214 de Gournay took part with the rebellious Barons and forfeited his lands, which were not, however, immediately restored to William de Fienes, but in lieu of them the sum of 60*l*. was assigned out of the royal treasury.[9]

---

[1] *Dug. Mon.* vi. p. 549. This is far from being a late record of a transfer of serfs; serfdom did not entirely cease in England until Tudor times.
[2] *Rot. de Ob.* p. 145.
[3] C. R. i. p. 372; she paid scutage in Surrey in 1217.
[4] *Ibid.* pp. 68, 79, 185, 228, 294.   [5] *Ibid.* p. 68.   [6] *Ibid.* p. 79.
[7] *Lip.* ii. p. 468.   [8] *Dug. Bar.* i. 430.   [9] C. R. i. p. 185.

On September 15th, 1215, the King granted Wendover again to William,[1] but as in the next year[2] he was deprived of his manor of Martok, and described in the warrant as 'being with the king's enemies,' 'qui cum inimicis nostris est,' the probable inference is that he had joined the standard of the French Prince Louis, to whom the Barons had offered the English crown. He evidently soon returned to his allegiance; for on September 5th, 1216,[3] full seisin of his manor of Wendover, which was probably forfeited at the same time with Martok, was restored by the King, who died some five weeks later.

One of the first acts of those who exercised the royal authority in the name of the young King Henry III. was to issue a warrant to the Bishop of Winchester, commanding him to allow W. de Fynes peaceable possession of his lands 'in bailla sua,'[4] so long as he rendered faithful service to the King. And the next year (January 27, 1217) such seisin in the vill of Martok is granted as he had before the war;[5] and in 1218 we find he had already paid 200 marks for having seisin of Wendover.[6] In 1221 he paid a hundred marks for having custody of the lands in Kent, which belonged to Arnold Earl of Guisnes.[7] Martok and Wendover were taken into the King's hand on account of William not coming himself or sending men to serve in the King's army in Wales,[8] but he soon made his peace with his feeble sovereign, and had re-seisin granted of his lands.

In the *Testa de Nevill*,[9] the name of W. de Fynes occurs as holding one fee in Gessick All Saints, and two fees in Somerset and Dorset, for which he paid scutage to the amount of 'liij^s iiij^d' in 1235-6; he also held a fee in Kersauton [Carshalton] and half a fee in Cheph'm [Clapham] of Hugh de Bohun,[10] and two years later, 1238, an inquest was held to determine whether he ought to do more service than that of one knight for the six

---

[1] *Ld. D. His.*; *Dug. Bar.* i. p. 430; *Baron Willis' MS.* on Bucks.—*Bod.*
[2] *C. R.* i. p. 278.   [3] *Ibid.* p. 286.   [4] *Ibid.* p. 294.   [5] *Ibid.* p. 297.
[6] *Ibid.* p. 367.   [7] *Excerp.* i. p. 65.   [8] *C. R.* i. p. 572.
[9] *T. de N.* pp. 160, 166, 168.   [10] *Ibid.* p. 221.

knights' fees he held of the King in Essex of the honour of Boloigne.[1] William de Fynes died 1240-1,[2] and was succeeded by his son Ingelram, who married a daughter of Jacques Lord of Condé, by whom he had two sons, William and Giles ; from the latter of whom Margaret was descended. Ingelram was knighted at Christmas 1247, and inherited his father's manors, and there are various references to him in the public records of those times.[3]

Ingelram fought in the Gascon wars, and also fitted out his brother with horse and arms for the same purpose. He was a most loyal adherent of Henry III. in all the troubles arising from the Barons' War ; in 1263 he apprehended and imprisoned young Prince Henry at Boulogne who had joined the Barons against the King,[4] and he is said to have distinguished himself at the Battle of Evesham. How highly the King appreciated his fidelity and other good qualities is shown by the fact that he ordered Ingelram's son William to be educated with the Prince Edward ; he also bestowed upon him to wardship of the son of William de Beauchamp, and after the Battle of Evesham he ordered that restitution should be immediately made to him of any of his estates of which he might have been despoiled during the confusion consequent upon the Civil War.[5]

The exact date of Ingelram's death is uncertain, but it must have taken place before 1269-70, when William de Fynes, 'who was in parts beyond the sea at his father's decease,' was found to be his heir.[6] There is a reference to him in the *Hundred Rolls*,[7] which I mention because it gives us a vivid idea of how great the value of money was in those days when it was thought worth while for a commission especially appointed to

---

[1] *Mad. Ex.* i. 648. His name appears also in the 'Red Book of the Exchequer.'
[2] *Dug. Bar.* ii. p. 243.
[3] *Ibid.* ; *Excerp.* i. p. 405 ; ii. pp. 250, 277 ; *Rot. Sc.* p. 265 ; *Cal. Rot. Chart.* i. pp. 64, 75, and 90 ; *Coll. Pro.* ; *T. de N.* pp. 221 and 229. In one of these entries the name is spelled 'Fednes.'
[4] *Blaauw.*
[5] *Dug. Bar.*
[6] C. R., 54 Hen. IV.
[7] i. p. 394.

place on record that the late King had granted to Ingelram a rent of sixpence a year issuing out of certain lands in Lincolnshire.

The public records contain not infrequent references to Ingelram's eldest son, William de Fynes, and to the latter's son John, who were both persons of prominent position, but it is not necessary here to refer further to this branch of the family because, as we have seen, Margaret's ancestor was Giles, second son of Ingelram. In 1278-9 Giles married Sibyl, the daughter and heiress of William Filiol, or Fillol,[1] of Oldcourt, in the parish of Wartling, Sussex. Some interesting particulars concerning Sibyl Filiol are to be found in 'Collins' Proceedings' of a suit brought by her and her husband, Giles de Fynes, against Richard de Pageham in 1278,[2] to recover forty pounds as a compensation for her violent abduction on August 30th, 1223. The account, which is in Latin, sets forth that on the morrow of the Decollation of S. John the Baptist, in the 7th Henry III. (August 30th, 1223), Richard de Pageham did take, or cause to be taken by some persons unknown, the said Sibyl by night at Wartling, and carried her off, and led her from place to place, until he imprisoned her at Rungeton, and kept her there for three years, to the grievous harm of the said Giles and Sibyl. De Pageham defended himself by claiming her parents' license for all that he had done, inasmuch as William Filiol her father and Cecilia his wife had granted him 'the marriage, guardianship, and nourishment [maritagium, custodiam & nutrituram] of Sibyl after her father's death for the sum of 200 marks. That, after her father's death, her mother gave Sibyl over to his care as before agreed on, and that he had done no harm to her nor imprisoned her.

It is difficult from this account to determine how far Sibyl and her husband were justified in the charges they brought

[1] *Coll. Pro.* p. 56. The Fillols were an Essex family, and held the manor of Kelvedon in that county; the name of their house—Fillols Hall—has been changed to that of Felix Hall. *Mo.* ii. p. 151.

[2] There must be some error as to this date. Were the date assigned to the abduction correct Sibyl would indeed have been an elderly bride.

SIR GILES DE FYNES

against de Pageham, at a period when the right to dispose of a minor's hand in marriage had a market value. At all events it is clear that Giles felt there was little chance of obtaining the desired satisfaction, for when the day of trial arrived he failed to appear, leaving himself and his bail at the mercy of the court, which ordered that the names of those who had stood his bail should be called, but eventually, finding that he had license to withdraw his charge, extended its pardon to him for his contempt.

In 1269 Giles obtained a license to go on a crusade to the Holy Land.[1] I do not know when he returned home; the next mention which I have found of him in the public records is in April 1281, when he obtained a royal warrant empowering him to take three does from Epping Forest, and in August, two years later, he obtained a similar warrant for three bucks;[2] in 1289-90, the name of Sir Giles occurs[3] as having free-warren at 'Veillecourt' (*i.e.* Oldcourt), and Mersham. For his good services the King made him a grant of the manor of E. Mersea in Essex during the minority of the heir, and the right to the customary fine payable by the latter on his marriage.[4] Sir Giles appears to have died before 1293, his estates being inherited by his son and heir John. His widow Sibyl had the quiet possession of her goods confirmed to her by royal warrant, dated St. Albans, January 24th, 1296; the deed expressing that it was in return for the good allegiance of her husband.

Their son John married Joan, daughter and heiress of Jordan le Forrester, son of Reginald le Forrester,[5] hereditary Forester of Windsor Park.[6] He died in 1331, and was succeeded by his son John, who married Maud de Monceux, heiress of Herstmonceux. I have no evidence as to the exact date of his marriage, but it could not have taken place later than 1329. John

---

[1] C. R. 54 Hen. III. m. 5 dorse.   [2] *Coll. P.* p. 55.
[3] *Cal. Rot. Chart.* p. 120.
[4] C. R. Ed. I. p. 168, and C. R. Ed. II. p. 117.   [5] *Coll. P.* p. 55.
[6] There are several references in C. R. Ed. II. 1313-18 to 'a John de Fienles,' but I am not certain that they refer to the above John.

was knighted and in 1343 was put in a commission to view and repair the river banks in the neighbourhood of Pevensey.[1] He died April 5th, 1351,[2] seised, amongst others, of the manors of Herst and Compton Monceux.

Camden says that 'soon after the Norman Invasion it [Herstmonceux] became the seat of a noble family, called from it "de Herst."' Waleran de Herst was the first to adopt the surname which has, since his day, formed the latter half of the name of the manor held by him and his lineal descendants till the commencement of the eighteenth century.

Mr. Venables says: 'Whence he derived the name Monceux is uncertain, and though I can confidently say that most of the statements which have been hazarded on this point are incorrect, I am unable to supply the true solution of the difficulty;'[3] and he then proceeds to give a full account of the predecessors of Maude de Monceux, to which I would refer anyone desirous of learning more details about that family.[4]

The heir of John de Fynes and Maud his wife was William, who, at the age of twenty-one, succeeded his father,[5] and marrying Joan, daughter of Geoffrey Lord Say, died 1359-60, seised of over fifteen manors.[6] His widow survived him some years, married a second time, and died on the Feast of SS. Peter and Paul, 1378.[7] There was issue of the marriage two sons, John and William; the former, who was three years old at his father's death, died on March 24th, 1375.[8]

His heir and successor in his manors and estates was his brother William, who was born at Herstmonceux on the Feast of St. Peter ad Vincula (August 1st), 31 Edward III. (1357). Some of the witnesses who attended the inquisition, held December 6th, 1378, for proof of William's age, gave quaint reasons for remembering the date of his birth: John atte Becke, because he was distrained in that year for his service of four chickens in arrear to the manor of Herstmonceux; W. Wylyng, because in that year Giles Parker stuck an arrow through his leg

---

[1] *Dug. Fens*, p. 90.   [2] *Add.* 5485, 117.   [3] *Ven.*   [4] *Ibid.*   [5] *Add.* 5485, 117.
[6] *I. P. M.* ii. p. 221.   [7] *Pat. R.* Oct. 20th, 1382.   [8] *Add.* 5485, 114.

THE DESCENT OF MAUD DE MONCEUX

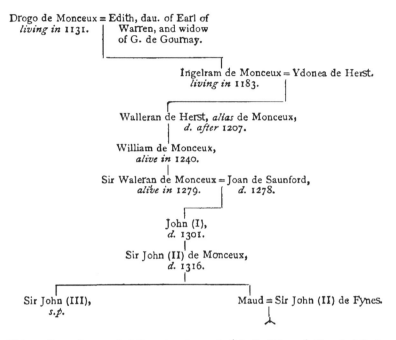

This pedigree is compiled from two sources, *Ld. D. Mis.* and *Ven.*, but I do not feel quite confident as to its absolute accuracy as regards the predecessors of Walleran de Herst.

in the churchyard; and W. Troymory, because in that year William de Fienles (meaning William de Fynes the father), then Lord of Herstmonceux, came to the house of the said Walter and wanted to beat him.[1]

This William, who became a knight, was sheriff for the county of Surrey in 1396 and 1398,[2] and his name appears in a commission of 'array' to resist the imminent invasion of the French in Sussex in 1387;[3] and later in more peaceful commissions to resist the invasion of the sea, and for that purpose to view the river banks and sea coasts near Pevensey, and the adjacent parishes, in 1391,[4] 1396, and again in 1401.[5] Sir William married Elizabeth, the daughter and heiress of William de Batsford, and widow of William Heron, whose mother Margery[6] was the heiress of Simon de Peplesham. Elizabeth died before her mother Margery, and on the latter's decease in the year 1407, all her estates passed to her grandson, Roger Fienes, the elder son of William and Elizabeth.

Sir William de Fynes died in the year 1405, and was buried in the chancel of the parish church beneath a very fine brass, still in a fair state of preservation. He is represented in full armour under a Gothic canopy, and the inscription when perfect was as follows :—

William ffienles chiauler qy morust le xiij jour de Janever l'an del Incarncon nr̃e Seigneur Jheu Cryst MCCCCV gist ycy. Dieu de sa alme eyt mercie : qy pur sa alme deuostement Pater noster et Ave priera vj^{xx} [120] jours de pardon en auera.[7]

He left two sons, Roger and James: the former was born in the manor-house of Herstmonceux, and baptized in the parish church on the 'Feast of the Exaltation of the Cross,' Sep-

---

[1] *S. Arch.* xii. p. 38.   [2] *M. & B.* i. p. xxxiv.   [3] *Pat. R.*

[4] *Pat. R.* Richard II. iv. p. 516 ; *ibid.* ii. p. 72.

[5] *Dug. Fens.* Referred to as 'Sir William Fienles,' p. 92; and as 'William Fenys,' p. 94.

[6] Mr. Venables says that Batsford was, when he wrote, still the name of a small farm in the Southern part of the parish of Warbleton.

[7] I have seen the date of his death stated to be a couple of years earlier. *Add.* 5485, 111.

tember 14th, 1384.[1] Both these sons served with distinction in the wars in France under Henry V. and the Duke of Bedford. James in consideration of his eminent services was created a baron,[2] and from him the present Lord Say and Sele traces descent.

His elder brother, Sir Roger, who was sixteen years of age at his father's death,[3] and who inherited the Herstmonceux estates, was a great warrior under Henry V. and VI.; he made expeditions into France with Henry V., and was possibly at Agincourt;[4] and he also went twice to the wars under Henry VI. Relating to one of his expeditions under Henry V. we have among our papers the following very interesting contract, or War Charter, between the King on the one part and Roger on the other, which is probably a fair specimen of the terms upon which the King obtained the help of his nobles to prosecute his wars in France. The original document is in greatly abbreviated Norman-French, and is difficult to put into English, but the following translation of it is, I believe, approximately accurate.

THIS INDENTURE made between our Sovereign Lord the King of the one part, and Roger Fienes, Knight, on the other. WITNESSES that the said Roger is retained towards our said Lord the King to serve him for an entire year on an expedition which our said Lord the King will make in his own person, if God pleases, into his Kingdom of France. At the beginning of the same year the aforesaid Roger, and his retinue, shall be at the sea ready there to make their muster; And the said Roger shall have with him on the said voyage for the whole of the said year ten men at arms, accoutred by himself, and thirty archers, of which archers, one third shall be on foot, and the others on horseback—the said Roger taking for the same wages, viz.—for himself 2s. 0d., for each of the said other men of arms twelve deniers,[5] for each of the said archers six deniers the day. Besides such wages, the said Roger shall take as well

---

[1] *Lansd.* 324, f. 244.   [2] *Dug. Bar.* ii. p. 245.   [3] *Add.* 5485, 111.
[4] In Sir N. H. Nicolas's *History of Agincourt* the name of Roger Fynes does not appear among those said to be present, but that of James Fenes (or Fynes) does.
[5] Denier, a silver penny.

for himself, as for the aforesaid other men at arms, the reward accustomed, that is to say according to the reckoning of 100 marks for thirty men of arms per quarter, of which wages and rewards the said Roger shall be paid for himself, and his said retinue, at the time of making of this Indenture for the first quarter of the said year, and similar wages and rewards shall also be paid to the said Roger for himself, and his said retinue, for the SECOND QUARTER, when he shall have made his muster of his said people at the sea port where they are bound to embark. And the said Roger will be bound to be with his said retinue well mounted, armed and arrayed according to their estate, at the port of the town of Southampton the first day of next May, ready to make muster there of his said Retinue before such person, or persons, as it shall please our Lord the King to limit and assign [appoint] for this purpose. At which port the said Roger shall then have for himself, and his said retinue, and their harness [1] and victuals, shipped at the costs of our said Lord the King: And also for a certain number of horses in the following manner, that is to say the aforesaid Roger for six of his own horses, and of ten other men at arms for the quarter year, and each mounted archer for one. AND after their arrival in foreign parts the said Roger will be bound to make the musters of the said people before such person, or persons, as shall be limited, and assigned, by our said Lord the King; as often as the said Roger shall be for this purpose duly notified, or required. And one month before the end of the said first half year the said Roger shall receive notice whether he, with his said retinue, is to serve our said Lord the King for the third quarter of the said year, or not.

AND in case it pleases our said Lord the King to have the service of the said Roger, and of his said retinue, for the said third quarter, then for that third quarter our said Lord the King will make with the said Roger for him, and for his retinue an Agreement such as should reasonably content him. AND similarly shall be done touching the last quarter of the first year.

AND if it happens that the said Roger shall, in the company of our said Lord the King, pass to the said parts of France, and return from thence to the Kingdom of England within the said year, or after, in the company of our Lord the King, or otherwise with his good leave, our said Lord the King will be

---

[1] Armour; obsolete.—*C. D.*

bound at his cost to pay for the use of the said Roger, and his said people, returning with him, their reshipping to them be delivered [the cost of their return journey], and afterwards for so many as he may want for his return to England within the term of six days after their reshipment for return to England shall have been delivered to them, (and he shall also be paid the costs of the passage of as many of his men as he may want to bring home if he gives notice of the number within six days of receiving orders to return). Provided always [toute voies] that the said Roger after such [order for ?] reshipment has been delivered to him does not make wilful delay on his re-passage.

AND if it happens that our Lord the King should countermand the said Roger his passage by sea, he will be bound for such a sum to make service to our Lord the King in such parts as he shall please, with so many of the men at arms and archers [1] [at the ordinary wages or such as the King shall decide upon ?].

AND the said Roger shall have all the prisoners if any shall be taken by him or his men on the said voyage, [? saving to the King] and Kings that may be sons of Kings, his . . . of France,[2] and also Lieutenant and Chieftains [before taken] of the said Adversary, who shall become prisoners before our said Lord the King, and for, whom there shall be a reasonable Agreement made to him, or those who have taken them. AND besides this our Lord the King shall have the third part of the spoils of war from the said Roger, as the third of the . . ? and the people of his retinue shall be answered [3] of their spoils of war in this voyage, also the gains of the prisoners, money, all gold and silver jewels, and other prizes, plunder shall not have been disposed of for the victualling of the host exceeding the value of the marks taken on the same voyage [expedition], and no other things concerning all right of prisoners and other spoils of war, which on the said voyage shall be taken by any of the retinue of the said Roger. There shall be certified to the Constable, or Marshal, or one of them, within eight days next after such was taken, the name or names of such prisoner or prisoners, and of their estate, as well as it can be known, and also the nature and quantity of the said spoils of war, and the value of the same by good estimation, and this under pain of

[1] This passage is obscure, but it may probably be paraphrased in the terms in following brackets.

[2] This passage also is obscure, but it appears to reserve to the King all rights of ransom for any royal personages who may be captured.

[3] To be accountable for; obsolete.—*C. D.*

forfeiture of the said prisoners and spoils to our said Lord the King.

AND our said Lord the King requires and grants that if any lands or tenements shall descend rightfully to the said Roger in England by any reasonable [rightful?] manner during the time that he shall thus be in the service of our said Lord the King; such lands, or tenements, shall not be retained in the King's hand, of the King by his Escheators, or any other ministers, [in] default damage or fealty, or any other personal service, BUT after due process ... affair in the Chancery shall be delivered to the Attorney of the said Roger, to do as he will without contradiction or impeachment of anyone.

AND the fealties and homages shall be respited till the coming back of the said Roger to England. AND our said Lord the King does not wish that during the aforesaid voyage any special or general assize [1] will be granted against anyone who shall press [2] with him in the aforesaid voyage.[3]

IN WITNESS of this thing to the part of this INDENTURE remaining with the said Roger our said Lord the King has put his privy Seal.

Given at Westminster the 8th day of February, the 4th year of the reign of our Lord the King [1417].

In December 1422, before Henry VI. had long been on the throne, he confirmed to Sir Roger a grant which his predecessor had made him, probably as a reward for his services in the French wars, of the custody of Porchester Castle, forest, warren; and also of two annuities, each of 20*l.*, the one charged on the King's free farms in the town of Cambridge, and the other on the custom on wool and woolfels in the port of Southampton.[4]

The *Calendar of Patent Rolls* for this period has many references to Sir Roger, who was nominated a member of a number of commissions appointed for various purposes; and in May 1425 he was ordered to have thirty men-at-arms

---

[1] Edict or judgment; obsolete.—*C. D.*
[2] In the sense of entering into the King's service.
[3] The meaning of these two paragraphs is to save Roger harmless against any legal process which might issue against him while away on the King's service.
[4] *Pat. R.* Hen. VI. p. 5.

and ninety archers in readiness at Dover for service in France; and in the same month he, together with some others, received a commission to take command of the men-at-arms and those who had entered into indentures to fight in France, and to conduct them to the camp of John Duke of Bedford.

On the occasion of New Year's Day, 1445, the King made several presents of jewels, and among the warrants for the delivery of these jewels is one for 'an ouche of gold, and in the middes a Flour de lys and yeven to Sir Rogier Fenys, knt. treasorier of our household on Neweyeris day.'[1] Being treasurer of the King's household he had to provide for many of the expenses connected with the coronation of Margaret of Anjou. The following warrant relating to this ceremony occurs in Rymer:[2]—

To ye tresorer and chamberlains, &c.

We wol and charge you that for such charges and expenses as now at this Solempnitee of Coronation of our right entirely Welbeloved Wyf ye Queene must be borne in the Office of our chief Botiller of Englande, ye make sufficient assignment unto oure trusty and Welbeloved knight, Roger Fenys, tresorer of oure household, of the some of a thousand pound to be had and received of the half xvth graunted to Us, by the Lay People of this oure Reaume nowe in this oure presen Parlement,'

and for the same purpose a further sum of 500*l*. of 'Prest' money[3] was assigned to Sir Roger, and also two sums of 2,000 marks each, and also 1,000*l*. for other expenses connected with the approaching royal wedding, which moneys were to be charged on the half xvth before mentioned, and on the fund called 'Prest' money respectively.

Sir Roger was Sheriff of Surrey in 1422 and 1434,[4] and in 1440 he obtained the King's license to fortify his manor-house at Herstmonceux, to enclose his manor, and to enlarge the park with six hundred acres,[5] and he then erected the castle, of which such fine ruins still remain.

---

[1] *Rym.* xi. p. 77.
[2] *Ibid.* p. 83.
[3] Prest: obsolete, meaning to lend; so 'prest money,' money borrowed.—*C. D.*
[4] *M. & B.* i. p. xxxv.
[5] *Add.* 6343, 321.

Roger Fynes [1] in the eighth year of Henry VI. (1430) obtained from Sir John Pelham a release from all feudal services due to the honour of Hastings, fealty only excepted, and Mr. Venables sets out this deed in his book on Herstmonceux,[2] and also a deed dated 1445, which confirmed this release.

Sir Roger Fynes married Elizabeth Holland, of Northamptonshire, whose arms (azure a lion rampant argent semée of fleur-de-lys) existed in painted glass in the east window of the Chapel of Herstmonceux Castle.[3] These arms show that this Elizabeth Holland was a branch of the family of the Hollands, Dukes of Kent and Exeter, whose predecessors also lived in Northamptonshire, at Brackley.

On Roger Fynes' death, which happened between 1444 and 1445, he was succeeded by his son, Sir Richard, who was Sheriff of Surrey and Sussex in the year 1452,[4] and afterwards Chamberlain to the Queen of Edward IV.; and who, as I have pointed out,[5] about 1446 married Joan, daughter of Sir Thomas Dacre, when she was about thirteen years of age, while his brother Robert married her sister Philippa. Philippa died without issue, upon which her sister Joan became sole heiress to her grandfather, Thomas Lord Dacre,[6] who died in January 1457-8. Thereupon Henry VI. accepted Sir Richard as Baron by the title of Lord Dacre by a patent dated November 7, 1458, and he was summoned to Parliament by writ dated October 9th, 1459.

---

[1] This spelling is the one most generally adopted in our family.   [2] *Ven.*

[3] This window and a few other fragments of glass formerly in the windows of Herstmonceux are all that now remain to our family of this property. Lord Dacre says that 'on the pulling down of Herstmonceux in 1777 I desired Mr. Hare to preserve for me this coat of arms, and 'tis now removed to Belhus and is in the South window of the Tower.' There is also a tradition in the family for what it is worth, that one chair now in the front hall at Belhus came from Herstmonceux. It is a very heavy chair of oak; there are several modern chairs there of the same pattern—a pattern known as 'Glastonbury chairs'—but this particular chair is to be distinguished from the rest, being much heavier, made of more solid oak, and much darker in colour.

[4] *M. & B.* i. p. xxxvi.   [5] *Ante* p. 57 *et seq.*

[6] *I. P. M.* (Henry VII.) i. Nos. 189 and 190. Lord Dacre appears to have thought that Sir Thomas Dacre had only one daughter, viz. Joan, and several old pedigrees speak of her as his only child, and so does the C. P.

SIR HUMPHREY DACRE

Richard did not obtain his wife's possessions without great contests and disputes during the next reign with Sir Humphrey Dacre, her uncle. The latter claimed as heir male of the Dacres; while Joan claimed as heir general being sole surviving daughter of Sir Humphrey's eldest brother.[1] Sir Humphrey had an initial disadvantage in this controversy, which was that both he and his brother had fought against Edward IV. at Towton; where the former was killed, and Sir Humphrey had escaped only to be attainted. He, however, was evidently not a person to voluntarily lose anything on account of his devotion to any particular cause or set of principles, if such loss could be avoided by a timely and abject submission. The King was fully aware he was not so safely seated on his throne as to afford to be indifferent to the allegiance of so powerful a baron as Dacre of the North; and in order to attach that Border chief to his dynasty was no doubt quite willing to forgive the devotion the Dacre family had shown to the cause of the White Rose.

Dugdale says:—

Sir Humphrey Dacre having deported himself obsequiously to the then triumphant house of York . . . was constituted master forester of Inglewood Forest for life, and continuing to enjoy the confidence of the King was summoned to Parliament as a Baron on 15 Nov. 1482 under the designation 'Humfredo Dacres of Gillesland chevalier.'[2]

Sir Humphrey, having succeeded in ingratiating himself with Edward IV., probably arranged some terms of compromise with Sir Richard Fynes previously to February 147⅔. On this date Sir Humphrey presented a petition to the King, in which he stated he was 'as repentaunt and sorrowfull as eny creature may be of all that which he have doon or committed to the displeasir of youre Highnes.'[3] And he goes on to beg that he may have

---

[1] Among our family papers is a document, not dated, endorsed—'A Supplication to the Kinge by Richard Fenys & Joan his wife for assurance of all Lord Dacre's lande.' It is numbered 5; also a copy of petition to the King by Sir Humphrey.
[2] *Dug. Bar.* ii. p. 23.   [3] *Par. R.* vi. p. 43.

restored unto him and his heirs all the family estates, except Holbeach in Lincolnshire, and Fyshwyk and Eccleston in Lancashire, which he suggested should be the property of Sir Richard in right of his wife.

Sir Richard and Sir Humphrey mutually agreed to leave all their differences to the judgment and arbitration of the King who then heard the cause which was laid before him and his Lords in Parliament. In 1473 he conferred on Sir Richard Fynes and the Lady Joan, and the heirs of their body, the same place and precedence in Parliament that her grandfather had enjoyed.[1] He also decreed to them part of the lands in dispute, but Gilsland,[2] the ancient seat of the Vaux, was adjudged, together with the greater part of the estates, to Sir Humphrey Dacre, with an ultimate remainder in default of heirs of his line to the heirs of his father, the late Lord Dacre. Sir Humphrey was ultimately created a baron, with place next beneath Sir Richard Fynes and the Lady Joan, and, by way of distinction, styled Lord Dacre of Gilsland. This was not a decision at all favourable to Richard, as the following entries in the *Cal. Pat. Rolls* show that he had already been granted the possessions of the late Lord Dacre :—

July 1st, 1461, Pardon to Richard Fenys & his wife for any entry they may have made upon possessions of Thomas, late Lord Dacre, in counties of Cumberland, Westmoreland, Northhumberland & Lincoln.

Jany 2nd 1462, Grant to Richard & his wife & heirs of her body of all the possessions of the late Lord Dacre in several counties said to be in the hands of the King by reason of a recent Act of Parliament :

And a similar grant to them in almost identical terms on October 13th, 1466.

---

[1] People do not appear to have been so anxious then, as now, to be styled by their titles, as Richard is referred to in the *Pat. R.* as 'Richard Fenys of Dacre Knight' more than once after the King's award had been made.

[2] *Par R.* vi. p. 44. This record speaks of 'Irthyngtone,' but this is the same as 'Gilsland'; Camden in his *Britannia*, p. 1033, calls Irthington the capital manor of Gilsland.

SIR HUMPHREY DACRE

We have an undated document which is a petition to Edward IV. in connection with this claim. It begins thus :—

To the Kinge our soueraine lorde Please it vuto youre heighnesse of youre moost haboundant grace to graunte vnto youre humble and trewe legees Rychard Fenys, Knyght and Johane his wife, cosyn and h^r to Thomas Dacre, Knyght, youre gracioux lettres patentes to be made in due fourme after the tenure that ensueth & they shall euermore praye to God for youre most honourable estatt.

Then follows in Latin the suggested form of letters patent.

The document which decided between these rival claims, of which I have an ancient copy, and which copy was produced in court on January 23rd, 1601, as appears from an endorsement on the back thereof, begins as follows :—

An Accord or agreement made by Edward the 4th in the 13 yeare of his Raigne [March 1473 to 1474] betweene Sr Richard ffynes as Lord Dacres, and homfrey Dacres Knighte, for ye Righte of the Dignity of the Barony.

EDWARD by the grace of god kyng of Englond & of ffrance & lord of Ierlond, to all crysten people sendithe gretyng yn oure lord god euerlastyng. fforasmuch as we consideringe that divers wariences, claymes, demaunds & debats had & like to have be contynued betweene Richard ffynes Knighte Lord Dacres and Joane his Wyfe cosene & heire to Thomas Dacre Knighte lat Lord Dacre and Philipe his Wyfe, that is to say daughter to Thomas, Sonne to the same Thomas & Philipe, one [on] that one ptye [part] And homfrey dacre Knighte, Sonne to the same Thomas Dacre Kn^t lat Lord Dacre on that other party [part], of and uppone, & for all Castelles, Lordshippes, Manores, Lands, & tenements, avousones, that some tyme weare the sayd Thomas Dacres lat Lord Dacres, & Philipe, his wife, or other of them, ffor the appeasinge of wch wariences, claymes, demaunds, & debats ether of the s^d partyes wear bounden to other by their escripte obligatory in the Some of x^m marks to abide our award, & arbitramente of the premisses, we thearuppon takinge uppon us the burden and charge of the said arbitramente have hard the tytles, evidenses, & intereste for bothe p̄tyes of the premisshes, and for more Riper declaracōn of the Same the tytle of bothe partyes of the premisshes our Judges have shewed & declared before us & the lords Sperituall & temperall in our Court of parleament, we will, & by thes presents awardethe upon the premisses.

The award then proceeds at some length to settle the dispute upon the terms I have mentioned, and the document concludes thus: 'Geeven att our palas of Westmester under our previe Seal the viijth daye of Aprill the xiij year of our Raigne' (1473).

As the descendants of Richard lived chiefly at Herstmonceux and those of Humphrey in Cumberland, they were commonly afterwards spoken of as Lords Dacre of the South and Lords Dacre of the North respectively.

In earlier times Barons were known merely by their own surnames, and the different ancestors of Joan Dacre, as they from time to time inherited the barony continued to use their paternal names. As we shall see, the Moultons, when they inherited the barony from the family of Vaux, did not cease to style themselves Moulton; and, in turn, their successors the Dacres, when they inherited it, also continued the use of their own patronymic. By the time of Edward IV., however, it had become the custom to annex some fixed appellation to peerages, and the King's award decided that Richard should be styled Lord Dacre, and thus take his title from the name of his wife's family.

The first person who held the barony which Richard Fynes claimed in right of his wife was Hubert de Vaux,[1] or de Vallibus, of Norman extraction, an individual of very considerable importance in the time of King Henry II., who gave him a grant of all that territory in Cumberland called Gilsland, a tract very large in extent, where he and his descendants chiefly resided and made their principal seat.

Hubert was succeeded by his son Robert, and to him King

[1] A pedigree among our family papers approved and warranted by Camden, and drawn up by Richard St. George, Norrey King-at-Arms. Among our papers are several documents drawn up for the use of Samson Lennard when he was proving his wife's title to the barony of Dacre. One of them states that 'This state & dignitie did annciently in the time of H. 2 belong vnto one Hubert de Vaux; as by an anncient booke of the Monastery of Lanrecost [Lanercost] doth appeare. But howe he came by it, by wrytt, or otherwise, beinge so Anncient, it doth not appeare.'

THE DESCENT OF JOAN DACRE

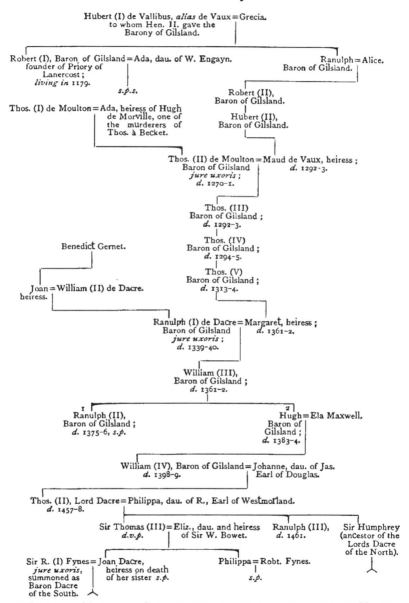

This is taken mainly from an ancient manuscript, endorsed in Samson Lennard's handwriting 'My wyfes pedigre by Talbot,' *L. P.* iv.; as to sons of Randolf de Dacre, *cf. post*, p. 179.

Henry II. granted several manorial privileges, such as soc and sac, tolls, infangthef, &c., throughout those estates in Cumberland which he inherited as heir to his father. His wife Ada, by her first husband, Symon de Morville, became great grandmother of the Ada who married Thomas de Moulton. In 1175 Robert was made Governor of Carlisle, which he successfully defended during a long siege against William, King of Scotland; and in the same year was also made Sheriff of Cumberland, which post he held until 1184. In 1177 he was one of the witnesses to the award made by King Henry between the Kings of Navarre and Castille; and in 1179 we find him appointed a 'Justice Itinerant' for Cumberland. In 1169 Robert founded the Priory of Lanercost in Cumberland, and it has been suggested that remorse for having treacherously killed a man named Gille Bueth, who had been his comrade in the wars, rather than mere piety, was the cause which induced him to this act of munificence.[1]

Robert de Vaux was succeeded by his brother Ranulph, but of him nothing is known except that he was in turn succeeded by his son, who was named Robert after his uncle.

Robert was granted the custody of the county of Cumberland and Castle of Carlisle in 1215; no doubt he was one of the Barons who took arms against King John, as before that year was out all his lands in Cumberland, Norfolk, Suffolk, Somerset, and Dorset were seized upon by the King. He was probably pardoned by Henry III. and reinstated in his possessions, as in 1222 he obtained a license to let his lands for three years for the purpose of going on a pilgrimage to Jerusalem. In 1234 he was Sheriff for Devon for part of the year. He had one son named Hubert, who died during his lifetime,[2] leaving one daughter named Maud, who succeeded her grandfather Robert.

In the reign of King Henry III. Maud de Vaux married Thomas de Moulton, son of Thomas de Moulton,[3] one of a

---

[1] *Dug. Mon.* vi. 236. *Cam. Brit.* iii. 204. *Denton's MS.* Cumberland.

[2] *Vide* before-mentioned pedigree by Camden and St. George; Sir William Dugdale says that Hubert outlived his father.

[3] *N. & B.* ii. p. 218.

family of great note in Lincolnshire [1] and Cumberland, and who by this marriage became a baron in right of his wife. He was hereditary Forester of Cumberland through descent from his mother Ada,[2] a daughter and co-heiress of Sir Hugh de Morville. Sir Hugh was a very powerful baron, and had vast possessions in both Cumberland and Westmoreland; he was one of the four knights that murdered Thomas à Beckett, and his sword with which he did that deed was said to have been preserved at his seat Isell in Cumberland until almost recent times. Thomas de Moulton was summoned with the other Barons to march into Scotland, and on another occasion to be at Chester to restrain the incursions of the Welsh. He died in 1271, leaving a son Thomas, who died in 1293, and who left Thomas,[3] his son and heir.

Lord Dacre says that this Thomas, who was twenty-six at his father's death, died two years later, leaving Thomas, his son and heir, thirteen years of age.[4] If this statement is correct he would have been the fifth Thomas in direct succession, and this system of naming a son after his father, if persisted in for several generations, is apt in after years to cause great confusion in tracing a pedigree.[5]

This fifth (?) Thomas de Moulton paid 100*l*. for his relief, and in 1303 was in the Scottish Wars, and again in 1306; the next year he received commands to fit himself with horse and

[1] An ancient document in our possession says that Thomas de Moulton of Gilsland had a grant for a market every Thursday in his manor of Holbeach, and of free-warren there and in Quaplode (Whaplode) on 31st Oct. 37th Hen. III. (1252).

[2] *N. & B.* ii. 217.

[3] 'Some writers leave out this Thomas entirely, and reckon but three descents of the Moulton family, Barons of Gilsland, whereas according to Sir William Dugdale and the best accounts there were certainly four.' *Ld. D. His.* Samson Lennard's MS. pedigree gives four Thomases, Barons, *ante*, p. 175.

[4] If these ages are accurate Thomas 3rd Baron must have begotten Thomas 4th Baron when he himself was only fourteen years old. There must be some mistake here; with all respect to Lord Dacre I think that either Thomas 3 was older at the time of his death or that there were only three generations of Moultons named Thomas who were Barons. These are all that are given in the pedigree, which is set out in the margin of the award of the title of Dacre to Margaret Lennard by the commissioners appointed by Queen Elizabeth to adjudicate upon her claim.

[5] I am now the fifth person in my family, in direct succession, whose only Christian name is, or has been, Thomas.

arms in order to assist in resisting the incursions of Robert Bruce of Scotland. In this same year he was summoned to Parliament among the Barons of the realm,[1] and in the next two years he was again fighting against the Scots. He died in 1313,[2] leaving issue by his wife Margaret an only daughter, named also Margaret, aged thirteen at her father's death.

In 1317 Margaret de Moulton married Randolf, or Ranulph, de Dacre, a son of William de Dacre and Joane, daughter and heiress of Benedict Gernet.[3]

Ranulph de Dacre was a member of a family, very eminent in the North, which from the time of William de Dacre (Sheriff of Cumberland and Governor of Carlisle 1235) had possessed the most considerable offices in the North, and were continually in the service of our English kings in their wars in Scotland and France.[4] Ranulph was probably a lawless and turbulent Border chief; and it has been said that he forcibly abducted the young heiress of the Moultons from a castle near Corby;[5] he was summoned to Parliament in her right in 1321,[6] and in 1325 took part in the expedition then made into France.[7] During Edward III.'s reign, in 1331, Ranulph de Dacre was, like his ancestor, made Sheriff of Cumberland and Governor of Carlisle, and four years later he was joined in commission with Robert de Clifford for defence of that town and the Marches of Carlisle. In 1336 he obtained a license to make a castle of his house at Naworth in Gilsland, and in 1338 he had an assignment of such wages as were due to himself and his men-at-arms for their services in Scotland.[8] Ranulph de Dacre

[1] Lord Dacre says it was the first Parliament after his coming of age.
[2] Many of these dates are taken from the C. P.
[3] Or perhaps Roger Gernet; it was no doubt from this family of Gernet that the Dacres obtained their Lancashire estates. *F. Aids*, iii. p. 91.
[4] *Ld. D. His. Dug. Bar.* ii.   [5] MS. by Mr. E. Sandford written *temp*. Car. II.
[6] The document belonging to Samson Lennard previously quoted from (*ante*, note p. 174) says that 'Ranulpe Dacre marryinge wth her in the time of E. 2, was likewise accepted to be a Baron of the Realme in her right for he likewise and his Issue by her enioyed the place in Parliamt and otherwise w̃ch Moulton helde and Vaux before him.'   [7] *Dug. Bar.* ii.
[8] Much of my information concerning this branch of the Dacres is taken from *Dug. Bar.* ii. pp. 22-25.

died in 1339, leaving four sons, William,[1] Thomas, Ranulph, and Hugh; his widow Margaret surviving him died in 1361.[2]

William, Thomas and Ranulph died without issue, and having each in turn succeeded to their father's title, and like him continually employed in the Scottish Wars, were in turn succeeded by their youngest brother Hugh, at the age of forty in 1375. The pedigree which I have printed, and which is perhaps more authentic, makes William to be the only son of the Ranulph who died in 1339, and does not mention Thomas. It gives Ranulph and Hugh as sons of William instead of brothers, but like this account shows Hugh to have succeeded to the barony in 1375.[3]

Some four years previously to succeeding to the title, Hugh (then a knight) got into trouble for having done wrong to William Earl Douglas, to the damage of a hundred pounds, contrary to the articles of truce between England and Scotland; and orders were given to the Sheriffs of London to apprehend him, and put him in prison until he should make good the damage. However, he was shortly after restored to the King's favour, as he was in the next year taking part in the wars in France, and in the following year engaged in the war in Flanders. From 1380 to 1382 he was one of the commissioners for guarding the West Marches. He was summoned to Parliament from 1376 to 1383, and died in 1384, having married Ela, daughter of Alex. Maxwell of Scotland, by whom he left William, his son and heir.

At the time of his father's death William de Dacre, who

---

[1] William appears to have died in 1361-2, as an ancient document in our possession says that the jurors made a presentment in 35th Ed. III. that William held the manor of Holbeach when he died, and that Ralf his brother was his heir. It is stated (*N. & B.* ii. p. 378) that William was succeeded by a brother Thomas, who died *s.p.*

[2] An inquisition, dated 36 Ed. III. (1362), held after her death found that she and her husband, Ralph de Dacre, held the manor of Barton, co. Westmoreland, *N. & B.* i. p. 407. I am not able to reconcile a statement in *F. Aids,* iii. p. 240, that in 1346 William Dacre held Holbeach, which Margaret, wife of *Thomas* of Gilsland, held formerly.

[3] In Sir Humfrey's petition (*Par. R.* vi. p. 44) the descent is given as being through Hugh, *son,* not brother, of Randolf, son of William.

was aged twenty-six, was in the King's service in Scotland, and on these grounds his homage was respited ; and in 1388 he was in the garrison of Berwick. William de Dacre married Johanne, daughter of James Earl of Douglas ;[1] he was summoned to Parliament from 1384, and died July 20th, 1398,[2] leaving Thomas his son and heir. Although William died in 1398, writs of summons to Parliament continued to be addressed ' Willo de Dacre' from 23rd Richard II. (1399) to 24th November, Henry IV. (1403).

The ancient document referred to in a footnote on a previous page says that William Dacre, Knight (meaning this William), entailed the manor of Holbeach on his son Thomas, and on his son's wife, Philippa, in the time of Henry VI., but this date cannot be correct, as Henry VI. did not begin to reign until September 1422.

Thomas, son and heir of William de Dacre, seems to have dropped the prefix of 'de' and to have been known as Thomas Lord Dacre. He was only twelve years of age at the time of his father's death, and was not summoned to Parliament until December 2nd, 1412. In 1417 he was retained by indenture to serve King Henry V. in his fleet for three months, with thirty men-at-arms and sixty archers, and in 1421 was constituted chief Forester of Inglewood in Cumberland. In 1424 he was one of the Barons appointed by Henry VI. to treat with James King of Scotland about peace, and in 1433 was again a member of a commission to treat with the Scots at Hadenstank about a matter then in dispute between them and the English. In the same year he held an important command in the army raised in the northern counties for the defence of Berwick against the Scots ; and in 1452 he was for the third time in a commission to treat with that nation. Thomas Lord Dacre died on January 15th, 1457-8, having married Philippa, daughter of Ralf Nevill, first Earl of Westmoreland. He had three

---

[1] In 1777 Lord Hailes expressed his opinion that Johanne could not have been a daughter of James 2nd Earl of Douglas, but that she might well have been a sister of his.—*F. P.*

[2] The date is given as 23rd R. II. (1399), in *N. & B.* ii. p. 379.

sons[1]—Thomas, who died in his father's lifetime; Ranulph[2] and Humphrey. These two younger sons both fought against Edward IV. at Towton, 1461, where the former was killed, and the latter, who escaped, was attainted in November of that year, although he was subsequently pardoned.

Sir Thomas, Lord Dacre's eldest son, was knighted; he married Elizabeth, daughter and heiress of Sir William Bowet, and Joan his wife, a daughter of Sir Robert de Ufford, a member of a very distinguished Suffolk family.[3] By this marriage he obtained, among other manors, those of Burgh, Hautbois, and Horsford, and the advowsons of Langley and of St. Michaels Mustowe (now known as St. Michaels at Plea) in Norwich, and also the manors and advowsons of Hurstpierpoint, and other manors in Sussex, which had come to the Ufford family by the marriage of Sir Edmund Ufford (the father of Sir Robert) with Sibil, or Sibilla, the heiress of the family of Pierpoint.[4] Sir Thomas died leaving only two daughters, Joan and Philippa.[5]

We have seen that after Joan Dacre married Sir Richard Fynes, and her sister had died without issue, he was summoned to Parliament in her right as Lord Dacre.[6] He and his wife appear to have had five sons—John, Thomas, Richard, William, and Roger; and one daughter, Elizabeth, who married Lord Clinton.[7]

Richard Lord Dacre took a considerable part in the public affairs of his time. In the reign of Henry VI., and also in that of his successor, Edward IV., Lord Dacre was on several

[1] This Lord Dacre had great disputes and litigation with the Abbot of Crowland; from Ingulph's account of this litigation it would appear that his eldest son was named John, or in any case that he had a son of that name, but I think the chronicler must be in error as to the Christian name of this son, as I can find only the above-named sons mentioned in any of our MS. pedigrees.—*Ingulph's Chronicle*, B. A. L. pp. 40 et seq.

[2] Ranulph wrongfully assumed the title of Lord Dacre of Gilsland, and was Summoned to Parliament by that name the year before his death.

[3] *Dug. Bar.* ii. pp. 47-50, and *T. & G.* i. p. 300.
[4] *S. Arch.* xi. p. 62.   [5] *I. P. M.* Henry VII. vol. i. Nos. 189 and 190.
[6] *Ante*, p. 172.   [7] Lord Dacre's will. *Add.* 5485, 119.

occasions appointed a Trier of Petitions in commissions composed of eminent persons, such as the Archbishop of Canterbury and other bishops, as colleagues.[1]

The name of 'lord Dakere of the Sowthle' appears among those of the 'barons and knytes beyng with owre soveryn lord Kyng Edward in hys jorny in to Scottlong at the fest of Seynt Andrew in þe month of Decembyr, Anno Domini M°.CCCC.LXij°.'[2] And a few years later, when in 1468 Margaret, sister to Edward IV., went abroad to be married to the Duke of Burgundy, Lord Dacre accompanied her as 'hur Chamberlayne.'[3]

In 1471 Edward IV. appointed Richard one of the administrators of Wales and the duchy of Cornwall, until the Prince of Wales should attain the age of fourteen, and two years later he was one of those appointed tutors and councillors to that Prince; and there are several more references to him in the Calendars of Patent Rolls for this period.

In 1472 he was in a commission of array in the county of Sussex for the purpose of defending the country against the 'King's enemies, the French, Easterlings,[4] and others.'

On November 24th, 1473, he was granted the Constableship of the Tower of London with all the profits belonging thereunto, after the decease of 'John lord of Duddeley';[5] as a reward 'for his good service to the King and his consort Elizabeth.'[6] This grant was complimentary to Lord Dacre, but was of no other use to him, as in fact he died before Lord Dudley.

In 1474 Richard's name was put into a commission for viewing and repairing the banks of the Thames from Greenwich to Wandsworth.[7]

[1] *Par. R.* v. pp. 373, 462, 496, 571.   [2] *C. S. P., Three*, p. 157.
[3] *Excerpta*, p. 228; Dugdale (*Bar.* ii. p. 24) says that it was Lord Dacre of the North who attended the Princess, but I think he is mistaken. He makes one palpable error in saying the marriage took place in '4 Ed. IV.,' while in fact the real date was four years later. At this period Humfrey had not received any formal pardon from the King, and had not been summoned to Parliament as Lord Dacre.
[4] The Hanse merchants of North Germany.—*C. D.*   [5] John Lord Dudley.
[6] *Pat. R.*   [7] *M. & B.* i. p. 226; *Dug. Fens*, p. 68.

Edward IV. esteemed him so highly that in more than one act of 'Resumption' in the time of that king it was specially provided that nothing in these acts should be 'prejudiciall or hurtyng' to Richard Lord Dacre, his wife, or his heirs.[1]

In alluding to Richard's good services the King probably referred to the part the former took in his campaigns against the supporters in the north of the Lancaster cause. I think it likely that it was to compensate Lord Dacre for the improbability of his living long enough to succeed Lord Dudley in his Constableship of the Tower that, in 1475, he was appointed one of the King's Council, having a grant of a hundred marks a year issuing out of the customs for that service.[2] At this period the system of appointing a body of laymen as a commission of oyer and terminer[3] to go round the country administering justice, although coming to an end, still obtained, and Richard Lord Dacre was appointed on several such commissions.

Lord Dacre died on November 25th, 1483,[4] and was buried at Herstmonceux, leaving his grandson Thomas, a boy of thirteen years of age,[5] his heir. On February 12th, 1484, a grant of wardship over this child was made to his grandmother Joan, and two other persons;[6] this Thomas was son of Sir John,[7] who died in 1483 during his father's lifetime.[8] Sir John married Alice, daughter and co-heiress of Henry Lord Fitz-

[1] *Par. R.* v. pp. 526, 625; vi. pp. 44, 202.
[2] *Pat. R.* Ed. IV. and Hen. VI. p. 534.
[3] A court or commission of 'oyer and terminer' is one whose duty it is to hear and determine suits brought before it.
[4] *Has.* ii. The C. P. says he died 1484, and an ancient abstract amongst our papers refers to his *I. P. M.* being 2nd Ri. III.
[5] Said to be sixteen years and more at the death of his grandmother Joan.— *Ibid.*   [6] *Pat. R.*
[7] *Ld. D. His.* gives his name as Thomas in error. His name is given as John in the pedigree forming part of the award signed by Lords Burghley and Howard, and also in his mother's will, *post*, p. 185, and *Cal. Inq.* No. 261.
[8] We have an old MS. pedigree endorsed in Samson Lennard's writing 'The auncient Petigree'; this says that John died in the time of Richard III., and as his father died in 1484 he must have died in 1483, as that King's reign only commenced in June of that year.

Hugh, by whom he obtained considerable estates, especially in Yorkshire,[1] and left issue at least two sons, Thomas and Edward, as appears from the will of Joan Lady Dacre.

An ancient copy of the will of Richard Lord Dacre in Latin is to be found in the British Museum, and it is of value from a genealogical point of view, as it shows that he had two more sons than appear in the pedigrees. By this will, which is dated September 20th, 1483, the testator first makes an adequate provision for his widow for the term of her life; he then goes on to dispose of the manor of Ewhurst, which he leaves to his son Thomas, and the heirs of his body, with remainders over to the heirs of his eldest son Sir John, already deceased; and further remainders in turn to his younger sons Richard, William and Roger, respectively, and lastly to his daughter Lady Clinton. He deals in a like way with his manors of Street in Sussex, Compton Monceux in Hants, and Wolfe le Fenis in Bucks, leaving one of them to each of his three younger sons, with remainders over (*mutatis mutandis*) similar to those he created in respect to Ewhurst; and he left all the residue of his estates to his grandson and heir, Thomas. Lord Dacre provided for the payment of his debts, and directed his executors to send his grandson Thomas 'ad scholas,' and to provide him with everything necessary to his rank. Lastly, he directed that four priests should offer up masses in the parish church of Herstmonceux for the souls of himself and his ancestors and for those of all faithful persons then dead, for the space of three years immediately after his death.

I think it was probably Richard who founded the Benedictine nunnery at Wallingwell, Notts, at the suppression of the religious houses; its founder was stated to be 'Lord Dakers of the South.'[1]

[1] *Ld. D. His.* The title of FitzHugh is now in abeyance; the two persons who could lay claim to it if the descendants of either of these co-heiresses became extinct, are Viscount Hampden through the Fynes, Lennards, &c., from the above Alice; and the Marquis of Bute from her sister Elizabeth; through the FitzHugh family there is also a claim to the barony of Marmion, in abeyance since 1335.

[2] *L. and P.* x. No. 364.

THOMAS (II.) FYNES LORD DACRE

Lord Dacre's widow, Joan, survived him, dying on March 8th, 1486;[1] by her will, dated October 13th, 1485, and proved June 14th in the following year, she directed that

My body to be buried in the quire of All Saints, at Hurstmonceux, between the high altar and the tomb of Sir Richard Fynes, knight, my late husband,[2] to Thomas, son of Sir John Fynes, knight, to Edward Fynes, brother of the said Thomas, to Elizabeth Lady Clinton, and Thomas Fynes, my son and daughter, all my chattels; and I appoint my sons, Thomas[3] and William Fynes, and Thomas Oxenbridge, my executors.[4]

As has been said, upon the death of Richard Fynes, Lord Dacre, the title descended to his grandson Thomas,[5] as the second Lord Dacre of the South, and he was admitted a member of Gray's Inn in 1492. It was probably at about this date he married Anne, daughter of Sir Humphrey Bourchier, eldest son of John Lord Berners, and by her had issue three sons and one daughter. His first and third sons were both named Thomas;[6]

---

[1] *I. P. M.* (Henry VII.) i. No. 189. Lord Dacre says she died 7th of Henry VII. (which would be 1492).—*Ld. D. His.*

[2] It is noteworthy that Joan refers to her late husband as 'Sir Richard,' and not as 'Lord Dacre.'

[3] Thomas Fynes, son of Richard and Joan, is probably the Thomas Fynes who was High Sheriff for Surrey and Sussex in 1508. We have a deed between him and a man whom he appointed 'Keper of the Kinges Gaole of Guldeford,' which is quite an interesting document, and has already been printed in the *Surrey Archæological Magazine.*

[4] *Test. Vet.* p. 390. A précis and part copy of this will, *L. P.* iv. quoting *P. C. C.* Logg, 182*a*, differs slightly from the version given by Nicolas. Sir G. Oxenbridge married as his second wife a granddaughter of Lady Dacre named Anna; she was a daughter of her second son Thomas.—*S. Arch.* viii. p. 231.

[5] It may be observed that here we again have four eldest sons in succession having the Christian name of Thomas, viz. Thomas Lord Dacre; Thomas who died in his father's lifetime; Thomas Lord Dacre who was hanged; and Thomas his son who died young; nor is this all, as Thomas, the first of these Lords Dacre, named two of his sons Thomas.

[6] Thomas Lord Dacre left Horsford and Hautbois to his third son Thomas and his heirs, with remainder over to Thomas, the son of his (Lord Dacre's) eldest son Thomas, and these estates did in fact become the property of this grandson; this would make one suppose that Lord Dacre's third son Thomas died young, and without issue. However, an ancient case for counsel's opinion, not dated, which from internal evidence appears to have been prepared about 1560, gives a short pedigree of the

his second son John, and his daughter Mary. The latter married Sir H. Norris, who was executed in connection with the charges brought against Anne Boleyn. It was their son who, we have seen, gave so much trouble to Margaret Fynes and her husband in after years.[1]

It is possible that they had another daughter of whom I have no record. Richard Londenoys of Brede is said to have married Catherine, daughter of 'Fines Lord Dacre,'[2] but the only daughter that Lord Dacre mentions in his will is Mary.

I have been unable to find out anything about Lord Dacre's second son John, who I presume died without issue, and all I know of his third son Thomas is that he had a son Philip.

Lord Dacre's eldest son, Sir Thomas Fynes, served in the war with Scotland in 1513 on board the 'Mary of Walsyngham,' a ship of 120 tons.[3] A few years after he married Joan, daughter of Edward Lord Dudley, who was grandson and successor to John Lord Dudley. Their marriage took place according to one of our documents, endorsed in the handwriting of Samson Lennard 'Notes of olde Mr Thorisbye,' in 1516. The 'note' is as follows :—

The date of the Indenture of Covenants for marryage ys dated the xvi of February A° vij of H. viij [1516] wherin yt ys covenantyd that the Lord Dacres sone shall marry Jane the L[ord] Dudleys daughter before the feest of thascencion of our Lord next comyng, and shall also before that day make assurance of lands accordynge to the covenants in the same indenture.

The assurance of the lands was mad the xx of Apryll next

Fynes family. From this pedigree it seems that Thomas the third son had a son Philip (no doubt the Philip referred to previously, p. 93). I am unable to reconcile this fact with the result of the limitations above mentioned of Horsford and Hautbois to Lord Dacre's third son Thomas and his heirs.

[1] *Ante*, p. 81 *et seq.*

[2] *S. Arch.* viii. p. 232, referring to a MS. in College of Arms; see also *Essex Visitation*, *Har. MSS.* 6065, fol. 76b, where she is described as 'Cath. dau. to ye Lord Dacre az. 3 lions rampt or,' which being the Fynes arms shows her to have been a daughter of some Lord Dacre of the SOUTH.

[3] *L. and P.* i. No. 4377.

after the datt of the indenture as that as yt ys to be thought yt was the viiij yere of H. viij or the maryage was.

Mr. Thursby must have made a mistake as to the date of this marriage in saying that it took place in April 1516; he mentions in his 'Notes' inquisitions held after the respective deaths of Sir Thomas Fynes and his father Lord Dacre ; and these inquisitions mention the age of the heir at the date at which they were respectively taken. From the inquisitions in question it is clear that the eldest son of Sir Thomas Fynes was born not later than August 1515, and therefore his parents' marriage could not have taken place later than November 1514.

Lord Dacre's eldest son Sir Thomas died October 26th, 20th Henry VIII. (1528), five years before his father.[1] Joan his widow, having married as her second husband Philip Audley, died August 1539.[2] By her first husband she had issue a son, Thomas—who as we shall see succeeded his grandfather in the title and estates—and a daughter christened Anne.

Anne married a Mr. John (or Walter) Mantell, who as we shall see was executed with his brother-in-law Lord Dacre. She seems afterwards to have married again, as a memorandum in the British Museum says :—

'Mr. Sampson Leonard of Kent tould mee . . . he sayeth lykewise that Mrs. Anne ffiennes daughter of my Lorde Dacres [he should have said granddaughter] was afterwards marryed vnto one Mr. Johnson of Northampton Sheir by whom shee had a daughter as hee hath beene formerlye towlde.[3]

Thomas Lord Dacre seems to have taken considerable part in public affairs. He was one of 'those of the Temporal Lords & Commons of the Diocess of Chichester who assented to, &

---

[1] 'Notes of olde Mr. Thorisbye.' Mr. Thursby was the third husband of Mary Lady Dacre, widow of the Thomas Lord Dacre who was hanged. *Post*, p. 207, *n.* 1.

[2] *Herst. Reg.* '1539 Aug. 9ᵗʰ Buried the Lady Jane Fynes mother of Lord Dacre.'

[3] *Add.* 5521, fol. 38.

signed the peace with France at Staples[1] on Sea near Boulogne, 3ᵈ November, 1492.'[2] In 1493 Lord Dacre was Constable of Calais; in 1495 he was made a Knight of the Bath; in 1497 he took part in the defeat of the Cornishmen at Blackheath in Perkin Warbeck's rebellion, and shortly after he marched against the Scots under the leadership of the Earl of Surrey;[3] while in November 1499 he was one of the peers who sat at the trial of the Earl of Warwick,[4] and in 1521 on that of the Duke of Buckingham.[5]

About this time Lord Dacre appears to have been spending more than he could afford, as in 1502 we find he conveyed the manor of Wandsworth, 'and all his lands & tenements in Wanesworth, Battersey, Puttenheth, Wymbledon, and other towns adjoining in the Shere of Surrey,' to Sir Reynold Bray for the consideration of 426*l*. 13*s*. 4*d*.,[6] and some eight years later he sold the Lancashire manors of Fyshwyke and Eccleston which came to his grandfather as a result of the compromise with Sir Humphrey Dacre.[7] In 1508 he was Sheriff of Surrey,[8] and on December 17th of that year he was one of the witnesses present in the great chamber in the Palace of Richmond when the espousals were contracted between the Archduke Charles and the Lady Mary, daughter of King Henry VII.; and he was one of the peers who signed a bond of 50,000 gold crowns to the Emperor Maximilian, and the Archduke, for the due performance of the marriage.[9] He was one of those peers who were appointed triers of petitions in 1510[10] and 1512.[11] He was also in a great many commissions for various purposes; several commissions of the peace, also commissions of array,[12] for inquiring what lands had of late years been imparked, and for

---

[1] Etaples. [2] *Coll. Let.* p. 16.
[3] *Dug. Bar.* ii. p. 244. [4] *Plumpton Correspondence*, C. S. P. p. 143.
[5] *L. and P.* iii. p. 493. [6] *M. & B.* iii. p. 350.
[7] *L. and P.* i. Nos. 1212 and 1965. Fishwick must now be a property of considerable value as it is one of the suburbs of Preston.
[8] *M. & B.* i. p. xxxvii. [9] *Hist. Com.* xi. App. Part iii. p. 113.
[10] *L. & P.* i. No. 811. [11] *Ibid.* i. No. 2082.
[12] Commissions of array were formerly issued in times of national danger for the purpose of calling out and training able-bodied men for defence of the country.

other objects. I do not think it necessary to specify all these commissions individually, but references to them will be found scattered through the first five volumes *L. and P.* There is one rather curious reference to Lord Dacre that may be mentioned, viz. that in 1518 he obtained a license to export 140 woollen cloths.[1]

Lord Dacre went with Henry VIII. when the latter made war with France in 1513, and appears to have had a troop of about 120 of his own men.[2] In 1517 he was a supervisor of the will of Sir Thomas Bryan, who had married his wife's sister, Margaret Bouchier.[3] In the 'Chronicle of Calais,'[4] in connection with the Field of the Cloth of Gold, there occurs this passage :—'The apoyntment for the Kynge to atend upon hym over the sea to Caleys in the xij yere of his reigne 1520,' then follows lists of peers and knights, and among the former occurs 'the lorde Dakers of the Sowthe.' On May 27th, 1522, Lord Dacre was one of those appointed to give attendance on the King at Canterbury on the coming of the Emperor Charles V.;[5] and a year later he was for a few months with the army 'beyond sea,' under the leadership of the Duke of Suffolk.[6] There is a very different sort of mention of Lord Dacre in the public records a few years after, as he appears to have been for some time a prisoner in the Fleet on the charge of receiving and harbouring suspected felons. February 7th, 1525 :

> The Lord Dacres hathe this daye knowledged and confesste the bearinge of Theuves, and his remysnes & negligence in ponyshem^t of them, and also his famylyer & conversaunte beinge wth them, knowinge them to haue com'ytted felonye, and dyvers others his mysdoinges in manner and forme as ys expressed in his confessyon & submyssyon subscribed wth his owne hande, wherevpon he ys comytted to ye keapinge of the warden of the ffleate, and his recognysaunce taken & knowledged the xxxth daye of Januarye last past, aswell for himself as for his sureties ys decreed by the saide most reverende father to be utterlye voide frustrate & cancelled.[7]

[1] *L. and P.* ii. Part ii. No. 4191.   [2] *Ibid.* i. Nos. 4306, 4477, 4534.
[3] *Test. Vet.* 553.   [4] *C. S. P., Ch. of C.* p. 20.
[5] *L. and P.* iii. No. 2288.   [6] *Ibid.* Part ii. No. 3288.   [7] *Lansd.* i. 105.

Lord Dacre was soon pardoned and in the King's favour again, as when Henry paid a visit to the Earl of Northumberland at Petworth, Sussex, in August 1526, he was one of the noblemen who went there to meet his Sovereign.[1]

Lord Dacre, like his ancestors, was in many commissions of sewers for taking care of the river banks in the neighbourhood of Pevensey, and he attended a meeting at Westham, close to Pevensey, in October 1532, to make regulations concerning the way in which fishing was to be permitted to be carried on there.[2] In July 1530 Lord Dacre was one of those peers who signed a petition to the Pope in favour of the King obtaining the divorce he had been striving so hard for.[3] Sir Goddard Oxenbridge, who died in 1531, appointed Lord Dacre a supervisor of his will, and left him a legacy of what nowadays sounds the ridiculous sum of 4*l*.[4] In January 1532 he was one of the many courtiers who gave plate to the King on New Year's Day,[5] and a year later the King returned the compliment.[6]

Lord Dacre died on September 9th, 25th Henry VIII. (1533),[7] and his will (dated September 1st, 1531) was proved 1534, an extract from which has been published by Nicolas.[8] The bequests of this will, which is an extremely long one, begin thus :—

I bequeath & recommend my sowle to Almighty God my maker & redeemer and to the Glorious Virgin our blessed Lady his moder and to all the holy saints in Heaven. And my bodye to be buried in the parish Church of Hersemonceux in the North side of the High Altar there where the Sepulchre is used to be made and one tombe there to be made and ordayned conveniente for the making and setting of the saide sepulchre. And apparel to be made and bought for the said sepulchre at my costes and charges in the honor of the most blessed Sacrament and my Saviour Jesus Christe. And I will that my executors give toward the light of the said sepulchre one hundred pounds of wax to be made in tapers of tenne poundes, one peece to burne about the saide sepulchre after the manner as the custom is nowe to burne abowte the same.

[1] *L. and P.* iv. No. 2368.   [2] *Dug. Fens*, 103.   [3] *L. and P.* iv. No. 6513.
[4] *S. Arch.* viii. p. 220.   [5] *L. and P.* v. No. 686.   [6] *Ibid.* vi. No. 32.
[7] 'Notes of olde Mr. Thorisbye'; *Has.* ii. 163; also *I. P. M.*   [8] *Test. Vet.* 653.

Item. I bequeath to the parish church of Hersemonceux ten poundes sterlinge to the use and intente to buy therewith one challice of silver and gilte if I buy neither give none to the same church in my lifetime.

And likewise I bequeath tothe said Churche tenne poundes toward a crosse of silver and gilte to be bought for the same Church to the honor of God and our Lady and all saintes in the saide Parish Church. If I buy none by ony dayes in my life.

Item. I bequeath to Sainte Richard's shrine of Chichester six shillings and eight pence.

Item. I will that my executors bury my body after an honest manner and degree of a Baron and to distribute in almes tenne poundes in silver or twenty marks to poore people the day of my buriall. And to distribute to every priest and clerke that singeth or sayeth dirge after the manner of the Churche there accustomed and also to ordaine meat and drinke for the honorable Lordes and gentlemen that cometh to my buriall. And if my sepulchre cannot be made in the place by me before appointed than I will that it be made in an honest and open place in the same churche in the sight of the people, that my sowle may be the better remembered and that there be made one tombe or other remembrance upon me that it may be known where my bodie resteth. And also I will that there be founden in the same Churche of Hersemonceux one honest secular priest being an Englishman borne, to sing for my sowle for the space of seven yeares next after my decease, to pray for my sowle, my father's sowle, my mother's sowle, and Anne my wife's sowle, all my ancestors' sowles and all Christian sowles the said priest to have yearely for his salary and to finde breade wyne and wax to sing with twelve marks sterlinge, and the same priest to be changed and removed if neede and the case so require by the direction and oversight of my executors.

Among our papers is a copy of the will of this Lord Dacre, and also an ancient copy of a deed made by him which recites that he had made his will on September 1st, and that this deed is intended ' to provide for the more sure execution of the same, and for performing divers other articles which are omitted in the said Will,' and then goes on to dispose of various of his manors. These documents are especially interesting in that they mention he had two sons named Thomas and also a son

John, and give other information as to his relations which are not alluded to by Lord Dacre in his family history. Among other provisions made by this deed is a legacy of five hundred marks as a marriage portion to his granddaughter Anne, whom he styles his 'niece'; his grandson Thomas he alludes to as 'my cosin & heir apparent.'

In pursuance of the directions of this will and deed, the fine and richly ornamented tomb, which is the chief architectural feature of Herstmonceux Church, was erected in 1534 to his memory and that of his eldest son. The monument from its position presents two fronts, one towards the church and one towards the chantry on the north. The material of which the tomb is built is of grey shell marble from the Petworth quarries, but the canopies of the niches and the more delicate tracery are executed in Caen stone. At one period it was 'restored,' the coat of whitewash with which it was covered was cleared off, and the coats of arms on the south side were fully emblazoned; but unfortunately the ignorance of those engaged on the restoration caused some serious mistakes to be made therein, which have made the identification of the coats a matter of some difficulty.

As we have seen from Lord Dacre's will, this monument was erected not only to commemorate himself, but also for the purposes of an 'Easter Sepulchre.' This means a spot where the ceremonies typifying the burial and resurrection of our Lord might be annually performed on Good Friday and Easter Day. For this purpose an arched recess formed in the north wall of the chancel above a low altar tomb without inscription was often employed; at other times the actual tomb was used for these ceremonies, as in this instance.

On the death of his grandfather in 1533 Thomas, the son of Sir Thomas, inherited the title when only about nineteen years of age.[1] Not only was he very young to succeed to so important

---

[1] 'An offyce was found the 26 of August in the 21st of Hen. VIII. at the wch tyme hys sone thomas fines was found to be of 14 yeres of age.' '9th January 25th Hen viij offyce after hys dethe [Thos. Lord Dacre] was found wherein hys

a position as that which he occupied on his grandfather's death, but it is probable he did not have the advantage of any education calculated to fit him for his responsibilities. We have seen that his father died while he was still very young, and that his mother married again; if upon her second marriage she left him in the care of his grandfather who had 'famylyer & conversaunte beinge' with 'Theuves,' the lad would most likely have associated with a set of men highly unfitted in every way to be the companions of any young fellow; and this bringing up may not improbably have been the cause of his adopting that wild and reckless career which was to bring him at an early age to an ignominious end upon the scaffold.

The young Lord Dacre, the third Thomas in succession, was summoned to attend Parliament in January 1534 when only nineteen years of age.[1] He married, apparently in 1536, just before his twenty-first birthday,[2] Mary Nevill, a daughter of George Lord Abergavenny.[3] She was one of the ladies appointed to assist at Queen Mary's funeral, and drove with three other peeresses in the 'fyrste chariot'; these ladies were directed to be 'apperelled accordinge to their Estates viz manteles and their Barbes [4] above their chines.'[5]

By her he had two sons: Thomas, who was fifteen years of age in August 1553,[6] and was therefore born in 1538, and Gregory, and one daughter Margaret. Gregory was christened on June 25th, 1539.[7] The document which gives his brother's age as fifteen in August 1553, says that Gregory at that date was aged thirteen years and a half, and, if so, he was about four months old when he was christened.

heyre was found of the yers of xviij & mor.' 'One other offyce founde in Sussex the ij day of September in the xxvj of H. viij. wherein hys heyre was found to be of the age of xix yeres.'—*Mr. Thursbie's Notes.*

[1] *L. and P.* vii. No. 55. [2] Private act, *post*, p. 206. [3] *Coll. Peer.* vi. p. 567.
[4] Barbe or barb, part of a woman's head-dress, still sometimes worn by nuns; it consisted of white plaited linen passed over or under the chin, and reaching midway to the waist.
[5] *Le. Coll.* v. p. 317. [6] Document referred to *post*, p. 207.
[7] *Herst. Reg.*

We have a document endorsed by Samson Lennard—'The Livery of Thomas lo Dacre my wyues Father,' dated Westminster, May 11th, 29th Henry VIII. (1537), which is a grant of his lands by the King to him upon his emancipation from wardship.

He appears to have had a good deal of trouble and some disputes with the executors of his grandfather's will. The two letters, written in February 1538, from Lord Lawarr (De la Warr), the one to Cromwell and the other to Lord Dacre, which are calendared,[1] do not explain the whole matter in dispute. It probably arose in connection with the charges the deceased peer had laid upon his estates. Lord Lawarr says in his letter to Cromwell 'We were content he [Lord Dacre] should have such lands as we have by his grandfather's will, he to have the profits and we the rent, till the will be performed. Threle to be receiver of these lands to the performance of the will, and Dacre to take all other profits to his own use.'

It was probably in order to enlist Cromwell's interest on his behalf that Lord Dacre gave the former the right of sporting over his parks of Danny and Hurst;[2] and with a like object when Gregory Cromwell, the powerful minister's son, came to live in Sussex, both Lord and Lady Dacre, he says in a letter to his father, welcomed him to the county and entertained him with presents.[3] In May 1536 Lord Dacre was one of the jury that sat on the trial of Anne Boleyn and Lord Rocheford;[4] and in June of that year he, with seventeen other peers, was summoned to a Council meeting at Westminster at what to us sounds a remarkably early hour, 8 A.M.[5] Other instances of very early hours for business are mentioned in this book. Probably, when artificial light was so imperfect, people were in the habit of setting a much greater value on daylight for all purposes of business than is the case at present.

The rebellion which broke out in the north this year was the occasion of Lord Dacre being one of those appointed to attend

---

[1] *L. and P.* xiii. Part i. Nos. 197, 198. [2] *Ibid.* No. 143.
[3] *Ibid.* No. 734. [4] *Ibid.* x. No. 876. [5] *Ibid.* xi. No. 5.

the King in person with a force of 200 men,[1] but in October, as the insurrection was so quickly suppressed, he was informed his services were no longer required.[2] In the following year he was one of the jury who found Lord Darcy guilty of treason;[3] and in 1538 he again formed part of the panel who tried and found guilty Lord Montagu and the Marquis of Exeter.[4]

In reading records of these times one is struck with what an absolute farce these trials were, and the docility of the peers in almost invariably finding guilty any nobleman that Henry chose to prosecute. They were no doubt panic-stricken and afraid of the King's wrath if they should dare to return a verdict of acquittal. At the same time each peer as he voted for the execution of one of his own order was making the probability of his own execution greater, and playing into the hands of the King, who, impatient at any obstacle to his absolute power, was anxious to have by his side a timid and subservient House of Lords.

In view of the fate which ultimately befell Lord Dacre, the following letter from him to Cromwell, written nearly four years before the event took place which caused his execution, is of considerable interest. I much wish I could have found the letter from Cromwell to which this is an answer; but from this letter we may, I think, fairly assume that it was no uncommon event for this young man to take part in what Stow calls 'stealing of deer in parks and other unthriftiness.'

December 4th, 1537, from Thomas Lord Dacre to Cromwell:

I have received your lordship's letters wherein I perceive your benevolence towards the frailness of my youth in considering that I was rather led by instigation of my accusers than of my mere mind to those unlawful acts, which I have long detested in secret. I perceive your lordship is desirous to have knowledge of all riotous hunters, and shall exert myself to do you service therein. I beg you give credence to Mr. Awdeley, with whom I send some of my servants to be brought

---

[1] *L. and P.* xi. No. 580.
[2] *Ibid.* No. 670.
[3] *Ibid.* xii. Part i. No. 1206 (20).
[4] *Ibid.* xiii. Part ii. No. 979.

before you; he can inform you of others who have hunted in my little park of Bukholt.'[1]

It is impossible to say how far young Lord Dacre enjoyed the favour of the King, but judging from the frequent mention of the former in the records of those times it may fairly be assumed that he had no grounds for complaining of his Sovereign's neglect of him. He was in the commission of sewers for Sussex; in a commission to 'search and defend' the coast of that county; in a commission for the peace; and in a commission for array.[2] When Prince Edward was christened Lord Dacre was appointed to bear the spice plates to the young Princesses;[3] and a month later, when the Queen, Jane Seymour, was buried, he was one of those deputed to bear the canopy over her corpse at the funeral.[4]

In 1539, upon the introduction of three newly created peers, one of them was led between Lord Cobham and Lord Dacre in the procession at Westminster.[5] A contemporary author gives the following account of what was, perhaps, the last post of honour filled by Lord Dacre.

On the arrival of Anne of Cleves in 1540, when

as she passed towards Rochester on Newyeares euen on Reinam downe met hir the Duke of Norfolke, and the Lord Dacres of the South, and the lord Montioie [Mountjoy], with a great company of Knights, and esquires, of Norffolke and Suffolke, with barons of the escheker, which brought hir to Rochester where she laie in the Palace all New Yeares daie.[6]

And Lady Dacre was one of those appointed to receive the Queen-bride.[7]

Lord Dacre's career, which had begun so brightly, came to a premature and tragic termination in the following year, when he and his only sister's husband, together with some others, were hanged in London. They went one night on a poaching

---

[1] *L. and P.* xii. Part ii. No. 1169.
[2] *Ibid.* xiv.   [3] *Ibid.* xii. Part ii. No. 911.   [4] *Ibid.* No. 1060.
[5] *Ibid.* xiv. Part i. No. 477.
[6] *Hol.* iii. p. 948; C. S. P., *Ch. of C.* p. 174; *L. and P.* xv. No. 14.
[7] *L. and P.* xiv. Part ii. p. 201.

expedition to hunt deer in a neighbour's park, when an affray with the keepers ensued, in which one of the latter was killed.

Judging from the letter Lord Dacre wrote to Cromwell this was not the former's first offence of this nature, and however much, to use his own words, he may have 'detested those unlawful acts,' he does not seem to have been strong-minded enough to shake himself free from the bad influence of some of his companions.

The following letter is written by one who was to a certain extent an eavesdropper of the Lords' proceedings when they were considering Lord Dacre's case; and it is to be regretted that both the doors of which he speaks were shut, so that he did not hear more of what went on, but it is refreshing to learn that Lord Cobham, who had been associated with Lord Dacre in more than one public function, had sufficient courage to show himself 'vehement and stiff' on his friend's behalf.

The letter, which is dated June 27th, 1541, only two days before Lord Dacre's execution, was written by William Paget, clerk to the Privy Council, to Sir Thomas Wriothesley, Garter King-at-arms. He tells him that the Lord Chancellor and the Lords Sussex, Hertford, Admiral Duresme, and St. John, with Mr. Baker, consulted in the Star Chamber upon Lord Dacre's case. They 'made great conscience' to find him guilty of murder, and sent for the indictment twice or thrice, and would rather have used some means to have made him confess; the writer knows not what they decided, but this day

he shall be arraigned . . . Sir, I am sent for to the Council, and must stay my writing until soon.

At my coming to the Star Chamber there I found all the lords, to the number of xvij assembled for a conference touching the lord Dacre's case; . . . To Council they went, and had with them present the Chief Justices, with others of the King's learned Counsel; and albeit I was excluded, yet they spake so loud, some of them, that I might hear them notwithstanding two doors shut between us. Among the rest that could not agree to wilful murder, the Lord Cobham, as I took him by his voice, was vehement and stiff. Suddenly and softly they agreed, I wot not how, and departed to the Kings Bench together; whereas the lord Chancellor executing the office of High Steward, the lord Dacre pledd not guilty to the indictment, referring himself to the trial of his peers, and declaring, with long circumstances, that he intended no murder, and so purged himself to the audience as much as he might. And yet nevertheless afterward, by an inducement of the confession of the rest already condemned, declared unto him by the judge, he refused his trial, and, upon hope of grace (as I took it), confessed the indictment; which he did not without some insinuation. His judgment was to be hanged. It was pitiful to see so young a man by his own folly brought to such a case, but joyful to hear him speak at the last so wisely and show himself so repentant. . . . To-day after dinner the Council was with the King to declare lord Dacre's humble submission, hoping thereby to move his Majesty to pardon him, which took no effect, for to-morrow shall . . . Mantel, Roydon, and Frowdes suffer, and the lord Dacre upon Wednesday. God have mercy upon them and give them grace to repent their evil doings and to take patiently their deaths.[1]

Holinshed gives the following full account of the circumstances which led to Lord Dacre's trial and execution[2]:—

There was executed at Saint Thomas Wateringe,[3] three gentlemen, John Mantell,[4] John Frowds, and George Roidon; they died for a murther committed in Sussex, in companie of Thomas Fines, Lord Dacres of the South: the truth whereof was thus. The said Lord Dacres, through the lewd persuasion of some of them, as hath beene reported, meaning to hunt in the parke of Nicholas Pelham, esquire, at Laughton, in the same countie of Sussex, being accompanied with the said Mantell, Frowds, and Roidon, John Cheinie, and Thomas Isleie, gentlemen, Richard Middleton, and John Goldwell, yeomen, passed from his house of Hurstmonceux, the last of April, in the night season, toward the same parke, where they intended so to hunt; and coming unto a place called Pikehaie, in the parish of Hillingleigh,[5] they

---

[1] *L. and P.* xvi. No. 932.
[2] *Hol.* iii. p. 954; the account in *Stow*, p. 582, is almost identical.
[3] In Camberwell, the place of execution for the county of Surrey, and criminals were also brought here from London to be executed.—*M. & B.* iii. p. 402.
[4] Lord Dacre's brother-in-law.
[5] Hellingly, a parish immediately joining Herstmonceux; it is probably the case still, and certainly a few years since, it was commonly believed in Hellingly that the

found one John Busbrig (or Busbridge), James Busbrig, and Richard Summer standing togither: and as it fell out, through quarelling, there insued a fraie betwixt the said Lord Dacres and his companie on the one partie, and the said John and James Busbrig and Richard Summer on the other, insomuch that the said John Busbrig received such hurt, that he died thereof the second of Maie next insuing. Whereupon, as well the said Lord Dacres as those that were there with him, and diuerse other likewise that were appointed to go another waie to meet them at the said parke, were indicted of murther; and the seauen and twentith of June the Lord Dacres himselfe was arraigned before the Lord Audleie of Walden, then lord chancellor, sitting that daie as high steward of England, with other peers[1] of the realme about him, who then and there condemned the said Lord Dacres to die for that transgression. And afterward, the nine and twentith of June, being Saint Peter's daie, at eleuen of the clocke in the forenoone, the shiriffs of London, accordinglie as they were appointed, were readie at the tower to haue receiued the said prisoner, and him to haue lead to execution on the Tower Hill; but as the prisoner should come forth of the tower, one Heire, a gentleman of the lord chancellor's house, came, and in the king's name commanded to staie the execution till two of the clocke in the afternoone, which caused manie to think that the king would haue granted his pardon. But neuerthelesse, at three of the clocke in the same afternoone, he was brought forth of the tower, and deliuered to the shiriffs, who lead him on foote betwixt them unto Tiburne where he died. His bodie was buried in the church of Saint Sepulchers. He was not past foure and twentie yeeres of age,[2] when he came through this great mishap to his end, for whom manie sore lamented, and likewise for the other three gentlemen, Mantell, Frowds and Roidon. But for the said yoong lord being a right towardlie gentleman, and such a one as manie had conceiued great hope of better proofe, no small mone and lamentation was made; the more indeed, for that it was thought he was induced to attempt such follie, which occasioned his death, by some light heads that were then about him.

ghost of the murdered keeper walked nightly in the meadows round Horselunges farm in that parish, which were pointed out as having been the scene of the fatal affray.

[1] The jury of peers consisted of the Marquis of Dorset, the Earls of Sussex, Derby, Rutland, Huntingdon, Bath, Hertford, Bridgewater, and Lords John Russell, Morley, Cobham, Powys, Stowton, Mountjoy, Windsor, Mordaunt, and St. John; of these peerages more than half have since become extinct.

[2] He must in fact have been twenty-six years of age.

This event is also referred to in other histories of that time.[1] Weever,[2] in mentioning that Lord Dacre was buried in St. Sepulchre's by Newgate, says that his execution 'happened in that bloudie yeare when Henry the eith unsheathed his sword vpon the neckes of the nobilitie.'

The 'London Chronicle'[3] says—

The xxix day of June Wensday Saynt Peturs day was my lorde Dakars of the Southe led be twene bothe the scherevis of London a foote from the Tow^r to Tiburn and there he was hanggid, and the said lorde Dakars a bove said was beryid in Saynt Powlkurs churche, and ye said lorde Dakars a bove saide was hanggid for robbre of ye Kyngges deer and murther of ye Kepars.[4]

The account by a contemporary letter-writer of any past event is of interest as showing how it struck persons living at the time. There are two such letters amongst the public records from foreign ministers referring to this case. The first in date is from C. de Marillac to Francis I. of France, dated June 30th, 1541; in it he tells the King that

the same day [Saturday, June 25th] was led to judgment a young lord called Dacre of the South, also allied with the greatest lords in England, and of 6000 or 7000 ducats income, who, for assembling armed men with the intention of seeking a park keeper whom they wished to slay, and slaying another in place of the man they were seeking, was condemned to be hanged, and yesterday was executed at the common gibbet of London, called Tyburn. His three companions suffered the like death, who were Mr. Mantel, one of the Kings 50 gentlemen whom he calls his Pensioners, a controller of his customs,[5] and one Reddyn, of a Kentish family; all gentlemen of a good house, aged 25 to 30, and much esteemed.[6]

---

[1] *God.*; *Stow*, p. 582; *Cam.*
[2] *W. A. F. M.* p. 436.
[3] *C. S. P.*
[4] There is a very similar account in *C. S. P.*, *Wrio. Ch.* i. p. 126.
[5] J. Frowds.
[6] *L. and P.* xvi. No. 941.

The other letter is from Chapuys, the Emperor's ambassador, written to the Queen of Hungary on July 2nd, in which he mentions that

Lord Dacres also, son of the Duke of Norfolk's sister [1] and cousin of this Queen, 23 yeares old and possessing a property of about 5000 ducats a year, was hung from the most ignominious gibbet, and for the greater shame dragged through the streets to the place of execution, to the great pity of many people, and even of his very judges, who wept when they sentenced him, and in a body asked his pardon of the King.[2]

On the back of an ancient copy of the Act of Parliament referred to later on, which provided for the jointure of Lord Dacre's widow, we have the two following endorsements:—

This vnfortunate L° Dacre herein mentioned did never committ wylful murder for it was generally known he was not at ye place; but in his imprisonment he was cunnynglye delt w^{t}all to confesse ye inditement for so he was persuaded he should saue his followers. And so by ye Tyranny of y^t tyme he was cast away through too privy counsellers y^t gaped after his lyving, wch yett they had not by reason of an intayle.

The above is certainly as I believe the handwriting of my ancestor Sampson Lennard.

1759, Dacre.

This note by Samson is really only a paraphrase of Camden's account, which says that 'the courtiers cunningly gaped after his inheritance.' However much these courtiers may have 'gaped' they got nothing for their pains, as the 'intayle' was, as Samson said, held to avoid forfeiture. Mr. Astle [3] gave Lord Dacre a copy of a record in the Paper Office which has the following endorsement :—

The Councill resident at London to the Lords of the King's Majesty's Councill at the Court 8th July 1541—opinion of the Judges and the King's Councill that the Lord Dacre's lands

---

[1] Chapuys is in error here. [2] *L. and P.* xvi. No. 954.
[3] Thomas Astle, 1735-1803, at one period Keeper of Public Records.

being intailed by the will of his grandfather ought not to be forfeited.

The document, after setting out that the late 'Lord Dacrez,' as it styles him, had been attainted, goes on to find that owing to the entail his lands ought not to be forfeited, 'but that the King's Highnes by reason of the nonage of the Heir may & ought to have the Wardship of the Body and the Custody of the said Possessions & Lands till the said Heir comes to his full age.'[1]

This report, which was a unanimous one, was signed by the Archbishop of Canterbury, Audley, Chancellor, the Bishop of London, and six others.

That industrious antiquary, Mr. Haley, says in his 'Collection of Divers matters concerning the County of Sussex,'[2] 'This case is carefully recorded in all the report books, ancient and modern, and has ever since been referred to in the courts of justice as a notable precedent. The truth might perhaps be that he was so far persuaded to take the thing upon himself as to say that he first proposed and induced his friends to go on that party, which declaration might have been made an ill use of with the King; and putting the matter in this light may reconcile the seeming disagreement between the historians and the lawyers in their relation of this affair.'

According to Stow, these poaching frolics were by no means unfrequent at that period. He says in his 'Annals,' under the year 1526 (p. 526) :—

In the month of May was proclamation made against all unlawful games &c. in all places, tables, dice, cards, and bowls were taken and brent; and when young men were restrained of these games and pastimes, some fell to drinking, some to ferretting of other men's conies, and stealing of deer in parks, and other unthriftiness.

This event took place before the days of regular law reports, and we are left without information as to the exact facts of the

[1] This is no doubt the document now calendared *L. and P.* xvi. No. 978.
[2] *Add.* 6343, 742-3.

case, and whether Lord Dacre was actually present when the affray took place.

Mr. Lower, in a very interesting paper,[1] has done much, however, to dissipate the web of romance which several writers had woven round the tragic end of Lord Dacre. He says that he himself once wrote some verse which, like Mrs. Gore's tragedy 'Lord Dacre of the South,' was founded upon the theory suggested by the early chroniclers, and by the notes of Samson Lennard, that this ill-fated nobleman, although himself guiltless of murder, being in a different part of the park from that in which it took place, was nevertheless executed ; and that this execution was the result of a conspiracy on the part of powerful courtiers then in favour with the King, who hoped, on his attainder, to obtain possession of the vast Dacre estates.

Mr. Lower in this paper dives deeper into history than did those earlier writers, and produces from the 'Baga de Secretis,' the official account of the trial, which at the time that Holinshed and Stow wrote, was no doubt not available to them.

From this it appears that on April 20th Lord Dacre assembled several persons at his castle of Herstmonceux, and they then conspired 'how they best could hunt in the park of Nicholas Pelham Esq. at Laughton with dogs and nets called buckstalls and bound themselves by oaths for such illegal purpose ; and also to stand against all lieges of the King, and to kill any of the King's lieges who might oppose them.'

The jurors found that the conspirators met again in the same place some ten days later, and having divided themselves into two bands, one under the leadership of Lord Dacre, sallied forth on their expedition. The band led by Lord Dacre came into collision with the keepers watching, and fearing lest they themselves might be recognised, at once attacked the former, with the result that ' John Busebrygge ' was killed.

If this was a true account of what did happen, Lord Dacre and his companions acted in a way not unknown to modern poachers, and he and they fully deserved the fate which they

[1] S. Arch. xix. p. 170.

met with at the hands of justice. Mr. Lower also explains that the affray took place at Hellingly, and not at Laughton, as although the latter place was Sir Nicholas's chief residence, there were some other local circumstances which made Hellingly a more suitable spot for a deer park.

Sir Matthew Hale in his 'Pleas of the Crown,'[1] written more than a hundred years after Lord Dacre's execution, in defining what acts amount to murder, says, 'If a person have no particular malice against any person but comes with a general resolution against all opposers, if the act be unlawful, and death ensue, it is murder; as if it be to commit a riot; to enter into a Park (Lord Dacre's case).' This pronouncement, although explaining when malice may be presumed in law, does not clear up the point as to where Lord Dacre was when Busbrig was killed.

The writ for this unfortunate young man's execution is as follows [2]:—

Henricus Octavus Dei gracia Anglie et Francie Rex, fidei defensor, Dominus Hibernie et in terra supremum Caput Anglicane ecclesie, vicecomes London, salutem. Precipimus vobis puniter iniungentes quod statim vlsis presentibus Thomam Fynes nuper de Hurst Mounseux in Comitatu Sussex, Dominum Dacre, alias dictum Thomam Dominum Dacre, de quibusdam felonijs et murdris Attinctum et morti adiudicatum ac in Turri nostra London detentum a dilecto et fideli Consiliario nostro Johanne Gage ordinis nostri Garterij milite, Constabulario Turris nostre London, seu eius locum tenente vel eius deputato, ibidem apud le Tower hill, per Indenturam inde inter vos et dictum Constabularium, locum tenentem aut deputatum, debite conficiendam recipiatis et eundem Thomam Dominum Dacre vsque ad furcas de Tyborne ducatis ducive faciatis, et super furcas illas suspendatis suspendive faciatis vsque ad mortem. Mandamus enim eidem Constabulario eiusve locum tenenti sive deputato ibidem quod ipsum Thomam Dominum Dacre vobis ibidem liberent vobisque in executione predicta fienda debite assistant. Teste me ipso apud Westmonasterium xxix° die Junij Anno regni nostri Tricesimo tercio.

LUCAS.

[1] P. 447.   [2] *Tan.* 168, f. 117*b*.

In view of what both Camden and Samson Lennard suggest, that his large fortune made some of the courtiers anxious to have him attainted of felony in hopes that the King might make grants to them of his estates, it is interesting to learn what the annual value of those estates were.

We have fortunately among our papers the following document drawn up a very few years after Lord Dacre's execution. Its contents throw some indirect light on the relative value of money then and now, and show us that his income was only a little more than a thousand pounds, which, however, in those days appears sufficient to have constituted an abnormally large fortune.

Thomas ffynes Lord Dacre
solde to Sr Antony Browne.[1]   Anno xxxvij Regis H. viij.
[1545–6]

The extent & cleare yerelye value of all the Manors Lands & heredytaments appertayninge to the inherytance of Thomas Fynes Lord Dacre the King's Majesty's ward sonne & heir of Thomas Fynes Lord Dacre attaynted and executed for murder in June Anno xxxiij H. viij wch said Thomas Lord Dacre [2] the sonne was three yeres of age at the death of his said father and his inherytance saved from forfeiture by reason of the intayle.

Then follows a list of his various estates with their rentals, the majority of which are said in a marginal note to be 'In the possession of the King's Majesty during the minority of the said Lord Dacre.' The total given as the yearly value of all the estates comes to 1,061l. 17s. 11d.[3]

Upon Lord Dacre's execution and attainder, his widow was left quite penniless, but no time was lost in obtaining an Act of

---

[1] These lands were not sold ; it probably means that Sir Antony had obtained a grant of them for the period of the infant's minority.

[2] As the attainder incurred by the conviction of Thomas Lord Dacre for felony was not reversed during the lifetime of his eldest son Thomas, it was not correct to describe the latter as 'Lord Dacre.'

[3] This total is about 120l. less than they are given in another rental of 1553. See also *L. and P.* xvi. No. 978.

Parliament in order to provide a dower for her from out of her late husband's estates. Among our papers is an ancient copy of this Act, which was passed in the same year as he was executed, and which runs as follows:—

'An acte whereby certen landes are passed to the Lady Dacres.

'Anno xxxiij Henry VIII.' [1541-2]

It recites that:

Mary Fynes widowe, late the wief of Thomas Fynes late lorde Dacres, commonly called Lord Dacres of the Sowthe lately atteynted of wilfull murther by the lawes of this Realme of England is not dowable nor oughte to be indowed of any the Manors lands &c. which were in the possession &c. of the said late Lord Dacres &c. nor yet had any Jointure in her late husband's lands for that the said Mary was espowsed & maryed unto her saide late Husband he being within the age of Twenty & one yeares & in the custody & ward of the King. The King's Majestie &c. according to his accustomable goodness of his liberalitie inclyned to mercy & pitty willing to extend his grace & clemency to the said Mary Fynes at the humble sute &c. of the said Mary for the relief of her and her children &c is contented & pleased that it be enacted by His Highnes with the assent of this present parliament, & by authority of the same, that the said Mary Fynes shall possess & enjoy for the term of her natural life, from Michaelmas last past, the Manors of Burham & Codham co. Kent—of Fromquinton & Belchwell co. Dorset, of Nashall co. Essex, & all their rights & privileges &c. the said attainder &c. not withstanding.'[1]

But on July 2nd the King ordered her to be paid 50*l.* at once, and directed that the Sheriff of Sussex should deliver to her 'All her apparel of velvet, satin, pearls, stones or goldsmiths work pertaining as well to her head as to the rest of her body.'[2] And during the course of the month the King, being 'moved with pity' for the destitute position of the widowed Mrs. Mantell, said that upon being fully informed as to her circumstances he would take order for her relief.[3]

[1] The then annual value of these lands was 140*l.* 17*s.* 5*d.*
[2] *L. and P.* xvi. No. 953.
[3] *Ibid.* No. 1019.

I am not able to state at what date Lady Dacre married her second husband, who was — Wootton, Esq., of N. Tuddenham, Norfolk, nor whether she had children by him. She outlived him and married, as her third husband, Francis Thursby, Esq., of Congham, in the same county;[1] by whom in 1559 she had living three sons and three daughters.[2] I believe that Lady Dacre died in or about 1576.[3] Thomas, her eldest son by her first husband, died on August 25th, 1553,[4] as appears by the following document in our possession:—

The extente & clere yerely vallew of all the Castelles Lordships Manors &c. late of the enheretans of Thomas Fynes Lorde Dacre of the South deceased; the xxvth of August anno I Q. Marie [1553] being then of the age of xv yeres & warde to her Majestie; all wch sayd Castelles &c. descended to Gregory Fynes Lord Dacre his brother & next heyre beynge of the age of xiij yeres & a half at the deathe of his sayd brother.

Then comes a list of his estates with their respective rents, the total of which amounted to 1,180*l*. 18*s*. 7¾*d*.

Among our deeds is one dated December 9, 1553, which is a grant by the Court of Wards and Liveries to John Fynes, gentleman, of the office of Keeper of the Park at Herstmonceux, parcel of the manor of Herstmonceux,[5] then in the hands of Queen Mary by virtue of the minority of Gregory Fynes, Lord Dacre; 'brother & heir of Thomas Lord Dacre deceased'; to hold the same during the minority of Gregory.

Gregory married Anne, daughter of Sir Richard Sackville, and sister to Thomas Lord Buckhurst, 1st Earl Dorset, by whom he had issue only a daughter, who died young, and whose effigy is

---

[1] This information as to Lady Dacre's second and third husbands is derived from *Ld. D. His.* In *Blom.* I can find no Wootton holding a manor in N. Tuddenham who could have been her husband. The same authority speaks of the family of Thursby (Thursbie) owning a manor in Congham from Henry VIII. till 39 Elizabeth, but does not mention a Francis of that name.

[2] MS. petition of his son Gregory (Lord Dacre) to the Queen.

[3] *Vide ante*, p. 50, *n*. 2.   [4] The C. P. says in error that Thomas died *v. p.*

[5] The fee appertaining to this office appears from our rent-roll of 1553 to have been 6*l*. a year.

on his tomb, although she is not mentioned in the inscription on that monument.

Anne Lady Dacre, in the course of the disputes with her brother-in-law Samson Lennard, speaks of herself and her husband as being very young at the time of their marriage;[1] and this must have been the case for, as we shall see, they were certainly married before the death of Queen Mary. The inscription on Lord Dacre's tomb supports his wife's assertion that they married at an early age as, although it does not give the date of their marriage, it says ' Quos ardens copulavit amor juvenilibus annis.'

When Elizabeth came to London upon her accession in November 1558, Gregory Lord Dacre was one of the noblemen appointed to attend upon the new queen, and his wife was made a Lady of Honour.[2] Strictly speaking he had at that period no right to the title, as the attainder of his father Thomas Lord Dacre was as yet not reversed, and therefore he and his sister were both attainted by his conviction. No doubt Gregory, or his young wife, took full advantage of the opportunity which their proximity to the Sovereign afforded them to make a good impression upon the Queen, and to induce her to look with a favouring eye upon his petition that the disabilities imposed upon him in virtue of the sentence passed upon his father should be removed. From the nature of things new rulers are apt to be desirous of ingratiating themselves with their subjects, and this was particularly the case with Elizabeth, who was ever desirous of popularity, and whose hold upon the throne was at that period none too secure. The claims to clemency which the Dacres put forward to their royal mistress were well received, and one of her earliest acts was to grant their petition.[3] Among our papers is an ancient copy of the document by which the attainder was reversed ; it runs as follows :—

In the Parliament held at Westm^r 5 January anno Elizabeth &c. 1st [1559] before the Lords Spiritual & temporal &c. this 40th Statute was enacted.

[1] *Ante,* p. 92.　　　[2] *N. Pro.* i. p. 37.　　　[3] *Cam.*

There was exhibited to the Queen's Majesty in parliament the act of petition[1] following—being the petition 'of Gregorie Fenes esqr. brother & heire unto Thomas Fenes esq. sonne & heire unto Sir Thomas Fenes Knight late Lord Dacres of the South'; recites attainder of last named Sir Thos Fenes, Lord Dacre in time of King Henry VIII ; whereby petiōner 'is a person in his blode lynage honor degree & dignitie corrupted' petiōner prays he may be restored in blood &c. to all intents & purposes as if the said Thomas Lord Dacre had 'neuer bene attainted.' To which petition, answer was made by the Queen & authority of Parliament—'Soit fait cōme il est desire.'

The entail created by the will of Gregory's great-grandfather was, as has been stated, of great service to him, inasmuch as it prevented the family estates from being forfeited to the Crown by virtue of his father's execution for felony. But when the entail had served its purpose, Gregory became anxious to have it modified so as to give him power to deal more freely with the properties comprised in the will. To this end, as soon as he had had the attainder reversed, he presented a petition to the Queen for a rectification of the terms of the will. He alleged that although he had at present 'but onlie one daughter yet for that both he and the Lady Anne his wife are of younge years he is like by God's help & grace to have manye more children both sonnes & daughters,' and that by the terms of the will he was unable 'to provyde lyvinge or other helpe or relief for anye his younger sonnes or for the advancements of the mariages of his daughters or yet to make his wife anye jointure or to redeme himselfe yf he should fortune to be taken Prisoner in the Warres in the service of your Majesty'; or to pay any debts he might owe at the time of his death, or 'to reward his true & faythfull servants.' He therefore prayed that certain manors mentioned in the petition should be held for the above-mentioned purposes. I have no means of knowing whether this petition was ever presented, and if so what its fate was, but as nearly all the manors named in it were dealt with subsequently in 1571 by

---

[1] This petition in slightly different words is also in *Rawl. B.* 58, 100.

the quadripartite Indenture,[1] it is not necessary to further consider here the terms of the petition.

One result of this settlement in 1571 was that in May of that year Gregory and his wife sold both the manor and the advowson of Beighton in Derbyshire, and Sir Henry Norris and his wife, and Samson Lennard and his wife, joined in the conveyance;[2] and on January 24th, 1582, Gregory and his wife sold Danny Park and other estates in Sussex to a Mr. George Goring of Lewes[3] for the sum of 10,000*l.*

At Elizabeth's Court there was a great system of giving New Year's gifts, and at that anniversary in 156½ Lady Dacre, not to be behind other folk, presented the Queen with a 'warming ball of gold,' weighing 3½ ounces; the Queen in her turn gave to Lady Dacre 'oone guilt bolle with a cover,' of the weight of 15¼ ounces;[4] and we read of gifts by each to the other on subsequent New Year's Days.

Gregory accompanied Lord Lincoln to France when that nobleman went there on an embassy in the 14th of Elizabeth [157½];[5] and in 1588, at the time of the threatened Spanish invasion, when Elizabeth made a proclamation calling on her nobles to arm and defend the country, among those to whom her Majesty's letters were directed requiring them to attend upon her person was 'L. Dacres of the South.'[6]

It has been said that Queen Elizabeth dined at Lord Dacre's house[7] at Chelsea on Michaelmas Day during her progress to review the forces assembled at Tilbury, and that the accident of goose forming part of her dinner on that occasion is the origin of our custom of eating roast goose on that day;[8] but I must say that I am not able to feel any confidence in the truth of this story.

---

[1] *Ante*, p. 82 *et seq*. [2] *D. Arch.*
[3] His son George, created Earl of Norwich, and who greatly distinguished himself on the Royalist side at the Siege of Colchester, built the present mansion of Danny.—*Hor.* i. p. 244.
[4] *N. Pro.* [5] *Hol.* iii. p. 1229.
[6] *Hist. Com.* xv. App. Part v. p. 44 (Foljambe).
[7] Once the home of Sir Thomas More.—*Faul.* i. p. 122. [8] *Play.* vii. p. 624.

The way in which Lord Dacre became possessed of his house and grounds at Chelsea is interesting. There is a State paper endorsed 'The just griefs of the Lord Marquis of Winchester against Winyfrede the Lady Marchioness of Winchester his late Father's wife.' This document alleges among a number of instances of undue influence on the part of Winyfrede that in 1575 the house at Chelsea, which cost 14,000*l.*, and land with it worth an equal sum, was sold to Lord Dacre for 3,000*l.*, 'whereof he payed in truth but 2,000*l.*'[1] The Marquis who presented this petition was the third holder of that title, and his stepmother Winifred (his father's second wife) was the third daughter of T. Ayloff, of Brittains Hornchurch, a member of a then well-known Essex family.

A contemporaneous writer refers to Lord Dacre in quaint terms when he says that in 1594 'he exchanged life for death he being a man of cracked brain.'[2] Beyond the above-mentioned instances I have found no record of his taking part in public affairs; and, judging from Camden's reference to him, it would appear that he was not very capable of so doing, for if he was not absolutely what the Scotch call 'wanting,' he was certainly a very weak-minded man, as I have shown in the previous chapter He died on September 25th, 1594,[3] and by his will, which, incredible as it sounds, is said to have been proved the same day, he left the whole of his property (except legacies of 100*l.* to Sir William Cecil, and to the Earl of Leicester, who were overseers of this will) to his wife absolutely, and he appointed her sole executrix.

Gregory was buried in the picturesque parish church of Chelsea, greatly beloved of artists, the interior of which is so old-world in appearance that many an American tourist spares time during his hurried rush round London to pay it a visit. One of the chief features of this interior is the imposing tomb of the

---

[1] *S. P. Dom. Eliz.* vol. cx. No. 30.   [2] *Cam.*
[3] 'Gregorie Fynes Lord Dacre of the South diede the 25th day of Septemb. beinge Weddensdaie whose funeralls and burial were kepte the 5th Novemb. here at Chelsey.'—*Faul.* ii. p. 127.

Dacres, a very fine specimen of late Tudor monumental work. It was restored in 1823 by the parish, as it is a condition by which the parish of Chelsea has a right to certain presentations to Lady Dacre's almshouses that this monument should be kept in repair.[1]

Gregory's widow did not long survive him, as she died on the 13th of the following May.[2] The terms of her will are noticed subsequently.

[1] *Faul.* ii. p. 104.
[2] *I. P. M. Rawl.* 433*b* (f. 309). A date two days later has been assigned by one author. 'The Lady Anne wife to the Right Honorable Lorde Dacres aforenamed was buried the 15th of May, whose funeralls were Solemnized at Chelsey the 19th of June followinge 1595.'—*Faul.* ii. p. 127.

THE DESCENDANTS OF SAMSON AND MARGARET LENNARD

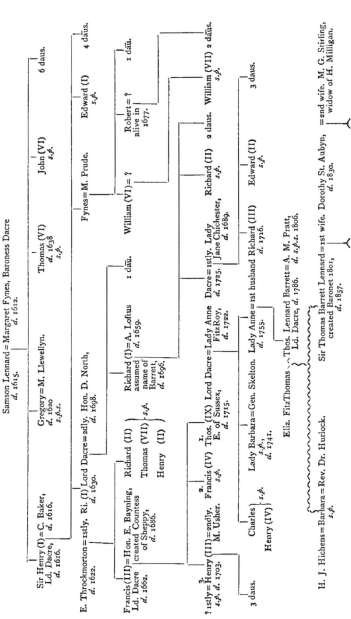

Note.—In this table are not included the issue of Dacre Barrett by his second or third wife, nor of Lady Anne Lennard by her second or third husband.

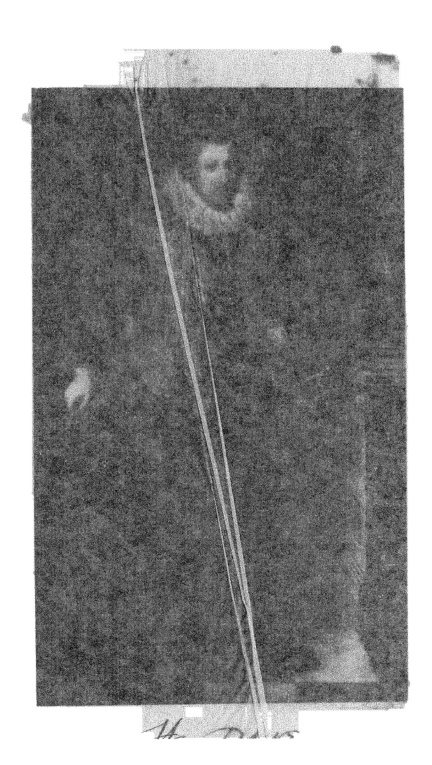

PEDIGREE OF SIMSON AND MARGARET LENNARD

· Dacre ·

CHAPTER III

SAMSON LENNARD—HENRY LENNARD, LORD DACRE— RICHARD LENNARD, LORD DACRE

As I have already shown, John Lennard's eldest son Samson was born about 1545, and he married, some twenty years later, the Hon. Margaret Fynes.[1] Camden, in his 'Britannia,' speaking of the death of her brother Lord Dacre, says: 'Whose sister & heir Margaret, Sampson Lennard, a person of extraordinary worth & civility, took to wife, & by her hath fair issue.' They had a considerable family, and if we may estimate the appearance of the rest of their children from the portrait we have at Belhus of their eldest son Henry, Camden's eulogy would not seem to be misplaced. Lord Dacre speaks of there being eight children,[2] but his copy from the parish registers of Chevening and Sevenoaks shows there to have been ten baptized in those churches; according to the inscription on Samson's tomb there were in all seven sons, of whom Henry, Gregory, and Thomas survived him; and six daughters, of whom five survived.

The following is a list of ten of these children, with the dates of their respective baptisms and marriages taken from the registers before mentioned; the other three children I am not able to trace, and they no doubt died in infancy. The

---

[1] It is remarkable that I am unable to fix the exact date of Samson's marriage. Lord Dacre does not mention it, nor, as far as I know, do any of the MS. pedigrees, nor do the commissioners in their award on Margaret's claim to the title of Dacre. The C. P. gives it as 1564, and this is confirmed by the inscription on her tomb, where it speaks of her and her husband having had forty-seven years of married life. *Cf. ante*, p. 95 *n.*

[2] *Ld. D. His.*

entries of the first four births are from the register of Chevening, the others, and all the marriages, from that of Sevenoaks, or as it was then frequently written 'Sen'nock.' In some of these cases the children are described as being the children of 'Sampson Lennard, gent.' It will be remarked that the daughters married at what we should now consider a remarkably youthful age :—

Henrie, baptized 25 March, 1569.
Anne, 1st August, 1572, married (age 18 yrs. 10 months) Herbert Morley, of Glynde, Sussex,[1] 25 May 1591,[2] died Sept. 19th,[3] and was buried at Chevening 20th Sept. 1624.[4]
'George *vel potius* Gregory,' baptized 25th October, 1573.
Mary, baptized 22nd October, 1574, married (age 19 yrs. 6 months) Ralf Bosville of Sevenoaks, 2 April 1594.[5]

Manning says, in his 'History of Surrey' (vol. iii. p. 54), that Thomas Onslow married Mary, daughter of 'Sir Sampson Lenard.' This Thomas died in December 1616 when in his 22nd year, leaving no issue.

Thomas, 23rd May, 1577.
Margarett, 28th September, 1578, married (age 15) Thomas Waller of Groombridge [6] 5 September, 1593.[7]
Elizabeth, 5th June, 1580, buried October 20, 1581.
Elizabeth, 26th November, 1581, married in 1597-8 (aged about 16) Sir Francis Barnham.[8] She had fifteen children (of whom ten survived) and died 18th Sept. 1631.[9]
Frances, 28th July, 1583, married (age 17 yrs. 10 months)

---

[1] Glynde Place belonged to the Morleys, a Lancashire family, for a considerable period, when in 1680 it passed to the Trevors on the marriage of John Trevor with the widow of William Morley, *Hors.* i. 345.

[2] *Sev. Reg.*   [3] *Har. So.* liii. p. 48.   [4] *Ch. Reg.*

[5] *Sev. Reg.* Probably a son of the R. Bosewell referred to *ante*, pp. 32; *ib. n.*; 40-1.

[6] Sir William Waller, the Parliamentary General, was a son of this Thomas and his wife Margaret.

[7] *Sev. Reg.*

[8] This marriage is in neither of the above registers, but is referred to in *Ld. D. His.*, and *post*, p. 226.

[9] *Has.* ii. p. 467.

Sir Robert Moore[1] of Lothesley or Loseley, Surrey, 12 May, 1601.[2] He was M.P. in the reigns of Elizabeth and James, and died February 162⅝, leaving six sons and five daughters.[3]

John, 11th October, 1584.

In no pedigrees have I found any mention of Samson having any son other than those just mentioned, but I have discovered a lease of lands by him dated 1605, and one of the witnesses to this document is a 'Richard Lennard.' This could hardly be his grandson Richard (afterwards Lord Dacre), who, we shall see, was the eldest son of his son Henry. This Richard would have been only nine years of age at the signing of this lease, and it is most improbable that he was one of the witnesses to it. Still, I know of no other Richard Lennard at this period, and it is possible that the boy had just learned to write, and that his grandfather, proud of his grandson's accomplishment, allowed him to be one of the witnesses by way of a joke. This explanation, I confess, does not satisfy me, but I cannot think of any better one; and in support of this theory it should be said that the signature in question, unlike that of the other witnesses to this deed, is in more of a printed than a written handwriting, and is at the side of, and not underneath, the signatures of the other three witnesses.

[1] One of our deeds dated December 1st, 11 Jas. I., shows that he had by that period obtained knighthood.   [2] *Sev. Reg.*   [3] *M. & B.* i. pp. 67 and 96.

Samson was admitted a member of Lincoln's Inn on May 9th, 1564, by 'special admission.' I might here remark that in all the documents I have seen signed by Samson he spells his name as I do here, but in Lord Dacre's writings, and indeed in almost every reference to him which I find, his name is spelt with a ' p.'

In the 33rd of Elizabeth (November 1590 to November 1591) Samson was High Sheriff of Kent; and he was elected a member of several Parliaments: in 1586 for St. Maws;[1] in 1588 for the borough of Christchurch, Hants; in 1592 for St. Germans; in 1597 for Rye; in 1601 for Liskeard; and in 1614 for the county of Sussex. In 1586 he appears to have wished to be elected for Southampton, as among the archives of that borough there is the following letter from a Mr. William Butler to the Mayor of that place:—

Oct. 12, 1586. Mr. Maior I have become an earnest sutor to you to have your favour & furtherance to make choyse of a Friende of mine to be one of your burgesses of your Towne in this parliament. The gentleman is a very sufficient man, and yf you make your election of a burgess, that is noe Townesman, you can not make choyse of a better, his name is Mr. Sampson Leonarde, dwelling in Kent, but yf yt please you, & the rest of your aldermen to grante me my sute, ye shall heare of him at my house at all times when you shall have cause to use him, who is a very sufficient gentleman in any matter for your Towne, & myself shall thinke myself greatly beholding to you.[2]

Samson was as public-spirited in taking part in the patriotic movements of that day for the defence of the country against the aggressions of Philip of Spain as he was in political matters, and in 1588, when the Spanish Armada was launched against England, we find Samson more than ready to take his part in repelling the invader. Among the MSS. of the Right Hon. Saville Foljambe there is a book in vellum covers endorsed 'The Book of Musters, 1588'; this refers to the warlike pre-

---

[1] His name in the Parliamentary return is spelt 'Leonerd.'
[2] *Hist. Com.* xi. Part iii. p. 120.

parations then being made throughout England to ensure the safety of the country. It gives a list of the 'chief captains' in the different counties of the kingdom, and among the list for Kent the name of Samson appears with fifty light horse ;[1] and eight years later, when Spain again appeared to be likely to attack England, we read that on November 10th, 1596, very careful preparations were made to guard the Medway from foreign aggression. A carefully thought-out system for sending the first alarm of the enemy's approach was adopted; a chain of stations was established whence signals were to be sent one to the other by beacon fires and gun firing, and places which were so situated as to be beyond reach of these signals were to be warned by means of hoblers[2] sent from Rochester by the Deputy Lieutenants. The Mayor of that town was to send notice to Sir J. Leveson, Thomas Walsingham, Mr. Style, Mr. Mayor of Maidstone, Mr. Lennard, and Mr. Rivers, and each of these captains was to give notice to the rest. On November 12th these five [sic] captains were to repair to Upnor[3] Castle with 1,080 men, and there be distributed in the five ships next the chain.[4]

The following letter from a Mr. Rowland Whyte to Sir Robert Sydney shows that Samson was active in doing magisterial work in his neighbourhood, and is also somewhat interesting, illustrating as it does the necessity that existed then, as now, for members of Parliament to conciliate their supporters :—

Euen now Mr. Lovelace of Kent came vnto me & desired me to procure hym some answer from your Lordship to a letter he sent you ; yt is about a Colt he says is vnduly detained from hym in Oteford park. His sute unto you is that you will direct your Lettre to Sir Thos Walsingham, Sir John Levison, M^r

---

[1] In 'The Abstracts of Certificates of able men and trained men in the several counties upon letters from their Lordships in April 1588,' under the heading of Kent, there appears the name of ' Sampson Leonard,' *Hist. Com.* xv. App. Part v. p. 37.
[2] Light horsemen.—C. D.   [3] Upnor is within two miles of Rochester.
[4] *S. P. Dom. Eliz.* cclx. No. 102.

Leonard, Mr Sidley or any two of them to examine the cause. I promised to write vnto you about yt for he is one of them that gaue you his voice in the Election, and I haue thanked hym for yt.[1]

Unfortunately we have no correspondence from Samson, except three drafts of letters to agents concerning his property at Horsford, Norfolk; but these are sufficient to show that he could express himself with great clearness and considerable dignity. There are in the British Museum two letters from Samson to a Mr. Hicks; I have not been able to identify the 'most vnhappye kynsman,' on whose behalf the following of these letters was written, which are addressed :—

To the Worshipful my very lovyng frend Mr Michael Hicks [2]

Good m^r Hicks I vnderstand by my brother how much we are all bound vnto yov for your frendship in procuryng the reprie of my most vnhappye kynsman for the wch I most heartylye thank yov. By a lamentable letter sent vnto me this nyght from some sisters of myne that remayne ther I am informed that the Quene hath lately sent Mr Wade [3] to the Kyng of Portyngall to require hym to leave his sute for Raulins [?] and that she is purposed the law shall haue his course for his execution, wch if it be true We have small hope our kynsman shalbe spared, I beseech yov affourd your best helpe at this pinche and I shall never forgett your kyndnes but ever be redye to requite to the vttermost of my power. And so w^t my most harty commendations in hast I leave yov
    Knoll this xvij of May 1592.
        Your very lovyng frend
            SAMSON LENNARD.[4]

In the second letter, also dated from Knole, but some two years later, Samson expresses a hope that Mr. Hicks 'wyll one day gett leasure to cum w^t your bedfellow to Knoll where you shall fynd the best welcome I can giue you.'[5]

---

[1] *Coll. Let.* ii. p. 67.
[2] Michael Hicks was Secretary to Lord Burghley, and had great influence and acquired a considerable fortune; from him Sir M. Hicks Beach is descended.
[3] Mr., afterwards Sir William, Waad was ambassador to Portugal, 1580.
[4] *Lansd.* 72, 166.   [5] *Ibid.* 77, 186.

Within a few years of his father's death, which, as I have said, took place in 1590, Samson received a very considerable addition to his fortune by the death of his brother-in-law, Gregory Fynes, Lord Dacre.

The estates which came to Samson through his wife by Lord Dacre's death were those of Herstmonceux, and many others which were settled upon her. As we have seen, Gregory left all his property, both real and personal, to his wife, not even mentioning his sister by name. I imagine that in making his will he bore in mind the disputes which had taken place between him on the one hand, and John Lennard, Samson, and Margaret on the other; and also the friction in the family which these disputes had caused. The following passage in his will seems to bear no other interpretation :—

and muche dowbtinge the hard measure that will contrary to my mynd & intencion be offred after my deathe to my said loving wife, if by any devise, pollicie or practize it may be had practized or compassed which danger & inconvenience I by all wayes & meanes beinge willinge & desirous to prevente.

As has been said already, Anne Lady Dacre did not long survive her husband, for she died within eight months of his death. She directed in her will that she should 'be buryed in one tomb with my lord at Chelsey,' where they both lie side by side.

Among the Salisbury papers there are some references to Lady Dacre's death, and to her testamentary dispositions. On May 14th, 1595, Mr. George Goring wrote to Sir Robert Cecil :—

I was ready this morning to come into the Court when I was sent for to my Lady Dacres who hath been this last night and morning more sick than before; as I understand more so shall you be advertised by Mr Moore, or myself. God deal in mercy with her; she is an honourable person.[1]

Goring had good reason to speak well of Lady Dacre, as he was

---

[1] *Hist. Com.* (Salisbury), v. p. 205.

one of the executors of her will, and not only he, but also his wife and his sister, benefited by the terms of it.

The same day Mr. Moore writes also to Sir Robert to inform him of Lady Dacre's death, that she has left 300*l.* to the Queen to buy a jewel ; to her own brother's eldest son and his other children what is thought to be worth 8,000*l.* or 9,000*l.* ;

also she hath given Mr. Leonard and his wife, who was my Lord's sister, and a child of his, that which is thought to be worth 6,000*l.* or 7,000*l.*, and the land which Mr. Leonard is like to have by the death of Lord Dacre & her, is taken to be worth, when it shall be out of lease, 2,500*l.* by the year, besides my lord's chief house, and the value of 2,000*l.* in woods ; whereby I doubt not it will be thought that both her husband's house, and her own are honourably remembered.[1]

A letter from Sir Thomas Sherley[2] to Sir Robert Cecil, referring to this devise to Samson, shows how intimate Cecil and Lennard were commonly supposed to have been. Sir Thomas writes on May 22nd, 1595 :

I understand that Lady Dacres hath bestowed her house at Dormans Well upon Mr. Sampson Leonard. I am also told you may command him in all reasonable things. I am therefore a very humble sutor that you will write your earnest letter to Mr. Leonard that I may be his farmer there paying yearly for the same as much as any other man will give.[3]

Lady Dacre's will, dated December 1594, was a very long and elaborate one, in which she made a great quantity of bequests—the first one, after the usual bequest of her soul to the Almighty, being to the Queen :—

And whereas next under god I doe acknowledge my selfe most bounden to the Queenes moste excellent M$^{tie}_a$ my dear and gratious Soveraigne for her manyfolde princly favors to my late lorde and my selfe, and am desirous to showe unto her

---

[1] *Hist. Com.* (Salisbury), v. p. 206.
[2] Sir Thomas Sherley, or Shirley, of Wiston, Sussex. There were two Sir Thomases, a father and son, living at this period.—*D. N. B.*
[3] *Hist. Com.* (Salisbury), v. p. 215.

highnes my loyall and thankeful minde by some token of remembrance, knowing (as I have seene by much proofe) that although my poore ability can present nothinge worthy her princly acceptacon, yet her royall clemency useth to enterteyne small guifts proceedinge from faythfull myndes, regardinge the givers affection above the value of the guifte. Therfore I will that my executors in convenyente tyme after my decease shall provide a Jewell of three hundred pounds value and deliver the same to her excellent M^{tie} as a poore remembrance of my humble duety to her highnes. Beseechinge almighty god that as hitherto he hath miraculouslie of his infinite goodnes preserved her highnes in happie felicitie from all her enemies to his owne glory and the greate comforte of this realme Soe that he will vouchsafe longe to contynewe the same And in the ende make her highnes a blessed member of his everlastinge kingedome.

Lady Dacre left money and lands for the 'buyldinge and edifienge' a hospital in Tothill Fields, Westminster, to be called 'Emanuell Hospital,' 'towardes the reliefe of aged people, and bringinge up of children in vertue, and good, and lawdable Arts in the same Hospitall wherby they might the better live in tyme to come by theyre honeste labor.' And she directed that her executors were to 'cause to be erected and buylte a meete and convenyent house, wth romes of habitacon for twentye Poore folks and twenty other poore children employing and bestowinge thereupon three hundred pounds.'

She left her house at 'Chelsey' and all other, her gardens, orchards, lands, and tenements, in 'Chelsey, Kinsington & Brompton,' to Sir William Cecil, Lord Burghley, for life, and after his decease to his son, Sir Robert Cecil. She devised her house 'called Dacre house nere Tuthill in Westm^r, and the gardens, lands, meadowes, and tenements thereunto belonginge' together with other estates to her relatives the Sackvilles.

The executors of her will were Lady Dacre's 'lovinge frinds,' Mr. Justice Fenner,[1] Sir Drewe Druery, Knight,[2] George

[1] He was related to the Goring family. A justice of the King's Bench for 21 years; he died 161½.

[2] Sir D. Drury had been tenant of Gregory Lord Dacre in respect of lands in Horsford and Hautbois, Norfolk; he was a gentleman-usher of the Privy Chamber during the reigns of Elizabeth and James, and also held other posts.

Goring,[1] and Edward More, Esqs., and to them, besides individual specific bequests or devises, she left her residuary estate. All her lands in Dorman's Well, Southall, and Norcott, in the county of Middlesex, Lady Dacre devised to Samson Lennard and his wife for life, with remainder to their daughter Margaret, who had married Sir Thomas Waller. This devise, however, was coupled with onerous conditions.

We have seen that there had been great disputes relating to the Fynes' estates, and that very strained relations existed between Anne Lady Dacre on the one side and Samson and his wife on the other. This being the case, coupled with the remarkable terms of Lady Dacre's devise to them, makes me think that her object in making them beneficiaries under her will was to ensure that Samson and Margaret should discharge the liabilities which she alleged they had contracted in respect of her husband's estate; and also to prevent them from attempting to dispute any portion of her testamentary dispositions.

The conditions of this devise were as follows: In the first place these lands were to be held by Lady Dacre's executors for four years after her death before Samson and his wife were to enter into possession of them. Four of the farms contained in this devise were to be let to certain persons she designated for twenty-one years, at rents which in three cases she fixed, and which in the other case her executors were to fix. The result of this was that for twenty-five years after her death Samson would have no power of selecting the tenants for these four farms, and no voice in the amount of rent which they were to pay for them. Then if either he or his wife were in any way to attempt to upset any assurance made by her of lands whether by will or deed, her devise to them was to be void, and it was also to be void if Samson neglected to pay to her executors the sum of 2,000*l.* in four yearly instalments of 500*l.*, which sum of 2,000*l.*, Lady Dacre says in her will, Samson had by an inden-

[1] The same G. Goring who purchased Danny from Gregory Lord Dacre, *ante*, p. 210.

ture with her late husband, agreed to pay to his executors within four years of his death.[1] From the evidence produced in connection with a bill in Chancery, which later on Samson exhibited against the executors of Lady Dacre's will, it would seem that Dorman's Well was variously valued at as much as 8,000*l*., and at as little as 5,000*l*.; and the papers in this case also show that Samson duly paid the sum of 2,000*l*. within two years of Lady Dacre's death. He also had to pay 1,200*l*. to Lord Burghley on account of Dorman's Well, but the reason for his being obliged to make this payment does not appear.

From the same set of papers we learn that the mansion-house of Herstmonceux had fallen into a very bad state of repair during the ownership of Gregory Lord Dacre, as one witness gives evidence that it appeared from the books of Roger Pulston[2] that Samson had had to expend 800*l*. on the house itself, and 200*l*. on the outbuildings, and that further necessary repairs would cost another 200*l*. There is in the British Museum a copy of a survey made of Herstmonceux on August 23rd, 12th Eliz. (1570),[3] which speaks of some parts of the building being in need of repairs; it says, 'the said gate & towers being defective, of separations of the embattlement thereof, and the watch towers wasted of great length, with violence of wind & weather, needful to be seen unto.' If these repairs 'needful to be seen unto' in 1570 were neglected for thirty years, it is not surprising that Samson was obliged to spend a very great sum —equalling more than 10,000*l*. of our money—in order to put the castle into a habitable state of repair.

In the Record Office[4] there is a reference to what must have been another source of expense to Samson, and that is that in 1610 he obtained a license for himself and his wife, Lady Dacre, to make a park with free-warren in 'Hethfield' (Heathfield), Sussex, and to enclose 600 acres of land called

[1] *Ante*, p. 82.
[2] Roger Pulston, a steward to John Lennard (*ante*, p. 140), evidently continued in the service of his son; he also appears among the list of Samson's tenants in the latter's rent-rolls.
[3] *Add.* 5679, 563.
[4] *Privy Seal, May 8th, Jac. I.*

'Baylee.' I have not been able to discover how Samson became possessed of Heathfield, as it does not appear in any lists I have seen of the estates belonging to the Fynes family; but in the before-mentioned survey of Herstmonceux, dated 1570, there is this reference to Gregory Lord Dacre's ownership of Bayly :—

There is in the parish of Hethfylde a wood called Bayly Wood containing 107 acres in the tenure of the Lord of Buckhurst which was stored with goodly timber trees of Oke and Byche whereof the one half is fallen by the lord of Buckhurst & his father and the residue is yearly to be felled by my Lord Dacre's grant & sale of the same woods;

and we shall see that Samson's grandson Richard Lord Dacre disposed by will of his lands in Baylee.

Before Samson obtained this license there were already Lennards of Bayly Heathfield, who, as has been stated, were second cousins of his by a common descent from the John Lennard who died 1530;[1] and we shall find references to this same branch of the family some thirty to forty years later in the account book of household expenses at Herstmonceux.[2]

At the time that Lord Dacre wrote his Family History there existed in the possession of Sir Thomas Rider, of Boughton, Kent, a MS. account written by his ancestor, Sir Francis Barnham, of his own family, of which Lord Dacre obtained a copy.[3] I give the following quotation from it, as Sir Francis mentions his marriage with Samson's daughter Elizabeth, and he also refers to his father-in-law's mode of living, and to his character :—

In the fortieth year of Queen Elizabeth my Father Martin Barnham served the Office of High Sheriff for the County of Kent and during his Shrievalty married me[4] to the daughter of Mr Sampson Lennard and the Lady Dacre in which match his

---
[1] *Ante*, p. 4. [2] *Post*, pp. 285, 287.
[3] This has been printed in full.—*Anc.* ix.
[4] As to parents arranging their children's marriages see *ante*, pp. 57, 64-5.

goodness sought rather to give me a Wife that might bring me a Noble alliance and promise the happiness of a good Wife (as being borne of a Mother that abounded as much in worth & Virtue as in honour) than to enrich himself or his other children by so great a Portion as it is probable he might have had in divers places, if that had been his Chiefest Ayme in my Marriage. . . . Within less than two years after my Marriage, I came to live in my Father's House tho' I had then by Covenant one Years Being more with my Father in Law (Mr. Sampson Lennard)[1] who tho' he kept a very honourable House and lived in all respects in so brave a Fashion, as might make the being there very delightfull, especially to me, who had always from all hands a very loving & Noble treatment, yet the happiness promised myself in the comfort of my Father's kind & familiar usage, & in his Advice & instructions &c made me hasten my coming to live with him.

I have a letter to Lord Dacre from Sir Thomas Rider, in which, speaking about his ancestress Elizabeth, Lady Barnham, he says :—

Of this lady there is a fine monument in my parish church. Tradition delivers her down as one of the Handsomest Women of the Age she liv'd in, & if the Sculptor, & Painter, did not flatter there is reason to believe that Account of her is just. She had fifteen children by Sr. Francis Barnham K^t; whose eldest son Robert was created a Baronet by James the 1st.

Among the letters in the published Sidney papers[2] there is an incidental reference to the hospitality of Samson's establishment. The letter, dated '27th Aprill, 1597,' is from Rowland Whyte to Sir Robert Sydney. He says :—

My Lady and the 3 greater children went vpon Monday morning towards Penshurst to see all Things well ordered there. She lay that night at Knole. Capt E^d Morgan, Charles Morgan and Capt Williams accompanied her Ladyship so farre and returned Yesterday to London hauing brought my Lady to

---

[1] This System of the parents of each of the parties to a marriage providing them in turn with so many years' board and lodging subsequent to the wedding appears to have been not uncommon ; *vide post*, pp. 439, 442, 453, 455.

[2] *Coll. Lett.* ii. p. 45.

the great Glasshouse[1] Hill towards Penshurst; and doe very much commend the Intertainment my Lady Dacres[2] gaue vnto my Lady & them.

The same publication has another reference to Lady Dacre, as it is mentioned that she and her daughter were present at the baptism of Robert Sidney, Earl of Leicester, on New Year's Eve 1595.[3]

Horsfield[4] thus mentions Samson's hospitality :—

This Samson Leonard [sic] & the Lady Dacre his wife lived much at Herstmonceux, and were remarkable for their noble housekeeping and hospitality, and embellished the house with costly chimney pieces in the best rooms, ornamented according to the fashion of those times with their coats of arms, crests, and supporters.

There can be no doubt but that Samson was more extravagant in entertaining and in spending money generally than having so large a family he could easily afford, as we have documents showing he owed money, and that he sold a considerable quantity of land, and I have found nothing to cause me to believe that, with the exception of one or two quite small parcels, he ever purchased any land with the proceeds of the estates which he sold. No member of our family has ever owned such large estates as he was possessed of, since he inherited not only nearly all his father's property, but also a very considerable portion of what had belonged to the Fynes. Unfortunately, however, he entered upon a course of dissipating his great possessions, conduct which has been only too zealously copied in the form of either sale, mortgages, or family charges by his descendants for nearly three hundred years, except in the

---

[1] I am unable to explain what this glass house could be ; see also references to John Lennard's glass house, *ante*, p. 140.

[2] It will be observed that Margaret is here styled Lady Dacres, a title to which we shall see the commissioners appointed by the Queen in the previous month of February found she was entitled ; but her claims were not formally acknowledged by the Crown until the succeeding reign.

[3] i. p. 386.   [4] i. p. 555.

case of Thomas Lord Dacre, who left his property in a better state than when he inherited it. It is thanks to his careful management of the family possessions that a small remnant of them still belongs to a descendant of Samson. Except Lord Dacre, every head of the family, and most of its junior branches also, have in turn in their respective generations, as entails were cut off and properties resettled, nibbled away at the splendid inheritance once theirs, which formerly extended into nine counties. Considering the family's systematic extravagance, it is remarkable it has been able to keep going for so many years; but now there is pressing need for a second John to arise, who, to use Samson's language when speaking of his father, might by 'his painfull & vertuous courses be the Authour of his owne advancement.'

I have a deed, dated May 17th, 1599, whereby Samson, described as of Knole, agreed to sell the manor of Scorton, Yorks, for 2,000*l*. in money, and the purchaser agreed also to 'give my Ladie Dacres his wife a good ambling geldinge' on the following All Saints' Day. I have also three deeds, dated in June 1602, in which he was still described as of Knole, whereby he sold parcels of land in Otford to three different persons. The sums he obtained by these sales, respectively, were 125*l*., 270*l*., and 103*l*. 6*s*. 8*d*.; in the last of these conveyances the property is described as 'the messuage called the signe of the Crowne' and six acres of land; in 1611 by a deed in which Samson is described as of Herstmonceux, he sold the manor of Wickhurst in Sevenoaks for 1,200*l*. These lands had all been bought by John Lennard in 1553 for 100*l*., subject to a rent-charge of 27*l*. issuing out of them, and this Samson bought up in October 1611 from the then owner, H. Lovelace, at a cost to himself of 540*l*. He also probably sold Ewhurst in Sussex.[1] Another reason for thinking Samson lived beyond his means is a deed in my possession, dated December 1st, 11th Jas. I. (1614), by which he conveyed his Norfolk estates of Horsford and Hautbois to trustees in trust to employ the rents derived therefrom in pay-

[1] *Hors.* i. p. 520.

ment of his own debts, and also the debts of his eldest son Sir Henry, for which Samson had become security. I have also a memorandum, dated May 8th, 1602, whereby Edward Rede promises to deliver up an obligation wherein Samson and Sir Henry were bound to him in 4,000*l.* as soon as the conveyance of the lands mentioned in this obligation is duly completed.

I have several of Samson's rent-rolls—viz. those for the years 1598, 1599, 1605, 1606, 1607, and 1608; and by these we see that his income in 1607 was 2,890*l.*, or nearly 3,000*l.* a year. At first sight it appears curious that his later rent-rolls show a larger total than do his earlier ones, although during the period which they cover Samson had parted with some of his estates. This, however, seems to be explained by the accounts being made out upon a different basis, and in his latter accounts he is credited with the estimated value of the lands in his own occupation at Herstmonceux; and also with the value of his rents in kind which are not included in the earlier accounts.

These rents in kind are set out very fully and are interesting, showing as they do the then estimated value of farm produce. They were due sometimes from copyholders, but we also find many instances of ordinary tenants paying a part of their rent in money and part in kind. On Samson's estates this system of some of the rents being paid in kind seems to have prevailed chiefly on those of his lands which were in the counties of Kent and Sussex. As an example we may take the case of his tenant at Burham in Kent, a Mr. Thomas Raines, who paid 80*l.* in money and thirty quarters of wheat at 24*s.* and twenty quarters of malt at 13*s.* 4*d.* Other values of farm produce which appear in these accounts are:—

A fatte weather 10*s.*; Lambs 4*s.* each; a Brawn 26*s.* 7*d.*; Conies per dozen dozen 5*s.*; Capons per dozen dozen 10*s.*; Geese per dozen dozen 12*s.*; Hens per dozen dozen 8*s.*; oates 6*s.* 8*d.* per qtr.

A tenant named Franckewell, who hired at a rent in money of 4*l.* 4*s.* two marshes in Peinsie (Pevensey?), Sussex, where he presumably had a decoy, had also at Christmas to furnish the following wild-fowl:—

viij Ducke & Mallerd . . . . iiij^s ⎫
viij Teales . . . . . . ij^s ⎬ ix^s iiij^d.
iiij Widgeons . . . . . xvj^d ⎪
ij d.d. (2 doz. doz.) Sintes[1] . . ij^s ⎭

The most striking feature of these rents in kind is the extreme relative dearness of wheat and cheapness of meat. Wheat was then making about as much as it was towards the end of the nineteenth century, but the price of mutton was very low, while rabbits at 5s. for 144, or less than $\frac{1}{2}d$. each, would not seem to pay for catching; and the price for poultry was but little higher in proportion.

There is also another point of interest in these rent accounts, and that is the insight they give as to the then value of lands in Sussex. As a rule, these accounts only mention the amount of rent paid by each tenant, and not the amount of acres in his holding; but in dealing with the lands in Sussex which Samson kept in his own hands, a different system is followed, and more particulars are given. Thus we see at Herstmonceux that the park is put at 500 acres at 5s. per acre, 'divers parcels of upland' at 10s. per acre, and 'divers parcels of mershe' at 15s. per acre.[2]

In the latter of these accounts the names of some estates which appeared in the earlier ones are missing, these having been sold by Samson. These estates, and the amounts of rents they produced him in 1599, are as follows:—

Kent	⎧ Knolle	. . . .	218	6 8
	⎨ Shorham	. . . .	4	6 8
	⎪ Otford	. . . .	22	0 0
	⎩ Crayford	. . . .	0	10 0
Wilts	Stanton St. Quinton	. .	145	0 0
Yorks	⎧ Thyme	. . . .	8	0 0
	⎩ Scorton	. . . .	37	12 0
Essex	Nashall	. . . .	7	15 0

[1] Stints (?).
[2] *Cf.* rentals in Essex about same period for lands belonging to the Barretts, *post*, p. 355 *et seq.*

I am not able to say when Samson parted with the lease of Knole, but it was probably in 1603. We have seen that the lease to Thomas Rolf was for ninety-nine years, from February 156⅝,[1] and that John Lennard obtained the residue of that term about 1570, when he granted a sublease of it to Samson for twenty years.[2] John's will, which is dated 1587, was made at Knole,[3] and Samson appears to have lived there in 1602,[4] and rents from Knole are credited in his rent accounts in 1598 and 1599,[5] but not in 1605, which is the next year for which we have these accounts. As he had inherited the freehold of Chevening, which is only three or four miles from Knole, and had also Herstmonceux since his brother-in-law's death, it is not to be wondered at that he was anxious to avoid having upon his hands another large country house so close to Chevening.

I do not find he had any house in London, but we have letters addressed to him there at the following addresses :—

'At the Sygne of the Catte & fidle in flete Strete nere St. Dunstone Church.'

'At his lodging in fleetstreete.'

'At Mr. Johnson his house neare the Horne in Fleet Street right over against Serieants Inn London.'

To the latter place we have letters addressed on various occasions from 1604 to 1615.

I have an account of moneys disbursed on his behalf, 'beginninge the xith of October, 1599, and endinge the xviijth day of the same.' This appears to have been on some occasion when he was from home, and from the rather frequent item of 'bote hier iiij^d' he would seem to have been in London. This week's outing cost Samson 10*l*. 3*s*. 1*d*., of which nearly half consists of 'Itm, delivered to yo^{r}selfe in golde v^{li}.' His food was not costly, being usually 'Itm, for yor dyet iiij^s,' but now and then he appears to have dined out with friends, and only had to pay for supper, as we have '14th Itm on Sonday yor

---

[1] *Ante*, p. 116.   [2] *Ibid.* p. 121.
[3] *Ibid.* p. 147.   [4] *Ibid.* p. 229.   [5] *Ibid.* p. 230.

dynner at Mr Barnhams[1] yor Supper ij^s.' On Thursday, October 18th, Samson must have given a breakfast party, or else, judging from the other daily charges, have indulged himself very greatly, as we find 'Itm on thursday for yor breakfaste at the white hart v^s iij^d.' 'Itm for horsemeat for vij horses on [one] night vij^s' is an entry at the beginning of his trip to London; and the only other mention of horses is the day he leaves, when we have 'Itm on Thursday for horsemeate for six horses on [one] nighte vj^s.' This shows us that he rode up from Chevening, and then sent his horses back there until he required them for the return journey. So also we see he had three servants in London with him who cost him iiij^s a day for 'boord wages,' while on the first night he was charged 'Itm for 6 of yor mens supper iiij^s,' which shows that three of these men were grooms, who came up to London in order to take the horses home. 'Itm to the footman to drincke going & coming x^d' explains how, with six horses who had to be taken home, he had three servants in London. Samson no doubt rode with five servants mounted and one on foot; three of these servants remained in town with him and three rode home, each leading a horse. In those days, when roads were so bad, the Thames was comparatively a more important means of intercommunication between London and Westminster than it has been of late years until the London County Council started their celebrated steamers, and this accounts for the frequent item of 'bote hier,' and also for his getting rid of his horses while in London.

Tips on leaving were no doubt universal then as now, and we find these two entries, 'Itm in reward to the horsekeapers vj^d,' and 'Itm in rewards to the chamberleine[2] iij^d.' The poor, the sick, and prisoners were also sharers in Samson's bounty, as we have 'Itm in reward to the poore iiij^d,' and 'Itm in reward at the thre [three] prisons & hospitall ij^s.' Samson was evidently determined to take the opportunity of being in London to hear music, as we have twice the entry, 'Itm in reward to Musitians

---

[1] Probably his son-in-law.   [2] Chambermaid.

ij^s'; while that he also went out into society is shown by the following, 'Itm in reward to divers noble mens trumpeters vij^s.' He also bought a book the better to enable him to fulfil his magisterial duties, as we find 'Itm for a tretyse of the office of a Justice of the peace compiled by Mr. Lamberte iiij^s vj^d,' which was the 'Stone's Manual' of the period.[1] That author gives a short epitome in verse of the duties of a justice of the peace, of which the following are the first four lines:—

> Do equall right to rich and poore
> As Wit and Law extends
> Giue none aduice in any cause
> That you before depends.[2]

It is probable that no subject during his whole career was of greater interest to Samson than his claim to the title of Dacre in right of his wife, which accrued to him in 1594 upon the death of his brother-in-law, Gregory Lord Dacre. The case is fully reported in Collins' 'Claims to Baronies.'

I have shown in a previous chapter that the title Gregory held had three times descended in the female line.[3] Samson's first step was to endeavour to get the Crown to acknowledge his wife as Baroness Dacre; in pursuance of which object she presented a petition to Queen Elizabeth,[4] who appointed Lord Burghley, the Lord High Treasurer, and Lord Howard of Effingham, Lord High Admiral, to inquire into and report upon her claim.

There is hanging in the Library at Belhus a long pedigree, beautifully written, and with several score of coats of arms illuminated. It is a remarkable example of heraldic work, and is in very good preservation, considering its age and the careless treatment to which it is inevitable it should have been subjected during the lapse of years, over three centuries, since it was completed. There are two MS. memoranda in panels

---

[1] William Lambarde (1536-1601), a Bencher of Lincoln's Inn and J.P. for Kent. He was a copious writer. His *Eirenarcha or of the Offices of Justices of the Peace*, published in 1581, and reprinted no less than seven times between 1582 and 1610, was long considered a standard authority.

[2] Book i. cap. 10.   [3] *Ante*, p. 170 *et seq*.   [4] *Har.* 6227, 15.

CLAIM TO TITLE OF DACRE

towards the bottom of this long roll. One is now impossible to decipher, and looks as if some one, possibly a child out of mischief, had purposely rubbed it out.

The other memorandum runs thus :—

This pedigree as it is of it self very honorable and auntient so by sundry noble families whose heirs by mariage hath bene incorporated unto this line the work hath bene the more techey [?] and the profe the more difficulte the conformation where of may be euidently disierned by the diligent peruser in justification where of I haue sette my hande. Richard St George. Norrey King of Armes of the North partes.

I think there can be no doubt but that Samson had this elaborate pedigree prepared in order to substantiate his wife's claim.

The commissioners made their report on the last day of February 159$\frac{8}{9}$; they found that Margaret had made good her claim to the title, and advised the Queen that she might 'at her good pleasure allow unto her the name stile and dignity of the said baronie.' This report, duly signed by the two commissioners, is among our family papers. It is in very good preservation, and sets out the pedigree in the direct line, with a few of the arms of the different families illuminated in proper colours, and is a fine specimen of a legal document of that period; but it is not one-tenth of the size of the large pedigree just referred to, measuring only about 2 feet 6 inches by 1 foot 6 inches. I have not been able to discover why the Queen did not act upon this report; Collins does not refer to the subject, so it may be presumed that in 1734, when his 'Claims' were published, the reasons were unknown that actuated Elizabeth in disregarding the finding of those commissioners whom she had herself appointed.

Lord Dacre says,[1] the Queen referred the matter to the Lords Burleigh and Howard to examine if Margaret's claim were good, which they both allowed it to be after mature consideration; but this not being quite finished before the Queen's

[1] *Ld. D. His.*

death it was again laid before commissioners appointed for such purposes in the succeeding reign. As the report in question was made seven years before Elizabeth's death, and as it left no point undecided nor requiring any further investigation, this explanation of Lord Dacre's seems to be an inadequate one. I think it probable that Samson had neither sufficient influence to successfully push his claim nor sufficient shrewdness to know whom to bribe to do so for him. If his father had been alive when the report was delivered, most likely he would so have managed matters that the Queen would not have long delayed giving effect to it.

The Earl of Essex wrote a letter to Samson about his 'homble petycone,' from which the latter appears to have claimed the title of Lord Dacre *jure uxoris* shortly after his wife's claim to it had been admitted. That he was not successful in this is shown by the subsequent proceedings which he took in the matter. There is a rather long MS. document in the Ashmolean Museum, headed 'Imperfections in Mr. Lenards Presidents,'[1] which has notes in the margin controverting the objections raised to his title in the text of the document. We shall see that these 'Imperfections,' whoever raised them, did not constitute a bar to his claims. The letter from Lord Essex is as follows :—

After my very harty comendatyones whereas hir M$_a$^{tie} upon yor homble petycone to enjoy by hir gratios favore the honore & tytle of the Barrony of Dacres of the Southe in the Righte of Margarete yor wyffe, sister & Sole beire to Gregory late Lord Dacres of the Southe affores^d bathe commanded mee as Earle Marshall of England to heare & Examene yor tytle & Clayme ther vnto ; I doe by these letteres require yo^w to appeare wth yor Counsell uppon Wensday 29 of this present Monthe of November at thre of the Clocke in the Afternoone at my house w^{t}hout Tempell Barre caled Essexe house & then & thear yo^w shalbe fully herde what yo^w cane saye for yor Selfe as also yf any thinge cane be sayd against yo^u by any other competytor, or what may be sayd by the Lawes of this Realme or the Lawes

[1] *Ashm.* 862, p. 151.

CLAIM TO TITLE OF DACRE

& Costomes of honore & Armes to barre yo^w of any suche clayme, to the end that hir Matie uppon suche a full hearinge & examenation maye knowe what Cause thear is to allowe or disalowe of yor Sute. And so willing yo^w to take knowledge of this citacon & warning by this Lettere and officere of Armes and not to faylle of yor appearance I comite yo^w to God. from the Courte at Whithall the 26 of November 1598.

Yo^r Loving ffrend
ESSEX.

To my very assured ffrend, Sampsone Leonorde Esquire.[1]

There is a published letter[2] from John Chamberlain to Sir Dudley Carleton, dated December 8th, 1598, in which, after referring to the Earl of Essex, he says :—

He kept a kind of Marshall's Court of late when the title of Nevill that claims to be Lord of Abergeny, and the title of Sir Henry Leonard that wold be Lord Dacres of the South was argued, but after divers hearings he left the matter as he found it, and so it is referred to the Quene.

And this is also mentioned in almost the same terms in the 'Calendar of State Papers (Domestic) Eliz.'[3] From this it would appear Samson was unable to substantiate his claim to the title through his wife; but upon what grounds it could be claimed by his eldest son, Sir Henry, during the lifetime of his mother Margaret, is not easy to understand.

Soon after the accession of James, Samson presented a petition to the King, again urging his wife's claim to the title of Dacre; and the matter was referred to the commissioners for the hearing of Marshal causes, who unanimously decided in her favour. We have their original report, which is dated December 8th, 2nd Jas. (1604), and is signed 'T. Dorset [Earl of, Lord High Treasurer]: Lenox [Duke of]: Nottingham [Earl of, Lord High Admiral]: Suffolke [Earl of, Lord Chamberlain]: E. Worcester [Earl of, Master of the Horse]: H. Northampton' [Earl of, Lord Warden of the Cinque Ports].

[1] *Har.* 6227, 108.
[2] *C. S. P.* p. 32. Chamberlain was a newsletter writer, and his letters date from 1598 to 1625.
[3] cclxix. No. 6.

I have also an original document endorsed: 'a declaration of ye state of the Barony under ye hands of the Haroldes.' This is signed by three heralds: William Dethick (Principal King-at-Arms), the celebrated William Camden (Clarenceux), and R. St. George (Windsor). It sets out how this barony had on three occasions been held by husbands in right of their wives; it refers to the finding in favour of Margaret by the commissioners appointed by the late Queen, and ends up thus: 'Wherefore she most humbly prayeth to be admitted thereunto as divers of hir Auncestors have in like case byn admitted.' This document is not dated, nor, as it has no other heading, can we be sure whether it was a petition to the King; it is more probable that it was put in as expert evidence before those commissioners to whom this matter had been referred.

James, unlike his predecessor, did not long delay acting upon the report of the commissioners, and Margaret was duly allowed the title of Baroness Dacre. As soon as she had been officially recognised as Baroness Dacre, Samson, having had children by her, put forward his own claim to be called to the House of Lords as Baron Dacre *jure uxoris*, as had been many persons before him; and notably in the case of his wife's ancestors, Thomas de Moulton, Randolph de Dacre, and Sir Richard Fynes.

Samson's wife died at Chevening on March 10th, 161½,[1] before his claim was adjudicated upon, and their eldest son Henry at once succeeded to his mother's title. The King, however, by Letters Patent, dated April 2nd, 1612, which are among our papers, gave Samson precedence as if he were the eldest son of Lord Dacre of the South, especially stating that he would have been summoned to the House of Lords had not the death of Margaret caused the title to descend to their son Henry, and so frustrate the King's intention.

Samson did not live long to enjoy this honour, as he only survived his wife about three years, dying in September 1615. At some period after his wife's death he appears to have

[1] *I. P. M.*

transferred most of his property to his eldest son, as, in an undated draft of a letter concerning the Norfolk property, he says : ' I have departed with the greatest part of my estate to my sonne Dacre.'

Samson and his wife lie buried under a remarkably fine tomb in Chevening Church, upon which are their life-size effigies, with the following inscriptions :—

Gloriosum Domini nostri Jesu Christi adventum expectans hic requiescit Sampson Lennard armiger, una cum charissima uxore Margareta Baronissa Dacre (sorore et proxima haerede Gregorii Fienes militis Baronis Dacre de le South) cui 47 annos, 4 menses, et supernumerarios aliquot dies, conjugali vinculo ligatus, suaviter et beate vixit ; suscepitque ex eadem 7 filios, Henricum, Baronem Dacre, Gregorium, et Thomam superstites, reliquis quatuor in infantia extinctis, et 6 filias quarum una periit infantula quinque supersunt ; Pietatis, comitatis, hospitalitatis, laude celebris et in commune bonus, praepropera nobilissimae uxoris morte ampliorem Regis gratiam anticipante, honore primogeniti filii Baronis Dacre de le South, diplomate illustrissimi Regis Jacobi decoratus, anno aetatis 71, ineunte salutis 1615, Sept. 20. ex hac vita migravit.[1]

On the other side :—

Margaretæ Fynes, Baronissæ Dacre, Filiæ Thomæ Baronis Dacre, Filii Thomæ Fienes militis, Filii Thomæ Baronis Dacre, Et Annæ uxoris ejus filiae Humfridi Bourchier Militis, filii Johannis, Baronis Bourchier de Berners, filii Gulielmi Bourchier comitis Essexiæ et Ewe, et Annæ uxoris ejus, filiæ Thomæ de Woodstock, Ducis de Glocestriæ ; ex materna stirpe filiæ Mariæ, filiæ Georgii Nevile Baronis de Bergaveny, filii Edwardi Nevile, Baronis de Burgaveny, filii Radulphi Nevile comitis Westmorlandiæ, et Johannæ uxoris ejus filiæ Johannis de Gaunt Ducis Lancastriæ. Amoris et honoris ergo posuit charissimus, idemque moestissimus conjux, quem cum felici prole beasset, exemplarque pietatis in Deum, obsequii in maritum, charitatis in pauperes, humanitatis in omnes, supra sexum exhibuisset ; tandem die Martii 10,[2] anno Salutis 1611, ætatis 70, cum summo bonorum omnium desiderio ; Supremum Spiritum libens lubensque Patri Spiritum, exhalavit.

[1] The *Ch. Reg.* records his burial on September 21st.
[2] According to the *Ch. Reg.* she was buried on this date.

Samson's three younger sons—Gregory, Thomas, and John—all died without leaving issue.

Gregory, who in July 1594 obtained a license to travel for 2 years,[1] married, about May 1614, Mawd, daughter of Richard Llewellyn; she was probably an orphan at the time of her marriage, and in the guardianship of her aunt, as the deeds by which Samson settled the manor of Apurfield, Apulderfield, or Apuldrefield, in the parish of Cudham,[2] as her jointure, are made between him of the one part, and Dame Margaret Hawkins of the other part, and recite that Mawd was a daughter of a sister of the latter. Lady Hawkins was the widow of the celebrated admiral, and her signature to one of these deeds is remarkable for its bold, clear handwriting. Samson obtained by Letters Patent a license, dated May 30th, 1614, enabling him to convey Apuldrefield, and this document shows that the lands he conveyed consisted of: 1 messuage, 5 tofts,[3] 3 gardens, 3 orchards, 300 acres of land, 13 acres of meadow, 300 acres of pasture, and 160 acres of wood. We have nothing to show what the fortune of the young lady was, but as her father-in-law made so good a settlement upon her, she no doubt brought her husband a respectable dowry. Lady Hawkins lived at Chigwell, in Essex, and in the

---

[1] *Docket book to Signet Bills.* Record Office.
[2] Formerly written Coldham and Caudham.—*Phil.* p. 123.
[3] A messuage giving rights of common; or land on which such a messuage formerly stood; old law term.—*C. D.*

GREGORY LENNARD

register of that parish there is the following entry of baptism dated August 31st, 1615: 'Jhon Leonard sonne of Mr. Leonard.' There is no entry in that register of his burial, but it contains many omissions at that period, and we shall see directly there can be little doubt that the child died quite young.

It has been already stated that it was not uncommon at one period for young married people to spend the first two or three years of their married life with the parents of each of them alternately, and as Lady Hawkins appears to have stood in the place of a mother to Mawd, she no doubt entertained the newly married pair for a year or two, which would account for her grandchild being born at Chigwell. By her will, dated 1619, she left to 'Mawde Leonerd' her best pair of Spanish 'borders,' enamelled black and trimmed with pearls, the upper border containing nineteen pieces and the nether border seven pieces,[1] and also a legacy of 200*l*.[2]

Gregory did not long enjoy married life, as he died in February $161\frac{8}{9}$ or $16\frac{19}{20}$, at Apuldrefield,[3] and his widow married, in or before 1621, John Wroth, of Loughton Hall, Essex, by whom she had no issue, and from whom she appears to have been divorced. During her first husband's lifetime Mawd, in May 1618, leased Apuldrefield for twenty-one years at a rent of 123*l*. 12*s*. for the first fourteen years, and 133*l*. 12*s*. for the remaining seven years of the term. She, however, reserved the timber and the right of sporting, and some other rights, and also three rooms in the manor-house—namely the great chamber with the old parlour under it, and the chamber called Duffield's chamber, and the use of the kitchen.[4] If it is correct that Gregory died at Apuldrefield, his death, no doubt, took place in this great chamber. Mawd died in 1635, and on September 14th was buried at Chigwell in accordance with her wish to 'lie neere her sonne,' who was the child of her first marriage.[5] Upon her death without issue the manor of Apuldrefield passed to Francis Lord Dacre by virtue of the terms of

---

[1] *C. H.* ii. p. 746. [2] *T. & G.* iii. p. 213. [3] *Ibid.*
[4] *Ibid.* p. 214. [5] *E. Arch. N. S.* viii. p. 346.

the settlement which, we have seen, Samson made upon her marriage with his son Gregory.

I have been unable to discover much about either of Samson's sons Thomas or John. An ancient MS. pedigree states that the latter died without issue, but does not give the date of his death. The same pedigree states that in 1628 Thomas was unmarried, and the Gray's Inn Register shows that he was admitted a member of that Inn on May 18th, 1596. We have some papers in a lawsuit brought more than a hundred years later against Thomas Earl of Sussex, by which it appears that Samson bought a farm in the parish of Sundridge called Oveny Cakett's, and this farm and twenty acres of land in Brasted he settled on Thomas, whom it there refers to as his 'youngest son,' and makes no mention of the existence of John, so I think we may assume the latter died while still a child.

An ancient copy of this Thomas's will [1] describes him as of 'Eveuns Green in the parish of Sundrish Kent.' He appointed his 'loving brother in law' Sir Francis Barnham his executor, to whom he left a legacy of 20*l.*, and all the residue of his property to his godson Thomas Lennard, who was his great-nephew, being second son of Richard Lord Dacre. Sir Francis Barnham was granted probate of this will in November 1638; and the parish register of Herstmonceux records the burial of Thomas on November 6th in that year.

Samson's eldest son Henry was, as we have seen, born in 1569. Like many others of his family he became member of one of the Inns of Court, and the Lincoln's Inn Register records that on October 15th, 1588, Henry Lennard, of Kent, was admitted to that Inn at the request of his uncle Thomas Lennard.[2] A year later, when only twenty years of age, he married Chrysogona,[3] daughter, by his second wife, of Sir Richard Baker, of Sissenhurst, Kent; and he obtained 2,200*l.* with her as a marriage portion.[4]

[1] *F. P.*   [2] Probably his great-uncle.—*Ante*, p. 4.
[3] This, to us, curious name, which in some of our papers is written Crysogon, she no doubt obtained from her mother's sister, Chrysogona Gifford, who married Lord Gray. These Giffords were a Hampshire family.
[4] The C. P.

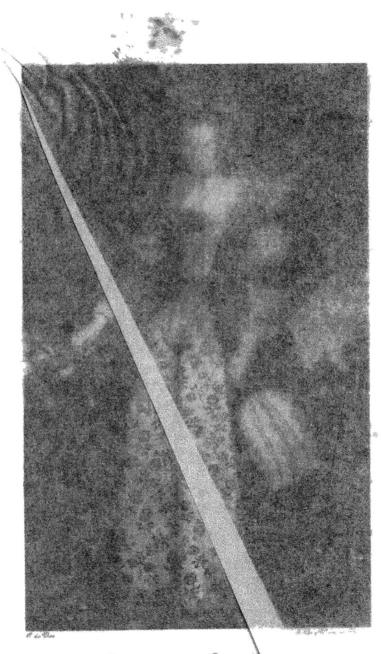

Chrysogona. Lady

the settlement which, we hav[e seen,] Samson [made upon her] marriage with his son Gregory.

I have been unable to discover much about either of Samson's sons Thomas or John. An ancient MS. pedigree states that the latter died without issue, but does not give the date of his death. The same pedigree states that in 1628 Thomas was unmarried, and the Gray's Inn Register shows that he was admitted a member of that Inn on May 18th, 1596. We have some papers in a lawsuit brought more than a hundred years later against Thomas Earl [of] Sussex, by which it appears that Samson bought a farm in the parish of Sundridge called Oveny Cakett's, and this farm and [tw]enty acres of land in Brasted he settled on Thomas, whom [he] there refers to as his 'youngest son,' and makes no mention [of the] existence of John, so I think we may assume the latter [die]d while still a child.

An ancient copy of this Thomas['s] will[1] describes him as of 'Evenus Green in the parish of Su[ndr]ish Kent.' He appointed his 'loving brother in law' Sir F[ranc]is Barnham his executor, [to] whom he left a legacy of [£], and all the residue of his property to his godson Thom[as] Lennard, who was his great-n[ep]hew, being second son of [the second] Lord Dacre. Sir Francis Barnham was granted probate [of this will] in November 1638; [and the parish register of] [M]aresorceux records the burial of [Thomas on November of th]at year.

[S]amson's eldest son [Henry was, as] we have seen, born in 1569. [Like many oth]er [sons of his family] he became member of [o]ne of the Inns of [Court, and the] Lincoln's Inn Register records that on Octr [1588,] Henry Lennard, of Kent, was admitted to th[e Inn at the r]equest of his uncle Thomas Lennard.[2] A ye[ar or two after, when only] twenty years of age, he married Chryso[gona daughter] b[y] his second wife, of Sir Richard Baker. [   ] and he obtained 2,200ℓ. with her as a [marriage p]ortion.

[1] [ ] [F.]
[2] This, [no] [   ] [   ] [   ] his great uncle.—*Ante*, p. 4.
[   ] no doubt [   ] [one] of our papers is written Crysogon, [   ] Chrysogona Gifford, who married Lord Cray.
[4] The C[   ]

Chrysogona, Lady Dacre

HENRY LORD DACRE'S CHILDREN

We learn by the papers in an action brought some years later that John Lennard and his son Samson settled on Chrysogona upon her marriage certain lands in Brasted for her life. Her father was son of Sir John Baker and Elizabeth his wife, widow of George Barrett, of Belhus, Essex.[1] The children of Henry and Chrysogona were as follows:—

1. Richard, born April 1596.[2]
2. Fynes, baptized at Sevenoaks December 27th, 1597.
3. Edward, baptized at Chevening November 17th, 1611.
4. Margaret, baptized at Sevenoaks October 27th, 1594. She married Sir A. Wildgoose, of Iridge Place, Salehurst, Sussex, and is buried in Willingdon Church of same county. The monument there was put up to her memory by her nephew George Parker. This monument states that she died at the age of sixty-one on August 16th, 1653, having been forty-four years a widow and having had three children, none of whom survived her nor had issue. If this inscription be accurate as to dates, she was born two years before she was baptized, and was left a widow at the age of seventeen, having already had three children, which, even in that period of youthful brides, sounds hardly possible.
5. Philadelphia, born about 1597. She married on December 1st, 1618, at St. Giles' Church, Cripplegate, London, Sir Thomas Parker, of Ratton, Willingdon, Sussex, and is stated in an old MS. pedigree to have been buried there on January 20th, 1661, aged sixty-four.
6. Pembroke,[3] baptized at St. Helen's, Bishopsgate, July 5th, 1602.[4] Married Sir William Brook, K.B., of Cowling Castle, Kent; they had an only child, named after her mother, who died *s.p.*[5]
7. Barbara. Lord Dacre says in his MS. 'History' that a pedigree in the Heralds' College shows her to have married

---

[1] *Post*, pp. 340, 354. [2] The *C. P.*
[3] So named after her father's friends, the Earl and Countess of Pembroke.— Ld. D. His.
[4] *Har. So., R.* xxxi. p. 10. [5] *Ld. D. Mis.*

a Sir Philip Stapleton, but he believes she died unmarried; in fact, she did so marry, as we read :—

Feb. 6th 1634 Sir P. Stapleton Widower 36 & Mrs Barbara Leonard [*sic*] of St. Anne's Blackfriars Spinster 30. dau. of the Rt. Hon. Henry Lord Dacres dec. & her mother also deceased at St. Anne's Blackfriars.[1]

Henry inherited to the full his father's public spirit and patriotism, and accordingly we find him, at the age of twenty-seven, taking part in the Earl of Essex's attack and capture of Cadiz. The following is Stowe's account of what happened after that town had been taken :—

The 27th of June [1596] being Sunday the Lords, Generals with all the chiefs & gentlemen of the Army heard a sermon at San Francisco when after dinner they made a great many Knights cuen all almost that did deserue it, or affect it, or not neglect or refuse it (as some did) this great indulgence of fortune and exceeding accesse of honor to them in this atchieuement made them not onely bountifull but prodigall of honour. . . . The rest which were Knighted at the Frierie, and afterwards, were :

Here follow the names of sixty-three persons, among which occurs that of 'Sir Henry Lennard.'[2] This somewhat cynical account of the great number of honours bestowed by Essex on his followers has its counterpart in some Army Gazettes of recent years, where apparently the names of nearly all those present in many of the engagements were selected for honours.

On September 27th, 1597, shortly after his return home, Sir Henry entered Parliament, where he represented West Looe. Mr. Courtney says : 'Sir Walter Raleigh had great influence at West Looe. R. Crosse who fought with him at Cadiz was elected in 1593, & was in the same class of Courtly Knights & Squires as Sir Henry Lennard of Kent.'[3] His portrait, which we have at Belhus, represents him as having been distinctly handsome, and doubtless this good-looking soldier and politician was a familiar figure in Court and fashionable circles.

[1] *Har. So.* xxvi. p. 233.   [2] *Stow*, p. 775.   [3] *Par. Rep.* C.

In 1612 Sir Henry was one of the lords who assisted at the funeral of Henry Prince of Wales; and Lord Dacre says that he was one of the peers appointed to sit on the trial of Robert Car, Earl of Somerset, at a period when the peers were not tried by their whole body, but by those specially appointed by the Lord High Steward.

We know that he was an intimate friend of William Earl of Pembroke, and of that Earl's brother-in-law, Sir Philip Sydney; and is said to have been with the latter when he was killed in the wars in the Netherlands. Sir William Browne,[1] writing to Sir Robert Sydney in 1601 and 1602, twice mentions meeting Sir Henry at Lord Pembroke's house. In one of these letters he says: 'Myself came the same day to London very weary yett made a steppe to my Lord of Pembroke, whom I found not within. There I mett with Sir Henry Leonard whose good company stayed me there so long till my Lord himself came in.' And in another: 'We dranke yester-nyght a health to your Lordship at my Lord of Pembroke's where was Sir Henry Leonard.'[2]

Sampson Lennard (the herald) published a translation from a French history of the prosecution of the Waldenses, published by J. P. Perrin in 1624, which he entitled 'Lvther's Fore rvnners,' and which he dedicated to the Earl of Pembroke, and in the 'Epistle Dedicatorie,' he requested his lordship's 'Honourable protection' for his work. In the dedication he says:

The reasons that embolden me to request this favour at your hands are principally these; First the loue you once bare to my honourable friend & deare cozen, Henry Lord Dacres of the South, the want of whom I feel the lesse, because I feel no want of loue in yourself towards me for his sake.

Although Henry's estates were so extensive, the life he led as a person of fashion seems to have been too costly a one for

---

[1] A poet of some note, and at one period in the retinue of the Earl of Pembroke.
[2] *Coll. Let.* ii. pp. 231, 257.

his income, and he appears to have suffered from that difficulty of living within his means which has pursued his descendants ever since. We have already seen that his father had become security for Henry's debts,[1] and later on the latter sold the manor of Northsted in Chelsfield, which had been part of his grandfather John's considerable Kent estates, to Lady Wolrich.[2] On June 6th, 1616, Henry conveyed the manors of Hautbois and Horsford in Norfolk to trustees, in order that they might sell the same so as to provide funds wherewith to discharge his liabilities.

At this period the manor of Horsford had a very narrow escape of being sold for the first time in its history. Henry consulted with his uncle Sir Samuel Lennard, of West Wickham, Kent, as to what price he should ask for it. Sir Henry Hobart appears to have been anxious to add Horsford to his St. Faith's estate, which it adjoined, and Sir Samuel writes that

seeing ye fines for ye copyholds are certaine & small & ye tenures by Knights service are almost all extinct, through the negligence of ye owners & their officers, I would think y^t twentie yeres purchase for ye present Rent of ye demesnes and tenants, and three yeres purchase for ye Improvem^t of Sir Dru Drurie's lease after 20 yeres, were a verie great Rate, wch would amount to 5148–7–0. ... I have sent your Lo. hereinclosed ye Inscription for my brother's Tombe wch I could wishe might be perused by my Lo. Byshop of St. Davids,[3] & so wth remembrance of my humble dutie I remaine alwaies

        Y^{or} Lo to be comanded
23° Novemb 1615.   SAMUEL LENNARD.

Edward Doyly, Lord Dacre's Norfolk agent, writes from Carrow Abbey, Norwich, on the 15th of the following month at considerable length on the subject of the proposed sale, and after narrating various points to be considered before arriving at a price says:

'Yf yor L$\overline{op}$ sett to hye a rate of the wholle yt ys a goode Fault, you may fale in yor P$\overline{ce}$ [price] & amend yt at yor

---

[1] *Ante*, p. 230.   [2] *Phil.* p. 111, and *H. K.* p. 71.
[3] Richard Milbourne, tr. to Carlisle. *Hay. Dig.*

Pleasure, but yf you be to lowe at the first, you can not wth credet ryse hyer.'

What, no doubt, saved Horsford from sale was the death of Henry, which took place in the month of August 1616, in his forty-eighth year. His wife did not long survive him, as she also died in the following month.[1] They were probably both carried off by some epidemic prevailing at that period, as Chamberlain wrote to Sir D. Carleton on August 24th, 1616, and says in the course of that letter: 'A new ague has appeared and Lord Dacre and others dead of it.'[2]

In 1861 there were exhibited, at a meeting of the Society of Antiquaries, inventories made on the death of Henry Lord Dacre of his personal effects in Chevening and Herstmonceux respectively. These inventories I have not been able to discover, but I take the following extract of their contents from the 'Journal' of the Society in question :—[3]

'Goods remayning & being in the house of Chiveninge in the County of Kent.'

First come the horses, of which the stock seems to have been small, which perhaps is accounted for by the statement immediately subjoined, that all the other geldings and 'naggs' were seized for heriots.

Then follows a list of

bedstids, canapyes, cushons, carpettes [meaning tablecloths], chairs, a newe seate, stooles, bedds, boulsters, pillows, flock bedds, hangings, ruggs, coverlids, blankets, tables, cupboards, joyned stooles, chests, presses, linen sheets, pillow beers, towells, bord cloths, napkins, cupboard cloths, dresser cloths, trencher cloths, diaper bord cloths, damaske˙ bord cloths, cupbord cloths, the silver plate, pewter vessels, brazen candlesticks, brass [pots &c.] iron stuffes, wooden wair, truncks, close stooles, a clock, hay, flax, yarn, &c.

One of the handsomest bedsteads is thus described :—

'Item one wainscot bedstedle, the testerne of stripte sattin of Bridges [Bruges] the vallence of the same beeinge fringed

---

[1] He was buried on August 9th, and she on September 30th.
[2] *S. P. Dom. Jac. I.* lxxxviii. No. 60.   [3] *P. S. A.* 2nd Series, ii. p. 32.

with silke. fringe, havinge fine watchet saie [1] curtens with matt and cord to the same being vallued and prised at xl^s.'

Several 'slope bedstedles,' 'trunk bedstidles,' and eleven 'livery bedstidles,' are mentioned.

'Item one old longe cushon of cloth of gold botkin with fower redd silke tassels to the same vallued & prised at x^s.'

Botkin is a late example of the use of the word 'baudekin' or 'bawdlekin,' which is frequently found in earlier inventories signifying an embroidered or brocaded silk fabric.

'Item two dornix curtens valued at iij^s iiij^d.'

Dornix (Tournay) frequently occurs in this inventory as the name of a stuff.

The 'carpetts' are of 'Turkey worke' for 'longe tables,' 'cupbord carpets,' carpets of 'green cloth,' 'needlework,' and 'dornix.'

Besides 'eleaven peeces of hangings of ymagery [2] vallued & prised at xlv^{li},' appear 'eighteen peeces of course varder [verdure] [3] hangings vallued & prised at iij^{li} vj^s viij^d.'

There were also five 'varder coverlets' valued at x^s.

The blankets consisted of 'Spanishe,' 'homemade,' and 'russet' [4] blankets.

'Item Lyvery cupbords [5] tenn vallued at xv^s.

'Item two chests with vyolls in them vallued & prised at ij^{li} xiij^s iiij^d.

'Item a clocke with a bell vallued at xxvj^s viij^d.'

The list of plate is a somewhat extensive one.

The Siluer Plate.

My Ladies Plate

Item one bason & ewer, two boyled meat dishes with my Ladies arms, two sallett dishes with my Ladies arms, two candlesticks, three potts with couers, one spowte pot with a

---

[1] 'Say,' a kind of silk or satin.—*C. D.*
[2] Or imagery, representation by images.—*Ibid.*
[3] Tapestry, in which scenery with trees or the like is the chief subject.—*Ibid.*
[4] Coarse cloth, often homespun.—*Ibid.*
[5] A stand with two or three shelves formerly used in the dining-room, on which the liveries (food, drink, &c.) intended for distribution were placed.—*Ibid.*

couer, fower porringers, one boate with two shells, and one suger box, one chafing dishe, one perfuming panne, one egg salte, one trencher salte, one pepper box, one ladle, one skywer, one tostinge forke, one grater, one pair of snuffers, five spoones with plaine handles, one little siluer bowle, two siluer plates with my Ladies Armes, one guilt cupp with a couer and a case for the same, one siluer pestle and morter all vallued and prised at lxvij^{li} vij^s.

My Lords Siluer Plate.

Item two siluer voyders,[1] three large guilded dishes, fower dishes of a lesser sort, tenn mutton dishes, tenn boyled meate dishes, two sallet dishes of the largest sort, eight sallet dishes, fiue saucers, two dozen of siluer plates, two dozen and fower siluer spoons, one large bason & ewer, two siluer candlesticks, two siluer bowles, one other bason and ewer, all vallued and prised at clxij^{li}.

Siluer plate in the pantry

Item one bason & ewer, two liuery potts, two colledge potts, three tankerds, fower bowles, tenn spoones, fower shells, fower candlesticks, two siluer salts all vallued & prised at lix^{li}.

The total value of the goods at Chevening was put at 550*l*. 5*s*. 10*d*.

In the case of the inventory at Herstmonceux the goods are enumerated according to the apartments of which they formed the furniture. These consisted of

The Hall, Parlor, Upper Parlor, my Lords Studdie, the lower Parlor Chamber, the Chamber where my Lord Richard Dacre laye, My Ladies closet, the next Chamber, the closet, my Lord Harrys Chamber, the Nurcery Chamber, the Stayerhead Chamber, the Ymbrodered Chamber, the With drawing Chamber, the Great Chamber, the Screene Lofte or Brushing roome, the Krimson Bedchamber, Best Chamber, Black bed Chamber, Music Chamber, Master Thomas Leonards Chamber, Yellow Chamber, Gate howse ditto, the five Chambers in the Yeomans howse, the Faulconers & Butlers Chambers, the Footman's Chamber, John Gardiner's Chamber, the Wardrobe,

---

[1] A voider was a tray or basket used for carrying away the remains of a meal, or for putting bones in before the use of forks was universal. It will be noticed that there is no mention of forks in this list.

the Bathing Chamber, the Plomery Chamber,[1] little ditto near the Gate, the Porters Lodge, the Gate house, the Spicery, the Still howse, the Butter howse, Wash howse, Milk howse, Brew howse, Kitchin, Bake howse and the Maides Chamber.

The list of plate was quite a short one :—

'16 pieces of plate guilte prised att lxxviij^{li}.'

The Hall contained (*inter alia*) 'fower peeces of Arras hanging cloth, one livery cupbord & turky carpett, one chair with three curtens of changeable silke, one paier of French virginalls with a frame,'[2] and 'certeyne picktures & mapps.'

In the 'Parlor' were 'two feather beds & a bedstead, fower peeces of Arras hanging clothe, two maps of heraldry, &c.'

The list of things in 'My Ladies Closett' is not without interest :—

Item one square table and divers sorts of glasses and some with stilled waters, some earthen and gally pots, some little pewter boxes, one stone morter, one allebaster morter, one little brasen pestle & morter, fower brass posnetts[3] or skillets,[4] one iron trevett, fower little boxes or little chests, one little still or limbeck, three bookes of accompt and certaine shelues, one hair sive, one little iron chain, all prised at xx^s.

In the 'Musick Chamber' were found 'one table, fower joyne stooles, seaven instruments of musick, one chest, one winde instrument or hoboie.'

Henry Lord Dacre was succeeded in the title and estates by his eldest son Richard, who was found by inquisition to be twenty years four months and eight days of age at the date of his father's death.[5]

Before considering any further Richard's career, it will be convenient to deal with what information I have been able to obtain concerning his two brothers.

---

[1] For the storing of plumes? Many plumes were associated with armour and civil costume.
[2] A spinet, or small harpsichord.—*C. D.*
[3] A small basin.
[4] A small vessel for cooking.
[5] The C. *P.*

Lord Dacre says[1] that Henry's two younger sons, Fynes and Edward, died without issue; and this statement appears in the printed pedigree to the folio edition of Collins's 'Peerage,' and in several of our MS. pedigrees. I have found no trace of Edward having been married; indeed, in all the pedigrees where I have seen him mentioned it appears as though he had died unmarried. The only references I have found to him are that he was admitted a member of Gray's Inn on November 26th, 1630, and that on June 25th, 1631, a license was given to 'Edward Lennard of Kent brother to the late Lord Dacres to travel for 3 years with 2 servants and £40 in money.'[2]

Edward was alive as late as October 1637, as documents in the Record Office[3] show that at this date he was engaged in a lawsuit respecting the manor of Burham, but I cannot say what was the date of his death.

In the case of Fynes Lennard I have found references to three of his children in two ancient MS. pedigrees which it is remarkable should have escaped the notice of Thomas Lord Dacre, and it is more strange still that he makes no reference to the following statements by Hasted and by Philipott. The former says that the manor of Burham, in Kent, was devised to Fynes, third son of Henry Lennard, Lord Dacre, by his father, and that this Fynes left issue a son Robert, who in the reign of Charles I. alienated the manor to Francis Barnham, of Hollingbourne;[4] while Philipott states that it was William, an elder brother of Robert, who had lately alienated it.[5] An inquest *post mortem*, taken at Maidstone September 24th, 1616, on the death of Henry Lord Dacre, shows that some months before his death he had settled on trustees the manor of Burham after his decease, as to one moiety on his second son Fynes and his heirs male, remainder to his third son Edward, and the other moiety on Edward, after he had attained seventeen years of age, and his heirs male, with remainder to his brother Fynes. The latter in April 1615

---

[1] *Ld. D. His.*
[2] *S. P. Dom. Chas. I.* cxcv. No. 5.
[3] *Chancery Pro. B. & A. Chas. I.* p. 56, No. 31.
[4] *Has.* ii. p. 161.
[5] *Phil.* 92.

obtained a license to travel for 3 years with 2 servants and £50.[1] Whether he married while on this trip I know not, but there is a mention of his children in the public records,[2] when in February 1647/8 William, Robert, and Mary Leonard (*sic*), children of this Fynes by his wife Mary, daughter of Prude, or Proude, of Canterbury, petitioned that they may be naturalised. The petitioners stated that, although born abroad, their parents were English, and that they had lived in this country from infancy and professed the Protestant religion, and their petition was granted. William and Robert were both beneficiaries under the will of their cousin, Francis Lord Dacre, which will was made in 1655, and Robert certainly was alive in 1677, as in the accounts of his cousin the Earl of Sussex in that year is an entry of a buck being sent to him.

From one of the MS. pedigrees above mentioned we learn that William had a son named after him, who died without issue, and that Robert had two daughters, who also died without issue. I have the following letter from Fynes Lennard to a Mr. Field, who was a steward at Herstmonceux, and to whose account book I shall draw attention later, which shows that the writer, like many of his family, was a keen sportsman. Why he should have required a pass for his 'houndes' is not clear. It sounds as if it were a license which might have been required a few years ago, when Mr. Walter Long, for the purpose of stamping out rabies, was putting so many obstructions in the way of dog owners :—

Deare Mr. Feilde

should I not render thankes to him I haue alwayes found soe true a frende, being I am noe otherwayse able to requite ȳr loue. I were not worthy of memory, but I hope thise shall make you an assurance both of my well wishes, and thankes to you for my houndes ; but as you were most carefull soe I am most unfortunate, for Carleton having not gott a passe for them, my man brought me noe more as three couple, and one of the best

---

[1] *Docket Book to Signet Bills.* Record Office.
[2] *Hist. Com.* vii. p. 10.

obtained a license to travel for 3 years with 2 servants and £50.[1] Whether he married while on this trip I know not, but there is a mention of his children in the public records;[2] when in February 1643 William, Robert, and Mary Leonard (*sic*), children of this Pynes by his wife Mary, daughter of Prude, or Proude, of Canterbury, petitioned that they may be naturalised. The petitioners stated that, although born abroad, their parents were English, and that they had lived in this country from infancy and professed the Protestant religion, and their petition was granted. William and Robert were both beneficiaries under the will of their cousin, Francis Lord Dacre, which will was made in 1615, and Robert certainly was alive in 1677, as in the accounts of his cousin the Earl of Sussex in that year is an entry of a buck being sent to him.

From one of the MS. pedigrees above mentioned we learn that William had a son named after him, who died without issue, and that Robert had two daughters, who also died without issue. I have the following letter from Fynes Lennard to a Mr. Fissit, who was a steward at Herstmonceux, and to whose account book I shall draw attention later, which shows that the writer, like many of his family, was a keen sportsman. Why he should have required a pass for his "bounties" is not clear. It sounds as if it were a licence which might have been required a few years ago, when Mr. Walter Long saw the purpose of examining his game, was putting so many obstructions in the way of ———

Dear Mr. Fissit,

Should I not render thankes to him I haue alwayes found soe true a frende. Being I am not otherwayse able to requite y'r loue. I were not worthy of memory, but I hope thise shall make you an assurance both of my well wishes, and thankes to you for your bountis: but we you were most carefull soe am most unfortunate, for Carleton hauing not gott a passe for them, my man brought me noe more as three cuple, and one of the best

---

[1] *Docket Book to signed Bills.* Rec. ——
[2] *Hist. Com.* XII. p. 10.

was lost at London, the other three couple I here Hemsley that dwells in Southwarke hath, and did I not dayly expect going into the feilde, I would send my man on purpose over for them an [1] a horse or two, but if I can I will see Sussex for a month or lesse when wee returne, els I will send my man to Hemsley. I have writte to Carleton about itt. Pray forgett not my loue to my Brother and Sister Parker[2] and lett her know if I come 'tis only to see her. I here my father Knoles is dead which I am hartely sorry for, God receave his soule.[3] if you will honor me with some lines Carleton or Mabs can send dayly to me. I shall not fayle to remember you ere itt be long, by the first convenient messenger with a couple of hatts, soe with my loue and prayer for you I rest

                                  Your faythfull freinde
May the 4th, 1634.   FIENES LENNARDE.
   Deosborgh.[4]

Pray if you see Hemsley tell him I hope he wilbe soe honest as when I send my man on purpose to lett me haue my Dogs I can but pay for the Keeping.

I have been able to find out no more than this about Henry Lennard's younger sons. My information about his heir Richard is also somewhat meagre. That he was living at Herstmonceux in 1617 is shown by a letter from Monsieur de Tourval, dated in July of that year, in which the writer mentions that he is going to pay a visit to Lord Dacre in Sussex.[5]

In the following November, within two years of his father's death, Richard concurred with the trustees in selling the manor of Hautbois in Norfolk for 900*l*. We have a deed dated May 5th in the following year (1618) which, after reciting that Lord Dacre had paid his debts or most of them, goes on to convey to him from the trustees the manor of Horsford, which, as has been stated,

---

   [1] Obsolete form of 'and.'—*C. D.*

   [2] Fienes's sister, Philadelphia, married Sir Thomas Parker, of Ratton, Willingdon, Sussex.

   [3] I cannot suggest to whom the writer refers.

   [4] Query, Desborough in Northamptonshire. If so, the writer may possibly have been on a visit to the Thomas Lennard of that county.—*Ante*, p. 3.

   [5] *S. P. Dom. Jac. I.* xcii. No. 107.

his father had conveyed to them, together with that of Hautbois, in order to provide means of paying his debts.

Richard rebuilt his house at Chevening from designs by Inigo Jones;[1] but that celebrated architect's design was greatly altered, and not for the better, by the first and the third Earls of Stanhope.

Richard's first wife was Elizabeth, third daughter of Sir Arthur Throckmorton, of Paulerspurie, Northamptonshire, son of Sir Nicholas, Queen Elizabeth's celebrated minister.

Elizabeth Throkmorton

We have a deed dated October 29th, 44th Eliz. (1602), by which Sir Arthur settled all his various estates, which were considerable, upon Sir Walter Raleigh (he signs this deed 'W. Ralegh'), Sir Edward Wotton and two others as trustees. The scheme of this deed of trust was to settle all Sir Arthur's estates upon himself for life, remainder to his wife during widowhood, with remainders to Sir Arthur's four daughters and his brother, in certain specified portions. The share of Elizabeth was to be the manors of Cosgrave (Cosgrove?) and Tighefield (Tiffield?) in Northamptonshire. The deed reserved to Sir Arthur a power of revocation, and this power he no doubt exercised. We have another settlement by Sir Arthur upon his family, dated 1610, which recites the revocation of previous deeds of settlement; this deed is signed by his three unmarried daughters in very bold signatures. From these two deeds, and from the recitals they contain of other deeds, it is clear that Sir Arthur was addicted to making settlements on his family, and subsequently exercising those powers of revocation which those deeds of settlement contained.

From the following extract of a letter quoted by Lord Dacre,[2] which was written in 1613 by Sir Henry Wotton to

---

[1] *Arch.* C. xvi. 128. [2] *Ld. D. Mis.*

Sir Arthur Throckmorton, the latter's daughters appear to have been unusually good-looking, so much so as to have attracted the King's attention. Sir Henry's object in writing this letter was to induce Sir Arthur to come to Court, in order to be present on the occasion of the marriage of the Princess Elizabeth to the Elector Palatine, and he concludes thus :—

I will add to these Arguments that, out of your own Store at home, you may very much increase the beauty of this Assembly ; and your daughters shall not need to provide any great splendour of Cloathing because they can supply that with a better contribution, as hath been well authenticated even by the King's own testimony of them. For though I am no longer an Ambassador, yet I am not so bankrupt of Intelligence, but that I have heard of those rural Passages.

The marriage of Richard to Elizabeth no doubt took place in June 1618, as I have their marriage settlement which is dated the 1st of that month. By this settlement Sir Arthur undertook to pay to Richard the sum of 3,000*l.* within one month of the marriage, and a further sum of 1,000*l.* within three months of the birth of the first child of that marriage. On his part Richard agreed to settle upon his wife, as a jointure, his estates in Cambridgeshire and Chevening in Kent; and he covenanted to leave her at his decease that house for her life, properly furnished. This eventuality, however, never arose, as Elizabeth died during her husband's lifetime—I think, almost certainly, from the result of childbirth. My reasons for saying this is that she was buried at Chevening on February 19th, $162\frac{1}{2}$, the same day as her son Henry was baptized.[1] Elizabeth, during her short married life, bore her husband no less than four sons :—

Francis, born May 1619.
Richard, baptized April 24th and buried 25th, 1620.
Thomas, baptized March 8th, $162\frac{0}{1}$.
Henry, baptized February 19th, $162\frac{1}{2}$, buried August 16th, 1624.[2]

[1] *Ch. Reg.*   [2] *Ibid.*

There are the following references to Richard in the 'State Calendars':—

In December 1620, upon inquiry made as to who had paid the contribution to the Palatinate, Lord Dacre said that he had done so;[1] and on March 25th, 1626,[2] there is mention of a 'Grant to Richard Lord Dacre, Thos. Letsome and Nicholas Page[3] of a privilege for making steele for 14 years invented & perfected by Letsome by the charge of Lord Dacre & assistance of Page being the first inventor thereof.'

In the Herstmonceux household account book there is an incidental reference to a 'steele forge' which probably was near that castle, and possibly the scene of this trio's attempts to become successful ironmasters. We know that there was an iron working on the estate nearly a hundred years earlier in 1574, as a return was made of the owners of ironworks in the counties of Surrey, Sussex, and Kent; and amongst these there is this entry, 'The Lord Dacres 1 fordg 1 furnace in Buckholt in the bandes of Jeffreys.'[4]

After a few years of widowerhood Richard married at St. Giles, Cripplegate, in January 162$\frac{4}{5}$,[5] his second wife, Dorothy North; a very clever and attractive young woman, then twenty years of age, the daughter of Dudley Lord North. John Chamberlain, the news-letter writer, in a letter to Sir D. Carlton, dated December 18th, 1624, mentions the approaching marriage, and says that it is 'no great preferment for so fine a gentlewoman to have a widower with 2 or 3 sons at least.'[6]

I have a draft of the settlement proposed to be made upon the occasion of this marriage, which is dated January 3rd, 22nd Jas. (1624-5). From this document it appears that Dorothy brought her husband a fortune of 2,500*l.*, and that he settled upon her for jointure a life interest in certain quit-rents,

---

[1] *S. P. Dom. Jac. I.* cxviii. No. 57.   [2] *S. P. Dom. Chas. I.*, Docquets.
[3] This man Page attested the codicil that Richard made to his will.
[4] *S. Arch.* iii. 241.   [5] The C. P.
[6] *D. N. B.* sub tit. North. Cf. *S. P. Dom. Jac. I.* clxxvi. No. 65.

There are the following references to Richard in the 'State Calendars':—

In December 1620, upon inquiry made as to who had paid the contribution to the Palatinate, Lord Dacre said that he had done so;[1] and on March 25th, 1626,[2] there is mention of a 'Grant to Richard Lord Dacre, Thos. Letsome and Nicholas Page[3] of a privilege for making steele for 14 years invented & perfected by Letsome by the charge of Lord Dacre & assistance of Page being the first inventor thereof.'

In the Herstmonceux household account book there is an incidental reference to a 'steele forge' which probably was near that castle, and possibly the scene of this trio's attempts to become successful ironmasters. We know that there was an iron working on the estate nearly a hundred years earlier in 1574, as a return was made of the owners of ironworks in the counties of Surrey, Sussex and Kent; and amongst these there is this entry, 'The Lord Dacres : fordg 1 furnace in Buckholt in the handes of Jeffreys.'

After a few years of … and Richard married at St. Giles, Cripplegat … wife, Dorothy North; a very clever and attractive young widow, then twenty years … the daughter of … John Chamber… dated … marriage, and … so fine a gentlewoman … to be made upon the occasion of … dated January 3rd, 22nd Jas. (1624-5). … appears that Dorothy brought her husb … of 2,500*l*., and that he settled upon her for jointure … terest in certain quit-rents,

---

[1] *S. P. Dom. Jac. I.* cxviii. No. …   *S. P. Dom. Chas. I.*, Docquets.
[2] This man Page attested the counsil that Richard made to his will.
[3] *S. Arch.* iii. 241.
[4] *D. N. B.* sub tit. North. *S. P. Dom. Jac. I.* clxxvi No. 65.

lands, and messuages in Cudham and Brasted, Kent; and among other provisions in the settlement was one giving to her, her tenants and assigns, a right to fell and take wood and underwood growing on these premises for 'fyerboote, houseboote, ploughboote, carteboote, hedgeboote, palebootes, and other bootes.'[1]

For the reasons I give later[2] I believe that the marriage settlement proposed to be made on Dorothy by Lord Dacre was altered, and that Chevening mansion-house was settled upon her for life.

The settlement of Brasted was not carried out until March 8th, 162$\frac{4}{5}$, about two months after this marriage, as I have a deed of that date made between Richard Lord Dacre and Sir Francis Barnham (his uncle by marriage) of the first part, and Dudley Lord North and Sir Dudley North of the other part, by which, after reciting the marriage settlement of the previous January, and that the marriage had taken place, Sir Francis assigns and grants the said manor of Brasted upon the trusts of the settlement.

Richard Lord Dacre and Dorothy had issue a son Richard, who was baptized at Herstmonceux on May 7th, 1626,[3] and a daughter Catherine, who married Chaloner Chute the younger, son of Chaloner Chute, of Sutton Court, and afterwards of the Vyne. It is probable that Dorothy did all she could to persuade her husband to settle property upon her children by him, and, as far as her son Richard is concerned, she was successful; as, when Richard the younger was barely five years old, Richard his father was induced to make a provision for him, and accordingly, in February 16$\frac{29}{30}$, he settled his Norfolk estate of Horsford on Thomas, his second son, and other trustees, to hold the same for ninety-nine years from Michaelmas 1647 (which would be when Richard the son would attain his majority), in

---

[1] 'Boote,' properly 'bote,' in old law, an allowance of necessaries for repair or support, *e.g.* fire-bote, enough wood for fuel; house-bote, enough wood to repair a house, &c.—*C. D.*

[2] *Post*, pp. 263-5, 307-8.   [3] Parish Register.

trust for himself for life, remainder for raising a convenient jointure for such lady as his third son, Richard the younger, might marry, and for providing a portion of 4,000*l*. for this son's daughters, if he should die without issue male.

Apparently not satisfied with this arrangement, on April 30th following Richard Lord Dacre had another settlement drawn up. The parties to this deed were, besides himself, his son Richard, his two elder sons Francis and Thomas, and also his brothers-in-law Sir William Brook and Sir Thomas Parker. By this document Horsford was settled on Lord Dacre for life, remainder to his son Richard and his heirs male, with remainder over to his brothers, but by the accident of 'company beinge then wth him' this deed was never executed, as 'he commanded his servant to bringe the deed for him to settle at another tyme this beinge in Kent from whence he not longe after went into Sussex and died, and soe was prevented frm̄ sealinge the saide deede.' It is, I think, worth calling attention to, the unusual occurrence of minors, as these sons of Richard then were, being parties to a deed.

It is fortunate for me that Dorothy's influence was so strong, as but for her Horsford would no doubt in course of time have gone to Richard's grandson Thomas, and by him have been sold, and the proceeds squandered in play, as were the rest of the Lennard and Dacre properties.

Although it is somewhat anticipating events, it may perhaps be conveniently mentioned here that from the last-mentioned settlement Richard did not reap the benefits that his parents intended without being obliged to have recourse to legal proceedings. His eldest brother Francis repudiated the last settlement on the grounds that it was never executed, and that his brother had already been sufficiently provided for. However, at last a compromise was effected, and in consideration of Richard giving up any claim he might have to certain property in Kent, his brother conveyed Horsford by a deed, dated August 1645, to Dudley Lord North and Sir Dudley North in trust for Richard and his heirs in tail male.

The death of Richard Lord Dacre, which took place on August 19th or 20th, was the result of some sudden illness, and feeling himself about to die, and there being no time to summon legal assistance, he made a codicil by word of mouth which he delivered to Sir W. Brook, the husband of his sister Pembroke, who chanced to be then staying at Herstmonceux. The Herstmonceux Register records Richard's funeral as taking place there on August 21st, 1630, and probate of his will was granted on the 30th of that month to Sir Francis Barnham, his executor.

His will, dated November 25th, 1624, or only a few weeks before his second marriage, begins with the usual declaration of faith and recommendation of his soul to heaven, which was still 'common form' in wills of those times. Richard then made provision for the portion of his youngest sister Barbara, which seems strange, as it might be supposed that she had been already provided for by his father; he left 1,500*l.* to his son Thomas, to be paid to him at the age of two-and-twenty; to his brother Fynes an annuity of 50*l.*; and he entreats his 'most faithful friend & loving uncle Sir Francis Barnham Knight to be a suitor for the wardship of my son who shall be my heir to whom, as much as in me is, I commit the education of my sons.' He appointed his two brothers-in-law, Sir William Brook and Sir Thomas Parker, and his cousin, Sir Samson Darell,[1] overseers of his will; and to every one of them, as a small token of his great love, a piece of plate of twenty nobles. A noble was a coin, then obsolete, worth 6*s.* 8*d.*, so that these legacies were worth less than 7*l.* each.

The will goes on to devise to his heir at common law all his lands at Herstmonceux, Old Court, Gotham, and Baylee, whereof he was seised in fee-tail; 'that thereby my dread Sovereign Lord the King's Majesty may be satisfied such duties as by my death shall belong unto him well assuring myself that the same are a full third part of all my hereditaments'; and he devised

---

[1] No doubt a descendant of his great-aunt Ann.

all his lands in Kent, Sussex, Lincolnshire, Cambridgeshire, and Norfolk to his eldest son and his heirs.

To this will there is added the codicil which is stated to have been expressed and declared by him by parole on Thursday, August 19th, 1630, at Herstmonceux, in his sickness whereof he died, his written will not being then there, which codicil was written after his death, and followeth in these words :—

My Lord called Sir William Brook unto him & said to him I give to my son Richard the lease of Aldermaston, and the stock upon it, and said more 'Will Brook I have noe friend here but you, my sonne is a child. I desire he should pay fifty pounds a year to this poor man' (speaking of Mr. Reginald Dacre [1]) 'during his life.' Item, he expresses & said my desire is that there should be 3,000*l.* raised for the portion of my daughter, by my uncle Barnham, as he thought fit. Item, he said now I give to my wife all the plate which is marked with my arms & hers, and her Chamber Cupbord plate, and after the decease of my Aunt Lennard [2] for the bettering of her jointure I give unto her that land which should come unto me for the bettering of her daughters portion. Item, he said now to Sir William Brook, you owe me 1,700*l.*, my will is it should go towards my sister Barbara her portion, and there is in my trunk money to make it up, and the rest which remaineth therein I give to my wife.

This is an instance of an informal codicil expressed when the testator was on the point of death, and reduced to writing

---

[1] Lord Dacre says in his *History*, 'Who this person was there remains a doubt, but by his Christian as well as surname it seems that he was somehow descended from the old Lords Dacre, and he appears to have been protected by this Richard Lord Dacre. It is probable, however, that Sir W. Brook mistook his Christian name, and that this person was Ranulph Dacre, last heir male of the Lords Dacre of the North; for he, amongst others, is witness, half a year before, of a settlement then made by my Lord of the Manor of Horsford, signing "Ranulphe Dacre." [I have not discovered this deed.—*T. B. L.*] In the parish register of Greystock, where he was buried, there is such a mistake, for therein he is named "Randal Dacre, Esq., last heir male of the Lords Dacre of the North."'

[2] I am at a loss to say who this aunt could have been, unless it was the widow of his uncle Gregory; but she had married Mr. Wroth as her second husband some years before this date.—*Ante*, p. 241.

after that event had taken place, being admitted to probate. Francis disputed his stepmother's claim under the codicil to the reversion of his great-aunt Lennard's estate, and from several little pieces of somewhat negative evidence I am inclined to think that the relations existing between Dorothy Lady Dacre and her stepson Francis were always strained. Sir William Brook was evidently worthy of the trust that his dying brother-in-law reposed in him, as by writing down Richard's words he put on record the fact that he owed him 1,700*l.*

Lord Dacre was also fortunate in having so kind and conscientious an uncle, by marriage, as Sir Francis Barnham proved himself to be, as he undertook the guardianship of Richard's two sons, Francis and Thomas, whom he brought up at his seat named Broughton, near Maidstone, and had them educated by a private tutor.[1]

I have discovered very little about Richard's second son Thomas. He succeeded, as we have seen,[2] in 1638 to the property of his godfather and great-uncle Thomas; he also had the Cambridgeshire property at Weston Colville, probably as a younger son's portion, and some little land in Sussex. This appears from some accounts drawn out in $167\frac{1}{5}$, some two years after his death; the object of these accounts was to show the total estate to which his nephew, also named Thomas (who, at the period these accounts were made up, had been created Earl of Sussex), was entitled upon his coming of age. Thomas's Cambridgeshire property produced then 202*l.* 10*s.* a year, and his lands in Sussex 65*l.* a year; the Earl of Sussex became entitled to these estates of his uncle, but subject to such heavy charges—viz. 4,800*l.* and two annuities of 20*l.* each—that there could have been very little margin of value in them. This Thomas does not appear to have ever married, and at some period subsequent to 1662 he was living at Chichester.[3] The

[1] Letter from Sir T. Rider (a descendant of Sir Francis) at Boughton to Thomas Lord Dacre, dated March 23rd, 1760.

[2] *Ante*, p. 242.

[3] Papers in action brought by Elizabeth Lady Dacre against her husband' executors, where Thomas is described as of Chichester.—*F. P.*

household account book of Herstmonceux shows that anyhow, from 1643 to 1649, during his elder brother's lifetime, he lived very much with him at that mansion, as among the strangers recorded as staying there 'Mr. Thomas Lennard and his 2 men,' and sometimes his '3 men,' is a very frequent entry; and he was on such affectionate terms with his brother Lord Dacre that the latter appointed him an executor of his will and guardian of his eldest son Thomas, afterwards Earl of Sussex. His burial is recorded in the Herstmonceux Register as having taken place on October 5th, 1672.

Pepys says that on February 10th, 16$\frac{59}{60}$,[1] he found at his office Mr. 'Lenard,' one of the clerks of the Council, and that he took him to the Swan and gave him his morning draft. This Mr. 'Lenard' may well have been the Thomas in question; if not he was probably some relative, as at that period a very large number of public appointments were filled by the younger sons of those families who possessed influence at Court.

The only letter we have from this Thomas shows that he had that devotion to sport which characterised so many members of his family. The letter was written to his half-brother Richard, who had assumed the name of Barrett, after Lord Newburgh's death, which had taken place in January 1645.

[Addressed] To his euer honoured and deare brother Richard Barett Esquier. these.

Derest Brother

I haue receaued by your man the [watch?] and allso apayer of pliers, for which I must remaine your debtor, and I haue sent backe to you your nagg, but not soe fatt as I could haue wished him, the reason is the yeare was to farr spent when he was sent downe to bee fatted in the marsh, but as longe as you meane to ridde him all this winter, and keepe him in the stabell, he will thriue the better for his not beeing so fatt, after amounths beeing in the house you shall doe mightie well to take some bloude from him. I am now hard a hunting euerie day with my littell doggs, which geue mee much sport, and I am onely unhappie not inioiyng your good companie. I shall not

[1] *P. D.* i. 51.

fayle god willing of waighting one my Noble Mother,[1] my deare Sister, and your selfe, att Christmas, if noe accident happen out to hinder me the contrarie, (whose most humble seruant I am) and all for yours remaining your most affectionat brother, and seruant, to bee commanded as longe as I am

THOMAS LENNARD.

Oct. 17th, 1650.

Bee pleased to present my humble dutie to my Noble Mother, and my Loue to my deare Sister.

It is unfortunate that Thomas did not address this letter more fully; had he done so we should have known where the Dowager Lady Dacre and her son and daughter were then living. Inasmuch as she married her second husband at Chevening Church some ten days after the date of the above letter, she was probably at that time living at the Hall there, and her two children were probably living there also. I feel sure that Dorothy Lady Dacre (Richard's widow) lived a very large portion of the sixty-eight years which elapsed between her own death, and that of her first husband, at his seat of Chevening.

I have seen it stated that for many years after the death of Richard Lord Dacre his widow lived at Kirtling with her brother, Lord North,[2] and this may have been the case; but I am inclined to think that Chevening was settled on her for life. We have seen that Richard Lord Dacre made such a settlement on his first wife; I have not found the perfected settlement which he made on Dorothy, but only a draft of an *intended* settlement, which may, quite likely, have been modified in her favour.[3] Moreover, we shall see later that in 1677 the Earl of Sussex paid some Lady Dacre—no doubt his grandfather's second wife Dorothy—rent for Chevening at the rate of a little over 200*l.* a year.

On October 28th, 1650, when about the age of forty-five, Dorothy Lady Dacre married, as his second wife, Chaloner Chute, of Sutton Court, Chiswick. I have already said

---

[1] His step-mother. [2] Third Baron North.—*D. N. B.*
[3] *Cf. Hist. Com.* xiv. Part vi. p. 319.

that Catherine, Lady Dacre's daughter by her first husband, married Chaloner, the son of this Mr. Chute by his first wife. I have not been able to discover the date of her daughter's marriage, but no doubt the earlier marriage, whichever it was, was the indirect cause of the subsequent one. Mr. Chute purchased that well-known house, the Vyne, in Hampshire, in 1653, and later on became Speaker of the House of Commons.

Dorothy Lady Dacre's married career with her second husband was not a very long one, as he died in 1659. During the years immediately succeeding her second marriage Dorothy probably did not live much at Chevening. We know that in each of the years 1657 and 1659 Francis Lord Dacre had a child christened in the church there.

As we shall see, sometime between 1653-9 her son Richard offered to lend Belhus to her and Mr. Chute, which offer they accepted, and furnished that house. Lady Dacre certainly spent the summer of 1664 there, as is shown by a letter to Richard from an agent.

Mr. Chute's son, Chaloner the younger, died in 1666, leaving three sons, Chaloner, Edmund (or Edward), and Thomas, and one daughter, Elizabeth.

I have not been able to discover when his wife Catherine died; I have found no mention of her in any letter or legal document, but I imagine she died before her husband, or very shortly after his death.

Dorothy Lady Dacre became guardian to her daughter's children, and managed the Vyne estates for several years. About 1677 she became engaged in a fiercely contested lawsuit with her eldest grandson Chaloner, concerning a sum of money left her by her late husband, Mr. Chute, and charged upon the Vyne.[1] This action brought up the whole question of her management of the Vyne estates during her grandson's minority; and so angry did Lady Dacre become with him that she constantly spoke of him as that 'Villianous Viper.'

In 1683 her granddaughter, Dorothy Barrett, stayed most of

---

[1] *Hist. Com.* xi. Part ii. pp. 152 *et seq.*

that winter with Lady Dacre at Chevening, and it was here too that another granddaughter of hers, Anne Barrett, married in 1688, while staying with her grandmother.

Another granddaughter, Elizabeth Chute, lived with Lady Dacre until the marriage of the former, which took place at Chevening on June 16th, 1691, to Charles Cotterell, widower.[1]

From the contents of some of his letters I feel sure that Lady Dacre's favourite grandson, Thomas Chute, lived with her also from the time that she left the Vyne. The christening of his eldest son as 'Thomas Lennard' took place at Chevening Church on July 20th, 1688, the Earl of Sussex being one of his godfathers, and his great-grandmother Dorothy his godmother. The christenings at Chevening of one more son and two daughters of Thomas Chute are also recorded in the register of that parish. No doubt at some period of her life Dorothy Lady Dacre had a house in London; she certainly had one there in 1696, as Roger North, writing to her that year, addresses his letter to her 'at her house in Bedford Walk neare Grays Inn London.'[2]

In her will Lady Dacre speaks of her house, 'which is called Chevening Place.' She was buried in the church of that parish on April 21st, 1698, and the register says of her, 'aged 93 years.'[3] From this somewhat circumstantial evidence I imagine that she lived at Kirtling and Chevening, from the date of her first husband's death until after her second marriage; that then for a time she allowed her step-son, Francis Lord Dacre, to live at the latter place, either having lent him the house or else as tenant, while she lived at Sutton, the Vyne, and also sometimes at Belhus. After 1666 she probably lived at the Vyne for more than ten years, and during some of this time let Chevening to the Earl of Sussex.

After the litigation with her grandson Chaloner she went back to Chevening and lived there, with occasional visits to her

---

[1] Sir Charles Lodowick Cotterell, eldest son of Sir Charles; he was Master of the Ceremonies, and was knighted February 168$\frac{8}{9}$; he died 1710.—*D. N. B.* and *Ch. Reg.*
[2] *Jess.* iii. p. 239. [3] *Ch. Reg.*

house in London, until the time of her death, having Thomas Chute, his wife, and children living with her.

Dorothy was possessed of very great energy and strength of character, and was in many ways a remarkable woman. She took the keenest interest in the doings of her descendants down to the last; and in the closing years of her life she exerted herself greatly to bring about a reconciliation between Dacre and his father, and after the latter's death between Dacre and his sisters.

Although Lady Dacre lived to an age so advanced as to see her step-great-granddaughter, Lady Barbara Lennard, attain the age of twenty-one years, she died in full possession of her faculties.

CHAPTER IV

FRANCIS LENNARD, LORD DACRE, AND THOMAS LENNARD EARL OF SUSSEX.

FRANCIS LENNARD, the eldest son of Richard Lord Dacre, according to the 'Complete Peerage,' was aged eleven years three months and eight days at the death of his father; and as the latter died on August 19th, 1630, that would make Francis to have been born on May 11th, 1619. According to the custom of those times he was sent to Oxford at an age which to modern ideas would have been more suitable to school than college, as he matriculated at Merton on October 15th, 1634, when only fifteen years of age.[1] He was fortunate in coming into a considerable property from his maternal grandfather before his father's death, as is shown by an inquisition taken at Shipston, Worcestershire, on March 30th, 3rd of Charles I. (1627), where it was found that Sir A. Throckmorton died June 21st, 1626, that his daughter Elizabeth was one of his co-heirs, and that Francis, as her son and heir, was entitled to a fourth part of his grandfather's inheritance—viz. the fourth part of the manor of Paulerspurie, and fourth of the manor of Silvester, in Worcestershire, and of divers lands in Northamptonshire, Bucks, and Oxon.

While Francis was still a minor he became entitled also to considerable possessions in the north of England in a very remarkable manner. Among our papers is an opinion of counsel signed 'Heneage ffinche,' no doubt the future celebrated Lord Chancellor, the Earl of Nottingham, or else his father Sir Heneage. The document is not dated, and the opinion is

[1] *F. A. O.*

written on a scrap of paper which consists merely of a very short opinion of counsel in favour of some claimant, who from the context appears to have been Francis Lord Dacre, and the claim to have been to some of the Dacre estates in the north.

Randolf, or Ranulph, Dacre, the last male representative of the Dacres of the North, died in the parish of St. Dunstan in Fleet Street, London, on December 10th, 1634;[1] and it was thereupon claimed on behalf of Francis Lennard that the large Dacre estates in Cumberland and Westmoreland should descend to him in virtue of the award made by Edward IV. in 1473. It will be remembered that Sir Richard Fynes did not obtain his wife's title and possessions without great disputes with her uncle, Sir Humphrey Dacre, and that upon the matter being referred to the King, he made an award which was in the nature of a compromise.[2] As regards those estates in the north, which he decreed were to go to Sir Humphrey, he directed that there was to be an ultimate remainder to the heirs of the grandfather of Joan Dacre, Sir Richard's wife, in the event of the male issue of Sir Humphrey becoming extinct.

It must be a most unusual occurrence for a remainder, contingent on the extinction of all the males of a particular branch, to take effect nearly two hundred years after it was created, and should serve as an object-lesson to persons interested in the future of their posterity never to forget in making wills or settlements, that remainders, however remote they may appear when created, do sometimes take effect in a most unexpected manner.

There is, however, a great difference between being entitled to property and absolutely obtaining possession of it, as Francis was to find to his cost. In order to understand his difficulties in this respect it is necessary to consider briefly the latter history of the Dacres of the North.

Thomas Lord Dacre of the North, great-grandson of Sir Humphrey Lord Dacre, died October 10th, 1566, leaving one son, George, and three daughters—Anne, Mary and Elizabeth.

[1] 'Brief for the Lord Dacre.'—*F. P.* [2] *Ante*, p. 173.

His widow Elizabeth, daughter of Sir Francis Leyburne of Cunswick, co. Westmoreland, married soon after his death, Thomas Duke of Norfolk,[1] who became guardian of her children. George Lord Dacre stayed some time at Thetford with the Duke, and the latter finding that the climate agreed well with the boy, when he went away, left him there under the care of Sir Richard Fulmerston, who was an intimate acquaintance of the Duke's, and lived at the monastery of the Black Nuns in Thetford, of which he had obtained a grant at the time of the dissolution. There was a long gallery in the monastery in which this young Lord Dacre met his death, and where Blomfield says in his time

they pretended to show you the blood of an unhappy youth who was here slain by a fall from a wooden horse that he used to vault or ride on, which they tell you Sir Richard was designedly the cause of, by having the pins of one of the wheels taken out for that purpose, in order that at his death he might enjoy his estate; and this is the occasion of the frightful stories among the Vulgar of that Knight's appearing so often to the terror of many: But 'tis mere fiction for the spots on the wall were nothing more than is seen on many plasterings.[2]

No doubt young Lord Dacre died here at the age of eight years, on May 17th, 1569, but there seems to have been no proof that he met with foul play, and Blomfield discredits that portion of the story altogether, which he declares to have been an invention of Leonard Dacre, the boy's uncle.

Upon the death of George, his sisters became co-heiresses to such large estates,[3] that the Duke of Norfolk, thinking it a pity that wards so rich should marry strangers, lost but little time in getting them all married to his three sons. His eldest son, Philip Earl of Arundel, married in 1571, when he was

---

[1] She died in childbed on September 4th, 1567, and was buried at Kenninghall, co. Norfolk.—The C. P.

[2] *Blom.* i. 434. The long gallery was pulled down more than one hundred years ago, and what remains of the monastery has been converted into a racehorse stable.

[3] In an ancient petition of Francis Dacre, dated 1626, he speaks of these estates being worth from five to six thousand pounds per annum.—*F. P.*

twelve years old, Anne, the eldest of the sisters, then seventeen years of age, who, surviving her husband, died in April 1630.[1] His second son, Thomas, afterwards Earl of Suffolk, married Mary, who died in April 1578, aged only fourteen;[2] and his third son, Lord William, married Elizabeth. Anne brought her husband Greystock Castle and other lands as her moiety of the large Dacre estates, while Lord William, in his wife's right, became possessed of Naworth Castle and other lands as her moiety.

In those days bloodshed and perversion of justice were so frequently committed with impunity by persons in influential positions, that I do not feel so sure as Blomfield was that there is not some truth in the tradition of young George's death being brought about at the instigation of the powerful Duke in order that he might secure these large estates for his own sons.

As soon as Lord Dacre's death became known, his uncle, Leonard Dacre, laid claim to the title and possessions, and appeared before the 'Councell at York' to make it good.[3] Leonard's claim rested largely on the award of Edward IV., and this he was unable to produce, and he alleged that the Duke had seized, and carried away to his house in Norfolk, all the Dacre evidences in order to prevent him from proving his right to the estates, which had he been enabled to do so, the Duke's sons would have been obliged to surrender to him. The award was very probably in duplicate—we have one among our family papers, no doubt the one delivered to Sir Richard Fynes, which, as is proved by the endorsement on the back, was produced on January 23rd, 1601, in order to support the claim of Margaret, wife of Samson Lennard, to the title of Dacre of the South. Had Leonard Dacre been able to produce this document, the course of his whole life and the fortunes of his branch of the family would probably have been entirely different; as it

---

[1] Notes of Inquisition on her death.—*F. P.*   [2] The C. *P.*
[3] Ancient document headed 'The accidentall delaies hindering the profe of the Lord William Dacres Intail,' and endorsed, 'Howe Francis Daker went from all his lande.'—*L. P.* vol. iv.

was, he was not allowed to assume the barony to which he was entitled, nor was he able to obtain possession of his estates.

It has been said that the Queen's minister, Cecil, being anxious to detach the Duke of Norfolk from the confederacy of the Border Barons,

offered Norfolk his influence to have the lawsuit about the Dacre inheritance settled in his favour. Norfolk accepted the offer, and a legal decision was given against Leonard Dacre on July 19. This had the effect of separating Norfolk from the northern Lords, who all sided with their neighbour Dacre.[1]

The descendant of a race of fighting Border chiefs, Leonard was not the man to tamely submit to being cheated out of his inheritance by Court intrigues, and, smarting under his injuries, he formed a scheme of raising a rebellion and rescuing Mary Queen of Scots. He seized the family castle of Naworth, and raised a body of 3,000 men, but his ill-armed and ill-disciplined levies were no match for the better-equipped garrison troops of Berwick, which marched against him under Henry Cary, Lord Hunsdon, and which, after a severe encounter, drove him and the remnant of his forces over the Border into Scotland. Elizabeth, in a letter of thanks to Lord Hunsdon for his victory, speaks of 'that cankred and subtil Traytor Leonard Dacres,'[2] and lost no time in having him attainted. Leonard after a time crossed over to Flanders, where he died at Louvain in great poverty and without leaving issue, on May 1st, 1578.[3] His brother, Edward Dacre, who was also attainted, died without children, on December 1st in the same year as Leonard.[4]

Francis Dacre, the youngest of the three brothers, now put forth his claim to the title and possessions of his ancestors, but in this respect was no more fortunate than was his brother before him, although he obtained a decision in his favour from 'Sundry the Lords of the Privie Councell & summ of the Judges,'[5] and

---

[1] *Q. E.*   [2] *Coll. Peer.* 'Lord Hunsdon.'
[3] 'Brief for the Lord Dacre for Lazonby,' &c.—*F. P.* Another of our papers puts his death as taking place in 1580.
[4] *Ibid.* Another of our papers puts his death as taking place in 1583.
[5] Ancient document previously cited, *ante*, p. 270.

for a short time enjoyed the rents of the lands in dispute ; but an action was immediately brought against Francis in the Court of King's Bench, and before that cause came for trial the Queen, by virtue of some former entail, was declared to be entitled to the Dacre estates. Francis being at last in despair of obtaining justice, and at the end of his resources, left the kingdom in September 1589—for doing which he was attainted of treason—and went to Spain, where Philip II. made him a captain of two hundred musketeers.[1] Before going abroad Francis wrote a long letter from Croglin in Cumberland to Elizabeth, dated September 17th, 1589,[2] in which he sets forth the reasons that had forced him to leave the country.

In the course of this letter he says :—

To beg I am ashamed, to work I cannot, to want I will not, therefore I am enforced to seek for maintenance where I with credit may gain the same, and am determined to employ that little that should have brought me to attend your Majesty to carry me elsewhere. I have taken my son with me for that I have left him nothing to tarry behind me with all ; If God hath provided living for us we will live together, if not we will starve together ; for my daughters[3] I commit them to God and such friends as it shall please him to provide for them.

Before many years had passed Francis appears to have desired to return to England,[4] but he probably did not do so until after the Queen's death. The *C. P.* states that his first wife is said to have been Dorothy, a daughter of John Radcliffe, of Derwentwater ; and that it is certain that in June 1607 he married, at St. Saviour's, Southwark, Mrs. Avis Downham. There was issue by his second wife a son Randolf, baptized March 8th, 160⅞, at St. Dunstan's in the West, as 'Son of Frauncis Lord Dakers.'

---

[1] *Hist. Com.* (Salisbury), v. p. 448. [2] *Ld. D. Mis.*

[3] *N. & B.* ii. p. 351, says that Francis left surviving him a daughter, Mary, who lived to a very great age, and who died without issue. He had also daughters named respectively Elinor and Elizabeth.—*Hist. Com.* (Salisbury), vii. p. 397.

[4] *Ibid.*

The eldest son of Francis Dacre was the one he took abroad with him, who was also named Francis; he died during his father's lifetime on February 10th, 163½; and his father died on February 19th in the following year, leaving Randolf, his son by his second wife, his heir.[1]

In the reign of Charles I. Randolf presented a petition to that King, in which he set forth his father's attainder in 36th Elizabeth, and said that King James had given his father a pension of 350*l.*, being 200*l.* for himself, 100*l.* for his wife, and 50*l.* for the petitioner; that this had been paid until February 1632,[2] when Francis died,[3] and goes on to pray that the King will grant him such of his family estates as still remain in the hands of the Crown. On October 14th, 1634, the King ordered that the matters set forth in the petition should be considered and inquired into; but, as has been said, Randolf died in that year. In the parish register of Greystock there is this entry:—

A.D. 1634. Randall Dacre Esq. (son & heir to Francis Esq. dec^d the youngest son of the late Lord William Dacre) being the last heir male of that Lyne, which said Randall dyed at London and was brought down at the charges of the Right honōble Thomas Earl of Arundell & Surreye & Earl Marschall of England.[4]

Thus, in poverty, ended the once powerful family of the Dacres of the North.

It is difficult to follow the devolution in ownership which occurred at the death of the young George Lord Dacre of all the lands owned by him. His step-father the Duke was

[1] 'Brief for the Lord Dacre.'—*F. P.*

[2] In fact, the payment of this pension had been irregular, as is shown by an ancient copy of a petition by Francis in 1626.—*F. P.*

[3] Aged about eighty-six; in petition of 1626 he speaks of himself as being above eighty years of age.

[4] *Ld. D. Mis.* This Thomas, Earl of Arundel, was a first cousin once removed to Randolf, being the son of Philip Earl of Arundel, and Anne, his wife, daughter of Thomas Lord Dacre. Philip Earl of Arundel was attainted in 1589, and died 1595. His son Thomas was restored to his father's title and lands in 1604.—The *C.P.*

attainted, and so was the Duke's eldest son, the Earl of Arundel; so also was George's uncle, Leonard Dacre, who had vainly laid claim to the estates; but, however these estates may have changed owners since the death of George Lord Dacre, we find that upon Randolf Dacre's death a considerable portion of them were in the hands of the Howards, the then Earl of Arundel and Charles Howard;[1] both being in possession of considerable portions of them. After many years of fruitless litigation an agreement was come to between the parties, to leave the matters in dispute to the arbitration of Sir Thomas Widdington and Matthew Hale, who at that period were both distinguished members of the Bar, and Francis Lord Dacre bound himself in a bond for 10,000*l.* to abide the result of this arbitration.

The award is not dated, but as Sir Matthew Hale is therein described as 'Matthew Hale Consellor,' and as he was created a serjeant in January 1654, it must have taken place at some period previous to that date. The result of this arbitration was to award to Francis the castles and manors of Dacre and Kirkoswald, and the manors of Blackball in Carlisle, Brackenthwaite, Newbiggin,[2] Bouskail, Soulby,[3] Mosedail, Staffol, Lazonby, and Glassonby in Gilsland, in the county of Cumberland; and the barony and manor of Barton, and the manors of Barton Martindaile and Patterdaile in Westmoreland; while Gilsland and the forest of Gelsdaile and Brerethwaite, seventeen manors, and the advowson of Stapleton in Cumberland, went to Charles Howard, who in the award is described as of 'Howard

---

[1] The conveyance of these premises in dispute gives incidentally this pedigree:—

F. P.

[2] This must not be confounded with the parish of this name, as that at this period, and for many years before, belonged to the family of Crackenthorpe.—*N. & B.* i. pp. 364 *et seq.*

[3] According to the same authority this manor since Edward II. has belonged to the family of Musgrave.—Vol. i. pp. 552 *et seq.*

Castle'; there is no mention in the award of the Earl of Arundel.[1]

In considering the annual value of this imposing list of lands acquired by Francis Lord Dacre under the award, it must be explained to readers not acquainted with real property law that a person may own a manor—that is, the manorial rights—without necessarily owning any land within such manor which he has power to let; and this was evidently the case here, as a rent-roll of the Cumberland and Westmoreland estates when belonging to the Earl of Sussex, eldest son of Francis, shows that from some of these manors only rents quite small in amount were due from the 'free & customary tenants'—*e.g.* in the case of Brackenthwaite and Newbiggin, the rents for which combined only amounted to about 5*l*. a year. There is one item of rent which is remarkable: after the entry of free and customary rents received from the manor of Glassonby there appears 'the Greenhues[2] there 6/3'; and like entries, though for different amounts, appear after the names both of Staffold and Brackenthwaite. The total gross rents amounted to about 800*l*. a year; but several deductions for repairs, fees to bailiffs of the different manors, arrears of rent and salary of 40*l*. to the agent, made a considerable diminution to the net amount received by the owner.

On May 1st, 1655, deeds were executed by Charles Howard and Lord Dacre for the purpose of carrying out the terms of the award, and the one signed by the former is among our papers. In 1657 Lord Dacre sued the Crown in the Court of Exchequer for the recovery of Lazonby[3] and other possessions, whereupon

the barons on mature consideration adjudge that the hands of the Keepers of the liberty of England by authority of parliament

[1] Ancient copy of the award.—*F. P.*

[2] A secondary meaning of 'greenhouse' is a house where green or unfired pottery is placed to dry before being put into the kiln.—*C. D.* I can find no mention of pottery being made in the Lake Country. It is possible that there was once a manufactory of rude local pottery in those parts, but I confess that this explanation does not satisfy me.

[3] *N. & B.* ii. pp. 416-7.

be amoved from the possession of the Manor of Laysingby with the appurtenances, & that Francis now Lord Dacre be restored to his possession thereof, together with the issues and profits thereof from the time of the death of Ranulf de Dacre.

So it would appear that even after his arbitration with the Howards, Francis had to take steps to make good his title against claims on the part of the Crown.

While on the subject of this litigation it may be worth remarking how very early in the morning people began business in the seventeenth century; one of our documents connected with this case bears the following endorsement: 'Indorse this faire for me & doe it very true letter for letter & word for word. I must have it at my chamber by seaven in the morning at the furthest to examine.'

In 1641, when about twenty-two years of age, Francis Lennard married the Hon. Elizabeth, a daughter of Paul, first Viscount Bayning. The Bayning family came originally from Nayland, Suffolk, and afterwards lived at Dedham, Essex. Elizabeth's grandfather Paul and her great-uncle Andrew were both citizens and aldermen of London, and accumulated such vast fortunes in trade that they might be described as merchant princes. Paul Bayning, the alderman, built a magnificent house at Bently, Essex, in the time of James I., which was pulled down by his descendants before it was fifty years old. He had great disagreements with his wife, from whom he obtained a divorce *a mensa et thoro* in 1600, and it was said that he retired from the office of alderman to spite her so that she might not become Lady Maycress.[1]

The Baynings were an early and conspicuous example of those rich mercantile families who for the last three hundred years have been constantly marrying into the ranks of the English nobility, and also been themselves made peers; and so by their wealth have tended to keep that class who bear titles in the prominent position which they still fill in the eyes of most persons. No doubt in Stuart times the wealthy and

---

[1] Chamberlain's Letters.—*C. S. P.* p. 132.

be amoved from the possession of the Manor of Laysingby with the appurtenances, & that Francis now Lord Dacre be restored to his possession thereof, together with the issues and profits thereof from the time of the death of Ranulf de Dacre.

So it would appear that even after his arbitration with the Howards, Francis had to take steps to make good his title against claims on the part of the Crown.

While on the subject of this litigation it may be worth remarking how very early in the morning people began business in the seventeenth century; one of our documents connected with this case bears the following endorsement: 'Indorse this . . . . for me & doe it very true letter for letter & word for word. I must have it at my chamber by seaven in the morning at the furthest to examine.'

In 1614, when about twenty-two years of age, Francis . . . and married the Hon. Elizabeth, a daughter of Paul, first . . . . Bayning. The Bayning family came originally from Wayland, Suffolk, and afterwards lived at Dedham, Essex. Elizabeth's grandfather Paul and her great-uncle Andrew were both citizens and aldermen of London, and accumulated such vast fortunes in trade that they might be described as merchant princes. Paul Bayning, the alderman, built a magnificent house at Bently, Essex, in the time of James I., which . . . . by his descendants before it was fifty years . . . . with his wife, from whom he . . . . them in 1600, and it was said . . . . a german to spite her so that he might not become Lady Mayoress.[1]

The Baynings were an early and conspicuous example of those rich mercantile families who for the last three hundred years have been constantly marrying into the ranks of the English nobility, and also been themselves made peers; and so by their wealth have tended to keep that class who bear titles in the prominent position which they still fill in the eyes of most persons. No doubt in Stuart times the wealthy and

[1] Chamberlain's Letters.—C. S. P. p. 132.

recently ennobled Baynings were the butt of many sneers, and were jeered at, as some brewers of late years made peers have been laughed at in 'Truth' for forming the 'Beerage'; but as the whirligig of time goes on Stuart creations have become quite old in comparison with the bulk of those of which the present peerage is composed.

The first Lord Bayning with his relatively huge riches, and with all his daughters well married, and himself, through his granddaughter the Duchess of Cleveland, destined to be the ancestor of more than one ducal house, could afford to laugh at those who circulated spiteful jokes at his expense, as do, no doubt, his modern prototypes. Christened Paul after his father, he was created a baronet in 1612, a baron in February 162$\frac{7}{8}$, and a viscount in the following year, and died at his house in Mark Lane, London, on July 29th, 1629; he left, besides enormous estates in the counties of Essex, Suffolk, and Herts, personal property of over 153,000*l.* Lord Bayning married Anne, Dowager Viscountess of Dorchester, a lady of very good family, daughter of Sir H. Glenham, and granddaughter of the Earl of Dorset; she died at Westminster on January 10th, 163$\frac{8}{9}$, and was buried at Gosfield, Essex, on the 31st of that month, under the title of her first husband.[1]

Paul, first Viscount, had issue one son, Paul, and four daughters. The son did not live long after succeeding his father, as he died in 1636, aged only twenty-three years: he left issue two daughters, married respectively to the Earl of Oxford and John Herbert, youngest son of the Earl of Pembroke. Neither of these daughters had issue, so that their father's great estates were ultimately divided among his four sisters, who were Cicely, wife of Viscount Newark; Elizabeth, wife of Francis Lord Dacre; Mary, wife, firstly, of Viscount Grandison,[2] and, secondly, of the Marquis of Anglesea; and Anne, who married Henry Murray, a Groom of the Bedchamber to Charles I., and who, after her husband's decease, was created Viscountess Bayning in her own right.

[1] The *C. P.* [2] By whom she had Barbara, afterwards Duchess of Cleveland.

The treaty for the marriage of Francis Lennard and Elizabeth Bayning was dated April 16th, 1641, and her portion was to be a sum of 20,000l.; while he, on his part, agreed to settle on his wife, as jointure, lands to the value of 1,500l. a year, and among the lands so settled was Cudham and Apuldrefield. When they married Elizabeth was only sixteen years of age, as appears from a decree in a lawsuit brought by her some twenty years later, and after her second marriage, against her first husband's trustees; his trustees also brought an action against her, and these actions were settled by a compromise effected by an order of the Court of Chancery in 1667. From the papers in these actions I have obtained several particulars concerning Francis and his wife, to which papers I shall refer subsequently as 'Lawsuit.'

Francis Lord Dacre and his wife had the following children:—

Philadelphia, baptized at Herstmonceux, January 29th, 1643;[1] married D. O'Brian, third Viscount Clare, and died 1662.[2]

Elizabeth, born March 15th;[3] baptized at Herstmonceux, March 20th, 164$\frac{3}{8}$; married before 1671 William Brabazon, third Earl of Meath. They had no male issue.[4] He died in 168$\frac{4}{5}$, and she married again, before October 1686, the Hon. William Moore;[5] and, dying in 1701, was buried at St. Paul's, Covent Garden.[6]

Thomas, born May 18th, 1654.[7]

Francis, baptized at Chevening, September 11th, 1657.[8]

Margarett, baptized at Chevening, June 25th, 1659;[9] died unmarried.

[1] Her mother was churched February 16th, 1643.—*H. A. B.*

[2] He espoused the cause of James II., and his large estates in Ireland were confiscated by William III. and granted to the Earl of Albemarle. Their descendants were in the service of the King of France, and their race became extinct in the seventeenth century.—The C. P.

[3] *H. A. B.* [4] *Vide post*, p. 433, *n.*

[5] He may have been a son of Henry first Earl and third Viscount Drogheda.

[6] The C. P.

[7] *Har. So., R.* xxxiii. p. 2. The title of 'Dacre' is in error here given as 'Varres.'

[8] *Ch. Reg.* and *Har. So., R.* xxxiii. p. 9, where birth and baptism are given as October 1657. [9] *Ch. Reg.*

Henry is said to have been born after his father's death,[1] and this was no doubt the case, as, a few days before Francis Lord Dacre died, he expressed a wish to 'make provision for the child the plaintif [Lady Dacre] then went with.'[2] Henry was certainly born by Michaelmas 1662, as he was then one of the parties to the Chancery suit.[3]

Lord Dacre at the time of his marriage, besides owning Herstmonceux and a reversion to Chevening, had also a house in London near Fleet Street, as is shown by a letter, dated May 7th, 1641, and addressed 'To my worthy good freind Mr. Willm Wood servant to the Right Honble the Lord Dacre at his house in Salisburie Court nere Fleet Street London.'[4]

As Lord Dacre had children born at Chevening in 1657 and 1659, I think it is probable that about this period he either hired that house from his step-mother, Dorothy Lady Dacre, or that she lent it to him. We have seen in the previous chapter that at this time she was living with her second husband (who did not die till 1659) at the Vyne and at Belhus.

They were stirring times when Francis Lord Dacre married, as troubles between the King and Parliament, so long brewing, were just developing into civil war. Like the Lords Suffolk, Wharton, and Willoughby, none of whom at that period had attained thirty years of age, young Lord Dacre, fired with enthusiasm for democratic ideals so especially attractive to youth, threw in his lot with the Parliamentary party.

It is quite likely that Francis was greatly influenced in his political career by the example of the Parliamentary general, Sir William Waller. Sir William was a first cousin of Lord Dacre's father, and his views on the dispute then raging between the King and the Parliament would probably carry great weight with his young relative, and we know that not only Sir William, but also his wife and children, were frequent guests at Herstmonceux.

In January 164½ the King sent a message to Parliament, to

---

[1] *Has.* i. p. 361. Notes by the late H. B.-L.
[2] 'LawSuit.' [3] *Ibid.* [4] *F. P.*

which the Lords replied by a message of thanks, and requested the Commons to associate themselves with it. The Commons wished to add as an amendment to such message of thanks a request that the Tower, and other forts, and also the Militia, should be put under the command of such persons as might be recommended by both Houses of Parliament. This amendment was rejected by the majority of the House of Lords, but the minority, of whom Lord Dacre was one, signed a protest against this rejection.[1] It was about this period that the Committee appointed by the House of Commons to place the kingdom in a position of defence recommended, among other things, that the Lords-Lieutenant nominated by the King should be superseded by others chosen by the Parliament, and suggested the name of Francis Lord Dacre to fulfil that post for the county of Herefordshire.[2] Two years later, when the King summoned the members of both Houses to hold their sittings at Oxford, Francis was one of the twenty-two peers who disregarded this summons, and continued to meet at Westminster.[3]

In 1646 he was appointed one of the Commissioners, fifty-one in number, for the maintenance of peace between England and Scotland.[4]

About this period the Parliamentary party appointed a Committee of Lords and Commons to attend to affairs in Ireland, and Francis appears to have been an active member of that body.[5]

Lord Dacre in his 'Family History,' when treating of his ancestor's political career, says :—

But in the end, finding that those who had got the power into their hands were running too great lengths and bringing everything into anarchy and confusion, he would by no means act with them, but set himself against their measures, and at length, perceiving that it was impossible to do any good there, absented himself from the House of Lords.

---

[1] *Rog.* i. p. 11.   [2] *D. N. B.*   [3] *Cla.*
[4] *Thur.* i. p. 79.   [5] *S. P. I.* 1647-60, pp. 739-40.

The following facts relative to his attendance at the House of Lords during those trying times are on record :—

On June 18th, 18 Car. (1643), a letter from Lord Dacre was read in the House of Lords, in which he expressed 'a great desire to attend this House but because his health is not good at this time to come in person & do his service to this House but hopes within a fortnight to come in person.' The following reply to this communication was approved by the House and signed by the Speaker :—[1]

My Lord.
  I am by the Lords now assembled in Parliament commanded to let you know that they take it in very good part those respects to the House which you express in your letter to Lord Wharton ; they will command nothing prejudicial to your health but they do expect that your Lordship will not fail to be here within the time prefixed in your letter, & seeing your service here is necessary, & much conducing to your own honour, the sooner you come it will be the better, thus bidding you heartily Farewell, I rest.[2]

That Lord Dacre did attend sittings in the House of Lords in the following months of August and September is shown by entries in the Journals of that House.[3] A little later there is the following letter from him among the Thurloe 'State Papers':—

To Lord Grey of Werke, Deputy speaker of the House of Lords.

            Herstmonceux
My Lord   Jan. 22, 1643.
  On Wednesday night last I received your lordships of the ninth of this month, and would most gladly have obeyed the commands of the House of Peers, by coming presently away to wait on the affairs of the kingdom on the 22nd, had not the ways ever since been so extremely clogged by a very deep snow, that men pass not without much difficulty and danger;

---

[1] Although on ordinary occasions the Lord Chancellor acts as Speaker of the House of Lords, during these disturbed times the Lords elected the Earl of Manchester as their Speaker.

[2] *H. L.* v. p. 143.   [3] *Ibid.* vi.

I beseech your Lordship to add to this reason the weakness of my own health, not being able to endure the rigour of the journeying on horseback in such exceeding cold weather as now it is ; and to represent this to their lordships favourable constructions ; not that I intend to make long use of any way to excuse myself from that duty, which I shall ever owe to the commonwealth, but very shortly shall give my attendance on their Lordships with all willingness and readiness. And so I rest your lordships most humble servant,

FRANCIS DACRE.

I have no knowledge whether Lord Dacre really did suffer from delicate health at this period, but as his career shows us no sign of any desire to shirk responsibility we may, I think, accept his reasons for non-attendance as being genuine ones, and not mere excuses to avoid being present.

During the winters of 1645 and 1646 Francis appears to have made journeys into the North,[1] but there is nothing to show whether they were made for private reasons, or for the purpose of taking any active part in the great struggle then going on between the King and the Parliamentary party. In the month of October 1647 Lord Dacre had a special summons to attend the House of Lords, as among the entries in the accounts for that month there is this one, 'Paid Mr. Baker a messenger that came to somon my lord to ye Parliam^t 01 li.'[2]

When the ordinance for the trial of the King was about to be introduced, and all the absent peers were summoned for December 28th, 1648, Francis was kept away by sickness, but he was in his place on January 8th following, when that bill was brought up from the Lower House, and was one of the twelve peers who had the courage to unanimously reject it.[3] Speaking of the rejection by the peers of this ordinance the author of 'The Parliamentary History of England' says :[4] 'In order to perpetuate if possible the names of those few noble peers who had courage in this dangerous time to meet and make the afore-

---

[1] *H. A. B.*
[2] *Ibid.*
[3] *Rap.* ii. Book xvi. p. 568.
[4] Vol. xviii. p. 492.

said Resolution we give the list of them from their Journal.' Then follow the names of only twelve peers, of whom Lord Dacre was one.

No doubt in acting as a rule with the Parliamentary party, and yet opposing them at this crisis, he and his companions on that occasion displayed far more moral courage than many who all along espoused the King's cause; if only a larger number of the peers had been on the popular side, and at the same time had, like Lord Dacre, sufficient strength of character to meet in the House of Lords, and offer strenuous opposition to the King's so-called trial, England might have escaped the dishonour of being numbered among those nations who, at some period or another in their history, have allowed their sovereign to be done to death. As a result of the independent line of conduct which Lord Dacre adopted in thus opposing the extreme members of his party, Sir James Harrington and others clamoured for his impeachment, and that of his companions, as being 'favourers of the grand delinquent & enimies to public justice & liberties of the people.'[1]

Collins says in his 'Peerage' that in

1654 Cromwell summoned a House of Commons in which Francis Lord Dacre sat as one of the members for the County of Sussex; and had he not been a Peer, as matters then stood, reasons might perhaps have been found to justify it, but as he was so, it seems that he and those other lords who submitted to sit in that assembly, were wanting to their own dignity, and to the interest of that noble body to whom they belonged. This convention, however, was dissolved in five months, not being favourable to the Protector's schemes, and we do not find that the said Francis sat in the next.

Although I think it probable that Francis gradually withdrew himself more and more from any active share in politics, we have in 1660 another proof of his moral courage. In that year a bill was passed by the House of Lords, which had for its object the vacating of some fines of lands which had been levied in due form. Lord Dacre, perceiving that such a measure

[1] *Par. His.* xviii. p. 493.

284   HISTORY OF THE LENNARDS

struck a blow at all security of property, and that this policy, if persisted in, would result in general anarchy, in spite of the risk he ran by so doing, was not afraid to record his protest against this attack on persons who, having bought land and had it conveyed to them with all legal formalities, suddenly found themselves arbitrarily deprived of that for which they had paid their money.[1]

As we have among our family papers no private letters to or from this Lord Dacre, I should not have been able to say much about his manner of life had I not been fortunate enough to find a large account book of his household expenses at Herstmonceux very carefully kept by a man named Field, who appears to have been a tenant on the estate, and also steward at a salary of £10 a year. Unfortunately the first few pages and the title page are missing. What remains, however, gives the weekly expenditure from 'the 19th daye of August 1643'[2] until December 1649, together with an account of the moneys received by Field for rents, &c. At the foot of each page appears the signature 'Fra Dacre' to show that he had passed these accounts, which sometimes showed a balance due to Field, and sometimes one due to himself. There are two points worth remarking about this signature; one is that at this period the custom, now universal, for a peer to sign himself by his title without any Christian name prefixed to it, although coming into fashion, had not then become general;[3] the other is that by the end of August 1645 we find Lord Dacre no longer signing himself in this account book

Fra: Dacre but *Fra: Dacre*

[1] *Rog.* i. p. 19.

[2] I had thought that these pages had got torn out in recent years, but I find that my cousin, H. B. L., mentioned some forty years ago that the account begins on August 19th, 1643.

[3] As to this, see facsimile signatures of Gregory Fynes, Lord Dacre; Margaret Lady Dacre; Lord Newburgh; and of Henry and Richard Lennard, respectively Lords Dacre.

I am unable to account for this whim of his, which was possibly owing to some passing fashion of the day. In recent times we have seen many instances of newly made peers choosing a title with 'De' prefixed; *e.g.* De Ramsey, De Freyne, De Mauley, De Vesci, &c., &c.

This account book is very elaborately kept, and a careful perusal of it gives the reader a considerable insight into the life in a large country house during the Stuart period. As, however, I have already published [1] an account of this book with many extracts of its contents, I only include a few of them in this work, and content myself with some remarks on the information derived from it, which helps to illustrate Francis's life.

The account book in question contains a weekly list of guests, in every week the names of some visitors to the castle are recorded, and these lists show that Lord Dacre was extremely hospitable, and kept pretty well open house. A great many of the visitors were related to him, as among their names, many of which often recur, are:

Lord and Lady Baltinglass.[2]
Mr. Lennard of Bayly, his kinsman.
Mr. Thomas Lennard, his brother.
Lady Wildgoos, his aunt.
Sir Thomas and Lady Parker, his aunt.
Lady Grandison, his sister-in-law.
Several of the Barnham family, his cousins.
Sir Stephen Lennard, his kinsman, of West Wickham, Kent.
Richard Lennard, his half-brother.
Catherine Lennard, his half-sister.

[1] *S. Arch.* xlviii.
[2] This Lord Baltinglass (second Viscount) married Anne, only surviving child of Sir Peter Temple's first wife, Anne. Anne Lady Temple was sister to Elizabeth Throckmorton, Richard Lennard's first wife, so that Francis Lord Dacre and Lady Baltinglass were first cousins. She was defrauded by her step-brother, at the instigation of her father, of the inheritance which she should have had as a result of her parents' marriage settlement. Her husband, Lord Baltinglass, was ruined by the effects of the disturbances in Ireland; he died in 1665, but she, although considered so delicate in her youth, lived on to a considerable age in poverty, and died in the Fleet, August 1696.

His step-mother's name is not among those of the visitors, so it seems not unlikely that there was a coolness between them, which was probably owing partly to Dorothy's efforts to have Horsford settled on her son Richard, and partly to the fact that she had Chevening for her life. Although Francis did carry out his father's intentions in respect to the settlement of Horsford, it was no doubt not accomplished without considerable soreness of feeling on his part, and it is likely that he always felt a grudge against his step-mother, the more so that her efforts on her son's behalf were crowned with success ; and judging from the terms of his will, referred to later, he had no great affection for his half-brother.

Among other visitors were the Lords Nottingham, Westmoreland, Montague, and Stamford, all belonging to the same political party as did Francis.

One of the Earl of Stamford's sons was christened 'Leonard,' possibly after Francis, who may not improbably have been his godfather.

As might be expected, Lord Dacre's house was somewhat a rendezvous for the Parliamentary army. We find the general Sir William Waller, and his wife Lady Anne (a daughter of the Earl of Winchelsea and Nottingham), and their boys, were often at Herstmonceux.

The following entries in the account book refer to the existence of three persons of the name of Lennard, whose relationship with Lord Dacre I am unable to trace :

'6th to 27th October, 1649. Paid Mr. Francis Lennard's widdow in part of 7^{li} due for one year's annuity 5^{li}.'

This lady, to whom I have found no other reference, was probably the widow of Francis Lennard, of Heathfield.

'December 12th to 19th, 1646. Paid Alexander Lennard by my lords assighnment for a frees sute 03^{li}. 05^{s}.'

There is no other reference to this person ; if a relation at all he was probably not a legitimate one : the Christian name of Alexander is not one as far as I can discover ever borne by a member of our family.

HERSTMONCEUX

There are constantly references in the account book to a 'Mr. Henry Lennard.' He evidently filled some position on the household staff of the castle. Such entries as these are not uncommon :—

Jan. 20th to 27th, 1643. P^d by my Lord's assighnment to Mr. Henry Lennard at his going to London 01^{li}.

Jan. 27th to February 3rd, 1643. P^d by Mr. Woods assighnment to Mr. Henry Lennard as appeareth for his bill for hors hire, his charges to & at London and back again 01^{li}.. 04^s.

August 22nd to 29th, 1646. Paid Mr. Henry Lennard disbursements for my lord 08^s.. 06^d.

This Henry was paid 10*l.*, a year, which was the highest scale of pay received by any of Lord Dacre's servants and retainers, but he evidently had the family difficulty in making his income suffice for his needs, as the accounts show that more than once he drew his pay several months before it fell due. I think that there can be no doubt he was a relation, but I am unable to suggest from whom he could have been descended.

The following note in 1644 was made while 'Mr. Thomas Lennard & 3 men,' were among the visitors at the castle :—

Memorandum. The 11th day of this February a view was taken of the bills and saults lying in Pemsie belonging unto my Lord as appeareth by marks stones there set up in the presence of Thomas Lennard Esq. James Field gent. Thomas Lennard ye squire's man and others.

The first Thomas mentioned was, probably, the Hon. Thomas, Lord Dacre's brother, who was a frequent visitor, and to whom Francis was very much attached; or it might have been 'Lennard of Bayly,' and the second Thomas was perhaps the latter's son.

The expression 'bills and saults' is not easy to understand in this connection; 'saults,' no doubt, meant salt marshes, which on the Essex marshes are called 'saltings.'

The following letter among the MSS. in the British Museum throws some light on the lawless state into which the country was then drifting, and on the position occupied by 'Lennard of Bayly' as regards Lord Dacre :—

To the honoured Knight my noble freind Sr Thomas Pelham present this.

Noble S^r I haue giuen charge to Thom Lennard my keeper of Bayly to bring before you certain deere stealers, by whome my parke, and as I am enformed most parkes neere it, haue suffered very much ; I doe therefore request you, that if there bee any lawe on foote, you would be pleased to take the strictest course with them that may bee, excuse mee I beseech you, for this importunity and trouble, and command mee as your most humble seruant.

Herstmonseaux.   FRANCIS DACRE.[1]
July 7, 1644.

The account book contains a good many references to hawking, coursing and shooting. At the present time, when so many persons turn out partridges purchased from Hungary and elsewhere in order to increase their stock, the following entry is of special interest :—

'Jan. 30th to February 6th, 1646. Paid Mr. Shoarditch for 5 partridges to be turned abroad 2s. 6d.'

In this connection I may mention that among some notes of business by J. Coke, dated June 2nd, 1649, there is the following :—

'Mr. Barrett's [no relation to our Barretts] warrant to take yearly 40 brace of partridges in the bush lands of Sussex to store Nonsuch fields.'[2]

Tame pheasants also appear not to have been unknown, as we find 'paid in reward to one that presented 3 tame feasants 01^s 00^d'; but there is nothing here to show whether they were turned off in the woods, or whether they were kept as pets in an aviary.

The above entries show that Francis Lord Dacre was much devoted to field sports, but there is nothing remarkable in this, as great fondness for sport has ever been a leading characteristic

---

[1] *Add.* 33084, fol. 60.   [2] *Hist. Com.* xii. Part i. p. 164.

of English landowners; what is remarkable is the particular form of sport to which he was chiefly addicted, and that was yachting. It is said that the word yacht was not known in England until 1660, when the Dutch presented one to Charles II., but even a casual inspection of the Herstmonceux account book would show this statement to be incorrect, and numerous references to the 'yought' show how fond Lord Dacre was of sailing.

Lord Dacre in his 'History' says of his ancestor Francis:—

It is said in the family that he took great delight in all matters relating to Navigation, and that he presented King Charles the second (who was himself very understanding in that art) with model of a light vessel, built in a new manner, invented by himself, which was greatly approved of by the King, and followed afterwards in the construction of ships of this kind.

It is not impossible that this entry 'Jany 164$\frac{7}{8}$ Paid Mr. Wyet for drawing a moddle 01^{li}' refers to this very model which Lord Dacre some years later presented to Charles II.

A letter from the Earl of Leicester to Mr. Secretary Coke, dated '$\frac{2\ \text{Nov.}}{23\ \text{Oct.}}$ 1636,'[1] shows that when seventeen years of age Lord Dacre had crossed to France and back to Rye, at least on one occasion when he and other passengers were in great danger from some 'Dunkerkers,' 'who used violence against them & robbed them & if the sight of a Holland man of Warre had not made them go away they had used them worse.' It is not improbable that, being near the sea, he frequently took little voyages in the Channel, and so early acquired that love for sailing which he appears to have retained all his life. In January 1660 he was nominated one of the Wardens of the Trinity House Corporation, and in June 1661, the year before his death, it was agreed by the whole Company of the Elder and Younger Brethren, that he, and the Earl of Sandwich, should stand for the election for Master. The election took place the same day, but it went against Lord Dacre, the Earl of Sandwich being chosen.[2]

[1] *Coll. Let.* ii. p. 435.   [2] Records at Trinity House.

How far Francis ventured in his yacht does not appear, but the accounts show that she certainly at times sailed as far as London. The entries in the account book referring to his ships are of interest as showing some items of what his hobby cost the first Englishman who is known to have been a yachtsman, but as they are already in print it is not necessary to repeat them here.

Francis Lennard, like so many of his family before and since, spent more than his income, and the account book shows that he was reduced to borrowing money from time to time from Field, the keeper of this account book; from Wood, who was also in his service, and from several other persons.

The first record I have found of his borrowing money is in 1646; Lord Baltinglass being pressed for money, as was usually his case, probably applied to Francis for a loan, and he, not being able to lend the money, borrowed it for him from Field, and no doubt made himself responsible for the repayment of principal and interest.

'March 21st, 1646, Paid Field interest on 50^{li} lent to my Lord Baltinglass 04^{li}.'

There are several entries later which refer to Lord Dacre's loans and his payment of interest on them. It is not easy to arrive at the amount of the loans, nor upon what terms they were made, as there is no specific account of them, only such references as the following entries :—

1647 March, Paid Mr. Smith & Field for the use of 500^{li} due ye 28 July last past 30^{li}.

April, Paid Kelly for the use of 150^{li} due at o^r Lady for one halfe yeere 6^{li}.

July 24, 1647, Paid Sr Thomas Parker for the use of 500^{li} one yeere 30^{li}.

October 1649, Paid Field for the use of 500^{li} halfe a yeere 20^{li}.

From these entries it would appear that Francis was able to borrow money at from six to eight per cent., which seems a low rate of interest considering the then scarcity of money, and that there is nothing to show that he gave any security for these loans.

I have not found many entries referring to Lady Dacre's allowance, and such as there are do not point conclusively as to how much that allowance amounted to; there is nothing to show for certain whether it was 50*l.* a year, or 50*l.* a quarter. We have such entries as these in 1646: 'May 16th. Paid in part of my ladies allowance due Midsummer 20^{li}.' 'July 4. Paid my lady the whole remainder of her allowance due at Midsummer 30^{li}.' There is, however, in the previous December this entry: 'Paid unto my Lady by my Lord's assignhment 50^{li},' and this I think makes it nearly certain that her allowance was 200*l.* a year.[1]

During the course of the year 1655 Lord and Lady Dacre were said to have had some serious disagreement, and Major-General Goff wrote on November 15th of that year to Mr. Secretary Thurloe: 'The Lord Dakers is gone beyond sea upon some discontent betwixt him & his lady. It is feared by many here that he should have had the *custos rot. (rotulorum).*'[2]

That some 'discontent' did exist between Lord and Lady Dacre we have evidence of a negative nature in the papers connected with the action brought by Lady Dacre against her husband's executors before referred to.[3] They show that he made his will in September 1655, and that in this will he made no mention of his wife, but appointed his brother Thomas, and his cousins Sir R. Barnham and Sir T. Parker, to be executors of his will and guardians to his son and heir, with legacies to each of 100*l.* If there had been no dispute, as alleged by Goff, it might have been expected Lord Dacre in his will would have made some reference to his wife; while the date of its execution, September 1655, is such as to give colour to Goff's statement made in the following November.

The evidence of Thomas Crompe in the suit throws some

---

[1] Lady Dacre alleged that Lord Dacre at time of her marriage agreed to allow her 500*l.* a year for her personal expenses.—'Lawsuit.'
[2] *Thur.* iv. p. 190.   [3] *Ante,* p. 278, and *post,* pp. 296–8.

light on this 'discontent.' Crompe says that for many years he had the management of Lord Dacre's affairs; he refers to his master going into France, though he does not mention the date of this journey, and says that he believes the reason that Lord Dacre did not by his will constitute his widow guardian of his eldest son was because he thought she would marry again; and that, had Lady Dacre been content to live in the country with her husband, the latter told him he would 'have done better for her in his will.'

The will was not a long one, but some of its provisions were rather remarkable. Lord Dacre left to 'my welbeloved brother Thomas 500*l.*,' but to his half-brother 'Richard Lennard als Barrett' only 10*l.*; and a like legacy to his cousin William Lennard. William's younger brother Robert must have been a great favourite with Lord Dacre, as after leaving all his landed property to his son Thomas and his heirs male, with remainder to his own brother Thomas and his heirs male, he devised the ultimate remainder to this Robert Lennard, to the total exclusion of his half-brother Richard. Probate of this will was granted in May 1662.

It is quite likely that Lord Dacre having taken an active part in political life, and not approving of the lengths to which his party had gone, preferred living in retirement at Herstmonceux, engaged in country pursuits and his favourite amusement of yachting, rather than spending his time in the capital, where he would not have been able to escape from the atmosphere of politics; and in those days to have refused to act with his party would have exposed a man of Lord Dacre's position to the suspicion of being a 'malignant,' a charge easily made by enemies and difficult to disprove, and one very apt to be followed by loss both of estates and liberty.

The return of the Stuart dynasty was an event calculated to increase Lord Dacre's wish for retirement, as the best he could hope for from the new King was that he would be treated with coldness by him or be entirely ignored, and either treatment would render the position of a rich and powerful peer an intolerable one were he to frequent London; while he might reasonably consider that living a retired country life was by far the safest course to adopt until time had somewhat softened the bitterness of party strife engendered by the Civil Wars; but for all that, as we have seen, in December 1660, when party feeling was running very high, he was not afraid to emerge from his retirement in order to protest against the action of the House of Lords.

A year later, on December 13th, 1661, Francis obtained a pardon under the Great Seal, and this must have greatly improved his position, and have rendered him safe against accusations of anyone who might have borne him a grudge. As was then the custom, the terms of the patent were wide enough to grant him exemption for almost any possible crime that he could have committed previously to the date of its taking effect, which was December 29th, 1660.[1]

Lady Dacre, being accustomed to mix much in society, no doubt found the country dreadfully monotonous, as in those times country life was far duller for women than for men, when the former had but little company to amuse themselves with, and probably took much less part in the sports in which their men-folk found occupation than they do in these days.

If Lady Dacre sighed for the amusements of town during the Commonwealth, how much more anxious she must have been to take a part in them after the Restoration, when her sister and brother occupied brilliant positions at Court, and where her niece Barbara was the reigning favourite of the King. The fact that her second husband was an ardent Royalist, and that she was given a life-peerage in her own right by Charles II., are in themselves indications that her political sympathies were not those of her first husband's; and so, reading between the lines, we can see sufficient grounds for easily believing that this 'discontent' really existed. Moreover, in the light of what we have seen Crompe deposed to, as to Francis thinking she would marry again, makes one apt to wonder whether Lord Dacre

[1] This deed is now framed, and hangs at Horsford Manor.

may not have seen or heard of some flirtations going on between his wife and the man whom she ultimately married as her second husband. But, however serious 'the discontent' may have been when General Goff spoke of it in 1655, some sort of agreement must have been arrived at between the parties in 1656, as we have seen they had a son Francis baptized in September 1657.

In 1662 Francis Lord Dacre, while staying at 'his lodgings in St. Martin's Lane,' was seized with a sudden illness,[1] from which he died on May 12th, before having time to make a fresh will providing for his youngest children born since 1655, which, as has been stated, was the date of his will. I have seen it said that he was 'probably buried at Chevening but that the burial register for that date is lacking.'[2]

Francis was unable to live within his income, large though it was for those times,[3] and this is shown by the instances already quoted of his borrowing money as early as 1646. The habit of living on borrowed money is, like other bad habits, easier to acquire than to shake off; and Lord Dacre found this to be the case; for when he died it appears, from the lawsuit before referred to, that his debts and the legacies he left amounted altogether to no less a sum than 18,000*l.*—an enormous amount for the seventeenth century.

From a decree, in another action against the executors to enforce payment by them of two legacies of 3,000*l.* each to the deceased lord's eldest daughters, Philadelphia and Elizabeth, we learn that the legacies Lord Dacre left amounted to 7,420*l.* and his debts to 9,834*l.*, and that the value of deceased's personal estate was only 8,449*l.* The papers connected with this last-mentioned action show that, not long before Lord Dacre's death, the Mr. Crompe before mentioned purchased lands worth respectively, 5,500*l.* and 800*l.* on behalf of his employer, and for the payment of the greater part of the purchase money thereof

---

[1] 'Lawsuit.'
[2] *Arch.* C. xvi. 120. His widow in her will speaks of his being buried there, and directs that she shall lie there also.
[3] The plaintiffs in the 'Lawsuit' alleged it was 6,000*l.* a year, and the executors put it at about 3,500*l.*

he said that he remained jointly liable. The court decreed that these recently purchased lands should be sold, and the proceeds derived from such sale should be applied in the first place in discharging the debts and engagements in which Crompe stood engaged with and for Lord Dacre, and afterwards towards discharging the latter's debts and legacies. I am unable to state why Lord Dacre bought land with borrowed money, but it seems that a considerable portion of his debts were connected with these and other purchases of lands. A deed dated 1664, to which the surviving executors of his will (his brother Thomas and Sir R. Barnham) were parties, shows that Lord Dacre had borrowed 1,600*l.* on mortgage of some of his marsh lands as early as 1655.[1]

Within less than two years of her first husband's death Lady Dacre married David Walter, as is shown by the fact that in Easter Term 1664 Mr. Walter was joined with her as her husband in an action which she brought in the Court of Chancery.[2] David Walter, the second son of Sir John Walter, Chief Baron of the Exchequer, was a devoted Royalist, and Charles II. rewarded him for the great valour and loyalty which he displayed during the Civil Wars by making him a Groom of the Bedchamber; and appointing him, in 1670, Lieutenant-General of the Ordnance, a post, however, which he appears to have occupied only for a short period.[3]

There were no children of this union, and Mr. Walter predeceased his wife, dying in London on April 22nd, 1679, in the sixty-eighth year of his age,[4] and leaving her a small property at Drayton, in Middlesex, worth about 75*l.* a year. I think it most likely that he also left her an estate in Oxfordshire, as her accounts show that she derived about 300*l.* a year from that county, where neither her mother nor her first husband had any property.

Lady Dacre's sister, Lady Anglesea, died in 1671, and by her will she left 'To my deare sister the Lady Dakers

[1] *F. P.*
[2] 'Lawsuit.'
[3] *Hay. Dig.* p. 259.
[4] Tomb in Wolvercote Church, Oxon.

my Emerod[1] Ring sett with two ffossette[2] diamonds and my Turky[3] Ring of the old rock sett with two ffossett Diamonds.'[3] It would be interesting to know where these rings are now.

The result of the litigation between Lady Dacre and the executors of her first husband's will was distinctly favourable to her, and although she did not win on every point put forward on her behalf, she was successful on quite as many of them as probably her legal advisers anticipated. Lady Dacre asserted that Lord Dacre had a marriage portion with her of 20,000*l.*, and that he agreed to settle on her lands worth 1,500*l.* a year for her life; part of this jointure was the house and estate of Gosfield, in Essex, then worth from 600*l.* to 700*l.* a year; and when Lord Dacre desired to sell Gosfield (for which he got 3,000*l.* more than he had given), Lady Dacre concurred in that sale, and he, by a deed dated May 19th, 1654, settled upon her Buckholt and other lands in Sussex instead, which he covenanted would be worth during her life not less than 660*l.*; the sum of 600*l.* being the assumed value of the Gosfield estate and that of 60*l.* the annual value of the house. Lady Dacre asserted that these lands had produced at least 100*l.* a year less than this sum of 660*l.*, and she required the executors of Lord Dacre's will to make up the deficiency. They, on their part, contended that Lord Dacre had only received 9,000*l.* or 10,000*l.* of his wife's promised dowry, and that, even if the Buckholt estate had fallen in value, some estates in Cambridgeshire, which Lord Dacre had settled on his wife to secure 900*l.* a year, had risen so much in value as to make the loss on one of these properties balanced by the gain on the other. Lady Dacre's view, which in the end was the one adopted by the court, was that whatever increase of annual value might have taken place in the Cambridgeshire estate, it had nothing to do with her claim to 660*l.* a year from Buckholt.

The interest of Lord Dacre in Gosfield arose in this way.

---

[1] Emerald.—*C.D.*   [2] Facetted or cut like a brilliant.—*Ibid.*
[3] Turquoise.—*Ibid.*

His mother-in-law, Lady Dorchester, seems—probably after her second husband's death—to have purchased Gosfield and other manors in Essex, and to have charged the former with 5,754*l*. 16*s*. for the benefit of two of her daughters—viz. Mary Lady Grandison and Elizabeth, afterwards Lady Dacre—in equal portions. This money was not paid at the time of her death in 1639, and Lord Dacre, in 1647, bought out Lady Grandison's interest in Gosfield so as to be able to deal with that property. We have a paper showing what moneys Lady Dorchester owed to these two daughters, and it is endorsed 'what I owe my daughters.' By this memorandum it appears that she had owed them 1,500*l*. each in March 1636 (of which 500*l*. had been repaid) and 1,520*l*. each from December 1637, and that these principal sums, together with interest, amounted on June 24th, 1639, to the sum of 2,877*l*. 8*s*. due to each daughter.

In the course of the litigation between Lady Dacre and her husband's executors, it was alleged that she had possessed herself of jewels and household stuff to the value of 3,000*l*. or 4,000*l*., but all that she admitted to have taken was a seal watch and other inconsiderable things ; there can be no doubt but that she anyhow took possession of several pictures, as by her will she disposed of family portraits, to most of which it is highly improbable she was entitled.

Lady Dacre made one claim against her husband's executors which to us would appear to be an extraordinary one. This was that, inasmuch as Lord Dacre's will was made in 1655, before the birth of his younger children, Francis, Margaret, and Henry, and his death being a sudden one, so that he had no opportunity of altering it and thereby providing for their maintenance, the court should order that some provision for their support should be made by their father's executors. In those days the scope of the Chancellor's equity jurisdiction was far from having become crystallised, as has long since been the case ; and this appeal on behalf of Lord Dacre's younger children was made only a few years after that great legal authority Selden had written, 'Equity is a roguish thing. 'Tis all one as if they should make the standard for measure the Chancellor's foot.' In this case the length of Lord Clarendon's foot was very long, as the court ordered the relief sought; but in respect that the estate could not afford so great a maintenance for the three younger children as their 'Quality' deserved, directed the executors to pay to Lady Dacre the sum of 750*l.* for the five years ending the following May, which was at the rate of 50*l.* a year for each child, and also ordered that this sum might be augmented in future, at the Chancellor's discretion, as the children should grow up.

Lady Dacre when a widow lived in a house in Covent Garden, no doubt for some years with her younger children. She must have been very well off for those times, as from an account kept for her by Mr. E. Stroud, dated 1678, her income was then nearly 3,000*l.* a year. Stroud's book for the half-year ending Michaelmas 1679 shows that he had received on Lady Dacre's behalf, after allowing 168*l.* for repairs and taxes, the sum of 1,252*l.*, and that rents to the amount of about 350*l.* were in arrear. These rents were derived from lands in the counties of Sussex, Kent, Cambs., Oxon., Middlesex, Lincoln, Suffolk, and Worcester. There are only a few items in the accounts which seem to call for notice; one is the payment of a rent at the rate of 200*l.* a year to the Governor of Dover, which I am quite unable to explain. It is rather curious that Apuldrefield was held of the King as of his castle of Dover at a yearly rent of 71*s.*;[1] but this, I think, can only be a coincidence, and can have no connection with the above-mentioned payment to the Governor of that place. The other point is that sums to the amount of 50*l.* were remitted to France in 1679, which probably Lady Dacre caused to be sent over there for the benefit of her son Francis, who, as we shall see, was in France at this period a fugitive and presumably in indigent circumstances.

I have also a book of Lady Dacre's household and stable

[1] *T. & G.* iii. pp. 1 *et seq.*

expenses in 1680-1. It is very carefully kept, showing what was spent each day in provisions, and each week for other household necessaries, and it deals with such small details as the amount of coals, charcoal, and candles used each week in each room. By this we see that Lady Dacre used charcoal to warm her room, probably in a brasier like those still used in Italy, and that a good deal was consumed both in the kitchen and pantry; but in Mr. Lennard's [1] room coal was burned, as it was indeed in most parts of the house.

The expenses for the year ending Lady Day 1681 are shown thus:—

	£	s.	d.
Household expenses	842	11	6
Stable do.	224	14	7
House rent (less 40s. taxes deducted)	215	0	0
Servants' wages	102	13	11½
	£1,385	00	00⅓

This expenditure would appear to leave Lady Dacre a very good margin out of her income for personal expenses.

In September 1680 Lady Dacre was created Countess of Sheppey in her own right; [2] it has been said that she owed this title to the influence of the Duchess of Cleveland and the Countess of Sussex; but although I am unable to say how she did obtain it, I do not think either of these ladies, who were her niece and grand-niece respectively, had at that period sufficient influence with the King to obtain from him such a mark of royal favour for the benefit of their kinswoman; and that the reason for her promotion in the ranks of the peerage must be looked for elsewhere.

In many cases where titles were bestowed on ladies by Charles II. the reason for his conferring such dignities upon them was notoriously obvious; but, as Lady Dacre had attained the age of fifty-five before she was made a peeress in her own right, it is not probable that she attained that dignity by the

---

[1] No doubt her youngest son Henry.   [2] The *C. P.*; *Lutt.* i. p. 55.

same line of conduct as led to the creations of such titles as those of Cleveland, St. Albans, or Portsmouth.

The Countess made her will on June 19th, 1684,[1] and died about two years later, it being proved on July 19th, 1686. After the usual bequest of her soul to the Almighty, she directed that her burial should be at Chevening, where 'Francis Lord Dacre my dear husband and some of my children are buried.' And she left 20*l.* to the poor of that parish, a like sum to the poor of the parish of St. Paul's, Covent Garden, and 40*l.* to those of St. Martin's-in-the-Fields, 'where I have a pew & usually go to Church.' She then went on to bequeath to her eldest son, by this time the Earl of Sussex, several family portraits by Sir Peter Lely, which she desired him never to part with but 'keep them in the family';[2] she also left to the Countess, his wife, a portrait of the Duchess of Cleveland, and the 'picture of the Lord Grandison her grandfather reputed to be drawn by Sir A. Van Dyke.'[3] After other bequests of portraits and 'mournings' (meaning mourning clothes), some of which were to be made up at the cost of the estate, she went on to devise to her son the Earl her lands in Sutton Marsh, and gave him all that he owed her on condition that he paid to his brother Francis certain moneys then due to him, and also 1,000*l.* to his niece Mary O'Brian; but if he shall neglect or refuse to do so, then 'my executors are to do their utmost to recover from my son Sussex all debts due from him to me.'[4] She left 100*l.* to the executors and the overseer of her will, one of the former of whom was Sir Charles Cotterell.[5]

I have not been able to discover very much about Francis and Henry, the two younger sons of Francis Lord Dacre. Francis, born at Chevening, matriculated at Queen's College, Oxford, on October 11th, 1675, at the age of eighteen, and became a

---
[1] The *C. P.* gives in error this date as 1686.
[2] Most of these are now at Belhus. [3] Now at Belhus.
[4] This seems to show that in spite of succeeding in her action against Lord Dacre's executors she had not been able to obtain payment of all the money decreed to her in that action.
[5] *Ante*, p. 265.

THE HON. FRANCIS LENNARD

student of the Inner Temple a year later;[1] and in 1678 his eldest brother the Earl was his guardian.[2] I think it not unlikely he was extravagant, or if not especially extravagant that he was without business habits, as his mother in her will, when directing her executors to take the entire management of what she left him, speaks of him as 'being very unknowing in business of that nature.' It is not improbable that he was delicate, as in 1678 he went to Paris and from thence to Montpelier—a place which, although no longer in fashion since the Riviera has been opened up, was at one time a great resort for persons with delicate chests. He stayed there anyhow until 1680, and while in France the Earl's agent Greenwood remitted him 200*l.* a year; but I have no means of knowing whether this was a voluntary allowance or the result of some family settlement. In May 1680 Greenwood remitted him a legacy of 100*l.*, which he enters as 'Received of Sir Wm Walter his Uncle's legacy,'[3] and it appears that Francis had a small estate in Kent producing about 70*l.* a year, the rents of which seem to have been received by Greenwood and credited to his employer the Earl.'[4]

Lord Dacre in his 'Family History' says nothing of this Francis except that he died unmarried; but I have found that he became a Roman Catholic, and a follower of James II. in his unsuccessful endeavours in Ireland to recover his lost crown; and although a MS. pedigree says that Francis went into France for the recovery of his health, where he died, I think it is far more probable that his chief object in going there was to escape from the executioner's axe.

The following letter from his brother, the Earl of Sussex, to William III., dated three weeks after the Battle of the Boyne, in which Francis probably took part, is in the British Museum. I cannot say that the letter reflects great credit on the Earl's

---

[1] *F. A. O.*, who says in error that he was seventeen years of age when he matriculated.
[2] *Green.*
[3] This legacy was possibly from David Walter, his mother's second husband.
[4] Most of these details are gathered from Greenwood's accounts.

brotherly affection, as it shows him to be so much more anxious to secure for himself his ward and brother's forfeited property than to obtain the pardon of his life :—

Sir,
  I am lately informed to my great sorrow & confusion that my Brother a rash young man hath soe much forgott his duty & allegiance to your $M^a y^{tie}$ as to be in the Irish Rebellion. By his horrid crime he hath most deseruedly Forfeited his life & fortune, the first is ye least of my fears, when your May$^{tie's}$ goodness and mercy is so well knowne ; his little fortune the law, without your May$^{tie's}$ further grace, may wrest from him ; wch being only for his life, & afterwards in mee and my Heirs, I become, Sir, an humble suppliant to you ; that if your iustice shall make him forfeit, you will be pleased to bestow the forfeiture on mee, that I may not only be better inabled to doe something towards the support of this miserable man, but preserue my owne inheritance from the wastes & spoyles that any grant of it to others may bring upon it ; this grace & bounty Si^r signyfied by your May^{tie} to my Lord President, who is pleased to write in my behalf to your May^{tie}, will for euer bynde me to be what, By inclination, as well as duty, I was allways, S^{ir}

  Your May$^{tie's}$ Most dutiful humble Ser^t
July ye $\frac{21}{1690}$ SUSSEX.[1]

Lord Sussex's greed for his brother's property does not appear to have been rewarded by success, as in December 1690 a bill was brought into the House of Lords to provide for the attainder of those rebels concerned in the rebellion in Ireland, and that their estates should be forfeited. On the same day the Earl, his brother Henry, his sister the Countess of Meath, and Elizabeth Coote, a kinswoman, presented a petition that Francis's property, in which they had reversionary interests, should be excepted from the bill. The petitioners expressed their great sorrow that Francis had become a convert to the Popish religion, and was seduced and drawn into the rebellion in Ireland. 'They say that they are all Protestants, & that they have contributed as much as in them lay to this happy Revolution.'[2] It is probable that Francis became a member of

---

[1] *Add.* 33924, fol. 80.   [2] *Hist. Com.* xiii. App. Part v. p. 234.

the Church of Rome between 1678 and 1680, when living in France.

Francis's brother Henry, no doubt, lived with his mother in her house in Covent Garden until his unfortunate marriage, which took place at some period between 1680 and 1684, the date of the Countess of Sheppey's will. It is from this will that we learn all that we know about this marriage, which Lord Dacre in his 'History' does not refer to at all.

What was the name and position in life of Henry's first wife does not appear, but no doubt the former was of no importance, and the less we know of the latter is perhaps the better. It should be remembered that at the moment of his taking this false step Henry was very young; he would not have been twenty until 1682, and being his mother's favourite child, I think it not improbable that he had been brought up 'tied to her apron strings,' as his name is not to be found among the lists of young men entered at either of the Universities or at the Inns of Court. The Countess of Sheppey expresses her views about her new daughter-in-law in no undecided manner in the following passages of her will:—

'My son Henry by his late marriage which is very distasteful to me hath drawn my kindness from him, having formerly given him the bulk of my estate.' In leaving him a small legacy of 100*l.* a year she takes special precautions in so doing, 'that the woman who hath so unfortunately ruined him may never have any benefit thereby,' as after directing that the proceeds arising from the sale of her properties shall be in trust as to one moiety for her son Francis and the other moiety for Henry, she goes on to say that the true meaning and intent of her will is that if at any time after her decease Henry shall live with 'her he hath been trepanned to marry then during such cohabitation' her executors are to pay him only 50*l.* a year, but 'if it shall please God that my Son Henry shall survive his now wife,' then he and his heirs were to be entitled to this moiety, which otherwise was to go to Francis and his heirs, with remainders over to her eldest son, the Earl of Sussex, and his heirs.

Henry did survive his 'now wife,' who probably died in 1695 :[1] he married secondly on May 11th, 1698, at St. Mary, Carlisle, Mrs. Mary Usher, a lady whose maiden name was Haddock. She probably came from Carlisle, as Henry in his will describes himself as of that city, and appoints his brother-in-law, Josiah Haddock, of Carlisle, guardian of his children in case his wife should die during their infancy, and if he should be dead also, then other persons, also of Carlisle. It is not unlikely that he made her acquaintance when staying at Dacre Castle with his brother the Earl of Sussex, and that having no tie to make him select any one place to live in, he settled down in his wife's neighbourhood. Henry had by his wife Mary three daughters, Margaret, Anne, and Catherine, who were all under age at the date of his death, which took place in 1703.[2] His second wife did not survive him many years, as probate of her will was granted in May 1707,[3] and by this will it appears that she had two daughters, Mary and Elizabeth, by her first husband, then living. It appears from Henry's will that up to the time of making it he had not received that share of his mother's estate to which, in accordance with the terms of her will, he became entitled upon the death of his first wife, nor had it been received at the date of his widow's death, as is shown by her will; but this property did come ultimately to his daughters, and a private Act of Parliament (8th Anne, 1710) was obtained to confirm an indenture dated June 24th, 1709, to which these three girls and their guardian, Josiah Haddock, were parties, and to give power to the infants concerned to agree to a partition. The estate seems to have consisted of property in the City of London and in the parish of Stock, in

---

[1] Letter dated December 1859 from Mr. G. S. Steinman, antiquary, to the late H. B.-L.   [2] *Le N. M. A.*   [3] *P. C. C.*

executors a[...] only 50l. a year, but 'if it shall please
[...] that my [son Henry] shall survive his now wife,' then he
[...] his heirs were to be entitled to this moiety, which otherwise
[...] to Francis and his heirs, with remainders over to her
[...] the Earl of Sussex, and his heirs.

[Henry] did survive his 'now wife,' who probably died in
[...] he married secondly on May 11th, 1698, at St. Mary,
[...] Mary Usher, a lady whose maiden name was
[...] probably came from Carlisle, as Henry in his
will describes himself as of that city and appoints his brother-
in-law, Josiah Haddock, of Carlisle, guardian of his children in
case his wife should die during their infancy, and if he should
be dead also, then other persons, also of Carlisle. It is not
unlikely that he made her acquaintance when staying at Dacre
[...] brother the Earl of Sussex, and that having no
[...] let any one place to live in, he settled down
[...] neighbourhood. Henry had by his wife Mary three
[...] Anne, and Catherine, who were all under
[...] death, which took place in 1703.[2] His
[widow did not] survive him many years, as probate of her
will was granted in May 1707,[3] and by this will it appears
that she had two daughters, Mary and Elizabeth, by her first
husband, then living. It appears from Henry's will that up to
the time of making it he had not received that share of his
mother's estate to which, in accordance with the terms of her
will, he became entitled upon the death of his first wife, nor
had it been received at the date of his widow's death, as is
shown by her will; but this property did come ultimately to his
daughters, and a private Act of Parliament (8th Ann. 1710)
was obtained to confirm an indenture dated June 24th, 1709, to
which these three girls and their guardian, Josiah Haddock,
were parties, and to give power to the infants concerned to
agree to a partition. The estate seems to have consisted of
property in the City of London and in the parish of Stock, in

---

[1] Letter dated December 1859 from Mr. G. S. Steinman, antiquary, to the late H. B.-L.   [2] *Le N. M. A.*   [3] *P. C. C.*

Essex, which latter they did not sell until 1745. They appear to have married as follows: Margaret to Colonel Lanoye; Catherine to Mr. John Jones, a barrister; and Anne to Mr. Jerome Tully.

Thomas, the eldest son of Francis, was only a child when he succeeded his father, and Lord Dacre, in his 'History,' speaks thus of his maternal grandfather. He

was Lord of the Bedchamber to King Charles [II.] & coming very young to Court fell (as was natural enough to do at his age) into the expensive way of living he found the fashion there, and through this unlucky setting out, and the neglecting afterwards to take a proper care of his affairs from an easiness & Indolence in his disposition : not to be excused (as he neither wanted parts or capacity), and by great losses at Play, he was so much entangled and distressed that at different times he was obliged to sell several of his Estates and at length some years before he died his Noble Seat at Herstmonceux in Sussex and lands in that County by all which he much diminished his Fortune tho' he had still a reasonable one left, being at the time of his decease possessed of Chevening and a good estate round it; and of the Manors of Dacre, Kirkoswald, and divers other Manors and lands in the North. As the first part of his Life was spent in the bustle of a Court, the latter part of it was dedicated to retirement, living almost entirely at his house at Chevening, in which parts he had always a considerable interest and influence, being very much beloved on Account of that good temper & affability for which he was remarkable.

The first public reference I can find to this Thomas Lord Dacre is that he matriculated at Magdalen College, Oxford, on November 23rd, 1667, when he was about fourteen years of age, under the description of 'Baron of Dacre Castell in the North,' and 'created' M.A. January 23rd, 1668.[1] He appears to have been in Paris in 1670.[2]

It seems rather strange that young Lord Dacre should have been as well received at the Court of Charles II. as he evidently was, his father having been a somewhat prominent opponent of the Stuart dynasty; and I think his introduction there must

[1] *F. A. O.*
[2] See mention of Lord Dacre's winning at cards from his cousin, *post*, p. 423.

TABLE TO SHOW RELATIONSHIP IN BLOOD BETWEEN THE EARL OF SUSSEX AND HIS WIFE

Paul Viscount Bayning, = Anne Glenham, = 2nd husband, D. Carlton, Viscount Dorchester.
d. 1629.   d. 1638-9.

                                   Mary = W. Villiers, = 2nd husband, the Marquis of Anglesea,
                                                 Viscount Grandison.

                                                      Barbara ~~~~~ Charles II.
                                                 Duchess of Cleveland.

Elizabeth = Francis Lennard,
created Countess   Baron Dacre.
of Sheppey.

              Thomas Lennard, = Lady Anne FitzRoy.
             Baron Dacre : created
                Earl of Sussex.

THE EARL OF SUSSEX'S ESTATES

have been the work of some member of the Bayning family, and probably that of his mother. Whoever it may have been that was responsible for bringing him at so early an age into the dissolute and extravagant Court set, it was a most unfortunate introduction for him, as it was the cause of his making an unhappy marriage, and of leading him into an expensive mode of life which he had not sufficient means to maintain. When he succeeded his father he came into a goodly remnant of the vast Dacre estates which his ancestor Samson had with his wife, although the lavishness of his father and other ancestors had done much to curtail its original proportions. I have an account of what his estates amounted to when he came of age, and from this account it appears that their annual value was as follows:—

	£
Cumberland and Westmoreland	647
Lincolnshire	798
Sussex	1,054
Quit-rents in Kent	26
Total from all estates	£2,525

Unfortunately the account in question is not perfect, as some of the front sheets are torn off, but on the other hand it contains a page which purports to be a summary of all the annual rents, and to the total income there shown is appended this note, 'The Totall Revenue.' The fact that the Chevening estate is not included in this rental account, and that in another account [1] a rent of about 100*l.* half-yearly appears as being paid to 'Lady Dacre' for Chevening in 1677, is evidence of the correctness of my theory, referred to in the previous chapter, that those properties were settled on Dorothy Lady Dacre for her life. In 1677 there were two Dowager Ladies Dacre, viz. Dorothy, the Earl's step-grandmother, and Elizabeth, his mother; the latter was created Countess of Sheppey, but not until 1680. There can be no doubt but that this 'Lady Dacre' means Dorothy, as we know the particulars of Elizabeth's marriage settlement, and there is no mention in it of Chevening. We have seen in the

---

[1] *Green.*

previous chapter Dorothy Lady Dacre was living at the Vyne in 1677, so she is not unlikely to have let Chevening to the Earl at this period. In yet another account[1] the rents from the Cumberland and Westmoreland estates are given as 785*l*. 15*s*. 4*d*., and those from Cudham and Apuldrefield, in Kent, as 457*l*.

The debts of his father were heavy, and so was his mother's jointure, and I think we may safely say that at the period when Lord Sussex[2] had his largest income it did not greatly exceed 3,000*l*.; still, in those days such an income would have been accounted a considerable one, and it is probable that when Lord Dacre was first introduced to Court there were but few unmarried noblemen mixing in society who were considered to be such an eligible match as the young, good-looking bearer of the ancient title of Dacre, and owner of Herstmonceux and the reversion to Chevening. It was presumably the prominent position which the possession of this title and these estates conferred upon him that caused him to be selected as husband for his cousin the King's daughter by Barbara Lady Castlemaine, afterwards Duchess of Cleveland. Thomas Lennard being under age and inexperienced, with no near male relative of whom to take counsel, it is not to be wondered at that he consented to a match which, although attractive in a way, had no substantial grounds to recommend it. No doubt the beauty of his child-intended rendered him willing to contract this marriage; we have no record of what she was like at that age, but the picture of her at Belhus when grown up, painted by the Swedish painter M. Dahl, represents her as a very lovely woman.[3]

Although Lady Anne was called FitzRoy, and was commonly spoken of as a daughter of Charles II., there is in a published pedigree of the Palmer family the following account of her birth and education :—

The Lady Anne Palmer daughter to the Earle of Castlemaine & Barbara Countesse of Castlemaine was borne the

---

[1] *L.P.* iv.   [2] To give him his future title.
[3] Dahl is said to have seen this picture some years after he had painted it, and to have declared that it was one of his best works.

previous chapter Dorothy Lady Dacre was living at the Vyne in 1677, so she is not unlikely to have let Chevening to the Earl at this period. In yet another account[1] the rents from the Cumberland and Westmoreland estates are given as 785*l*. 15*s*. 4*d*., and those from Cudham and Apuldrefield, in Kent, as 457*l*.

The debts of his father were heavy, and so was his mother's jointure, and I think we may safely say that at the period when Lord Sussex[2] had his largest income it did not greatly exceed 3,000*l*.; still, in those days such an income would have been accounted a considerable one, and it is probable that when Lord Dacre was first introduced to Court there were but few unmarried noblemen mixing in society who were considered to be such an eligible match as the young, good-looking bearer of the ancient title of Dacre, and owner of Herstmonceux and the reversion to Chevening. It was presumably the prominent position which the possession of this title and these estates conferred upon him that caused him to be selected as husband for his cousin the King's daughter by Barbara Lady Castlemaine, afterwards Duchess of Cleveland. Thomas Lennard being under age and unsupported with no near male relative of whom to take counsel, it is not to be wondered at that he consented to a match which, although attractive in a way, had no substantial grounds to recommend it. No doubt the beauty of his child-intended rendered him willing to contract this marriage; we have no record of what she was like at that age, but the picture of her at Belhus when grown up, painted by the Swedish painter M. Dahl, represents her as a very lovely woman.[3]

Although Lady Anne was called Palmer, and was commonly spoken of as a daughter of Charles II., there is in a published pedigree of the Palmer family the following account of her birth and education :—

The Lady Anne Palmer daughter to the Earle of Castlemaine & Barbara Countesse of Castlemaine was borne the

---

[1] *L.P.* iv.   [2] To give him his future title.
[3] Dahl is said to have seen this picture some years after he had painted it, and to have declared that it was one of his best works.

25 Feb[r] being Shrove Munday about 10 of the clock Anno 1660.[1] In the yeare '68 she was sent to a French Monastery at Challieau near Paris & was brought home the following yeare. Anno 1671 she was sent to my Lady Neville (Daughter to Lord Abergavenny) Abbesse of Pontoise in Normandy to be bred & returned againe to London November 1672. 3 yeares after she was married to Thomas Lennard Lord Dacres & Earl of Sussex.[2]

The old saying that "'Tis a wise child that knows its own father' was singularly applicable to Lady Anne's case. Her mother did not separate from her husband for some years after her birth, and he acknowledged Anne as his child; and though he does not in terms describe her as his daughter in his will, by that document he appointed her to be one of his trustees, and he left her both real and personal property, and also jewels. It is well known that the King and her mother passed the night of the Restoration (May 29th, 1660) together,[3] and her birth took place just nine months later; the King claimed her as his child, and granted her the royal arms with the baton sinister; while the Duchess in a letter written to Charles some eighteen years later, when she had broken with the King and was quarrelling with her daughter, says:—

Though I am so good a Christian as to forgive her, yeat I can not so fare conquer myself as to see her dayly, though your Maty may be confydent that as she is yours, I shall allwayes haue som remains of that kindness I had formerly for I can hate nothing that is yours.[4]

On the other hand many persons believed her father to have been the Earl of Chesterfield, who was her mother's first lover, and whom she is said to have much resembled both in face and person.

In August 1674, when only thirteen years and six months of age,[5] the Lady Anne was married at Hampton Court.

---

[1] 1661 of our reckoning.
[2] *Mis. Gen.* i. footnote, p. 110.
[3] *Stein.* p. 22.
[4] *Ibid.* p. 169.
[5] The C. P. states that she was born February 29th, 166½. For information about child-marriages *vide Chester Child-Marriages* by *Dr. Furnival, E. E. T. S.*

There exists the following contemporaneous account of the wedding:

About 9 in the morning, the Lord Dacre was conducted to the Dutchess of Cleveland's lodgings from his own by Mr. Onslow (tutor to the Dutchess's children) Sir John Baker and some other gentleman attending him, where the bride was ready dress'd to receive him. The King came from Windsor, a little after 12 o'clock, and, immediately repaired to the said Dutchess's lodgings and, having stayed a while, he led the bride out by the hand ; after them, came the bridegroom, then the Duke of York, leading the Dutchess of Cleveland, then, Prince Rupert, then, the ladies of kindred to the bride and bridegroom. In this manner they proceeded through the gallery; at the upper end thereof, in the antecamera to the King's bedchamber, they were married by Dr. Crew, Bishop of Oxford, after of Durham, according to the Book of Common Prayer, half an hour after 12 o'clock, where were present the King, the Duke of York, Prince Rupert, the Duke of Monmouth, Dom Carlos, Marquis del Fresno, Spanish ambassador, Earl of Suffolk, Earl of Arlington, Lord Keeper Finch, and Lord Treasurer Danby.

When the marriage was celebrated, the King first kissed the bride, and, by and by, the bridecake was broken over her head, which done, the married couple retired till dinner was ready.

The King led the bride to dinner, which was provided in the presence chamber, and placed her on his right hand, he sitting in the middle of the table, and the Dutchess of Cleveland on his left, the ladies of the kindred on both sides of the table, and at the end, on the King's left hand, the Lord Keeper and Lord Treasurer. The Duke of York, and the rest of the nobility had a table provided for them in another room.[1]

To provide for the wedding clothes of Lady Anne, and of her sister Lady Charlotte, who married the Earl of Lichfield,[2] the Duchess purchased of William Gosling & Co., lacemen, gold and silver lace to the value of 846*l.* 8*s.* 6*d.*; of Benjamin Drake, milliner, wares to the amount of 315*l.* 18*s.* 6*d.*; of Nicholas Fownes, mercer, wares to the amount of 642*l.* 14*s.* 6*d.*; of John Eaton, lace and other things to the amount of 1,082*l.* 8*s.* 10*d.*; of Peter Pretty & Co., mercers, wares to the amount of

---

[1] *Ashm.* 837, f. 214. [2] Sir E. H. Lee, Bart., created an Earl ; he died 1716.

55*l*. 11*s*.; amounting in all to 2,943*l*. 1*s*. 4*d*.; and of this amount the King paid out of the secret service funds 1,599*l*. 18*s*.[1]

In the same month as the marriage took place, Charles II. granted the bridegroom from his secret service fund an annuity of 2,000*l*. as a dower with his bride; and in the month of September following, he charged in his favour a sum of 20,000*l*. upon a specific fund, viz., on the indemnity of 200,000 'patacoons,'[2] which was due from the States-General of the Netherlands in accordance with the then recent treaty of peace, which sum of 20,000*l*. was to be in lieu of the annuity;[3] and when the Duchess went to live in France the King granted the Countess those lodgings in Whitehall which her mother had previously occupied.[4] The annuity was only paid for a very few years, and the lump sum of 20,000*l*. is still owing, although the Earl of Sussex, and after his death his daughters, in vain made efforts to obtain payment of it. In the December following Andrew Marvel writes: 'Some ladyes tell me that there is a collection of pearls making in all parts to make a necklace of 8,000li. which the King presents to the Countess of Sussex.'[5]

It could not be expected that Lady Anne, the child of such parents, would prove a satisfactory wife. 'What's born in the bone will come out in the flesh,' and never could the proverb apply more accurately than it did in her case, and anyone who may have hoped for any better result must have been entirely devoid of any belief in the teachings of heredity. How much the poor girl deserved blame for her subsequent profligate behaviour is difficult to say, as from the point of view of morals she had everything against her. Not only was she born of parents remarkable for their licentiousness, but being married when still a mere child, she enjoyed the freedom accorded by custom to married women at a period when of a tender and

---

[1] *Stein.* p. 148.
[2] A Portuguese dollar formerly struck for use in Brazil.—*C. D.*
[3] We have the warrant to the Earl of Danby and others directing its payment.
[4] *Beauties.* [5] *Hist Com.* vi. App. p. 473.

impressionable age she ought to have still been in the schoolroom. One can imagine no worse education for a young girl than that which she would receive at the Court of the 'Merry Monarch'; and mixing in the society in which she did, it is no wonder that such references to her as are to be found in the publications of that day are far from being to her credit. Of all her profligate women friends, the Duchess of Mazarin was probably the worst, and Rochester's lines which refer to their friendship and to the Duchess's negro—'That loathsome ugly black,'[1] as he calls him, are perhaps too coarse to print in the present day.

The Countess was still only a child, not much more than fifteen years of age, when, on July 12th, 1676,[2] she gave birth to a child, who was christened Barbara after her grandmother the Duchess. Barbara married Charles Skelton, lieutenant-general in the French army, and Grand Croix of St. Louis; she died in Paris, 1741, leaving no issue.[3]

Lady Sussex's other children are as follows:—

Charles, baptized at Windsor Castle, June 3rd, 1682; he is said to have died aged only eighteen months;[4] in fact, he was a little older, as he died 'bout 10 att night 13th March 168¾.'[5]

Henry, died an infant.

Anne, born August 17th, 1684;[6] married as her first husband her cousin, Richard Barrett.

In October 1674 the King raised Lord Dacre to the dignity of an Earl by the title of Sussex; a news-letter of September 8th mentions that his patent is passing the signet;[7] he received his writ of summons on May 19th, 1675, and was introduced to the House of Lords two days later.[8] The Earl was appointed a Gentleman of the Bedchamber. Among our papers is an ancient copy of a grant to him by the King of a pension of 1,000*l.* for life upon this appointment in the place of

---

[1] *Poems*, i. p. 167. There is also reference to the Countess, *ibid.* p. 143.
[2] *Stein.* p. 224.
[3] MS. pedigree.
[4] The C. P.
[5] *Green.*
[6] *Stein.* p. 224.
[7] *Hist. Com.* xii. App. vii. p. 113.
[8] *Hist. Com.* ix. p. 62.

Thomas Earl of Ossory, deceased; and the document is endorsed, 'Passed here 5th Aug. 1680.' But some three years previously the Earl appears to have obtained the reversion to Lord Ossory's post, as among Greenwood's accounts for 1677 I have found the following entries on September 22nd in that year:—[1]

<pre>
Pd Mr Vice Chamberlaynes man for
  Certificat of ye Bed Chamber Place
  for his LordP 00 10 00
Given to ye Ringers at Chevening by
  order 00 05 00
</pre>

The latter entry, no doubt, refers to a peal rung at the Earl's parish church in honour of the occasion. It should be mentioned that Greenwood appears to have been a sort of confidential steward or secretary to Lord Sussex.

Evelyn mentions that in December 1674 Lady Sussex acted at the Court in a masque called 'Calisto or the chaste Nymph.'[2] This play, or masque, was written by John Crowne, and published by him in 1675. Turning as it does upon the sudden passion of Jupiter for the nymph Calisto, it is perhaps rather less coarse than might have been expected for a play at that period dealing with such a subject. At the beginning of the play the author gives what we should now call the 'original cast,' but which he presents to his readers in the following high-flown strain:—

It having been the manner of all those who have had the Honour, before me, to serve the Court in employments of this nature to adorn their works with the names of those Great Persons who had parts in the Representation, I hope I shall not be condemned if I, following their Examples, Consecrate this of mine to Posterity by the same Policy.

The Persons of the Play.   The Personators.

Calisto a chaste & favourite Nymph of Diana beloved by Jupiter. } Her Highness the Lady Mary.

---

[1] *Green.*   [2] *Eve.* ii. p. 94.

Nyphe, a chaste young nymph friend to Calisto.	Her Highness the Lady Anne.
Jupiter in love with Calisto .	The Lady Henrietta Wentworth.
Juno	The Countess of Sussex.
Psecas, an envious nymph enemy to Calisto, beloved by Mercury.	The Lady Mary Mordaunt.
Dianna Goddess of Chastity.	Mrs Blagge late maid of honour to the Queen.
Mercury in love with Psecas.	Mrs Jennings Maid of Honour to the Dutchess.

Nymphs attending on Diana who also danced in the Prologue, and in several entries in the Play.

      The Countess of Darby.
      The Countess of Pembroke.
      The Lady Katherine Herbert.
      Mrs FitzGerald.
      Mrs Frazier Maid of Honour to the Queen.

The part of Juno was one of the most important in the play, and the fact that it was allotted to the Countess shows that she was a prominent member of what we should now call 'the smart set' in the fashionable society of those days. Nearly two years later, in September 1676, when Evelyn supped at the Lord Chamberlain's, he records that the Duchess of Mazarin and the Countess of Sussex were among the company present.[1]

This great intimacy of the Countess with a person so notorious as the Duchess was, as might be expected, extremely distasteful to Lord Sussex, and there are references in several letters written by Lady Chaworth[2] to the attitude of remonstrance the Earl adopted towards his giddy young wife on the impropriety of her conduct, and his determination to get her away from London in the hopes that in the comparative seclusion of Herstmonceux she would shake off the bad influence of Madame Mazarin, and that of her other fast

---

[1] *Eve.* ii. p. 108.
[2] Daughter of the Seventh Earl of Rutland.

THE COUNTESS OF SUSSEX

friends about the Court. In giving an account of the Lord Mayor's Show on November 2nd, 1676, she says :—

I was in Cheapside and had the good luck to escape the squibs which were very plentifull, especially directed to the balcone over against me where the Duchess of Mazarine, Lady Sussex, Prince of Monaco, and Portingall Embassador stood, one of them lighting such [sic] on Lady Sussex's which forced [her] presently to put on a huge patch. They say her husband and she will part unless she leave the Court and be content to live with him in the country he disliking her much converse with Madame Mazarine and the addresses she gets among that company.[1]

About a month later, on December 12th, she writes : —

Lord Sussex is well again and continues peremptory to take his wiffe out of towne and she is to conclude dancing with the ball tonight att the Dutchesse's and goes out of towne they say tomorrow or next day.[2]

And again, on December 25th :—

Lady Sussex is not yet gone but my Lord is better, and holds his resolution of goeing as soone as the weather breaks up to make good travailing. She and Madam Mazarine have privately learnt to fence, and went down into St. James's Park the other day with drawn swords under their night gownes, which they drew out and made several fine passes with, to the admiration of several men which was lookers on in the Park.[3]

In the following month—viz. January 167⁶⁄₇—Lady Chaworth, who appears to have taken a deep interest in Lady Sussex's doings, mentioned in a letter of the 19th that 'Lady Sussex continues very ill and phisitians are gone down to see her';[4] and recurring to her favourite topic, says on the 28th : 'Lady Sussex is mightily pleased with fox hunting and hare hunting but kisses Madame Mazarine's picture with much affection still.'[5]

How conspicuous a figure the Countess cut in fashionable

---

[1] *Hist. Com.* xii. Part v. vol. ii. p. 31.
[2] *Ibid.* p. 33.
[3] *Ibid.* p. 34.
[4] *Ibid.* p. 36.
[5] *Ibid.*

circles at that period is shown by the fact that in the Verney correspondence, Sir John Verney, writing to Edmund Verney about that period, says: 'Lady Sussex is at last, tho' unwillingly, gone with her Lord into the Country.'[1]

We have by no means such complete accounts of the household expenses of the Earl of Sussex as those of his father, previously referred to[2] and to some extent quoted from in this chapter. I have only found some fragments of an account book for part of the year 1677; still, these are sufficiently full for us to learn from them something of the life which the Earl and his Countess were then leading at Herstmonceux.

What in these accounts were described as 'Household expences' for the seventeen weeks over which these fragments extend show that the average expenditure under that head was somewhat over 14l. a week, or between 700l. and 800l. a year. I am not able to state exactly what items were included under this heading, but servants' wages were not, as they are entered separately; and some of these appear to have received much higher wages than were paid at Herstmonceux in the time of the Earl's father: especially was this the case in respect to the cook Francis and his wife—the former had 12l. 17s. for wages due at midsummer, and the latter 25l.; but as these fragmentary accounts extend to only one entry of wages paid to any one servant, it is impossible to tell whether such wages were paid for three months or for some longer term. The wages at Herstmonceux do not appear to have been paid very punctually, as those due at midsummer were not received until well into August. While on this subject of servants' wages it may be noted that the gamekeeper Clark must have held a very important position in the establishment, as his wages were 12l. 10s. a quarter, or nearly as much as a Norfolk head keeper's wages are in the present day: besides this he received a fee of 10s. for bucks killed and given away; thus, 'p^d Mr Clark two ffees one for ye Buck sent to my Ld Treasurer and one sent to

---

[1] *Hist. Com.* vii. App. p. 468. [2] *Ante*, p. 284.

Mr Robt Lennard.'[1] What seems very curious is that in May we find: 'paid to my Lord at ye death of ye first buck 00..10..00.' Out of whose pocket did this payment come? It appears as a debit, and, if so, the Earl's steward in making this payment merely paid his employer 10s. with which he was subsequently to debit him.

We have heard from one of Lady Chaworth's letters how kindly Lady Sussex took to hunting on her arrival at Herstmonceux; the only reference to this sport in these accounts is that in April 2s. 6d. was given to the man 'that brought ye hounds from Sir R. Parker.' When hunting was over cricket matches helped to pass away the summer, and we see that in June the keeper of the accounts 'p^d to my Lord when his Lord^p went to the crekitt match at ye Dick^{er} 03..00..00.' It is not clear why Lord Sussex wanted so much money in order to attend a cricket match; one can only suppose that he, being the principal person in the neighbourhood, considered he ought to entertain all the players. Dicker Common was of considerable extent previous to its enclosure in 1819, and was situated about five or six miles from Herstmonceux, in the parish of Chiddingly. They also played other games, for we find in August: 'Lent to my Lady at Nyne pinns 00..01..00.'

The only other entry I have found connected with sport is in September, when 1s. was 'given to Richard pook for finding of partridges'; this may have been paid to 'pook' for finding birds for hawking, or possibly in order to shoot at them with one of the 'birding pieces' or 'snaphaunces' which the household account book shows that they had in the castle at the time of Francis Lord Dacre.

They seem to have been fond of music, as such items as 'pd to ye Musick' are fairly frequent; as a rule the sums chronicled as paid on that account are so small—2s. or 3s.—as to suggest village bands or itinerant players, but on one occasion no less a sum than 2l. 5s. is recorded as 'p^d to ye musick.'

[1] Robert was a first cousin once removed of the Earl, being a son of Fynes, and grandson of Henry Lord Dacre, *ante*, p. 251.

Every lawyer who remembers his 'Smith's Leading Cases' knows from the 'Six Carpenters' case how common a drink wine was in Stuart days, and in these accounts we have an instance of this in the following entry: 'ffor a bottle of wine for ye officers of excise at Battle & for my horse 00..01..02'; and in those days of cheap living tobacco was also much less expensive than now, as we read, 'P^d for 1 lb. of Tobacco 00..03..06.' Farming stock was ridiculously cheap also, as is shown by, 'P^d for 50 Cows 26..00..00,' and 'P^d for a bull 02..05..00.'

The young Countess was no doubt very smart, being attended everywhere by her page, for whom a silver-hilted sword was bought at a cost of 1*l.* 7*s.* 6*d.* and an embroidered belt and silver buckles for 16*s.*; but, in spite of her luxurious surroundings, she appears to have become terribly bored by her life in the country alone with her husband, which the delights of hunting, 'nyne pinns,' and 'crekitt matches' were not powerful enough to counteract. It may be that, after leading so gay a life at Court, she pined for the society of the Duchess of Mazarin and other kindred spirits whom she met there, or it may have been that she found the company of the Earl was not congenial. Whatever the cause, being discontented at home, and not being able to return to the Court without an open breach with her husband, it was only natural that her thoughts should turn to France, where she had been brought up, and which she had only quitted some five years before. I have no evidence to show exactly when she did go to Paris, but not until after the latter part of September 1677, as we have these entries towards the end of that month: 'P^d for 2 Paire of French gloues 11^s; for one Trimed 1^{li} 5^s; for Lady Sussex 01..16..00.' 'P^d for 3 paire of Large knitt stockings for Lady Sussex 01..17..06.' On the 18th of the following December we find Lady Chaworth writing about the Countess again as follows: 'Lady Sussex is put by her Mother into a religious house in France, and she means certainly to come hither in the spring either to ajust things better between her and her

Lord or to get his consent that her daughter may goe into orders.'[1]

When the Countess did go to Paris she left her infant child behind her. This is shown by such entries in Lord Sussex's accounts as 'Paid for a night gown &c. for Lady Bab 01..16..00' in February 167¾; the child had been learning to walk before her mother's departure, as in the previous June we find, 'P^d for a goe cartt for Lady Bab 00..04..00.'

The King appears to have given christening plate to 'Lady Bab,' the little bearer of his favourite's name, as we see, 'Oct. 1677, P^d at ye Jewell office ye fees for Lady Bab's christening plate 1^s per ounce; office keeper 5^s; 06..15..00'; and again, 'March 167⅔ P^d att Sr Robt Vyners[2] for Exchange of Lady Bab's plate and for engraueing 01..09..06.'

After the Countess had left her husband to go to France he gave up their lodgings in Whitehall; indeed, from the entries in the accounts, he appears to have given them up a few months before she had left, as we read in the accounts: 'Aug. 1677, P^d Tom the Porter for helping to cleane the Lodging att Whitehall when delivered up 00..09..00'; and later on the Earl sold chimney-pieces out of that house which were presumably tenant's fixtures, 'Nov. 1677, Rec^d for a Marble chimney Peece from Whitehall 07..00..0,' and again, 'Apl. 1678, Rec^d of Mr. Cromp for a Chimney of Marble sold from Whitehall 05..00..00.'

I think it also probable that Lord Sussex either sublet Chevening, or attempted to do so, during the autumn that his wife went to Paris. In no other way can I explain this entry: 'Nov. 1677, P^d for putting Chevening house into ye City Mercury & upon ye Change 00..12..06.' Unfortunately, there is not a copy of the 'Mercury' for that date in the British Museum, and so I am unable to say positively that the house was advertised, but the above entry seems to bear no other construction. The

---

[1] *Hist. Com.* xii. Part v. vol. ii. p. 44.
[2] Sir Robert Vyner was one of the Masters of the Mint, and 'King's Goldsmith.' —The C. B.

following two entries also look as if they record expenditure in connection with attempts to sublet Chevening :—

Jany 1677, P^d & Expended to wait on Lady Vane in & about London for Chevening—02..00..00.

July 20, 1678, Sp^t upon Mr Mann goeing to view Chevening 00..03..00.

It is clear that Lord Sussex wished to cut timber at Chevening, and possibly did so, as his right to timber is one of several matters upon which the celebrated Serjeant Raymond was consulted on his behalf, and the fees paid to him are recorded in these accounts.

The Earl at this period seems to have made habitable, and occasionally lived at, Dacre Castle, near Penrith; over the principal entrance are the arms of Lennard quartering those of Fynes, Dacre, and Moulton, carved in white marble and surmounted by an earl's coronet, which he no doubt had set up when he repaired the old building. Among the accounts of Sir D. Fleming is this entry: ' 20 Sept. 1680, Given at my Lord Sussex's at Penrith being invited by Sir J. Lowther to dine with his Lordship there—00..03..00.'[1]

Judging from the following extract from a letter written to Thomas Lord Dacre in 1784 by Mr. J. C. Brooke, Somerset Herald, there appears to have been remarkably little accommodation in Dacre Castle :—

We were two or three days at Dalemaine the seat of Mr. Hasell, the present owner of the Castle and Manor of Dacre wch gave me an opportunity of being much at that place: It excites one's wonder to imagin how a family of such note as the Dacres, who were Barons when they resided there, cou'd possibly accommodate themselves in so small a building as the Castle, which, except one large room on each story, contains only a small closet, hardly large enough to hold a bed, in each angular tower.

One of the reasons which probably made Lord Sussex more inclined than otherwise he would have been to sublet Chevening

[1] *Hist. Com.* xii. Part vii. p. 395.

THE EARL OF SUSSEX'S DEBTS

was that, being a Groom of the Bedchamber, he had no doubt to spend a good deal of each year in attendance on the King. The accounts I so often refer to show that he went to Windsor in September 1679, and that while there became ill, so we find, 'P^d porter to carry his Lord^p trunk sent to Windsor—01..00'; and in the same month 'P^d Coachire & expences at Windsor for self when his Lord^p was sick 01..15..00'; 'P^d for oranges & Lemonds for his Lord^p 01..00.'

All this time Lord Sussex was, no doubt, greatly exceeding his income, but the accounts, although they show that he was constantly borrowing money, do not throw much light on his gambling propensities:—

'October, 1679, P^d Fynlo his journey to Herstmonceux 00..04..00 P^d more for cards he carried down . . . . 00..11..00'

show that the Earl liked to be provided with the implements of gaming, but does not carry the matter much further. An entry a few days later—' Returned into Sussex for his Lord^p by note 100..00..00'—suggests that the cards sent down did not bring luck to the head of the Lennards; and such an entry some two years earlier, as 'P^d to my L^d when Sir Thos Dyke dined here 02..03..00,' looks as if the dinner had been followed by an unsuccessful night's play, and this amount possibly represents the host's losses after he had parted with all his ready money to his guests.

The borrowings were on a much larger scale; one sum of 5,000*l*. Lord Sussex appears to have paid interest on at the very moderate rate of six per cent.; but besides this, and other large sums, there is continual reference to money in smaller amounts being borrowed in a hurry, such as—'Nov. 1678, P^d a messenger out of London for money 00..01..00'; 'coachire & charges to fetch £100 of money 00..02..06.'

At this period Lady Sussex was still living over in Paris with her mother the Duchess, who then resided there; and the King himself seems to have attempted to bring about a reconciliation between the young couple. We have a letter

Y

dated June 4th[1] by Ann Barrett[2] (who was a cousin of the Earl), in which she says :—

My Ld Sussex has received a message by Sr. Thomas Bond,[3] and Colonel Villars[4] from his Lady to receive her again, and 'tis believed if he should refuse, which he has not yett, but defers his answer till she has writt to him herself, the Dutchess will prevaile wth the King to stopp his pension of 2,000 li a yeare, and by that means force him to it ; I hope the hearing she is much handsomer than ever will revive my Ld's old Love, and without trying rough meanes they may come together and live as affectionately as Sr. John Williams[5] and his Lady, who are now as fond a couple as your faire Mistress and Mr Finch who have been married 3 weeks.

The Duchess had occasion to come over for a short period to England in the spring of 1678, and during her absence she left her daughter under the care of the Abbess of Conflans, near Paris ; but on her return she found that her wayward child had left Conflans and moved into the religious house of the Holy Sepulchre in the quartier of St. Germain within that city.[6]

During the residence of the Duchess in Paris she had carried on an intrigue with the Hon. Ralph Montagu (afterwards Duke of that name) who was the English Ambassador there ;[7] and perhaps the most revolting episode in Lady Sussex's career of profligacy occurred during her mother's visit to England, as she then took the opportunity of her mother's absence to supplant her in the affections of Montagu.

Henry Savile, writing in July 1678 to the Earl of Rochester, is full of the news, and says :—

[1] The letter does not bear the date of the year, but the context proves it to be 1678.
[2] Daughter of Richard Barrett the elder.
[3] Controller to the Dowager Queen's household, created baronet, 1658, in Brussels. Bond Street is said to have been named after him.
[4] Villiers, eldest son of Viscount Grandison and nephew of Duchess of Cleveland ; he died *v.p.*, 1690.
[5] Probably Sir J. Williams, of Marnhull, Dorset, second and last baronet. He married, 1673, Susan, daughter of Sir Thomas Skipwith, Bart.—The C. B.
[6] *Stein.* p. 156.
[7] Mr. Fea states that the Ambassador had secret instructions from the King to get her away from her mother.—*Beauties.* See also footnote, *S. T.* xi. p. 599.

THE COUNTESS OF SUSSEX

There are terrible doeings att Paris betwixt my Lady Cleaveland and her daughter Sussex. As I am a friend to the family, till the storey bee more compleate I will not venture at sending you the whole relation, but whilst the Mother was in England the daughter was debauched by our Embassador Mr. Montaigue, who has lived with her in the most open scandall, to the wonder of the French Court and the high displeasure of this, the King being very angry with the Embassador, and his friends and ennemyes now struggling at Court to support or ruine him.[1]

The Duchess wrote a long letter to the King complaining of her daughter's behaviour, of which the following is an extract:—

Paris, Tuesday [May 16] 78.

I was never so surprized in my holle lifetime as I was at my Comming hither, to find my Lady Sussex gone from my house and monestrey where I left her & this letter from her which I now send you a copy of. I never in my holle lifetime heard of suche government of herself as She has had since I went into England. She has never been in the monestery two daies together, but every day gone out with the embassador; and has often layen four daies together at my house, & sent for her meat to the Embassador, he being allwaies with her till 5 a'clock in ye morning, they two shut up together alone, & w^d not let my maistre d'hostel wait, nor any of my servants, onely the Embassador's. This made so great a noise at Paris, that she is now the holle discourse. I am so much afflicted that I can hardly write this for crying, to see that a child that I doated on as I did on her, sh^d make so ill a return, & join with the worst of men to ruin me.[2]

I am not able to say what King Charles wrote to the Duchess in reply, but from the tenour of a second letter from her to him, it is clear that his letter was quite satisfactory to her, as she says : 'I reseud your Ma^{ty} letter last night with more Joy than I can expres for this prosiding of yours is so jenoros and obliging that I must be the worst wooman aliue ware I not sensible.' She goes on to say that she had sent Lady Sussex the King's letter, which she refused to return; she also repeats

---

[1] *Hist. Com.* (Marquis of Bath), ii. p. 166.   [2] *Stein.* pp. 156 *et seq.*

her story about her daughter's intimacy with the 'Embassador' and begs the King to have her put into the Abbey of Portroyal, for whar she is now all pepell uisits her, and the Embasodor and others, caryes consorts of museke euery day to entertan her, so that the holle disscores of this place is of nothing but of her, and she must bee ruend if you doe not tacke some spedy cores with her; this Portroyall that I propos to you is in great reputation for the piete and regularety of it, so that I thinke it much the best place for her.[1]

There is the following letter in the British Museum [2] from the Earl of Sussex, which is only dated 'July ye 20,' but from its context it seems safe to assume that it was written about the same time as these letters from the Duchess, viz. 1678; there is nothing to show to whom it was addressed, but, from a reference in the postscript, it would appear that the King had taken the advice the Duchess had given as to where her daughter was to be made to take up her abode, and had given up the idea of compelling the Earl to take his wife back again:

July ye 20.

Since your depart from hence I recieued a letter from Lady Sussex wch I haue sent a copy to my Lady Duchesse and like wise my answer to her letter; where she may see how ungratefull she is for all her past favours wch I hope will disabuse her of those ill impression she had of me, and now y^t her actions has declared her guilt it will be a iustification; that I were not capable of those ills her daughter would haue rendered me to the world. S^r I am confident your good word was neuer wanting in the seruice of y^r friend, and to y^t end I beg your assistance and interest to her Grace, wch I am sure is such as will soone establish her good opinion of me, wch will bring Noonday to him y^t has so long endured night, and euer oblige S^r your faithful serv^{ant} SUSSEX.

I showed ye King her letter who was enraged at y^t part of it y^t touched her Mother; and for ye rest swore it was lyes, and y^t she was ye worst of women and should suffer by it: for y^t in case she came hither he would send her back by the same Voiture without seeing her; and for the future would take care she should be neither a scandal to himself or me and had giuen

---

[1] *Stein.* pp. 164 *et seq.* *Add.* 21505, 32.   [2] *Eger.* 1169, fol. 21.

order to my Lord Sunderland[1] for ye placing of her a La Porte Royal. I suppose you may easily haue a sight of these letters I send my Lady Cleaueland, wch I would willingly you should haue, y^t I may haue y^r opinion of w^t I haue done, and w^t ressentments they haue with her.

Before her death in 1709 the Duchess appears to have become reconciled with her daughter in spite of their rivalry about Montagu, as by her will she left the Countess her 'striking watch' and other trinkets, and made bequests of a similar nature to the Countess's daughters, the Ladies Ann and Barbara Lennard. Moreover in a letter from the Duchess, afterwards referred to,[2] she expressed much concern on her daughter's behalf for the extravagance of Lord Sussex.

Greenwood's accounts show that during Lady Sussex's stay in France there were not infrequent letters sent to and received from that country by Lord Sussex, as such entries as: 'June, 1679, P^d for a ffrench packett 00..02..06.' 'September, 1679, P^d postage to Paris for his Lord^p l̄res 00..00..10,'[3] are not of uncommon occurrence. It would seem, therefore, as if the Earl and his Countess did not lose touch of each other; but I have found nothing to show what led them to become reconciled, nor when they again began to live together. It presumably was not later than the autumn of 1681, because, as I have said, in 1682 she gave birth to a boy who was christened Charles.

The King was not improbably an active agent in bringing his daughter and her husband together once more, and it is not unlikely that he permitted the christening of this child to take place at Windsor, and himself stood sponsor, in order to show that he at least did not choose to believe her guilty of that freedom of conduct which, according to her mother, was such as to make Lady Sussex the 'holle discorse of Paris.' In a letter from the Countess of Northampton, written on June 10th, 1682, there is

---

[1] Principal Secretary for State.—*Hay. Dig.*   [2] *Post*, p. 332.
[3] Among these accounts there is an item of 1*s.* 6*d.* for postage of a letter to Ireland; it is therefore difficult to understand how *more* than *one* letter could have been sent to Paris for less than the cost of one to Ireland.

a reference to the favour with the King in which his daughter, whom he seems entirely to have forgiven, then stood. She says: 'Cleaveland has not yett seene the King tho' he is so kind to her daughter Lady Sussex as to bye Lord Falkenbridges house for her.'[1]

We have no evidence as to how the Earl and his Countess got on together after her return, but the following lines by Rochester, written about this date, show what sort of reputation Lady Sussex then enjoyed :—

> And here would time permit me I could tell
> Of Cleveland, Portsmouth, Crofts & Arundel,
> Moll Howard, Su – – – x, Lady Grey and Nell.
> Strangers to good, but bosom Friends to ill,
> As boundless in their lusts, as in their will.[2]

It shows a remarkable state of public taste then prevailing which made it possible for a person like Rochester, constantly mixing in the society of these ladies, to publish such scurrilous lines about them, let their conduct be what it might; and, as I have already mentioned, there are references to her in other verses by the same author which are hardly possible to print.

In January 1682 Evelyn again mentions the Countess, whom he says he met at the entertainment of the Morocco Ambassador at the Duchess of Portsmouth's, where 'there were at a long table a lady placed between two Moors and amongst these Lady Lichfield & Sussex, the Duchess of Portsmouth, Nelly, &c. concubines, and cattle of that sort, as splendid as jewels & excess of bravery could make them.'[3]

Among other extravagant tastes of Lord Sussex was that of horse-racing; I have not been able to discover how far he indulged in this sport, but he certainly gave the Newmarket Challenge whip which bears his arms and is still occasionally competed for.[4] It is not likely that the Countess would exert any influence she might possess over her husband to induce him to pause in his extravagant way of living, which was fated

[1] *Hist. Com.* xii. Part v. vol. ii. p. 75. [2] *Poems*, vol. ii. p. 131.
[3] *Eve.* ii. p. 162. [4] *Bad. R.*

to bring him to ruin; indeed, from what we know of her breeding and bringing up, she might have been expected to encourage rather than curb his expensive tastes. We have a statement of accounts between the Earl and some person not named therein, and in these it appears that he was debited in a sum of 200*l.* for moneys paid to Lady Sussex at Newmarket on October 23rd, 1683; the mere payment to her at Newmarket of this sum is not in itself an absolute proof that the money was spent in gambling, but I think it is fair to conclude that this was probably the case.

In October 1684 Lord Sussex was at Newmarket, as an item in Greenwood's accounts is 'Lres to Newmarket for his Lord^p 00..00..09'; and as the item before that is 'Expended in Coach hire to fetch £200 out of London at tymes— 00..04..06'; and the one after 'To his Lord^p by note as appears—120..05..00,' it does not look as if the Earl, to use modern slang, had 'had a good week' there.

A little earlier in that year, in the month of August, Greenwood charges 12*s.* 6*d.* 'for copping [copying] a Perticular of Lord Sussex estate for ye King'; which looks as if the Earl had been driven to ask his father-in-law for pecuniary assistance, and for the purpose of making clear his need of such help, had furnished him with a full account of his financial position; it may not improbably be that he merely petitioned to have paid him what was owing on his annuity now greatly in arrear.[1] To get payment of money due from a Stuart was pretty well as hopeless a task as to get blood out of the proverbial stone, and it is hardly likely that he was successful in his appeal; in any case Lord Sussex appears to have been getting more and more straitened for money, in spite of his mother's death in 1684, by which he benefited financially, as in April 1685 we read: 'P^d Porter & charges about selling the Plate table & stands to Mr Child 00..08..00.'

In the month of June 1685 there was a sum of 1,090*l.* 16*s.* 5*d.* due to Greenwood from Lord Sussex on a balance of accounts

[1] *Add.* 33054, f. 51.

which had been running since 1677, and as the Earl appears to have been unable to pay him the whole amount then due, he granted him a lease for thirty-one years of Dacre Castle, Park, and of a parcel of woodland, all in the county of Cumberland, and paid him 90*l.* 16*s.* 5*d.*; and in consideration thereof obtained a receipt in full for the debt. There is no mention made of any rent being reserved, so it is to be supposed that Greenwood obtained possession of these premises free of rent for the extent of his term.

I think it quite probable that the cause of the final separation between the Earl and his wife was a difference in opinion arising out of the change of dynasty. The Earl was a staunch Protestant, and on December 11th, 1688, he was one of those peers who signed an order to the Earl of Dartmouth bidding him offer no opposition to the Prince of Orange's fleet, and to remove all papist officers from their commands.[1] Lady Sussex not unnaturally took the side of her uncle, the fallen King, and determined to follow his fortunes on the Continent. She had obtained permission from the Prince of Orange for a passage to France, when on December 26th Pepys wrote to the Earl of Dartmouth to say that,

The Prince was pleased this day to hold his hand from signing a warrant I had by his order prepared for the Mary yacht's transporting the Lady Sussex to France, saying that he was likely very suddenly to have an occasion of his own to make use of all his yachts, & therefore should not let any of them goe abroad on other occasions.[2]

Although foiled in her attempt to go in the 'Mary,' this rebuff did not prevent the Countess from joining her exiled sovereign, as soon after she went to France accompanied by her two daughters, and attaching herself to the Court of King James, was made a Lady of the Bedchamber to his Queen, Mary of Modena. Lady Sussex was an early arrival at the Court of St. Germains, and it was said by Danjean that

there are four ladies of the Queen of England whom she will have seated when there are either Princesses, or Duchesses of

[1] *Hist. Com.* xi. Part v. p. 229. [2] *Ibid.* p. 241.

LADY BARBARA

France present. These are Lady Powis an English Duchess, Madam Montecuculi, & the Ladies Sussex and Waldegrave as daughters of King James.[1]

I think it probable that Lady Sussex continued to make France her home until her husband died, but she was over in England, possibly only for short periods, in 1705, 1707, and 1711. In 1705 she proved the will of Lord Castlemain, who in the eyes of the law was her father; in 1707 she was a party with the Earl to the conveyance of Apuldrefield; and in the latter year she executed a deed by which she and her husband came to a settlement about some property which Lord Castlemain had left her.

Barbara Lennard

While at St. Germains an attachment sprang up between the Countess's eldest daughter, Barbara, and General Skelton, and they were ultimately married, though her father showed considerable reluctance in giving his consent, as the General was a Roman Catholic, and by his adherence to James had rendered himself an alien to England.[2] I am not able to give the date of this marriage; in October 1704 Luttrell writes: "'Tis said the Lord Tenham is to be married to the Lady Barbara Leonard [*sic*] daughter to the Earl of Sussex.'[3] There is apparently a curious confusion in this statement, because some years later Lord Teynham did marry, as his third wife, Barbara's sister Anne. It is, of course, quite possible that in 1704 Lord Teynham was paying attention to one of the sisters, and that rumour coupled his name with the elder one; or it may be that he did become engaged to Barbara, that the match was broken off, and that years after he married her sister, then a widow;

---

[1] *Strick.* ix. p. 295, who says that the first of the two last named was, however, a daughter of Charles II.

[2] *Coll. Peer.* His father was Bevill Skelton, second son of Sir John, an ardent Royalist, to whose memory there is a monument in the old church at Plymouth. Bevill served as page-of-honour to Charles II. during his exile, and after the Restoration filled several posts of importance. He followed James II. when he went to St. Germains, where he was Controller of the Household.

[3] *Lutt.* v. p. 474.

but in the absence of more knowledge of the facts speculation on this matter might be endless. Lady Barbara cannot have married until 1711, as in one of our deeds dated that year she is described as 'Lady Barbara Lennard.' It is said that Barbara's sister Anne became a Roman Catholic in 1698,[1] and it is probable that the sisters changed their religion at the same period.

Much harassed by increasing debts, and with his income greatly diminished, as since the death of Charles II. his wife's annuity had ceased to be paid, it is no wonder that the Earl, being so put to it for ready money, should take steps to have the entail cut off on some of his lands. Accordingly a bill was brought into the House of Lords in January 169$\frac{2}{3}$[2] to enable him to sell Herstmonceux Castle and his Sussex estates, and to modify the existing settlements which affected those in Kent, Cumberland, and Westmoreland, which, it was mentioned, amounted in value to 1,200*l.* a year.

The bill recited that the promised dowry of 20,000*l.* had never been paid, that the Earl's debts amounted to a like amount, and that these debts had been in part contracted by his father and in part by himself, occasioned by the great expenses he had been put to by his marriage. The bill was only read once, and Herstmonceux was not sold until some years later; but I have no means of knowing how Lord Sussex contrived to make both ends meet in the meantime. It may have been by sales of other properties; in Lord Dacre's History there is the following note:—

Estates sold by Lord Sussex (inter alia).	
To Mr Naylor Herstmonceux	£38,000
Mr Woodnot Bucks	6,500
The house in Town in Warwick St. Charing Cross	3,400
Mr. Glover part of Apurfield	1,090
Thos Know another part of Apurfield	3,030 [3]
Henry Powell another part of do.	395
Thos Stratfield Cowdham [Cudham] Court & Manor	1,760
	£54,175

[1] *Lutt.* iv. p. 466.   [2] *Hist. Com.* xiv. Part vi. p. 319.
[3] Sold in July 1707.

It will be observed that this list does not give the date of these various sales, and from the words *inter alia* in brackets it would appear that the Earl sold other properties not mentioned here, of which probably Lord Dacre had not been enabled to obtain particulars.

In 1698, by the death of Dorothy Lady Dacre, Chevening, and the rest of the Kent property which had been subject to her jointure, came to Lord Sussex. Towards the end of Dorothy's life there arose some coolness, or misunderstanding, between her and the Earl. In her will, dated July 1691, she made a bequest to him, which she revoked by a codicil dated March 1694, in which she said she had bequeathed to him her own picture 'now at my house at Chevening drawn by Sir Anthony Van Dyke . . . as a memorial of me.' Lady Dacre then goes on to say that since then she has 'found very unexpected neglect and disesteeme' from him, 'which have assured me that my bequest would have been valued by his Lordship for the painter's sake more than my owne, I having formerly hopes that his particular obligacons to me would have pcured [procured] better acknowledgem[ts] from him than any consideracon of my haveing been his grandffathers wife.' Lady Dacre then goes on to bequeath the portrait in question to her grandson Thomas Chute. It was at about this period that Lord Sussex enfranchised from fines and manorial charges Blackhill at Carlisle, for which he received thirty-six years quit-rents, which was some little temporary help; and about the same time the common was divided and granted in fee to the tenants of the manor, the lord reserving to himself as his share 150 acres, which was afterwards called Blackhill Park.[1]

When the Stuart dynasty vanished from England any reasonable hopes which Lord Sussex may have entertained of ever getting paid the dowry which Charles II. had promised him with his wife must have vanished also. It is said that a drowning man will catch at a straw, and so anyone ruined by his own extravagance will, like a gambler, neglect no 'outside'

[1] *N. & B.* ii. p. 247.

chance in the hope that luck may favour his desperate condition, and a happy turn of the wheel of fortune place him once more in a position of solvency. Accordingly we see that, undaunted by his previous unsuccessful efforts to induce his royal father-in-law to keep his promise, Lord Sussex presented a petition to William of Orange setting out the orders given by Charles II. as to payment to him of an annuity of 2,000*l.* a year until the principal sum of 20,000*l.* was paid, that the latter had never been paid, that there had been great irregularities in payment of the former, that arrears to the extent of 1,800*l.* were due to him at the death of Charles II., that nothing had been paid him since then, and that there was due to him at midsummer 1698 for principal and arrears of the annuity a sum of 32,600*l.*[1] As well might Lord Sussex have thrown his money into the sea as to spend it in drawing up, and presenting his petition, for as he had not been able to obtain payment during the Stuart dynasty, there could have been but little hope of inducing a King of another and a hostile line to pay what he may fairly have considered was a private debt due from his predecessors, and one which they themselves had not scrupled to leave unsatisfied.

In 1703 the Earl's financial position was evidently going from bad to worse, as on May 23rd of that year his mother-in-law the Duchess of Cleveland writes[2] to Sir Thomas Dyke avowing her concern 'for the position of her daughter Sussex & her childerne,' whom the extravagances of Lord Sussex, she says, threaten with ruin; and the writer urges Sir Thomas, as trustee of her daughter's marriage settlement, to exercise his powers for her protection and that of her children.

In 1708 came a great crash in Lord Sussex's fortunes, and Herstmonceux, that splendid specimen of an early brick building, for the first time in its existence was sold, and so passed away from the descendants of its builder, Roger Fynes. The purchaser was 'Counsellor' Naylor, who gave for it 38,215*l.*, and some ninety years later it was valued for sale at 62,932*l.*[3]

[1] *Add.* 33054, 51.   [2] *Hist. Com.* (Morrison), ix. p. 466.
[3] *Add.* 5679, f. 699 (333 ?) *et seq.*

Although the Castle of Herstmonceux has been so often described that there is nothing fresh left to be said about it, still it seems necessary to give a brief description of that building so as to enable anyone reading this book to form some idea of what the house was like which was the home of so many of the persons with whom this work deals.[1]

The castle built by Roger Fynes in 1440, at a cost, it is said, of 3,800*l*.,[2] a huge sum in the fifteenth century to spend on a house when money was of so much greater value than it is to-day, was constructed of brick made by Flemings brought over by Sir Roger Fynes, and has been said to be the earliest known brick building of any importance erected in England since the days of the Romans. The art of brickmaking, like many other arts, became lost in England when the Romans returned to the Continent, and it was many years before bricks were again employed for building in this country. In Holland, however, bricks of a first-rate quality had been made continuously from a very early period; and, as those of which Herstmonceux was built are very good and hard, the tradition that they were manufactured by Flemings is not improbably true, as it is hardly possible Englishmen at this period could have constructed bricks of so good a quality. Herstmonceux was so solidly constructed that, had it not been gutted more than three hundred years later in order to satisfy the whim of a foolish woman, acting under the advice of an incompetent but once popular architect, it might still have been inhabited, a splendid monument of the period when fortified castles were gradually giving way to those large country houses which, during the great epoch of building under the Tudors about a century later, were to become so great an ornament to many parts of England.

Francis Naylor Hare, nephew of the Mr. Naylor who bought the castle from the Lennards, lived there very seldom, and on his death in 1775 it came to his half-brother, the Rev. Robert Hare,

[1] Those requiring more details will find a full description of the castle in Mr. Venables' monograph on this subject.
[2] *Ven.*

second son of the bishop of that name. As the castle had been greatly neglected during his brother's ownership, when Mr. Robert Hare came into the property, he found that the building required very considerable repairs, and he allowed his wife to call in the then celebrated architect, Wyatt, in order to report what had better be done to it. Wyatt was no respecter of antiquity, and lived at a period when architectural taste was at its lowest ebb, so he advised that this magnificent specimen of mediæval building should be pulled down, and the materials employed in building the modern house now known as Herstmonceux Place, and, except as far as the outer walls were concerned, this advice was unfortunately followed.

It is sad to reflect that if Mr. Hare had not been well enough off to employ an architect the old castle might still have been standing, and had this been the case there are many architects in the present day to whom a wealthy owner might have safely entrusted the task of restoring this fine old building to its original splendour.

It is said that the castle possessed a window for every day and a chimney for every week in the year; while its oven was so large that tradition says that on one occasion twenty-four women sat down in it for tea. The building was a regular parallelogram enclosing four open courts, each angle strengthened by an octagonal embattled tower rising about fifteen feet above the main building. Grose, writing before the house had been dismantled, gives the following description of it :—

The Castle encloses three courts, a long one and two smaller ones ; the entrance is on the South front through the great gate house, which leads into a spacious court, cloistered round. On the North side is the hall, which is very large, & much resembling those of Oxford & Cambridge that have not been modernized ; the fireplace being in the middle of the room, & the butteries at the lower end. At the upper or Eastern side of this hall lie three handsome rooms, one of them 40 feet long ; these lying one within another constitute the best apartments in the Castle ; beyond them is the Chapel, some parlours for common use, with rooms for upper servants, composing the East front. The grand stairs which lie beyond the hall occupy an area of 40 feet square. The Kitchen which is beyond the staircase to the West, is large, & as well as the Hall & Chapel, goes up in height to the upper storey of the house. The offices belonging to it are very ample; and the oven in the bake house is 14 feet in diameter. The left side of the South front beyond the great Gate house is occupied by a long waste room, like a gallery in old times, and seems as if it were intended for a stable, in case the Castle was beseiged, or it should be found necessary to bring the horses and other cattle into a place of safety. Underneath the Eastern corner tower, in the same front, is an octagonal room which was formerly the prison, in the midst is a stone post with a large chain. Above stairs is a suite of rooms similar to the best apartments over which it stands; the Chambers on this floor are sufficient to lodge a garrison; & one is bewildered in the different galleries that lead to them; in everyone of the windows of which is painted on glass the alant or wolf dog, the ancient supporters of the family of Fynes. Many private winding staircases, curiously constructed in brick work without any timber, communicate with these galleries. The towers on each side of the Gate house on the South, are 84 feet high. The South & North fronts of the Castle are 206½ long and the East & West fronts measure 214½.

In August 1752 Horace Walpole visited Herstmonceux, and his letter to Mr. Bentley describing it has been printed on several occasions. He says, speaking of the castle:—

it is seated at the end of a large vale five miles in a direct line to the sea with wings of blue hills covered with wood, one of which falls down to the house in a sweep of one hundred acres. The building, for the convenience of water to the moat, sees nothing at all; indeed it is entirely imagined on a plan of defence, with drawbridges actually in being; round towers, watch towers mounted on them, and battlements pierced for the passage of arrows from longbows. It was built in the time of Hen. VI, & is as perfect as the first day. It does not seem to have been ever quite finished, or at least that age was not arrived at the luxury of whitewashing, for almost all the walls except the principal chambers are in their native brickhood. It is a square building each side about 200 ft. in length; a porch

& cloister very like Eton College; & the whole is much in the same taste, the kitchen extremely so, with three vast funnels to the chimnies going up on the inside. There are two or three little courts for offices, but no magnificence of apartments. It is scarcely furnished with a few necessary beds & chairs. One side has been sashed, & a drawing & dining room, & two or three rooms, wainscoted by the Earl of Sussex, who married a natural daughter of Charles the Second. Their arms with delightful carvings by Gibbons, particularly two pheasants, hang over the chimneys. Over the great drawing room chimney is the coat armour of the first Lennard Lord Dacre with all his alliances. . . . The Chapel is small & mean; the Virgin and seven long, lean saints, ill done, remain in the windows; there have been four more, but seem to have been removed for light; and we actually found St. Catherine, and another gentlewoman with a Church in her hand, exiled into the buttery. There remain two odd cavities with very small wooden screens on each side the altar which seem to have been confessionals. The outside is a mixture of grey brick & stone that has a very venerable appearance. The drawbridges are romantic to a degree; & there is a dungeon that gives one a delightful idea of living in the days of soccaye & under such goodly tenures. They showed us a dismal chamber, which they call Drummer's Hall, & suppose that Mr. Addison's comedy is descended from it. In the windows of the gallery over the cloisters which leads all round to the apartments is the device of the Fienneses, a wolf holding a baton with a scroll le roy le veut.

If Lord Sussex had any feelings of sentiment it must have been a bitter pang to him to find himself obliged, largely by his own folly, to sell the home of his ancestors, where he had lived so much, and on which he had spent so much money. It is said that he 'ornamented the best apartments with handsome ceilings of stucco work, and with a great deal of fine carving by Gibbons.'[1]

One of the contributory causes of the Earl's continual pecuniary embarrassments was the frequency of the litigations in which from time to time he found himself involved. I have shown that before he came of age he was a defendant in an action

[1] *Grose*, v.

brought by his mother against himself and the executors of his father's will; afterwards he had considerable litigation about Halton, in Lancashire, and other properties in the north; and towards the latter part of his life he was much troubled and put to considerable expense by actions brought against him, both in the Court of Chancery and at common law, by the guardian of the three daughters of his brother Henry, the latter of whom is mentioned by a contemporary writer, who, however, in error speaks of Lord Sussex's nieces as his nephews.[1] The claim on their behalf was based upon the Kentish custom of gavelkind, and it was attempted to show that the lands which the Earl owned in Kent were subject to that custom. Lord Sussex was successful in this litigation, which was really of a frivolous nature; but the victory to a man so much embarrassed as he was proved a severe tax upon his then scanty resources.

So much 'pent' for money (to use a Norfolk expression) was Lord Sussex while this litigation was in progress, that he had recourse to asking his cousin, Dacre Barrett, for the loan o 100*l*. Dacre obviously did as he was asked, as among our letters to him is one signed 'Sussex' thanking his cousin for some favour received, and dated very shortly after the following letter in which the Earl requested this loan; it was addressed:—

To Mr. Barret Lennard att Bellhouse, In Essex.

Octobr. 29th, 1710.

I cannot deare Cousin but acquaint you how I am plagued wth him y^t is guardian to my Neices. I had you know last year a tryall at ye Queens Bench, and upon a full hearing a Verdit, this year he has brought another, wch is to be tryd in ye same place this ninth of November; and for some years last past I haue had noe less then 4 suits in Chancery wch wth making out my title for 23 different purchases has cost me £3,000 at least, wch has very much incomoded me & run me in debt (as I beleiue you are but to sensible of from the trouble y^r Sister gaue you) this beeing the case wth me at present I shall take it for a particular fauour if you could lend me a £100; or two vpon

[1] *Lutt.* vi. p. 504.

this emergency for a Year. I would not haue taken this liberty but you beeing the nearest relation I haue now liueing I thought I might presume ye more freely. I haue but two daughters liueing, & both prouided for, and it's possible you or y^r Sonne may not repent the kindness you doe me, wch shall allways be acknowledged by, S^r. y^r Kinsman and Ser^nt,

SUSSEX.

P.S. I lodg in Cooks court by Lincolns Inn.

There is the following reason for supposing that the Earl of Sussex may have been acting as deputy Earl Marshal for the Duke of Norfolk, but his name does not appear in the list of those that have served that office, although that of an Earl of Sussex, of a different creation, does in 1725.[1] On May 24th, 1711, Sir S. Harcourt wrote to Robert Harley to congratulate him on being made a peer, and said: 'It is necessary y^r Lordship should give note to the Earl Marshall (my Lord of Sussex) of y^r intention and desire to be introduced tomorrow that he may order the Heralds to be at the House of Lords to attend you';[2] Mr. Harley took the hint, and wrote to the Earl requesting the attendance of the Heralds.[3]

Lord Sussex died at Chevening in November 1715, and was buried there on the 11th of that month.[4] Soon after his death his widow and her daughter, Lady Anne, returned from France, and stayed for short periods at Chevening until June 1716, but they made their headquarters in London, where they lived in lodgings, for six weeks of the time in Rider Street, and for twenty-seven weeks in what was then called 'Pel Mel.'[5] It would appear that the family party then living together in London consisted also of Lady Barbara Skelton and her husband, and in any case the latter certainly spent some of this period at Chevening.

During 1716, at some date which, however, I am not able

[1] *Hay. Dig.*   [2] *Hist. Com.* xv. (Portland), iv. p. 696.   [3] *Ibid.*
[4] The date is in error given as October 11th.—*Arch. C.* xvi. p. 120.
[5] For this and other information as to the whereabouts of the Countess and her daughters during this period, I am indebted to some very elaborate accounts concerning the Chevening property, which commence immediately after the death of Lord Sussex.—*F. P.*

to exactly fix, the Countess and her daughters sold the Dacre properties in Cumberland and Westmoreland to Sir C. Musgrave for 15,000*l*.;[1] and they also parted with the advowson of Hever, which had been purchased by John Lennard.[2]

In the month of June 1716, Lady Anne married her cousin Richard Barrett, and her subsequent career is treated of in another chapter. The Countess of Sussex lived with her daughter Lady Anne during those two brief episodes in the life of the latter—viz. her marriage with Richard Barrett, and her period of widowhood after his death; and when Lady Anne married, as her second husband, Lord Teynham, the Countess appears still to have remained living with her. She was buried in her son-in-law's vault at Linstead, Kent. There appeared the following contemporaneous notice of her death in 1722:

'May 16, dy'd Anne Fitz Roy natural daughter of King Chas. II by Barbara Villiers Dutchess of Cleveland and Relict of Thomas Lennard Earl of Sussex.'[3]

From the contents of her will it appears that at the time of her death the only property the Countess was possessed of was 4,050*l*. stock of the South Sea Company; of this she left 1,000*l*. to her daughter Lady Barbara Skelton for life, with remainder over to her granddaughter Anne Roper; 1,000*l*. to her daughter Lady Teynham for life, with remainder over to the children of the latter by Lord Teynham; 1,000*l*. to her grandson Thomas Barrett Lennard (afterwards Lord Dacre), provided he was brought up by his mother, but if withdrawn from her care, then to the latter; she also left some smaller legacies, and made Lord Teynham residuary legatee and executor.[4]

---

[1] *N. & B.* ii. p. 380.   J. C. Brooke, the Herald, writing to Thomas Lord Dacre in 1784 says: 'It will give your L^p. no satisfaction to be told that it is said in Cumberland the Musgrave family have a clear £1,000 ₱ ann. profit by the purchase they made of your mother's Cumberland estate.'

[2] *I. K.*   [3] *H. R.* vii.

[4] As the South Sea Bubble burst in 1721, the Countess's 4,050*l*. stock in that concern could have been of no great value at the period of her death.

MALE DESCENDANTS OF ROBT. BARRETT.

SHOWING RELATIONSHIP BETWEEN E. LORD NEWBURGH AND THE HON. RICHARD LENNARD.

```
Robt. (I.) Barrett, of Hawkhurst,        Ri. de Norton, of Aveley,
       temp. E. III.                          d. before 1346.
                                                   |
                                   Thos. de Belhus = Elizabeth, heiress to
                                                  alive in 1390.   her father.
                                                   |
              John (II.) = Alicia,
              settled in Aveley  co-heiress.
                   in 1400.
                       |
              Thomas (II.) = Matilda, dau. of J. Pointz, of N. Ockendon.
                     d. 1440.
                       |
              Robt. (II.) = 2ndly, Margaret, dau. of Robert Knolles, of Herts.
                     alive 1453.
                       |
J. Harpsfield.   John (III.) = 1stly, Elizabeth, dau. and heiress of Ri. Braytoft.
                        d. 1526.
                           |
Thos. Dineley = Phillipa. = 2dly,   George.         5 sons
       1st husband.                d. v. p. 1525.    d.s.p.
                    |
Sir John Baker = Elizabeth = George.
        2nd husband,   |
                       |
                 Edward (I.) = 2ndly, Anne, dau. of Sir G. Somerset,   Arthur   } d.s.p.
Sir Richard.          d. 1585.          d. 1568.                    Robert (III.)
                          |
Crysogona = Sir H. Lennard,  Charles = Christian, dau. of Sir W. Mildmay.   Edward (II.)
               Lord Dacre.    d.v.p. 1584.                                     d.s.p.
                  |                     |
Ri. Lord Dacre.              Sir Edward (III.)              Walter
                             created Baron Newburgh,         d.s.p.
Hon. Ri. Lennard,
to whom Lord Newburgh left Belhus,
```

CHAPTER V

THE FAMILY OF BARRETT

HAVING traced the history of the elder branch of the Lennards descended from Richard Lord Dacre down to the death of the Countess of Sussex in 1722, we must go back some years and consider that of Richard Lennard (youngest son of Richard Lord Dacre) and his descendants. But before doing so it is necessary to go back still further and give some account of the ancient family of Barrett, whose name and arms were assumed by this Richard, and have ever since been borne by his descendants. Accordingly it is to the consideration of the Barrett family that this chapter is devoted.

The name of Barrett is one which occurs often in England; the family of that name, from whom Sir Edward Barrett (Lord Newburgh) was descended, came originally from Hawkhurst, in Kent, where Robert Barrett was living in the 23rd of Edward III., as is proved by a deed mentioned by Lord Dacre.[1] There was a family named Barrett who owned Perry Court in the parish of Preston, near Faversham, as early as the time of Edward II., and Lord Dacre suggests that Robert was probably one of these Barretts, and that he possibly owned both Hawkhurst and Perry Court. The pedigree in Lord Dacre's book traces Robert's descent from Thomas Barrett (9th Edward III.), son of John Barrett.[2] Robert, of Hawkhurst, had a son John,[3] and here we

---

[1] Grant from Simon de Secele and John Recford to Robert Barrett in 23rd Ed. III. of three acres of land lying *super domia* [*sic*] *de Secele.* Secele is one of the twelve manors of Dens in Hawkhurst.—*Ld. D. Mis.*

[2] This is the pedigree in *Har. MSS.* 1541, 21*b*.

[3] A pedigree by a nameless writer, probably copied *circa* 1650, gives Robert Valentyne (*temp.* Henry IV.), son of Robert, as father of John of Aveley.—*Ibid.* 1408, fol. 184.

get on to surer ground, as from his time down to that of Lord Newburgh we have a record of the entire descent of the Barretts and their alliances.

We have a deed dated the last of October, in the 21st of Richard II. (1397), by which John Dran, rector of the Parish Church of Hawkhurst, quit-claims 'John Baret *firmarius meus*[1] of all suits, actions, &c., which he has against him from the beginning of the world' (*a principio mundi*), and this shows that John Barrett was then living at Hawkhurst. It may well be that at this period John was about to marry and move into Essex, and that before leaving his native place he wished to have it placed on record that he had paid his rector all that he owed him. I have not discovered in what year he married, but he was married and settled in Aveley within the next four years, as we have a deed by 'John Baret de Alvythlee,' dated the Sunday after Purification (February 6), 2nd Henry IV. (1401), whereby he grants and confirms a meadow called 'Belhous mede,' in the parish of Stifford, for the term of ten years, commencing from the previous Michaelmas.

Lord Dacre says :—

John Barrett marrying Alicia Belhouse transplanted himself to Aveley ; For this family of Barrett before that time were settled at Hawkhurst in Kent for several generations, as appears by ancient Deeds, & probably came into England with William the Conqueror, their name being in the Roll of Battle Abbey.[2]

This assertion that the name of Barrett, so essentially unlike a French name, should have appeared in the Roll of Battle Abbey has always struck me as being on the face of it most improbable. Mr. Guppy, in his 'Homes of Family Names,' says that 'Barratt, Barrett, or Baret, was a personal name of Teutonic origin, occurring in England in pre-Domesday times';[3]

---

[1] Probably meaning farmer or collector of tithes.
[2] *Ld. D. His.* The name of Barrett appears in the copy of the Roll given in *Hol.*
[3] P. 26 ; *cf. Bar.* The name Barretti is not an uncommon one in Italy.

THE DE BELHUS FAMILY

and more than two hundred years ago Dugdale, in the preface to his 'Baronage,' referring to that celebrated Roll, says :—

It might be expected, that I should have ascended much higher in my discourse of some Families than I have done; perhaps from the Norman Conquest, presuming them to have been Originally French ; and that there is some colour for it in regard their names are found in divers Copies of that Memorial commonly called the Roll of Battail Abbey. To this I answer ; that there are great Errors, or rather Falsities in most of those Copies ; by attributing the derivation of many from the French, who were not at all of such Extraction ; but meerly English ; as by their sirnames taken from several places in this Realm is most evident. But such hath been the subtilty of some Monks of old that, finding it acceptable unto most to be reputed descendents to those who were Companions with Duke William in that memorable Expedition whereby he became Conqueror of this Realm ; as that to gratify them they inserted their names into that antient Catalogue.[1]

Before going on with the account of the Barrett family some mention must be made of the family of de Belhus, or Belhous, which appears to have been one of considerable importance. As early as 1240 a branch of them owned estates in Norfolk, in the parishes of Bodney, North Tuddenham, Hockering, Bilney, Wrenningham, and other places ; and in 1290 Richard de Belhus was Sheriff of both Norfolk and Suffolk. In 1360 his grandson, Sir Richard, died, leaving only daughters, so that the family became extinct in Norfolk. In Essex the de Belhuses owned lands in Rayleigh, Ramsden, Stanway, and elsewhere ; and one of them, 'Sir Thomas de Belhus alias Bellus,' who lived at Stanway, was for many years ' Vice Comes,' or what would now be called Lord Lieutenant of Cambridgeshire.[2]

Although all the branches of this family appear to have entirely died out long ago in the male line, they left their name behind them attached to the land, as there are manors of 'Belhouse' in both the parishes of Tuddenham, and of

---

[1] See also *Bar*.   [2] *Le Coll*. i. Part ii. p. 440.

Wrenningham, in Norfolk; and in the parishes of Aveley and of Gosfield,[1] in Essex; and not only so, but in the latter county the parish of Ramsden Bell House bears their name to distinguish it from the adjoining parish of Ramsden Crays, and Newington, near Folkestone, was at one time called Newington Belhouse to distinguish it from the other parish of the same name in Kent.[2]

The dates at which those members of the Belhus and Barrett families lived, from whom we are descended, can in many cases be ascertained by referring to our family deeds.

The first de Belhus to settle at Aveley, or as it was then called 'Alvethley,' was Nicholas de Belhus, second son of the before-mentioned Sir Thomas de Belhus, of Stanway, who was Constable or Seneschal of Ponthieu, *temp.* Edward I. We have two conveyances to this Nicholas by his nephew Thomas, who was a son of Sir John de Belhus, both made in the 13th of Edward III. (1339), the one dated June 7th and the other St. Thomas the Martyr (August 5th). Lord Dacre considers that there can be no doubt Nicholas married a lady of the name of Odingsel, and that he and his wife lie buried under an ancient marble before the altar in Aveley Church, 'for though the Inscription is torn off yet the Arms remain in brass at the four corners and are those of Belhus impaled with Odingsel.'[3] The name of Oddyngselis appears in one of our deeds dated Thursday before St. Peter ad Vincula (August 1st), 16th Edward III. (1342), which is a grant to a Sir John of that name of a manor in the county of 'Nothyngham,' with its 'villains and their issue & chattels.'

Nicholas de Belhus was succeeded by his son Thomas, who married Elizabeth, daughter and heiress of Richard de Norton and Margaret his wife, of Aveley. Our deeds show that Richard was alive in December 1342, but he must have died not long after, as four years later Margaret is in another deed described 'quae fuit uxor Richardi de Nortune.'

[1] *Mo.*   [2] *Phil.* p. 245.
[3] *Ld. D. His.* The arms in brass are there no longer.

Richard Norton's daughter Elizabeth brought her husband a considerable amount of land, and no doubt the manor since called Belhus, as in the old Court Rolls and deeds it is styled 'Nortons alias Belhouse,'[1] and the Alicia de Belhus who married John Barrett was one of the children of this marriage. Thomas de Belhus was a great benefactor to the Abbey of Stratford Langthorn, in Essex, to which he left the manor of Bumsted, or Bumpsted, in the parishes of Aveley and Upminster. All trace of the manor-house is long since gone, and for very many years there have been no manor courts held, but the name still survives in the 'Bumpsted Meades,' which is the name of some meadows on the north side of the park at Belhus. Among our deeds is a grant by William Bumpsted, son and heir of Sir William Bumpsted, of a rent of 9s. 4d. payable for lands in 'Alvethlie,' dated St. Peter ad Vincula, 11th Edward III. (August 1st, 1337).

Lord Dacre says that Thomas de Belhus died towards the latter end of Richard II.'s reign;[2] we know he was alive in the 14th of that reign, as we have a release of lands to him, dated Michaelmas of that year (1390). Besides two daughters, Alicia and Isolda, Thomas left a son named John, who was buried in the Abbey of Stratford, and as he died without children his sisters became his co-heiresses.

Alicia's sister Isolda[3] married, firstly, Gilbert at Lee, by whom she had no issue; and, secondly, Walter Sergeant. Lord Dacre says:— '

There remains a Curious Deed of Partition of this Manour of Belhouse, dated the 21st of Richard II, between the two sisters, wherein it appears that there must at that time have been a Capitall Mansion here, for mention is therein made of the Hall, and great Chamber, and upper and lower Chambers thereunto adjoining; of the Gatehouse which had two chambers in it above and below; of the Gardens, Stables, Pidgeon House, &c.

---

[1] *Ld. D. His.*   [2] *Ibid.*
[3] Both pedigrees in *Essex Visitations, Har. So.* xiii. p. 145 and *ibid.* xiv. p. 548, give Alice as the only daughter.
Ld. D. His. I have not found this deed.

John Barrett and his wife Alicia had a son and heir, christened Thomas, who married Matilda, a daughter of John Pointz, lord of the manor of N. Ockendon.[1] Both Fuller and Weever give an interesting account of the death in 1461 of a Thomas Barrett, who, having taken sanctuary at Westminster to escape the fury of a mob, 'was from there hayled forth, and lamentably hewyn a peces.' I do not repeat their account, because although they considered it referred to this Thomas, it must in fact have related to some other Thomas Barrett, for, as Lord Dacre[2] points out, the Thomas we are concerned with died at least as early as 19th Henry VI. (1440–1), as we have a deed of that year in which Matilda Barrett of 'Avethlie' is described as a widow.[3]

The son and heir of Thomas Barrett was Robert, who married twice; he had no children by his first wife, who was Margery Chichley; his second wife was Margaret Knolles, daughter of Robert Knolles, of Mimms, Herts. Lord Dacre believed Margery to have been a daughter of John Chichley, citizen and chamberlain of London, by Margaret, a daughter of Sir Thomas Knolles; and was of opinion that she and Robert Barrett's second wife were first cousins to each other, and granddaughters of that Thomas Knolles who was twice Lord Mayor of London during the reign of Henry IV. Lord Dacre states that the only reason for doubting their relationship to each other is, that previous to the Reformation the Church would not allow a man to marry a woman who was first cousin to his former wife, but he goes on to remark that this difficulty could have been got over by obtaining a dispensation from the Pope.[4] Robert's widow Margaret married John Edwards, citizen and salter of London,[5] but I have no record of when her second marriage took place,

---

[1] The Pointz family was one of considerable local importance, and there are a number of remarkable monuments to their memory in N. Ockendon Church. The last of the line died 1643, a bachelor.—*Mo.*

[2] *Ld. D. His.*

[3] That he was alive in 1439 is proved by a deed of release to him, dated 'last of March, 17 Henry VI.'—*F. P.*

[4] *Ld. D. His.*; *Ld. D. Mis.*   [5] *Ld. D. Mis.*

nor of the date of her first husband's death. He was alive as late as October 11, 32nd Henry VI. (1453), as is shown by a deed of that date, by which he made a grant of lands called Gossards in 'S. Wokendon' (S. Ockendon);[1] and Lord Dacre says that five years later, in the 37th Henry VI. (1458-9), Walter Sergeant (son of Walter of that name, his father's uncle by marriage) released to him his moiety of the manor of Belhus, *alias* Nortons.[2]

Robert's son and heir was John, who 'applying himself to the Study of the Law, and particularly the Civil Law, became eminent therein.'[3] I have not been able to find out that John was ever admitted a member of the Inns of Court; if so, it was no doubt previous to 1500; and none of the records of these Inns, nor of Doctors Commons, go back to such an early date. The celebrated writer Leland included among his epigrams the following one addressed to John :—

Ad Joannem Barretum jurisperitum.
Sic tua Budaei divina volumina magni
Saepe manus verset, verset et Alceati,
Sic tua sollicitos facundia rara clientes
Sublevet, et medio stet tua caussa foro.
Perlege quaeso meas Barrete Epigrammata nugas
Censorem quoniam te statuere suum.[4]

which may be thus translated :—

To John Barrett learned in the law. Thus may your hand often turn over the divine volumes of the great Budaeus[5] And turn over those of Alceati.[6] Thus may your rare eloquence lift up [cheer up, or help] your anxious client, And may your cause stand in the middle of the forum. Pray Mr. Barrett read through these trifling epigrams of mine since they have [I have] appointed you the censor of them.

John Barrett may be considered the founder of this branch of the family of Barrett. He succeeded in his profession, and

[1] Gossards is a detached portion of the parish of Stifford.
[2] *Ld. D. His.* ; *Ld. D. Mis.* [3] *Ibid.* [4] *Le Coll.* v. P. 107.
[5] Bude or Budaeus, 'le plus savant homme de France au commencement du XVIe. siècle,' born 1467, died 1540.
[6] A. Alceati, a great writer on jurisprudence, born near Milan, 1492, died 1550.

must have made a considerable sum of money, as he added greatly to the estate he had inherited, and rebuilt his mansion-house which is now known as 'Belhus.'

He commenced acquiring land round Belhus in 1495; we have a deed dated in April of that year by which he purchased the reversion to a farm in Aveley called Culverhouse; in this deed he is described as 'gentilman of London,' so that probably at this period of his life, being actively employed in his profession, he spent most of his time in town. During the next thirty years he bought several more farms in the neighbourhood; among others Lawrence's, Quintin's, a farm adjoining Bredal Street, 'Somers at heth,' and the manor of Noke.[1]

John married several times, having had no less than four wives, but I regret to be unable to give the dates of any but his last marriage.

His first wife was Elizabeth, daughter and heiress of Richard Braytoft and Elizabeth, daughter of Sir Edward Dodingsells;[2] by her he had the following six sons and one daughter:—

George, who married a daughter of his father's second wife, and died in 1525, a year before his father, leaving issue.

Thomas, who became a priest; he died later than January $152\frac{4}{5}$, as he is mentioned in his brother George's will of that date.

Four other sons, who all died young;[3] and Elizabeth, who married Thomas Cumberford.

John Barrett's second wife was Phillipa, daughter of John Harpsfield, and widow of Thomas Dinely; in 1509 he purchased a farm then known as Blaches, and the deeds connected with this purchase show that at this period he was married to Phillipa, and in two of these deeds John Harpsfield is described as 'pannarius,' or clothier.

[1] I have treated more fully of his purchases of land round Belhus in an article in the *E. R.*, July 1906.

[2] *Ld. D. Mis.* The Barrett pedigree in vol. xiii. *Har. So.* contains many errors as to John's wives.

[3] In the Aveley Register there is this entry of a burial: '1593 Bartholomew s. of John Barret."—*P. m. St.* p. 141. It is just possible that this entry refers to a son of the John Barrett whom we have been considering, but it is not probable that it does so.

JOHN (II.) BARRETT'S CHILDREN

By Phillipa he had the following six daughters :—

Cicely, married William, son and heir of Walter Culpepper, about January 4th, 1530; from the directions contained in her husband's will she appears to have been dead before November 1559, and to have been buried in the parish church of Salehurst.[1]

Muriel, married Sir John Champneis, or Champneys, of Hall Place, Bexley. He became Lord Mayor of London in 1534,[2] in which year she died.[3]

Anne, married Martin Bowes.

Joyce, married Sir James Wilford.

Margaret, married Walter Crompton.

Bridget, who died unmarried.

I do not know when Phillipa died, but her father was alive in 1520 even if she were not, as in that year he was party to a fine, by which John had lands in Aveley and Upminster conveyed to himself.

John's third wife was Margaret,[4] daughter of Sir Edward Norris; of Ricot, Berks, and sister of that Sir Henry Norris who married a daughter of Thomas Fynes, Lord Dacre.[5]

In one of the codicils to John's will he speaks of an indenture he had made in July 1526, in order to secure a jointure to his wife 'Mary,' so presumably he married his fourth wife about that date, and from an expression in his will she appears to have been either a daughter or a widow of a 'Mr. Blague.'[6] He had no children by this last, and, indeed if I am right as to the date of his fourth marriage, he could only have had

---

[1] *S. Arch.* xlvii. p. 62. The Culpeppers were an ancient family, and were using arms as early as 1329. *Ibid.* p. 48.

[2] *Hay. Dig.*

[3] Monument in Bexley Church, Kent.—*Ld. D. His.*

[4] I have seen her name given as Mary in MS. pedigree.—*F. P.*

[5] *Ante*, pp. 152, 186. The arms which the Norris family then bore as their paternal coat (which were really the arms of the Ravenscrofts)—viz. ar. a chevron between three ravens' heads sa.—are in one of the painted windows at Belhus.

[6] Lord Dacre. says that from the agreement of names and dates there is reason to think that she was widow of Robt. Blague, of Dartford, Kent, one of the Barons of the Exchequer, *temp.* Henry VIII., and daughter of John Brook, Lord Cobham, and Margaret Nevill, his wife.—*Ld. D. Mis.*

posthumous issue by her. Lord Dacre says it is doubtful if he had any by Margaret, although one pedigree gives two daughters, Elizabeth and Frydswid,[1] both said to have died unmarried.

John Barrett died on October 24th, 1526, and his inquisition was held on October 21st in the following year; this shows that he died possessed of rather less than 1,400 acres of land round Belhus; small properties in Hornchurch and Havering atte Bower, and about 600 acres in Sutton, near Rochford. Lord Dacre remarks that this inquisition was carelessly taken, and contains several inaccuracies.

From John's will we learn that he had a house in St. Vedast's Lane, London, and that his brother-in-law, Lewes Harpsfield, had been the cause of his losing considerable sums of money for which he appears to have become security. The directions the will contains as to his funeral are interesting, and so are his bequests of furniture and jewellery, for which reason I have given some of them in full.

This will is dated October 14th, 1526, and was proved on February 23rd following. In it he describes himself as 'John Barrett Esquire Register.'.[2] He orders his body, if he dies in London, to be buried by the bodies of his well-beloved wives Phillipa and Margaret, and if he dies in Essex, by the body of his wife Elizabeth. He also gives somewhat minute directions as to the way in which his funeral is to be conducted. He says:—

I will charge myne executors that my body be buryed w^{t}out any pomp of the worlde oonley w^t xij torches, and no mo, except iiij or vj hand torches to be borne by my servants, beinge my household servants, and to have their Lyvery, or my tenants about my corpse at the tyme of my buringe;[3] wherof after the same my buringe don, I bequeath two of the sayde torches to

---

[1] Friswid was the Christian name of Margaret's mother.
[2] '1526-7 Barrett Register of Prerog. Court London Alvethely et Essex.'— *P. C. C. Porch.* 22. Lord Dacre suggests that he was probably a registrar of the diocese of London, wherein he dwelt for some years.
[3] Meaning that his household servants, dressed in their livery, or his tenants were to carry the torches.

JOHN (II.) BARRETT'S WILL

St. Leonards churche, two to Alvethley, ij to Lamehith churche, on to St. Barthilmews churche, on to the churche of o^r Ladye of Strethall [?], won to Sutton churche, callyd Sutton Magna, wherof I am patron, one to the churche of Welneton [?], one to the churche of Stanford Dyneley, and one to the chapell of St. James of Foxcot, where my sone George Barrett, whose soule God pardon, was patron in the right of my foresaid good doughter his wif.

He makes certain bequests of small sums of money to several churches, and the will then continues:—

Item. I have had so great losses by my late brother in law Lewes Harpisfield, brother to my wife Phillipa, whose souls God pardon, that I can not make such bequests to my wife & children as my mind was to do, nevertheless I bequeath to my well beloved daughter Elizabeth, late wife to my good son George, whose soul God pardon, to occupy at my place called Belhouse Hall alias Barretts, which I have newly builded, and at suche tyme as it shall fortune hir to lye there, and if she be sumwhat rulyd by me in hir marriage, as I trust she will for the comforte of her & her yonge children ; these parcels following. Imprimis. The hangange of my hall there stayned, the great standinge table in the great wyndowe, the grate aundyrons with the Grate fyer forke my greatt fier showell of brasse, my grate lattyn chaffer nowe beinge in London w^t formes, stooles, tables, testryls as it nowe is at Belhouse, to occupie as longe as my said place doth remayne in hir custodye with, and after hir death, to Edward Barrett, or to suche of my sonnes children & hers, as shall fortune to be my heirs and hers. Item. the hangine of buckram, and the tables new and olde, the carpitt work of beyonde seeworke of verdures, all my cushions therof carpett worke, and other w^t forms stolys and other necessaries. It^m the story of romayne[1] of tapystry, cont iiij peces for the Chambre over the parlor, with chests cupbourds & other things there. It^m My hangings of the storey of Sheppards, accustomed to hange in the Chambre over the Ketchin, of tapystry, cont iiij peces some greatt some small, the hanginge in the chamber over the larder of roses paned, cont iij or iiij pieces of coarse tapystry ; It^m my greatt bedds of tapystry sellor[2] and

---

[1] *The Romaunt of the Rose* (?), a translation of the *Roman de la Rose* attributed to Chaucer. This tapestry probably represented a scene from the poem.

[2] A bed canopy.

testor & counterpoynt of wedlock[1] lined with fyne canvas, and all the hanginge of tapystry of hawkinge & huntynge, whiche was accustomed to hange in my greatt chambre in London, and my great cheste w^t yron chains in my great chamber in London to remayne at Belhouse for ever as longe as it will last for one heirelome, & also all the resydue to remayne.

Then follow the directions as to his funeral already mentioned, and bequests of 100*l.* to each of his four daughters by his wife Phillipa. The will then continues :—

It^m I bequeath unto my wyf Mary all such plate stuff of household & juells as were hers before the spousals betwixt hir and me, and also all suche juells & plate as hereafter followyth, That is to saie a chayne w^t greatt crosse sett with stone & perell of the value of L^{li} at leaste, an image of our Lady Assumption sett w^t stone & perle, twoo paire hedys of gold, an harness w^t gold w^t an hanging perle, a lytte dumsent [*sic*] sett w^t perle w^t certayne knotts of golde to sett ouer a rybbon, & a dyamonte w^t a hanginge perle callyd an horte,[2] and divers other small juells, and besydes that as moche plate as shalbe valued at one hundred marks suche as myne executors shall thinke conuenyent, whiche is moche as Mr. Blage dyd leue hir to my knowlege.

It^m I bequeath to myne eldyst doughter unmaryed my cuppe called the Mulbury. . . . Item I bequeath to every of my said daughters Anne, Margaret, Cicely, & Joyce, one rynge of golde for their weddynge ryngs, of suche as remayne in my closett. It^m I bequeath to my daughter Champneis my ringe with the Turkeys[3] for a remembraunce. It^m I bequeath to my sonne Thomas Barrett a layer [?] silver & gilt, vi spoons with raven hedds,[4] one of my best custs [?] silver and gilte with a cover, and a standinge cuppe silver & gilt.

John devised Belhus, and the farm called Culverhouse, to Elizabeth, the widow of his son George, for life, remainder to their sons Edward and Robert in tail male, and the other farms

---

[1] An allegorical representation of marriage woven into the 'counterpoynt.'
[2] Hort is a name for the bilberry. Possibly this pearl was so called from its resemblance to the fruit.
[3] Turquoise.
[4] These spoons no doubt had belonged to his third wife ; *vide ante*, p. 349 note 5, as to the Norris arms.

at Belhus called respectively Bumpstead, Blaches, Drivers, Quintons, Somers, Lawrence's, and Noke, &c., &c., and also his land at Hornchurch, to trustees for payment of the debts 'which I owe to the Kinges Highnes for Lewes Harpsfield,' and all his other debts; and to provide for his daughters until they marry, with remainder to his above-named grandsons in tail male. He directed that Sutton, in Essex, and the advowson of that church, as well as his house in Vedast Lane, in the parish of St. Leonards, London, were to be sold to pay his debts; and by a codicil he devised his estate at Sutton, if not sold for that purpose, to Robert, whom he describes as 'youngest son of his son George.' He also devised lands in Staffordshire to his son-in-law John Champneys, subject to certain charges then existing upon them. The probate to his will was granted on February 28th, 152⅔.

When John Barrett died, Edward, his eldest grandson, was found by the inquisition to be of the age 'of 5 years & more.' This Edward's father, George, had married Elizabeth Dinely, only daughter and heiress of Thomas Dinely by his wife Phillipa, who had married as her second husband, and as his second wife, John Barrett, George's father. The Dinelys were an ancient Lancashire family, and by her George obtained lands in Berkshire and Hampshire; she being the heiress of the Dinelys, he also became entitled to blazon the arms of the various families of FitzHerberts, de Fortibus, and many others from whom her family traced their descent.

George Barrett's will, dated January 18th, 152⅘, was proved in August of that year.[1] He left various bequests of apparel and other personal belongings; among others his

gowne of Damask lyned with velvet to be made into two vestments, wherof I geve the oon to saint James Chapel at Foxcot in Hampshire, where I and my wife be patrons, and thother to our lady Church of Strethall, where my father is Lord and Patron, Praying my tennts and the pishens of the foresaid Churches

[1] '1525 George Barrett Graye Freres London Alvetbely et Essex Wolverton et Hants.' 36 Bodfelde.

to pray for my soule and all $\overline{X}$pen soules. . . . I bequeath to my said wyfe my bedde of crymsyn sattyn and tawny velvet, a bedde of Downe, ij pylowes, ij paire of the fynest shets, the bedstede of beyonde see making belonging to the same, Item another bedde of blue and orange tawney Bruges satyn with a couerlett of the same and curteyns of sercenet of the same colour, a bedde of Downe, ij pylowes w^t their bere,[1] two pair of shetts and the beyond see bedde for the same.

He also left directions in his will that coloured glass with his 'Image' and that of his wife should be put up in the several churches of Wolverton, Stanford, and Foxcote.

After the death of George, his widow Elizabeth married, as her second husband, Sir John Baker, of Sissenhurst, Kent, who was a Privy Counsellor to Henry VIII.; and one of their grandchildren, Crysogona, became wife of Henry Lennard, Lord Dacre, and grandmother of that Richard Lennard who succeeded to Belhus, and assumed the name of Barrett.

George Barrett had three sons, Edward, Arthur, and Robert; the two latter are said to have died without issue. He had also one daughter, Katherine, who married a man of the name of Kelway.

I have not been able to find out much concerning George Barrett's eldest son, Edward, but he was probably a person of some considerable position, and was High Sheriff for the county of Essex in 13th Elizabeth (1570-1).[2]

William Bulleyn, a very eminent physician and botanist, dedicated one of his works to Edward Barrett, which he would not have been likely to do had he not occupied a somewhat prominent position. The book, which is printed in black letter, is entitled, 'A Dialogue bothe pleasaunt and pietifull wherein is a godlie regiment against the Feur [fever] Pestilence, with a consolation and comforte againste death.' The dedication begins as follows : ' To the Right Worshipfull & his singuler good friende Maister Edwarde Barret of Belhous of Essex Esquier, William Bulleyn sendeth salutations.' The dedication

---

[1] Bere or bear, a pillow-case.—*C. D.*   [2] *Mo.*

is somewhat verbose, but the following passages may be worth quoting :—

Euēso (Evenso) I do commende vnto you this little boke (wherein I writte parte thereof in youre owne house) whiche doe intreate[1] of sonderie thynges, to you I dooe hope not vnprofitable. . . . . And as I doe well consider a gentle manne of your good nature can but take your frēdes (friend's) simple token in good parte, euen so I am sorie that it is no better to pleasure you, yet giuyng God most humble thankes for the same, who kepe you in good healthe & worshippe   This twelfe of Marche 1564 yours euer   WILLIAM BULLEYN.

Edward was careful in money matters, and, like his grandfather, took great interest in his estate, to which, by the purchase of the manor of Bumpstead in 1541, and of Bretts fourteen years later, he added some thousand acres.

We have two rent-rolls of his, one of which describes 'Belhus' as 'The Capital Mansion or Manor house called Belhouse alias Barrett's Hall in Avethly.' The earlier of these documents gives the acreage of his Essex lands, and is dated 1566; and from this I gather that the Belhus estate then consisted of a little over 1,700 acres, and that he had also a small property at Hornchurch in the same neighbourhood. It was not without a considerable amount of trouble that I arrived at the acreage of the estate, as in the original document it is not easy to make out the figures, which are often corrected and scratched out, and the castings given in it are not unfrequently inaccurate, so that a great deal of checking was necessary in order to arrive at the correct total. At that period the use of Roman numerals was still common, and were used here, so that such amounts as, e.g., 80 and 399 are expressed respectively thus—iiij̄, and ccc iiij̄ xix, which, although easy enough in principle, makes it somewhat troublesome when casting up long lists of such figures. In order to obtain the rentals of Edward Barrett's estate I have used the second rent-roll, dated 1574, because this one gives the rents of all his lands, whether in Essex or elsewhere.

---

[1] Obsolete form of 'entreat,' which in the sense used here is also obsolete.

The rents for the Belhus estate came to 320*l.*, which for 1,700 acres works out at about 3*s.* 9*d.* per acre. In one case, in addition to a money rent, the tenant had to give the landlord every year a boar, or an additional sum of 1*l.* 6*s.* 8*d.*, at the option of the latter; and in another the tenant of the warren, in addition to his rent, had to render to his landlord every year 240 couple of grey conies and twenty-four dozen of '*sucking rabbits*,' of which the former were reckoned at 3*s.* 4*d.* and the latter 1*s.* 8*d.* a dozen, which together equalled 8*l.* 13*s.* 4*d.* in money.

The value of the rents due to Edward Barrett from his other estates were as follows:—

The manor of Northouse in Hornchurch	£30
„ „ „ Stanford Dyneley in Berkshire	71
„ „ „ Wolverton in Hampshire	71
„ „ „ Haywoods in Hampshire	34
„ „ „ Foxcot in Hampshire	44
	250
From the Belhus estate, as we have seen	320
Total	£570

To which must be added the properties belonging to his third wife, the rents of which were as under:—

The manor of Shrubland in Suffolk	£167
„ „ „ Norweys Hall, alias Lyttles Hall in the parish of Bray, Berkshire	50
	£217

So that his total revenue from land (and he had probably no other source of income), including his last wife's estates, was a little under 800*l.*, which was then a considerable fortune.

Ever since I can remember I have heard a tradition that Queen Elizabeth stayed at Belhus on her way to review the troops at Tilbury Fort, and a bedroom there is called 'Queen Elizabeth's room.' This is, I think, the place to notice the tradition, for if her Majesty were ever at Belhus her visit would no doubt have taken place during the ownership of this Edward Barrett. The walls of the room in question are hung

QUEEN ELIZABETH AT BELHUS? 357

with the remains of what must once have been very fine silk brocade, with an elaborate gold pattern on a blue ground, and the bed canopy, curtains, and valance, as well as the chairs, are of the same material. The suggestion is that these were the original hangings put up in honour of the Queen's visit. I think that there can be no doubt at all that this is entirely nonsense, and that whether the Queen were ever there or not, these old hangings belong to a very much later date than that of our last Tudor sovereign. I am inclined to think that the tradition itself is not more than a hundred years old at most, and that it is based upon a passage in Nichols's 'Progresses of Elizabeth.'[1]

In describing a progress she made in 1578, that author says: 'The Queen after visiting Mr. Baches at Stanstead Abbas proceeded to Mr. Barrett's at Bell-house, a fine old mansion in the parish of Aveley, in the way to Wanstead in Waltham Forest, which was the Earl of Leicester's seat.' To this is appended a footnote which, after a short description of the house, concludes: 'Bellhouse is now the property of Sir Thos Barrett Lennard Bart who has carefully preserved the original appearance of the apartments occupied by the Queen in an adjoining farm house.' Of this farmhouse I know nothing, nor, except from this footnote, have ever heard anything. If the Queen did go round by Belhus when on her way from Stansted Abbas in Hertfordshire to Wanstead, on the western borders of Essex, everyone must admit that she, or her advisers, selected a most remarkably circuitous route, and one which would have more than doubled the necessary length of that journey. As far as I know, Lord Dacre nowhere mentions this hypothetical visit, which he would surely have done had he ever heard of it; neither does Morant, and Nichols quotes no authority in support of his statement.[2]

[1] Vol. ii. p. 94.
[2] In *Literary Illustrations*, vii. p. 797, Nichols says, speaking of Belhus, 'In the stables of this mansion is a large vacant stall where it is said the palfrey of Queen Elizabeth stood when she came there to review the troops at Tilbury.' I have never heard of this tradition, and do not believe that it has even the authority of age to support it.

Edward Barrett, like his grandfather, was fond of the wedded state, as he also married several times. His first wife was Katherine, daughter of Alexander Culpepper, of Bedgbury, Kent, whom he must have married in 1543, as a deed of settlement of part of the Belhus estate which he made upon that marriage is dated in July of that year. He does not appear to have had any children by Katherine, and he certainly had by her no son to survive him.[1]

His second wife was Anne, only daughter of the Hon. Sir George Somerset, of Suffolk, third[2] son of Charles Earl of Worcester. By her he had two sons—Charles, who died in his father's lifetime, leaving issue, and Edward, who died without issue; he had also one daughter, Margaret, who married as her first husband Sir H. Forster, of Aldermaston, Berkshire.

The death of his wife Anne, and the names of her children, are recorded thus in a MS. in the British Museum:—

The worshipfull Ann Barret late wief to Edward Barret of Belhowse in the parish of Aveley in Essex Esquire, died at[3] London the vij of February in Anno 1568, et R Reginæ Elizabeth xj, and from thence conveyed to Belhowse in Essex aforesaid, and there buryed the xiij day of February, by Hugh Cotgrave Richmond Herauld. The said Ann Barret was daughter of Sr George Somerset, sonne to the Right Honble Charles Erle of Worcester, and had issue by her husband, Charles, Edward, and Margaret. The certificate of the truth of theis presents being taken by the said Richmond Herault the xiij day of February abovesaid, and signed by the hands of Edward Barrett her husband, & M[r] Charles Somset.[4]

Edward's third wife was Elizabeth, daughter and co-heiress of Sir Robert Litton, of Knebworth, Herts,[5] and widow of

---

[1] The Essex Visitation pedigree, *Har. So.* xiii. p. 145, makes no mention of this wife.

[2] Some pedigrees say second son.

[3] As showing the greater relative importance now of London over all other towns, it may be remarked that anyone writing in the present day would say 'in,' not 'at,' London, in the same way as he would say 'in England'; but he would use the word 'at' before all other towns.

[4] *Har.* 1408, 184. [5] *Ld. D. His.* says of Shrubland.

Thomas Little, of Shrubland, Suffolk, and Bray, Berks, Esquire.[1]

By her he had two daughters: the eldest, Anne, was christened at Aveley on June 21st, 1572;[2] she married Sir Thomas Corbet, of Sprowston, Norfolk, High Sheriff of Norfolk 1622 and 1635, and he and his wife lie buried under a fine tomb in the church of that parish. The second daughter was Elizabeth, who married, as his first wife, Brampton Gurdon, of Assington, Suffolk, High Sheriff for that county 1585; she died April 5th, 1605, having borne her husband six sons and three daughters.

Edward Barrett may possibly have also had a son by his last wife, as there is this entry in the Aveley Register under the head of 'chrystenings': '1583 Water [sic] s. of Edward Barrett.' There is no such child mentioned by Lord Dacre, nor in any of the pedigrees I have seen is there any reference to such a one; and as that was the year in which Walter, Edward's second grandson, was born, we may safely conclude this entry refers to him. The same authority shows that Edward's widow Elizabeth died in 1594; as the 'Buriall' on July 31st in that year is recorded of 'Mrs. Elizabeth Barrett of Bellhouse, widow.'

After his third marriage Edward Barrett lived sometimes at the manor-house of Lyttles, at Bray, which was his last wife's jointure by her first husband.

He was buried in Aveley Church with this inscription on a brass:[3] 'Here lyeth Buried the bodie of Edwarde Barrett Esquier of blessed memorie, who beinge a faithefull pfessor of the Gospel lyvinge moste Christianly hierein depted this liffe the laste of Januarie A° Dm 1585[4] and now restethe in the Lorde.'

By his will, which was proved February 15th, 1585,[5] he left all his personal effects at Belhus to his wife Elizabeth,

---

[1] By her first husband she had a daughter, Helen, who married E. Bacon, of Shrubland, third son of Sir Nicholas Bacon, Lord Keeper.—*Vis. S.* Mr. Bacon probably obtained Shrubland from his wife Helen, while her mother had Bray as her jointure.

[2] Aveley Registers.

[3] A brass with his arms now (1908) on the floor of the chancel.

[4] This would now be reckoned as 1586. [5] *P. C. C.*

except certain tapestries, ceiling, wainscot, and glass in windows; these she was to enjoy the use of for twenty-one years, and then they were to pass to his grandson Edward. I presume that by the expression, glass in windows, he meant coloured glass; and in the dining-room windows there is some armorial glass, which Lord Dacre says was no doubt made for John Barrett, the builder of the house. He left a year's wages to all his servants who had been in his service for two years, or more, at the time of his decease, and sums of money varying from as much as 5*l*. in the case of Aveley, to 10*s*. in the case of Wennington, to be distributed among the poor in eleven different parishes in Essex, Suffolk, Berks, and Hants, in which he held property. He directed that the funeral was to be without 'any vain pomp or superstition used nor any mourning apparel worn,' and for the funeral expenses he left his executors 30*l*.

I have heard an eminent antiquary[1] say, that in order to arrive at the present value of any specific sum mentioned in the sixteenth century, you should multiply it by twenty or twenty-five. This would give 600*l*. to 750*l*. as the present value of the sum Edward provided for his funeral, which does not seem to be in accordance with his expressed wish that his funeral should be a plain one.

In September 1569, Edward Barrett granted a piece of land in Wennington situated in Lander's Lane, containing about an acre of land, to George Uphevering and Ri. Saunders, churchwardens and husbandmen, and their successors, for ever, upon trust to apply the proceeds in relieving the poor, and in repairing the parish church, these yielding to the said Edward and his successor yearly, one red rose at the Feast of the Nativity of St. John the Baptist; and this acre was given up to my father in 1872, in exchange for some other land, with the authority of the Enclosure Commissioners.

Edward's eldest son, Charles, died at the age of twenty-nine, in August 1584, nearly a year and a-half before his father. We know next to nothing of his life, except that in 1578 he

[1] Mr. St. John Hope. It is stated in *Toone's Chronology* that when Charles I. came as a boy to England in 1604, and was created Duke of York, he had £40 per ann. settled on him that he might more honourably maintain that dignity.

married Christian, daughter of Queen Elizabeth's eminent statesman, Sir Walter Mildmay. After the marriage had been arranged an agreement, dated June 12th, 30th Elizabeth (1578), was made between Sir Walter Mildmay, Chancellor of the Exchequer,[1] of the one part, and Edward Barrett of the other part, whereby they covenanted that their respective children, Charles and Christian, should marry each other before July 1st then following. Sir Walter was to pay 800*l.* to Edward Barrett, who on his part was to settle the manors of Bretts, Noke, and divers lands on Christian for her life, with remainder to her children by his son Charles; and Belhus and other portions of that estate, and other lands in Essex, on Charles and his heirs. Edward Barrett signed his name to this document with only one 'r,' although his name in the deed is written with two.

There was issue of this marriage :—

Edward, born June 21st,[2] was christened at Aveley, 1581.
Walter . . . . . 1583[3]

and a daughter named Anne, who, on February 13th, 1602, married Sir E. Harley, K.B., and dying on December 1st, 1603, lies buried at Cuxton, Kent,[4] in which church there is an elaborate monument to her memory, and that of her infant son.

Muilman, in his 'History of Essex,'[5] says, speaking of Aveley: 'The manor of Bretts hath a mansion house about 1½ miles N.W. from the Church. Tho' long since converted into a farm house retains signs of it's having being once a gentleman's seat. Charles Barrett Esq. father of the Lord Newburgh lived in it'; and Lord Dacre confirms this statement,[6] which may be the foundation of the assertion by the late Henry Barrett Lennard[7] that Dacre Barrett had lived there.

[1] He is so described in this deed, although he appears to have resigned in 1572. —*Hay. Dig.*

[2] *Inq. P. M.*; *vide* deed 688, Essex Abstract.—*F. P.*   [3] *Ante*, p. 359.

[4] From some of our deeds it appears that she had a charge of 500*l.* upon Belhus, and possibly other charges secured upon the timber there. 687 and 690, Essex Abstract.—*F. P.*

[5] Vol. iv. p. 345, published 1770. The account it gives of Belhus bears traces of Lord Dacre's hand.

[6] *Ld. D. His.*   [7] *Post*, p. 586.

Bretts, although dreadfully spoiled during the last two hundred years by most tasteless alterations, still bears inside some traces of its antiquity, and has the remains of a moat on two sides of the house. Some years before it was bought by E. Barrett it belonged to the family of Cely, and was known indifferently as Brytys, Bryttes, and Bryttys Place. The Cely family was important in the mercantile world, being merchants of the Staple at Calais, and some of their letters which have been published [1] give considerable information about the life led in England during the fifteenth century. The last Cely to live at Bretts died there in 1494.

At the time Charles Barrett died a brass was put over his tomb at Aveley, and the subsequent history of this brass, and the brass itself, is remarkable; a very full account of both has already been published, from which the following abridged narration is taken.[2] When the Rev. W. Holman, of Halstead, visited Aveley Church about the year 1710, the brass was *in situ* and perfect. He said that this escutcheon was on a stone of grey marble :—

Party per pale (argent and gules) barry of four counterchanged, for Barrett. Effigy gone. Underneath on a plate of brasse this Inscription in Gothick Letters :—' Here vnder lyeth Charles Barett, sonne and beire to | Edward Barett, esquire, who maryed Christian, daughter | to Sir Walter Mildmay, Knyght, and had by her ii sonnes | and on daughter. he deceassed in the xxix yere of his | age, the viii daye of August An° Dñi 1584.'

In 1856 the late Mr. H. W. King visited Aveley for the purpose of rubbing it, when he found the dexter half of the brass plate with the inscription gone, having been broken off.

In or about 1878, during the building of a workshop at Romford for a Mr. Booth, the lost dexter half of the inscription plate was dug up. This fragment remained in the possession of Mr. Booth until 1892, when he gave it to a Mr. Kennedy. In the course of time Mr. Kennedy ascertained that the brass came originally from Aveley, and shortly after two clerical

---

[1] *C. S. P.* [2] *E. Arch. N. S.* vii. p. 4.

gentlemen from Romford, with Mr. Kennedy's permission, took his portion of the brass over to Aveley, where they found the other (sinister) half of the plate still in its original matrix on the floor of the church. These gentlemen, assisted by the church clerk, tore up from its stone and carried away to Romford the remaining half of the plate. Mr. Kennedy protested against this proceeding, and ultimately deposited his portion of the brass in the museum at Colchester, upon condition that it should remain there until arrangements were made by some competent authority to refix it in its original matrix in Aveley Church. The other portion came into the possession of the vicar of Aveley, and the writer has lately arranged for the two portions being once more fixed in their original position in that church.

The plate (which measures 19½ by 5 inches) is palimpsest; and the side which may now be regarded as the reverse bears a fragment of a marginal inscription in Low German, and of about the year 1425, placed between longitudinal foliated borders of simple but very elegant design, both being alike. The fragment of the legend (which is in bold black-letter characters) gives the end and the beginning of a memorial inscription, and reads as follows: '*xxiii. ste. dach, i. meyie* ✠ *hier legh.*'[1] The groundwork of the beginning of the legend (the two words coming after the cross) has been hatched, probably preparatory to the inlaying of enamel; but that of the concluding portion (preceding the cross) has not been similarly hatched. This suggests the probability that the brass was never finished, and therefore never laid down, and controverts the belief expressed by Mr. H. W. King that the plate was stolen from some desecrated German cathedral in which it had been originally laid down. The fragment is quite unique so far as Essex is concerned; but fragments of similar inscriptions, of Flemish origin and of more or less similar date, have been discovered in other parts of England.

This brass is, therefore, of uncommon interest; few have

[1] XXIIIrd day of May ✠ Here lyeth.

undergone such adventures, and its reverse side is an excellent example of Flemish art at the beginning of the fifteenth century.

After Charles Barrett's death Christian married Sir John Leveson, of Halling, Kent,[1] and they were both alive on May 3rd, 1609, as appears from the marriage settlement of her son Edward.

Charles's second son, Walter, matriculated at Queen's College, Oxford, March 17th, $1599\tfrac{7}{8}$, aged fourteen; B.A., October 20th, 1601; student, Lincoln's Inn, 1602.[2] He died at Braintree, Essex, aged thirty-five, having been married only a few months, leaving no issue; and was buried at Aveley in 1618. As will appear from his brother's correspondence, he travelled with him in 1605 from Spain to Italy.

Of all those persons whose lives I have in this book attempted to sketch, there is no one who so much distinguished himself as did Edward, Charles's eldest son, who, being merely the son of a country gentleman with no special family interests, was able by means of his own ability to attain to considerable eminence in the domain both of politics and of diplomacy. I much regret that I have only such meagre details of his career as are quite inadequate for the purpose of chronicling with any fulness the events of a life spent in the public service at such an important period of the nation's history, when the power of the royal prerogative was being broken down, to be succeeded by that system of a constitutional monarchy which has been, and still remains, both the wonder and envy of Continental nations.

Two writers of the seventeenth century make slight references to this Edward Barrett. Weever says:—[3]

The surname of Barret [sic] is at this day of exemplarie note and doth greatly flourish by that worthy gentleman Sir Edward Barret Knight Lord Baron of Newburgh chancelour of the Dutchie of Lancaster & one of his Maiesties most honourable privy Councell;

---

[1] Ancestor of the Leveson-Gowers, Dukes of Sutherland. According to the Visitation of Essex 1614 (which is I believe in error), Christian's second husband was John Leveson, of Kent, and not Sir John Leveson.

[2] F. A. O.   [3] W. A. F. M. p. 447.

undergone such adventures, and its reverse side is an excellent example of Flemish art at the beginning of the fifteenth century.

After Charles Barrett's death Christian married Sir John Leveson, of Halling, Kent,[1] and they were both alive on May 3rd, 1609, as appears from the marriage settlement of her son Edward.

Charles's second son, Walter, matriculated at Queen's College, Oxford, March 17th, 159¾, aged fourteen; B.A., October 20th, 1601; student, Lincoln's Inn, 1602.[2] He died at Braintree, Essex, aged thirty-five, having been married only a few months, leaving no issue; and was buried at Aveley in 1618. As will appear from his brother's correspondence, he travelled with him in 1605 from Spain to Italy.

Of all those persons whose lives I have in this book attempted to sketch, there is no one who so much distinguished himself as did Edward, Charles's eldest son, who, being merely the son of a country gentleman with no special family interests, was able by means of his own ability to attain to considerable eminence in the domain both of politics and of diplomacy. I much regret that I have only such meagre details of his career as are quite inadequate for the purpose of chronicling with any fulness the events of a life spent in the public service at such an important period of the nation's history, when the power of the royal prerogative was being broken down, to be succeeded by that system of a constitutional monarchy which has been, and still remains, both the wonder and envy of Continental nations.

Two writers of the seventeenth century make slight references to this Edward Barrett. Weever says: [3]

The surname of Barret [sic] is at this day of exemplarie note and doth greatly flourish by that worthy gentleman Sir Edward Barret Knight Lord Baron of Newburgh chancelour of the Dutchie of Lancaster & one of his Maiesties most honourable privy Councell;

---

[1] Ancestor of the Leveson-Gowers, Dukes of Sutherland. According to the Visitation of Essex 1614 (which is I believe in error), Christian's second husband was John Leveson, of Kent, and not Sir John Leveson.
[2] F. A. O.
[3] W. A. F. M. p. 447.

and Fuller,[1] after mentioning his name, says : ' These Barretts received much wealth by the daughter & heir of Bellhouse of Bellhouse an ancient & fair seat in the parish of Aveley.'

Edward Barrett was educated at Queen's College, Oxford, where, at the age of sixteen, he matriculated the same day as his brother, on March 17th, 159$\frac{7}{8}$, and in 1600 he became a student at Lincoln's Inn.[2] During his long minority the Queen, by the advice of the Court of Wards, granted his wardship to his maternal grandfather, Sir Walter, by Letters Patent dated October 1587, and assigned the sum of 10$l.$ yearly for his 'exhibition'[3] until he attained the age of ten, and after that age the amount was to be doubled. On March 24th, 31st Elizabeth (1589), Sir Walter assigned this right of wardship to his daughter Christian and her second husband, Sir John Leveson. I am not able to prove the date of the marriage of Sir John to Christian, but it not improbably took place about this period, as it would be likely that as soon as his daughter married again Sir Walter would hand over the wardship of his grandson to the child's mother and step-father.

On June 22nd, 1602, when Edward Barrett came of age, Sir John Leveson assigned to him the wardship of himself by deed, only stipulating that he paid his sister Anne her portion of 500$l.$, and also that he held Sir John harmless against a claim for 1,000$l.$ by the executors of Elizabeth Barrett, Edward's grandfather's third wife.

Soon after he came of age Edward obtained a special livery of his lands under the Great Seal on November 27th, 1602 ; but in order to obtain this he had, on October 28th previous, to be a party to an indenture made between Sir Robert Cecil, on behalf of the Court of Wards, and himself, whereby he covenanted that if the schedule annexed to this indenture did not set out the full annual value of the lands to which he was entitled as heir to his grandfather, that then he would pay to the Queen the double annual value of any such lands as might have been omitted from or wrongly valued in the said

---

[1] *Full.* [2] *F. A. O.* [3] Allowance for Subsistence.—*C. D.*

schedule. I cannot believe that the schedule was accurate, for it gives as the total acreage of the Belhus estate only 1,220 acres, and the annual value of it is set down at 55*l*. 13*s*. 4*d*., while we have already seen that in 1574 the estate consisted of 1,700 acres, producing a rent of 320*l*.[1]

In spite of heavy feudal imposts upon inheritance, which in some ways are not altogether unlike our much-abused 'death duties,' young Edward found himself fairly supplied with ready cash when he came of age, as no sooner had he obtained livery of his lands than he started off to travel on the Continent, and, expecting to be away for some little while, he executed a letter of attorney, dated November 30th of this same year, by which he appointed his step-father and his mother to manage all his affairs during his absence.

I have no means of knowing where Edward's travels took him first, but in 1605 he went with the Earl of Nottingham [2] on his embassy to conclude peace with Spain, whence he wrote to his step-father from Valladolid. The letter is not without interest, showing as it does how much richer in those days Spain was than England. The young traveller says that he has spent 1,000 ducats (a ducat being worth there 5*s*. 6*d*. in English money) between Seville and Valladolid; and that the exchange between Seville and London was eight in the hundred. He goes on :—

This countrie is so full of money that they esteem less of 5ˢ than we do in England of 6ᵈ; and after this rate all things are valued here. . . . my lodging here will cost me 23 ducats a month and I have only 3 chambers for my money. I hear by some gentlemen that are already arrived that my brother cometh along with Sir Richard . . . and next winter if it be yͬ will I shall be ready to carry him into Italy. My Lord Amiral[3] is expected here within these two days and I am to go and meet him, there was never Prince nor Embassador entertained with half the respect and magnificence that this shall be.[4]

Before the end of the year Edward and his brother arrived in Italy, where they stayed for a time at Florence, and also

[1] *Ante*, p. 356.   [2] First Earl, perhaps better known as Howard of Effingham.
[3] Sir R. Leveson, Marshal of the Embassy to Spain.—*D. N. B.*
[4] *Hist. Com.* v. p. 140.

LORD NEWBURGH'S MARRIAGE 367

visited Venice. This is shown by some letters in the British Museum[1] to Edward, written by Sir Henry Wotton, Ambassador at Venice in December 1605, and in the spring of the following year. They were on intimate terms, as Sir Henry signs himself 'your deere freind to serue and Loue you.' These letters refer chiefly to politics in Venice, and the question of electing a new Doge in the place of Grimani, who had then just died.

In one of these letters Sir Henry speaks thus of the Gunpowder Plot, of which he had then only recently heard:—

From home I haue had indeed as you imagine, besides priuate Letters, a very large and particular dispatch from my L. of Salisbury about the late practises, wch arriued somewhat late in my hand haueing beene sent by the way of ffrance a day after the departure of the Anwerpe post. And it appeareth therein what the fruites are of that viperous brood nourished in forrein semenaryes under the Coulers of Religion & Charity, and the holy vse of their absolution, by wch a Priest had assured the Conscience of that Johnson or Vaux (for hee hath diũse names) some two dayes before hee should haue putt fier to the trayne.

I have no evidence as to when Edward Barrett returned to England, but we know he was knighted on April 17th, 1608,[2] and I have seen it stated that James conferred this honour on him at Newmarket;[3] and on April 22nd in the following year he was a party to a deed in which he is described as 'Knight.'

The object of this deed was to provide a proper jointure for his intended wife Jane, who was one of the daughters of Sir Edward Carey, and sister to Sir Henry, afterwards Earl of Falkland and Lord Deputy of Ireland. The marriage must have been solemnised just about this period, as a further deed entered into for the same purpose, dated May 3rd following, recites that the marriage had then taken place. By this deed he settled Belhus and some of the adjoining lands on his wife as her jointure, with remainder to his heirs, and divers remainders over; and for further securing her jointure he charged it also on his manor of Wolverton in Hants. If the age—thirty-eight—assigned to Jane when she died in 1632[4] is correct, she was

---

[1] *Har.* 1579, f. 125 *et seq.*
[2] *F. A. O.*
[3] *Par. Rep.* C.
[4] The *C. P.*

only fifteen years of age when she married. She had only one child, a daughter named Catherine, who died young.[1]

Sir Edward soon after his marriage entered political life, and represented Whitchurch in 1614, and Newport in 1621-2. Such records as we have of his public life show that he devoted all his abilities to the Stuart cause. The following is an indication of his leanings in that direction.

When the Elector of the Palatinate, Frederick V., accepted the crown of Bohemia, his father-in-law, James I., in order to provide funds for his assistance, again imposed on England the obnoxious system of taxation called 'Benevolences'; the Privy Council wrote to the Sheriffs requesting them to solicit subscriptions for that purpose in their respective counties; and although Sir Edward was not Sheriff of Essex, he went out of his way in order to collect moneys with that object from some of the parishes in the neighbourhood of Belhus. In this connection there is the following document in the British Museum:—

A note of all such Moneys as haue bin Pay[d] vnto me Sir Edward Barrett, Kt. for the Affaires of Bohemia by theis Parises here vnderwritten.

Wenington	.	.	.	.	.	00	13	06
Vpminster	.	.	.	.	.	05	07	06
Alueley	.	.	.	.	.	24	10	02
Chaldwell	.	.	.	.	.	01	07	00
Westherrock	.	.	.	.	.	03	06	00
Thorrockeparua	.	.	.	.	.	01	00	00
Grayes Thorrocke	.	.	.	.	.	05	11	00
Stifforde	.	.	.	.	.	01	13	00
Orsett	.	.	.	.	.	10	03	08
Northockingdon	.	.	.	.	.	12	02	00
Southockindon	.	.	.	.	.	04	02	00
Raynham	.	.	.	.	.	05	14	00
East Tilbury	.	.	.	.	.	04	03	10
						79	13	08

Received the 14th of Jully 1620 of Thos. Milner serv[t] to S[r] E. Barrett, k[t] to the vse of the King of Bohemia the summe of } £79 13 8

WARWICKE.[2]

[1] Ld. D. His.   [2] Har. 1579, f. 163.

THE BELHUS ESTATE

It will be observed from the foregoing that Aveley, where Sir Edward lived, contributed vastly more to this fund than any of the other parishes whose names occur in the list.

During the first ten years which succeeded his marriage Sir Edward appears to have taken great interest in his estate at Belhus, and to have had funds available to both increase and improve it. In November 1617 he purchased for 1,100*l.*, from a member of the then prominent Essex family named Ayloff,[1] the farm then, and still, known as Courts; and a couple of years later he bought the farm known as Kenningtons for 1,700*l.*

It may be of interest, as giving some evidence of the value of money in those times, to mention that directly he had bought Courts Sir Edward let it, and its sixty-eight acres of land, for 40*l.* per annum for ten years, reserving to himself only the dovecot, the tenant covenanting to do all necessary repairs, being allowed gate-bote, house-bote, and fire-bote[2] from the timber growing on the farm.

That part of Essex near Belhus, and probably indeed the whole of Essex, must have presented a very different appearance then from what it does now; and its cultivation, if such an expression can be properly applied to land in a state of nature, being nearly all meadow or pasture, caused it to resemble somewhat the appearance which the country now presents to a traveller on, say, the Great Western line as he goes from London down to Exeter. Moreover, at the period when this survey was made there existed many hedgerow belts, which are still common in parts of Sussex and Kent, which must have given the face of the country a very wooded appearance.

Courts farm is practically now all arable, while in 1619 fifty of its sixty-eight acres were pasture, and only five were arable. This very large predominance of pasture over arable obtained over the whole estate. We have a very carefully made map of

---

[1] This family should not be confused with that of Aylet, once also an important one in Essex.

[2] *Vide ante*, p. 257, *n.* 1.

the estate, and also a 'Booke or Terrar showynge particularlie the measure, name, Kynde, Tenure, and parish, of all the demeane landes & tenementes belonging to the Mannor of Belhouse ... made by Samuell Pierse of Maidstone in the Countie of Kent 1619.' I have three copies of this 'Booke,' one of which is most elaborately bound in gold tooled white binding. The 'Booke' in question shows that in 1619 the estate contained 2,249 acres, and that of this only 700 were arable, the rest being pasture (889 acres), meadow (327 acres), 'reedes' (23 acres), and 'woode' (308 acres).

Besides this change of so much of the land from pasture into tillage, no less than ten of the then existing eighteen farmhouses which the estate contained at this period have not only entirely disappeared, but their names are lost also; and the manor-house of Noke has long since been converted into a four-tenement building. The names of all of these farms appear in every case to have been derived from that of some previous owner whose name can be traced in our deeds.[1]

On December 23rd, 1618, Sir Edward obtained a grant from the Crown of free-warren, and a license to make a park round Belhus, which he proceeded to do by adding to the pastures which already surrounded the house, parts of those farms known respectively as the Warren, Culverhouse, and Bumpstead; and by stocking his new enclosure with deer. The rights conferred under this charter of free-warren were upheld by a legal decision in 1777;[2] and in 1823, when a trespass upon the free-warren was committed and an action commenced, it was only stayed upon terms of the defendants making a written apology, paying all costs, and making other acts of restitution.[3]

In 1630 Sir Edward obtained legal sanction for stopping up a public road which led from Aveley Mill to the present high road to Stifford and Ockendon, and which ran quite close to the south boundary of his newly enclosed park. This stopping up

---

[1] I have treated more fully of this subject in an article in the *E. R.* July 1906.
[2] *Ld. D. Mis.*
[3] *L. P.* iv.

of a public thoroughfare was not accomplished without opposition on the part of those accustomed to go that way, and, from the terms of an order made by the House of Lords [1] in that connection, it would seem that Sir Edward had also stopped up some other public road, probably the one marked in the before-mentioned estate map as leading from Aveley to Upminster on the west boundary of the park, and which is now only a right of way as a foot-path.

The names given in the 'Booke' to some portions of the park are to a certain extent descriptive of their respective characters at the present day; thus the south-east corner was 'the Warren,' and is of a dry gravelly nature well adapted for rabbits, and when a small boy I remember my father being at some trouble to fill up the rabbit holes there, and exterminate their inhabitants, in order to provide a safe exercising ground for his hunters. The portion of park lying between the house and the kitchen garden was called 'Sheeps Leaze,' or sheep's pasture, and being much of the same nature as the Warren just referred to, was, and still is, more suited for running sheep on than most other land in the immediate vicinity. That portion of the park to the north-west of the house, where there are two small ponds, was called 'Brickfields,' and I think there can be no doubt but that the origin of these ponds was that John Barrett made excavations there in order to procure clay with which to manufacture bricks for building Belhus. Even in these days of good roads it is a costly matter to cart such heavy goods as bricks any distance, but in times when roads existed only in name it must have been almost impossible to do so, and the obvious course for anyone to adopt who intended to build a large house was to dig clay and burn bricks as near to the site of the house as circumstances would permit.

It must not be thought from what I have written about Sir Edward and Belhus that he was what may be called a typical seventeenth century country squire, whose chief or only interests were confined to his house and property, and in whose

[1] *H. L.* vii. p. 157.

eyes local events assumed a magnitude quite out of proportion to their real importance. He had travelled too far, and seen too much of men, to be contented to settle down as a 'Squire Western,' and no doubt the fact that he had twice sat in Parliament stimulated his ambition.

In 1622 he wrote to the Marquis of Buckingham, then the most powerful subject in England, to solicit some post. The exact nature of the employment he desired to obtain does not appear from the letter, which, indeed, is of a very involved nature, and fawning in its tone beyond belief. There is no reason to suppose that Sir Edward was of a servile nature, and no doubt the terms in which he couched this letter were just the same as any other person in those days would have used when writing to so important a personage to solicit an appointment; he was connected by marriage with the Duke, as the latter married a granddaughter of Sir Henry Knyvett, of Charlton, Wilts, and Lady Barrett's maternal grandfather was another Sir Henry Knyvett, of Buckenham, Norfolk; both these Knyvetts were members of the same family, and when Buckingham married in 1620, Sir Edward would naturally have a good opportunity of becoming acquainted with the husband of his wife's cousin. As Sir Edward was ambitious, he no doubt made the most of this opportunity, and ingratiated himself in that powerful minister's favour. Both warmly attached to the sovereign, and in the public service, I think they were most likely on terms of great friendship, as Sir Edward by his will left a considerable legacy to Lord Francis Villiers, the Duke's youngest son.[1]

The letter above referred to, which was addressed 'To the most excellent Lord my lo. the Marquis of Buckingham Lo. High Admirall of England,' is as follows :—[2]

My Lord,

Yo^r lo: is so farre remooued from y^{or} friends, and seruants that they subsist onelle vpon the strength of that fayth, wch y^{or} lo: noblenes, and good fortunes supporteth, yet if in this

[1] *Post*, p. 396.   [2] *Har.* 1581, f. 254.

absence, I suspect, that I maye well bee shutt out of y^{or} lo: thoughts, when so manye affayers of greater consequence, haue taken up the roome, I presume yt would not argue so much weakeness in mee, as yt would negligence not to put y^{or} lo: in minde how great a character of y^{or} greatness yt would bee, at this distance, to effect that wch y^{or} lo: promyses haue engaged my hopes to aspyer vnto, yet these thoughts keepe not back that tribute of deuotion and good wishes wch is due to y^{or} lo: happines. And I haue tyed my selfe to y^{or} lo: seruice wth such a knot, that if I could giue ouer hoping to receaue some fauo^{r} woorthie of y^{or} lo: noblenes my first request must bee to bee commanded something woorthie of my deuotions, that I might at the least appear woorthie though lesse happie, and not conclude in so poore a state of neglect that maye make y^{or} lo: noblenes fatall to mee; I hope if y^{or} lo: absence bee lengthned out you will preuent[1] my hopes by some effectual Lettre to the King, that may cut of all hazards, and that y^{or} lo: fauo^{rs} will sooner arryue to me then my suit to y^{or} lo: who knowes yf not the merrit, yet the faythfullness of
                    Y^{or} lo: humblest Seruant
London March 3. 1622.   E. BARRETT.

I am not able to say whether this obsequious letter was effectual, and if Buckingham did bestow any office upon Sir Edward; but he was appointed Ambassador to France very soon after Charles came to the throne, and I think it is almost certain that he owed this appointment to the Duke's influence. Lord Dacre suggests that Sir Edward never did in fact take up his duties as Ambassador, and says: 'It is to be supposed that some accident intervening prevented the Embassy from taking place.'[2]

Among our papers is a certified copy, dated February 5th, 1645, of an indenture, dated April 30th, 1625, between Sir Edward and his wife of the one part, and the Dowager Lady Leveson, his mother, and others of the second part. This deed begins with a recital that Sir Edward 'is forthwith to take his Voyage into ffrance & there to remayne and contynue Ambassador Leiger';[3] and further recites that he owed moneys to the

---

[1] Meaning 'anticipate.'—*C. D.*   [2] *Ld. D. His.*
[3] Obsolete for ledger, meaning a resident minister.—*C. D.*

parties of the second part, and was desirous of settling his debts before his departure. He then proceeds by this deed to covenant to levy a fine of his estates in Berkshire and Hampshire to their use, upon trust to pay his debts, with divers remainders over, amongst which were remainders to the heir of his grandfather's son-in-law, Sir H. Forster, husband of his grandfather's daughter Margaret by his second wife, and to the heirs of his grandfather's sons-in-law, Brampton Gurdon and Sir John Corbett, respectively, who, as has been said, had each married a daughter of Edward Barrett by his third wife Elizabeth.

Sir Edward certainly expected to set out about May 1625, as there is an application from him as Ambassador to France to Sir J. Coke, dated May 11th in that year, in which he requests 'praviledge & security for his mariners.'[1] A letter in the British Museum[2] from William Boswell,[3] a well-known diplomatist, shows that Sir Edward had applied to him for hints as how best to discharge his new duties; in replying Mr. Boswell certainly spares himself no trouble, as he writes at very great length, dividing his letter into no less than eighteen paragraphs. This letter is dated May 29th, 1625, and is addressed 'To the Right Honorable Sir Edward Barrett Knt his Mat^ies Ambassador to the French King.' As usual at that period the letter is couched in very humble terms, and he constantly refers to his correspondent as 'your lordship' as if he were a peer. This letter, which is far too long to give in full, begins thus:—

My very good Lord,
Rather in obedience to your Lordshipps expectacōn than hope of adding anything to y^or knowledge I take leave to put y^or Lordp in minde of some few pticulars concerning your negotiacon in ffrance, as also psons who may happily be of vse to y^or Lordp for the better aduancem^t thereof: my occasions which are many att this present and my long absence from such Employm^ts or almost thought of any thing in that kinde, make me come shorte of what I should.

[1] *Hist. Com.* xii. App. Part i. p. 193.   [2] *Har.* 1579, f. 56.
[3] Knighted 1633.

The first thing that Mr. Boswell advises Sir Edward to do is to settle 'a Ciphre wth Mr Secret^{rie} before you goe,' and he gives a list of several Italian authors on this subject, and then says, 'And the best for the practise herein that I haue heard of in England is Mr. Phillips an auntient man, prisoner in the King's Bench.' Then follow names of prominent men in France with whom it would be advisable for him to become well acquainted, and those of Englishmen resident in that country who are to be trusted.

Other heads of advice are :—

'Y^{or} L^dps secretarie to keepe a journal, or the minutes of euery day as materialls of dispatches.'

To send dispatches to English ministers abroad so as to keep them well informed on what was passing in France.

To keep in touch with English merchants at Lyons, ' Marseillis, Bourdeaux,' Rochelle, Rouen, &c.

To watch the movements of what we now call the money market and the exchange.

To observe the doings of the mercantile marine.

To study carefully the position of the rival religious parties, and 'whether the last Warres haud added or abated the number & courages of the Prot.'

To know all the details of the questions of precedence between Spain and France as it is desirable to keep these countries 'at odds, for soe oure King shall holde the Balance of Europe, & his owne Kingdom in Peace, and withall doe good offices vnto ffrance.'

The relations of France with Holland and the Empire are also to be carefully noted, and so are the

pceedings & disposition of the ffr: in the p̃sent league with Engl: Ven: Savoy, &c which they may bee suspected to hold onely for, & dureing the Pursuit of theire owne ends, which beeing compassed, wee may bee left to seeke anew how to attaine ō^{rs}. C'est tousiours l'honneur de la France de faire bien ses affaires.

Mr. Boswell concludes this long letter, for which he apologises as 'abrupte & disordered' with a list of books such as 'Grotius,' &c., which he advises Sir Edward to obtain, and finally ends 'I beseech you burne these imptinent pieces and couer my faults.'

On September 24th in this same year another prominent person who wrote to Sir Edward as being Ambassador in Paris was Sir Thomas Roe, our representative at the Court of Turkey, who dated his letter from 'Halchys nere Const^{ple}.'[1] He writes on diplomatic business, but he begins by congratulations on Sir Edward's appointment :—

I am soe assured of the dearness of y^r nature y^t my congratulations shall not bee less acceptable for their latenesse ; 'hee comes betime that lost none' ; and ȳ^r Ldship will measure mee by youre Selfe. As soone as I knew of your employment I was glad of the occasion to present you my service, and wish that I may continue this still with ȳ^{or} increase of honour.

He then proceeds to urge Sir Edward to press the French Government to cause payment to be made to certain merchants for debts incurred to them by the French Ambassador, the Baron of Cicy.

Among other pieces of news he thus quaintly mentions the progress of a fearful epidemic :—

The sickness that hath raged as though it would repeople Hell, and dispossesse the fallen Angells of their auncient Kingdome, begins to yeeld to the season ; from the first of August to the end of the third [week?] there fell 8900 in the whole. Since fiuer 140^M [2] besides the out townes and villages adjacent. It hath concluded with so vyolent storme of winde as many ages hath not knowne ;

and he concludes, 'Thus presenting ȳ^r Ld with my wiues service & presuming both to kisse the fayre hands of ȳ^r Noble Lady I commite you to the blessed keeping of our gratious God.'

If Sir Edward did not go to France in 1625, there was evidently at that time a widespread belief that he was about to

[1] *Har.* 1579, f. 77. Catalogued as from Roe, but the signature is difficult to read thus.
[2] Since February, 140,000.

do so; and a letter from Mr. Thacker to Sir J. Coke,[1] dated November 23rd, 1625, points to this expectation when he says: 'Your honour may be exceedingly well furnished with 4 dapple grey horses of Sir E. Barrett, will cost little under £100, they may be seen at his house in Marbone [Marylebone] Park'; this looks as if it was thought that Sir Edward had gone, or was just going, abroad, as otherwise he would not have been likely to have wanted to dispose of, what sounds to have been, his state team of horses.

It is probable that the reason Sir Edward's departure for France was delayed was that his patron the Duke went there himself as Ambassador, which post he filled during the months of May and June 1625.[2] On Buckingham's return it was no doubt intended that Sir Edward should succeed him, and until it was decided to despatch an Ambassador hither Sir Edward would have had a strong claim for any mission of importance that it was proposed to send to a European State. Such an opportunity soon arose as a mission to the King of Denmark and Holland was in contemplation, and there are in the British Museum instructions indexed as being for Sir Edward Barrett 'When passing by the Hague to the King of Denmark.'[3]

However, he was again forestalled by the Duke, who in the autumn of 1625 went for a short period to the Hague as Ambassador.[4] Disappointed a second time within a twelvemonth of occupying one of the most important and responsible posts that a subject can attain to, Sir Edward's claims became almost irresistible; and accordingly we find four documents in the British Museum[5] which are 'Instructions for our trustie and welbeloued Sir Edward Barrett K^{nt} our Ambassador Leger to our deare brother the most Christian Kinge.' They are not identical word for word; for instance, their references to the seizure of British merchant ships are in one less conciliatory than in the others, but the gist of their contents are substantially

---

[1] *Hist. Com.* xii. Part i. p. 230. [2] The *C. P.*
[3] *Har.* 1584, 98. [4] *D. N. B.*
[5] *Har.* 1584, 89, 93, 133, 195, 198.

the same. Three of these documents have no dates, but the first one is dated 'Whitehall Apl 30 1626,' and is endorsed, 'receaued May 4, 1626,' and are therefore, presumably, the ultimate directions given to Sir Edward. These directions are to the following effect :—

The King says that Mr. Secretary Conway shall furnish Sir Edward with copies of all treaties and negotiations recently concluded by the Earl of Holland and Sir Dudley Carleton, the late Ambassadors. There are three matters to which Sir Edward's attention is especially directed, and which he is urged to have carried through as early as possible. They are—

1. The execution of the 'Main Leue.'
2. The returne of our owne shipp the Vauntguard and our Merchants shipps.
3. The Ratification of the Treatie in 1610 according to Articles agreed by our Ambassadors & the Ministers of that King.

Sir Edward was to acquaint himself with the causes pending in the English Court of Admiralty concerning French ships which had been seized, and to pay special attention to the state of things then existing between the French Government and the Protestants, more particularly those of the town of Rochelle, and to urge the latter to dutiful behaviour towards their King; at the same time, these Huguenots were to rest assured that the King (Charles) would do all in his power to protect them in the exercise of their religion, as he had already promised by his Ambassadors; and Sir Edward is exhorted as occasions offer to press upon the French King in a tactful manner his obligation to observe towards his Protestant subjects all those edicts concerning them made by himself, or by his predecessors.

Sir Edward is reminded that it was part of his duty to keep his 'ears open to all men and of all sorts' whereby he might come to the knowledge of anything which may be to the King's service. He was to watch carefully all political movements in France, and all foreign treaties whether open or secret ones. In case of any public meetings or functions, when questions might arise as to the precedence of the representatives of other nations,

CHANCELLOR OF EXCHEQUER

Sir Edward was to remember that he does not yield place to any, except to the Emperor's Ambassador; but in the case of the Pope's Nuncio, in order to avoid all scandal or dispute, he is to have no dealings with him. One of these sets of instructions [1] bids him especially support the Grisons, and when their Ambassadors come to the French Court

You are to take notice of them as Ministers from a State not only in Amitie wth us, but whose conservacōn wee have cause, in justice & reason of state, to wish and indeavour, for the furtherance of o^r owne iust dessignes, the support of the good partie, and the benefitt of Christendome.

Yet a third time, when all seemed really settled, was Sir Edward doomed to disappointment, as diplomatic relations between England and France were in such a state of tension that it was considered wiser to delay sending an Ambassador to that country, until at length, in the month of November, Buckingham again went himself.

It is not improbable that it was in order to compensate Sir Edward for the disappointment caused him by his reasonable expectations of serving his King and country being so continually frustrated that on October 17th, 1627, he was raised to the peerage under the title of Lord Barrett of Newburgh, county Fife.[2] In July 1628, owing to the influence of his patron the Duke, who sent warrants to that effect to Sir J. Coke, Lord Newburgh was appointed Chancellor of the Exchequer.[3] He has left the following MS. account of the ceremony of his being sworn into that office :—[4]

July 1628. I was sworne a privy Cōncellour at whitehall.

Aug. 1628. August 11 I recieued a reference from the L^{ds} of the Privy Councell to the M^r of the Rolls.

And me, to examine, call to account, & Procure the expediting of all the business of Prizes ther, or hereafter, to be taken, the reference dated 8th Aug. at whitehall.

[1] *Har.* 1584, 197.
[2] Lord Newburgh obtained a grant of supporters in February 16$\frac{29}{30}$ from the Lyon office, Edinburgh.—*F. P.*
[3] *Hist. Com.* xii. App. Part i. p. 360.   [4] *Har.* 1579, 164.

Aug. 15. I receiued my Pattents vnder the Great Seale For the offices of chancellor of the excheq^r, & vnder Treasurer.

Aug 20. I tooke the severall oaths of chancellor of the exchequer and vnder Treassure^r at druery house[1] Before my Ld Treassure^r[2] and Baron Vernon,[3] and the exheqr seals then deliuered vnto me vpon Satterday the 23rd of Aug.

The Fearfull and Horralbe [*sic*] Murder was committed vpon the D. of Buckingham's Person at Porchmouth by one Leaurtenant Felton vpon Tuesday 14th of Octo. My Lord Treassurer & I took our oaths at Wesminster in this manner following.

My Ld Treassurer was accompanied wth a great Troop of L^{ds}, privy councello^{rs} officers and other K^{ts} and Gent ; to Wesminster on horsback he rideing foremost in the Middle betweene my Ld Keeper[4] and my Ld Privy Seale[5] and all the rest following according to their Places and Degrees; being ariued at Wesminster he went to the farther end of the Hall, and theire stayde vnderneath the Chancery Court till my Ld Keeper was placed in Court and had heard a motion. Then he was called into ye Court, wheare he stood Bare headed dureing the Tyme my Ld Keeper made a speache to him, concerning the quallitie, charge, and Duty of his place, wch being ended, kneeling on Cusshion in the Court vnderneath my Ld Keeper, he took the oath of Allēagenc and supremacy, and then the oath of his office, wch being done, My Ld Keeper deliuered him his Pattents and accompanyed him from thence into the Cheq^r Court, wheare I mett him at the stayers head, and we went togather to the Excheq^r Barr, where we stayd Bare headed, and my Ld Keeper being sett. In the court, the Marshall of the Court cam to my Ld Treass^r to know whether it was his pleasur to haue his Pattent Read, and vpon his desireing of it The Pattent was deliuered to M^r Jo West, Deputy to the K^s Remembrancer, who read it. And then my Ld Treass^r was called into Court where

---

[1] Drury House, in Drury Lane, was for a considerable period the property of the important family of that name. At the time when Essex was attempting to organise the revolt against Elizabeth's authority, which was to prove abortive and to lead to his execution, Drury House was the headquarters of himself and his adherents.

[2] Sir R. Weston, of Skreens, Essex, created Baron Weston and afterwards Earl of Portland ; title extinct.

[3] Sir George Vernon, appointed Baron of Court of Exchequer, 1627.

[4] Sir Thomas Coventry, afterwards Baron Coventry; title extinct.

[5] Henry, first Earl of Manchester.

againe he took the oaths, the two first kneeling, and the last standing, and then was he placed in his place, and my Ld Keeper returned into the Chancery. Then I remayned still at the Barr: The Marshall cam to me and demanded whether I desired to haue My Pattents read, and vpon my desire signified, they were delivered to Ca^r West who read them both; then I was called into ye Court, and kneeling vpon a Cushion read the 2 first oaths, and after that standing vp took the oaths of My two places, Mr West Reading them, and then affter saluting of ye Barrons, was placed in My Place aboue my Ld Treass^r, from whence after a Motion wee arose, and went and vissited the offices of the receipt, and so departed.

It does not appear how long Lord Newburgh was Chancellor of the Exchequer, but his name as holder of that office is recorded as late as 1641.[1]

On April 15th, 1629, he was appointed Chancellor of the Duchy of Lancaster, a post which he held until his death in 1644.[2]

Among other public duties fulfilled for a time by Lord Newburgh appears to have been that of Keeper of the Records at Whitehall, as in the British Museum there is a document [3] which begins thus:—

| Sr Thos Wilsons office.[4] | The Generall heads of things in the office of his Maties Papers & Records for business of State & Counsell established att Whitehall. |

This is a catalogue of various documents in some Government office, apparently made by some person retiring for the benefit of his successor; towards the foot of this document is this memo.: 'For the service of the right honorable ye Lord Barrett.'

In 1628 Lord Newburgh entered into a great speculation, but I regret to say I have no means of knowing how it turned

---

[1] *Hay. Dig.*   [2] *Ibid.*   [3] *Har.* 1579, fol. 83-85.
[4] Sir Thomas Wilson was Keeper of the Records at Whitehall, 1601–29.

out. Sir William Alexander (afterwards Earl of Stirling) had obtained from James I. a grant to Nova Scotia, but he does not seem to have taken any active steps to dispossess the French, who had already got a slight footing in that country. Lord Newburgh was taken with the idea of becoming a great colonial landowner, and associated himself with other persons to send out there a person styled Captain Kerck, furnished with letters of marque, in command of a small fleet. Kerek's voyage was very successful; he defeated the French, took several of their ships, and set up King Charles's arms in place of those of the French near Tadousac. Upon this freebooting captain's return, Lord Newburgh asked the King, for himself and his partners, to grant them a patent for the exclusive rights to trade with and to plant that country, and this the King promised to do. Sir William Alexander then asserted his prior claim under the patent granted to him by James; but at last terms of compromise between Sir William and Lord Newburgh seem to have been arrived at. The latter and his partners declared themselves prepared to find 30,000*l.* for sending out a fleet, merchandise, and forces for reducing the country, and trade with the savages, and they petitioned the King to sanction the agreement which they had come to; but whether or not their petition was granted does not appear.[1]

In connection with this scheme of colonisation, Lord Newburgh, already a peer, was, on or about October 2nd, 1628, created a baronet of Nova Scotia, and received a grant of, presumably, 16,000 acres in that region, whereof he obtained seizin in the following January.[2]

The next we know of Lord Newburgh is that towards the end of 1632, after twenty-four years of married life, he sustained the loss of his wife, who was buried at Aveley on January 11th, 163$\frac{2}{3}$. After making due allowance for the highflown language which often distinguishes testamentary documents, I think we may say with confidence that her death was a very great loss, and a very deep grief to her husband. In his

[1] *Hist. Com.* xii. Part i. p. 375-7.   [2] The *C. B.*

will, made some ten years after her death, he speaks of her thus :—

my late deare, and now blessed wyfe, the comfort, blessing, and vnexpressable happiness of whose fellowship and companie it pleased God iustlie for my manifold and enormous sinns to depryue mee of.

Lord Newburgh gave a more practical proof of the attachment he felt to his wife, and to her family, than by merely writing a laudatory account of her in his will, as he did not scruple to uphold the cause of one of her nephews against Strafford, Lord Deputy of Ireland, then in the zenith of his power. Lord Newburgh's brother-in-law, Lord Falkland, was Strafford's predecessor in Ireland, and the latter regarded the friends of Falkland with suspicion, for he looked upon this nobleman as his secret enemy.[1] When Falkland was recalled from Ireland in 1629 and Strafford sent to replace him, he at once deprived Lord Falkland's son of the command of a company which he held in Ireland. Lord Newburgh, regardless of the risk he ran in incurring the wrath of so powerful an adversary, did not hesitate to support the claim of his wife's nephew. How much Strafford was annoyed at this action on his part is shown by the following letter :—[2]

That my Lord Newburgh should move for the father's company for the Lord of Falkland's son, a boy, I can only say thus much it was, and is at this instant, so ill ordered as in a meaner man might well have been the turning him out of his captainship . . . the conclusion therefore is I am confident his Majesty will not debar me of what belongs to my place for all the solicitation of the pretty busy Lord Newburgh, who if a man would move his Majesty for anything in the gift of the Chancellor of the Dutchy, would as pertley cackle, and put himself in the way of complaint, as if he had all the merits and ability in the world to serve his Master.

However sincerely Lord Newburgh may have deplored the loss of his wife he came of an uxorious stock, and so, like his

---

[1] *Le. His.* iii. p. 11.   [2] *Straf. L. & D.* i. p. 128.

predecessors, Thomas, John, and Edward, he soon took to himself a successor to her whose loss he so touchingly lamented. In August 1635 he married Katherine, daughter of Hugh Fenn,[1] of Wootton, Gloucestershire, and widow of Hugh Perry, Sheriff of London 1633. She brought him 10,000*l.*, in those times a very considerable sum, and he on his side settled his Belhus estate upon her for the term of her life, after his decease. Katherine was singularly badly educated for a woman of her position, even making all allowance for the small amount of education which in Stuart times was considered to be necessary for women. I have found a bond signed by her which she entered into with Chalonor Chute in 1653, no doubt in connection with the lawsuit with Richard Barrett, and which is referred to later.[2] To say that she has signed her name badly to this document would be to indulge in gross flattery; she has printed rather than written it, and this in a fashion which any very young child nowadays would be ashamed of.

Lord Newburgh had no issue by this marriage, but when she married him Katherine had four daughters by her first husband, and to these children Lord Newburgh proved a most kind step-father, of which we have evidence in a somewhat curious manner. All these step-daughters married persons of title. The youngest one, Mary, as her second husband, married Sir William Fermor, Baronet, and died in 1670; her funeral sermon was preached by the celebrated Puritan divine, the Rev. J. Dobson, and in the course of this sermon he said :—

The place of her birth was the great City and this also was the School of her education in the Family, & under the Eye of

[1] The C. B. calls him Richard; Richard was her brother, and was Lord Mayor of London 1638.—*Hay. Dig.*
[2] *Post*, p. 398.

the Honourable the Lord Newburgh, then Chancellor of the Dutchy, who in his Love & Care was indeed the second Father to the Children, as by marriage he was become a second Husband to the Mother; which I the rather mention because it was not fit that he should be passed over, whom for this good office she could never speak of without honour.

A remarkable testimony to the Chancellor's virtues, the more so as when this sermon was preached there was nothing to be gained by singing his praises, as he had then been dead many years.

As Lord Newburgh filled a public position, it is only to be expected that there should be many references to and some letters from him in the reports of the Historical MSS. Commission, but a quantity of these relate only to details of official business, and are not of sufficient interest to quote from; but it may be mentioned that one of these letters is dated from 'Belhouse.'

One letter, however, written to his old friend Sir J. Coke, soon after the latter's retirement from public life, in which he gives an account of the flight of the Chief Secretary, Windebank,[1] and speaks of the approaching trial of Strafford, is perhaps of sufficient interest to be inserted:—[2]

Dec. 7th 1640 Duchy House.

Presuming that you & I are long since passed beyond the bounds of ceremony, I was loth to answer your letter with idle lines, till I could send you a warrant for a doe, which this paper shall present unto you; and I shall always be studious upon all occasions to preserve the correspondence of that good friendship which hath long been betwixt us. I believe you have much of the troubles of these times, which will prove unto the happiness of your safe retreat to a plentiful fortune and a life of freedom & quietness. Your brother Mr Secretary Windebank hath lately made a retreat also, but upon ill terms, for being sharply prosecuted in the Lower House he is fled

---

[1] Sir Francis Windebank fled to Calais, 1640, and died in Paris six years later.—*D. N. B.*

[2] *Hist. Com.* xii. Part ii. p. 266.

beyond the seas; I hope not distrusting his innocency for great crimes, but his good nature & willingness to please having made him either neglect that warranty who should secure him, or adventure upon the transgressing of those laws which he did not know or think could be so dangerous to him in his place. And the King at this time being under the advice of the worst consellor, necessity, which takes from him all power to defend any servant of his whom his own innocency, or the opinion of it in Parliament shall not protect. . . . I presume you have long since heard of the condition my Lord of Strafford is in, who is like to be the greatest example of these times.

There is a letter from Lord Newburgh to his kinsman, Sir R. Leveson, written from the 'Dutchie House' on November 29th, 1642, which gives some account of public affairs and the struggle going on between the King and the Parliament.[1] He says that he hopes that the example of the Staffordshire justices in providing guards for the safety of the county will be followed in other places; complains of the pillaging round about, particularly in Essex and Suffolk; he says that the fatal encounter at Braynesford[2] has dispelled the hope of an accommodation between the King and the Parliament; and that the King's army is about Reading and Oxford. He also alludes to the burdens which will arise by the contributions for the support of the armies on both sides, the daily messages between the King and the Parliament, and says that to the last sent by the Parliament inviting the King to return, the King gave an answer which in the first place was very sharp, but in the end invited them to send propositions.

The King's fortunes continued to go from bad to worse, and his adversities were naturally reflected not only upon his adherents in the field, but also upon his supporters in civil life, and among these Lord Newburgh suffered along with the

---

[1] *Hist. Com.* v. App. p. 147.

[2] Brentford, sometimes written Brainford or Braynesford. The King won a victory there over a small force of the rebels, which put an end to all hopes of an understanding taking place between the opposing forces. For full account of this affair, *Rush*, ii. Part iii. p. 58 *et seq.*

rest of those who threw in their lot with the Stuart dynasty. His persecution, so far as I have discovered, commenced on August 30th, 1641, when he, together with others, was impeached by Sir John Corbet for their action respecting himself.[1]

On November 25th, 1643, the House of Commons sent a message to the House of Lords to desire their concurrence on several matters, one of which was that 'Lord Newburgh an assistant of this House may be assessed for his twentieth part.'[2] On December 23rd following the Lords appointed 'the following Thursday for considering the question of assessing the Assistants of this house for the twentieth part.'[3]

The same day a direct attack was made on the property of Lord Newburgh and some others by the Earl of Stamford, the Parliamentarian General, who petitioned the Lords, saying that in spite of all his services to the Parliamentary party, they had in no way been rewarded, and that his necessities with his servants and troopers 'are now so extreme that unless some immediate care can be taken they must either plunder or starve,' and he prays that, owing to his miserable condition and past services, the twentieth part of the estates of the Earl of Arundel, the Countess of Rutland, Lord Newburgh, and Baron Trevor may be allotted to him for his present succour.[4]

Lord Newburgh did not, to use a recent public expression of Mr. Chamberlain's, take this attack upon his property 'lying down,' but on December 30th he petitioned the Lords, and prays leave to represent to their House his sufferings and the condition he is reduced to by the miseries of these times before any further charge is laid upon him. He says that he has been compelled to sell his plate, has been deprived of the benefit of his office, and of so much of his estate as abates two-thirds of his yearly revenue; he has now no personal estate, but some

[1] *Hist. Com.* iv. App. p. 99.   [2] *H. L.* vi. p. 311.   [3] *Ibid.* p. 351.
[4] *Hist. Com.* v. App. p. 118. By an ordinance dated November 1642, commissioners were appointed to assess those persons who had not contributed to the Parliamentary Army to the payment of 'such sums of money according to their estates as shall be thought fit and reasonable, so as the same exceed not the twentieth part of their estates.' *Rush*, ii. Part iii. p. 71.

ordinary and necessary goods which he is engaged by marriage contracts to leave to his wife after his death. His debts are three times the value of his estate, and increase daily as he is compelled to borrow at interest to defray the ordinary expenses of his family. Notwithstanding this he has ever since the beginning of this Parliament attended at very great charge as an assistant upon their Lordships' House.[1]

At this period the King's adherents—especially if they were in any way brought into notice by holding positions in the public service—had a very hard time to pass through; anxiety about the success of their Sovereign's cause could never have been absent from their minds, their private fortunes were constantly being subjected to various extortions at the hands of the Parliamentary party, and even their lives and liberties were in the greatest jeopardy. No wonder if the strain of such times proved too much for some to bear; and it is probable that these constant worries were the cause of Lord Newburgh's death, which took place, no doubt, in December 1644, as he was buried at Aveley on January 2nd, 164$\frac{4}{5}$.[2]

That his fortune had already greatly suffered by the course of public events as early as two years before he died, is shown by the statement he made in his will that his means had been 'soe much lessened' owing to the 'Publique Miseries'; and no doubt it suffered still more during the interval intervening between then and his death.

Lord Newburgh published his will, all written in his own handwriting, on March 17th, 1643, in the presence of Sir Robert Bindloss (or Bindlosse)[3] and six other witnesses. He began with a more than ordinary elaborate disquisition on the uncertainty of life, and then made the usual bequest of his soul to the Redeemer—'buylding my Saluation onlie vpon the merrits of his passion, wch ransome is onlie suffitient to redeeme mee from the second death, and the roabe of his righteousnes onlie,

---

[1] *Hist. Com.* v. App. p. 119.   [2] Aveley Register.
[3] Sir Robert, created baronet 1641, had married Rebecca, third daughter of Lord Newburgh's second wife by her first husband.—The C. *B.*

large enough to couer the nakednes, and deformitie, of my sinfull soule.' He directed his body to be buried without any 'vaine and costlie pompe of Heraldrye' in the vault he had made in Aveley Church. He directed that 'blacks' were only to be given to his dear wife and her children, and to his family and servants ; and that

my chaplayne, or some other graue religious preacher, to bee appoynted to preache at my buryall, and him to bee seriouslie and strictlie enjoyned not to dawbe ouer my sinfull lyfe wth any prayses, nor to waste anye tyme in the relating of anyethinge els concerning mee ; But that I dyed laying holde vpon the merrits of the death and passion of my Lord and Sauiour Jhesus Christ, and anchoring the hope of my Saluation onlie vpon him, who, beeing both my Aduocate and my Judge, my cause cannot miscarrie, mercye being his, and by him layed vp in store for those that wth true fayth repose vpon him. . . . And whereas my Creddit and the reputation of my conscience & honestie lye at pawne for the payment & discharge of my just debts w^{ch}, beeing the fruits of an vnthriftie vaine and wastefull lyfe, I most humblie beseech my God out of the riches of his mercye to forgiue.

Lord Newburgh then proceeded to direct the payment of these debts, and charges his lands in Berkshire and Hampshire for that purpose, and also to provide annuities of 20*l.* each to two of his servants, or in lieu thereof a lump sum of 200*l.* to each of them. He then mentions that he had agreed by his marriage articles to leave his wife 1,000*l.* worth of plate, and the like value of other goods and household stuff, but that 'by the publique miseries of these tymes my owne necessities have enforced mee to sell allmost all my plate' ; Lord Newburgh bequeaths to his wife instead not only all the plate he still possessed, but also sundry articles of jewellery, and all his household possessions and live stock, whether at Belhus or the Duchy house, 'excepting the ould suite of tappistrie hanguings in the great Parler at Belhowse, and the ould suite of tappistrie hanguings now vsed in the chamber ouer the Hall at Belhowse wch I desire maye still continue their.'

This bequest to his widow was saddled with a charge of 200*l*. 'for the charges of my Funerall in that pryuate waye and manner as I haue herein directed'; and 30*l*. to provide 'two playne Siluer fflaggon potts' for the Church at Aveley;[1] and she was also to pay two legacies amounting to 150*l*.

Lady Newburgh was named executrix of the will, and if she accepted the office her executors were to receive the rents of the Belhus estate for five years after her decease; if she refused to act then Robert Brisco was named, who was to take the advice of 'my very good freind Mr Chalonor Chute of Sutton Court' as to the best means of satisfying all debts and legacies by sale of the lands in Berkshire and Hampshire.

In his will Lord Newburgh again reverts to the troubles and unsettled state of things caused by the Civil War, and says:—

and for the satisfying of my Debts and Legacyes seeing the Publique Miseries of these tymes haue soe much lessened my personall estate & means, and haue, and dailie doe, soe much encrease, and adde vnto my debts that I cannot leaue such an estate for the satisfying of them, as I heretofore might haue expected, nor haue the meanes to enlarge the respect to my freinds, and seruants, as I haue desyred and intended (wch I hope shall not lessen mee in their good thoughts).

He left 10*l*. to the poor of Aveley; 5*l*. to those of the Savoy parish,[2] and 5*l*. to those of the parishes in Berkshire and Hampshire, where he had property. Then follows a long list of gifts to his widow of specific articles, beginning with 'my dyamend hoope ring wch I vsuallie weare'; other gifts follow to her daughters, and to her grandchild, Edward Perry; to 'my Noble and deare brother Sr Richard Leveson my gold clocke; to Chaloner Chute 20*l*. and a bay gelding called Bay Aloffe';[3] and amongst many other bequests that of a picture of a pot of flowers 'which hangs usually in the wthdrawing

---

[1] These are no longer among the Aveley Church plate, if, indeed, they were ever purchased as directed.

[2] The Savoy, London, where the offices of the Duchy of Lancaster were situate.

[3] Probably named after some member of the important family of Ayloffe, of Braxted.

chamber at the Dutchie house,'[1] to 'my noble and most honoured friend the Ladie Dacres widdowe.' He bequeathed to 'ffrances now the wife of Benjamin Blackhead the choyce of any of my night gownes,' and unto his servant, Edward Ridley, 'all the rest of my Apparell and Twenty pounds,' and a few other specific legacies to servants; he gave to the rest of his servants 130*l*.: of which 30*l*. was to be distributed among the undermaids, and the residue to be divided 'among the rest of my servants as my Executors shall think fit, and according to the tyme and merit of their seruice.'

The devise of the Belhus estate upon ' my Cosen Mr Richard Leonard the sonne of the Ladie Dacres widdowe' is fully treated of in the next chapter.

Lord Newburgh finishes his will with the following final pious exhortation:—

And so I recomende my spirrit into the bandes of my most mercifull and Glorious Redeemer Jhesus Christ, in full fayth & confidence that when it shall please god to call mee out of this world, my death, by the merrits of his death and passion, wilbee to me a bridge and passage to eternall happiness.

After the entry in the Aveley Register which records his burial, the vicar has appended the note, 'Vir sanctissimus,' which the Reverend William Palin says was honourable to both parties, the deceased squire being a devoted Royalist, and the vicar a reputed Puritan.[2]

[1] In the Savoy, London.   [2] *Pal. M. St.*

CHAPTER VI

RICHARD (I.) BARRETT

Down to 1687, when his son Dacre and his family came to live with his father at Belhus.

RICHARD, the only son of Richard Lord Dacre by his second wife, was not five years old at the time of his father's death, and, when little more than seven, was admitted to Gray's Inn on August 12th, 1633.[1] His great-grandson, Thomas Lord Dacre, in his ' History' says of him :—

This Richard in his youth had travelled for several years ; his oeconomy and way of Living was such as became a Man of fashion, and his House frequented by the best Company, that truly great James Duke of Ormond in particular used ev'ry summer to pass some days with him at Belhouse ; [he was] a Man of great learning and well versed in Natural Philosophy[2] of a fine Taste in all the Polite Arts and an Encourager of Ingenious Men. He was a firm Royalist or Cavalier as they were then called ;[3] I have heard that he was a man of warm passions prone to Choler, and of an amorous disposition.

In this account, in which he also mentions that Richard was

[1] *G. I. R.*

[2] I have a small volume which consists of such part of Collins's *Peerage* as refers to the barony of Dacre, with MS. notes on interleaved pages. These were made either by Thomas Lord Dacre or more probably by his son Sir Thomas. The above passage about Richard is set out in the *Peerage*, and after the words 'natural philosophy' there is this MS. note : ' There was formerly at Belhouse the remains of a Laboratory where he often used to employ himself in a variety of chemical experiments.' I doubt the accuracy of this statement, and think that the laboratory in question was not that of Richard, but of his son Dacre.

[3] There is a secret hiding-place in the upper room of the tower at Belhus, which perhaps was constructed in those days. This hiding-place is behind a wall of lath and plaster, and cannot be approached except by a wicket in the wall of an adjoining room on the upper storey of the house. The wall of this other room does

CHAPTER VI

RICHARD (I.) BARRETT

Down to 1687, when his son Dacre and his family came to live with his father at Belhus

RICHARD, the only son of Richard Lord Dacre by his second wife, was not five years old at the time of his father's death, and, when little more than seven, was admitted to Gray's Inn on August 12th, 1633.[1] His great-grandson, Thomas Lord Dacre, in his 'History' says of him:—

This Richard in his youth had travelled for several years; his oeconomy and way of Living was such as became a Man of fashion, and his House frequented by the best Company, that truly great James Duke of Ormond in particular used ev'ry summer to pass some days with him at Belhouse; [he was] a Man of great learning and well versed in Natural Philosophy[2] of a fine Taste in all the Polite Arts and an Encourager of Ingenious Men. He was a firm Royalist or Cavalier as they were then called;[3] I have heard that he was a man of warm passions prone to Choler, and of an amorous disposition.

In this account, in which he also mentions that Richard was

[1] *G. I. R.*

[2] I have a small volume which consists of such part of Collins's *Peerage* as refers to the barony of Dacre, with MS. notes on interleaved pages. These were made either by Thomas Lord Dacre or more probably by his son Sir Thomas. The above passage about Richard is set out in the *Peerage*, and after the words 'natural philosophy' there is this MS. note: 'There was formerly at Belhouse the remains of a Laboratory where he often used to employ himself in a variety of chemical experiments.' I doubt the accuracy of this statement, and think that the laboratory in question was not that of Richard, but of his son Dacre.

[3] There is a secret hiding-place in the upper room of the tower at Belhus, which perhaps was constructed in those days. This hiding-place is behind a wall of lath and plaster, and cannot be approached except by a wicket in the wall of an adjoining room on the upper storey of the house. The wall of this other room does

High Sheriff of Essex in 1679, Lord Dacre has probably said all in his ancestor's favour that was possible, and has only touched lightly on his defects. Beyond what he says of Richard we have no proof he was of a specially amorous disposition, but we have abundant evidence that he was 'prone to choler,' and I think there can be no doubt he was an almost impossible man to live with. He treated his devoted wife with great neglect; he quarrelled with his son Richard, who appears to have been a very amiable young man; he was on bad terms for some time with his eldest son, and then, after a reconciliation, he quarrelled with him worse than ever. His daughter Anne was for years a devoted slave to her father's caprices, but in a fit of rage he turned her out of the house, together with her invalid sister, and he does not appear to have got on very well with his mother. The story of his life is the most sad and painful one of our family history, but, whatever his faults may have been, the last years of his life were so wretched and lonely that they cannot but excite the reader's pity. His wife, who appears to have been passionately fond of him, died after about six years of married life; his second son was killed before his eyes, and his eldest son endeavoured to have him confined as a lunatic.

Richard, after he ceased to be able to walk about to give orders to the workmen on his estate, went on horseback as long as he could do so; but for the last six years of his life he was bedridden, having what was then described as 'palsey or scurvey in the nerves.' In July 1684 a Mr. Waldron, writing to Ireland about him, says:—

and for his state of body he has the palsie and cannot feede himselfe, he gets vp early in a morning, and in his coach goes about till eleauen a clock, then home to dinner, and after that to bedd againe.

not join up to the wall of the tower, and the wicket opens into a deep lead valley in the roof; on the other side of the valley is another wicket which gives access to the hiding-place. Our generation did not know of this hiding-place until it was recently discovered by the accident of the wall-paper which covered the wicket in the other room peeling off.

Later on his hands became bent nearly double, he could not move in bed without help, he had one or more fits of apoplexy, and was unable to speak so that persons could understand him. In this miserable state he passed the last years of his life, attended only by servants, and having merely occasional visits from his daughter Anne, who married soon after he had turned her out of his house; possibly his daughter Dorothy visited him also, as she appears to have lived with her married sister.

To add to his misfortunes, he was no doubt greatly worried by the violent disputes and intrigues which went on towards the end of his life between his children Dacre and Anne, as to which of them was to succeed to such of his property as was in his power to dispose of by will; and constant litigation, which from one cause and another he was almost always engaged in, would have tried the temper of a man blessed with a more serene disposition than fell to his lot. He died un-reconciled to his son, who was then in Ireland; and his daughters, although living only six miles off, do not appear to have been with him at the last.[1]

This, however, is anticipating events, and I will now return to the story of Richard's life.

As has been stated, his father left him as his portion the manor of Horsford.[2] Lord Newburgh by his will left him the Belhus estates upon condition that he assumed the name of Barrett by which designation he was afterwards known. He usually signed himself 'Ri. Barret,' with only one 't'; curiously enough his wife always signed herself 'Anne Lennard,' as until her marriage did also his daughter Anne. His youngest daughter likewise signed herself Lennard,[3] while his son Richard signed indifferently 'Ri. Barrett,' 'Ri. Lennard,' and even

Richard's father and Lord Newburgh were cousins by a common

---
[1] Carew Mildmay's letter to Dacre.—*Post*, p. 519.   [2] *Ante*, p. 257.   [3] *Post*, p. 433.

descent from Elizabeth Dinely.[1] Lord Dacre in his Family History says there was a tradition in the family that the reason Lord Newburgh left his Essex property to Richard was that

when he was single he was in love with Dorothy North, but that she preferred Richard Lennard Lord Dacre who was the younger man, and had the largest estate, notwithstanding which Lord Newburgh always preserved such a regard for her that it was the principal motive for his leaving her son his Family Estate.

This is a romantic story which it seems a pity to attempt to destroy, and I do not wish to discredit it, but only to point out that, whether this were so or not, there were other causes which caused Lord Newburgh to act as he did. Among our papers are a good many of the pleadings in the different lawsuits in which Richard became involved as a result of his being left Belhus; a careful perusal of these papers, fragmentary though they be, throws much light on this devise, and shows that it was not nearly as valuable a one as it appears to have been supposed. Although both Lord Dacre and my cousin, Henry Barrett-Lennard, allude to Richard having been left Belhus, neither of them point out that really he was only left a reversion to the estate, burdened with a heavy charge, and that to secure even this he had to contest several lawsuits. From different portions of the pleadings in these actions I am enabled to construct a tolerably consecutive account of the whole matter, but as unfortunately most of the documents bear no dates, these can only be given approximately.

Lord Newburgh seems to have been much addicted to making his will, and for several years he made a fresh one 'as his pleasure was set to his relations'; and on one occasion, during his first wife's time, he left Belhus to his heir-at-law, Sir Humfrey Forster.[2] When he heard this news Sir Humfrey was

---

[1] *Vide* pedigree, *ante*, p. 340.
[2] First baronet, created 1620, also spelled Foster. In Lord D.'s pedigree of Lord Newburgh's family. Sir H. Foster is given as husband to Margaret, a sister of Lord Newburgh's father; and Lord D. says: 'Sir Humphrey Foster of Aldermaston,

so ill-advised as 'to boast and glory'; and when this attitude of his came to the ears of Lord Newburgh, that old statesman, greatly displeased at such behaviour, revoked this will, and we have no reason to believe that he ever mentioned Sir Humfrey's name again in any other of the wills which he made subsequently.

In March 1643-4 Sir Robert Bindlos, the husband of one of Lord Newburgh's step-daughters, was staying at Belhus, and on the 17th of that month Lord Newburgh 'came out of his closet into the Green Parlour[1] where Sir Robert and others were,' and made a publication of his will to those present. By this will he declared that his wife by her jointure was entitled to Belhus, and the rents of his estates there, for the term of her life, and on condition of her accepting the office of sole executrix to his will he gave to her executors these rents for a period of five years after her decease. He directed his trustees[2] immediately upon his death to convey the Belhus estates to Richard and his heirs, whom he described as 'my cosen Mr. Richard Leonard sonne of the Lady Dacres widow, daughter of my Lord North,' subject to the above-mentioned interests of his wife in them, upon condition that Richard and his heirs should assume the name of Barrett.[3] This devise, however, was accompanied by a charge of 500*l*. a year upon the estates in

Berks, was heir at law to Lord Newburgh, and the present Earl of Radnor (anno 1776) is, thro' the Pleydels, heir to the Fosters.' One of the pleadings, where the name is spelled Forster, says 'that Sir Humfrey Forster grandfather to him this defendant and whose heir hee, this Defendt. is, which sayd Sir Humfrey Forster was Sonne to Sir William Forster, Sonne to Sir Humfrey Forster, by the sister of the said Lord Newburgh.' This is a discrepancy of a whole generation, making the alliance with the Forsters through Lord Newburgh's sister instead of through his aunt; moreover, the C. B. states that William, father of Sir Humfrey, second baronet, died *v. p.*

[1] The word closet, meaning an inner chamber, and sometimes used for bedroom. I have not been able to identify the green parlour.

[2] By a deed dated considerably anterior to his will Lord Newburgh conveyed his estates to trustees, who were to hold these estates upon such trusts as he should by will declare.

[3] I have an ancient copy, undated, of an enactment by Parliament that Richard and his heirs should bear the name and arms of Barrett.—*F. P.*

favour of Lord Francis Villiers, to be paid to him for the first ten years after Richard should succeed to them;[1] and he left to the latter the furniture and tapestry hangings of only two of the rooms at Belhus.

In 1644, when Lord Newburgh died, his trustees, Sir R. Leveson[2] and Mr. R. Charlton, refused to convey the estates to Richard in accordance with the terms of the will until so directed by the Court.[3] Richard, at that period a minor, petitioned 'The Commissioner of the Great Seale of England' by Dudley Lord North, his guardian, that the trustees might be directed to carry out the trust for his benefit as declared in the will.[4] He obtained a decree in his favour at some date subsequent to January 164$\frac{7}{8}$, and, in pursuance of this decree they conveyed the estates to him. This, however, was only the beginning of the litigation in which Richard became involved in connection with Belhus.

At the time of Lord Newburgh's death the park at Belhus was well stocked with deer to the number of 300 or more, and it was full of oak, ash, elm, and other timber, planted into walks and 'places of pleasure convenient for beautifying a noble and ancient seat, as the same had long bein wherein Lord Newburgh & his ancestor had resided.'

On September 29th, 1653, Lady Newburgh[5] married at St. Giles-in-the-Fields, as her third husband, William Morgan, Esq., of Cawthropp, Oxon., and these two persons, in order to raise money for

his supply and expences, to the utter defacing and destroying of said house, park, and premises, are cutting down trees in the park, and made great havock, & spoil, & destroyed great

---

[1] Lord Francis died in 1662, and his brother the Duke of Buckingham sold his reversion to a Mr. Pennington.

[2] Son of Lord Newburgh's mother by her second husband.

[3] Recitals in a deed dated May 29th, 1683.—*F. P.*

[4] This was so stated in a draft petition when drawn, but the references to Richard's minority and Lord North's guardianship are struck out, so that he was probably just of age when it was presented. He came of age in May 1647.—*F. P.*

[5] Described in the register as 'Lady Kath Newberry of Bellowes Co. Essex.'

quantities of deer, and much lessened the number thereof left at the time of the death of Lord Newburgh, and they give out they will cut down more trees, till they do not leave a tree standing worth /6d. or a deer in the Park ; they have already cut trees to the value of £2000 ; they also suffer the house and premises, which were in good repair at the decease of Lord Newburgh to fall into decay.

These were some of the grounds upon which Richard prayed for an injunction to restrain Lady Newburgh and her husband from committing waste, but I have no record as to the result of this petition. Soon after this Richard brought an action for waste against Lady Newburgh and Mr. William Morgan, on account of timber they were cutting in a wood indifferently described in the pleadings as 'Brannards' and 'Baniards,' which wood is now known as 'Brannetts.' Richard recovered from them in this action a sum of 1,500*l.* as treble damages, but he ultimately agreed to relinquish his right to payment of these damages, and also paid them the sums of 800*l.* and 300*l.*, and in consideration of this, Lady Newburgh, and her husband Morgan, conveyed the house and park of Belhus to Richard.

A large country house, with only two rooms furnished, except to a person who has a considerable amount of ready money, is a possession resembling somewhat the typical white elephant, and no doubt Richard felt in much perplexity as to how to turn his new acquisition to the best advantage. He was not to receive the income derived from the estates until five years had elapsed after the death of Lady Newburgh, and she was, probably, at this date, comparatively speaking, a young woman ; and even upon the expiration of her interests in the property he was only to succeed to it subject to a heavy charge on it for ten years. Richard's interests were chiefly in Ireland, where his wife's property was, and which demanded his closest attention, that country being then distracted with the Cromwellian wars ; and as Belhus was unfurnished and produced him no revenue, he hit upon the expedient of offering the house to his mother and step-father for three years. This is shown by the following unsigned and undated draft of a letter, which from the context appears to have been written in Ireland by his wife's hand, and is certainly endorsed by her: 'Mr. Barret to my la. Dacre.'

The letter begins 'S^r,' so it was no doubt intended for Chaloner Chute, Lady Dacre's second husband. As we shall see, Richard married in February 165$\frac{2}{3}$, so this letter must have been written at some period between that date and April 1659, when his wife died:—

S^r.

Y^{rs} of y^e 15th, of y^e last month came nott to my hands till yesterday by wch I perceaue my intentions concerneing y^e disposall [of] Belle house are misunderstood, for since there is none vpon whose care & friendship I may so confidently rely as your selfe, you may be sure I would nott venter y^t place to further preiudice since you were pleased to undertake ye protection of itt; and therefore you nott being in towne y^{r}selfe I deliuered ye keys and care of itt to my brother[1] who employed Baldwin for ye present, who had noe farther trust from mee y^n to looke after ye woods as formerly hee had done, & as for ye Warener, vpon better information, I found hee p^d but 31^{lb}, & being an ancient servant of my Ld Newburghs I was willing to bate him 15^{lb} a yeare, & allow itt to you, as long as hee continues a servant there.

S^r my aime is nott to benefitt my selfe by anie profitts from y^t place, more y^n what may conduce to ye preservation of itt selfe, & therefore shall referr itt to you, & iff you please to cause mr. Haughton[2] to specifie in writing what shall seeme convenient to you for vs both, for 3 yeares time comenceing either from midsumer last, or this michelmas next ensueing (though iff my affaires here occassions my longe continuance in this Countrey tis nott my intentions to comitt itt to ye [care of?] anie person butt y^r selfe) lett itt bee sent me ouer I shall perfect itt by hand & seale, wch may suddenly be done, & wch I had nott omitted had you beene in towne att my comeing away, wch my affaires here obliged me to set some speede.

[1] He probably alludes to his brother-in-law, Mr. C. Chute, the younger.

[2] This mention of Mr. Haughton conclusively proves this letter to have been written by Richard, as the former's name more than once occurs in Anne's letters to her husband; there is also a letter to Mr. Haughton from the then Norfolk agent. He was, no doubt, a Solicitor, or else a business agent acting for Richard.

I hope itt may bee a recreation to y^r selfe, & my mother, sometimes to see itt, wch I assure my selfe will bee advantageous to itt, & a greate satisfaction as this, and all expressions of y̓r freindships, are to

Your verie obedient & affectionate Sonne.

my wife presents her most humble service to you.

There is no doubt that Mr. Chute and Lady Dacre accepted this offer; and that they did furnish Belhus is proved by a paper drawn up soon after Richard's death, and headed : 'An Inventory of my Lady Dacre's goods at Bellhouse May ye 11, 1696,' and also by the fact that by her will Lady Dacre left all her furniture at Belhus to Richard for life; after his death to her grandson Dacre for life, and after him to her great-grandson Richard. I am unable to say how much Lady Dacre lived at Belhus, but in 1664, after her second husband's death, she certainly spent some months there.[1]

The inventory of Lady Dacre's goods at Belhus is not without interest as throwing some light on the way country houses were furnished at this period. I give as a specimen the contents of the room which is described as the 'best chamber.'

One Bedstead, & 1 Bed, one Bolstre, 2 Quilts, & one silke Quilte, one Suite of Curtaines, 3 Bed Carpets, 4 chairs, 6 Stooles, & 1 table, & carpet, 2 Stands, 1 Suite of Gilt leather & plush hangings, one paire of brass andyrons, one paire of iron doggs, one brass fireshovell & Tongs.

The only fuel used was evidently wood, as iron 'doggs' and fire-backs are mentioned as belonging to almost all the rooms; tongs, and also often a fire-shovel, but never a poker, which is required only when coal is used.

There is no mention of any easy- or arm-chairs, nor of washing-stands,[2] sofas, dressing-tables, nor looking-glasses. There

---

[1] *Post*, p. 414.

[2] In this connection I may mention that an inventory of my great-grandfather's furniture at Hactons, taken as recently as 1800, makes no mention of any washstands in the servants' rooms; but in the housekeeper's bedroom there seems to have been 'a jug and bason'!

is only one chest of drawers mentioned, a few cupboards, and a couple of presses for 'cloathes'; carpets are found in only a few rooms, the number of chairs specified as being in each room seems somewhat inadequate, and only one couch is mentioned in the whole inventory. There are a considerable number of pictures, but no glass or crockery of any sort appears in the list, except under the head of 'Still House' where the inventory mentions '9 earthen dishes, 6 pewter dishes, a pye plate & pasty plate.'

There is no mention of any books, nor bookcases, nor of any sort of ornaments except pictures. No doubt there were some things in the house which, Richard having acquired, would not appear in this inventory of his mother's furniture; but I think we may safely conclude that those ordinary articles of present day use which we miss in this list, such as washing-stands, &c., were at this period to be found only, if at all, in the houses of persons of very great wealth and importance.

The glimpse this inventory affords us of life in the seventeenth century is calculated to make us indeed thankful that we did not live in the days of the Stuarts. If any of us could be transported back to those times in order to pay a visit to our forefathers, how inexpressibly uncomfortable and dull we should find their lives. Nowhere to put one's clothes when unpacked, no washing arrangements, no looking-glass; but worst of all would be sitting in an unwashed company during the long evenings of winter on straight-backed chairs, with nothing to read, in almost darkness, except for the light of the wood fire, or what could be derived from the flame of a stray flickering candle. No wonder if people gambled and drank then in order to pass away the monotony of such an existence.

Some time later Richard Barrett had to petition the Court of Chancery that a writ might issue against a certain Pennington and others, who were assignees of the interest of Lady Newburgh in the Belhus estates, to answer his complaint that they had granted leases, cut down timber, and otherwise committed waste on the estate; and Richard appears to have succeeded in this petition. The petition bears no date, but the date can be approximately fixed because it is presented to Lord Chancellor Clarendon, and he held that office from 1660 to 1667.

Some years later, when Lord Shaftesbury was Chancellor (he took office in 1672), an action was brought against Richard by some other assignees of Lady Newburgh, who claimed a right to fell timber; and about 1670 to 1672 he was engaged in defending a suit brought against him by Sir Humfrey Forster (or Foster),[1] who claimed as heir-at-law of Lord Newburgh,[2] and who was grandson of the Sir Humfrey previously referred to.[3] I feel no doubt Richard was successful in these actions also; indeed, I doubt if Sir Humfrey ever carried his action very far. At last, on July 22nd, 1674, Lady Newburgh died, and, five years later, Richard entered into an agreement with Pennington, who was not only her assignee, but had also acquired the annuity of 500*l.* payable to Lord Francis Villiers [4] out of the Belhus estates upon the determination of Lady Newburgh's interests in it.

The object of this agreement was to settle terms of compromise between Richard Barrett and Pennington as to a claim of the former against the latter for repairs to buildings which had been neglected. Pennington died in 1679, and his representatives assigned his interest in the annuity to Sir Peter Parravicinni Knight, merchant of London. In October 1691 Sir Peter acknowledges to have received by R. Owen, on behalf of Richard Barrett, the balance still due to him for this

---

[1] Second baronet.
[2] We have a document dated May 20th, 1672, signed 'Ri Barrett,' which is a receipt from him to Richard Owen for the will of Lord Newburgh, which will, the receipt states, was delivered to Owen according to an order of the Court of Chancery made on 6th of said month. The device with which Richard sealed this receipt is 1st and 4th Lennard, 2nd Fynes, 3rd Dacre, and over all on escutcheon of pretence his wife's arms.
[3] *Ante*, p. 396.   [4] *Ante*, p. 397, n. 1.

annuity, which should have been paid in July 1689, and he then released to Richard his charge on Belhus. Thus at length, forty-seven years after Lord Newburgh's death, the last of the charges with which he saddled his devise to Richard came to an end.

I am not able to show what was the annual value of the Belhus estate in 1679, when it passed out of the hands of Lady Newburgh's trustees into those of Richard; we have, however, two 'Particulars' of the estate dated 1651, showing the acreage and annual value; and for the purpose of this valuation the mansion, park, garden, and hop ground, which are stated to contain 337 acres, were valued at 200*l.* The acreage of the Manor of Belhus and the lands and farms belonging is given as 2,247 acres, producing 855*l.*; and that of the land in the adjoining parish of Wennington as over 300 acres, producing 225*l.*, the annual value of the whole being put at 1,080*l.* 3*s.* 4*d.* This 'Particular' does not show what the land in Wennington consisted of; much of it was, and is now, marsh meadows. But the 2,247 acres of Belhus are thus divided:—

Meadow	327	
Reed or Salt Marsh	23	
Pasture	889	
		1,239 grass.
Woods		308
Arable		700
		2,247

This description is interesting, as it shows how much larger in Stuart times was the proportion of grass to arable land in Essex than is the case at the present day.

Richard married Anne, only surviving child of Sir Robert Loftus [1] and his wife Eleanor, daughter and eventual co-heiress of Sir Francis Rushe. Eleanor died on May 27th, 1639,[2] and Sir Robert died on October 25th of the following year.

[1] Knighted November 5th, 1619.—The C. P.

[2] *Cf.* letter from Lord Strafford in August of that year referring to her recent (?) death, *post*, 441.

Their only son Henry, who was five years of age at his father's death, died November 9th, 1640, whereupon Anne, their only other child, who was then fourteen years and three months old,[1] became the heiress of her family.

Sir Francis Rushe was descended from a family who lived at Sudbourne, in Suffolk; a great commander in the wars against the Irish in the time of Elizabeth, he was knighted by Essex, and made a Privy Councillor of Ireland. He married Mary,[2] only surviving child of Sir Henry Duke, by whom he had four children, Thomas, who died unmarried November 17th, 1629, and three daughters, Eleanor, Mary, and Anne, who then became his co-heiresses. At the time of his death, which took place June 18th, 1623,[3] he was lord of the manor of Clones, county Monaghan, and possessed the lands formerly belonging to that Abbey, which extended into the adjoining county of Fermanagh; he also owned Dunsink and Scribblestown in county Dublin, and some estates in England.

Sir Henry Duke, who married Elizabeth, sister to Edward, first Lord Brabazon, was one of Queen Elizabeth's fighting captains in Ireland. In the course of his campaigns he discovered that there existed a suppressed Abbey at Clones, and that that town was an important spot, from a strategical point of view, in which to plant a garrison. He wrote a letter from Dublin on February 29th, 158$\frac{8}{7}$, to the minister, Lord Burghley, in which he said:—

In my trauell in those ptes I founde owte for her M$_a$^{tie} th' abbay of Cloneys in Dartrey in McMahowns countrey, wch was concealed from her highnes ever since the Suppression, and is the onlie place to laie a garrison for the brydelinge and refourmynge of McMahowns Countrey.[4]

As a result of this letter Sir Henry was sent to Clones in order

---

[1] Inquisition dated April 15th, 1641. *Vide Irish Abstract.—F. P.*
[2] At the time of her marriage to Sir Francis she was widow of Richard Gifford, by whom she had one son, Sir John, who inherited his father's property of Castle Jordan. After the death of Sir Francis she married Sir John Jephson, of Frowle, Hants.—*Hist. Com. in V. C.* iii. p. lx.
[3] *Shir.*
[4] *Ibid.*

to conquer and hold it, against the turbulent natives of that district. Lord Dacre mentions [1] the following note concerning Sir Henry, but unfortunately he gives no reference as to whence he derived these particulars: 'A Memorial given unto Queen Elizabeth concerning the then state of Ireland.' In this paper mention is made of advice given to Sir William Fitz-Williams, the Lord Deputy, to send Sir Henry Duke as Sheriff of Monaghan to be placed in the Abbey of Cloonis, 'which is your Majestie's, and himself the farmer there, with his own company of light foot, & his own band of 100 men more to be left there in Garrison.' And in another part of the same paper :—

when your Majestie's garrison soldiers were first planted in the County of Monaghan there was great service offered to Sir William FitzWilliam by Sir Henry Duke for his setting down at the Abbey of Cloonis, whereof he is farmer, with his own company of light foot etc. At that time there were at the same Abbey good & defensible buildings to succour your Majestie's garrison which are defaced & pulled down by the traitors.

On September 20th, 1587, the Queen granted to Sir Henry a lease for twenty-one years of the lands which, before the Dissolution, had belonged to the monastery of Clones. Sir Henry died in February 1595,[2] and by the time James came to the throne his only surviving daughter had married Sir Francis Rushe, as appears from the recitals of a fresh lease of these premises granted to him by the King for a second term of twenty-one years. This lease, which is among our papers, is dated '14th Sept. 1 Jas.' (1603), and is remarkable in that it is sealed with Elizabeth's seal, as presumably the new Sovereign's seal had not been delivered in Dublin at such an early period in James's reign. The lease contains some other points of interest worth noting. Among the parcels demised is

the scite or precincte of the late Monasterie, or Religious house, of Clonies in the dartrie in McMahownes countrie, conteynynge

[1] *Ld. D. Mis.*   [2] *Shir.*

halfe an acre of lande wherein standeth one church halfe covered with strawe, the stone walls of one cloister, a hall, a Kitchen, & divers other edifices now uncovered & ruynous.

The rent reserved was 5*l.* a year, but Sir Francis had also to keep at its own proper charges in Clones 'a compotent and sufficient garde to the number of six persons able men of English nation.' Moreover, he had to covenant not to alienate without licence to any but persons born within the pale, and of English parents; and he had also to covenant not to charge any of the inhabitants 'with any exactions called cony, or liverie, or like unlawful impositions.'[1]

Some five years later the King granted all these lands in fee, subject to this lease, to a person of the name of William Bruncker, who sold the reversion of them in the following month to Sir Francis.

Clones was from earliest times the scene of many a bloody conflict, and the town was several times burned to the ground. As recently as 1641 the great rebellion, which in that town broke out on October 23rd and 24th, was the occasion of the massacre of most of its Protestant inhabitants, and the almost entire destruction of all the buildings of which the town was composed.

The Abbey at Clones which, on more than one occasion, was destroyed by fire, was established for regular Canons of the Order of St. Augustine. It was founded by St. Tighernach, and he removed the see from Clogher here, where he died of the plague on April 4th, 548, having attained a considerable age. The Abbots of Clones who succeeded the saint were in many instances distinguished for their learning or piety.[2] The following account of the antiquities of Clones is taken from a very interesting and exhaustive paper by Mr. Wakeman, who records

---

[1] The billeting by Irish chiefs of their military followers upon private persons was called 'coney and liverie'; and an ancient writer has quaintly explained the former term to mean 'man's meat,' and the latter one 'horse meat.'

[2] *Archd.*

in it some of the local traditions which still existed when he wrote some thirty years ago:—[1]

The Ancient town, or rather city, of Clones, now presents few objects of interest to the antiquary. War, fire, and the vandalism of centuries, have all but obliterated the landmarks of history, which formerly rendered the city of St. Tighernach one of the most interesting spots in Ireland. The round tower, however, still stands, and near it may be seen a precious relic of ante-Norman architecture, mutilated and dismantled indeed, but still exhibiting features of no common interest. Of the church and monastery founded here in the sixth century no vestige remains, but in 'the Diamond,' a site anciently appertaining to the monastic enclosure, one of those wonderful evidences of the artistic taste and mechanical power of our early cross-builders may still be studied. This monument, however, is far from perfect, and may be noticed as consisting of portions of two separate crosses. Upon a massive shaft representing, in quaint sculpture, several passages in Scripture History, has been placed the head of a smaller cross no other portion of which is known to be extant. . . . A magnificent fort stands on the skirts of the town, a little to the north-west of the less ancient structures. This earthwork which may well be described as stupendous consists of a central mound extremely high and steep, in the form of a truncated cone, the surface of which is quite flat, and amply sufficient for the accommodation of a right royal house. Surrounding the central *dun* or *les* are three concentric *raths*, also extremely steep, so much so that to climb them is in some places a matter of no little difficulty. Dr. Joyce suggests that this fort was raised by a Pagan chief named Eos, and that the name 'Clones,' anciently written 'Cluain-Eois' [Cloonoce], should be translated 'Eo's meadow.' . . . The round tower may be regarded as one of the earliest structures of its class remaining in Ireland. . . . There can be no question that the Clonis tower, like all other buildings of its class, terminated in a conical stone roof. This, however, no longer remains, and at first sight the wall, as at Kilkenny, Cloyne, Kildare, and elsewhere, would appear to terminate in a mediæval parapet. The building called the Abbey appears to have formed the nave of a highly finished church, dating most likely from the close of the XI. or

[1] *J. R. H. A. I.* iii. Part ii. 4th series.

beginning of the XII. century. . . . The most striking and original feature of this interesting ruin is a carving which appears upon its northern wall. . . . In it we have a perfect representation of our ancient Irish crosses, such as those of Kells, cut in relief. . . . Nothing like this cross, in its position at least, has been observed in connection with any other church in Ireland. . . . Situated upon a line between the round tower and the Abbey, and directly facing the doorway of the former structure, occurs a monument in some respects unlike anything which has elsewhere been noticed in Ireland. It is formed of a single block of hard red sandstone, five feet ten in length by three feet in height, which has been fashioned into the form of an early Irish church. The interior is artificially hollowed, so that the work forms a shrine, in form exactly like that of St. Ethelreda, preserved in Ely Cathedral.

There are in other places somewhat similar monuments, but built of many stones, ' but this being a monolith may be looked upon as *sui generis* at least in Ireland.' The ground over which it stands is regarded as specially holy, and much contention has taken place for it as a burial-place: one or two families have from time to time appropriated the stone, and carved eighteenth-century inscriptions upon it, which have been purposely defaced.

I have said that Eleanor Rushe was one of three co-heiresses of her father's estates. The way in which the sisters arranged the partition of these estates is not easy to follow, as only some of the deeds remain, and I have seen neither deeds nor recitals referring to any property in England, so I am unable to say to whose share that fell. I think it is clear that Sir Robert Loftus and his wife as early as 1633[1] bought the third share of her sister Mary, who had married Sir Charles Coote, and it is said that they raised the purchase money by a mortgage on these lands.[2] In November, 11th Chas. I., the Ulster properties were settled on Sir Robert, and his wife, and the heirs of her body

[1] *Irish Abstract* deed dated Michaelmas, 9th Chas. I. (1633). *Hist. Com. in V. C.* iii. p. 227, where the date is given in a recital as 'about 1635.'

[2] *Ibid.* This Sir Charles was the second baronet, and was created Earl of Mountrath. His wife Mary could not have lived very long, as Sir Charles married a second time before May 1645.—*The C. B.*

with remainders to his, then unmarried, sister Anne, afterwards wife to Sir George Wentworth.[1] The consideration which induced Anne to exchange her interest in these properties for a remainder, contingent on her sister having no children, does not appear, nor are the dealings with the Dunsink and Scribblestown property easy to unravel. It is sufficient to say that, by some means or another, the properties which had belonged to Sir Francis Rushe in the counties of Dublin, Fermanagh, and Monaghan respectively, all came to his granddaughter Anne Loftus, but not improbably burdened by some charges for the benefit of her two sisters. Indeed we know that Richard Barrett paid altogether 2,600*l.* to the Wentworth family (who seem to have acted as trustees) in connection with Dunsink and Scribblestown only.[2] Anne Loftus also inherited from her parents a claim to the estate of Monesterevan, co. Kildare, which her grandfather Viscount Ely had promised to settle upon her father. This proved to be indeed a 'damnosa hereditas,' as it was the cause of a lawsuit which lasted for over forty years, and in which our family were at length defeated,[3] after the expenditure of very large sums of money.

It is difficult to fix the exact date of Richard and Anne's marriage, which Lord Dacre does not mention. The papers in connection with the above-mentioned great lawsuit afford some information on this point. They were probably married in February, in what we should reckon 1653, but which in those days was called 1652, and sometimes written $165\frac{2}{3}$.[4] One of the documents dated January 1652 was signed Anne Loftus; while another dated February 26th, 1652, refers to

[1] Third brother to Thomas Earl of Strafford.
[2] *M. & B. v. B.* See also letter from Anne Mildmay, *post,* p. 522 *et seq.*
[3] *Post,* p. 437 *et seq.*
[4] One of our documents relating to this lawsuit states that Richard married Anne at Clones on May 1st, 1651 ; but I believe that this is not the date of their marriage. Several of the dates given in this document are certainly not accurate ; among others, that of the death of Anne, which is there given as having taken place on May 2nd, 1655. We have a letter from her written in 1657, and, in fact, she died in April 1659. *Post,* p. 413. This document quoted from is printed in vol. iii. p. 251.—*Hist. Com. in V. C.* 1904.

them as if married, and one dated March 5th, 165⅔ does so in a most unmistakable manner, speaking of them as 'Richard Barrett and Anne his wife.' It is true that another document in this case, dated March 31st in the same year, orders attendance as witness in the cause of Edward Lord Loftus, and Anne *Loftus*, but this was probably owing to the clerk who drew it up not being aware of her then recent marriage.

Lord Dacre says [1] that Anne Loftus was a 'woman of great merit and learning as may be seen from her compositions still remaining in Latin, French, & Italian.' I regret to say that the only writings of hers which I have been able to find are some letters to her husband. The spelling and handwriting of these letters certainly show that she was better educated than most ladies of her day, though hardly themselves of such merit as to justify all Lord Dacre's encomiums upon her learning.

Anne became an orphan when little more than fourteen years of age, and Lord Dacre says that he has heard she lived as one of the family with the Earl of Strafford until his execution.[2] Whether this be so or not, the fact that ever after her father's death she lived in England was put on record in a suit brought against her husband by some persons of the name of Stanley.[3]

In a letter we have from Viscount Drogheda [4] to Anne's grandmother, Lady Jephson, written from Mellefont, December 7th, 1640, he says that

Sir Robert, by one of his last acts did constitute myself, Mr. Barnewell, and my cozen Nichās Loftus [5] gardians unto my Cosen Anne Loftus, and accordingly the Prerogative Co^{rt} hath directed lr̄ees [letters] of tutall [6] to us, an office of troble, yet for

---

[1] *Ld. D. His.*

[2] This may well have been so, as the Earl was greatly attached to her mother, *vide post*, p. 441, and, moreover, one of his brothers married her mother's sister.

[3] *Hist. Com. in V.* C. iii. p. 227.

[4] It is Signed 'Moore'; his proper style was 'Viscount Moore of Drogheda.' He married Alice, youngest daughter of Chancellor Loftus, and was therefore uncle by marriage to Anne. Formerly the word 'cousin' was not so restricted in meaning as it is now, and was used to express relations or kinsfolk in general.

[5] Nicholas Loftus, of Feathard, died 1666, was a somewhat distant cousin of Anne's.

[6] Tutelage, guardianship.

them as if married, and one dated March 5th, 165⅔ does so in a most unmistakable manner, speaking of them as 'Richard Barrett and Anne his wife.' It is true that another document in this case, dated March 31st in the same year, orders attendance as witness in the cause of Edward Lord Loftus, and Anne *Loftus*, but this was probably owing to the clerk who drew it up not being aware of her then recent marriage.

Lord Dacre says [1] that Anne Loftus was a 'woman of great merit and learning as may be seen from her compositions still remaining in Latin, French, & Italian.' I regret to say that the only writings of hers which I have been able to find are some letters to her husband. The spelling and handwriting of these letters certainly show that she was better educated than most ladies of her day, though hardly themselves of such merit as to justify all Lord Dacre's encomiums upon her learning.

Anne became an orphan when little more than fourteen years of age, and Lord Dacre says that he has heard she lived as one of the family with the Earl of Strafford until his execution.[2] Whether this be so or not, the fact that ever after her father's death she lived in England was put on record in a suit brought against her husband by some persons of the name of Stanley.[3]

In a letter we have from Viscount Drogheda [4] to Anne's grandmother, Lady Jephson, written from Mellefont, December 7th, 1640, he says that

Sir Robert, by one of his last acts did constitute myself, Mr. Barnewell, and my cozen Nichās Loftus [5] gardians unto my Cosen Anne Loftus, and accordingly the Prerogative Co't hath directed lrēes [letters] of tutall [6] to us, an office of troble, yet for

[1] *Id. D. His.*
[2] This may well have been so, as the Earl was greatly attached to her mother, *vide post*, p. 441, and, moreover, one of his brothers married her mother's sister.
[3] *Hist. Com. in V. C.* iii. p. 227.
[4] It is signed 'Moore'; his proper style was 'Viscount Moore of Drogheda.' He married Alice, youngest daughter of Chancellor Loftus, and was therefore uncle by marriage to Anne. Formerly the word 'cousin' was not so restricted in meaning as it is now, and was used to express relations or kinsfolk in general.
[5] Nicholas Loftus, of Feathard, died 1666, was a somewhat distant cousin of Anne's.
[6] Tutelage, guardianship.

mine owne p[ar]ticular, and I presume soe for the rest, I assure yor La^{pp} [Ladyship] the care I have of mine owne children shall not bee more than of her.

I am unable to say who arranged the marriage between Anne and Richard; nor have I found their marriage settlement: at the date of their marriage he was in the twenty-eighth year of his age, and she about a year younger. They must have been a very attractive-looking couple; the portrait of Richard at Belhus represents him as extremely handsome, although with rather a melancholy expression, while a miniature 1 of her shows Anne to have been a remarkably good-looking young woman with a very great profusion of light-coloured hair. It is difficult to say with certainty where they lived during their married life, which was only a short one, as Anne died in 1659.

In 1653 Richard had a house in London, but none of the letters in our possession are written from or addressed to him there, and in none have I seen any reference to his ever living in London. All the references I have found to his London house is the following note by Lord Dacre:— [2]

The present Lord Dacre's cousin M^r. Mildmay told him, that his mother informed him that her father, Mr Richard Barrett Lennard's London house was in Newport Street near St. Martin's Lane & that it was a large one and looked into the Fields; Leicester House standing then as it were in the Country. Sir Nich^s Pelham had also a house in the same street.

And also the fact that an answer in one of his lawsuits was 'taken & sworn at the house of Richard Barrett Esquire in St. Martin's Lane in the parish of St. Martins in the Fields on May 26, 1653.' [3]

[1] This miniature was given to me by my cousin, Francis Barrett-Lennard, and is thus described in Lord Dacre's catalogue of his portraits: 'A miniature in water-colours, being a copy by Mr. Cosway from a miniature in the possession of Carew Mildmay, Esq., probably by Cooper.'
[2] *Ld. D. Mis.*
[3] *Hist. Com. in V.* C. iii. p. 227.

I have not found any of the letters which were no doubt written by Richard to his wife while away, indeed the only reference to her which we have of his occurs in a postscript to a letter to his agent in Ireland, written in December 1655, where he says, 'Pray forgett nott to enquire for some pearl for my wife.' He probably referred here to the small seed pearls found in mussel shells in Ireland, and especially in those taken from the river Blackwater.[1]

I doubt if the marriage proved a very happy one, anyhow from Anne's point of view. The ten letters of hers to her husband which are preserved are all of them very affectionate, but most of them reproach him for his continued absences from her: she says in one letter that out of four years of married life he has been absent from her eighteen months. Then during the first portion of their union she bore him children in abnormally quick succession, which must, to say the least of it, have been very inconvenient to herself. No fewer than two boys and one girl (none twins) were born to her between November 1653 and May 1655. An undated letter of hers indicates that she did not nurse the children herself, but sent them away to be reared by a wet nurse, and from occasional references in other letters this would appear to have been the usual custom in those days for people of means. More than twenty years later, in October 1682, Fletcher, the Clones agent, writes to her son Dacre, 'The Country Nurs my Lady was speaking about is dryed up since her childs death.'[2]

A careful perusal of Anne's letters to her husband enables us to fix the dates of the births of her children approximately, which seems to have been as follows:—Dacre, in November 1653; Richard, August 1654; Anne, May 1655; and Dorothy in the spring of 1659—in giving birth to whom it seems to be not improbable that her mother died. In 1657 Anne speaks of her 'poore girle' as if she had then only one girl, and in a letter, dated September 1658, she evidently refers to herself as being enceinte. Writing to Richard in Dublin, in

---

[1] *Wake*, ii. p. 125. [2] *Cf. T. S. E.* iv. p. 494.

July 1655, Anne speaks of a man named 'Francis' who had evidently been recently appointed agent at Clones, and advises Richard not to build a house there. She probably had in her mind the idea that they would before long be living at Belhus, little thinking that another twenty-four years would elapse before her husband would obtain full possession of those estates.

From the superscriptions to some of her letters, and from references in others, it is clear that Anne and her children paid frequent visits to Mr. Chute and her mother-in-law, Dorothy Lady Dacre, at Sutton Court; which is evidence of the very friendly, if not even affectionate, terms which subsisted between the mother and daughter-in-law. A further indication of Lady Dacre's feelings towards Anne may be found in a letter she wrote, nearly twenty years after the latter's death, where she says, 'for the sake of the deare wife that is gone, and brought you a Noble fortune, doe not neglect her children.'

We know from a letter of Anne's, dated July 22nd, 1657, that at that date Richard was in London and she in Dublin, and that she was losing patience with him on account of his delay in joining her there, and she says, 'iff you stay anie longer I shall absolutely conclude this storie of my lo of Barkeshires [1] money is a meere pretence.'

In August of the next year Anne Barrett was again at Sutton Court, and in the following September back in Dublin, whence she writes the last of her letters that has been preserved. She died on April 4th, 1659 (in one pleading her death is said to have occurred at Dunsink), and was buried at St. Audoens Church, Dublin;[2] as had been her mother, Sir Francis Rushe, her grandfather, and Sir Henry Duke, her great-grandfather.

We know that Richard was elected a member of the Irish Parliament to represent Carrick-on-Shannon in April 1661, and I think it is probable that he remained in Ireland for some

---

[1] Thomas Howard, created Earl of Berkshire, 162$\frac{5}{6}$.—The C. P.
[2] Funeral entries in office of Ulster King-at-Arms, Dublin; also in the *Irish Builder*, December 15th, 1886, vol. 28, p. 334.

years after his wife's death, but sent his children over to England to live with his mother. The following letter is addressed to him 'att his house ouer the Bridge in Dublin this d d in Ireland,' by a Mr. 'Jo Jenkins,' who writes from the Temple on December 10th, 1664 :—

'My Lady[1] hath spent most of this summer at Belhouse, & her Ladyship like it soe well had it nott beene for takinge care of her bisnesse in Chancerie she would have staid longer. . . . my Lady & your children are all in good hellth God bee thanked for it ; the greate bisnesse of the Parlem^t is now how to Rayse the fines, & twenty hundred thousand pounds the deate [debt], & for Carreinge one [sic] the Dutch Warres.[2]

Richard was probably still living in Ireland in 1670, when in the May of that year he sent his two sons, Dacre and Richard, then aged respectively nearly seventeen and sixteen years, abroad for the benefit of their education[3] under the care of a Mr. Van Bobbart, from whom we have the following letter :—

[Endorsed] From Mr Van Bobbart[4] The Travelling Tutor to Mr Dacre Barrett & his Brother.

24 Jul.
Orleans the 7 Aug. 1671.

Honorable Sir,
it is not about 6 weeks, when according to your honn^r command's we left Paris and returned for Orleans. we did intend to haue gone for Blois, but thought to haue first y^r hon^{rs} order whether the Gentlemen, y^r Sons, should learn to ride the great horse.[5] wherefore we are resolued to stay here till your honn^r answear, which we waite for impatiently. Both Mr Dacre and Mr Richard, doe find themselues, God be thanked, very well, & in good health and, as they are wont, follow theyr studies, & exercises. Mr Dacre grows very much, & lookes now like a man, & i would wish to know y^r honn^r pleasur how long y^r

---

[1] Dorothy Lady Dacre.
[2] War was declared with Holland in the following February.
[3] How greatly this was then the custom vide *T. S. E.* iv. p. 496.
[4] There was a professor of Botany at Oxford of this name who died there in 1679, aged eighty-one ; this was probably his son or grandson.
[5] Probably a system of riding of which the modern example is what is called in a circus *haute école.*

honn^r intends we should stay yet in France, and whether we shal doe the Tour de France, & come through Holeand back again into England (which j confesse would coste some monny), and j shall not be wanting to shew my utmost obedience to y^r honnors least commands. What in my former letter j told y^r honn^r of buying of Lawbookes, & of our monny, since j doubte not but y^r honn^r hath receiued them, j shall supersede[1] to trouble y^r honn^r with it again.
So expecting y honn^{rs} commands
humbly (take my leave)
      y^r honn^{rs} Most humble & most obedient seruant
            HENRY VAN BOBBART.

Mr Dacre, & Richard remember theyr duties & humbly ask y^r blessing.

Not long after the date of this letter Dacre wrote one to his father in Latin; the burden of his letter being the old, old story, a request for money, so frequently the chief object of a boy's epistles to his father:—

[Endorsed] Viro Honorabili Dno Richard Barrett Parenti meo aeternum colendo. Dublinij.
   Venerande Domine Pater,
      Quamvis nulla mihi suppetat scribendi materia, quae aut tibi prodesse, aut tuum tam gravibus, ut scio, curis implicitum animum delectare possit, non tamen moveor quo minus hisce te affari audeam; ea parentum solet esse conditio hi more [sic] nihil gratius ijs contingere videatur quam intelligere ut valeant, ut vitam agant quibus vitam dedere, neqe de hoc paterni tui amoris effectu dubitare licet, qui tot quotidie benevolentiae tuae certissima argumenta accipio. Non evagabor hic, quanta in nos studia tua fuerint dum absentes et remotos indies maioribus cumular [sic] beneficiis et modo proficiamus nec sumptibus nec industriae parcis. Longa haec sunt; longiora tamen, si quanta animi submissione quanta cum reverentiâ haec recordemur, exponere vellem. Fateor infinita sunt quae recepimus et flagitamus semper nova eorum instar qui cum se solvendo esse non vident priora debita novis adaugere non erubescunt. Quid velim, coniectu haud est difficile. Saepius pecuniae opem a te imploravimus et toties obtinuimus: atque tamen sollicitare iterum tuum auxilium non pudet; scilicet peregrinantibus quam

---
[1] Meaning 'desist' or 'leave off.'—C. D.

argentum nihil magis necessarium est; in eo vis virtusqe consistere videtur; ex eo animum alacritatemqe capiunt, tanquam unico et solo ad bene agendum proficiendumqe remedio. De prospero quem optamus causae tuae successu tibi nobisqe gratulamur; facit Deus, ut detectis iniquitatis iniusti possessoris velis splendore suo prodeat iuris tui aequitas et ut tandem pressa hactenus triumphet bona causa. ardenter haec precor votumqe hoc quo epistolam finio certissimum sempeterni [sic] fidelis mei obsequii indicium accipias velim qui sum

    Tui obsequentissimus filius et humillimus servus [1]

DA: BARRETT.

  Aureliae VII Cal
    Septembris Anno 1671.

Translation: To my ever-respected father the Honourable Richard Barrett. Dublin.

  Honoured Sir and Father

    Altho' I have nothing particular to communicate which may be of advantage to you, or even amuse your mind, already occupied by so many cares, & anxieties, still I am not the less emboldened to address you on the subject of my own concerns, being fully aware, that the nature of parents is such, that nothing can at any time be more agreeable to them than to be made acquainted, as much as possible, how those fare to whom they have given life. And least of any should I doubt this fact, who daily receive such proofs of your fatherly affection, nor shall I exaggerate in saying how great your care for us has been, when being absent, and at a distance from you, we are from day to day loaded more and more with benefits by you, and if only we make progress you spare neither expense nor trouble. This is a long letter, but it would be longer if I could record those things with as much submission of mind, and as much reverence, as I should wish to express them with. I confess that I have received very much, and I am always asking for fresh benefits, like those who, when they see that they are insolvent, do not blush to increase their former obligations by fresh ones. It will not be difficult for you to guess what I now require. Often have we requested from you assistance in money, and as often received it. In the present instance however I am not ashamed to demand it again; nothing being so necessary to travellers as money, in which indeed their moral and physical

---

[1] Some of these words are almost impossible to make out with certainty, the original being torn.

strength consist ; from its possession they derive both spirit and energy, and lastly it is the one and only means of enabling them to make good and satisfactory progress. We congratulate ourselves as well as you on the favourable progress of your law suit which I hope you will be cautious about. God grant that the veil being drawn aside, which at present hides the iniquity of the unlawful possessor of your property, the justice of your suit may prevail with transcendent splendour, and that the good cause, which till now has been stifled, and pressed down, may ultimately triumph. I earnestly pray for these things, and pray accept this wish, with which I finish this letter, as the surest indication of my eternal faithful duty to you.

I am your most obedient son & most humble servant

DA. BARRETT.

Orleans[1]
7th September 1671.

The two boys and their tutor returned to England[2] at the end of December 1671, having been abroad about a year and a-half. Among our papers I have come across a most interesting document endorsed by Lord Dacre:—

Mr. von Bobbarts Account of the Expences of my Grandfather and Great Uncle Lennard in the year 1670 when they were in France for their Educations Completion. He was their travelling Tutor. This account is addressed to their father Richard Barrett Lennard. D——.

The account is made out in livres and sols—a sol or sou = one penny, and a livre = 20 sols, or 1s. 8d. (at par).

The total expenses for tutor, boys, and a man-servant for a year and seven months came to about 500l., which, even allowing for the difference in the value of money, seems not to be an

---

[1] Aurelianum.
[2] That they went to Belhus on their return is shown by an item in Van Bobbart's accounts of coach hire to the 'Three Nuns' and to Hornchurch. The 'Three Nuns' in Whitechapel, now a sort of hotel, was formerly one of the great coaching inns in London whence the Essex coaches started. Hornchurch is a village some four miles from Belhus. The fact that the boys went to Belhus in December 1671 does not prove that their father was then living there, as the house might then still have been occupied by their grandmother Lady Dacre.

excessive one, particularly as the account included the costs of various sight-seeing, such as 'three men broken on the wheel,' and other sights and amusements which the tutor apparently considered to be instructive and edifying for his pupils. The total amount expended in washing for all this period is, as might be expected, a shockingly small sum, being only 22 livres, 16 sols, or less than 2*l*. of our money. The cost of each pair of shoes that they bought was little enough, being only 3 livres each, but they purchased no less than fifty pair. The account is beautifully made out under different headings for each class of expenditure, and will be found interesting reading, as it throws light on the fashions and customs of those days :—

Account of expences made by Mrs Dacres and Richard Barretts dureing theyr stay in France till theyr return into England from the $\frac{23}{13}$th of May 1670 till the $\frac{3}{8}\frac{1}{1}$ of Decemb. 1671, haueing with them a Gouverneur and a Lacquay ; diuided into Seuerall particullars, viz.

R. (I.) BARRETT'S SONS 419

	JOURNEYS AND VOYAGES WITH THE CHARGES.	L.	s.	L.	s.
A. C. 1670.					
May 22, 29.	from London to Paris	189	4		
Jany. 4.	going to St. Clou	12	0		
16, 17.	from Paris to Orleans	54	0		
Aug. 12, 17.	to See the Court at Chambourg.	30	0		
1671.	at the church at Bion diuers times	36	8		
Jan. 30. Feb. 2.	from Orleans to Paris	53	9		
Jun. 12.	to St Bois Vincenne	8	0		
July 1, 3.	Seeing the rest of the King's houses about Paris	23	10		
5, 9.	from Paris to Orleans passing through Veau: VizCount & Fountenbleau	56	9	740	17
Septemb. 3.	going à la Terté	9	10		
Novemb. 26, 28.	from Orleans to Paris	57	0		
Decemb. 13, 19.	from Paris to Cales	98	0		
	I stayed there three dayes and the Gentlemen 1½.	21	0		
21.	the Gentlemen went for Dunkerke	15	17		
23, 26.	from Cales to London with the duties on the roade	70	0		
30.	hireing a coach to goe to the three Nunnes and soe to Hornchurch	6	10		

	DIET AND PENSION.				
1670					
May 30. Jun. 30.	at Paris & à la crois blanche at Orleans	133	0		
July 1 till Jan. 30, 1671.	at Orleans in Madm. Rousseletts house	918	0		
Feb. 3. Apr. 1.	at Paris at Mr. Vosier	266	0	2376	16
Ap. 1. Jun. 30.	at Mr. Gaudrys in Paris	407	6		
July 3, 5.	at Paris	15	0		
July 9. Nov. 25.	at Madm. Rouseletts at Orleans	565	0		
Novemb. 28.	at Paris	72	10		
Decemb. 13.					

	SICKNESS.				
	at Paris to the Apothecary and the Physicien for Mr. Dacres.	54	0		
	twice at Orleans	16	0		
	for cureing the Lacq^s foot being broken by a cart running ouer him	23	0	95	
	twice for draweing out of Mr. Richard tooth	2	0		

L. 3212 13

	1670	Clothes.	L.	s.	L.	s
Jun. 1.		Twoe Sutes of Stuff mixed with Silk lined with white tabby, and couered with Silk laces	212	0		
		a Coat for the Lacq. together with ribbands, linnan, hatt, stockins	36	0		
Octob. 4.		twoe Cammelot Cloakes	137	0	1146	7
	1671	a Sute for me	104	0		
May 15.		twoe Silk Sutes with Pantaloons	232	13		
		twoe Sutes of cammelot with Silver laces, and Silver buttons	279	14		
Novemb. 18.		three Sutes of droguet a l'imperiale, with makeing up the Silk Sutes	145	0		

	Stockins.				
	four payr of silk for Mr. Dacres	38	10		
	three payr of silk for Mr. Richard	28	0		
	1 payr for me	10	0		
	a payr of woollen, and a payr of thred for Mr. Dacres	5	6	93	16
	3 payr of woollen for me	10	10		
	for mending of them at diuers times	1	10		

	Shoes.		
	fifty payr of shoes a. 3.l. a payr		150

	1670	Hatts.				
May 20.		three hatts a 6.l.	18	0		
Septemb. 4.		three hatts a 5.	15	0		
	1671					
Febr. 8.		2 hatts for Mr. Dacres & Richard	10	0		
May 15.		twoe Bevers	22	0	83	18
Novemb. 18.		twoe gray hats	12	0		
		a gray one for me	4	0		
		3 Couerts a. 15.s.	2	5		
		for dressing of Mr. Richards hatt at Douer	0	13		

By the precedent page . 1474 1
3212 13
L. 4686 14

THEIR EXPENSES 421

	GLOUES.	L.	s.	L.	s.
	22 payr	15	19	20	4
	3 payr of double chamois	4	05		

RIBBANDS.

the Gentlemen besstowed on Madm Rousselett . . . 5 0 } 16 0
for theyr own use at diuers times 11 0

PEEREWIGS AND TRIMMING, &C.

Twoe perrewigs . . . 44 0
Mr. janvier dressing of one, . 2 0
cutting of hair, Shauing, knifes,   } 59 0
Scissars, musk dalie, and Comes 13 0

BELTS.

Twoe green Silk belts . . 36 0
one for me at orleans . . 15 0
twoe wast belts . . . 5 0
twoe of leather giueing mine in   } 69 0
change 8 0
one of black cloth for me . . 5 0

SWORDS.

Mr. Dacres haueing lost his, j gaue him mine, and bought another 9 0
one for Mr. Richard his being   } 16 15
stolen at Luxenbourg . . 3 0
Mending of them at diuers times 4 15

1670
May 25.

LINNEN.

4 half Shirts laced, 4 payr of cuffs laced, 4 Cravettes laced, 2 payr of drawers, twoe payr of stockins 90 10

1671
May 15.

2 half Shirts for me, a cravette, 2 payr cuffs 32 0
4 half Shirts with point de Paris,   } 234 4
2 payr of cuffs, twoe Cravettes with point de Paris . . 68 4
6 whole Shirts, each of us twoe, 4 payr of drawers, 2 payr of linnen stockins for Mr. Richard, 4 handkerchief with buttons . 43 10

of the precedent page .

415 3
4686 14
—————
L. 5101 17

422　HISTORY OF THE BARRETTS

1670	WASHING.	L.	s.	L.	s.
May 30. juin 30.	at Paris	4	0		
1671 Febr. 3. Jul. 3.	paying euery month 3.l.	15	0	22	16
Nov. 25. Decemb. 13.	at our last being at Paris	2	19		
Decemb. 27.	at London	1	6		
	for fyre and candles at Paris for torches at Orleans			20	1

EXERCISES.

		L.	s.	L.	s.
To the Dancingmaster for tenn months & a half, the first a. 20 l., the rest a. 12		134	0		
Fiue months for me a. 5 l.		25	0		
To the master of the Guitarre and the Viol [1] for fiue months and a half a. 20 l.		110	0		
Twoe months upon the Lute [2] a. 14 l.		28	0		
playing on the castaniettes		11	0		
for musick books		2	10		
for twoe payr of Castaniettes		11	0		
at Paris for hireing a Viol, and Guitarre, and mending the Viol broken, for 3 months whilst they learnt upon the Lute		9	0		
hired a Viol and Guitarre at Orleans a. 4 months, as also bought a Viol at Paris		8	0	615	10
for strings		2	0		
To the Musick master a month and a half		19	0		
To the master of the language 3 months a. 20 l.		60	0		
To Master Makarmite Professor of Philosophie		45	0		
To the Fencingmaster 2 months for us three together with files and Shoes		45	0		
To the Tennis master for teaching of 4 months; playing of parties, tossing of balles		106	0		
				658	6
of the precedent page				5101	17
				L. 5760	3

[1] A mediæval muSical inStrument now represented by the violin, viola, &c.

[2] A mediæval muSical inStrument which continued in use in Europe until about 1750, and is now represented by the guitar, mandoline, and banjo.

OF A TRIP

DIUERTISSMENTS.	L.	s.	L.	s.
Going to a Ball in masquerade	10	10		
To see Playes, a l'opera, and a l'hostel de Burgoyne at Paris &c. and at Orleans	28	0		
We was invited at a Christmass supper, but payed for it	9	0	131	10
at Bowls; and soe lost collations	25	0		
at cards in our house after supper and elsewhere	15	0		
Mr. Dacres lost unto my Lord Dacres[1] the day before we went out of Paris	44	0		

BOOKS.

	L.	s.	L.	s.
Corpus Canonicum	10	0		
Twoe Institutiones Justinianeæ	3	0		
Pacii Commentarius in instituta	1	0		
Ejusdem Isagoge in Jus Ciuile and decretales	1	0		
Mendorie Philosophia	1	10		
Quintilianus	1	5		
Quintilian in French	0	10		
Terence	1	5		
Femmes fortes	1	15		
Lucain	1	15		
Mr. Ouden French Grammar twice	1	10		
Mr. Chiflet	1	0		
An English & French Grammar with dialogues	1	15		
Tacitus and Suetonius	0	16		
Persius	0	9		
Tursellinus	0	8	52	19
Buchanani Poemata	0	8		
Farnabii Rhetorica	0	10		
Gemmulæ 4. linguarum	0	13		
a French Arithmetik	0	15		
La conformite des ceremonies modernes avec les anciennes	1	0		
Voyage en Nova Zembla &c.	1	0		
Pomona	0	15		
French airs of Ao 1670	0	13		
Mappe of Paris	0	15		
La Vie et le thresoir de St. Denys &c.	0	5		
Twoe paper books to write the Philosophie in, as also paper for to write letters, and for other use	9	7		
for the newes books	8	0		

of the precedent page . 184 9
5760 3
L. 5944 12

---
[1] His cousin Thomas, afterwards Earl of Sussex.

		L.	s.	L.	s.
	for letters receued out of England	12	0		
	Receiued out of Germanie, Holland, &c. for me	18	0	30	0
	because we stayed at Orleans j was obliged to immatriulate meeself, and administer some offices in the German nation which comes to			20	0

	NEWYEARS GIFT; and in Going				
1671	away to the MAIDS.				
Jan. 30.	In Orleans to the maids	6	0		
	to the Pedell of the German nation for presenting us with almanacks	3	0		
	to the Musicien and the Tennesmen	6	10	24	10
July 1.	at Paris to the maids	3	0		
Novemb. 25.	at Orleans to the maids	6	0		

TO THE POOR.

	To twoe English Soldier at Abbeville	1	10		
	to Twoe Irishmen	2	5		
	To an English woman	1	10		
	To an English Capucin	1	10		
	To three Dutchmen	2	0		
	to the Frenchman yt came with us from Cales	0	13	35	8
	To the Poor in general	8	0		
	in the Tirelire[1] for to learn French	12	0		
	Going away to the Minister of Bion	6	0		

PHILOGRAM WORK, which the Gentl. bestowed on my Lady Dacres and theyr sisters.

	a box to put essences in	17	18		
	for the fitting of it	3	10	37	2
	a knife with a fork and spoon	12	0		
	for twissars	3	6		
	for three fanns			19	10
	Seeing of the Louvre; the Machines at the jesuits; going to the Steeple of St. Croix at Orleans; of St. Eustache at Paris, to the Apothecarie garden			5	0
				171	10
	by the precedent page			5944	12
				L. 6116	2

[1] Money-box.

		L.	s.
Seeing three men broken upon the wheel and one shot to death .		2	10
Seing of St. johns fire a la Graive twice		7	10
Repaying a Visit to Mr. Widders in a coach and from thence a la Cour de la Reyne . . .		2	15
A Sneesebox for Mr. Richard .		0	15
The monny of Mr. Page, which his Uncle gaue me, not reaching j lend him, (which noe doubte he will repay unto your Honnr) as by the account appear . .		15	12
		29	2
By the precedent page .		6116	2
Summa of all Expenses .	L.	6145	4

1670	RECEIUED.	L.	s.
May 22.	hundred ninety eight pound sterl. whereof j took in bills £183. a. 51, the rest in English monny a. 13 s. a shilling, amounts to	2506	12
1671 Jan. 22.	j drew for hundred pound upon Mr. Owen and receiued for it of Mr. Charon in Orleans	1260	0
May 22.	by a bill of £100 upon Mr Owen j had for it of Mr. Alexandr at Paris . .	1266	12
Novemb. 27.	again of Mr. Alexandr, for a bill of 100 .	1260	0
Decemb. 12.	more of Mr Alexandr, payed by Mr. Owen at our comeing to London .	126	0
Decemb. 27.	j took from Mr. Owen twoe pound, a. 13 Sols a Shilling makes . . .	26	0
	Summa of receipts . . .	6445	4
	whereof being deducted the Summe of disbursements	6145	4
		L. 300	0

I remain debtor unto yʳ honnor, which debt yʳ honnr bestowed on me the 12th, for which and all other favours, (as they are infinite) soe doe j acknowledge myself for euer obliged
    yʳ honnrs
   most humble most devoted Servant
salvo errore calculi.   HENRY VON BOBBART.

In 1672 Richard was admitted to the freedom of the Borough of Lancaster, but what his connection was with that part of the world I am unable to discover. In 1674 he went over to Ireland, as is shown by the following letter from a man of the curious name of Porkrich, who was his agent from 1659 until September 1674.[1]

[Endorsed] For the Hono^ble Richard Barrett in Dublin, These.

H_o^ble S^r

I am glad of yor safe arrivell in Irland I would haue writt sooner but eury day expected yor Hon^r in Clownish, to be short such times I neuer hau. I dout not but yo^u heere enugh theare, but I am Confident ytt is much woorse heere. I protest I was neuer affrayd to see yor Honr untill now. How- euer I hope yo^u wilbe pleasd to com into ye cowntry with what conuenient speed yo^u may, (although I cannot as formerly salute yo^u with a bagg of mony), truely not only yor Hon^rs estate, but many others is likely to bee much wast, ye tenants dayly crying upon mee, som for abatement of rent, othors throwing up theyr lands for y^t theyr goods is dead, & I only giue them good woords & referr to yo^u, which in short is all from

Sr Yo^r Hon^rs most Humble servant
Aghanamallatt   MICH. PORKRICH.
May the 22th, 1674.

I am unable to fix the exact date at which Richard left Ireland and took up his abode at Belhus—probably about 1673, as in the recitals to a bill which he filed against Swann, at one time his agent at Clones, he speaks of being in constant residence there in 1674; and we have a letter from Dorothy Lady Dacre to her granddaughter Anne, dated March 1673, addressed to her 'att Belhous.'

At this period, or very shortly after, Richard's sons were both in Ireland, Dacre looking after his father's estates there, and Richard employed in some capacity at the Viceregal Court at Dublin; we have an unsigned deed, dated 1678, by Richard the elder, appointing his son Richard, in conjunction

[1] He was dismissed before September 1674. Recital in papers relating to action against E. Swann, Successor to Porkrich.—*F. P.*

with his son Dacre, his attorneys for the purpose of letting, and otherwise managing the Clones property. There are several letters from a man of the name of Fifield to Richard the son, about some legal business which he appears to have been assisting the writer in. Those which are dated 1677 are addressed to Richard 'at the Castle in Dublin.' The Duke of Ormonde was at this period Viceroy of Ireland, and, as I have said,[1] he was a friend of Richard the elder. Among the Marquis of Ormonde's papers connected with his governorship of Ireland there is the following entry: 'September 1677 Gentlemen that now ride in the guard that are in the family'[2] (here follow some names, and then this note), 'Mr. Barrett does not desire it.'[3] In a letter by Richard the younger written from 'London ye 7th, 81,' to his brother Dacre in Dublin, he no doubt refers to his employment at Dublin Castle.

One thing I must beg of you is that you would wait on my Lord Duke, and my Lady Duchesse, and tell them what is happened unto me, that I am fallen into my fathers Displeasure, and that now I despond of being able to serve them any longer or return into my former Station in such an Equipage as would be Creditable for them, wch I allwayes made my greater end then any thing of my own advantage, and you may then speak to my Couzen Cornwall, to Enquire what it is that is in bank for me amongst my fellow bed Chamber men. I hope my old freinds will be just to me notw̄thstanding my Long absence, at least if they have forgotten me, they will not forget themselves to be gentlemen, your man James will be a fit instrument for to be Employed in ye prosecution of this affaire wⁿ [when] you have thus mov'd it. if I get any thing t'will serve to Quit of some scores that may be claim'd on my account there; if I get nothing I shall be sorry to be so ill dealt wth.

We have seen that Lord Dacre says that Richard the elder was 'prone to Choler,' and during his son Richard's stay in

---

[1] *Ante*, p. 392.

[2] The word 'family' is used in another entry just before this, meaning belonging to the household of the Duke.

[3] *Hist. Com.* xiv. *Marquis of Ormonde*, ii. p. 208; advanced to the dignity of duke in peerage of Ireland 1661, in England 1682.

Ireland he appears, as regards his feelings towards him, to have fully lived up to the character ascribed to him by his great-grandson. I am not able to state with certainty the cause of his anger with his son, or when it began, but he appears to have been on good terms with him as late as February 9th, 1677, as on that date R. Fifield writes to Richard the younger and says, 'Y^r father did me the honour lately to be merry at my house where he talked only off you.'

I have discovered some of the pleadings in a lawsuit in which Richard the younger was one of the defendants, and I think it not unlikely that being involved in this action was the cause of his father's anger against him. The only papers I have found relating to this suit are headed 'The several Answers of Richard Barrett Junior Esq. to ye bill of Complnt of John Desminers, Alderman of ye Citty of Dublin,' and obviously this is not sufficient material from which to follow the whole of the story. Richard the son seems to have been sued by the Alderman for two sums, one of 48*l*. 9*s*. 3*d*. and the other of 38*l*. 16*s*. 1½*d*., and also for money due for board, lodging, and washing, and his father was made a co-defendant. Richard the younger says in his answers that the first sum of money was advanced to him for the purpose of carrying on his brother's litigation with the Loftus family; and that the second sum was for his own use, and that he never denied his liability, and intended to repay it when able to do so. As to the claims for board, lodging, and washing for two years, he said that when he came over to Dublin with the Duke of Ormonde, as 'one of his family,' his lodgings in the Castle were not ready for him, and that upon the earnest solicitation of the Alderman, who was much indebted to his father, he did stay with him some three weeks, but never stayed at his house after except as a guest, now and then, of his brother Dacre who lodged there, and occasionally he also dined there as guest of the Alderman himself As to the washing, he said he did send his washing there, and agreed to pay 4*l*. a year, but as Mrs. Desminers very kindly refused to take any payment for this, he had intended to give her a piece of plate as a present, had he remained longer in Dublin. But the fact that he had this action brought against him, and that his father was joined in it as a co-defendant, may very probably have been the cause of his father's anger against him. We have some undated letters to Richard the younger from his sister Anne, which no doubt refer to the estrangement between the father and the son, and show that she was forbidden by her father to have any intercourse with her brother upon pain of his most severe displeasure, or, as she quaintly puts it, 'without ye hazard of my last Stake.'

Letters written by Richard the younger to his sister Anne, and to his brother, tell us that his father was treating him with considerable harshness, and show what a wretched life he was leading during what proved to be the last years of his existence. In September 1680 he tells his brother that he cannot leave Belhus to go to London on account of the 'meanness of his garb'; that his father is 'implacable,' and that he hopes he will 'very suddenly think fit that I should have my nakedness covered, if not from first keeping the house, and next keeping my chamber, I shall at last be forced to keep my bed.'

In the following February he writes from London to his sister Anne at Belhus about some 'dougges' (drugs) that his father wanted, but which poor Richard said would cost 'more than he was worth either in money or in credit.' In June he was still in London, and writes to Dacre in Dublin, when he says, 'that lately my father had seem'd inclinable to a reconciliation for me to his favour,' but that hearing from a banker in Dublin that he had drawn upon his father for 38*l*., his father is in such a rage against him that 'my hopes are almost quite dasht again.' He writes again in that month to his brother saying that matters with his father stand in the same position that they did, and that 'my Lord C. Justice North has all along promised by his interest to restore me to his [the writer's father's] favour, and to that end went down to Bellhouse, but when he came there his Intentions were diverted by his own interest for that time.' In July he says that his aunt, Lady Sheppey,[1] has invited him to go into the country with her for some long time; and that 'my Lord C. Justice North (who is the only man who can byasse my father with reason) declines the speaking one word in my behalf, and since I told him my Condition seems to fly me as one would an impertinent beggar,' and that his grandmother, Lady Dacre, who had come to stay at Belhus for the summer, only aggravated matters between him and his father. In the following November Richard the younger was again back in London, having spent all the summer with his aunt. He was still as hard up as ever, but his father had become reconciled to him. There is a vein of dry humour running through many of Richard's letters. He says, writing to Dacre:—

the other day I recieved a message from my father by w$\bar{ch}$ he not only promised me his blessing, if I would come for it, but his favour; the advantageous proffer was too welcome to necessitous me to be refused; the first I have obtained: the latter remains unconfirm'd, as not having enjoy'd any effects of it.

In the month of January 1682 he says he has still only obtained from his father a blessing, and that he sees no hope of getting anything more tangible. Any money he has is from his aunt, and he is ashamed of receiving obligations from her which he has no chance of repaying, and that he has asked his father in vain to give him enough money to enable him to go to the East Indies. His father, he says, 'will endure the sight of me and speaks pretty freindly to me,' and so he hopes that he may relent, if only he receives good remittances of rent from Ireland.

Richard writes later on in the month in the same desponding manner, saying that he hopes Mr. Slone (the Irish agent) will not continue to spread the report that he is empowered by his father to sell the estates of Scribblestown and Dunsink, in county Dublin, lest his father should be induced to part with them, tempted to do so by some of the offers that may be made

[1] Widow of his uncle Francis Lord Dacre.

to him. Richard evidently considers that if his father did sell these estates, which he had promised to settle on him, the money derived from such sale would not be set aside for his benefit, but would be otherwise disposed of, for he writes :—

were it not for some small sparks of hope remaining to me on this account [*i.e.* becoming owner after his father's decease of Scribblestown and Dunsink] nothing could alter my resolution from taking any course to dispose of my self, being plunged into ye utmost dispair by meer want, and necessity, the effects of which must have been long ago starving, had not my Lady Sheppe's kindness in commiserating my condition been my relief.

In May he tells his brother that he has at last obtained a reconciliation with his father, upon condition that he asks the latter for no money to discharge the debts which he contracted during his displeasure, and that he is to have a future allowance, but only to the extent of 20*l.* a year. He begs Dacre to lend him 20*l.*, 'for I protest to ye living God if I receive not this favour from you I am for ever ruin'd; for upon this alone depends either my happiness, or utter misfortune, ye Jayle being ye only thing I can expect.' Just a month after writing this last letter he writes another one to Dacre, this time in good spirits; he has unexpectedly received something (no doubt money), and he says, 'unless you are ye Author of my happinesse, I know not where to direct my thanks for the favours that providence has bestowed on me.' It is well to think that something had occurred to cheer him up in June 1682, for on the 26th of that month his life was prematurely cut short at Belhus by a fall from a horse[1] in the twenty-eighth year of his age.

The tradition is that he was breaking in a horse, and his father watching him from the windows of the north drawing-

---

[1] The date of his death is mentioned in the pleadings in the lawsuit respecting the ownership of Dunsink and Scribblestown, which took place between Dacre Barrett and his sisters.—*F. P.*

room, when he was thrown on to his head and killed on the spot. I remember as a boy the remains of a very old lime tree near the north side of the house; this tree, or what remained of it, was held together by iron rods and chains, and it used to be said that at it's foot this fatal accident took place. Lord Dacre says of Richard that he was

a young man of great hopes, was killed in the prime of Life from a fall from an Unruly Horse, which he was breaking in the Park at Belhus, having been only a few days returned from France where he had been passing some time in one of their Academies, and died a Batchellor.

Lord Dacre wrote his History less than a hundred years after Richard's death, and Richard was his great-uncle, so that one would expect his account of him to be fairly accurate. I can only suppose that Lord Dacre had not read the numerous letters from Richard that I have referred to, and which prove that he had not been in France for several years before his death, if indeed he had ever been in that country, except when he and his brother were there under the care of Mr. Van Bobbart.

Richard the younger, from the tone of his letters, appears to have been of a very affectionate nature, and much attached both to his sister Anne and to Dacre. His affection for the latter was most disinterested; he took great pains to plead his brother's cause with his father and his sister Anne when the question arose about Dacre's proposed marriage with Lady Jane; and after that marriage he more than once expresses his anxiety that his brother should have an heir, which, of course, would have been most prejudicial to his own chance of succeeding his brother. On July 12th, 1681, he says, 'Pray present my humble service to your Lady, whom I should be glad to hear from your own self that she were wth child.' And on the 19th, 'Pray present my most humble service to your Lady whom I hear I may give Joy of a great Belly'; and in the following February he refers to a hope that she should 'be with child.' In May he hopes that she may have a 'happy delivery and that it may be to both your satisfactions,' and in June 1682 he says: 'Pray present my humble Service to your Lady. I expect every day to hear of her having made me an Uncle.'

Before treating of Dacre and his relations with his father, it is convenient to say something of Richard's daughters, Anne and Dorothy. Of the latter we know little; she was

[1]

a delicate girl and died single, and she appears after her sister married to have lived much with her. In one of her letters Anne speaks of Dorothy as being 'Very Lame both of her hands & Leggs,' and of her having been obliged to use a stick to walk with at Belhus before she had gone for a change of air at Chevening, where, however, she was able to walk without its assistance. We have no letters from or to her; and, although she was a party with her sister in the lawsuit against her brother Dacre, I imagine that she acted under Anne's influence, and took no active part herself in that matter.

Anne appears to have been quite a different character, very accomplished in the French and Italian languages and in music; she was a witty and even brilliant letter-writer, as appears from her correspondence. Her cousin Roger North says that she 'was as good company as one could desire.' In 1677, when she was about twenty-two years of age, she appears to have nearly been married to a Mr. Coote, son of Lord Coloony, which would have been 'soe noble and worthy a mach.'[2] We have no means of knowing why the marriage did not take place, but probably

---

[1] As to her signing herself 'Lennard,' *vide ante*, p. 394.

[2] Letter, dated 1677, from Dorothy Lady Dacre to her son Richard urging him to arrange for this marriage. The Coote family was much connected with the Lennards, as Sir Charles Coote (created Earl of Mountrath) married, as has been stated, Mary Rushe, a sister of Anne's grandmother; and Elizabeth Brabazon, a granddaughter of Francis, Lord Dacre, married, as his second wife, Sir Philips Coote, of Mount Coote; while Charles, a son of Sir Philips, married Kath Newcomen, daughter of Sir Robert (sixth Baronet) and Lady Mary Newcomen, which Lady Mary was a sister of Lady Jane Barrett.

F F

her father refused to make the necessary settlements; she occasionally mentions the name of Mr. Coote in letters to her brothers in connection with some songs he was to have sent her, and in 1678, in a letter to Dacre, speaking of him as a prophet, she says: 'Since you are good att foretelling future things, informe me what will become of me, since ye knowledge of my Fortune depends as much upon your will, as your prescience.' This is probably an allusion to the proposed marriage and to the negotiations going on about the settlements. After this marriage was broken off Anne spent some eight or ten years very unhappily at Belhus, being tyrannised over by her father, to whom she appears to have always behaved as a most dutiful and devoted daughter.

Such letters as we have from her written during that period are much more depressed in tone than those written later, when no doubt time, that great healer of all sorrows, had caused her regrets for the loss of Mr. Coote to become less vivid. Writing to her brother Richard, she speaks of the miserable poverty and unquietness from which she suffers, but says that all thoughts of her own concerns, 'though they be as near as my Shifts, or to speak more plainly my no Smocks,[1] are buried in my grieffs for you.' And when forbidden by her father to see Richard she writes a most loving letter to him, concluding, 'Deare Deare Brother lett me hear from you for without y^t comfort, though my Father has laid absolute Command on me to be Chearfull, and banish greif, there will be nothing butt cloudes in ye face of your most aff^t Sister Anne.'

There are several references among our letters which show how dull and disagreeable the life at Belhus must have been for a young girl, and how greatly it was aggravated by her father's selfish and inconsiderate conduct. Her grandmother, Dorothy

---

[1] 'No Smocks.' Whatever Anne intended, it is clear she did write 'no,' perhaps for new. The first meaning of 'Smock' is a woman's Shift. From the context it would appear that in those days the word 'Shift' was considered more elegant than 'Smock'; while now, to some persons, the French word 'chemise' is considered more elegant than 'Shift.'

Lady Dacre, writes: 'I am very sorry that you are very sollitary in a place wher you have noe neighbours to deuvart you.' And in a letter to Dacre, not dated, but written between 1682 and 1687, Anne says:—

Bellhouse is such as you knew itt, and my manner of Living ye same you formerly had here, or rather worse. My Father's Distemper making him very Uneasy: most of his Time spent in Bed where I am for some houres in ye day, on ye same duty we used to pay in ye Parlour by ye Chimney Side, and which is yett worse. I have 40 journeys up & down stairs with his orders to ye Familly,[1] which is all in his own management to ye minutest part of it.

The autobiography of the Hon. Roger North, printed in Dr. Jessopp's edition of 'The Lives of the Norths,' gives the following vivid picture of Anne, and of her father's conduct towards her, and the life then being led at Belhus:—

I used to make frequent visits to Bellhouse to my relations there, because it lay near Purfleet, from whence I could walk thither. And this I did more out of respect to a lady, Mistress A. Barrett als Lennard, daughter of Mr. Barrett my cousen german, than any diversion his company afforded, who, though ingenious, and in general of a very good understanding, was of such a morose wilful spirit that it was very fastidious[2] to be in his company, especially considering his infirmities, which had disabled him as to all action; and he spent his whole time either in bed or in a chair, and was carried from one to the other. But his daughter was bred with my Lady Dacre's own Aunt[3] who was a lady of an extraordinary character, and particularly well bred, and of an undaunted spirit, one whom I would choose to breed[4] a young lady, and to give the tour of honour. Here she stayed till her father, like a beast, took her away to be burried with him alive in the country; where, by the tyranny of his temper, being always cross & perverse, especially to his children, he had broke her to the greatest degree of submission and obedience that I ever observed.

[1] For previous use of this word *vide ante*, p. 427.

[2] Such as to cause disgust or loathing.—*C. D.*

[3] Roger North did not write an easy hand to read; there must be a mistake in this passage. Dorothy Lady Dacre, Anne's grandmother, brought her up, and not some aunt of Lady Dacre's, who would have been Anne's great-great-aunt.

[4] To form by education, to train.—*C. D.*

Although she was there for the most part alone, and without company fit for her, she found ways to entertain herself so that her time was not lost. For she mastered that puzzling instrument the lute ; and having a good voice, and the instruction of an Italian, one Signor Morelli ; she acquired to sing exceedingly well, after the Italian manner, to her own playing upon the lute or guitar. She was also addicted to books, and was mistress of French, & Italian, as well to speak as read ; and withal of an exceeding obliging temper, which, with the advantage of her first breeding and the assurance by that, softened by her mortified life in the country, together with a more than ordinary wit and fluency of discourse, made her as good company as one would desire in a relation.

It was believed that I made addresses to her, in order to match with her, and I do not wonder at it, because it was notorious that I took frequent and great pleasure in her company. I must profess myself a lover of virtue in any one, either with or without the -osi, but she had both. However, if she had not been so near a relation I could not in honour have done so without a justification that way ; and it will also be believed that such constructions did not escape my thought, and I had well considered the matter, whereupon I must own I should have esteemed myself happy in a settlement with so worthy a person, and despair (out of my too near relation) to meet with the like within the sphere of my pretensions. But her fortune, and mine, were not enough to support that outward form of honour in the way of living, according to the esteem of the world, which I thought became the quality I should take her into. And whatever philosophy I might pretend to, and by the strength of it to defy the censure of small or great vulgar, I could not expect that a woman should cordially concur with me, but on the contrary it was reasonable to believe she should retain the little emulations and pride incident to her nature, which, however prudent to conceal it, would, if not gratified by outward splendour of living, inwardly grieve her. I knew it would me, to think, as I certainly should, that it did so. Therefore I never made any experiment to know if my service that way would be accepted by ; but applied myself to serve & oblige her all other ways that fell in my power. But I may perhaps speak more of the case of matching elsewhere. In the mean time I can not omit one passage in the history of this lady, for whom I had so much honour, to show that virtue, early or late, will find a reward beyond what never fails to attend it,

Although she was there for the most part alone, and without company fit for her, she found ways to entertain herself so that her time was not lost. For she mastered that puzzling instrument the lute ; and having a good voice, and the instruction of an Italian, one Signor Morelli ; she acquired to sing exceedingly well, after the Italian manner, to her own playing upon the lute or guitar. She was also addicted to books, and was mistress of French, & Italian, as well to speak as read ; and withal of an exceeding obliging temper, which, with the advantage of her first breeding and the assurance by that, softened by her mortified life in the country, together with a more than ordinary wit and fluency of discourse, made her as good company as one would desire in a relation.

It was believed that I made addresses to her, in order to match with her, and I do not wonder at it, because it was notorious that I took frequent and great pleasure in her company. I must profess myself a lover of virtue in any one, either with or without the -osi, but she had both. However, if she had not been so near a relation I could not in honour have done so without a justification that way ; and it will also be believed that such constructions did not escape my thought, and I had well considered the matter, whereupon I must own I should have esteemed myself happy in a settlement with so worthy a person, and despair (out of my too near relation) to meet with the like within the sphere of my pretensions. But her fortune, and mine, were not enough to support that outward form of honour in the way of living, according to the esteem of the world, which I thought became the quality I should take her into. And whatever philosophy I might pretend to and by the strength of it to defy the censure of small or great vulgar, I could not expect that a woman should condescend or occur with me, but on the contrary it was reasonable to believe she should retain the little emulations and pride incident to her nature, which, however prudent to conceal it, would, if not gratified by outward splendour of living, inwardly grieve her. I knew it would me, to think, as I certainly should, that it did so. Therefore I never made any experiment to know if my service that way would be accepted by; but applied myself to serve & oblige her all other ways that fell in my power. But I may perhaps speak more of the case of matching elsewhere. In the mean time I can not omit one passage in the history of this lady, for whom I had so much honour, to show that virtue, early or late, will find a reward beyond what never fails to attend it,

I mean, (besides a quiet mind), a happy settlement. The old man, upon the revolution of some unaccountable perverseness, (for he never was friends with all his children at once), fell out with this daughter, & her poor weak sister. It was thought his reason was, that they had mutually given to each other their fortunes, (which had been secured to them and not to him), but notwithstanding the merit of so many years slavery to his humour, and an unmatched obedience, he was implacable, and would by all means turn her out of his house to shift for herself as well as she could. And, concurrent with this displeasure, an overture of an honourable match came, which grew up with it, and as the one was desperate, the other took place, as if Providence had provided a husband to succeed a father. This match I treated for her, adjusted a full jointure & provision for children, and as a father gave her [away],[1] and within a few years an estate fell to her husband in Somersetshire of 600*l.* per annum. She has several sons, and lives happily, and is able to protect her sister, who was to be discarded with her. This I look upon as a happy catastrophe after a desolate life, and I should be glad for the sake of the world (if they deserve so much mercy) that all instances of virtue and vice were as conspicuously remunerated according to their deserts.

For some years after he came of age Dacre appears to have lived in Ireland, partly, probably, for the purpose of looking after his father's estates in that country, and partly for the purpose of prosecuting the great lawsuit against the Loftus family. The action was commenced many years previously by Sir John Gifford, to establish the claims of his half-sister, Dacre's maternal grandmother, to important estates in Ireland. It was carried on by Dacre's mother before her marriage, and after her marriage both his parents took some proceedings in the case, but they do not appear to have persevered much in the matter; and it seems to have been left by them to their son Dacre to prosecute the action with any vigour. It is not easy to understand why Richard did not contest the case himself instead of allowing his son to do so. It may be that, having been obliged to prosecute so many actions in regard to Belhus, he had no energy left to embark on this one concerning estates

---

[1] As to her marriage *vide post*, p. 490.

in Ireland, and that but for the determined character of his mother, Dorothy Lady Dacre, he would have acquiesced in the last judgment which was adverse to his claims. Letters from Lady Dacre to both her grandsons show how deeply interested she was in this case, and it was no doubt largely owing to her pertinacity that her son Richard allowed the action to proceed in his son's name, and consented to find the money necessary for its prosecution. Anne, writing to Dacre in 1678, says, speaking of her father, 'I can assure you he does protest with a great deale of earnestness that you shall never want money to prosecute your Right whilst he has any.'

This lawsuit against the Loftus family[1] in one form or another lasted for more than forty years, and had a far-reaching effect of a public nature. The conduct of Lord Strafford in respect of the early stages of this suit formed part of the eighth article of his impeachment,[2] and it is not too much to say that Strafford's execution paved the way to the impeachment and execution of Charles I.

As has been said, Richard's wife was Anne, daughter of Sir Robert Loftus; Sir Robert's father was Adam Loftus, nephew of Adam Loftus, the Archbishop of Dublin. He was born 1568, appointed Chancellor of Ireland 1619, and in 1622 created Viscount Loftus of Ely.[3] The Chancellor was anxious to have his son Robert married to Eleanor, daughter and eventual co-heiress of his former colleague, Sir Francis Rushe.[4] In order to negotiate this marriage he employed Sir William Colley, whom he considered 'so understanding & so honest a gentleman that he could repose full confidence in him,' and who was a friend of the parents of both the young people; and the marriage took place, in July or August 1621, at Castle Jordan, in county Meath. It was agreed

[1] Most of the documents concerning this lawsuit which have been the chief source of my information are in print.—*Hist. Com.* ix. App. Part ii., and *Hist. Com. in V.* C. iii.

[2] *Tryal*, p. 221.

[3] The district formerly styled Eile, Ealie, Ealy, and Ely is now included in King's Court and the county of Tipperary.

[4] In 1613 they were both returned as members for King's County.

that Sir Francis should pay 1,750*l.* to the Chancellor as a marriage portion for his daughter. 'Sir Francis was with much difficultie wrought & persuaded' to the match, and at first proposed to give his daughter a portion of 1,200*l.* only. The Chancellor having promised that he would settle upon Robert and his heirs the manor of Monesterevan,[1] co. Kildare, and such other lands in England and Ireland as were worth 1,500*l.* per annum, at the same time expressing a hope that he might be able to settle a still larger estate upon him, Sir Francis agreed to make Eleanor's portion up to 1,750*l.*, upon the understanding that the Chancellor's settlement should be to the heirs of Robert and 'Dame Elynor,' even if their issue should be daughters only. The Chancellor also promised to settle 200*l.* a year on Robert for his present maintenance and 300*l.* a year on his wife Eleanor should she survive her husband; and he further undertook that he would not settle more than a rent-charge for 200*l.* upon his second son, Sir Edward. It was also part of the agreement that Sir Robert, his wife, children, and servants should live with the Chancellor 'at his charge, or otherwise have from his lordship competent satisfaction in lieu thereof.'

Apparently the Chancellor would not have been able to carry out his undertaking to settle lands worth 1,500*l.* a year on his eldest son even had he been desirous of so doing, as a commission, appointed for finding what lands he was possessed of immediately after his son Sir Robert's marriage, found on October 16th, 1638, that they amounted to 1,145*l.* a year only. These lands, situated in Kildare, King's and Queen's Counties, consisted of:—

	£
Monasterevan	357
Coshagoolie, Harristowne, Richardstowne and Moylesstowne	165
Kilpatrick & Kilbegg	15
Fontsland	130
Crew Eustace	80
Irregan	60
Ely O'Carroll	258
and lands in England	80

[1] Now known as 'Moore Abbey.'

The Lord Chancellor being desired by Sir William Colley to put the said agreement into writing, his Lordship being then in the Country, sayed his writings were in Dublin, but promised to perform the said agreement, and which being made known unto Sir Francis Ruisshe, and his Lady, by Sir William Colley, the marriage by the consent of all parties was solemnized, and the 1750[1] payed to the Lord Chancellor, and land worth 5000 li. is descended to the Lady Loftus sythence the said marriage, by the death of Thomas Ruisshe, brother to the said Lady Loftus.

The Chancellor did not carry out his share of the agreement beyond allowing Sir Robert and his family to reside with him. Sir Francis Rushe during his lifetime attempted to induce the Chancellor to keep his promise about the settlements, but his efforts were not successful, and he 'often complained greviously against his dealings, and Sir Francis upon his death bed expressed himself very much grieved thereat.'

After the death of Sir Francis, 'friends and relacions of Dame Ellinor' also tried to persuade the Chancellor, but found that not only was it impossible to get him to make the settlements he had promised, but that he 'had discovered rather an intention to confer a great, if not the greatest, part of his estate on his second son and his heirs, who yet had none, to the disherison of his eldest son the said Sir Robert & his heirs.' Thereupon Eleanor's half-brother, Sir John Gifford, in the month of February 1636, presented a petition to the King setting forth his version of the case, and praying that the matter might be referred to the Lord Deputy of Ireland and his Council, because if it were proceeded with in the Court of Chancery in Ireland the Lord Chancellor would 'become both Judge and party.' The King, by a letter dated February 9th, $163\frac{6}{7}$, granted this petition, and ordered the matter to be referred to the hearing of the Lord Deputy and his Council.

At this period the Lord Deputy was Wentworth (afterwards Lord Strafford), who had been appointed in 1633. For a short time the Deputy and the Chancellor got on fairly well together, but two men, each so obstinate and high-handed in their methods as they both were, could not continue long in their respective posts without disputes occurring between them sooner or later, and this wrangle in the Loftus family was the means of precipitating such a collision.

From the Chancellor's point of view, he was most unfortunate in the tribunal appointed to hear the petition against him, for not only had Sir George Wentworth, the Deputy's brother who was one of the Council, married a sister of Eleanor's, but the Deputy himself was an interested party, as he was a very great friend of that lady. Leland, writing about the disputes between the Chancellor and Strafford, states that Sir John Gifford had married a daughter of the former, and claimed some settlement of fortune on his wife which her father was not disposed to grant. This careless mistake as to the relationship of the parties is not calculated to inspire any great confidence in the rest of Leland's account of the matter. He goes on to say that Loftus declared that the sentence of the Council against him had been dictated by Strafford, and adds, 'His suggestion had the greater weight when letters were divulged written by the Lord Deputy to the wife of Sir John in a strain so affectionate, and gallant, as raised suspicions of an unlawful intercourse between them.'[1]

This scandal is also mentioned by Clarendon, who in his account of Strafford's trial says :—

In the pressing this charge many things of levity as certain letters of great affection and familiarity from the Earl to that lady [Eleanor Loftus], which were found in her cabinet after her death, for she was lately dead ; others of passion were exposed to the public view to procure prejudice, rather to his gravity and discretion, than that they were in any degree material to the business.[2]

Whether this statement of Clarendon's was founded on fact or upon gossip, the following extract from a letter written by Strafford to Lord Conway in August 1639,[3] shows how great a

---

[1] *Le. His.* iii. pp. 39, 40.   [2] Vol. iii. 117.
[3] *Straf. L. & D.* ii. 381.

regard he had for her, and how unfit a person he was therefore to decide a case in which her interests were concerned :—

> We have sadly buried my Lady Loftus, one of the noblest persons I ever had the happiness to be acquainted with, and, as I had received greater obligations from her Ladyship than from all Ireland besides, so with her are gone the greatest part of my affections to the country, and all that is left of them shall be thankfully and religiously paid to her excellent memory and lasting goodness. That cause then which hath given so much entertainment to the Court all this while is like forthwith to fall before the King in judgment; and thereupon I have been an humble Suitor I may come speedily over, to be present and assisting in the defense of the Proceedings, and acts of this state therein, which trust will be granted mee before you receive these: so shall I have the high contentment also to minister, the best of my endeavours at least, to the preservation of the innocent children of that gentile Person who, to have procured the whole world, could not have moved a dishonourable or unrighteous thing to me, no tho' she had known aforehand that I would have yielded thereunto.

Shortly after the King's order of February already referred to, Sir John Gifford, finding it impossible to get counsel to appear for him against so powerful an individual as the Lord Chancellor, presented a petition to the Lord Deputy, dated February 27th, 163$\frac{4}{5}$, praying that Mr. Sergeant Catlyne, Mr. Solicitor General, Mr. Plunckett, and Mr. Sambach might be required to act for him; and this petition was acceded to by Strafford.

I think it is probable that Sir Robert was of weak intellect, or else in very weak health, although the evidence for this statement is rather negative than positive, and it is only by putting together all the little indications that we have of his character, none of them convincing in themselves, that I come to this conclusion. In the first place, although in those days a newly married couple often lived for the first year or so with the parents of one or other of them, it was, to say the least, unusual for a man, together with his wife and children, to live for thirteen or fourteen years in the same house with his father and mother. Then, again, the Chancellor said that Robert never gave him any cause for 'disaffection,' 'having ever demeaned himselfe dutifull unto his parents, except in one particular wherein he was mislead by others,' which seems to amount to a suggestion that he was somewhat weak-minded.

Sir Edward, speaking of his brother, said that he had 'only one son, who was from his birth a very weak and infirm child, and not like to live long, and one daughter, & that he was not likely to have any other children.' As Sir Robert and his wife were then quite young people, this seems to be a very bold assertion to have made, except upon the supposition that there was something wrong with him. Again, it is difficult, except on the hypothesis of some mental weakness on the part of Robert, to account for Lord Loftus's strong preference for settling the estates on Edward, his second son, to the exclusion of his eldest son Robert, who, he himself says, did not give him cause for 'disaffection.'

But the point I rely upon chiefly is, that Robert appears to have taken no steps himself to assert his rights, but allowed his wife's half-brother, Sir John Gifford, to initiate and carry on the litigation on his behalf. It was said that Sir John Gifford exhibited his petition to the Lord Deputy and Council 'with the previty of the said Sir Robert Loftus who gave a stipend to a sollicitor to sollicite in that cause'; but Sir Edward in his petition of 1678 suggested that Sir John preferred his petition 'without the consent and contrary to the good liking of Sir Robert.' Whichever of these statements is true, it is clear that Robert took no active part in the matter, and what is certainly remarkable is that he does not appear to have given any evidence in support of his claim.

The marriage between Sir Robert and Eleanor was proved, not by the production of the marriage certificate, or by the evidence of the chief parties themselves, but by replies to interrogatories administered to two of their old friends, only one of whom was present at the marriage.

Upon hearing the petition the Lord Deputy and his Council found for the petitioner, which, being so prejudiced in Eleanor's favour, Strafford would no doubt have done had her case been as weak as in fact it was strong; and it was decreed on February 1st, 163⅔, that the Chancellor should settle the house of Monesterevan, and so much of the lands as were worth 1,250*l.* a year, 'to the use of the said Lord Chancellor for life, and after his death, to the use of the said Sir Robert, and the heirs of his body begotten on the body of the said Dame Elynor,' free from all incumbrances, except the right of the Chancellor's wife, Lady Sarah,[1] to her 'thirds,' and 'the joyncture of the said Lady Elynor, and the said annuitie of 200*l.* a yeare to Sir Edward Loftus during his life.' It was also decreed that the Lord Chancellor should pay to Robert the arrears of his promised allowance of 200*l.* a year with interest at the rate of 10*l.* per cent. per annum, subject to some question of account between father and son as to allowances made already to the latter, and that Robert was to retain possession of the lands and house of Drumnoe worth 200*l.* a year, and that a sum of 2,000*l.* lately paid by the Chancellor towards Sir Robert's debts was not to be set off against the arrears of the promised 200*l.* a year, 'as that somme was payed upon other subsequent causes and consideracions which had noe privitie with the covenants betwixt his Lordship and Sir Francis Ruisshe.'

Lord Loftus refused to obey this decree, and was, in the month of April following, committed to prison in Dublin Castle for contempt and not paying the costs of this petition, and there he remained for sixteen months, and in June 1639 his whole revenue was sequestrated by order of Strafford and his Council. It is impossible not to admire the courage with which Lord Loftus held out against the pressure brought to bear upon him by the Irish Government, supported by the King himself. The Chancellor was at this time about seventy years of age, a period of life when few men would display such tenacity of purpose. His confinement in the Castle, where 'the prison was very close and pestered with many prisoners,'

[1] Sarah, widow of R. Meredyth, Dean of St. Patrick, and afterwards Bishop of Leighlin; he died 1597, and she in 1650.

was so rigorous that, after a letter dated March 1638/9 from the King to the Lord Deputy and Council, ordering that the Lord Chancellor be kept a 'close prisoner,' neither his wife, children, nor servants were allowed to remain in the prison with him. On March 21st he petitioned the Government in vain, saying

your petitioner being committed close prisoner & thereby deprived of the comfort of wife, children, and servants, whereby to preserve his health & life, most humbly beseeched your honours to be graciously pleased to afford him the comfort of so ancient & dear a companion as being man & wife these forty years.

Nor was a petition more successful which he presented shortly before Easter, in which he said, 'there is a holy time approaching wherein the Acts of piety ever practised, that your Lordships will be so far pleased to release the strictness of this restraint as that my chaplains may perform their duty unto me in that behalf.' The Lord Deputy and Council replied, 'the petitioner's contempts have justly drawn upon him that condition in which he now stands, and do render him incapable of the favour he desires.' Sarah Lady Ely also petitioned that, as her husband had been forty-six weeks a prisoner in Dublin Castle, she 'may have the liberty of one of the next convenient rooms, where she may be near to give directions upon such fit of weakness as he is very often troubled withal, and for the provision of that small sustenance whereby nature is preserved.'

The Chancellor was very anxious to go to England in order to appeal to the King, and on June 19th, 1638, the Lord Deputy and Council sent to Mr. Secretary Coke a letter pointing out that, before the Chancellor is allowed to do so, he ought to be compelled to obey the orders of the Board, as well for the sake of justice to the petitioner, 'as least otherwise this Cause might Chance to trench in Consequence very much upon the uniuersall peace of these Affaires, and due Settlement of the Regall power ouer this stirring and unruly people.' The following passages from this letter are the most important ones:—

His Lo^p before all carryed himself personally towards ye Lord Deputy in such a manner as we ye Councell were very much scandalized thereat . . . His Lo^p questioned, and charged at ye Boord, wth greevous and foule misdemeano^{rs}, coming to answer in his priuate and naturall capacity only, is required to Kneel; wth Austerness enough Replye, hee will dye first. In this particular wee humbly offer whither this Appeale, as hee terms it, ought to be admitted, or hee much rather commanded to submit for soe much, and confesse his Errour, and seeke his pardon from this boord, where ye Affront was soe rudely given and pursued. Where wee can not Choose but obserue how Cautiously his Lo^p indeauours to sett ye ground of his Contempt, and Consequently his Committall, upon the not deliuery of the Seale wthout special warrant. Where in truth it was his Lo^{ps} not kneeleing appearing at ye Boord Chardged Criminally, and there Commanded to offer his defence in his priuate Capacity.

In the end the Chancellor was permitted to go to England upon the terms that he, his wife, and his son Edward, should levy fines of his several manors in Ireland to trustees, who were to hold the same to the uses declared in the above-mentioned decree, subject to a proviso for alteration thereof if his Majesty should think well to alter the same. In November 1639 the matter came before the King in Council, and after hearing the Lord Chancellor and his son Sir Edward, the appeal was adjudged to be without cause, and the decree was affirmed.

I have said that Sir Robert died in 1640, leaving two children, Henry and Anne. Henry died in less than a month after his father, whereupon Anne became sole heiress to her father. The Lord Chancellor was not slow to take advantage of his orphan granddaughter's tender age, and consequent inability to protect her own interests; this and the general sense of uncertainty and instability which then prevailed throughout the country, owing to the fact that the disturbances which ultimately culminated in the rebellion, and execution of the King, had already made some considerable head, encouraged him to make an application to the House of Commons complaining of the decree. That House sent a paper to the House of Lords entitled 'Declaration and desire of the Commons in Parliament concerning an illegal decree against the

Lord Loftus'; and in May 1642 the House of Lords ordered that the decree be reversed, and that all conveyances made pursuant thereto be made void, and all moneys received by virtue of the sequestration be paid over to the Chancellor; but that such lands as had been bought by him for the sum of 2,000*l.* descendible to his heirs general, should descend and come to Anne Loftus, daughter and heir of his son Sir Robert, and his own grandchild and heir general, and that if the Chancellor had bought no such land for her, then 2,000*l.* of the moneys to be restored to him by virtue of this order should be deposited in the hands of Sir George Wentworth for her benefit, when she should marry or attain the age of twenty-one years. The surviving trustees of those to whom the Lord Chancellor, in obedience to the order of the Lord Deputy and Council of Ireland, had conveyed his estates, reconveyed these estates to him in pursuance of the above order of the Lords; but he did not live long to enjoy his triumph. He died at Middleham, co. York, about 1646,[1] and was succeeded by his son Edward.

Anne Loftus presented a petition against the order of the Lords, the chief ground of which was that it had been made after her parents' death while she was under age, and was not represented by any guardian; and her petition was referred to a committee of the Parliament. The reason that neither Lady Jephson, Anne's grandmother and guardian, nor her uncle, Sir John Gifford, appeared before the House of Lords to support her case is set out in the following communication from the Lords Justices and Council of Ireland:—

1642, May 11. Dublin Castle.—Not long after the breaking out of this hideous and cruel rebellion in this kingdom the Lady Jepson and her son Sir John Giffard, knight, were constrained to betake themselves to their house or castle of Castle Jordan in the county of Meath, about thirty miles from this city. Standing upon their guard and necessary defence against the rage and fury of the bloody rebels, and having been dispoiled by the rebels of all their estates, which they could not keep within their gates, and their English tenants being robbed

[1] The C. P.

of all their substance, they were forced for preservation of the persons of these poor English (their tenants) to take them home to them, and have all this time (out of the little left to themselves) preserved them alive, and relieved them to their great and insupportable charge. And they with those English have been this long time so beleagered by the rebels, as they have been and still continue in great danger, yet sometimes Sir John Giffard took opportunities to sally out with some parties of men, and slew and wounded at several times divers of the rebels, and with much difficulty and danger (notwithstanding many threatening messages and menaces from the rebels) hath hitherto preserved against them that place and those English there with him, who had been otherwise ere this time destroyed by the rebels. And the ways and passages between that place and this have been these five months past, and still are, so blocked up by the rebels (who swarm in great multitudes in all the passages) as there is yet no possibility for the Lady Jepson or her son Sir John Giffard to come hither, without the strength of an army to guard them, or if Sir John should depart thence it might beget very great prejudice to the public service in that part of the country, and give too, too much advantage to the rebels towards destruction of that place and all the English there. All which particulars at the humble suit of Sir George Wentworth, knight, son-in-law to the said Lady Jepson, we do hereby certify to your Lordship, to the end you may be pleased to take an opportunity to make the same known to that most honourable House.

    Signed : WILLIAM PARSONS, JOHN BORLASE, ORMOND OSSORY, CH. LAMBERT, AD. LOFTUS, ROSCOMMON, RO. DIGBYE, J. TEMPLE, FR. WILLOUGHBY, JA. WARE, GEO. WENTWORTH.[1]

Anne's petition at such a period of civil strife had but a poor chance of being considered upon its merits, as her uncle, by his action on behalf of Cromwell, was then in high favour with the rebels. In May 1648 Edward Lord Loftus fortified and held Middleham Castle at considerable expense, and, as a result, had to go to prison for debt. Lambert, the Parliamentary general, reported that Lord Loftus had served well, and must have

[1] *Hist. Com. in V.* C. iii. p. 213.

expended on the defence the 500*l*., which he claimed to have done.[1]

Somewhat later, after Anne had married Richard Barrett, they presented a joint petition 'to the right honoᵇˡᵉ Comᵗᵉᵉˢ of Parliamᵗ for tryall of Peticōns' that they might be discharged of attending any longer some other Committee of Parliament, appointed in August 1652 to consider a petition by the then Lord Loftus, and that they might 'be left to attend ye Judgm̄t of parliam̄ᵗ upon the said Report.'

Richard and Anne appear to have become resigned to not inheriting any estates from the late Chancellor; so much so that we have a draft agreement, dated May 12th, 1656, whereby Richard and his wife agreed with Edward Lord Loftus to give up all their claims against him in Kildare, King's and Queen's Counties, in consideration of being paid by him the sum of 1,000*l*. This draft agreement is signed by Chaloner Chute (Richard's step-father) with this reservation: 'I doe approve of the deed in the form thereof, but the agreement I leave to the p̄rties themselves.' I have not been able to discover why these negotiations for a compromise were broken off; it is more than likely Lord Loftus could not pay the money; anyway the 'p̄rties themselves' do not appear to have signed the document.

About August 1662 Dacre Barrett presented a petition in Ireland setting forth that Lord Loftus had, by disingenuously concealing material facts, obtained letters from the King dated July of that year for passing a bill to vacate the decrees of 1637 and 1639 in his family's favour, and praying for an Act to confirm those decrees.[2] And a letter, dated May 1663, from a P. Brian shows that underhand influences were being exerted against Dacre, and in favour of Lord Loftus, whose 'business' the writer says 'is very just.'[3]

In 1666 Richard Barrett put on record a claim to these estates on behalf of his son Dacre; and in 1668 Dacre, still a minor, proceeded, by his grandmother, Dorothy Lady Dacre,

---

[1] *S. P. I.* 1647–60, p. 577. [2] *Ibid.* 1660–2, p. 692.
[3] *Ibid.* 1663–5, p. 75.

by bill in the Irish Court of Chancery, to have the settlement decreed by Strafford and his board carried out, but on hearing the cause the court made no order. Nothing daunted, four years later, in 1672, Dacre presented a petition to the House of Lords in England to have the order of 1642 reversed, but before hearing this petition Parliament was prorogued.

In 1673 Dacre petitioned the King, who, by a letter, dated March 16th of that year, ordered Arthur Earl of Essex, Viceroy of Ireland, to report upon the whole case. The report, which is a very full account of all this litigation, was dated August 1674 ; but Dacre was not satisfied with the report, and preferred to the Viceroy a petition of exceptions to certain of the findings which it contained. The Earl of Essex, however, refused to alter the report, which is thus endorsed :—

My Lord Lieutenant made not any order upon this but had his secretary acquaint him [Barrett] that he had consulted the Judges therein, but did not think fit to give himself, or his Lordship further trouble therein, nor alter the same, and would stand by the report as the same was signed, and since wee have heard noe more of it.

The case was gone into again by the House of Lords in 1678, when Dacre petitioned for a reversal of the decree of 1642 ; but in spite of the fact that this decree was made when the rebellion had already begun, the Lords affirmed it, and dismissed the petition. ' Youth lives on hope,' and Dacre being young, and feeling confidence in his cause, did not entirely despair of obtaining justice until, in the Irish Courts, he had made one last unsuccessful effort to obtain possession of those lands which the first Lord Loftus had undertaken to settle on Robert Loftus and his descendants.

The following letters to Edward Lord Loftus[1] show what strange ideas as to justice prevailed in those days. The writer evidently considered it a matter of course that personal influence and friendship with the jury, or perhaps even with the judge, and not mere justice, should decide the case. This letter and another, written a few months later by the same person, are the

[1] *Hist. Com.* ix. App. part ii. p. 329.

BARRETT v. LOFTUS

last record we have of the lawsuit which had gone on at intervals from time to time since 1637 till 1680 :—

London, 4 March [16]79-[80].

Sir,—I have yours of the 21th of February, and am sorry that Mr. Barrett gives my deare Lord so much trouble in a business decided long since, and lately confirmed by the highest judicature in England. I do not understand after that how an ordinary judicature in Ireland can or dare meddle in itt. However, itt is fitt to provide for the worst. I send you one for Sir John Bellew, and do write that [*sic*] another to him. I send you another for a brother-in-law of mine. He will be mett with by any att Clunihane, where hee is well knowne. I send you another for Mr. Coghlan, the lawyer, who may be very usefull. He is my relacion, a King's County man, and related to some of the jury, and well acquainted with others of them. I write to him by this poste about this business, and in answear to a letter I receaved from him by the last packett. He writt to me that he was goeing on the Connaught circuitt, and that he would be at Molingar assise the 18th of this monthe. You have severall good men on the pannell. Mr. Forth is one, and he is my relacion. His sister, Madam Stepworth, is here. I hope to gett her to write to him. Captain Baldwin is my tenant, and his daughter is here, who will write to him and to her brother, being both on the pannell. Sir William Pettie is here. If one man of the jury stand out against the rest (as I hope some will) itt will do well. I hope Mr. Coghlan is not feed against you. If he be not, he will get his two kinsmen of the Coghlans, and mine, to appeare. However, I mind my brother Atkinson being in their neighbourhood to goe to both. If I can think of any other thing for your advantage, I shall studie it and write to one friend or other next post. I acquainted my Lord Privy Seale with this proceeding. I am sorry you did not send me the names of the Judges who go on that circuitt of Leinster. I wish my deare Lord and Lady health and happiness, and the rest of your relacions att Monasterevin, and do assure you that none is more att your service than

Your most affectionate and most humble servant,

GARETT MOORE.[1]

[Addressed] For the Lord Viscount Loftus, or Francis Loftus Esq.

[1] Doubtless a member of that family of Moore of which Henry, third Earl of Drogheda, was then the head. The name of the first Viscount Drogheda was Garrett. The families of Moore and Loftus twice intermarried.

London, 18 May, 1680.

My Lord,—Your Lordship's last letter brought me the ill tydeings of my Lord your noble father's death, which was truely unwellcome to me; but this is a tributt we must all one time or other pay to nature. His Lordship hath lived to a good age, and carryed the reputation of a worthy, just, and good man, to his grave; which is noe small comfort to your Lordship Had itt been in my weak power to serve him in his lifetime, I am certain he believed I would have done itt; and my Lord, I give your Lordship the same assurance in behalf of me and mine, and shall to the utmost of my weak endeavours performe itt to my dyeing day. I see Mr. Barrett would loose no time in his prosecution; butt I hope and doubt he will fall shortt of his expectation. I intend, God willing, to be in Dublin next tearm, and shall be as ready to serve your Lordship as any man, and with much realitie.

I suppose that you have the opinions of learned counsell here employed by your father, which may fortifie your counsell there, and if you had Sir William Jones, Serjant Pemberton, and one or two more of the best counsell here, their opinions under their hands uppon the printed state of the case, it would be a great leading both to the judge and your lawyers there. I doe not doubt your Lordship takes care to procure an honest, indifferent jury, which is a maine matter; and if the tryall goe by a jury of the King's Countie, itt will be hard if wee have not good friends amongst them. I think Judge Jones[1] is an honest man. . . . Thus, wishing your Lordship may live as long as my Lord your father hath don, and with as much honour and reputacion, I kiss your Lordship's hands, and subscribe with the satisfaction that you will owne me to be, my Lord, your lordship's most affectionate and most humble servant,

GARETT MOORE.

[Addressed] For the Right Honourable the Lord Viscount Loftus, Dublin.[2]

In the year 1680 Dacre, having made the acquaintance of the widow of Arthur, second Earl of Donegall, and having ascertained what fortune her eldest daughter, Lady Jane Chichester, would have, determined to become a suitor for the hand of the latter. He induced some mutual friend to sound the Countess on

---

[1] Oliver Jones, Justice of the King's Bench in Ireland, 1672-82.
[2] Arthur Loftus, third Viscount.

this subject, and learned from him that Lady Donegall had said she would prefer Dacre as a son-in-law to anyone in the kingdom, on account of his not being guilty of many vices then most common. What vices she referred to we are not told precisely, but Richard speaks of his brother's 'sobernesse & temparate-nesse' being the great attraction to the Countess. Gambling with cards and dice was much in vogue during the period immediately succeeding the Restoration; and from this vice Dacre seems to have been entirely free. In his account book the entries which refer to losses at play are extremely uncommon, not half a dozen in as many years, and then they only chronicle the loss of nominal sums, such as 'to my Cosen Chute lost 1^s'; 'To Maior Batement at play 6^d'; the largest sum that I have discovered he lost at any one time was 8s. 6d.[1]

Dacre ascertained that Lady Donegall was so favourable to the match that she was prepared to give her daughter 1,000l., in addition to the sum of 3,000l. to which she was entitled under her father's will upon her marriage; and at the time Lady Donegal made this offer she was aware that Sir Hercules Langford[2] was anxious that his son should marry Lady Jane, with only the 3,000l. settled on her by the late Earl's will as her portion and 1,500l. a year after his own death.

The Countess, besides offering to give this additional dowry of 1,000l. if Dacre married her daughter, also proposed that the young couple should live for two years 'in ye house wth her where they shall be at noe cost for neither meat, drink, nor Lodging &c.'

Dacre wrote long letters about this proposed alliance to his father and to a Mr. Bateman, who appears to have been one of his father's intimate friends. He reminds his father that he had ordered him to look out for some suitable match; and he says that in Lady Jane he has found a person 'endowed with all

---

[1] Possibly losing 44 livres to his cousin was a lesson which he laid to heart.—*Ante*, p. 423.

[2] First baronet; of Kilmackevett, co. Antrim; creation 1667.—The *C. P.*

those qualities which I have ever wisht to meet with in a wife when it should be my chance to have one.' He mentions how well she has been brought up, and lays considerable stress on the advantage such an alliance would be to him, as well on account of her fortune as of her social position.

To Mr. Bateman he writes in the same strain, urging him to use his influence with his father to obtain his consent to the marriage, for he says, 'I know how great the esteem my father has of your reason is, and the deference he has to it,' and he also writes to his sister Anne a short letter to the same effect. She replies in most affectionate terms, saying that he 'deserves all the good Fortune the world can afford,' and giving her love and service to Lady Jane.

There is a sentence in this letter of Anne's that shows Dacre had not then given up all hopes of being successful in the great lawsuit, as she says, 'I am nott so unreasonable as to spinn my Letter to a greater Length, knowing you can have no idle time that are at once to Solicite a Suite in Law, and one in Love, pardon me ye naming the most generous Passion last.'

Richard, Dacre's brother, also writes both to his father and to Anne upon this subject, urging the former to agree to the marriage, and to the latter begging her to use all her influence with their father to induce him to do so. I think that Lady Jane was probably a somewhat plain child (she was only sixteen years old), as Richard, though he says much in favour of her fortune, birth, and education, is not so enthusiastic about her appearance. To his father he says :—

All I can say of her is that her humour is more to be admired than her beauty wch though it be not extraordinary, yet is Sufficient for any Modest vertuous wife wth whom my Brother may live as happy as ever married pair did, if her fortune be as well liked by you, as her person & genius is, by all that know her.

Richard's letter to his sister is written at much greater

those qualities w'ich I have ever wisht to meet with in a wife when it should be my chance to have one.' He mentions how well she has been brought up, and lays considerable stress on the advantage such an alliance would be to him, as well on account of her fortune as of her social position.

To Mr. Bateman he writes in the same strain, urging him to use his influence with his father to obtain his consent to the marriage, for he says, 'I know how great the esteem my father has of your son is, and the deference he has to it,' and he also writes to his sister Anne a short letter to the same effect. She replies in most affectionate terms, saying that he 'deserves all the good fortune the world can afford,' and giving her love and service to Lady Jane.

There is a sentence in this letter of Anne's that shows Dacre had not then given up all hopes of being successful in the great lawsuit, as she says, 'I am nott so unreasonable as to spinn my Letter to a greater Length, knowing you can have no idle time that are at once to Solicite a Suite in Law, and one in Love, pardon me ye naming the last generous Passion last.'

Richard, Dacre's brother, also writes both to his father and to Ann upon this subject, urging the former to agree to the marriage, and to the latter begging her to use all her influence with their father to induce him to do so. I think that Lady Jane was probably a somewhat plain child (she was only sixteen years old), as Richard, though he say much in favour of her fortune, birth, and education, is not so enthusiastic about her appearance. To his father he says:—

'All I can say of her is that her humour is more to be admired than her beauty wch though be not extraordinary, yet is Sufficient for any Modest virtuous wife wth whom my Brother may live as happy as ever married pair did, if her fortune be as well liked by you, as person & genius is, by all that know her.

Richard's letter to his sister written at much greater

LADY JANE CHICHESTER

length. His description of Lady Jane's appearance is as follows :—

As to her person I can only say this, that as Shee is not in beauty ye most exquisite of her Sex, so shee is not any wayes defective, her stature though one cannot Ghesse [1] well what it may be by what appears now, shee not being above Sixteen years of age, promises to be a good mean, though rather inclining to be tall than low, her body well shaped, her face ovall, her haire dark brown, her Complexion clear and healthy, and through all her features appears an extraordinary sweetnesse and goodnesse.

To this Anne replies with a most cordial letter, in which she says that in twenty-four hours their father was quite reconciled to the idea, 'and tells every one he's going to be a grandfather.' She says he seems to be particularly pleased with the proposition of the Countess to keep the bride and bridegroom with her for two years, which he declares will be worth a thousand pounds to Dacre, and he promises to hand over to him the Clones estates immediately upon his marriage, and to entail Horsford and Belhus upon him and his heirs. Anne then goes on to chaff Richard, saying, 'you who are quickened with ye sight of the Faire, and are I find att least half a lover.'

The marriage took place in July 1680, and marriage articles, dated the 28th of the previous June, were drawn up between Richard Barrett and his son Dacre of the one part, and the Dowager Countess of Donegall, Lady Jane, Richard Earl of Ranelagh,[2] Viscount Massarene,[3] and Sir John Cole[4] of the other part, by which it was agreed that the Clones estate, which was then valued at about 900*l.* a year, should be settled on Dacre and his wife for their present maintenance, and for her jointure, and afterwards to their male issue in tail; that

---

[1] Early form of 'guess,' used by Spencer.
[2] Richard Jones, third Viscount, first Earl of Ranelagh.—The *C. P.*
[3] John Skeffington, Second Viscount.
[4] Sir J. Cole, first Baronet, was connected with the bride, his wife being a daughter of the Hon. John Chichester; he was ancestor to the present Earl of Enniskillen. The two last-mentioned parties to this deed were all connected with Ireland.

Richard was to retain Belhus and Horsford without impeachment of waste for his life, but after his decease they were also to go to Dacre and his heirs in tail male. It was also agreed, in consideration of all the lands Richard was settling on Dacre, that the latter should by deed relinquish to his father his reversionary interests in his mother's property of Dunsink and Scribblestown, so that Richard might be free to deal with them as he chose.

On Lady Jane's part it was agreed that 3,000*l.* of her marriage portion should be paid to Richard Barrett at once, and that he was to be given good security for the payment of the remaining 1,000*l.* This dowry of Lady Jane's was to provide portions for Dacre's two sisters, and in consideration of this sum they were to release the Horsford estate from charges to that amount which had been laid upon it in their favour.

It is not easy to determine the exact dates of the respective births of the children Lady Jane bore to Dacre, nor, indeed, how many children she did have. The printed pedigree gives as their issue one son, Richard, and three daughters, Jane, Dorothy, and Henrietta; so, no doubt, no more lived to grow up.

I have found a pedigree with the following pencil note, 'now living 1754,' after several of the names, and as this was made by, or for, Thomas Lord Dacre, it ought to be correct as far as it goes; but, unfortunately, it gives dates of neither marriages nor births. As far as it refers to Dacre's children by Lady Jane, it is as follows:—

| Henrietta *s.p.* | Dorothy wife of Hugh Smith now living 1754. | Jane married Anno 1730 to Mr. Ranby now 70 years of age 1754. | Richard died in lifetime of his father 1716. |

On page 221 of Lord Dacre's History there is an entry written in a handwriting different from that in which the whole MS. volume is written, and (from the fact that it records Lord Dacre's own burial) obviously written in after his decease,

LADY JANE'S CHILDREN

which purports to give a list of those members of the family who were buried in a vault in Aveley Church. Amongst the entries in this list there are the following :—

Mrs. Henrietta Barrett died March 29th, 1725, in ye 26th year of her age.

Richd Barrett Lennard Esqr died Dec. 24th, 1716, aged 26 years.

These entries are obviously not accurate as regards the ages they assign to Henrietta and to Richard respectively, for, as we shall see, their mother, Lady Jane, died as early as 1689, and these mistakes have given me an infinity of trouble. When writing an account of a family it is of the first importance to ascertain, if possible, the dates of the marriages, births, and deaths of its various members; if there are any doubts as to these dates those doubts should be stated, and no mere guess be put down as if it were an undoubted fact. For a long time I had discovered no evidence to cause me to suspect these entries were not correct, and therefore I supposed that Lady Jane must have died several years after the date at which she did in fact die. Unfortunately, the Aveley Register for the years between 1646 and 1718 is lost, and therefore the most valuable source of evidence is not available.

Some of the witnesses in the lawsuit Dacre had with his sisters concerning Dunsink and Scribblestown speak of Dacre bringing with him five children to Belhus, when he went to live there with his father. Dacre himself says, in the pleadings to that case, that he took two sons and one daughter with him to Belhus, and that two girls were born there. We know that the son who lived to grow up was named Richard, and that he was the eldest of the two sons mentioned by Dacre as being taken by him to Belhus. He was probably born in 1682, about the end of September or beginning of October.[1]

The previously quoted letter to Dacre from his brother Richard alludes to Lady Jane being enceinte in July 1681, and

[1] I am unable to obtain any evidence from the Public Office in Dublin as to the date of his birth.

the result of her then condition was possibly a child still-born, or one who only lived a very short time. In May 1682, in another letter, he alludes to Lady Jane being again in the same state; and in June of that year he says, 'I expect every day to hear of her having made me an Uncle.'[1] This expression he could not have used if they had had a child born in 1681, and still living when this letter was written. The Irish agent, Fletcher, writes to Dacre 'the 16th, 1682,' saying, 'now Sir I wish you joy of y^r new son & y^r lady a good recovery.' This letter was probably written on October 16th, although no month is mentioned, as on October 20th, 1682, Fletcher writes the letter already quoted[2] about a wet nurse; and, moreover, we have a letter to Dacre from Lady Longford, dated 'October ye 8th,' in which she says, 'I am glad to here my Lady is so well after her delivery.' It is true that of these letters one does not mention the month nor another the year in which they were respectively written, but I think there can be little doubt they were all three written in October 1682. As Fletcher's first letter speaks of a 'new son,' it would seem that one had been born in the previous year, and this can only be reconciled with the passage, 'Make me an Uncle,' which occurs in Richard's letter, by the supposition already suggested that that child did not live long, if, indeed, it were not still-born.

The second of the sons whom Dacre mentions that he took with him to Belhus when he went there in 1687 was named Edward. We have only indirect references to him; he was born at Liverpool in 1687,[3] and probably died when quite young.

Dacre's account book of household expenses from 1683 to 1690 shows that he had children born during the years 1684 and 1685. The entries which refer to this are:—

1684 Dec.	fruit when my wife lay in	.	0	6	0
1685 Oct. 10.	Mrs Taylor ye Midwife	.	5	15	0
—	for christening ye child	.	0	3	0
— Oct. 21.	To ye Wet Nurse	.	1	3	0

[1] P. *Ante*, p. 433.   [2] *Ante*, p. 412.
[3] *Post*, p. 474.

At this period he was living at Smithfield, Dublin, in the parish of St. Michans. I have had the register of that parish searched for references to these children, but the only one to be found is as follows: 'June 1684, Jane, daughter of — Barrett Esqre and Jane his wife.' I have not been able to find any mention of the death of the second child, nor any entry for funeral expenses; but, having regard to the number of children which we have seen Dacre says he took with him to Belhus, I have no doubt but that it died an infant. Dacre and Lady Jane had also a daughter named Dorothy, who, we shall see, married Mr. Hugh Smith. The monument erected to her memory states that she died on February 1st, 1755, in the seventy-third year of her age. The age there assigned to her is obviously not correct, as, if so, she must have been born in 1682. Mr. Walter Rye tells me that he has not infrequently discovered errors of this class. I believe she was born in 1688. The only reference I can find to her, which possibly throws some light upon the date of her birth, is this entry in Dacre's accounts: 'Nov. 10th 1688, to Dolls nurse, 10 weeks £2.' I think she was probably born in June or end of May in that year. In the account book we find 'June 2^d for a cradle 6..0; for a swathe 2..0.'

Speaking of the time of James I. Miss Strickland says:—

At this period a child as soon as it was born was swathed or swaddled in a number of rollers, their arms were bound down to their sides and their legs straight and close together after the exact pattern of an Egyptian mummy ... this frightful custom prevailed in England at the beginning of the last century.[1]

Lady Jane's youngest daughter, Henrietta, was born in the autumn of 1689, as we find in the account book 'Sept. 16 to Mrs Clark ye Midwife 1..1..6'; and I am disposed to think from a statement of Dacre's[2] that the birth of this child was the predisposing cause of Lady Jane's death.

I think for the reasons above stated that we may assign the

---

[1] *Strick.* vii. p. 313.   [2] *Post*, p. 501.

following respective dates to the births of those children of Dacre who survived infancy :—

Richard, September or October 1682.
Jane, June 1684.
Dorothy, September (?) 1688.
Henrietta, September (?) 1689.

We have some evidence that the young Richard was a good-looking but delicate child. His grandmother, the Countess of Donegall, writes on 'ye 20 June 83': 'Pray let them haue a greatt care of Dicky.' And his aunt Lady Mary says on 'May ye 15, 86, pray remember me to my brother Barret & to prety dicky.' In a letter dated 'ye 2 of No^{br},' and which has on the back an ancient endorsement '1685,' the Countess begins thus: 'Becaues Dere Mr Barret y^r wife has taken phisik, and not well able to Rite, I giue y^u this trobole to let y^u know all y^{rs} are well, and pritty Dicky very good Company.'

Lady Jane in her letters to Dacre makes the following references to her son: 'I would not carry Dicky with me to knockbelymore[1] for feare he should get sum mischef with mrs fosters rude boy'; which looks as if he were not over-strong; and so does this passage in another, where she says that his sister, more than a year younger than himself, 'runs almost as strongly' as he did. He seems at some period to have had a bad arm, for she writes: 'Pray remember to bring sum of ye grene sercloth[2] for Dicky's arm.'

I think it is most probable that, in pursuance of the marriage agreement, Dacre and his bride immediately after the wedding went to live with Lady Donegall in her house in Aungier Street, Dublin.[3] It is not in the nature of things that

[1] Miss Elizabeth Moore, of Knockballymore, was eventually Lady Jane's successor, as we shall see Dacre married her after his first wife's death.

[2] Cerecloth; perhaps this was in August 1685, on the 15th of which month Dacre enters among his payments: 'For Physick for Dick, 2s. 7d.'

[3] Aungier Street, once one of the most fashionable streets of Dublin, has, since Lady Donegal's days, greatly come down in the world, and now many of its houses, then the abode of the best society, have fallen so low as to have become ruinous tenement dwellings. The same transformation in the character of localities is often

a man should live for any long period in the house of his mother-in-law without friction arising between them, as the mother naturally likes to continue to regulate her household according to her own ideas, and it is equally natural that a man when married should wish to be the head of his own establishment. I have no means of knowing how long Dacre and Lady Jane did live with the Countess, but probably not for a whole year. In a letter to Dacre, dated July 12th, 1681, his brother Richard says:—

Nothing can be so satisfactory to me amidst my griefs as to heare from you that your fortune is more favourable to you in your concerns on that side, for indeed I am not more sensible of my own adversity, than I am that there should be any differences continue betwixt you and your Mother in law my lā Don.

And he makes another reference to this subject in a previous letter dated about a month earlier.

There was a very considerable delay in paying Lady Jane's portion, owing, it was said, to the difficulty in settling the late Earl's debts, which it was necessary to do before his trustees could pay legacies. In the meantime Dacre, in order to get the settlements effected, was obliged to pay his father the promised sum of 3,000*l.*, and to give him good security for the 1,000*l.* left owing. Towards this amount he had only received the sum of 1,000*l.* promised to him by the Countess, and he had to borrow the remaining 2,000*l.* Early in 1682 Dacre and his wife took proceedings in the Court of Chancery in Ireland against the Countess of Donegall, Sir John Cole, Viscount Massarene, and the Earl of Ranelagh, trustees of the will of the late Earl Donegall; and by an order of the court, dated February 5th in that year, the matters in dispute were referred to Mr. Justice Keating, Chief Justice of the Common Pleas in Ireland.

Dacre alleged that as only 1,000*l.* of his wife's portion had been paid, he was obliged himself to borrow 2,000*l.* to pay his

enough to be seen in London; to cite an example, Seven Dials may be mentioned, which at the period we are now considering was among the best and most fashionable quarters of the town.

father, and also had to give him security for the further sum of 1,000*l*.,[1] and he demanded that her portion should be paid, and that she should have a share in a sum of 400*l*. per annum which the late Earl of Donegall had directed should be allowed for the maintenance of his younger children. The Countess objected to Lady Jane being allowed any portion of this 400*l*., saying that, besides giving her daughter a sum of 1,000*l*. as an additional marriage portion, she had given her daughter clothes, linen, and other necessaries for her marriage, of the value of 400*l*., and that she never expected she would claim any more from her. Mr. Justice Keating ordered that from the date that Dacre and his wife ceased to live with the Countess until they presented their petition they should be allowed at the rate of 50*l*. per annum, and from the date of the petition until March 25th, 1685, at the rate of 60*l*. per annum out of the sum of 400*l*. allowed for maintenance of younger children. He also ordered that on March 25th, 1685, 1,000*l*. should be paid to Dacre, and that the remaining sum due of 2,000*l*. with interest should be paid within two years of that date.[2]

It is not easy to say how far this lawsuit was what is called a 'friendly' suit; no doubt there was a certain amount of friction between the parties to it, but the following passages in an undated letter from Lady Jane to her husband shows that Dacre and the Countess were again on good terms: 'All that comforts me is that you are likely to get ye portion, & that my Mother and you agree so well. . . . I hope in god they will pay all my portion which will end all disputes.'

A relation of Lady Donegall's, whom she alludes to as 'my cozen Gorges,' appears in 1683 to have offered to take in Dacre and his family as what we should now call 'paying guests,' for the Countess writes, 'the Rate she setts is 40 shill aweke for 5

---

[1] Dacre paid his father this 1,000*l*. on June 21st, 1685.

[2] Dacre's book of household accounts shows that on July 25th, 1685, he was paid on account of his wife's portion, 1,138*l*. 15*s*. 9*d*.; and on following August 1st, £23 16*s*. 8*d*., being the balance of 60*l*. per annum due March 25th, 1685. On June 24th, 1686, he received 7*l*. 6*s*. 5*d*., which 'Said sum compleats the payment (both principall & interest) of two thousand pounds due the 25th of March, 1685.'

of you, if you kepe y^r Coch Horses there she has ether hay or gras, but noe otes.'

Dacre was admitted to the freedom of the City of Londonderry on September 12th, 1684, and to that of Carrick Fergus on October 20th in the same year,[1] and no doubt he and Lady Jane lived in Ireland until 1687, when, on account of the troubles in that country, they came to Liverpool. Ireland was at that period in a terrible condition, a most bloody war being in progress; Dacre's town of Clones was nearly entirely destroyed, as the war raged greatly in that portion of Ireland, and most of his farms were deserted.

We have no less than twenty-two letters from Lady Jane to Dacre and from him to her, which were probably written between 1680 and 1687, but those of hers are not dated, and they relate almost entirely to the smallest matters of domestic interest, with scarcely any allusion to public affairs. The spelling of Lady Jane's letters is extremely bad even for those days, in spite of what was said before her marriage about her good education. Certainly her correspondence contrasts very unfavourably with that of her sister-in-law, Anne Barrett—indeed, her spelling is so erratic that at times it is difficult to guess what she does mean. Such words as 'sum fisich,' 'ginge,' 'deats,' 'chorch,' 'maluncoly,' 'pediges,' 'aporpus,' 'foling sickness,'[2] and 'hipecret' which, among other original forms, occur in her letters can be easily guessed by their context, but 'enchouos,' 'haue lost my haue stomak & was forst to drae blisters behind my ears,' 'sidebobs glasses,' and 'Miss rider's Capt.' are expressions some of which would probably puzzle most readers to explain.

Lady Jane's letters may indicate a want of education, but they show no lack of affection, and indeed they, like those of Dacre's mother to her husband, are evidently inspired with the warmest and most tender passion. There is a letter to Dacre dated only 'the 22 of feb.' signed 'Eli Cole,' no doubt written in 1681 by the wife of Sir John Cole, which speaks of Lady

---

[1] The certificates of these admissions are among *F. P.*
[2] Falling Sickness, epilepsy.

Jane's great love for her husband. It is obviously a reply to one from Dacre, who had written to her in a fit of depression, and had, perhaps, expressed in it some doubts as to his wife's love for him. She tries to cheer him up, saying, 'I am uery sorry for your cous of malincoly, but I know allsow that you are so apt to indolg your self in it, and I wish I cold preuell with you not to dew it'; and, after expressing a hope that the business which has taken him to London will soon permit him to return to his wife in Ireland, the writer continues :—

for I am shuer you have a wif heere that is mity impasont for it. I did not thinke she had that great fondnis as now your absans maks her shue to a great degre, for after you went nowthing cold sattisfy her, for a weke she was in that sad condison that now body cold spake to hir but she wept, and was in pashen of weping. I found she wold dow hirself hort, and wold not dres hirself, but went in black in the malincole Way that euer I saw, a poere thing she is still, neuer at rest but when she hears from you, and we haue had of latt much delayes of packts for we haue had sens you went all wayes thre or fore to gether, wich maks hir mity impasont, this I only tell you to sattisfy you that I dow belaue you haue a wif that laus you to a great degre.[1]

During the period which immediately followed Dacre's marriage his father became much irritated against him, possibly on account of some delay which arose in paying him Lady Jane's marriage portion in accordance with the terms of the settlement; however, whatever the cause may have been, there is no doubt but that for some time there existed a considerable coolness between the father and son, which was not dispelled until Dacre made his 'submission' to him, which presumably means that he made a very humble apology.

In order to try and arrange matters Dacre went over to England; he probably went in January 1681, as the following letter to his bride appears to have been written after his arrival

[1] The phonetic system of spelling employed by the Chichester family shows, as might be expected, that they spoke with a strong Irish accent. No English person, however erratic in spelling, would write such a word as 'Sure' with an 'h.'

in London. The mention of Lord Conway enables me to fix the year in which it was written :—

My Dear

The expectation of finding a letter here from you, caused me to hasten my iourney, that I might the sooner receive that satisfaction, but I perceive you have not been mindfull of me, nor remember the promises you made me at parting, or which is worse are soe uniust to me as to beleive I cann enioy my self with out some assurance from your self, that you yet think on me ; though I cannot but blame my self for entertaining these fancyes, as not suiting with that excellent goodness I ought to be better acquainted withall, yet such is the continuall disquiet I have been in ever since I parted from you, that I am not wholly able to banish them, if you have still the same thoughts of me that you seem'd to have entertain'd, you will ascribe it to the excess of my love, which has render'd me impatient : & pardon

My Dearest Dear

Your most affectionate   D. B.

there is noe greater news here at present then that my Lord Conway is made Secretary of State, & takes possession of his place on Thursday next.[1]

London. January ye 25.

While in London Dacre lodged 'at Mr Francis Coolyes house in Henrietty Street ouer against ye Cross Keys,' and to that address Lady Jane sent several letters, of which the following will suffice as a specimen. She had evidently not expected that Dacre would have been obliged to remain so long in England as was the case ; but no doubt legal business was at least as slow in those days as it is now, and we shall see he did not succeed in bringing it to a conclusion until the middle of the following April.

I receuid you kind letter my Dearest Deare life, and know not what to say to you in retourn, but I doe asshoure you that you may be confedent that my loue is as great as yours can be thought I cant expres it so well as you. I am much trouble that you haue not received my letters for this is ye forth letter I haue writen to you. I am mightyly over joyed to heare that

[1] Lord Conway was Secretary of State for the North from January 1681 till 1682-3.

you and your father doe agree so well, which puts me in hops of seeing my Dearest soon, when you left you tould me that I should see you within six wicks, and I am sure I think ye time is alredy past; I know noe nuse but that my Lord Cheife Justes bouth is deid this morning.[1]

my unkel chichester gives his humble serus to you, and all the rest of your frinds heare

but my Deare yours most intirly
J. BARRET.

Dublin ye 12 (or 22) [February].

I think there is no doubt but that the following letter to Dacre from Lady Donegall relates to the coolness which we have seen had arisen between the father and son; the former probably delaying to make the promised settlements because Lady Jane's portion had not been paid over to him:—

Dub $\frac{the}{26}$ of March

I have had soe ill helth Mr Barret for this munth past that I haue not bin in acondistcōn to make any Returns to y^u for the fauor of y^r letters. I did hope by the last post to have hard all things was soe well agreed between y^u & y^r father that we might have had y^r Company by this in Ireland, but then found he had maid anew objection which we thought not of before, but Sr John Cole and I, though we knew twas ahasard to us to part with the mony, yet we would Run itt rather then yu should be preiudist, but we found Allderman Desminere soe scrupolus that we had much to doe to get the mony out of his hands. I hope when y^r father perfects his part yu will y^{rs}, and signe anew dede of Joynter to y^r wife, for I know not how far this may binde that is drawn, yu not being then invested in an estate, and though I Question not but yu will be auery good husband, yet tis not fit for me to part with my mony, and leue her to y^r Mercy. I think Mr Slone was much in the rong in persuading y^r father not to Com over, for shure itt might haue bin much to yr advantage, yu being now to settle in the world he would have seen ye necessity of asupply, which he cannot soe well study of att this distance. Y^r wife I thank God is well, but uery impatiant to see yu: I know I nede yuse noe argumtts to

---

[1] Sir Robert Booth, Lord Chief Justice of the King's Bench in Ireland, was buried March 2nd, 1680-1.

yu to hasten to her, yu being I hope well asshured of her affect to yu which is much to the sattisfaction of y^r

humble saruant
J. DONEGALL.

My humble saruis to y^r ffather, and to both y^r sisters, though I haue not the honor to be known to them.

After spending at least three months away from his bride, when he probably at first did not anticipate having to be absent more than as many weeks, Dacre at last, in the words of the poet, was able to say,

> The heavy hours are almost past
> That part my love and me,
> My longing eyes may hope at last
> Their only wish to see,[1]

and had the satisfaction of seeing all the legal formalities complied with and the last of the marriage settlement documents duly signed. The letter he wrote to Lady Jane on the conclusion of this business expresses how relieved he is to be able to return to her again:—

London Aprill 15.

This day having put an end to my tedious buisness[2] has likewise restored me to part of my satisfaction, wch [I can] never think myself truly to en[joy] whilst I am absent from all that I hold dear to me in ye world, you may believe me Dearest that nothing can equall my impatience till I have fully compleated it, which cann onely be in the enjoyment of yourself. I should not need to tell you how soon I mean to hasten to that could you measure your owne by my love, which, in the meantime, hardly permits me to rest

I am My Dear Yours
D. BARRETT.

We know by letters to Dacre from Fletcher, his agent at Clones, that he and Lady Jane were staying in Dublin, 'att Coll Shapcotts neere Smithfield,' in the autumn of 1682. They had no doubt gone to the capital on account of Lady Jane's expected confinement; and two years later they were also

---

[1] George Lord Lyttelton.

[2] The marriage settlements in pursuance of the agreements made on occasion of the marriage were signed, some on 14th and some on 18th April, 1681.

residing in Dublin, when letters were addressed to him 'att his house in Smithfield.'

In a letter dated ' 9^{ber} 21st 1684' Fletcher mentions an early instance of that emigration from Ireland to America which was in later years to assume such large proportions. He says that ' Wm Mills the tenant to halfe of Killigurmy, by the maggott of his wife, is persuaded to sell all his stock and goe for Carolina,[1] which I am sorry for, he was an excellent ten^t.' More than thirty years later Dacre was to hear further complaints of the increasing tide of emigration from Clones, as his then agent writes on December 18th, 1718, ' Yo^r Hon^r never saw how many is goeing for New England out of this countery, there is nea^{re} fforty ffamillys goeing out of this parish of Clownis, and the fforsters[2] all goes.' This agent writes again in the month of March following:—

I have noe newes, but here is a hundred ffamilleyes gone through this towne this weeke past for New England, and all the fforsters as I gave yor Hon^r acc^t; Mr Bellffore of Lisinskey has sett us fifty Tates of land on the Cross of Clownis this day that is all wast, the Tenants being all gone to New England, I believe we shall have nothing left but Irish att last; but I hope yor Hon^{rs} Estate will be safe enough, for they complayne most of the hardshipps of the tythes makes them all goe, which is true, for the Clergyes is unreasonable.

This is, however, anticipating events. In the letter from Fletcher already quoted from he mentions the severity of winter in quaint terms, saying: 'We have had a very severe winter hitherto and I think without a new Creation we shall never in this County see Cock blackbird or thrush.'

On February 21st, 168$\frac{4}{5}$, Fletcher, writing again from Clones, says, 'I hope the death of our good King[3] will make no alteracon we proclaimed James ye second in this town on Thursday last.' And a little later in another letter he says, '. . . there's noe money now stiring in the Country, I have not rec^d one farthing from the ten^{ts} since the King's death, and to drive these

---
[1] The State of Carolina was formed in 1663.
[2] Obsolete form of 'forester.'—C. D.   [3] Charles II. died February 6th, 168$\frac{4}{5}$.

Cath^{cs} is to noe purpose. I am ashamed to tell yor Honnr how much they are in arrear.'

Much of the material for this family history, from the date of Dacre's marriage in 1680 down to that of his father Richard's death in April 1696, I derive from the pleadings in the lawsuits which, immediately upon the decease of the latter, were commenced between Dacre and his sisters, Anne and Dorothy. Dacre's account-book also furnishes information by which several dates can be determined.

Richard, from about the date of Dacre's marriage, was probably becoming more and more dictatorial and tyrannical towards his children; we have seen how harshly he was treating his son Richard, and no doubt his conduct was gradually developing that eccentricity which, later on, encouraged Dacre to endeavour to have him declared incapable of managing his own affairs.

While Dacre and his young family were living in Ireland, looking after his estates at Clones, he alleged that his sister Anne 'made use of that advantage to lessen him in the esteem of his father,' and 'for the better carrying out of this design gott one Richard Owen, formerly a servant in the family, into ye confederacye'; and that Owen did all he could to create a breach between the father and son, by writing to the latter several letters giving a very 'od account' of his father, and that 'he was no better than a brute, with a design to move him [Dacre] to a prejudice to him, and at the same time was lessening Dacre to his father meerly with designe to create a difference between them.' There is evidence that while Dacre was in Ireland Owen was employed by his father in the management of his affairs, though we have no absolute proof that he then cut timber and committed other waste, still less that he was employed by Richard at the instigation of Anne, as Dacre says was the case.

The career of Owen seems to have been a very remarkable one. There was a 'R. Owen,' described as 'of London,' who was admitted student at the Inner Temple in 1675, and called to the Bar there in 1686, and there can be no doubt but that it was the same Owen who came to have so great an influence over Richard. Dacre speaks of him as 'one Richard Owen who is now Rich Owen Esq.'; Richard in his will describes him as 'my faithfull friend and servant Richard Owen of the Inner Temple Esq.,' and in the probate to that will he is described as 'armiger.'

Both the handwriting and the contents of a letter which he wrote to Dacre in $16\frac{78}{80}$ show him to be a man of a superior education, and it is difficult to reconcile this letter, and these descriptions of him, with the following account of his origin as given by Dacre in his pleadings :— [1]

He had beene a menial serv^t to yor or̃s [orator's] father, in Station or degree of his valett de chambre, to shave, and attend him in his chamber, & waite at his table, and goe of errands for him, and for these purposes was entertained by him as his Servt at the wages of 4^{li} per ann.

And Dacre goes on to say that Owen, having served his father in Ireland, was discharged for some misbehaviour. He then came to England, and for a time was employed by 'a Taylor' as a clerk to keep his books and get in his debts, but thinking this post to be 'of too little grandeur' 'he insinuated himself into the acquaintance' of Dorothy Lady Dacre, who took him into her employment as a domestic servant to wait at table and go to market to buy provisions for the family. Owen having persuaded Lady Dacre that he knew something of law matters, she gradually employed him to go errands to her solicitors and persons conducting her affairs. While so engaged in this more or less confidential capacity there were matters of business pending between her and her son Richard (possibly about her occupation of Belhus), and Owen so managed 'to encourage differences' between them that for some time great misunderstandings arose between the mother and son.

When Lady Dacre became involved in her great dispute with her grandson, Chaloner Chute,[2] Owen's misconduct in the

[1] *B. & M. v. B.*   [2] *Ante*, p. 264.

matter was such that, upon it coming to her ears, she discharged him, and he at once took service with her opponent, Mr. Chute, who employed him as his agent in this lawsuit against Lady Dacre. Owen afterwards contrived to again obtain the confidence of Richard, who employed him both to pay and to receive money for him, and to keep his accounts and transact a variety of business matters for him in London and elsewhere, for which he paid him a salary of 20*l.* a year. The pleadings from which I get this information about Owen's career do not mention the dates at which he was in the service of these different employers, but I think it probable that Richard employed him as a sort of agent at some period subsequent to 1675, when Owen entered the Inner Temple—a rise in social position which even now would be most unusual, and which in those days, when education was restricted to so small a number of persons, must have been in the highest degree uncommon. It shows that he must have been a man of very remarkable capacity and industry to have raised himself from the humble position of a domestic servant to that of barrister-at-law, and to become entitled to be described as ' armiger.'

Anne declared that on the very day the fatal accident happened to her brother her father promised that, as Richard the younger was killed, he would leave Dunsink and Scribblestown, which was to have been his portion, to her and to her sister Dorothy. Shortly after the tragic death of his son, Richard did settle these properties on his daughters; but the deed of settlement contained a power of revocation, and as Dacre was then in Ireland, and his sisters living with their father, it is probable that, as Dacre said, Richard was persuaded to do this by Anne. Previous to Dacre's marriage settlement Richard was only tenant for life of his estates, and Dacre said that he was persuaded by his father to convey to him Dunsink and Scribblestown in order that the latter might be able to make some provision for Richard the younger.

I think that the contingency of Richard (the son) dying without issue was probably never contemplated by either his father or his brother, and that, therefore, nothing was done to provide for the future destination of these properties in case of the happening of such an event as did in fact take place. The absence of any such provision was the cause of great family bitterness and quarrels, which might have been avoided had it been agreed, when Dacre conveyed his right in these properties to his father, whether, in the event of his brother's death without issue, the properties in question were to come to him after his father's decease, or to go to his sisters.

The fact that Richard had settled Dunsink and Scribblestown on his daughters was probably not long in reaching Dacre's ears, and he was, no doubt, greatly annoyed at this intelligence; anyway, we find by two letters to him from Anne, one dated November 8th, 1683, and one, though not dated, evidently written about the same time, that he had written to her, as she says: 'of a Style differing much from what I have formerly had of yours. . . . I am Curious in Observing your Expressions, & must own to you yourself I found that Cold.' These letters of hers are most affectionate, and, unless Anne was a thorough hypocrite, show a sincere desire to convince her brother that he has misjudged her, and, to use her own words, that she was 'still ye same you heretofore call'd an Affectionate Sister.'

In 1686, Richard being in arrear with the annuity of 500*l.* charged by Lord Newburgh's will[1] upon Belhus, resolved to cut timber in order to raise funds for paying it. Anne says that she endeavoured to persuade her father not to take trees out of the park, as she thought Dacre would not be so much annoyed at the timber being cut in the woods as he would be at the park trees being felled. Richard was quite angry at this remonstrance of hers, saying that she had 'too much care not to displease a brother who deserved no regard either from him or from her.'

As has been stated, the disturbances in Ireland during the spring of 168$\frac{8}{9}$ caused Dacre to move with his family to

[1] *Ante*, p. 396.

Liverpool, where he appears to have hired a house for a time from a Mr. Warren.[1]

I have found an account headed 'The Honorble Dacre Barrett's accompt for moneys paid from the time of leaving Clownish till his going for England 1686.' The first date is February 28th, and the last date that is mentioned is 12th, presumably of March; but, unfortunately, almost all the items have no date prefixed. The route taken was by Cavan, Kells and Dunshaughlin, and at all these places, no doubt, the party slept as among the entries are the following: 'att Cavan wn going to Dublin 02–12–02, att Kells 01–17–00, att Dunshaughlin 01–08–04.'

Dacre probably rode on horseback and Lady Jane in a coach, as these items occur: 'pd Mr Brady for yor horses att severul times as he sayes 03..01..06,' and 'pd ye coachman yt carryed my lady up 04..11..00.' The luggage was taken by carrier: 'pd the carryer yt carryed ye goods to Dublin 02..04..06.'

The party started off to the strains of music, as we find: 'to the Hoe boyes [Hautboys] when you were going away 00..02..03'; and also, 'to ye Musick then 00..02..03.'

The not infrequent entry of 'pd for mending ye coach' gives one an idea of the frightful state that the Irish roads were in during the winter months at that period.

From Dacre's account book they appear to have stayed at Ringsend[2] before sailing for England. Their bill there amounted to 1l. 14s. 2d. for 'diet & lodging,' and on February 26th they sailed in a ship owned by a man of the name of Edwardson, to whom they paid 3l. 4s. 6d., and 10s. to 'ye seamen.' That they were safely arrived before March 1st is shown by this entry on that date: 'To a woman for shewing ye church at Leverpool 1s.'

On their arrival at Liverpool they stayed at a Mr. Fisher's two or three nights, paying him 2l. 3s. 11d. for 'diet &c.,' and

---

[1] Letter from Lady Jane, *post*, p. 480. Dacre's account book has the following entry: '1687 June 10 To Mr Warren a ½ years rent paid him aforehand £8.'

[2] Formerly within Municipal Dublin City boundary, and near to the mouth of the Liffey.

then they went into lodgings with a Mr. Norris at the cost of 1*l.* per week ; and here they stayed till June 10th, during which time their housekeeping cost them only 19*l.* 8*s.* 10*d.* for the three months. On that day they left Norris's lodgings to take up their abode in the house they had hired, giving 10*s.* as tips to his servants.

It was while they were staying in Norris's lodgings that Lady Jane gave birth to a son, who was christened Edward. Neither in Lord Dacre's History nor elsewhere had I seen any reference to such a child, but in Dacre's account book there are occasional entries of shoes and other clothes for 'Neddy.' There is also an entry on May 25th, 1687, 'to ye Midwife £4..6;' and the day previous, 'to ye Clark at Leverpool 2^s..6^d.' I therefore had search made in the register of St. Nicholas parish church there, with the result that the following entry was found : ' May 6th Edward son of Dacre Barrett Esq.' This boy probably died when quite a child; I have found no reference to his death, but he was alive in June 1690, as in that month one of the last entries in Dacre's account book is ' Shoes for Neddy 1^s.'

While at Liverpool Dacre kept three coach horses and one nag horse, which he brought from Dublin at what seems the extremely small cost of 7*s.* 6*d.*, and 2*s.* 6*d.* to ' ye seamen,' and he appears to have had several servants in his employment while there.

Possibly Liverpool had by then already become the centre of the wild beast trade in England, and that it was from a 'Cross' of the period that Dacre bought on April 10th a 'flying squirrel' for 6*s.*, whose box cost an additional 2*s.* 2*d.*; and on May 14th a ' Red Bird,' which cost the then very considerable sum of 1*l.*, besides his cage, which came to another 5*s.* 6*d.* Items for 'bird seed' and 'canary seed' are not uncommon in these accounts, so that someone of the family must have been fond of keeping pet birds.

During their stay at Liverpool Dacre was a somewhat frequent visitor to Knowsley, the seat of William, ninth Earl of

DACRE BARRETT

Derby, as appears from several entries in his account book, of which the following are specimens :—

		s.	d.
June 10th	To my Ld Darbey's Coachman	10	0
	To ye Postilion	2	6
25.	To my Ld Darbeys Keeper [1]	10	0
August 20th	To ye pantry boy at Knowsley	1	0
October 1st.	To ye groom of ye Chambers	5	0
.. 6th.	To ye Keeper at Knowsly	2	6
October 8th.	To ye 2 Cooks	10	0
.. 15th.	To ye under groom of ye chambers at Knowsly	2	6
	To ye kitchen boye		6
November 11.	To Pocket at Knowsly	3	0
	To ye groom of ye chambers	2	6

Some of these tips seem to have been on a very liberal scale, allowing for the then value of money. While on the subject of tips to servants, it may be remarked that in the time Dacre lived it appears to have been quite common for guests to tip the cook employed at the houses where they visited; thus we find in January 168$\frac{7}{8}$ Dacre, when staying with Sergeant Rebow in Essex, gave 2s. 6d. to 'ye cook maid'; and on the occasion of two other visits he rewarded the cooks with a similar amount. It always seems hard on cooks, who have it in their power to add so greatly to a guest's comfort, that they should be almost the only servants in the present day who do not receive from a departing guest any acknowledgment for the pains they have been at to render his visit an agreeable one.

The cause of the intimacy between Dacre and the Earl was probably due, in the first instance, to the latter's wife, who before her marriage was Lady Elizabeth Butler. She was a granddaughter of James Duke of Ormond, a friend of Dacre's father,[2] and, moreover her uncle, the Earl of Gowran, had married an aunt of Dacre's wife. It may be worth remarking here that Dacre was to become an ancestor of one of the successors to his friend's title, for, as we shall see, his daughter Dorothy in course

---

[1] Probably Lord Derby had sent Dacre venison.   [2] *Ante*, p. 392.

of time became the maternal grandmother of the twelfth Earl of Derby.

It was while they were at Liverpool that Dacre received a civil letter from his father, inviting him to bring his family and come and live with him at Belhus. Anne says that R. Pigott and Mr. Henry Mildmay, by her father's direction, wrote to Dacre to that effect. The chief interest in this observation of hers is that it shows how intimate at Belhus the Mildmay family must have become by then to have been asked by Richard to write on his behalf a letter of so private a nature. This remark does not apply to his having told Pigott to do so also, as Pigott appears to have acted in some business capacity for Dacre. Dacre says that Anne did all she could to oppose this visit, even going down on her knees to beg him not to give this invitation; but her father was not to be turned from his purpose of having his son's company, and complained to him of 'the great hardships he lay under,' by which Dacre suggests his father referred to the way in which he was being managed and ruled over by Owen and Anne.

That there was some truth about Anne's intrigues against her brother appears by a letter dated October 26th, 1687, from Pigott, where he says :—

On Wensday last was deliuered yor Letter to yor father, which I hope in time may produce some good efect, but with all you must be asistant to yor owne afaire, haueing now such an opertunitie, as itt may be hardly the like : yor Sister Madam Anne being vnder some displeasure, by her recomending a bayly, whome yor ffather is now very angery w^t, soe if you will venter a iorney itt may be worth yor time ; . . . I asuer you [that your] ffather, when I dined w^t him, calld for a glass of wine, and dranke to all at Leuerpoole, and comanded mee to see itt goe rounde, wich I did.

On the other hand, the following letter from Dacre's cousin, Lord North and Grey, shows that he at least did not believe that Anne was in any way acting contrary to her brother's interests; but one could wish that the style of his Lordship's letter had been somewhat less involved :—

These to Dacres Lennard Esq. Alias Barrett at his house in Liverpoole, Lancashyre present.

S^r

I had not presumed on your privacy without Command, yett am to hope the care of a parent Entrusted to an Intyre friend may not be the lesse acceptable. A letter was wrote to y^{ur} father, & sent by one Mr. Pigotts. After many Indearings as of his sons kindnesse, & frequent joys in the letter Opned it was, & presently Wth indignation all torn, & burnt. Dear Cousin I presse not into privacyes, yett am sollicitous in your concerns & for your good solely. May I begg a return to this informing of the Contents. A sister has been almost at deaths Door, I assure you most faithfully as your friend, that she is intyrely in all respects at all tymes ffirmly doing good offices for you to your father, without care of her own Concerns. Living wth him gives jealousy of another way of demanour, but tis an Errour to think so. A letter to her would asswage Greif wch seriously afflicts her, for I know not you have the sad inheritance of rejoicing when another can be in plague by reason of yours. I adde no further but in all sincerity this 4th Dec. 1687 subscribe my Selfe & hope for a return hearto at my house in Laycester fields

NORTH & GREYES.

Dacre did not lose much time in availing himself of the fact of his father being in so amiable a mood towards himself, but started at once for Belhus, by way of London, with a couple of menservants. On November 15th he left Liverpool by boat for Rockferry, now a part of Birkenhead, for which he paid 2s. 6d., and hired two horses to take him to Chester for 5s. There he slept two nights, and then started in the coach, for which he paid 2l., with his two servants riding after him. The places he slept at on the road are as follows: Whitchurch, Newport, 'The 4 Crows,' Castle Bromwich, Coventry, Northampton, Dunstable; and on the night of the 23rd he arrived in London, on the eighth day after leaving Liverpool. He did not stay there long, but shortly went down to Belhus, only delaying in town long enough to get some necessary clothes, as is shown by the following letter to Lady Jane:—

My dear Life

The greatest satisfaction I met with at coming hither was the recieving y^{rs} by Mr Piggot . . . I came hither but last night & have seen no body as yet, so am able to give you no account of anything, I designe as soon as I have made me some cloaths to goe down to Belhouse; pray let me hear often from you . . . .

I am My Dearest y^r

London Nov. 24
[16]87.

D. BARRET.

After Dacre's departure from Liverpool, but before Lady Jane had heard of his reception at Belhus by his father, she became greatly perplexed as to whether or not she was to follow her husband, owing to the arrival of the preceding letter from Lord North and Grey. She sent it on to Dacre with the following remarks:—

December ye 6.

My Dearest life

this morning when I receiued this letter I was in the greatest trouble in the world for fears y^r jorney would be to noe effect, & then I thought it was som body got him to writ it for feare of y^r coming, & I receiuing neare a letter from you, I could not tell what to think, or whether I should preper for my jorney, or noe: . . . I haue all thinges in raedines to be sent away, but stay tell I heare from you an anser to my leter of the 2 of December. the Carrier goes 3 times a week to worinton,[1] & Carries goodes their, but goes from thence to London onest a week, that is evry wensday. I hope to haue a letter from you afrieday, & then hope I shall be out of my fears.

I am my Dearest y^r

J. BARRET.

For Dacre Barret Esqr.

Dacre evidently was not convinced by Lord North's letter that his sister was well disposed towards him, as he thus replies to Lady Jane:—

Belhouse Decr. 13th, 87.

My Dear

I receivd this day four letters wth seaverall enclosed from you, their comming alltogether was occasioned by Mr. Piggot's

[1] Warrington.

having been for some time out of towne; I find you were surprised at reading my Lord Norths letter, you made a right iudgement that it was to hinder my comming up to my father, for it was contriv'd by the whole knot for that end, finding him inclinable to have me with him. I read it to my father who storm'd at it, but of that more when wee meet; he continues extreamly kind to me, the particulars would be to tedious to relate here, but I have a great deal of good news for you, & I believe y^r prayers have not been without their effect. I hope by that time my two men come to you you may be ready to come away. I think the best way will be to hire the stage coach wholly to your self, the price to take it altogether is tenn pounds,[1] if you send to Adams, the clerck of the coach, who knows me, he will secure it; you may for more assurance write to Mrs. Anderson; in this case you must send the chariot by sea with the other goods you designe that way; my father is very earnest with me to write to you to bring him some servants, but more especially a good dairy maid, with you out of Lancashire, for the servants wee have at present here are to, say the truth abominable: if Betty[2] makes great promises of amendment, and is desirous of it, bring her with you (for shee may be of use to us here), but not otherwise. . . . I think Fishers & Mr Nuttals advice for sending up your necklace &c. will be the safest way but you must not let any body, so much as of y^r own family[3] know it. pray write me word what day you will be in towne, which you may do when you have agreed for the coach, that I may meet you there, and provide you a lodging.

Pray write back to Mrs Browne that I agree to let Mr Hays have the house. I choose to have you doe it that you may not loose the broad peices.[4] . . . I am glad to hear the children are well   I am
My Dearest y^{rs}
D. BARRET

if the carriage of our owne coach to London by sea comes

---

[1] In fact the coach seems to have cost 12*l.*, *post*, p. 483.

[2] In Dacre's accounts there are several entries referring to Betty; as February 15th, 168$\frac{5}{6}$, 'for a pair of shoes for Betty 1^s 8^d.' Her wages appear to have been 4*l.* per annum, as we find, 'To Betty a quarter's wages 1^{li}.' That Betty did go to Belhus is shown by this entry: 'Betty & Moll's passage by water [from London] to Belhus with goods, 5^s.'

[3] Note again obsolete use of this word.

[4] Coins first issued in 1619, and then worth 20*s.*—*C. D.*

to as much as it is worth, as I fear it will, you must make use of it up, if possible hiring horses, but be sure in the agreement let them be to find them with meat on ye road

[Addressed] For the Right Honble the Lady Jane Barrett at her house in Liverpool, Lancashire.[1]

The following letter crossed the previous one, and it shows how much the poor lady was worried as to what course to take in order to get rid of the remainder of their lease of the Liverpool house, and how best to arrange for her journey to London; which is not to be wondered at when it is remembered that she was then only about twenty-three years of age, quite inexperienced in business, and probably had never been out of Ireland before. Moreover, bad roads and the terrors of highwaymen made such a journey in those days a somewhat serious matter for more experienced persons:—

December 14 (1687).

My Dearest life.

I was in hopes that the theirty pound from Chester would haue discharged all thinges, but I find it will not doe. I haue aknafe to deal with that warrin he will haue all the rent.[2] If I can get a tenent I will, or els I will luck up the doors. I haue sent you a note of what is due I am so perplext I know not what to do to think to stay heare longer then I desired. Mr willis has a mind to his 07.06.00 which I will pay him, & all the rest of ye people, as far as it will goe. willis will let me haue mony, if you can let him haue it in Dublin, pray recken what is due, & what will hire 6 horses, & what will beare my charges, & order him to let me haue it; he proferd it of himself. I hope you let me haue ansar atusday next, & then that uery day fisher will goe to Chester to heir the horses for the monday after, for I must not haue them hired till I am sertin of the day; if I leaue Chester on munday cum senit, I will goe fhrom hence a frieday, or saterday, which will be the best day to goe ouer the water, mr. fisher teles me he is sure I will find it impossible to hire horses to London for that their

[1] There is this endorsement on the letter: 'From Mr. D. B. L. to Lady J. from Belhus w^h shows he had ill offices done him with his father.'

[2] In fact she seems to have paid him 5*l.* 15*s.* only for the second half-year in ieu of notice, whereas the half-year's rent was 8*l.*

is none that will let horses goe such a jorney, & the stag horses I cant haue under a [v]uast sum, he says he would aduise you to send the choch up by sea, but what you haue ordered me to doe I will do, if their is horses to be got in Chester; what ever they aduise me I hope I shall doe evry thing to please you, & shall I hope order evry thing as if you wear heare now I know y^r mind, the 30 00 00 pd [30*l*.] will pay most, pray if it is possable let me not be disapointed of goeing when I desire, for I shall neuer haue any satisfaction tel I am with you, for I doe cry, & fret, all the day at all their imposabiletyes, after all these [v]uexations I shall heaue the joy of seeing my Dearest which if they were six times more it will make me amens

I am my Dearest y^r
J. BARRET.

My humble duty to y^r father, & seruis to y^r sisters.

Since I writ my letter mr. fisher came hear he presents his seruis to you, & will doe you all the seruis lyes in his powre, but he sayes he is asured by seueral that he will neuer get any chochman to carry up the choch this time ayeare, the wayes being so bad, under 20 pd [20*l*.], & if he takes the stage choch he may haue it for 10 he beliues, he says the pole is roten, & it will be neuer be fit so great a jorney without breaking it all to peces; what euer they say, I will doe what you think fit.

willis will not take his 07 06 00 out of the 30 pd for feare I might had use for it but out of ye mony he lends me.

We have one more letter from Lady Jane at Liverpool before she began her journey; it is obviously in answer to her husband's letter to her of December 14th :—

My Dearest Life   (1687)

I receiued your letter, & am extreamly glad to heare of y^r fathers kindness to you. I asshure you it is noe smale satisfaction to me to think that after all y^r misfortunes you will heaue sum cumfort; if I did not sheare it my self yet it would be my greates joy to haue you happy, & I wish with all my soul I may neuer lesen it by any folt of mine, whilst I liue I shall make it my studey to deserue yr loue, & I heaue more reson than ever woman had to be greatfull which I shall be whilst I haue breath. . . . I sent for mr. fisher asoon as I got y^r letter, he saye the carrier is a uery honest man, but if you please he will goe himself, he will inquire aboute a ship bound for London, though he beliues their is none redy as yet, he will teak care of my thinges & se them shipt. I know not when to send away my thinges be [*sic*] the carrier not knowing when I must leaue this pleace. I know not by what safe hand to send my wach, and necklus, mr. fisher sais the Carriers is the safest. I was thinking to haue got them sent by my L. Derby, but I heae noething of him goeing; pray send me wourd what I must doe in it, what must I doe about the house if I must get a tenent for our time in it, & what I must doe with the Coles, & tourf that is left. I entend to speak to bety[1] & giue her worning of her sorcy fites, & withal tell her upon the first I will turn her away, if she promises amenment for the time to cum I will bring her;

         I am Dearest yr
of Decbur.   J. BARRET.

I am not able to fix the exact day of Lady Jane's departure from Liverpool. The account of what she expended is headed thus: 'Here follows an account of money laid out by my wife from ye 15th of Nov^b being the time I left Leverpool to ye 4th of Jan being ye time shee come to London,' but no dates are given. From the items of the accounts she appears to have taken longer on the journey than did Dacre; indeed I imagine that it occupied her from December 23rd till January 4th—or twelve nights on the road. The fact that she was a woman travelling with young children may be the sole reason that her journey to London took longer than her husband's, but it also may be that the weather was worse, and that therefore the roads were even more execrable than usual. We have among her travelling expenses items which do not appear in Dacre's case—namely, on two occasions payments for a guide, and once 'for drawing ye coach out of ye dirt 1^s'; while between Newport Pagnell and Dunstable she was charged 1*s*. for 'passage through a gate,' which possibly means a toll-gate over some private road. That she broke the journey at Coventry and

---

[1] References to 'bety,' *ante*, p. 479; she does not appear to have been able to control her 'sorcy fites,' as, in an undated letter to a Mrs. Longland, Lady Jane says: 'bety behaued her self so ill I was forst to discharg her she grow so socy I could not bear her & shod her houmer more than I euer I saw before.'

LADY JANE BARRETT

had a good rest there is shown by this entry: 'At Coventry 2 nights £1..5..6.'

It appears that 12*l*. was paid for the coach for Lady Jane, her children, and her servants, who no doubt occupied the whole of it; the entries which refer to this are 'Jany 4. To ye Chester stage coach £6'; and among Lady Jane's disbursements there is also, evidently at Chester, 'To ye stage coach in hand £6.' These items, however, by no means covered the expenses of the move from Liverpool, as we find on January 6th: 'To ye carrier for bringing my goods from Liverpool £4..2..6'; and the more bulky goods were no doubt sent round by sea, as we find 'To bringing my goods from Liverpool £7..' For 'wharfage and porteridge 17^s 3^d'; and 'To a waterman 1/-.'

Lady Jane stayed a few days in London to rest after the fatigues of the journey, and to get some clothes so that she might look her best when making the acquaintance of her father- and sisters-in-law. Some of the entries in the account book show that she was buying some finery, as we read 'for gold galoon £3..2..9,'[1] and 'to Mr Brinsley ye Clothier £2..19,' and other items of that nature.

On January 7th they went down to Belhus, as we find on that day they paid 'To a hire of a coach to Belhouse £1..5.' It must have been a trying drive in the middle of winter for the young Irish wife coming so far from home, and knowing that at the end of it she was to make the acquaintance of her cantankerous father-in-law, of whose severity to his children she had, no doubt, heard a great deal, both from her husband and from her brother-in-law Richard.

[1] In our portrait at Belhus of Lady Jane the neck of her dress is trimmed with gold galloon.

CHAPTER VII

RICHARD (I.) BARRETT
Down to the time of his death, 1696.

DACRE BARRETT

WHEN Dacre arrived at Belhus he found himself in high favour with his father, and the latter very shortly after his son's arrival made a will, dated January 26th, 168$\frac{2}{3}$, by which he left to him everything he possessed absolutely.

Mr. Pigott and J. Seacome were two of the witnesses to this will; it was no doubt executed when Richard was very ill, and not improbably thought himself shortly about to die. He only signed himself 'R. B.,' and this in a very shaky handwriting, and by his signature is written 'The Marke of Richard Barrett.'

Among those Dacre brought with him to Belhus was one J. Seacome, who was in his service as footman and groom, at the wages of 4*l*. a year and livery. Seacome gradually became a sort of factotum to Dacre's father, to whom he transferred his services, and ended by ultimately managing not only his master's property and household, but also his master as well. In all the subsequent controversies which arose he opposed Dacre's wishes and interests in every way, and played a chief part in turning him out of Belhus, and it is stated that he swore that if Dacre tried to come back he would shoot him through the head.

The accounts of Seacome's conduct, like the rest of the evidence as to what went on at Belhus during the closing years of Richard's life, are somewhat contradictory. However, there can be no doubt but that he acted in an overbearing manner, like a beggar mounted, and that he feathered his nest during the time he was in Richard's service; he himself admitted that he owned land worth 20*l.* a year, and had besides cash to the amount of 150*l.* On some occasion Seacome robbed a fish-pond at Rainham, and is said to have been protected from the consequences of his act by Mr. Mildmay's interference. Seacome and his associates, who had netted a quantity of carp, which they put into a pond at Belhus, were had up before a justice of the peace, but Seacome made some compensation to the owner of the pond, and by Richard's permission sent him a haunch of venison. Robbing a fish-pond is a class of offence one would seldom or never hear of now, but when, owing to the bad state of the roads, it was difficult to obtain sea fish while fresh at any considerable distance from where they were caught, fresh-water fish were preserved in ponds for the table.[1]

It was said also that Seacome gave orders to the servants and discharged them when he thought fit, and that he and his wife occupied Richard's own pews in church, just as if he had been the squire; he admitted occupying these pews, but said he and his wife did so by Richard's direction.

During Dacre's stay at Belhus he was much inconvenienced for money, as owing to the troubles in Ireland his rents from Clones became smaller and smaller, until at last they must have nearly entirely ceased. He wrote on February 14th, 168$\frac{4}{8}$, which was soon after his arrival at Belhus, to Mr. Westgarth, who was either a solicitor or agent in Dublin, complaining of his Clones agent, Fletcher, and asking Westgarth to remit what he had received from Fletcher, 'with all the speed you can, my occasions being extraordinary,' and he continues:—

I am almost weary of writing still on ye same subject, therefore begg you would as soon as y^r occasions will permit doe something as to taking his accounts, and what shall be necessary

---

[1] There is a considerable amount of information relative to the care formerly bestowed upon ponds containing fresh-water fish in the 'Marchant Diary.'—*S. Arch.* xxv. p. 163.

therupon that I may discharge him, my affairs going to wrack more and more every day through his mismanadgement ... You will please from time to time let me know what the charge is in both these buisenesses, not that I am unwilling to be at any that shall be convenient, but that I may the better order my affairs ... pray S^r let me have an answer to each particular of this and continue to sollicit my good freind Mr Fletcher, for these little driveling sums are of no use to me.

And in another letter, dated February 27, he complains greatly of Fletcher's being remiss in his duties in getting in rents. He says:—

I doe very well remember that when I was there myself I never could get him to distrain, or take any course to recover what was due .... It is impossible for me to subsist on 40*l.* to 50*l.* a year which at this rate of management is all that is likely to come to my share .... I hope he [Fletcher] has sent you up more money for my account, if he has pray return it as speedily as may be for I never wanted in my life till now ; it must go hard with me to have recieved no more than Twenty pounds out of my All^{sls} [All Souls, November 2nd] rents.

As matters in Ireland became much worse before they in any way improved, so did Dacre's financial difficulties increase, and on October 9th, 1688, we find him again writing to Westgarth about Fletcher and his overdue rents, when he says : ' I should be glad to hear of more money coming in, I never wanted it more.'

A few months later Westgarth made a journey to Clones at Dacre's request, and on January 29th, 168$\frac{8}{9}$, the former, on his return, writes him a long report of the state of things prevailing there. In the course of the letter he speaks of Fletcher being ill, which was perhaps the cause of the poor man not being sufficiently zealous in his duties to satisfy Dacre. It is difficult in these days of fast trains, good roads, and motor cars to realise the very great difficulties and hardships that beset a traveller in Ireland in the seventeenth century, especially during the winter months, but this following letter gives a vivid account of them :—

January the 29° 1688   Dublin.

Hon^{rd} S^r

According to your desire & commands I have been in the Country, & made a stay for some days at Clownish in order to settle your affayres : I must confess such a journey I never went in my life, for I scarce rid ten yards without danger of my bones; my M^{ns 1} I believe gott above thirty fals, & the snow was so deep that I am confid^t I went through Snow heaps much higher than my horse in many places, and in one place I am confid^t neare a Quarter of a mile, w^h was for most p^t as high as any horse in Irel^d, but thanke God I gott noe harme, only made a tedious jorney, riding one day only 3 Miles. In the Country I found the British for the most p^t had quitted y^r houses, & were gott into little sort of garrisons Capt. Townleys one, Red Hill another, Mr Montgomeryes a third, and several other places ; the Irish on the other side were raysing a vast number of soldiers 30 Companyes, as I believe, in the Countyes of Monaghan & ffermanagh.

Mr. ffletcher I found not well as I believe still he is & doe thinke he will not live many yeares being, as he app^rhends, & soe indeed appears, in a very depe consumption, notw^{th}standing, as his sickness gave him leave, he fell upon your acc^{ts} wch are I think settled very fayrely . . . .   As to the estate in general I find more disorders yn I know well how to redress, y^r Ten^{ts} are for any thing I can pieve very miserably poore, & almost every towne a nest of beggars that destroy the corne that grows ; till times setle my advice is, if you please, to make a generall abatem^t except in very pticulr cases . . . . the abatem^{ts} ought I think to beginne from Alsls[2] 1687 ; & this I desire you will write further ab^t for I fear several of them will leave the land for want of ym wch they plainely threatened I not being impowered as they expected to give y^m . . . . as to the Ten^{ts} yt have noe leases, theres noe way but to take what they will give, if they will but stay on the lands till times mend, ffor that country & soe indeed generally all the North, is pfectly in armes.

Westgarth goes on to say that he would prefer to give up acting for Dacre, 'as the times are so bad that I know not whether I can venture down any more. . . . Now the North is so generally in armes that I am told none are suffered to travell

---

[1] Messenger, in the sense of guide or attendant.   [2] All Souls.

w^th^out passes, & besides it very dangerous on account of robbing.' He says that if he is to continue the agency he must be paid a salary of 50*l.* a year and some other allowance, which he estimates as not worth 40*s.* a year, or else Dacre had better 'employ Mr. Fletcher who is now still on the place and will I thinke really serve you honestly, and as he did before, I mean upon the same terms, and to whom I will willingly resign,' and he goes on :—

I hope you will not judge hardly of me in this matter for you are sensible times have changed much since Sumer last, & if I could have managed itt, w^th^out too much disadvantage, I would not soe suddenly have complayned, but if I had lost had expected y^r^ favor in some other matter, but really the p̄rjudice is too Considerable to undergoe, besides the hassard of my life, wch forces me to acq^t^ you that I cannot be at any loss in case I should be robe of yor money in bringing it up to Dublin; you know theres no constant returne, & on that acc^t^ I believe your money has often layde; now the last time I was y^r^ I brought up yor money I gott, but dare not venture to doe soe any more, if I am to be at any other hassard y^n^ venturing my self wth itt, & therefore desire you will lett me know your pleasure as to this particular.

Other letters of Westgarth's written to Dacre during the year 1690 (any he may have written in 1691 are missing) give a vivid description of the miserable state of Ireland during that disturbed period.

Dacre's relations with his sister Anne after he had arrived at Belhus were no doubt far from cordial. He came there under the impression that she had done her utmost to prevent his visit, and probably made no attempt to disguise his annoyance with her. Anne at last one day asked her father, in Dacre's presence, if she had ever endeavoured to cause differences between them, to which Richard replied, 'No, you never did,' and, turning to Dacre who was standing behind him, he said, 'You know, Son, I told you so when you came into the house'; which Dacre admitted to be the case, and there and then begged

Anne's pardon for his unjust suspicions of her.[1] This apology of Dacre's was probably only a formal one, and did not signify that the former affectionate terms which used to subsist between him and his sister had been restored.

In March 1681 Richard, having occasion to go to London, entrusted Anne to pay and receive money on his behalf, and, finding that this plan saved him much trouble, he made her continue to act as paymaster for him after he returned home. She often asked him to look through her books, but he, with characteristic indolence, refused to be bothered with accounts. Not long after Dacre had arrived at Belhus, Richard, no doubt instigated thereunto by Dacre, told Anne to give up her accounts to her brother, who would go through them on his behalf; and Anne says that, although a balance of 24*l*. was then owing to her, she had all the difficulty imaginable to obtain repayment of this sum from Dacre.

On April 16th, 1688, about three months after Dacre's arrival at Belhus, Anne and her sister were at Chevening, where they had probably taken refuge with their grandmother, Dorothy Lady Dacre, after their father had turned them out of Belhus, which event has been already referred to.[2] In a letter to Lady Jane from Anne at Chevening, dated April 16th, 1688, which was written in quite affectionate terms, she says:—

I am very Indifferent as to any other Message or Account of things from Bellehouse, tho' it should be ye Seizour of my Cattle, & ye stopping of my Goods; Yett whatever shall be of that sort, pray lett me know it. It may serve for an Occasion of smileing, which I want often.

I have no evidence that Dacre had anything to do with this quarrel between Richard and his daughters; but as it took place so shortly after the arrival of Dacre at Belhus, and as we know that the brother and sisters were not on the best of terms, I think there can be little doubt Dacre took advantage of any little circumstances which may have arisen causing friction

---

[1] *B. & M. v. B.*   [2] *Ante*, pp. 393, 437.

between his sisters and his father to foment his father's displeasure against them.

It must, however, be said, in fairness to Dacre, that there is nothing in the above-mentioned letter from Anne to Lady Jane, nor in one she wrote to him two or three weeks later announcing her marriage, to indicate that she considered him to be even remotely the cause of her father's displeasure with her and her sister.

A. Mildmay

On May 1st, 1688, while Anne was on this visit to Chevening, she married a Mr. Carew Mildmay, she being then about thirty-three years of age.[1] We have seen what part Roger North says that he took in connection with this wedding. Anne asked her father to give her some money in order to buy clothes for this occasion, but this Richard refused to do; Dacre, however, gave her 30*l.* towards the cost of what we now call a trousseau,[2] and she wrote to him from Chevening very soon after her wedding, expressing her regret that some illness had prevented him from being present at that ceremony and giving her away.

Carew Mildmay was son and heir of Henry Mildmay,[3] of Marks Hall, near Romford, only a few miles from Belhus; and it is therefore probable that he and Anne had been acquainted with each other for several years, and it is more than likely that

---

[1] In the 'marriage allegations' of Canterbury she is described as of being 'abt. 24,' and her intended husband as 'abt. 29.'—*Har. So.* xxxi. p. 56. Assigning such an age to her was no doubt a piece of delicate flattery on the part of Mr. Mildmay, who, being a near neighbour, was probably acquainted with her age.

[2] *B. & M. v. B.*; also entry in Dacre's household account book, April 1688: 'To my sister Mildmay a little before she was married given 30..0..0.'

[3] Carew was High Sheriff for Essex in 1713. The Mildmays were an important family, and in the reign of James I. there were no fewer than nine branches of that name in Essex, all springing from the same stock; but in the course of a century and a half the last male representative died. They greatly inter-married, which may have been one of the causes of the family's disappearance.

Richard's harshness in turning his two daughters out of his house was the immediate cause that brought Carew to the point, and induced him to propose when he did, as Roger North says: 'As if Providence had provided a husband to succeed a father'; and in this case it seems as if the marriage was arranged by the young people themselves instead of by their respective parents, as was then the usual custom.

The following is a description of Marks Hall in 1803, since when it has entirely disappeared, and even its site has become difficult to trace :—

Marks Hall about 2 miles W. of Romford, a very ancient fabric forming a quadrangle, is now falling to decay. The foundations are of brick, but the superstructure is of timber and plaster, at two opposite angles is a square brick tower embattled & the whole building is surrounded by a moat. This mansion has been uninhabited many years.[1]

Charles Dickens once told a friend of his that he took Marks Hall, then in ruins, for the scene of the fire in Mr. Haredale's house in 'Barnaby Rudge,' which novel he wrote while staying in that neighbourhood.[2]

After her marriage Anne remained for some time, nominally at least, on good terms with Dacre, as she writes very bright, chatty letters to him in November and December 1688, and in the following January, giving him many items of public news of those exciting times which witnessed the flight of James II. from London.

When James II. determined to repeal the Penal Laws and Test Act Macaulay says :—

a proclamation appeared in the Gazette announcing that the King had determined to revise the commissions of peace and of lieutenancy, and to retain in public employment only such gentlemen as should be disposed to support his policy. . . . Every lord lieutenant received written orders directing him to go down immediately into his County. There he was to summon before

---

[1] *B. & B.*   [2] *Ex relatione* the Rev. J. J. S. Moore, Vicar of Dagenham.

him all his deputies, and all the justices of the peace, and to put to them a series of interrogatories framed for the purpose of ascertaining how they would act at a general election. He was to take down the answers in writing and transmit them to the Government.[1]

The Lord Lieutenant's return for the county of Essex has been printed from the original documents in the Bodleian Library, and is as follows :—

The Answers of the Deputy Lieutenants and Justices of the Peace for the County of Essex as they have beene separately examined to the three following questions :—
 1. If in case he shall be chosen Knight of the Shire or Burgess of a Towne, when the King shall think fitt to call a Parliament, whether he will be for taking off the Penal Laws and the Tests.
 2. Whether he will assist or contribute to the Election of such Members, as shall be for taking off the Penal Laws and Tests.
 3. Whether he will support the King's declaration for Liberty of Conscience by liveing ffriendly with those of all Perswasions, as subjects of the same Prince, and good Christians ought to doe.

After this come the names of men of position in Essex with their respective answers, and among them is 'Richard Barret.' To the first two questions he answers that 'His condic'on is such as renders him incapable either of serving as a Member of Parliam[t] or being assisting in Elec'on : To the third that with living friendly with those of all p'swasions, he should ever comply.'

During the course of 1688, probably soon after Anne and Dorothy had been obliged to quit Belhus, Dacre persuaded his father to revoke the deed by which he had settled Dunsink and Scribblestown on his daughters, and by a fresh deed executed in August of that year he resettled these properties upon himself and his heirs.

[1] *Mac.* ii. p. 318.

In the spring of 1689 Lady Jane went up to London three times in order to try to obtain some post for her husband through the influence of Lady Derby with the Queen,[1] to whom she was Mistress of the Robes. Her first visit to London was from February 27th to March 25th, and it cost 12*l.* 9*s.* 7*d.*; she stayed 'at Mr. Wroth's over against ye Diall in Panton Street.' While she was in town William Moore wrote the following letter in order to induce Dacre to come up also and try for himself:—

London March the 3d.
Dears Cousin
    Lady Jane acquainteing my wife this day of Lady Darby's readinesse to serue you in geting some ciuill employm^t for you, makes me thinke it absolutely necessary for you to come to towne if you intend to doe yrselfe any good, for so kinde a profer aught not to be reiected at this time, therefore pray make all the hast to towne you can, for euery thing is got up euery day

I am y^{rs}
W. MOORE.[2]

[Addressed] ffor Dacre's Barrett Esqr.

Dacre, however, was not willing or not able to come, but stayed on at Belhus, perhaps fearing lest his sisters, being quite near at hand, should obtain too great an influence over his father if he were to leave the coast clear. Richard becoming unwell, Dacre wrote to his wife on March 22nd, telling her to come down quickly as 'the Mildmays have already taken the alarm & sent yesterday a long compliment, & I expect they will be here to-morrow'; and the next day he says:—

My Father growing worse and worse is I doe really believe in great danger, which makes me desire you would come away with all the haste imaginable ... The Mildmay & Doll are expected here by the Coach this day, & I suppose there will be a great deal of double dilligence used.

---

[1] As to the intimacy between Countess of Derby and Lady Jane, *ante*, p. 475.

[2] The Hon. William Moore, already connected with Dacre through the Loftus family, married Dacre's first cousin Elizabeth, daughter of Francis Lennard, Lord Dacre, and widow of third Earl of Meath, *ante*, p. 278.

This attack, however, passed off, and in May we find Lady Jane twice again in London upon the same errand. The first of these two visits was from April 30th to May 7th, and cost 3*l*. 16*s*. 7*d*., and the second was from May 13th to May 24th, and cost 7*l*. 4*s*. 8*d*.

In one of Lady Jane's letters to Dacre, she says she had good hopes given her of being able to get him a post in the 'Aliation offis' (*sic*) but not one in the 'Costom house.' I have no doubt but that her efforts were in vain, as I have never come across any letters or documents to show that Dacre ever held any position which carried payment with it.

We have an undated fragment of a letter from Dacre to his wife, evidently referring to this attempt to procure him an appointment, and saying that he would be willing in accordance with the custom of those days to pay a substantial bribe for such a post. He says :—

endeavor to inform yrself further by putting Mr. Cooly upon making enquiry what other places though of less value there may be, for such there are ; could my Lady procure us a commissioners place it would be well worth the giving 4 or 5 hundred pound. I am sure I am as capable of serving the King in it as anyone that could be employed . . . Lady comes to towne, and you have the least encouragement from her, I will be with you out of hand. Pray get Mr. Cooly to enquire further, and hear out for other plans, in case these should be thought to great for [me]

Dacre had suffered, and was still suffering, so much loss as a result of the disturbed state of affairs, and the almost entire destruction of Clones, that he may well have hoped for some Government post to help him along till times should become more settled in Ireland. No doubt the following statement of his losses at Clones was drawn up in order to substantiate his claims to some office of profit from the Government :—

The Lossess which Dacre Barret āls Lennard Esqr. hath

susteyned in Ireland by Tyrconnel, or by means of the Governm^t comeing into Irish hands

He hath lost his whole Mannor of Clownish, and Baroney of Dartry, in the County of Monaghon in ye Province of Ulster, all his Tenants being gone, & the Land lies wast, or enjoyed by Tyrconnel and his Adherents. The yearly value whereof when the said Dacre Barret left Ireland, about two years agoe, amounted P.Annu. to . . . . } li 818 00 00

The losses he susteyns at p^{r}sent in Particular by ye meanes aforesaid

Arreares for May halfe Year 1687 . .	86	09	6½
Arr͞es for All Saints halfe Year's 1687. .	114	16	07
Arrears for May halfe Years Rent 1688 .	295	15	01
The halfe Years Rent for All Saints 1688 .	416	01	06
	913	02	8½
The halfe Years Rent at May day now at the dores	391	19	06
In all	1305	02	02½

The said Dacre Barret hath not one penny of Estate more in ye world at p^{r}sent to mainteyne himselfe, his lady, & four Children, other than what is before mentioned.

It was a considerable while before times showed any improvement for the unhappy Irish landlords.

They were, and are, an unfortunate class with everyone's hand against them, and during the last twenty-five years have suffered much at the hands both of the tenants and the legislature, but during even the darkest period of Mr. Gladstone's rule their condition was prosperous compared to what it was at this period of Dacre Barrett's life. Mr. Walter Dawson, writing on March 16th, 168⁸⁹⁄₉₀, said : 'Most of Clownish is destroyed,' and as to the tenants, 'If a man should offer to demand rent from y^m they would be reddy to beate one'; and the following letter written in July 1690, more than a year later than the date of Dacre's petition, draws a lamentable picture of the state of affairs then existing at Clones:—

Dublin July the $\frac{30}{31}$ 1690

Honord S^r

Upon the rc^t of a late letter from Mr Owen I went immeadiately for Clownish from whence I returned this very day; I had in my jorney hard lodgeing, & cold fare, & found little better there, the whole country from Kels to Clownish, except a few at Cavan, being only a wilderness wth a few houses uninhabited; the Towne of Clownish is something beter, what escaped burning being for most p^t [part] inhabitted either by Towne's people, or Strangers, the acc^o on the other Side will informe you how the Towne is; as for yor estate itt is alsoe waste, except Mr Hammiltons land, & one Andersons wch they live on, the cabbins are much ruind, butt most of those in the country standing, those in the towne that were ruined in pt are much destroyd by the Towne people for fireing; the mill of Cumber is quite destroyd, that of Anlore standing but the front gone, the castle wants a deale of Slating, and one of the Joysts above the dining room floore is come from the wall, it was I am told full of dung, but is now cleane, & a pt of itt inhabited by Ensigne Lee, Tom Morgan is in another pt for a while wch is much better ӯn if empty; Having found yor concernes in the condition above m:^{d} I thought fitt to affix the paper, of wch on the other Side there is a copy, on the cross wch I left there sticking; the contents are Such as I hope wilbe Satisfactory to you, & I am sure Such as the necessity of yor concernes obligd me to thinke fitt to offer, & though you may thinke them very large, yet I am confid:^{t} they must be enlargd yet, for the country is soe totally wasted that I know they will purchase ten^{ts} upon any termes, & noe Sooner were these proposals on the cross than one Welsh, as I am told, offerd house, garden, & grasing for as many cattle as some would bring, for nothing, only to be neare him : I am confid:^{t} alsoe there wilbe a necessity of enlargeing yor orders to 5 if not 7 years for Setting,[1] for I am sure none will Sitt downe upon the encouragem:^{t} of bare 3 yeares, as to the Tenem:^{ts} I have sett 2 or three, rather for introduccōn to setting then anything else, for the people doe not looke upon themselves under any obligacōn to pay for any thing at p^{r}sent, the other Tenem:^{ts}

[1] Letting.—C. D.

wilbe I hope soone inhabitted by the old ten:ᵗˢ or yʳ wives, & being for most pt upon leases I thought not convenient to medle with, but lett yᵐ come in & then deale wᵗʰ them as well as can be, I thought to have lockt up yoʳ house, as Mʳ Owen writt, but could nott, it being the Lˢ Store house, besides the doore was not hung, & wanted both lock & hinge. I made a carpenter goe abᵗ hanging itt, & left money wᵗʰ Ensigne Lee to buy lock & hinges & pay for the hangeing, & obliged him at his leaving itt to dlr [deliver] the key to none but Mʳ Hammersly if at home, or his brother in Law, whoe is now in the house where Mʳ Hammersley livd, whoe I desird dlr it to noe one but my order, besides which I writt to Mr. Dawson, whoe I was told was coming to Clownish wᵗʰ his family, & acqᵗᵉᵈ him wᵗʰ pt of ye contents of Mʳ Owens letter relating to him, & told him, till he was on better termes wᵗʰ you, I judged he could neither doe you, nor himself service; this is wʰᵗ I have done and w:ʰᵗ I thinke is possible to be done at pʳsent till the Law opens, wᶜʰ wilbe I hope next terme, & then theres an absolute necessity of having an honest intelligent pson [person] fix on the place, & there remayne, & if you thinke nott fitt Mʳ Dawson be concerned, whose imploymᵗ nor noe mans else I will God willing desire otherwise then fayrely, I doe hope by that time to provide you a pson, if it please God he lives, that wilbe found both honest and able to mannage yoʳ affayres, & from whome you nede not question to finde fayre dealing wᵗʰ. I shalbe every way obligd for designing till the affayre, though mannagd by another hand shalbe under my owne pticular care, & for the Sallary, as to ᵂᶜʰ I hope you will judge my last proposall reasonable, itt shall beginne when he comes up to the place, & for the trouble of this or any other jorney I may in the interim have, I will take it upon accᵒ of my Sallary here, wᶜʰ I hope you will allow me since my coming to Dublin, wᵗʰ my charges of this jorney to Clownish, or any other I may have, wᶜʰ is all I will desire, though I protest I have had a misfortune this time being forced to give a mayre wᶜʰ lyved wᵗʰ me on the mountaynes worth 3 or 4ˡⁱ, for one not now worth 3 cobs,[1] but this my last jorney I shall leave to yʳ owne consideration, & desire the favor of yoʳ answere, wᵗʰ what convenient spede you please. My humble Service to Mʳ Barrett I am Honorᵈ Sʳ

      Yoʳ humble Servᵗ
          W̅: WESTGARTH.

[1] A Spanish dollar, formerly current in Ireland.— C. D.

I have not bin in Towne since I came home soe have little newes. The K. is at Chappelllizard [Chapelizod] but goes I heare towards the army tomorrow. Douglass is removed from Athlone ab^t 10 miles w^bt occasions it I know nott.

Though the country be terribly wasted yet, there being continuall plundering, & many people having gott Stock whoe never had any before, I hope wth prudent managem^t your concernes may be sooner planted y^n expected. I hope you will pardon my freedome in advising in this letter abt enlarging time for setting, ^Wch I am sure I doe wth noe other designe y^n yor Service, & doe assure you the pson I designe for yor concernes, if it might be any inducem^t, understands country affayres better y^n my self, & may phaps be a ten^t to some of yor land.

An acc° of the tenem:^ts Standing in Clownish.

A tenem:^t formerly George Hammerslyes now in possession of Walter Murphy.

Edward Fields house & garden sett to Jane Grame for 15^s till May 1691.

Archdeacon Smiths house standing, & he expected home.

Hugh Roe o Simmons house now possessd by one Welsh, but if he will leave itt, sett to Alexr Johnston till May 1691 for 10^s : who is alsoe oblig'd to see the timber of the cabbins be nott burnt, & they will nott forbeare to give an acc° of y^m.

John Clearke is dead, but his wife is come to his house, wch is burnt, only a little crate built wth in the wals.

James Makarray has built a sort of a new cabbin wch I offered him for 5^s as an acknowledgm^t till May, but I feare he will leave itt, for he sd he would goe into the country.

Wm Byers a sort of a house built by himself last yeare, not knowne whether he will come to it or nott.

Joseph Clegs house Standing, he at Enniskillen & expected back. Wm Johnston comes to his house againe.

The list contains the names of eighteen tenants altogether and the state of their houses in the town.

The following is the Notice which Westgarth says he affixed to the market cross at Clones :—

Whereas by the goodness of God almighty, & theire Matyes care a Setlem^t of this country is now likely to ensue ; Dacres Barrett Esqr having appoynted me his Agent for mannagem^t of his concernes of the Towne & Manno^r of

Clownish. These are to acq^t all psons whoe now or hereafter may be concernd in the s^d Towne or Manno^r that, as to such prsons as have formerly had leases wch are not expired, Mr Barrett does desire, & expect, they returne to theire holdings & Setle as formerly, he being willing to give such abatem^t of the rents contracted by y^r leases as the misfortunes of the times shall make appeare to be reasonable, as alsoe to have such consideration of the arrears wch they, or any of them, are in arreare to him before the wars, as may be reasonable, and as for such lands where noe leases are in being off, or the ten^{ts} destroyd & gone, if either the psons whoe live on the same, or any other, be disposed to setle thereon they shall, from the first of Novemb^r next, have liberty to settle for one yeare from thenceforth upon paym^t of the 4th Sheafe of what graine they Sow, they having allowd them upon the land graseing of one cow for every acre sowne, & grass for theire plow horses, And shall alsoe have p^{r}ference to purchase the sd 4th Sheafe att reasonable rates, And such as are desirous to erect any cottages in the Towne of Clownish shall have y^m for a terme at reasonable ground rents, And all psons of the Towne are hereby desired to take notice to provide y^m selves wth fireing, soe as not to be necessitated to burne the timber of any houses in Towne, either standing or decayd, wch if they p^{r}sume hereafter to doe, notice wilbe taken, & they cald to an acc^{tt}; And lastly Mr Barrett desires they may have notice that noe other pson, except such as may be appoynted by Mr Barrett hereafter, only my self, & those appoynted by me, have any authority to make any contracts relating to Mr. Barrett's estate; And in order to the clearer Satisfac͞con of all psons that may be concerned of what lands are in lease what nott, I designe God willing, soe soone as conveniently I can, to send an acc^t y^{r}of to Mr Hammerslyes house, where the same wilbe ready to be shewd any may be desirous to see itt; Witness my hand this 28 of July 1690.

It was probably about now, soon after the Battle of the Boyne (January 1st, 1690), that Dacre drafted an address to William of Orange in the name of the inhabitants of Clones.

The loyalty of the address leaves nothing to be desired, but I could wish that my ancestor had been in the midst of the troubles, and had written it in Clones, instead of doing so from his safe and distant retreat at Belhus.

The spirit in which it is conceived reminds one of what a titled Irish absentee landlord is said to have remarked when his Irish agent was shot: 'If my tenants think that they will intimidate me by shooting my agents they are very much mistaken.'

The draft address, which is so torn as not to be legible in places, is as follows:—

To the King's Most Excellent Maiety

The Humble Address and Association of ye Inhabitants of ye Towne of Clones, Mannour of St. Tarn and parts adiacent, in ye Barony of Dartry etc. etc.

Sir

The many miraculous deliverances y^r Maiesty has had from ye hellish contrivances of y^r enimies, are as many evidences that you are ye particular care of heaven; it created you a savier to these nations, and to all Europe; and it preserves you to compleat the glorious work in which you have already made so great a progress, and bring down that Gigantick power which has dared to warr against heaven itself. Wee are all unanimous in our resolution of sacrificing those lives we owe to yr Maiety in defence of . . . . which we are . . . . seal with our blood.

Whereas there has been a horrid and detestable conspiracy found and carried on by papists, and other wicked and traterous persons, for assassinating his Maities royall person in order to encourage an invasion from France to subvert our religion, laws and liberties, we, whose names are hereunto subscribed, do heartily sincerely, and solomly profess, testifie, and declare that his present Maiesty King William is rightfull and lawfull King of these Realms; and we do mutually promise and ingage to stand by, and assist each other, to ye utmost of our power in ye support, and defence of his Maiesties most Sacred person, & government, against ye late King James and all his adherents, and in case his Maiesty come to a violent and untimely death (which God forbid); we do hereby further freely & unanimously oblige ourselves to unite, assosiate and stand by each other, in revenging ye same upon his enemies, & their adherents, & in supporting, & defending ye succession to ye Crown, according to an Act made in England in ye first year of ye reign of King William & Queen Mary intitled etc. etc.

It is, I think, tolerably certain that Lady Jane died at Belhus in September 1689, soon after the birth of Henrietta;[1] unfortunately Lord Dacre does not mention the date of her death, and we have no letters which refer directly to it; and, as has been stated, the Aveley parish registers for this period are missing. A letter from Dacre to his agent, William Westgarth, written from Belhus on March 3rd, 169$\frac{0}{1}$, however, supplies this missing date within a month or two. Dacre's letter refers to his dispute with Mr. Walter Dawson, whom he had appointed his agent at Clones, and whose appointment he was anxious to revoke; and he was taking the opinion of Sergeant Osborne as to what his legal position was as to such revocation. He says:—

I am much troubled or rather ashamed the Sergeant, or indeed anyone else, should see how much I have fooled myself in the affair, but it was done soon after the death of my wife wch did deprive me of all consideration.

Now Dacre appointed Dawson his agent on November 19th, 1689, so that Lady Jane must have died some day previous to this date.

Dacre, in his pleadings in the litigation he carried on with his sisters about Dunsink and Scribblestown, speaks about the barbarous usage which his children were subjected to by Owen and Seacome while at Belhus, and goes on to say that his

wife having recieved such like usages in her life time was grieved thereat, and being there delivered of another daughter, and in great afflic͞con to see the Poor Children and her self so barbarously used, and continuing soe to doe even in the time of her child bedd, noe longer able to beare the same, shee then dyed in great trouble and afflic͞con.

One of the witnesses who gives evidence for Dacre in that lawsuit deposes 'That after Mr. Barrett's wife dyed deponent heard that Dacres Barrett Esq. was turned out of the house etc.'

It was in the spring of 1691 that Dacre was compelled to

[1] *Ante*, p. 459.

leave Belhus. It could not have been until some date subsequent to March 3rd, 169⁸⁄₉, for, as I have said, we have a letter written on that day by him at Belhus to Westgarth; but we have evidence in another letter to Westgarth, which he wrote in the previous December, that the relations between father and son were greatly strained. He says in the course of this letter:—

to deal plainly I have met with such illusage from my father in return for all that care, charge & pains I have taken, and been at on his behalf that I have put on a full resolution to meddle no further.

The fact that Dacre was obliged to leave Belhus is referred to in the pleadings in the action against his sisters, and the reasons we are given for this departure are, of course, divergent. Dacre said that Richard, becoming weaker both in mind and body, Owen and Seacome, instigated by Anne, caused him, in 1689 and 1690, 'to withdraw his kindness' from his son, and also told his father that Dacre intended 'to cut his throat, or poyson him.' Dacre also said that his children were refused bread and butter and the milk necessary to sustain nature, although the poor children cried for it, and the servants asking for the same were told that 'if any milk was left after the hogs, dogs, and ferrets were fed,' they might have some, but not otherwise. Dacre also stated that, although he bought two cows to provide his children with milk, these cows were not allowed to graze in the park, but, by Seacome's orders, they were driven away and pounded. Finally, Dacre says that, taking further advantage of his father's increasing weakness, Owen and Seacome, in a most insolent and barbarous manner, came to him one day and turned him out of the house, and so misused his children and the servants who attended on them that he was forced to take them away, which he seems to have done, according to one of the witnesses, at some date before midsummer, when some man came and took them away in a cart.

It is difficult to say for certain how Dacre's children were treated, but I am afraid it is more than probable that the poor little things had a very unhappy time at Belhus. We know from the evidence of some of the witnesses that a young woman named Susanna Robarts was in Dacre's service about December 1690, and that he dismissed her because, one day hearing his child Dolly cry, he had reason to believe she was beating her. During the period which intervened between Dacre being turned out of Belhus and his children following him, which seems to have been about two months, Susanna, then Mrs. Seacome, was again at Belhus, this time in Richard's service, and had the care of the children given over to her. With no one to protect them from her spite, it is nearly certain that these two months, at any rate, must have been two months of wretchedness for these unfortunate children, whose mother was dead, and whose father had left them in the tender care of those avowedly hostile to him.

Anne's version is that Dacre might have stayed on at Belhus had he behaved himself properly, but that after he had succeeded in getting his father to execute the deed of revocation and to make a will in his favour, he behaved so badly to his father that the latter sent for Owen to come down from London in order to turn Dacre out of his house; and she further said that, coming some three weeks after on a visit to Belhus, her father then told her of Dacre's bad conduct, and said that he had 'miscalled him to his face, and told him he would make him know he had as much to do in ye house as himself, and that if he did not behave himself as he should, he would use him as he deserved.'

One of the witnesses against Dacre said that one day, when writing at table, some words of anger passed between the father and son; that Dacre rose up in a passion, and called his father 'old beast, and old rogue,' and told him, making use of a filthy expression, he did not care what he could give him, nor what he could give away from him. Whereupon Richard said, 'Sirrah, hold your tongue, or else I'll turn you out of the house.'

Another witness gave evidence that Dacre spoke of his father in her presence as 'old dog, old knave, etc.,' and that he once said 'the old beast deserved to be strangled.' This witness's evidence should be received with great suspicion, as she admitted she had been in Dacre's service, and had been discharged by him on a charge of ill-treating one of his children.

Whatever may be the truth of these stories, it is obvious that the relations between Dacre and his father were strained to breaking pitch.

We know from Roger North's account that Richard must have been a most trying person to live with; we have seen how harshly he treated his son Richard; and that he once turned Anne, and perhaps also her sister, out of his house. At the same time great allowances must be made for him owing to the afflicted state he was in; to be unable to move hand or foot, and only able to eat that which his servants put into his mouth, was a situation calculated to try the temper of a saint. I cannot believe that Dacre, even supposing the evidence as to the abusive expressions he was said to have used was not true, behaved to his father with that consideration which his relationship and the feeble state of the latter's health demanded. I do not suppose anything would have induced Dacre to have gone on living at Belhus had not the state of his property in Ireland been so desperate.

It must have been a most disagreeable position for him to have had a man like Seacome, who had actually been in his own service, managing his father and his affairs, and occupying his father's pew in church, although that may perhaps not have taken place until after Dacre had left Belhus.

It is difficult, under any circumstances, for a father and a grown-up son to live together in harmony, and in this case, where the father had such tyrannical ways, and was allowing the property to deteriorate so much that more than one of the farmhouses fell into so great decay as to become deserted, the position must have been intolerable.

Without attempting to apportion the exact amount of blame which attaches to each of them, I do sincerely pity both the bedridden father, a prey to the schemes of Owen and Seacome, and also the son, recently bereft of his young wife, thwarted and insulted by Seacome at every turn, and this at the moment when he was so harassed by the appalling state of his property in Ireland, and had the greatest difficulty to make both ends meet.

What an endless fund of gossip and speculation to the people of Aveley these quarrels at Belhus must have afforded! Even now, when people have so great a number of papers and other publications to read, the doings at the house of the squire are the engrossing topics of conversation at the local public-house tap-room in every country district; and how much more so must this have been the case when public news, even of the greatest importance, filtered down into the country in the most leisurely manner. Then, as now, there was a 'Ship' at Aveley, and no doubt the stories, many of them fabulous, that have been told of my family within its walls would make a far larger volume than this I am now writing.

Dacre stated in his evidence that his father's income was about 1,500*l.*, besides the profits derived from timber and woods, which Owen and Seacome sold and disposed of at their pleasure, and that there was not spent in housekeeping or otherwise expended upon his father above 200*l.* a year, 'the family being very small, and a very little table of no great expense kept for him or them.' He said that the park and warren also yielded them 'things of advantage,' and that 'no accounts were kept, except what they pleased to do amongst themselves by accounting to & releasing each other'; and that his father was not capable of looking into or examining any accounts, and he calculated that Owen and Seacome must each have owed to his father at the date of his death 5,000*l.*, or some such large sum.

How far these stories are true cannot now be determined, but the evidence of one of Dacre's witnesses, if it may be considered trustworthy, goes to show that there was some conspiracy between Owen and Seacome to get rid of Dacre, so that they might be the better able to manage the poor dying Richard and his affairs for their mutual advantage.

Mary Kemp, who was a servant at Belhus, deposed that on some occasion, when she was going to London from Purfleet by water, Seacome gave her a letter to Susanna Robarts, 'whom he courted in the way of Marriage.' Mary being possessed of a full share of curiosity, so often said to be in a special degree an attribute of her sex, became very inquisitive as to what might be the contents of the letter entrusted to her charge, which she says she believed was 'all about Love.' In those days very few women in her position were what in Norfolk are called 'Scholars,' which expression, by the way, only means that the person so designated is able to read and write more or less; and so Mary in order to satisfy her curiosity had to have recourse to a male fellow-passenger she was fortunate enough to find on board the boat, who was learned enough to be able to tell her what this letter really did contain. A recital of the love that John Seacome bore for Susanna occupied, as Mary anticipated, the chief portion of this epistle, of which she was the untrustworthy bearer; and no doubt she and her scholarlike fellow-passenger indulged in many laughs at the expense of John's admiration for the charms of the fair Susanna.

Although a lover's admiration may be a very serious matter for himself, and even for the object of that love, there is something about it that is irresistibly comic to the minds of a certain class of people, especially if they are persons not endowed with a fine sensibility—as witness the roars of laughter that are always excited in a law court, when the love-sick effusions of a defendant in an action for breach of promise of marriage are read aloud by the counsel for the plaintiff. John's letter did not, according to Mary's evidence, consist only of rhapsodies about Susanna; but in order to incline her to view his suit with favouring eyes he held out to her the solid inducement that, if she would come down to Belhus and be housekeeper, she should have everything under her management, as 'he & Mr Owen had soe contrived matters betwixt them to turn the said Dacre Barrett and his children and family out of doors.' Mary Kemp then goes on to depose that 'some short time after, the said Mr. Barrett, his children, and family, were turned out of the house, and Seacome went to London and marryed the said Robarts and brought her to Belhouse where she lived with him' till Richard's death. Much of this evidence sounds to be true, but at the same time it does not do to give too great credence to Mary and others of Dacre's witnesses, who were all of more or less the same class of persons; because whatever might be the result of this lawsuit—which it must be remembered did not take place until after Richard's death—at the time these witnesses gave their evidence it was Dacre who was the new master of Belhus, and so it would have been in his power to reward or punish them according to whether their evidence was in his favour or in that of his sisters.

In the month of April or May 1691 Dacre obtained a commission of lunacy in order to rescue his father, and his father's estates, out of the hands and management of Owen, Seacome, and their confederates. This, he said, he did upon the advice of several relations and persons of note with whom he consulted. Amongst the evidence upon which Dacre relied to obtain this commission were the following statements. That his father caused 'his calves to be curreyed & dressed like running, or hunting horses,' and also caused a 'great mastiffe dogg' to be brought into his parlour, and washed and curried like the calves. Anne said that some of her father's calves having got lice, he ordered them to be curried or combed, as the best way to prevent their being spoiled. Richard was, perhaps, in this matter ahead of the times in which he lived, as it has been a common custom now for years to dress, with brush and currycomb, both show cattle and show dogs.

Dacre also said that his father, after his sows had littered, would make some servant attending on him 'bring in ye young piggs, and lay them on his bed where they would crawl about and commit nastyness at which he seemed very well pleased, and then called them Sir Thomas, and Sir Robert, and the names of Gentlemen & Captains [1] in the County'; and that 'he caused a great quantity of cheeses to be brought into his bed room, & kept there until they became rotten, & nauseus, as he said, in order to preserve them from the rats.' And Lee, one of his witnesses, says that he saw 'a flasket [2] of the rottenness of these cheeses brought out of Richard's room for the hounds.'

Anne denied these stories about the pigs, but said that before Dacre had come to live at Belhus, his father had some 'outlandish swine given him whose piggs were spotted, and that when gentlemen dined with him, he often had them brought into his room to show them, when they were admired by all,' and that he had 'had 2 Portugall Piggs given him by Sr Thomas ffanshaw [3] and y^t the Serv̄ts to distinguish y^m from other Piggs called them ffanshaw Piggs'; and as to the cheeses, she said that a complaint having been made to her father by the other servants that the dairymaid had made bad cheeses, he had some brought up into his room that he might see for himself, but she knew not how long they were suffered to remain there.

These stories may perhaps show some eccentricity on the part of Richard, but even if we had not had Anne's explanations, and had accepted Dacre's version of them as not being at all exaggerated, such conduct does not amount to a proof of lunacy; if it were enough to do so, who amongst us would be safe?

Possibly public opinion was less tolerant in those days of any oddness of behaviour, or it may be other evidence as to Richard's physical and mental weakness which may have been produced was deemed sufficient; but, anyhow, the commission found an inquisition of lunacy against Richard, and his custody and the management of his affairs was committed to a 'William Moore Esq.' [4] Anne seems to have exerted herself greatly to prevent this order being carried into effect; whether it was

---

[1] Chief persons.   [2] Obsolete; a long narrow basket.—*C. D.*

[3] Of 'Jenkins' Barking, Essex, a near relative to Sir Richard Fanshaw, Ambassador to Spain and Portugal.

[4] I have no evidence that this was the Hon. W. Moore already referred to.

affection for her father that prompted her action or self-interest it is impossible to say, but we have no grounds for supposing that Richard would have been less cared for by Mr. Moore than by his own servants, and he was clearly in a state of health to require some one's care. Anne wrote to her father that she 'would secure him from those attempts to the utmost.' After her letter had been received Dacre and his friends attempted to seize his father, but were prevented; and upon an application by Owen to the Lords Commissioners of the Great Seal, this commission and inquisition of lunacy was ordered to be set aside and superseded.

It was no doubt after Dacre's unsuccessful endeavours to have his father declared incapable both of looking after himself and his affairs that he wrote, but apparently without any good result, the following two letters to Richard, the second one of which was probably written from Ireland:—

Sr May ye 1st 1691

With all humbleness I present my duty and submission to you, and begg leave to let you know tis no small greif to me to find myself under y^r displeasure. I am not conscious of any willfull occasion for it, but doe not iustifie myself in all things that have past, And I am perswaded were there not some who, by aggravating passages farr beyond truth have greatly provokt you, ye goodness of y^r nature had long since pardond all my faults, and now it is my humble request upon my knees to you, that yu will accept of this my submission wch I doe wth all humbleness begg, and be reconcild to me, & I doubt not but by my future carriage, I shall demonstrate that I am y^r dutyfull son; you have oft said you were satisfied of my duty, & how comfortable it was to y^r mind living or dying, but now again to fall under y^r displeasure is an affliction insupportable to me, therefore I must humbly repeat my request on my knees that you would be so good to pardon me and receive me into y^r favor again him who shall ever behave himself as with all dutyfullness becomes

S^r
Y^r most dutyfull & obedient son
D. BARRET.

A Coppy of ye letter I sent to my father.

S^r

With the greatest humility I am capable of, I throw my self at y^r feet, & assure you, nothing in the whole course of my life has been so great an affliction to me as to find my self so much under y^r displeasure as I perceive I am, & that which aggravates my unhappyness above measure is, that I should have given occasion for it, Tho I am perswaded that had not some former passages been aggravated farr beyond truth, ye goodness of y^r nature had long since pardond all my faults ; & receiv'd my most humble submission wch with a heart full of greif I now humbly offer, & earnestly beseech you to accept : and May I now find credit with you as what I here write is free from Interest, or any other designe then a sincere desire to be reconciled to you, which with all ye earnestness of a truly penitent Sonn I humbly begg, w^{ch}, if granted, my future behaviour shall demonstrate how sensible I am that you have by this action, so generous, and so like a Christian, layd on me ye greatest obligation, next that of nature, to be for ever y^r most obligd, Most dutyfull, and obedient Son

D. BARRET.

Feb: 19th 9½

In connection with the litigation between Dacre Barrett and Owen and between the former and his sisters, some facts relating to the wages then paid to domestic and to out-of-door servants appear incidentally in the evidence ; and as wages in former days are of general interest I give the following examples of some of the wages then paid at Belhus.

A man who worked on the home farm, and 'did thrash, hedge and ditch,' &c., had 8s. a week all the year round, and a park-keeper had 12*l.* a year ; while an indoor man-servant said he received 6*l.* a year and his clothes. A woman washed Richard Barrett's linen and cleaned his chambers for wages of 4*l.* 10s. a year ; and one who was a cook had 5*l.* a year. Another woman who was housekeeper had 8*l.* a year, while Seacome's wife said that her husband had a *salary*, not *wages*, of 15*l.* a year.

I am unable to say where Dacre and his children went to immediately after being turned out of Belhus, but he was at

DACRE BARRETT'S SECOND MARRIAGE

Clones as early as April 16th, 1692, as we have a letter of that date from Westgarth addressed to him there.

The year 1692 was an eventful one for Dacre, as during the course of it he was put in the Commission of the Peace, and on September 27th elected member of Parliament for co. Monaghan. He moreover married a second time in that year. Dacre's second wife was Elizabeth Moore, daughter and co-heiress of Thomas Moore, of Knockballymore, co. Monaghan,[1] and by her he had one son, who died an infant, and a daughter Elizabeth, who lived to grow up. I am able to fix the approximate date of this marriage, which doubtless took place about August 1692, by finding a copy of a bond dated the 18th of that month, made in contemplation of it, by which Dacre covenanted to pay to William Barton, of Thomastown, co. Louth, the sum of 4,000*l.*, unless he paid to Mr. Barton within one year of that date the sum of 500*l.*, and within two years after the death of his father the further sum of 1,500*l.*, which two sums, making together 2,000*l.*, were to be laid out, and settled as a jointure, upon Elizabeth for her life, and after her decease for her children.

The following extract from a letter written by John Smith, who acted in some way as an agent at Clones, shows that Dacre was having the castle done up for the reception of his new bride, and that they took up their abode there in the autumn of 1692:—

Clonis, Oct. 13. 92

.... I Rec[d] the things you sent by Daniel & am glad to heare of your safe ariuall at Dublin : we are getting all things in a readiness for the reception of your family : your chamber is ready, the door Hanged, so is the rooms ouer it, the dineing roome ceyled and once washed over, & the staircases in good order .... wee got good store of turfe home.

Dacre's second wife lived less than two years after her marriage, and we know nothing of their short married life,

---

[1] He was descended from Lieut.-Colonel Brent Moore, a younger brother of Sir Edward Moore, of Mellefont, ancestor of the Earls of Drogheda.—*Ld. D. His.* Lady Jane appears to have been on visiting terms at Knockballymore.—*Ante*, p. 460.

which was probably spent chiefly at Clones; the following letter from Dacre to her, and one from her to him, is all the correspondence I have found of theirs. The cordial invitation to come partridge hawking contained in the letter, which follows these, is no doubt intended for Dacre, and written by the same person that he covenanted with to provide the above-mentioned jointure.

>   For Mrs Barret
>   at Clones near Belturbet,
>   (Frank)[1]   D: BARRET.
>   My Dear Life
>   Since I came to town I have not wanted employment in looking over my things, which are much spoil'd, & many missing: I am mightily at a loss to know how to send them down, there being no carrs here from the North, nor any expected, & the rates they ask to goe from hence are excessive, but there is no remedy; you had an account by Daniel of the disappointment I met with at Navan about the cows, at my return, if they are to be had for money in the countrey, wee will not want them. I am heartily weary already of being here, & have more than once wish'd my self with you, meeting with no satisfaction but where you are, for I am
>   My Dearest
>   Y^{rs} intirely
> Dublin   D: BARRET.
>   May 6th 1693.
> My Love & service to all our friends.
>
> [Endorsed] ffor Dacre Barret Esqr.
>   att his Lodgings ouer against the coach & six Horses in Capell Street.
> Free   Dublin.

Your letter, my dearest life, I receaued which was the only satisfaction I haue had sine you left me, I shall not fail to preform that promis you claime, tho I fair you will laugh at my scribbling, but you must excuse that, and beliue all the kind and dear things imaginable, for I know not how to expres it,

---

[1] As has been stated, Dacre was then an M.P. in the Irish Parliament.

and all that I can say more is I long to be again happy in my dears company and that I am dear, dear
Your one entierly
ELIZA BARRET.

I hope your little wons are all well, And I long Mighttyly long to see them, my duty to my father, my lord, and uncle barton, my mother, aunt, and sisters gieus ther seauis.

Oct. 13th
Balle Thomas 7$^{br\,1}$ 4th 93.

Dear s^r

If you'll be so kinde to make me a Visit I will show you as much sport as partridg Hawking affords, & if you'll bring my Cousin with you shall be glad of it, & need not tell her she'll be welcome, & at cock hawking I will come & see you, y^e latter end of this weeke we shall haue Venison & claret & glad of y^r company who am
Y^r affect humble servt.
W. BARTON

my seruice to my cousin.

The following letter from John Smith from Clones fixes the date of Elizabeth Barrett's death.[2]

[Address] ffor Mr William Westgarth Liueing upon Ormond Key.
Clones: June 28.
1694

I am heartily Sorry I haue occasion to write to you upon this Sad & dismal account which so troubleth me that I scarsely know how to set pen to paper: it hath pleased God to take to himself Madam Barret which occasions A great deal of distraction & sorrow in the family; the Esqr: desires you would order hls Taylor McDonnell to make him A black Coat Lyned with Crape, & black wastcoate of Crape, also to make his man A Coate of ordinary black Cloath & Lyne it with shalloon:[3] he hath pd 20^{li} here which you may Receiue in 2 or

---

[1] September.

[2] The parish records now at the Four Courts, Dublin, throw no light on the matter, as, although they begin in the year 1667, they only continue without interruption until 1671, after which a break occurs in their continuity until 1722, when they commence again.

[3] A light woollen stuff used for lining coats, and for women's dresses.—*C. D.*

3 dayes of M^r fforbus, & indeed sooner if this important ocasion had not hapned, he desires you would order it to be returned ouer to Mr. Moor his relation: the Taylor may take up the things of Mr Walker, Liueing upon Blind Key, & he will take order to Satisfie him for them as soon as conuenience offers. He also desires you would get him, A paire of black worsted Stockings, & A fashionable Mourning Hat band, & Mr. Wells [?] will pay you for them: this being all that offers at present onely the tender of best Affections ffrom Sr

Your Humble Seruant,

JOHN SMITH.

We have a tradesman's account for cloth 'creap' at 2s. 5d. per yard and black cloth at 12s. per yard, sold to 'Esqre' Barrett on July 2nd, 1694, which no doubt formed part of the mourning bought by Dacre on the occasion of his second wife's death.

I think from the terms of a letter to Dacre, dated July 16th, 1695, written by his kinsman Mr. Coote, that the former stood again for Parliament about that time, and that opinion is confirmed by a receipt to him dated April 22nd, 1696, for 'A sum of twenty pounds & the beeing in full of what money hee owed mee att the election.'

Dacre did not take his son Richard to Ireland with the rest of the children, as he was sent to Eton about June 1692. Richard's grandmother, Lady Donegall, appears to have sent the boy to a Dame's house, which was kept by Mrs. Detton, and to have arranged the terms upon which he was to be received; amongst others he was to provide himself with 'two pare of sheets, and siluer spoone, and siluer poringer.' During the first few years of Richard's being at Eton his father was much pressed for money, and both the boy's letters to his father, and those of his Dame, show how difficult they found it to obtain even necessaries from him.

In a letter from Clones, dated March 169¾, Dacre speaks of sending over some money 'for my boy at school at Redding.' I am not able to explain this, and have no other reference to a son being at school there, and can only suppose that Dacre meant near *Reading*, from which place Eton is only about fifteen miles distant.

A letter from a Mr. Nicholas Sanderson, dated 'Dub^l ye 12th of X^{ber} [1] 93,' was sent to Dacre at Clones pressing him to pay the writer the interest due on some loan, and if possible to pay off the loan itself. One of Westgarth's accounts shows that Dacre's debt to Saunderson was only 100*l.*, and that interest was charged on it at the rate of ten per cent. But besides borrowing money of Saunderson and others, who were probably men of business, Dacre's necessities drove him to borrow from his friends, as is shown by the following from Lord Blaney:—

Jan^v ye 18th 1693

S^r

I send the bearer to wait on you & troubel y^u for ye small sum between us, I hope y^u will lett mee have it by him, I send y^u inclosed y^u Lett^r wherein y^u assured me to pay it att Alls^{lls} last. I would not give y^u these many troubels but my occasions urgently requires it, and my land is wast, and yours planted : I hope now y^u will not disapoint.

y^r aff^{tt} Kindsman & Ser^{tt}

BLANEY.[2]

It is to be hoped that Lord Blaney's confidence in Dacre, as shown by sending him his promise to pay before receiving his money, was not ill-founded, and that he did receive that which his 'occasions so urgently required.'

It is quite likely that Dacre, being pressed for money, did not go to the considerable expense of having Richard over to Clones from Eton for his holidays, and in a letter of the latter to his father, dated 'July 16 1693,' he says, 'be pleased to give my duty to my mother though unknown'; this refers, of course, to his first step-mother, and tends to bear out my theory that Richard remained at school in England.

Mrs. Detton writes a letter to Westgarth in October 1694, from which it appears that it was proposed to withdraw Richard

[1] December.
[2] Richard, fourth Baron Blaney. The first Baron married a Loftus, and the Second Baron a Moore. Dacre was related, or connected, with both of those families, which explains Lord Blaney's form of subscribing himself.

from Eton, and I believe that this plan was carried into execution, but I am not able to say for certain whether or no this was the case.

We have no letters from Richard nor from Mrs. Detton during the years of 1695 and 1696, but in December 1695 Lord Donegall[1] writes a letter to Dacre at Clones in which he says :

I have one request to make to you, y^t y^u will lett my Nephew dick come and keepe his Chrismas wth me at Carickfargus,' and this seems to show that at that date, at any rate, young Richard was at Clones.

Westgarth writes from Dublin on August 24th, 1696, to Dacre, then in England, and in the course of his letter says :—

If it were not for feare of the small pox, yor children might I am confid^t, be much better, and as cheape this winter in Dublin as at Clownish, if yor honour do not send for y^m to England. I would gladly heare from y^r honour ab^t Mr Richard, the season now being far spent.

We have a draft letter from Dacre, probably to Westgarth, and in answer to this letter of his. Dacre's letter is not dated, but it bears internal evidence of being written when he had left Ireland after his father's death in 1696, and he says in it :—

The more y^n ordinary buisness y^t I have of late [2] had on my hands has made me extreamly remiss as to my buisness on y^r side, & more particularly in w^t relates to my children. I wish you could have found an opportunity to have Dick sent over, whose loss of time will be irreparable, & as to those at Clones whose condition (I fear) is infinitely worse, I beg you would bring y^m up to town,[3] but so y^t you accompany y^m y^{r}self.

In the years 1697, 1698, and 1700 we again have letters of Richard and Mrs. Detton from Eton, so we know, if he did leave that school in 1694, he went back to it again, probably after his father's means had improved owing to the death of Richard the elder, and also owing to Dacre's third marriage, which we shall see took place with a richly dowered widow.

[1] Arthur, third Earl.   [2] No doubt alluding to his third marriage, *post*, p. 528.
[3] Meaning Dublin.

Some time about August 1693 Anne Mildmay, her husband, and Dorothy her sister, went into Somersetshire, where Carew Mildmay had inherited an estate, and they remained there for about twelve months, returning to Essex in September 1694. In the previous month of May, during their absence in the west, Richard made a will,[1] which was ultimately, by his directions, given into the custody of Anne, and by this will he directed that the sum of 100*l.* only was to be spent upon his funeral; he left several legacies, among them one of 30*l.* to Seacome and one of 2*s.* 6*d.* to his son Dacre; to Anne he left all his household goods, furniture, pictures, pewter and brass plate, jewels, books, &c., except farm stock, ready money, and arrears of rent, which he bequeathed to R. Owen, whom he made sole executor. Dunsink and Scribblestown he devised half to Anne and half to Dorothy. It was admitted that, owing to palsy or 'scurvey of the nerves,' Richard was not able to sign this will without the assistance of Seacome to guide his hand. Soon after the will had been made Richard wrote to Anne, or more likely caused a letter to be written to her, to tell her what he had done for her and for Dorothy; and as soon as they came back out of the west they went to visit Richard at Belhus, and thank him for his kindness to them.

During the course of another visit they paid their father in October 1694, he told Anne that her grandmother, Dorothy Lady Dacre, had made a journey to see him in order to persuade him to leave Dunsink and Scribblestown to Dacre's children, or to one of them, and that in order to induce him to do so she told him of a letter which Anne was said to have written to Dacre as long ago as 1682, and in which she used 'unhandsome expressions of her father.' Richard also said that Mr. Rooth,[2] who was the second husband of Lady Donegall (Dacre's mother-in-law), showed him some such letter, and brought with him little Richard, Dacre's only surviving son, and did all he could

---

[1] This will was republished March 12th, 1695.
[2] Richard Rooth, son of Admiral Sir Richard Rooth, of Sutton, Surrey. The C. P. in error calls him *Booth*.

to persuade Richard to make his will in favour of his grandson, saying that Anne had shown herself to be unworthy of his favour, having written a letter so disrespectful in its contents.

Anne was most indignant at this report, and declared she did not believe she had ever written such a letter, and that it was probably a forgery, but avowed her intention of attempting to see this pretended letter of hers the next time she went to London. Poor Richard, no doubt wearied out by his bad health and these constant family disputes, begged Anne to take no further notice of the matter, saying that the letter was very likely a forgery, and that even if it were genuine, he quite forgave her for writing it, and that the production of this letter had in no way changed his feelings of affection for her.

This was probably the last attempt actually made to induce Richard to change the disposition of his property in favour of Dacre or of his children; but the following letter to Dacre from Mr. W. Moore[1] shows that Dorothy Lady Dacre, with wonderful energy considering she was over ninety years of age, had still some hope of bringing about a reconciliation between her son and her grandson :—

[Addressed] ffor Dacre Barrett Esqr.
    At
      Clones.
        London Aprill the 14th
          1696

D^{re} Cousin

  Y^r grandmother has very earnestly desired me to write to you to come, I told her it was long since I had heard from you & therefore did not know well where to finde you, but being satisfied she has a minde to doe you w^{ht} good she could before she dies, I thought fit to let you know that she is uery desirous you should come over, & that she will doe all she can to reconcile y^r father to you, wch I thinke would be a hapinesse for you in all respects, & may prove for y^r advantage. You know y^r owne concearnes best, but were I as you, I would lose no time in waiteing on y^r grand mother, & endevor all I could to be

---

[1] As to this Mr. Moore, *vide ante*, p. 278.

reconciled to y^r father. I desire you will give me an answer to this for I promiced her to write to you.

I am y^r aff: kinsman & Servt:
W, MOORE.

Consider y^r grand mother is old, & if she should die I doe not see who would endeavor y^r reconciliation to y^r father, & I doe not, but upon y^r submission, dout she will doe it.

It is impossible to say whether this letter, had it been written a little sooner, would have prevailed upon Dacre to come all the way from Monaghan to Essex on the chance of his grandmother being successful in her endeavours to make peace between him and his father. As it was, he could not have received it many days before he had the following from his brother-in-law, telling him that the death of his father had put an end to the possibility of that reconciliation taking place which his grandmother had been so anxious to see accomplished :—

Marks Ap^{ll} 29th 96

S^r

Yesterday we were surprised with ye News of my Father Barretts [1] sudden death : I thought it convenient to acquaint you with it, that you may take some Care about your concerns here. If there is anything that I can be serviceable to you in, I hope you will comand.

S^r
Your very Humble Servt
CAREW MILDMAY.

My wife is very ill, and has kept her Chamber this fortnight. She and my sister Lennard give their Humble service to you. Mr. Owen is left sole Executor.

There are always plenty of people ready to worship the rising sun, and Mr. Mildmay was not the only, or indeed the first, person to inform Dacre of his father's decease. John Deane writes the day before :—

London. Apl. 28th 1696

Honnoured S^r

It hath pleased God to take yor Father away Esqr Barrett who Dyed this morn about Eleven o'Clock after ye 3^d fitt of an

---

[1] Meaning his father-in-law, and his 'sister Lennard,' meaning his sister-in-law, Dorothy Barrett.

Apopexly; and I Imediately, asson as Recd ye Newes of it, came away for Londⁿ, not makeing publick my Intentions of coming, Expresly to let you know ye same; but after I came here consulting some friends, and finding how difficult it is to obtain a Pass [1] without which it is not safe, considering ye difficulty of tymes alsoe, I desist from coming.

He goes on to urge Dacre to come at once, 'for Mr Seacomb as I am Informed is Disposing of ye Cattle & all what he can to his owne Interest:' in a P.S. he says: 'S^r you may please to direct for Jno Deane a Barber att Hoⁿ Church in Essex,' and under Deane's signature in the following note in his handwriting: 'Who hath wrote at all times before according to yor Commands for yor Poore & Ready Ser^{vt} Jo. Lee.'

The same day the following letter was written:—

Wapping 28th Aprill 1696

S^r
  These with my humble respects to you, and friends, is to acquaint you that John Lovell at the time of my putting pen to paper was with me, who came on purpose to inform me of your father's death, who died this morning between the hours of ten and eleven o'clock, and the Bell rung for him about one o'Clock, which was a sufficient Sattisfaction, and therefore made it his business to come to me to acquaint me with it, Soe I thought it my Obligacon to give you this Narative, and Beg Leave to Conclude myself S^r

Your humble Ser^{vt}
JOSEPH CRANE.

In those days communication between London and that portion of Essex in which Belhus is situated was largely carried on by water,[2] and Wapping was no doubt one of the ports from which the boats that took passengers sailed, therefore it is not strange that one of Dacre's correspondents should write from there.

[1] Just at this period several trials for treason were being held in London in connection with a plot to restore James II.
[2] As is shown by several allusions in letters from Richard (Dacre's brother) and Richard (Dacre's son); also Mary Kemp's evidence, *ante*, p. 506.

The next day, April 29th, Seacome also writes, in a remarkably good hand, to inform Dacre of his father's death, and promises to 'preserve everything to y^r advantage till y^u can wth leisure come y^{r}self,' and he offers him his services in anything he is capable of doing.

Dorothy Lady Dacre wrote to Seacome on May 13th, 1696, asking him to send certain of her pictures to London, and she says: 'as for the rest I leave 'em there, and shall think it a kindness done to myself if you will take care of y^m, and the rest of ye goods, till my son [1] Dacre comes over.'

No doubt Dacre lost little time in coming to England on hearing the news of his father's death, and he was naturally greatly incensed when he found that his father hath left him only the nominal sum of 2s. 6d.

By the time he arrived at Belhus he found that Owen, to use a Norfolk farm expression, had 'taken the fore horse by the head,' and sold all the farm stock left him by the will, and no doubt the household goods, &c., were gone also.

Dacre brought an action against Owen to upset the will, and produced evidence to show that his father was unfit in 1694 and 1695 to make a valid will, but his witnesses were chiefly servants now in his own service, or tenants on the estate. On the other hand Owen produced a formidable array of witnesses, some of whom had witnessed the will, to prove that Richard, although quite incapable of moving hand or foot, was perfectly clear in his head up to the time of his death. These witnesses were persons of some position, and were in no way interested in the result of the action. Among them were the Rev. — Robertson, rector of Stifford, and his wife, and the Rev. Sam Kekewick, vicar of Rainham. William Palmer, lord of the manor of Grays, the founder of Palmer's School in that parish, a justice of the peace, and a person of considerable local importance, was also a witness to the will, and gave

---

[1] Another instance of the more elastic way words expressing relationship were used formerly than at present. Dacre, as we know, was Dorothy Lady Dacre's grandson, not her son.

evidence in support of it. The learned Dr. Derham, rector of Upminster, said that he had known Richard for about a year before his death, and that he was quite in possession of all his mental faculties, and that he had discussed with him 'ye Art of Clockworke and talked, and discoursed very rationally and gave a good account thereof'; and 'had discussed with him of Physick in which he always discoursed very pertinently, rationally, and with good understanding to the great satisfaction of the Witness who hath some understanding and judgment therein.'

In this connection it may be observed that Susanna, Seacome's wife, deposed that Richard 'was a very curious [1] man about Clocks and kept three clocks in his chamber'; and 'when these clocks wanted anything to be done to them he would desire Mr. Derham to put them in order and told him what they wanted and where the fault lay.' She also said that Richard had 'great insight, skill and judgment in Physick and did order himself as to his own distemper'; and she 'scarce ever knew him to take any Physick but what was of his own ordering, and hee did also prescribe Physick and give his advice to others that came to him, and did several cures.'

The evidence of these independent witnesses in support of the will was too strong for Dacre, and the will was admitted to probate. When Dacre arrived at Belhus, and found how he had been treated by his father, largely, as he considered, at the instigation of his sister Anne, he was so angry that he appears to have sent no reply to Mr. Mildmay's letter telling him of his father's death. In spite of this Anne determined to make one more effort at a reconciliation, as is shown by the following letter, which, although not dated, was obviously written soon after her father's death :—

Deare Brother
    (which is a style I am unwilling to alter)
    Tho' ye little notice you have taken of Mr. Mildmays Letter to you, might Discourage me, yett being very desirous

---

[1] In the obsolete sense of fastidious, precise.—C. D.

that yᵉ Unhappy Differences in Our Family shou'd have an End, I venture to send this, which doth not proceed from any Feare of what I hear you threaten Us with, butt from Love of Peace, and the due regard a Sister ought to have of a Brother's Reputation, and Interest. Moved by this, (and nothing else), I begg of you that before you are too far Ingaged, you wou'd Consider if yᵉ Person who perswades you to a Sute of Law, doth not Consult his own profitt more then yours, and if a Man who Deserves The Character, you your self have so often given of him, is to be Trusted in such a Case. As to my Fathers power to dispose of the Estate he has given to my Sister & I, you know he as good as Purchased two parts in three of it, paying 2000 lb to Sʳ George Wentworth, & 600 lb to Ld. Strafford & Mr. Carr, and redeem'd the other third part from a Mortgage to Pigott, and what Title cou'd remaine to you as Heire to my Mother affter this you gave up to my Father upon your Marriage, as by The Deed in Our hands will apeare.

If you are prevail'd upon to Plead my Father a Lunatick now, when you failed in it before, it will Certainly injure your Reputation more then his, for we can, and will, produce more witnesses of his being of sound Mind, then you can of the contrary, and those of more Creditt too.

If you pretend he was importuned to make this Will, the very Will it self shows yᵉ contrary, for if Mr. Owen had Urged him to it, without Doubt we shou'd have had nothing ; if we had, a Stranger shou'd have had less, besides att the makeing of it we were above a 100 Mile from him, & had not seen him in ten months ; if you say Mr. Seacome did, all yᵗ hear it must beleive if he cou'd have influenced him, he wou'd have provided better for himself, then so poor a reward as 30 lb for a painfull seven years service.

As to what we might Deserve from my Father, Remember that Horsfford was charged with 4000 lb. for younger Childrens portions by my Mothers mariage Settlements, and that upon yᵉ Payment of your Wives Fortune, 300 lb. of that was sunk by yᵉ Returne of Mony out of Ireland, and yett We signed a Writing clearing that Estate from the whole Sum, and can it be thought Distraction in my Father, to add to what was designed for us before we were borne, when we had lived 16 years with him and payd that Duty, which you thought Intolerable in a year or two ?

Reflect Seriously how the ready mony that shou'd have

made Our Fortunes was disposed of; That besides the 2600 lb for Scribblestown, and Pigotts money, there was a good sum laid out for ye Settleing of Clonis after my Mothers Mariage, that 1200 lb was paid to Morgan for to keep Bellehouse Park & woods from Wast; and what was expended in ye Long & Chargeable Sute against Ld: Loftus for your Interest, may better be guest at then counted, so that you have had as good a share of my Fathers Personall Estate as we shall have, when we have made the best of what is left Us, and injoy a clear Estate of above Two thousand pound a year, and have it in your power to provide as well for your daughters, as my Father has done for his.

I might add here, without Arrogance or Vanity, that I deserve a kinder Usage from you then to Disturbe Us in ye Injoyment of what is left Us; I was for many years happy in your Freindship, and thought myself so, and accordingly imployed all ye Interest I ever had with my Father in doing you Service, and that sometimes to the hazard of my Fathers Favour; I know the power that was in my Father to Charge, or dispose of Bellehouse, and Concealed it for your advantage; I promoted your Mariage with Lady Jane with my whole Indeavour, and brought my Father to consent to it; for which I have your thanks in Letters with ye highest Acknowledgments; I prevailed with him to forgive ye 200lb. you had of Desmyniers affter My Sister and I were made Executrixes, which was giveing so much from our selves; and affter your last comeing into the House, I had the Testymonie of my Father to you before me that I never did, nor Indeavour'd to do you injury with him in my Life; Nay affter that ill Advised Act of yours against my Father, my Extenuating of it and pleading to him for your Children, gave Ocasion to my Father to Creditt those, who for their own Interest perswaded him I took your part, and that He owed his being free from ye Custody of Mr. Moor to their zeale for him, and not to Us; and as farther proof of it made Use of what you said, that I advised you to it; Which was the most Unjust and Unkind Thing that ever you did, and I cannot give a greater Testymonie of my Desire of Peace, then to assure you I am ready to forgive & forgett it. Since my Father's Death you have had from Mr. Mildmay not only Fair & Gentlemanlike Usage, butt what was very Kind, so that if there be any Differences the Fault must be in you. I again begg of you to Consider all these things.

To Consult your own Reason, Conscience, Honour & Interest which are all Concern'd, before you Ingage in a Law Sute, and Expose your self againe in a Court of justice, which will not be Byasst,[1] nor Imposed upon by Mr. Sloanes Confidence, butt will judge according to Right & Reason which, I am assured by good Lawyers, is on our side.

I think in sending this Letter I have Acquitted my self of all that is Necessary on my part toward an Accomodation. If I am so unhappy as not to succeed in my Indeavours, I shall be much Greived, and shall most Unwillingly Ingage in a Law Sute against an only Brother. Butt no Action of yours shall take away my Charity, & the Service of Nature, which has and ever shall be the Rule of

Your most afft: Sister &
Humble Servant
A: MILDMAY.

Anne's letter makes out a very strong case against her brother, but we should remember that we do not know what answer he was able to make to her, and how far he was able to justify his actions. We shall see from Roger North's letter that opinions among their relations, as to whether Dacre or his sister were in the right, appear to have been divided; and we shall also see that their grandmother, Dorothy Lady Dacre, took his part in the controversy. If persons then living, who presumably were acquainted with all the facts, were divided in opinion on the subject, it would be rash for anyone in the present day to decide positively which of the parties is entitled to his sympathy.

This is the last letter we have of Anne's, and we know it was written in vain, as soon after his father's death Dacre plunged into litigation with his sisters concerning Dunsink and Scribblestown. The following letter from Roger North shows that he did his best, but without success, to make peace between brother and sister. It may be remarked that Roger's style was somewhat involved, and that he wrote a difficult hand to read, so I am not sure that two or three words in this letter are correctly given here.

[1] Obsolete form of 'biased.'

17. Jul. 1697. M. Temple.

S^r

I meet with so many Reflections Every where, among the Indifferent of o^r Relations concerning the suits depending between you, & y^r sisters, some blaming one side, & some another, according as Conversation hath accidentally Inprest upon them, but mostly agreeing in opinion, that it were well some way were found out if possible to Reconcile you, and many Insinuating that It becomes me to Interpose in the Matter, that I hope you will Excuse this officiousness, wch goes no further than to beg to know If I may for any thing serve you, wch I am most ready to doe in process towards an accord, tho Not in Exasperating as Some may, whose profit ariseth by it. I am sure you are Judg ennough competent to determine touching probability of success, as well in y^r owne as y^r freinds concernes, therefore I desired [?] not to Informe you, nor were I disposed, could doe it, having kept my self as farr off knowing the grounds [?] of y^r case as I could, and am sufficiently Ignorant of y^r share [?] of it, & so desire to Continue. So setting aside all ye Matter If you think I may by any Mediation obtain what you shall desire, or think reasonable for you to expect, pleas to communicate it, & I assure you I will act as one y^t values y^r freindship as—Relation, and desire to appear as he really is

Sr Y^r Most faithfull &
affectionate humble servant,
R^{OR} NORTH.

It appears from the following extracts of letters to Dacre, written to him by his son from Eton, that Dorothy Lady Dacre took the part of her grandson against his sisters, and that the latter were unsuccessful in the early part of these law proceedings :—

January ye 24 1697-8 Lady Dacre . . . saies she believes y^t ye goods that Mildmay has are but in huckersters hands, she saies y^t Mildmay comes there often, but she saies nothing to her, neither will she have any thing to do with her.

Sept ye 1st 1700 . . . I believe y^t ye Mildmays are quite down in ye mouth for I never hear Cottrell bragging as he used.

Sept ye 24th 1700 . . . Sr Charles Cottrell [1] & his wife was

---

[1] *Ante*, p. 265.

here this week & told a boy that was with him y^t Mrs Mildmay does not think to come from Ireland till after next Hilary Term, & y^t she will have another tryall.

Nov ye 21st 1700 . . . I was told that Mrs Mildmay designed if she had cast you to sell ye Estate to one Medlicot an Attorney in Ireland.

However, whatever success Dacre may have had in some of of these legal proceedings he was in the end entirely defeated, and his sisters were put in possession of Dunsink and Scribblestown, the annual rents of which then amounted to about 180*l*.

The final decision in this suit did not take place until Trinity Term 1701,[1] and I have found among one of Westgarth's accounts particulars of all the costs incurred by Dacre in connection with this litigation, which amounted to 540*l*. The counsel on his side included the Attorney- and the Solicitor-General for Ireland,[2] Sir Stephen Rice, Sir Toby Butler, and Mr. Saunders.

A noteworthy item in the bill of costs is 'spent att the taverne with Mr Saunders & Sir Toby Butler 00..07..03,' which seems a strange disbursement to be charged by a solicitor in his bill. In those days it was not uncommon in Ireland to give some fees to the Bar of a 'Luidore' (Louis d'or), which equalled 1*l*. 1*s*., but fees calculated in guineas were also given.[3]

I have been unable to trace any further the lives of Anne and her invalid sister Dorothy; the latter did not marry, and I expect she continued to live with her married sister.

Anne died on January 18th, 1718, and was buried at Romford. Her husband, baptized at Romford on November 23rd,

---

[1] I have a long document beginning 'Readings in the King's Court in Michaelmas term in II. Wm. III. (1699).' This was an action for trespass and ejectment by T. Tilson, lessee of Mildmay, against R. Hamilton, lessee of Dacre, concerning Dunsink and Scribblestown. Verdict for plaintiff, with 6*d*. damages.

[2] Robert Rochfort, afterwards a judge, and Alan Brodrick, afterwards Attorney-General, appear at that period to have been respectively Attorney-General and Solicitor-General.—*Hay. Dig.*

[3] To persons not conversant with the system of barrister's fees, there may seem to be no difference between 1*l*. 1*s*. and a guinea; but in practice a guinea fee to counsel may be either 1*l*. 3*s*. 6*d*. or 1*l*. 6*s*. as the case may be.

1653, was buried in the family vault in that church on May 1st, 1743.[1] He was succeeded by their eldest son Carew, who was a considerable friend of Thomas Lord Dacre, and who died in 1780 at the advanced age of ninety-six.

When Dacre hurried over to England on hearing of his father's death, as travelling was then such a difficult and tedious business, it is not to be wondered at that he left his children behind at Clones. The company of several young children would have been a source of considerable delay and embarrassment when a speedy journey was necessary; but once having arrived at Belhus it does seem to have been somewhat remiss on his part not to have made arrangements for having them sent over during the summer months instead of leaving them in a remote part of Ireland with no relations to look after them.

Dacre, however, at that period had matters nearer to his heart than his children's welfare and happiness, as his own affairs called for his undivided attention. The business of getting into order the neglected estates to which he had succeeded must have taken up much of his time; and, besides this occupation, he indulged in the more pleasing one of courting a rich young widow in the neighbourhood. With both these matters on his hands, no wonder he had little time in which to think of his children; and to such good use did Dacre put the three months which elapsed after his return from Ireland that on August 4th, 1696, he married, by license at Blackmore, Essex, as his third wife, Sarah Saltonstall, who, born in 1668, was therefore in the twenty-eighth year of her age, while he was nearly forty-three. She was a daughter of Sir Capel Luckyn, Baronet, of Messing, Essex,[2] and widow of

[1] *Mis. Gen.* ii. p. 265.
[2] The family of Luckyn, or Lucking, was a very old one in Essex. Sir Capel was the eldest son of Sir William, created a baronet 1628. A grandson of Sir Capel took the surname of Grimston, and is ancestor of the present Earl of Verulam.—*Mo.* ii. p. 177. The probable reason for Sarah being married at Blackmore was that her sister Muriel had married a Mr. Thomas Smyth, who was the Squire of that place.—*Ibid.* ii. p. 57. In some MS. notes Anne Lady Dacre, widow of Thomas Lord Dacre, speaks of Sarah as being 'by all account low & vulgar.'

Philip Saltonstall, of Groves, South Ockendon, in that county.[1] Their marriage settlement shows that she was life-tenant of lands in the latter parish consisting of about six hundred acres, and her interest in this was settled to her separate use, and so was also all her personal property. On his side Dacre covenanted to pay to trustees the sum of 800*l.* within one year of the birth of each child which might be born to them of this marriage, and survive its birth for that length of time, the interest arising from such sum or sums of 800*l.* to be paid to Dacre during his life, and after his decease the capital to be divided among such children of the marriage as might live to survive him.

The marriage settlement shows that, at time of her marriage, Sarah Saltonstall had two children, Richard, born 1689,[2] who died young,[3] and Philippa, who married a Mr. John Goodere, of Claybury, Essex, and whose descendants lived at South Ockendon within the memory of persons still living or only recently dead. Towards the end of the eighteenth century the family was represented by Mr. John Goodere, who seems to have been a typical ' Squire Western.' Before Lord Dacre's death he had entered into negotiations with Mr. Goodere about purchasing some of his estate, and after his decease these were carried on by Lady Dacre, his widow, but no purchase seems to have resulted. Mr. Goodere wrote to Lord Dacre on April 1st, 1782, when he said :—

as to the estate ... my grand point is to sell it being so very unwholesome a country, and destitute of fox hunting, which is the only sport I really like ... I amm now A hunting in Cambridgeshire, and cannot be up this fortnight.

---

[1] The family of Saltonstall was an old one in Ockendon; Gylbert Saltonstall was married there 1583. Philip, the father of this Philip, was said to have been killed by a fall from his horse at Belhus in 1668, the same year in which Sarah Luckyn was born.—*Pal. M. St.* p. 101 ; *Mo.* i. p. 101. Lord Dacre says in error that Sarah was widow of *Richard* Saltonstall. The settlement made on the marriage of Dacre to Sarah proves that her first husband's name was Philip.—*F. P.*

[2] *Pal. M. St.* p. 107.   [3] As to his illness and death, *post*, pp. 545-6.

A few years later, in 1790, an agent named Wiggins, employed occasionally by Lady Dacre, who had seen Mr. Gepp [1] at Chelmsford about this matter, wrote: 'Mr. G—— is not a steady regular man to do business with, if Mr. Gepp sees him it is but for a minute, & with difficulty gets a regular answer from him.'

Lord Dacre says that Dacre Barrett had issue by this third marriage a daughter named Catherine,[2] but he appears to have made an unaccountable mistake as to her name, as among the entries of baptisms for South Ockendon is the following: '1697, Iva Sarah, daughter of Dacres Barrett Esq, & Sarah his wife, bap.'[3] and Dacre in his will speaks of his daughter Sarah as being his only child by his third wife.

We have a letter dated September 25th, 1696, from Mr. Walter Dawson, asking Dacre to appoint him his agent at Clones, in which he says:—

Lately my wife & I have hard of your marriadge, which wee much Rejoiced at, and that $\overline{w}^t$ adds to it is that you have got a fine Lady of a good family, and a noble fortune with her, to whom wee wish you much Joy, & now I am wholey out of hopes of your ever living with us againe in Ireland, of whose good neighbourhood we are deprived, your family at Clownish are well, I am tould that you designe to remove your familly this winter.

We have also a letter from him to Dacre containing a somewhat belated congratulation on his third marriage written from Ireland in the March following that event. The writer begins: 'I doe heartily congratulate your happy marriage wth soe fine a lady as fame reports her to be.'

A letter from Dacre to Westgarth already quoted from [4] shows that, although he left all his children, except perhaps Richard, at Clones during the winter which succeeded his third matrimonial venture, Dacre was not altogether without some

---

[1] Evidently his Solicitor, and an ancestor of the present firm of 'Gepp & Sons,' solicitors, at Chelmsford.
[2] *Ld. D. His.* p. 59.   [3] *Pal. M. St.* p. 107.   [4] *Ante*, p. 516.

qualms of conscience for his neglect of them; and the following letter shows that the children were not left without some provision being made for their education :—

[Addressed] ffor the Honble Dacre Barret att Belhouse in Essex in the Kingdom of England
　　　These
To be left in Rumford Bagg to be sent as aforesd.

Cloneis ye 24th of December 1696

S^r.

. . . . As for myself wth in aweek after yor going away I came to this towne, and did my endeavor to teach the children to write before they went over, as yor honor may see that I did my best to teach them, and indeed it was very difficult att first, but now they are admired by all, that being so young & little should do so well, but they would be in more Awe if they were w^th .yor self I taught them every day, and went to James Learys house every night, I never endured more inconvency when I was teaching in my life for I could get none else to teach, and I was waiteing dayly when yo^u would send for y^m, and Now I am going away half naked for want of clothes, and has not a whole shooe to my foot, for yor Stewards would not give me not so much as would buy me a pair of shoes, and if I could get any Schollars w^thin 4 or 5 miles to get me som clothes, I would see the children once a week, least they should forget that wch I wth hardship taught them, they are very well. . . . . thus remaineing yor hono^rs
　　　　　　　　　　humble Servt till death
　　　　　　　　　　JOHN MC COLLIN.

On March 1st, 1696, McCollin was paid 3*l.* 10*s.* by Dacre Barrett's order for teaching his children to write for seven months;[1] and it is pleasant to think that he was not forgotten by Dacre after the latter had left Clones. There is a long account of Westgarth's made up since his account in 1698, in which there appear several entries of payments to this indignant teacher on his behalf, such as 'paid for Cloathes for John McCullin 0001..016..11'; 'a paire of shoose for John McCullin

---
[1] McCollin's receipt.—*F. P.*

00..04..11,' and we have a receipt from this John dated 'this 4th day of Feb 1710,' which is as follows:—

For a Druged coat & making	. . .	0 14	7½
For a shirt	. .	0 03	0
One pair shoos	. .	0 3	6
2½ of flanen and necessaries	. .	0 2	0
		1 3	1½

We have some accounts relating to the children's journey from Clones, as there is a receipt among our papers from one Dannell McCernus, 'March 13th 1696 Rec^d of Mr Westgarth to board charges of ourselves & horses to Clownish when wee came up with ye children 00-13.3.' By 'came up,' McCernus means 'came to Dublin,' where he was paid by Westgarth, who lived in that city.

Besides the difficulty of travelling in those days, another reason which may have induced Dacre not to bring these children with him to Essex when he first returned there is suggested by the address on the following letter. This address would seem to show that for some little time after his third marriage Dacre lived at Groves, his newly married wife's house, which was only about two miles from Belhus. It is almost certain that after his father's death Belhus stood in urgent need of some repairs, and it had to be refurnished to a considerable extent, for, as his father had left all his own furniture to his daughter Anne, all that remained there was what belonged to Dorothy Lady Dacre.[1] It is more than likely that Groves did not offer sufficient accommodation for Dacre and his wife, as well as the children of his three wives, and that therefore, until Belhus was ready to move into, he was obliged to let the children, who were in Ireland, remain there. The letter in question is as follows:—

For the Honble Dacre Barrett Esqr. att Groves These.
Deare Cosen
   This is to make a Proposall to you from my Ld. Lovelace, Mr. Horkins, and my selfe that if [you] can lend us

[1] *Ante*, pp. 400, 401.

y^r House for a fortnight we will go a great way toward destroying that subtle Species (calld foxes) out of y^r Countrey in wch we think we shant only divert our selves, but do the Countrey Service, since att y^t time of ye grase they are bigg, & in killing one you kill 5 or 6 often.

If y^t be reasonable I will Assure you we will be no Charge to you, for I have sent money by ye bearer to buy Corne, Straw, hay, Mutton, drinke &c. but if it be any way inconvenient to you, One line from you shall fully Satisfie

S^r y^r Aff humble Servt
T. CHUTE.[1]

My Gr. sends her Love & Service to y^r Lady & y^r Selfe.

My wife sends her humblest to ye both, as allso dos y^r T. Chute 9 March 9$\frac{8}{7}$

This letter is interesting as showing the vast difference between the way in which hunting men of those days regarded foxes and the way they do now. Then foxes were looked upon as vermin, as we now look upon rats or stoats and such like, to be killed at all seasons of the year, as the primary object then in hunting was not sport, as we now understand the word, but the destruction of a noxious animal. In an old pocket account book of Dacre's for the years 1704-5 there are several entries of payments for killing foxes, as, for example, 'To a man for killing a fox 1/-.' Foxes, in the times of which I am writing, were far more scarce than now, when in most parts of England the majority of persons regulate their behaviour towards them in accordance with the sentiments thus expressed by the immortal Mr. Jorrocks: 'In the summer I loves him with all the bardour of affection; not an 'air of his beautiful 'ead would I hurt . . . . but when the hautum comes . . . . 'ow I glories in pursuin' of him to destruction.'

While on the subject of the scarcity or otherwise of foxes in England in Dacre Barrett's time, it may not be without interest to remark that wolves were still fairly common in Ireland as

[1] The writer was the youngest son of Chaloner and Catherine Chute, *ante*, p. 264. Thomas Chute, when aged about twenty-four, married, in September 1687, Elizabeth Revett, of Ufford, Suffolk, about eighteen, and had several children.—*Har. So.* xxxi. p. 15.

late as 1696, as in November and in December of that year John Smith, writing to him from Clones, says in one letter: 'There are 5 wolves seen in Slebah which hath done much harm there, and in the College lands the last weeke they killed A Man which shot at them'; and writing about three weeks later he says:—

the wolves are increased to 14, & haue done much harme in the College land, & Sleabah, Capt Mongumry sent some Dragoons to Hunt them but could not meet with them, and within 2 or 3 nights after they Droue away of Coll Ecclin Bullocks & his aboue 120, which were tracked & found in A River nere the 5 mile town all but 24, which are not yet heard off.

That Dacre kept wolf-dogs appears from his accounts, when several entries occur which refer to them, such as 'Aug 15 1685 To ye man yt carried y^e Wolf bitch to Clones 8^a-6^d'; 'Feb 168$\frac{6}{5}$ meat for ye wolf doggs 9^d'; and so on. When Dacre was living in Liverpool he evidently lost one of these dogs, as we find: 'Aug 15th 1687 to ye Bellman for crying ye Wolf dog 1/-.' The efforts of the bellman were no doubt crowned with success, as there is the subsequent entry: 'Oct 15 1657 for meat for ye wolf bitch -:-: 4.'

Before treating of Dacre's life after he went to live at Belhus as its owner, it will be well to see what Thomas Lord Dacre says about his grandfather.[1]

Dacre was High Sheriff of Essex in the year 1705; he was a person of great Understanding and universal Learning, and was very much respected and Esteemed in the County he lived in, a true and Zealous friend of Liberty and of the Protestant Religion, for which he was an avowed Advocate in the most dangerous times (especially in the Reign of King James Second) and had he (as he at first seemed to intend) Engaged himself in Publick affairs, for which he had all the Necessary qualifications, he would most likely have distinguisht himself, particularly had he come into Parliament; But being naturally serious, and having met with many Vexations in his Youth, this disposistion

[1] *Ld. D. His.*

increased with Years, and inclined him (especially in the latter part of his days) to give himself over much to Retirement (which Course of Life indeed insensibly clouded and soured his Temper). His love of Solitude however did not prevent his endeavouring to be serviceable to mankind; he was in particular a most knowing and impartial Magistrate, and as such applied to from all parts of the County; his advice and Decisions being held in great Estimation by the Gentlemen of the County, and regarded in a very singular manner by all sorts of people. In the winter when he was in London (where he had a good house in Great Russell St Bloomsbury) he frequently attended the meetings of the Royal Society, then in its Meridian, of which he was an useful member, and the learned Dr Derham makes honourable mention of him in his philosophical Essays. He died at Belhouse anno 1723, and lies buried in the parish church there, where he has a monument set up by his eldest daughter, who was his Executrix. The Epitaph on it a very paltry one in ev'ry respect, and full of pedantic flattery, which he did not need having many real good qualities.

The date assigned to Dacre's death is not correct, and the mistake probably arose in copying Lord Dacre's MS.; it is incredible that he should not have known the date of his grandfather's death, especially as he succeeded him, and it is remarkable that Collins's 'Peerage,' which Lord Dacre corrected, as far as related to his own family, should also give the date as 1723. The entry of Dacre's burial in the Aveley Register is as follows: 'The Honble Dacre Lennard Barrett Lennard was buried Jan 13. 1724.' The entry has the name Lennard inserted twice as above. What was then called January 1724 would now be reckoned 1725. I have had Dacre's tomb in Aveley Church opened, and the inscription on the coffin is 'The Honourable Dacre Barrett Lennard died Jan 24 1724 74 years.' It is clear that neither the date of death nor the age assigned to Dacre on his coffin-plate is accurate, although it is not easy to understand how the persons responsible for the inscription should have made these mistakes. I have shown (*ante*, p. 412) that he was born in November 1653, so that in November 1724 he would have been seventy-one years of age. In the following January (still 1724 by the then system of reckoning) he must have been in his seventy-second year, and not '74 years.' The date of his death is shown by the finding of the Master in Chancery, who after Dacre's death had the administration of his estates, to have been January 1st, 172$\frac{4}{6}$.[1]

In reference to Dacre being High Sheriff, it may be remarked that in those days it was the custom for the Under Sheriff on his appointment to agree to undertake many more of the responsibilities, duties, and expenses connected with the office of High Sheriff than is now the case. Mr. John Cooper, of the Middle Temple, was Dacre's Under Sheriff, and in addition to covenanting to hold him harmless for any errors he might be guilty of in carrying out his duties as Under Sheriff he also agreed

to pay for the dinners of the Justices of the Peace attending Quarter Sessions, and to defray the charges of treating the Justices of Assize, and their retinue on the road to and from the Assize, in case they think fit to stay anywhere in their passage; and at his own cost to execute, whip, or put in the pillory any persons so sentenced, and to pay any reward payable by the Sheriff by Act of Parliament for the apprehension of any Highwayman, Clipper, or Coyner; and also to be at all costs for elections for Knights of the Shire, and of making all Proclamations.

As has been stated, Dorothy Lady Dacre survived her son Richard two years, dying in April 1698. The following letter from her grandson, T. Chute, to his cousin Dacre shows how little ninety-three years of an active life had done to destroy the vigour, or crush the powers of sympathy, existing in that very remarkable old lady. We see that almost in her dying moments she still interested herself greatly in the quarrel among her grandchildren, and did all she could to induce Dacre to become reconciled with his sisters.

Deare Cousen
    What we had just reason to feare is now come to pass, my Gr. dyed on Saturday about 6 att night whilest Prayers

---

[1] This finding is in an account book, which accounts were, year by year, passed by Master Francis Elde, and signed by him (*F. P.*); and an inscription in Aveley Church under the monument to him states that he died on January 1, 1724, aged 74.

were readeing to her: I never Saw a more patient resigned Creature, and Sensible to the last moment.

Soon after you went away my C. Mildmay, & C. Lennard,[1] came in, and after they were gone my Lady calld me, and asked whether ye mett here or not, I told her No, She wishd ye had (she replied) for she woud have recomended Peace and Unity to ye both, and Commanded me to acquaint ye both wth it, I promised her I would, and likewise endeavour to accomplish it by all ye Assistance in my power. This gave her great Satisfaction and I would go a great way to effect it, for her, and both y^r Sakes, but I know it is very little I am Capable of doing more than laying these, allmost last dying words, of our Grandor before ye, for she scarce ever spoke to be well understood afterwards, I have told C. Mildmay ye Same and I hope ye both will consider of it.

My Lady perticulurly ordered a private funerall, & to be buried att Chevening, No relation (it seemes according to Custome now) goes wth ye body but my wife, who she has made her Executor, and the Gentlemen of the Countrey to Carry her Lp. to the grave. I am realy very much afflicted for the death of so true a good Gr. & friend and therefore I hope you will pardon me for only adding that I am

      Deare Causn y^r most
        Aff^{te} humble Servt
          T. CHUTE.

I beg mine & my wifes humble Service to y^r Lady &c.
Ap. 19. [16]98.

As I have shown, this pathetic expression of Lady Dacre's dying wish for a reconciliation was in vain, and Dacre and his sisters fought the matter out to the bitter end; even the verdict in the lawsuit between them does not appear to have terminated their disputes, as a letter from a Mr. White at Brentwood to Carew Mildmay shows that two years after that lawsuit was ended there were still disputes going on between Dacre and Anne about the furniture at Belhus. Richard left all the furniture there that was his to Anne, but we have seen that a considerable portion of it belonged to Lady Dacre, and had been there over forty years when Richard died. Anne, living so near

[1] Cousin Mildmay and Cousin Lennard: no doubt alluding to Dacre's sisters Anne and Dorothy.

Belhus, directly after her father's death came to take possession of what he had left her before Dacre had time to arrive from Ireland. Under these circumstances further disputes and quarrels were inevitable, as neither Anne nor Dacre could have been absolutely certain as to the ownership of some of the articles of furniture; and Anne, being first in the field when any doubt occurred to her mind, probably decided the point in her own favour, and promptly carried off the article in question.

The letter from Mr. White is as follows :—

S^r
    pursuant to the desires of yor selfe and Lady, I waited upon Mr Barrett, on ffryday last; and imparted to him, what you desired me to doe; he was surprized at the errand, and not only acquainted me wth the Lady Dacre's Will; but Deed of Gift: by her Will she gave the use of all her goods to her Sonn for his life; and after his decease to M^r. Barrett her Grandsonn for life &c, and by Deed of Gift (many yeares subsequent to her Will) she gave her goods to Dacres Barrett Esqr. (her Grandsonn).

Mr Barrett saith a great many of the Goods, soe devised, and given to him by the Lady Dacres, are imbezelled, and never came to his hands: and he apprehends himselfe to be the injured pson: I wish I was capable of reconcileing this affaire, or that providence would direct some good friend to interpose soe far, as that this misunderstanding may be adjusted wthout any expense, wch is the hearty desire (and as far as I am capable, and have an opportunity) shall be the faithful the endeavor of S^r

                                      Yo^r humble serv^t
Brentwood.   THO : WHITE.
  17, August, 1703.

Dacre Barrett appears to have taken an interest in gardening, as there are several references among the letters of his Irish agents as to the condition of his garden at Clones which they would probably not have mentioned had he not taken a personal interest in it. Then, in the course of a letter to his agent Westgarth in Dublin, written from Clones on July 13th, 1693, he says: 'You will oblige me by letting your man call at one Artons a seedsman's shop in Thomas Street, I think his sign is the Orange tree, for a few seeds.' Then follows this list of the seeds he required :—

> Collyflower twelve pennyworth.
> Clove Gily flower ½ once, if dear ¼.
> Carnation about as much
> Cabbidge seed an ounce
> Sparrowgrass an ounce.

And a year later he asks Westgarth to send him leek, onion, and French bean seeds, also Cardus,[1] Scorsonera,[2] and 'a small quantity of ye seed of ye Sun flower.'

Three years later a lady writes to him :—

Sr   Carrow Arill ye 6th 96.

> I am very much out of Artichokes I onderstand you haue great store of good ones tharfore I entreat you will be so kind as to spair what you can of them and a few clove gilliflower slips to
>
>   Yo^r most affect^{te}
>   gossipe & hum^{ble} Sar^t
>   ELIZA BLANEY.[3]

We have also this receipt from a nurseryman for fruit trees which from the date were probably supplied for Belhus :—

> ther is 2 peachs trees at 2/6   .   .   0   5   0
>   3 apricocks[4] at 2/-   .   .   .   0   06   0
>   5 cherritrees at 10   .   .   .   0   04   2
>   In all   0   15   2

And at the foot when receipting the bill the seller appends the following guarantee :—

> I oblige myself hereby in case the above trees or any of y^m doe not grow, or be not right fruit, that I will give good trees for any of them that shall fail in one year from the date hereof, witness my hand 4th March 1697   GEORGE X ADDISON.
>   his / mark

---

[1] Carduus, a genus of erect herbs resembling thistles; in former times it was held in high esteem as a remedy for all manner of diseases.—C. D.

[2] Scorzonera, not much cultivated in England.

[3] No doubt one of the family of Lord Blaney, but from the Christian name and date not a Lady Blaney.

[4] Obsolete form of spelling apricots.—C. D.

This is a great contrast to the notice which modern nurserymen usually put in their catalogues : ' That we give no warranty, expressed or implied, as to description, quality, or productiveness, or any other matter relating to the seeds or plants we supply, and will not in any way be held responsible for any failure of crop.'

We have some evidence that Dacre was fond of horses and of sport; a letter written in a very good hand, dated 1693, from a certain 'Char Eccles,' who speaks of himself as being but a 'younge jocky,'[1] shows that Dacre then owned a stallion so good that the writer considered it worth while to send one of his mares to him from a distance of thirty miles. Then we have Mr. Barton's invitation to come partridge hawking,[2] and Mr. Pigott, in the P.S. to a letter previously quoted from,[3] says that he is staying with friends 'for hunting on the edgs of Cambridgeshire where we have had verie strong chases, but the graye gelding rides hartely'; this argues a knowledge of the 'graye gelding' on the part of Dacre, and an interest in his doings. In his accounts there were three entries during November and December 1689 'for powder & shot,' so presumably he was interested in shooting as well as in hunting. Very soon after Dacre had succeeded his father, while he was still living at Groves, he was in search of a good gamekeeper, as a Mr. Nicholas writes to him to say, ' I have my choyse of two jolly[4] fellows for keepers, the one was bred up in the Lord petre his park, neere you in Essex, and knows all the Country round,' and he goes on to say that he will accept the wages Dacre offered—namely, 15*l.* a year. A little later, in 1705, that distinguished statesman, Sir Stephen Fox, writes to recommend a man to him as 'a very good keeper of a Parke both for the skill he hath in Deer, and the care he takes of 'em.'

It is noteworthy that Sir Stephen addresses Dacre as 'the Honourable Dacre Barrett Esq.,' and so also did a Sir Thos. Littleton, as well as many persons of less social position. This

---

[1] Then meaning a person connected with or dealing in horses.—*C. D.*
[2] *Ante*, p. 513.   [3] *Ante*, p. 476.   [4] Brave.—*C. D.*

may have been merely an error on their part, or it may be that in those days the descendants of a peer were commonly styled 'Honourable,' while in the present day we apply that title only to peers' children. On the other hand his cousin the Earl of Sussex, when writing to Dacre,[1] addresses the letter to 'Mr. " Barret " Lennard,' not even 'Esq.'; so possibly there were formerly less strict rules than now as to how to address persons, as certainly was the case in respect of spelling.

In the early part of Dacre's career as owner of Belhus he seems to have taken a considerable interest in politics, and possibly had some idea of standing for Parliament in England, as he had already done in Ireland. In December 1700 a Mr. Lamerton writes to tell him that he hears writs are getting ready for calling a new Parliament, and that the existing one will be dissolved as soon as they are ready. This Mr. Lamerton, from whom we have other letters, appears from them to have been much interested in politics and public matters, and to have been in the navy, as one of his letters is dated 'Copenhagen Rode,' giving an account of the English bombardment of that city in support of Charles XII. A Mr. James Sloane also wrote three letters to Dacre in 1700 about election matters; one dated in December of that year refers to the impending new Parliament, and there he says:—

therefore I hope you will forthwith apply all y^r strength and diligence towards y^r election for y^t is ye general work all over ye kingdom, and a day's neglect may loose what is not to be regained in such cases, therefore either give itt quite over, or goe about itt immediately wth all y^r might.

I imagine that Dacre adopted the former of the alternative courses which his correspondent suggested, and gave 'itt quite over,' as I have found nothing to lead me to believe he ever did stand for any constituency in England. Another of Dacre's correspondents on political matters was a Mr. Clarke, who in a letter which bears no date, but from its context was evidently written just before 1700, tells him a good deal of the Essex

[1] *Ante*, p. 337.

political gossip which was current at the end of the XVIIth century. The persons he mentions are Sir William Luckyn,[1] Mr. Bullock,[2] Mr. ffitch,[3] Sir Charles Barrington,[4] Sir Francis Marsham,[5] Lord Maynard,[6] and Sir Anthony Abdy.[7] Most of these names which then represented families of importance in Essex have disappeared, anyway from that county, during the two hundred years which have elapsed since this letter was written, and there is no descendant in the male line of any of those families still remaining in the county who resides at what was in 1700 the family seat of his ancestor.

I do not know who this Mr. Clarke was; possibly he was a music-master, as in a letter, dated September 19th, he speaks of having been to see a harpsichord which he says he thinks is a bad one, and he goes on to say that he proposes to come to Belhus on Sunday evening and teach ' ye Ladys on Monday.'[8] Whether music-master or not, he was more or less a breeder of horses, as the following quaint extract of a letter from him to Dacre's son Richard shows that he wanted to sell to them at Belhus a colt of his own breeding :—

When last wth you I speak something of the Coult y[r] fine Horse gott, but then itt was little ; but now it is growne to that incredible greatness that everyone Admires him that sees Him ; and say if you wold make a Horse of Wax there can not be a finer shape, others say a very Topping Horse was his Sire, and that he will growe to be worth forty guineas. This makes me I can not satisfie myself without bringing Him for the Hono[rd] Esqr. Barrett, and y[r] self to see ; and I hope you will think

---

[1] Of Little Waltham, second and last baronet of the creation of 1661, who died in 1700. The first of these baronets was second son of Sir William Luckyn, first baronet, and brother of Sir Capell, second baronet of the creation of 162$\frac{8}{9}$, ancestor of the Earls of Verulam.

[2] Bullock of Falkborne Hall, Witham.

[3] William Fytch, M.P., Maldon, January 1700 and November 1701 ; probably of Woodham Walter.

[4] Of Hatfield Broadoak, fifth baronet; extinct 1832.

[5] Of High Laver, third baronet; extinct 1776.

[6] Of Easton ; now represented by the Countess of Warwick.

[7] Of Fillols (now Felix) Hall, Kelvedon, second baronet ; extinct 1868.

[8] In an account book dated 1704-5 there is this entry : ' For ye harpsechord, £5 15s.'

him fitting for y^r bringing up; and his purchase shall be no more than he is worth to any man.

Another of Dacre's friends was Mr. Cheek, who claimed the title of FitzWalter; he wrote him several letters [1] about political matters in Essex. In one of them dated March ye 15, 1705, he says, 'on Thursday next my Ld Rivers,[2] Ld Manchester,[3] Ld Gray [4] [sic], Ld Walden and y^r humble serv^t Desire y^r good companie at Chelmsford in Order to consult matters about Elecons.'

Dacre appears at times to have suffered a good deal from ague, which formerly was very prevalent in those parts of Essex which border on the Thames. John Norden in his 'Essex discribed'[5] says: 'I can not comende the healthfulness of it [Essex] and especiallie nere to the sea coastes ... and other lowe places about the creekes which gave me a moste cruelle quarterne fever.'

Arthur Young[6] also refers to ague as being a terrible scourge in Essex in his time, but now, although some persons still suffer from it there, it is greatly declining in frequency. Some one of the name of Nickolls wrote to Dacre in September 1703, saying that he had written to Dr. Slare 'about ye return of ye ague,' and that by that doctor's direction he sent him '6 specifick Draughts; 3 cordial night draughts; and one bottle of Pearle Cordial.' These remedies did Dacre good, or else he got better in spite of them, as we have a letter to Dacre from Dr. Slare, dated some two months later, in which he expresses himself glad to hear that the former continues well in health, and goes on to say that persons suffering from quartan fever are very apt to have relapses 'at this time of ye year until

---

[1] Robert Cheek, of Pyrgo, near Havering, claimed in 1660 the barony of Fitz-Walter, and signed these letters 'FitzWalter.' He was succeeded by his nephew, E. Cheek, who died in 1707. Letters I have from both R. and E. Cheek show that they wrote their name without the final 'e' which is attributed to them in the C. P.

[2] Richard Savage, Earl Rivers, of St. Osyth, Essex, succeeded 1694, died 1712.

[3] Lord Manchester then owned estates in Little Lees and Great Waltham, Essex.

[4] Lord Grey of Werke owned the manor of Epping, and died there 1706.

[5] C. S. P.   [6] A. Young, born 1741, died 1820.

ye sun begins to make a return towards us, viz December the XI.'

In one of his letters to Dacre, his neighbour Dr. Derham says: 'I have gotten an ague y^t batters me bitterly ... my head is so bad y^t I hope you excuse me for forgetting divers things I have to say, as I am sure I have done.'

Richard, Dacre's son, also writes to him to say that he has a fever which has turned to an ague, and that he intends to take 'ye Bark if it continues,' and in another, 'I am now going home with my ague fit.' We have another undated letter, apparently about that period, to some man in Aveley advising him to take bark for his ague; so that its use as a cure for that illness appears to have been very general in Essex as long ago as the early part of the eighteenth century, although the discovery of it as a drug, which was first made in Spain, only dates from about sixty years earlier.

In the small interleaved volume already referred to,[1] there is a note to the effect that Dacre had 'a curious and valuable collection of Books, Medals, and Natural and Artificial Curiosities.' That he was fond of his books is shown by a draft letter from him, no doubt to Westgarth, his agent in Ireland; in this letter, after giving directions about the household things he wants sent from Clones, presumably to England, he says: 'my China wares be packt up with extreme care but above all my books.'

When once settled at Belhus, Dacre discovered in a neighbour at Upminster Rectory a person whom he must have found thoroughly congenial, in spite of the fact that he gave evidence as to Richard Barrett's capability of making a will. This was the learned Rev. William Derham, D.D., F.R.S., a prolific author, and a person who enjoyed very considerable reputation for his scientific researches. Dr. Derham was presented with the living of Upminster, about four miles from Belhus, in 1689, and he lived there until he died in 1735. The first letter we have from him to Dacre is dated 1697, but it is of no interest, being only

[1] *Ante*, p. 392, n. 2.

a formal request for payment of tithes. But besides this letter we have nineteen more from him, ranging in date from 1704 to 1710; several of these letters, however, are not dated, and their contents are not such as to enable their respective dates to be fixed with any degree of certainty. The correspondence shows that Dacre and the learned doctor were most excellent neighbours one to the other, and that in their tastes they had a great many interests in common. It was owing to Dr. Derham's suggestion that Dacre joined the Royal Society, of which he was elected a member in 1705. In one of his letters, dated August 5th and no doubt written in 1704, the doctor says

one thing I had intended to say, but had like to have forgotten is, that I shall be glad to persuade you to be a member of the Royal Society. That you may see how honble and ingenious persons many of them are, wth which you are to asociate, I have sent you the last year's List of them.

In another letter, February 3rd, 170$\frac{4}{5}$, he tells Dacre that he is elected a member, and that 'P. George,' obviously meaning the Prince Consort, had become a Fellow. Some five years later he gives Dacre an account of the disputes between the doctors Sloane and Woodward, and of 'our unhappy squabbles at Gresh Coll.[1] which are very prejudicial to the honour of our most famous Society.'

Among the letters we have of Dacre's son Richard to his father there are some which relate to the fatal illness of Richard Saltonstall, the son of Dacre's third wife by her first husband. These letters are not dated, but one of them contains this passage: 'He told me Dr. Blackall will not be made a Bishop this time.' Dr. Blackall was made Bishop of Exeter 1707, and so we know that they were written previously to that date. Poor young Saltonstall was, no doubt, taken by his mother to London in order to obtain good medical advice, and was attended by Drs. Sloane and Ratcliffe, the most fashionable physicians of the time. He suffered from some sort of fever,

[1] In those days the Royal Society used to meet at Gresham College.

for which, among other things, he was given bark, and Richard says that

Dr. Sloane who was here just now gives us hopes of his recovery but does not like some of his symptoms and saies y^t all People in ffevers are best in the morning. He adds y^t these sort of ffevers swarm in the town, and out of scores of his patients he has had but one infirm girl who died.

When Dr. Ratcliffe was called in he gave very small hopes of the patient's recovery, but he changed the treatment, and ordered him 'to eat chicken Brothes, and drink as much sack whey as he pleases, which was denied him all along by Doctor Sloan, for he often asked for it to eat.' In spite of this, however, the poor fellow continued to get worse, and one day Richard writes: 'He is continually raving of Bellas [*sic*] and askt very often, when sensible, for some preserves made there, My mother desires you to order Mdm Jane[1] to send up some cherry and currant, made up with half wait of sugar.' I am unable to find anything by which to fix the exact date or place of his death, which no doubt followed shortly on the receipt of this letter, which is only dated 'Monday 4 o'clock.'

On July 25th, 1715, Dacre was appointed a Deputy Lieutenant for Essex by the Earl of Suffolk and Bindon, who was the Lord-Lieutenant of that county, and on the following day the Earl appointed him to be Colonel of the Green Regiment of Foot of the Trained Bands.

In those days the Lord-Lieutenant was the head of the Militia of his county, and those he appointed Deputy Lieutenants became *ipso facto* highly placed officers of that Militia, and therefore the position of a Deputy Lieutenant was one which carried with it duties and responsibilities at times sufficiently onerous. Now that the post of Lord-Lieutenant has ceased to have any connection with the Militia, his duties and responsibilities are very greatly diminished, and practically none at all are left to his Deputy Lieutenants, who are his deputies

[1] The writer means his step-mother and his sister Jane Barrett.

THE MILITIA

in name only.[1] So great, however, is the objection in England to abolish any institution or system, unless it is considered to be actually harmful, that the nominal rank of a Deputy Lieutenant has been retained and commissions to that rank given by the Lords-Lieutenant of the various counties to persons having no connection with the army. As a relic of his long-vanished military importance the modern Deputy Lieutenant still wears at levées and such-like functions a cocked hat and a uniform of a more or less military nature, in which he not infrequently looks as ill at ease as he often feels.

I have a long muster-roll of the soldiers serving under Dacre, and also several earlier rolls; one of them made for his wife's former husband, Major Philip Saltonstall, when he commanded the 'souldiers raised within the hundred of Chafford and part of the hundred of Barstable' in 1690; and one for Richard Saltonstall, an ancestor of the Major's. The latter is not dated, but appears, from the style of writing, to be not later than the end of the sixteenth or early in the seventeenth century.

This Richard was probably a son of Sir Richard Saltonstall, who was Lord Mayor of London 1598, and died 1601. The list is very carefully made, and at the end contains this summary of the men and their arms :—

Musketts	xxxi	
Pikes	lxvi	cclxxiiij
Callivers[2] . . .	lxv	
Bills & Halberds . . .	cxii	

We have also a notice dated 'this xij of September 1605 Southockenden,' and signed 'Ric^R Saltonstall,' to the High Constables of the hundred of Barstable, that they cause all persons in the hundred who

were or have been chardged wth the findinge of anie Armor or weapons That theie, and everie of them, doe make in redines and sufficient order for service, the Armor and weapons wherwth theie have beene so chardged as aforesaid against the xxvj daie

---
[1] Written before Mr. Haldane's Scheme for Army reform was made public.
[2] Calliver, or caliver, was a sort of light musket not fired from a stand.— C. D.

of this moneth, and that by viij of the Clocke in the mornynge of the same daie, theie do appeare before mee.'

The notice goes on to say that these persons are to appear 'in theire owne persons yf theie bee fitt, and of Abillitie of bodie so to doe, or otherwise such as are not, to provide such men, as are sufficient in that behalfe, to beare the same for them.'

I found all these rolls in one bundle, and I think they may have been given to Dacre at the time he took command of the regiment in order to assist him in seeing that all the parishes in his district sent their proper quota of men to serve in the Militia. There are also several lists for different parishes got out by their respective constables. They are somewhat curious documents, and the following short one for a small parish will serve as a specimen of the others :—

> The returne of ye Constables of Northockend^n June 3^d 1691.
> Sr Tho Littleton findes a horse for all his estate.[1]
> Sr William Russell findes part of a horse.[2]
> Mr Herbert findes half a horse for his Rectory & other lands.[3]
> Edward Sikes findes halfe a foote, & is joined with one out of Childerditch.[4]
> There are two other bargaines about nine pounds p. annum.
> WILLIAM WARD } Constables.
> RICHARD DAWSON }

Dacre had not been long in command of the 'Green Regiment' before Queen Anne died, and very soon after King George's accession we see by the following letter it was thought well to have the Militia in readiness for any emergency that might take place :—

> S^r
> I having received Letters from Mr. Secretary Stanhope wherein the putting the whole Militia of the County in a readiness is very much expected, I must desire you, & the rest of my Deputy Lieutenants, to loose no time in getting them in such

---

[1] Third and last baronet. A distinguished man, for two years Speaker of House of Commons. His grandfather, Sir Adam, married the heiress of the Pointz family, so long the Squires of North Ockendon.
[2] Of 'Stubbers' in this parish, now the property of C. B. Russell.
[3] Edward Herbert, rector 1658-1697. [4] A parish adjoining North Ockendon.

order for his Maj^{ties} Service when'ere they shall be required. And that upon your General Meeting you forthwith dispatch your Returns to me that I may lay them before the Councel., which meeting I hope will be as soon as possible as the p^rsent posture of affairs will admitt of

      I am
       S^r.
  Your most humble and obedient Servant
Audly end   SUFFOLK
 17 Octobr. 1715.

The attempt of the Pretender caused the greatest alarm in Ireland in 1715–6, as we see from the letters remaining from Edmund Kaine, who was then our Irish agent. He wrote in February 1715 (1716 of our style) :—

I can not but giue yor Hon^r an acc^t how I am tormented about the Militia, since the p^rtender landed in Scotland makes all afraid of an invasion in this Kingdom which is much talked of here, and the p̄lyment [parliament] has a vote in the house to make an act to make the Militia of this Kingdom more useful, so that all stiring very much, being there is Armes Come into all the Counties of this Kingdom, and an order from the Government to all officers to Exercize there men once euery week.

Kaine seems to have been most anxious that Dacre should obtain a commission to raise an independent troop of horse composed of his tenantry at Clones. There was no doubt some local jealousy about this, and it would appear that, although Lord Blaney and Colonel Montgomery obtained commissions for raising independent troops of horse of their tenants, Dacre was, in the first instance, only offered an independent company of foot. Kaine was evidently very indignant, it being no doubt a matter of dignity with him, although in one of his letters he gives as a reason for desiring Dacre's men to be mounted, that 'I am too old now to walke affoot'; and he mustered up one hundred and fifty-two horsemen well mounted, whom he took to 'an array.' In the end his efforts were crowned with success, and Dacre obtained the desired commission to raise his own troops of horse.

We have seen how pushed for money Dacre was at one

time, and it is satisfactory to know that he was ultimately in easy circumstances, and that financial worries were not among those he had to contend with in his latter days. At some period after he came to live at Belhus he purchased between three and four hundred acres of land in the neighbourhood, which he could not have done unless his income was then more than sufficient for his needs. I am not able to show what was the value of these lands, nor what was their exact extent, but we get some information on this head from a deed of conveyance by Dacre's daughter Jane, to whom, as we shall see, he left most of this property. A Mr. Freeman made him an offer of his Moor Hall[1] estate at the rate of twenty-three years' purchase on a rental of 216*l.* I imagine that this purchase was never carried through, but he bought some fields of Freeman adjoining the Romford Road, which contained forty acres and were called Bretts.

Very shortly after the death of his cousin the Earl of Sussex, which took place in November 1715, Dacre had a petition to the King prepared, but I have no evidence that it was ever presented; and I think it probable that the marriage of his son, which, we shall see, took place in 1716, prevented him from pursuing the matter further. The petition set forth a few facts concerning the title of Dacre, the death of the late holder of it, and the fact that his only surviving children were Lady Barbara Skelton and Lady Anne Lennard, who were both Catholics. It then goes on to assert that petitioner had sufficient means to support the title, and he prays the King to grant it to him rather than let it fall into abeyance between his two nieces, who are both Catholics, and so 'hinder ye said Honour & Dignity from being either extinguisht or ever coming to any papist to the prejudice of the Protestant Interest of this nation.'

During those politically exciting times which preceded the death of Queen Anne, and continued for a while after the accession of George I., when no man knew for certain whether

---

[1] I do not think that this can refer to the Moor Hall in Aveley, which my father purchased some fifty years ago.

time, and it is satisfactory to know that he was ultimately in easy circumstances, and that financial worries were not among those he had to contend with in his latter days. At some period after he came to live at Belhus he purchased between three and four hundred acres of land in the neighbourhood, which he could not have done unless his income was then more than sufficient for his needs. I am not able to show what was the value of these lands, nor what was their exact extent, but we get some information on this head from a deed of conveyance by Dacre's daughter Jane, to whom, as we shall see, he left most of this property. A Mr. Freeman made him an offer of his Moor Hall[1] estate at the rate of twenty-three years' purchase on a rental of 216*l*. I imagine that this purchase was never carried through, but he bought some fields of Freeman adjoining the Romford Road, which contained forty acres and were called Bretts.

Very shortly after the death of his cousin the Earl of Sussex, which took place in November 1715, Dacre had a petition to the King prepared, but I have no evidence that it was ever presented; and I think it probable that the marriage of his son, which, we shall see, took place in 1716, prevented him from pursuing the matter further. The petition set forth a few facts concerning the title of Dacre, the death of the late holder of it, and the fact that his only surviving children were Lady Barbara Skelton and Lady Anne Lennard, who were both Catholics. It then goes on to assert that petitioner had sufficient means to support the title, and he prays the King to grant it to him rather than let it fall into abeyance between his two nieces, who are both Catholics, and so 'hinder ye said Honour & Dignity from being either extinguisht or ever coming to any papist to the prejudice of the Protestant Interest of this nation.'

During those politically exciting times which preceded the death of Queen Anne, and continued for a while after the accession of George I., when no man knew for certain whether

[1] I am apt to think that this can refer to the Moor Hall in Aveley, which my father purchased some fifty years ago.

the Stuart dynasty would return or not, Dacre's son was much in London, and, no doubt, wrote many more letters to his father, telling him what was going on in the metropolis, than have been preserved ; several of them, however, are in my possession, and are not without interest as containing observations on events then taking place, and on the rumours with which the air was thick.

The father and son appear from their correspondence to have been on the best of terms with each other, and the latter seems to have done his utmost to conduct satisfactorily the various matters of business with which his father entrusted him ; and it is sad to reflect how grave a source of discord was soon to arise between them.

When the Earl of Sussex died his wife and her unmarried daughter Lady Anne returned to England. They had not been long in this country before Richard Barrett made his cousin's acquaintance, and having done so fell in love with her. She was then about thirty-one years of age, and, unless the portraits of her at Belhus by Wissing and by Murray greatly flatter her, was a very lovely young woman. Richard was probably some two years older, and a few years before this he had evidently, when over in Ireland, been courting a lady, as Kaine, the agent, said to him, in a letter dated October 10th, 1712 :— ' I declare by my Maker that I am concerned you should louse y^r M^{rs}, but I fancy it has been y^r owne fault' ; and then goes on to tell him of another young lady possessed of a good fortune. Except that Richard and Lady Anne were cousins, a marriage between them was exactly what anyone, interested in the welfare of the family, would have striven to bring about. Lady Barbara was then married, childless, and nearly forty years of age ; and unless she did have issue the title of Dacre would, upon her death, descend to Lady Anne if she survived her, and after Lady Anne's decease to her heir.

The old family place of Chevening was still unsold, and Richard, as his father's only son, would, upon the latter's decease, have become entitled to properties of considerable value in Essex, Norfolk, and Ireland. Unfortunately, Lady

Anne had become a Roman Catholic, and Richard's father was a Protestant, more bigoted than it would be easy to find in the present day, except perhaps in Ireland, where religious animosities are still bitter, and where Dacre had spent so much of his life.

He must have been acquainted with many persons who remembered the bloody rising of the Roman Catholics in Ulster in 1641, and had no doubt frequently heard from eye-witnesses stories of those dreadful times.[1] He himself had seen his town of Clones destroyed, and had been nearly brought to ruin by the Roman Catholic rising in favour of James II., and in common with most English landlords in Ireland he viewed Roman Catholics with the utmost detestation. Dacre, holding the very strong views that he did on the subject of the Roman Catholic religion, refused absolutely to consent in any way to this proposed alliance of his son's. It was all in vain that Richard wrote most imploring letters to his father, and got Dr. Hough, the celebrated Bishop of Lichfield and Coventry, whom no one could accuse of having any leaning towards Rome, to intercede on his behalf, Dacre remained quite hard and unmoved to all their prayers and remonstrances.

It is not improbable that Dacre's objections to his son's marriage with Lady Anne were fostered by his wife, who it is likely enough wished her step-son to marry Philippa, her daughter by her first husband. I think it is pretty clear that Richard was at one time attracted in that quarter, as in 1710, when on the eve of setting out from Ireland for Belhus, he wrote thus in a letter to his sister Jane :—

I think myself obliged to you in a particular manner for sending me word of Miss Phyllys welfare than which nothing could be more welcome ; with almost the same difficulty I have refrained writing to her as it was not visht [? wished] by her when at Bellas, & tho' I dare swear she has quite forgott me, I can assure you it is not so with me whom failure of hopes, and not affection has kept so long silent ;

and he asks her to give his ' humble service to Miss Phil.'

[1] For depositions on oath as to the awful cruelties perpetrated on that occasion see *Rush*, i. pt. iii. p. 405 *et seq.*

In another, undated, letter to this sister he says :—

Pray pay my respects to dear Miss Phill, & tell her that I drank her health yesterday in several places where everybody wished her present. I wish a line from me had been acceptable to her, but I despair of ever gaining that favour. However assure her that spite of all her frowns I shall ever Persevere to be her humble serv^t.

I am unable to say whether 'Miss Phill' continued her 'frowns,' or whether Richard having gained her favour proved inconstant; but certain it is that we have no further evidence of his attachment, which probably melted away when the attractions of the country belle were contrasted with the more cosmopolitan manner and charms of Lady Anne, who had spent so much of her time in France at the Court of the Grand Monarque, then the great centre of European cultivation.

Whether or no failure of this match was one of the causes for Dacre's resentment at his son's proposed marriage with his cousin Lady Anne, the fact remains that he was inflexible in his opposition to it. Lady Anne says in the pleadings in the action which subsequently took place between her and her father-in-law concerning the guardianship of her boy, that when she married his son Dacre refused to give him a larger allowance than 40*l.* a year, which no doubt was what he had been allowing him previously; and that when Richard's death took place he stopped even this small allowance, and would allow nothing towards a maintenance of his grandchild.

It is interesting to see that Dacre's daughter Jane took her brother's part, in much the same way as her aunt Anne Barrett (afterwards Mildmay) had taken her brother Richard's part in his disputes with his father. The two letters we have from Jane Barrett[1] on this subject are quite in the style that, some thirty or forty years previously, Anne had written to her brother.

One of them dated Aprill ye 9th, 1716, begins :—

Dear Brother. When my father commanded me on his Blessing not to see nor speak to you the Unhappy day you

---

[1] It is Somewhat remarkable that she signs herself in one of these letters 'Jane Lennard Barrett' and in the other 'Jane Lennard.'

were here, I took a resolution to write to you the offtener: and, with your permission, maintain y^t way a Friendship he endeavours to dissolve. .... never any Accident of my Life toucht me nearer to the heart y^n our last parting.

The letter continues in the same strain of most affectionate regrets for what had taken place between her father and her brother; and in the course of another undated letter, evidently written at the same crisis, she says:—

I would say more but tremble at what I have already done, for godsake burn this as soon as you have read it, and do not hazard to the Air (nay your own pocket for a minute) a paper that may ruin me; for my satisfaction let me have it upon Oath that it is no more in being, or I solemnly Vow I will never mention what concerns us.

There is a note of pathos in this disregarded injunction to destroy a letter that has survived now nearly two hundred years since it was written.

Richard was evidently too much in love with Lady Anne to be swayed from his purpose on account of his father's determined opposition to the match, and they were married at St. Martin's-in-the-Fields, on June 15th, 1716. In the register of that parish they are respectively described as 'Richard Barrett Lennard Esq. of St. James' Westminster, and Lady Anne Lennard of Chepsted in Kent.'

That they intended to be married in spite of Dacre's violent opposition is shown by the following letter to him from his Irish agent, dated some ten days before the marriage actually took place:—

Clownis, June the 5th, 1716.

Honrd S^r. I Receiued Yo^{rs} of the 24th of may last, which is the Greatest Soprise to me that euer I mett with in all my life, for I am troubled out of Measure for the Missfortain of yor only Son and the Great trouble yor Honr lyes vnder on that accasion which I am Sure must be very Greatt, I thought in the first place that he neuer would doe that with aney, without yor Honrs ffull Consent, and Secondly that he would Consider the Greatt and worthy ffamily that he is of, and the Greatt ffortain that yor Honr Could make him, and besides I thought if he

Could Gett the Greatest ffortain and ffamily that Could be gott, he would not Joyne with that profession,[1] I am sure he is much altered Since he was in Dublin, for then he Could not Indure them, I cannot tell what to say I am soe troubled, but yor Honr may depend vpon me, that I will ffully observe yor Honrs directions you mention vpon all accasions that offers.....
Yo^r Hours most Dutyfull Servant,
EDMOND KAINE.

A settlement, dated June 15th, 1716, was made on this marriage, whereby, after reciting that Lady Anne was entitled to a considerable portion in money, and considerable estates of land, as one of the co-heirs of the late Earl of Sussex, and that Richard Barrett was entitled to an estate tail in lands in England and Ireland worth upwards of 2,500*l.* a year expectant on decease of his father Dacre, but was not then capable of making any provision for benefit of his future wife or children, he therefore agreed that if Lady Anne should survive him she should be paid 10,000*l.* in lieu of any dower or jointure, and that he would settle lands to the value of 1,500*l.* a year on the issue male of this intended marriage in tail male, with power of appointment to younger children. This deed is duly signed by Lord Quarrendon (eldest surviving son of the Earl of Lichfield), the Countess of Sussex, Lady Anne, and Richard, who there signed himself

Richard and his bride went down to Chevening to spend the honeymoon, and within a week of this marriage received a very disturbing message from Lady Sussex, who was then in London. She wrote to say that 'Mr. Secretary Stanhope has a mind to be a purchaser to this Kent estate, & is to come & see it next week.' The debts of the late Lord Sussex amounted to 4,000*l.*, and Lady Barbara was then also pressing for payment of her portion. Richard was so anxious to avoid a sale of the

---
[1] Meaning Roman Catholics.

family property that he again wrote to his father on June 22nd, to implore him to make some arrangement whereby this domestic calamity might be avoided.

I have not Dacre's reply to his son—perhaps he never sent one—but if he did it was not of a favourable nature, as the negotiations for the sale of Chevening proceeded, although, as we shall see, those estates were not absolutely conveyed to Mr. Stanhope until a year later.

It was, no doubt, sound wisdom on the part of the Lennard family to make the intending purchaser comfortable when he came down to view the property, and this they appear to have tried to do, as there is an entry of 'More for 6 Bottles of Sack, & 6 of french wine given at several times to ye Purchaser when ye family was away & given to Mr Jones.' This is taken from some very elaborate family accounts which extend from the day after the Earl of Sussex's funeral in November 1715 until Chevening was sold. As soon as the Earl died his widow, and her two daughters, became interested financially in Chevening, and these accounts are made up with the view of showing exactly what expenses connected with that estate should be apportioned among these three persons respectively.

When Lord Sussex died the home farm was in hand; and a tenant having just given up his farm in so bad a state that no one would take it, this farm had to be farmed also by the executors. The farming stock seems to have been the property of the Countess, and she was entitled to a third part of the rents derived from Chevening, but those from Cudham were the property of her daughters. The accounts show that many of the expenses of the establishment were divided into three equal parts, and borne by each of these ladies, but some items were charged specially against the Countess, or Lady Anne, or Lady Barbara, as the case might be; as when General Skelton would have his apartment hung with grey cloth, for the hire of which an undertaker named Williams charged 6*l*.

In these accounts, those of the family who stayed at Chevening, besides paying their share of the establishment expenses, were debited 10s. each per week for board, and 5s. per week for each of their personal servants, of whom Richard and Lady Anne seem to have kept three. From these charges we learn something of the movements of the members of the family during this period: so we see that Richard and his bride came to Chevening directly after their marriage, and stayed there until late in December; Lady Sussex came on June 27th until 5th of the following July; and General Skelton and his wife came the same day, and stayed to August 28th.

When Richard left Chevening he went to London; it is not improbable that, feeling unwell, he came to town in order to be medically treated; anyhow the next we know of him is derived from two letters written to his father by the celebrated doctor Sir Hans Sloane: they are dated December 18th and 22nd respectively. In the first of these letters Sir Hans says that he 'apprehends it will be the small pox'; and in the second one he speaks of the appearance of further bad symptoms, and mentions that he had been in consultation over the case with Sir Samuel Garth, the eminent physician.

The united efforts of these distinguished practitioners did not avail to save poor Richard, who died on December 24th, 1716, and his death is thus recorded in a publication which appeared in the following month:—

The Honourable Mr Barrett of Essex who married the only daughter of the Earl of Sussex
The Lady Henrietta de Grey
The Countess of Berkley
The Lady Teinham [1]
The Lady Molineux

N.B. All these dy'd of the small pox, save that the last two Ladies being both with Child Miscarried also.[2]

[1] It is remarkable that a publication should chronicle in the same issue the death of Lady Anne's first husband, and also that of the second wife of him who was to become her second husband.

[2] *Ann.* iii. 309. It is interesting to note how frequently inaccuracies are to be found in books of reference when one knows about the persons to whom reference is made. In this short reference to Richard there are two: he was not 'the honourable,' and Lady Anne was not the Earl's only daughter.

It is said that Richard was buried in the family vault[1] under Aveley Church, but there is no monument to record his death, and, as I have stated, the registers for that period are missing.

A letter to Dacre from his Irish agent, condoling with him on the loss of his son, is the only letter I have found referring to Richard's death.

Four months after her husband's death, on April 20th, 1717, a son was born to Lady Anne, who was baptized in the following month, and named Thomas after his grandfather the late Earl.

About two months later the sale of Chevening was accomplished, and on June 15th, 1717, John Lennard's house, and the last of his lands consisting of about 3,350 acres, passed to the Stanhope family for the sum of 28,000*l.*, or a trifle more than 8*l.* an acre. The absolute handing over of the property took place a little later, as in a letter from Lady Katherine Taylor[2] to her niece Jane Barrett, dated Tuesday, August 27th, 1717, the writer says that Lady Anne 'Tould Lady Donegall that Schenevy (Chevening) was sould to Lord Stanop last Fryday to her great sattisfaction, & a Saturday my lord went to take possesion of it; that has been the busness which has keept her in Town.'[3]

The following undated letter by Lady Anne to Jane Barrett was no doubt written during the summer which succeeded the loss of the former's first husband:—

Dear sister.

I receiued yrs & reteurn you thanks for yr kind inquiery affter my health & familys wch are all uery well, except my self yt cant bragg of being perfectly recouerd; & allmost despare I euer shall, for malloncoly is not to be forgott, & I find it dayly increas; as to my little boy he is uery well & thriues finely, wch is a great satisfaction & comefort to me; for I hope in my old days to liue to see him a fine man to make me amends for all the troubles & afflictions I have gone through; ye town is uery hott & disagreable but hope soon to be in ye

---

[1] As a young man I remember my great-grandfather's second wife being buried there, and being told that it was then full.

[2] A sister to Lady Jane Barrett.   [3] *P. S. A.* ii. Second Series, p. 30.

country; as for news I know as little as you do for I go to no publick place, nor see non but near relations, & neuer think to inquier affter any; I beg pardon for not sending the receit sooner but could not find it, & was forcet at last to writ it by memory, but am sure tis right, if there is any thing else I can be seruicesable to you in let me know, I shall be allways ready of my side to show you how much I am dear sister
yr most affectionat sister & hum:^{ble} seruant
ANNE BARRETT LENNARD.

My Lady[1] giues her hum:^{ble} seruice to all yr family, pray my duty to my father, & seruice to all ye rest.

saturday morn.   12 a cloke.

Although Lady Anne says that 'malloncoly is not to be forgott,' she appears to have been able to banish it in the following spring, as in March 171¾ she married, as his third wife, Henry, eighth Lord Teynham. By him she had three children—Charles, Richard Henry, and Anne.

Charles married Gertrude, sister and co-heir of John Trevor, of Glynde, Sussex. He died in his mother's lifetime, on February 4th, 1754, leaving a son, Trevor Charles, and a daughter, Gertrude, who married Thomas Brand, of the Hoo, Herts. After the death of Thomas Lord Dacre he was succeeded in the title by this nephew, T. C. Roper; he died without issue in 1794, whereupon the title went to his sister Gertrude, who carried it into the family of Brand, where it still remains.

Richard Henry, upon the presentation of his half-brother, Thomas Lord Dacre, became Rector of Clones in Ireland, and had a considerable family; he was succeeded in this then valuable living by his son Henry.

Anne married in Ireland, probably about 1753, Mr. Peter Tyler, 52nd Regiment. I have no exact knowledge of the date of this marriage, but I believe that their eldest son was born about 1754. Mr. Tyler served as a lieutenant in General Johnson's regiment in Flanders, but, owing to his wife's loss of fortune, he was obliged to sell out and retire from the service.

---

[1] Her mother, the Countess of Sussex.

Anne had issue: Francis Henry, a solicitor in large practice;[1] Charles, who became an Admiral and was knighted; George, a successful East India merchant; Fanny, married a Mr. Wilder, and had a numerous family; and Molly, a great beauty, married Major Cronin, and is buried at Bathwick.

Lord Teynham committed suicide on May 16th, 1723, about five years after his marriage with Lady Anne.

Two years later, on October 16th, 1725, at the age of forty-one, she married at St. James's, Westminster, as her third husband, who was 37, being born 1688, the Hon. Robert Moore, of West Lodge, Enfield Chase, a son of Henry, third Earl of Drogheda. For this marriage, Lady Anne being a 'papist,' Mr. Moore received a pardon, dated February 3rd, $172\frac{5}{6}$, which was enrolled June 1727.[2]

Previous to his marriage Mr. Moore had been a member of the Irish House of Commons, representing Belfast in 1713-4, and Louth 1715-27.

I think it is almost certain that this marriage was an unsatisfactory one; in any case, it was clouded by financial difficulties, and when that is the case it often means an unhappy married life.

In February 1755, Lord Dacre, when writing to the Duke of Newcastle on behalf of his half-sister's husband, Captain Peter Tyler, in order to explain why Peter so much needed a civil post under the Government, said that, after the death of Lord Teynham, upon his mother marrying again, his step-sister's fortune fell into the hands of her Father in Law [stepfather]; who after she came of age, put her off from time to time with promises of giving her security for it upon his Estates; But when his circumstances came to light, it appeared that all he had was so incumbered with mortgages that there was not anything left to reimburse my Sister whose whole Fortune was in this manner lost.[3]

---

[1] Francis Henry, himself a grandson of the eighth Lord Teynham, married in turn two daughters of the eleventh Lord Teynham.   [2] The C. P.

[3] F. H. Tyler, writing to his brother George in 1787, speaks of their family as having 'been robbed of a good fortune by his Lordship's [Ld. D.'s] own mother.'

Lord Dacre was not a person at all addicted to 'washing his family dirty linen in public'—indeed, quite the contrary—and I feel sure that, in saying as much as he did, he left a good deal unsaid as regards his step-father's conduct.

I much regret I cannot fix for certain the date of the death of Robert Moore, which is given in the peerages as having taken place in 1728; it is certain that he lived for many years later, and I believe he did not die until 1762. Lord Dacre, in a memorandum about some family pictures, says that he bought them of Mr. Moore, whom he calls there his 'father in law,' after his mother's death, and this we know did not take place until 1755.

In 1762 a Mr. Morgan wrote a letter to Lord Dacre, dated September 30th, of which the following are the material portions:—

I had this morning a packett brought me by a messenger from Reading, and a letter from one Ann Hansard, which I send your Lordship, together with a copy of a will all of Mr. Moore's own handwriting, but so Scratch'd & Disfigur'd that I take it for granted, without any Comment on the Stile & Matter of it, that it was Composed at a time that he had made very free with his Bottle. I did not hesitate a moment (after I had coppyed the will) to return it (with two Letters to Lady Ranelagh one from Moore dated ye 29 of January last, and the other from Mrs. Hansard dated a Tuesday last) to Mrs Hansard by the same Messenger, and wrote her word that I would by no means be concerned in any of Mr. Moore's affairs, and must leave her to dispose of his Corpse & Will as she might be advised. The Messenger would have proceeded to town in Quest of your Lordship, had I not prevented him by possitive assurances, from what I've heard your Lordship declare, that you would not see him, or be any wise concerned in his Rediculous Executorship.

A few days later, on October 9th, Selina Lady Ranelagh,[1]

[1] She was aunt by marriage to Robert Moore, as he was a son of her first husband's sister Mary, who married Robert's father, the third Earl of Drogheda. Lord Ranelagh, the husband of Selina, must not be confused with the Earls of Ranelagh; he was Sir Arthur Cole, Bart., and created a baron 1717.

wife of Sir J. Elwill, Bart., wrote also to Lord Dacre on this subject. She said :—

The occation of my troubleing you with this is on the death of poor Robin Moore, the inclosed letter he left behind him which they did not send till two days after his death, & it was directed to London, by which means I did not receive it till near a week after his death, but upon the receipt of it I sent our Steward emediately to Redding, who got there just time enough to bury him, otherways he would have to be buryed by the Parish. I have like wise inclosed your Lord^{sp} a paper which he call'd his will, our steward brought away some Keys which they say belonged to some boxes of his that are at Sutton Courtney, if your Lord^{sp} thinks there may be any writings, or any thing of consequence there, I will send you the Keys on recieving your commands, otherways I shall send them back to the woman at Redding, as I will have nothing to do with them, the House that he died at at Redding is a poor Widow Womans who had been in jail with him, and they both came out of jail together, he had been there seven weeks before he died, the poor Woman made great complaints that she had had nothing for his board, but I gave my seruant only orders to pay the Nurse that sett up with him after his death, and the funeral.

The register of St. Lawrence's parish, Reading, amongst its records of burials, has the following : 'Oct. 5. 1762. Robert Moore Esqre.'

I think it is nearly certain that the references in Morgan's letter to 'Mr. Moore,' in Lady Ranelagh's to 'poor Robin Moore,' and the above entry in the register, all relate to the death of the Hon. Robert Moore. I much regret that I have been unable to find the copy of the will to which Mr. Morgan refers, or the letter from Mrs. Hansard, either of which would probably settle this point.

Assuming that this death was that of the Hon. Robert Moore, it points to a very sad fall in social position. A peer's son, for some time a member of Parliament, and married to a lady of very old family and high position, misappropriates his step-daughter's fortune, and, falling lower and lower, at last gets into prison.

It seems useless, in the absence of any evidence, to speculate as to the reason of his being sent to prison. Debt was in those days a very common cause for gentlemen being put in gaol, and they were sometimes released by their creditors when there appeared no hope of being able to obtain payment from them of their debt.

Mr. Moore came out of prison with, presumably, a very low class of woman, who had been his fellow-prisoner, but who was kind-hearted enough to give him shelter in her wretched cottage, where he, a victim to drink, ends his misspent life at the age of seventy-four in such a state of destitution, and so estranged by his own conduct from all his relations, that but for Lady Ranelagh he would have been buried in a pauper's grave.

Mr. Moore and Lady Anne had one child, Henry, who served on the Continent in the Scots Greys, then called the R.N.B. Dragoons, under the Duke of Cumberland during the Seven Years' War.

While abroad he showed symptoms of insanity, and was for a time in hospital at Nienburg, in the duchy of Anhalt. He returned home about 1761, and was placed under the care of various mad doctors, being for some years at Egham, at a private asylum kept by Mr. Irish. His step-brother, Lord Dacre, had the care of him, and when he came into some property put the estate into Chancery. Mr. Moore ultimately had property to the value of 1,000*l.* a year, of which the Court allowed half for his maintenance, which permitted him having a carriage and a private servant; while the rest of his fortune was paid to Lord Dacre, who divided it among those of Mr. Moore's relations whom he considered most had need of it. Mr. Moore never recovered his senses, but lived on for many years, dying at some date later than 1814.

With respect to the character of Anne Lady Teynham, we unfortunately know very little; but, in spite of the bad example given to her and her sister by the conduct of their mother, I have never seen any reference to cause me to imagine that either of them conducted herself otherwise than with the strictest propriety. Her education must have been very greatly neglected; besides the letter already given, we have a piece of a letter which she wrote to her eldest son, who had evidently been inquiring of her whether she had any old family letters or papers in her possession. Her reply, which is written in a terrible scrawl, is as follows:—

If there was any old letters of Samson Lennard or Henry Lord Dacres, yt was any way curious, or other papers my father burnt um; for there was trunks that no bod know what was in um, nor had not been opened in any bodys memory, so he brook um opened & burnt seuerall papaer w̄ch he after wards wanted, & cost a great deall to secharch for um, besidess ye trouble he had to find where to looke.

Although Lady Anne, upon her sister's death, became entitled to the title of Baroness Dacre in her own right, it is said that she never assumed it, but continued to style herself Lady Teynham. She died on June 26th, 1755,[1] when, as we shall see, the title of Baron Dacre passed to Thomas Lennard Barrett, her son by her first husband. Lady Anne was buried at St. Anne's Church, Soho, near to the tomb of her mother-in-law, the Countess of Drogheda, where her husband intended himself to have been buried.[2]

I have searched Somerset House in vain for her will, and think it most probable that she never made one; indeed, being a married woman at the time of her death, she probably, in the then state of the law, had nothing she could dispose of. We shall see later that some of the family portraits she possessed were sold by her third husband; and that the others, which he probably thought were not worth selling, passed in undivided shares to the children of her different husbands, and that Lord Dacre eventually obtained them from his half-brother and sister.

In 1719 Elizabeth—Dacre's daughter by his second wife—married Mr. William Sloan the younger, who was a most desirable match in respect of his prospects. The marriage settlements are dated April of that year, and by them Dacre agreed to pay 2,000*l.* to Mr. William Sloan, senior, and 1,000*l.*

---

[1] Given as June 28th in the *Gentleman's Magazine*.   [2] *Ld. D. His.*

to William Sloan, the prospective bridegroom. In return for this, and for some small Irish property which had belonged to Elizabeth's mother, and which Dacre brought into settlement, Mr. Sloan, the father, and his son, after providing for life-interests for themselves and Elizabeth, settled upon the heirs that might be born to the young people estates in county Down, in Ireland, and, what was of far greater value, land in Chelsea. One of the many parcels of land there was called the 'Park,' and consisted of forty acres of meadow surrounded with a brick wall, and then let for 200*l.* a year. This alone, now all built over, and in the centre of one of the most fashionable districts of London, must be worth a huge sum, and although I cannot identify its exact position, it no doubt forms part of the Earl of Cadogan's property there.

Among the trustees of these settlements were the bridegroom's uncle, Sir Hans Sloane, and Mr. Charles Cadogan, who married the heiress of the latter. He afterwards became Baron Cadogan, and was a predecessor of the present Earl of that title.

I have found the following bills for lace, which, no doubt, formed part of the bride's trousseau. One is from Eliz. Hayne for lace supplied to 'Mrs. Eliza Barrett,' dated 'May ye 16th, 1719.'

	£ s. d.
2 yds ¾ ½ of Lace at £4 10s.	12 18 09
5 yds 2 ell of narrow at 9/-	02 10 07½
	15 09 04½

And the other from Mrs. Pitronello De Huger, dated as paid 'ye 18 feb. 1719,' is for

	£ s. d.
3 yds Vall Lace & 4li	12 00 00
5¼ yds Vall Lace @ 23s	06 00 09
1¾ yds Vall Lace @ 17s	00 19 01½
	18 19 10½

It is to be hoped that poor Elizabeth's married life was as

happy as it was to prove brief, for she died in the month of November following her marriage, in the twenty-fourth year of her age, and was buried in the family vault in Aveley Church.

Henrietta, Dacre's youngest daughter by Lady Jane, who died unmarried, was buried at Aveley on March 31st, 1721. We have no letters to or from her, nor have I been able to discover anything about her life.

In 1722 Sarah, Dacre's daughter by his third wife, married Philip Hall, of Upton, Essex, and her father gave her a marriage portion of 4,000*l*. Her husband Philip, who served as High Sheriff for Essex in 1727, and was knighted upon that occasion, died in January $174\frac{6}{7}$.[1]

There were issue of this marriage one son, named Philip, and three daughters. The son had a most unsatisfactory career. His father died while the former was still a boy, and a Mr. Groce, a solicitor, appears to have been his guardian, and to have induced Lord Dacre to become a guardian jointly with him. Young Philip was, under Lord Dacre's advice, sent to Eton, but was not long there before he ran away. When he came of age he found himself possessed of an estate worth 1,000*l*. a year, besides several thousand pounds of ready money, all of which he soon ran through. It is said that at one period of his life he was often heard of as wandering about Epping Forest without food, and almost without clothes. At length he gravitated to the Fleet prison, where he remained to the day of his death, which took place in October 1801. A friend of the Hall family told Lord Dacre of the wretched plight into which Philip had brought himself, at the same time warning him that the young man was so drunken and worthless that if he had good clothes he would pawn them, and said that the only kind thing to be done was to allow him a trifle each week. This Lord Dacre did until he himself died.

Before Lord Dacre's death Philip Hall laid claim to the Belhus estates, basing his claim upon the fact that he was a direct descendant of Dacre Barrett, and after his death he

[1] *Mo*. i. p. 63.

proceeded to bring an action of ejectment against Lady Dacre, and put her to some trouble and expense in proving her title.

Notwithstanding this conduct on his part, she is said to have continued to him the allowance that Lord Dacre had made him. When Philip died in October 1801, Lady Dacre, upon the intercession of a Sir John Peshall,[1] who was a fellow-prisoner paid 10*l.* in order to have him decently buried. Sir John Peshall then in turn made more than one abortive effort to obtain possession of the Belhus estates, claiming under a will which he declared Philip had made in his favour.

Philip's eldest sister Sarah had a portion of 5,000*l.*, and married the Rev. — Thornton, a clergyman in Essex, who died in 1773, by whom she had issue. The two other sisters had as portions a like sum each; the elder of them is said to have been a very beautiful girl, and was supposed to have had a very unsatisfactory career; the younger one married a Mr. Haighway, who has been described as 'a low petty-fogging attorney.'

Dorothy Barrett

Dorothy, Dacre's second daughter by Lady Jane, was married in 1724, after long negotiations, to Mr. Hugh Smith. The match was in every respect a good one for her, and as she was about thirty-four years of age when Mr. H. Smith wrote to Dacre in November 1722 asking leave, as he terms it, to 'Make my Addresses to Her,' it is difficult to understand why her father was so procrastinating about this marriage. Ill-health may have been the cause, as Mr. Smith in a letter to Dacre, dated June 27th, 1723, mentions the fact that when he had called on him at his house in Great Russell Street 'you were then so ill y*t* you saw no Company'; and he goes on to say, 'But being now informed It is turned to the Gout (which I hope S*r* will prolong yo*r* Life) I beg leave to acquaint you with the Particulars of my Circumstances.'

---

[1] Creation of 1611; third baronet died *s.p.m.s.* 1712; title assumed from 1770 1838.—The C. *B.*

As to the 'circumstances,' we have a letter from Mr. Bell, who appears to have acted for Dacre, dated January 172¾. This letter shows that Mr. Smith had from London and Irish properties about 750*l.* a year, and that Dorothy's fortune was 250*l.* a year. Besides this he seems to have had very considerable expectations from his elder brother, who informed Bell that they (Hugh and Dorothy) should be welcome to his house as long as they pleased, and that he had no intention of marrying again, and believed he should not. Hugh Smith was the third son of Erasmus Smith, alias Heriz, Alderman of London. Erasmus's ancestors since the time of Henry VIII. had styled themselves Smith alias Heriz, and quartered the arms of both of these families. Erasmus, towards the end of the seventeenth century, bought South Weald from Sir William Scroggs, and after his death it passed successively to his sons Erasmus and Samuel, who both had no issue; and, the latter dying in 1732, it came into the possession of Hugh, the husband of Dorothy.

In June 1724 Hugh again wrote to Dacre in order to endeavour to induce him to allow the wedding to take place without any further delay. He thus begins his letter:—

S^r It is recorded of Jacob y^t he served two seaven years for Rachel; but then as he lived in the Age of the old Patriarchs those years to Him were, in Proportion, not so much as the Time I have worn yor Daughters chains.

On July 14th, 1724, he writes:—

The Impatience of a Lover will I hope plead my Excuse for this Trouble, It being very painful to live in Suspence; and as this Affair has already been two Years depending, which has exposed me to the Raillery of all my Acquaintance, & is still the Tea Table Talk of both Town & Country, that alone will I hope be sufficient Motive to excite you no longer to postpone it.

In the following month he writes:—

The month of August is now begun, but will I hope not be far advanced before my Happiness is compleated; and in order to it I beg leave to remind you y^t Wedding Clothes will necessarilly take up some time the Making, & therefore beg you will permit the Young Lady to go up to Town this Week to provide them.

Lord Dacre by some curious error says that this marriage took place in 1722, but in fact their marriage settlement is dated September 4th, 1724. Dacre,[1] in consideration of the brothers Smith bringing considerable properties into the settlement, which were situated respectively in Yorkshire, London, and Ireland, paid over to them as Dorothy's dowry the sum of 5,000*l*. In the church of South Weald there is a fine tomb to Hugh and Dorothy, with the following inscription —:

In a vault under this place lyeth the body of Hugh Smith Esq: late lord of this Manor descended from the antient family of Heriz, now Smith of Edmundthorpe in Leicestershire.

He married Dorothy the daughter of the Hon: Dacre Lennard Barrett of Aveley in this county Esq: by whom he had issue, only two daughters; Dorothy, the Elder, the wife of the Honourable John Smith Barry Fourth Son of the Rt: Hon: James, Earl of Barrington of the Kingdom of Ireland, and Lucy, the Younger, the wife of the Rt: Hon: James Smith Stanley, Ld. Vis^{ct} Strange only son and Heir Apparent of the Rt: Hon: Edward Earl of Derby.[2]

He departed this life the 8th day of May 1745 and in the 73^{r1} year of his age. Leaving his great estates and possessions in England and Ireland to his said daughters in equal shares.

He was always zealously affected to our present happy establishment both in church and state.

He was a tender husband and affectionate father, a sincere friend a kind landlord, good to his servants and charitable to the poor. Dorothy, his sorrowful widow survived him and departed this life on the 1st day of Febuary 1755 and in the 73rd year of her age and her body also lyeth in the same vault with her husband.

She was of exemplary piety and most properly discharged her duty in all relations of life, and in grateful regard to the

[1] It is noteworthy that Dacre signed the deed 'D. Barrett Lennard,' which is the earliest occasion that I have seen these two names so assumed in this order. His brother often signed 'R. Barrett als Lennard,' and his sister Ann signed herself usually 'A. Lennard'; but Dacre and his son always signed themselves D. and R. 'Barrett,' or 'Barret,' respectively.

[2] So that from Dorothy are descended both the Smith Barrys (now Lords Barrymore) and the Earls of Derby.

memory of so good an husband, she by her will directed a monument to be set up. And this monument is accordingly set up by her executor in the Year 1757.

Towards the close of his life Dacre Barrett was greatly worried by the litigation he embarked on in respect of the education and bringing up of his grandson and heir, Thomas.

It is impossible to say how much he was actuated in the course he adopted by feelings of resentment against Lady Anne for marrying his son in defiance of his express wishes, and how much by religious bigotry. In these days when, in England at least, there is so much toleration, if not absolute indifference, as to the form of religion held by others, it is perhaps difficult to believe that the position taken up by Dacre was not determined by vindictiveness towards his daughter-in-law, who in vain attempted to retain possession of her child by undertaking to bring him up in his father's faith.

It was not until Lady Anne had become a widow for the second time that Dacre attempted to interfere with his daughter-in-law's care of her child. Lord Teynham had become a Protestant before he married his third wife, and it is possible that this was the cause that induced Dacre during the life of the former to acquiesce in Lady Anne having the care of her boy, but that when Lord Teynham's death had removed his restraining influence he may then have considered it necessary to take steps to prevent any danger of his heir being brought up in the Roman Catholic religion.

On December 13th, 1723, Dacre petitioned the Court of Chancery that, as his own health was not sufficiently good to undertake the guardianship of the child, it should be confided to his nominees, Mr. Milner and Mr. Baynes, and he offered to allow 200*l.* a year for his maintenance. Dacre won his cause, and he was also successful in a second application to the Court on the 18th of the following March.

Lady Teynham appealed to the House of Lords against these decisions, and prayed that, if she were to be deprived of the care of her child, his guardianship might be confided to his godfather, the Earl of Lichfield,[1] and to the Duke of Grafton. Dacre strained every nerve to have the decisions of the Court of Chancery upheld; he had for his leading counsel the most successful man in his day at the Bar, the Attorney-General, Sir Philip York (afterwards Lord Chancellor Hardwick), and one who was known to have the greatest influence over the then Lord Chancellor;[2] while the letters we have to Dacre written from London by his daughter Jane show how much intriguing was going on, and what an amount of religious prejudice was being imported into the case in order to secure a decision in his favour. In his efforts he was entirely successful; and on April 16th, 1724, the House of Lords decided that Dacre should have the care of the infant, who was at once to be delivered over to him, or to such person as he should appoint.[3]

In one of Jane Barrett's undated letters to her father she says: 'I carry'd Master to Greenwich a Tuesday, & left him in great affliction, which I understood did not last long.' It must have been indeed a great grief to poor little Thomas to have been taken away from his mother's care by an aunt none too good-tempered, whom he had possibly never seen before, and to be placed by her at a strange school at the early age of seven. One is glad to see in a subsequent passage in the same letter that some person has sent Jane word that 'he is well and very well reconsiled to his school,' and we must hope that this was the case.

The boy no doubt spent his holidays at Belhus, as Todd, the Irish agent, in a letter dated July 11th, 1724, which he wrote to Jane Barrett, says, 'I am very glad to hear your nephew is at Bellhouse.'

This dispute about his grandson's education was the last great struggle in which Dacre was engaged; his life from his earliest days had been passed in a series of litigations and disputes with various members of his family. As a minor he was

[1] Geo. Hen. second Earl; as Viscount Quarrendon he had been a trustee of Lady Teynham's first marriage. *Ante*, p. 555.
[2] Lord Macclesfield; as to his partiality for Sir Philip, *Camp*. iv. p. 508.
[3] *H. L.* xxii. p. 321.

engaged in the great Loftus lawsuit; later on he had constant disputes with his father and his sisters Anne and Dorothy, and afterwards with his only surviving son and his son's widow. Besides these, he had several less important lawsuits with the Bishop of Clogher and other persons concerning his estate at Clones. This continual state of altercation no doubt greatly soured his disposition and depressed his spirits. It is not improbable that, being in bad health and tired out with that ceaseless strife which had ever beset him, Dacre was so weary of life's worries that his last illness found him in a condition in which he was unable to make any effort to rally.

Dacre was buried at Aveley on the 13th of January,[1] and his death is thus mentioned in the 'Whitehall Evening Post,' dated 'From Tuesday January 5th to Thursday January 7th. 1724-5.' 'On Friday last died Nicholas [sic] Barrett Esq: of Bellhouse in Aveley in Essex, a gentleman worth about 4000 l per Annum. To which his Grandson succeeds, a Minor now at school at Greenwich.'[2]

Dacre made his last will on October 21st, 1724; it was not a favourable one for his grandson and heir, but, considering how much Dacre's temper had been tried by his son's marriage, and how he himself had been treated by his father's will, I do not think the will can be considered to be a vindictive one. Shortly before his death he supplemented his will by a codicil dated December 14th, 1724. The joint disposition by these two documents was to charge his estates, under the powers in his first marriage settlement, with 4,000*l.* for the benefit of his daughters Jane and Dorothy, and with another sum of a like amount for his daughter Sarah under the powers contained in his last marriage settlement. He left his leasehold house in Great Russell Street, London, with its furniture, &c., to his wife, and to her he left also for her life all the lands he had himself purchased in Essex, with remainder in fee to his daughter Jane, subject to a charge of 1,000*l.* in favour of his daughter Sarah; to this devise he excepted a field of ten acres

---

[1] Aveley Register.   [2] Also in *P. S. G. B.* xxix.

close to the Aveley gate of the park, and this, after his wife's death, he left to his grandson. He also left to him as heirlooms the picture of his grandmother, Dorothy Lady Dacre, 'drawn by Sir Anthony Vandyke,' and those of his grandfather, Richard Lord Dacre, and of Edward Barrett Lord Newburgh. He bequeathed to Jane all the residue of his goods, chattels, and personal effects. This was very hard on his heir, as it meant that, but for the few pictures already mentioned, he inherited a large house absolutely empty.

Dacre appointed Jane guardian of his grandson, whom he directed to be brought up 'In the Protestant faith and attached to the Protestant succession.' He gave instructions about his own burial, which he directed was to be under the family seat in Aveley Church on the right hand going towards the chancel, not in a vault, but in a brick grave, and a marble monument to be put up close by. He also directed that new family pews were to be erected with 'Right wainscott.' It is perhaps rather unusual, but all his wishes in this respect were carried out, and until a recent 'Restoration' of the church the two pews were there, and one still remains.

The monument in Aveley Church to Dacre's memory is a good specimen of funeral monuments of that period. The inscription on it, which Lord Dacre says is 'full of pedantic flattery,'[1] is as follows:—

Hic positae sunt
Reliquiae DACRE BARRETT LENNARD Armigeri,
Viri, si Generis Vetustas et Claritudo Spectentur,
Illustris,
Si opes et praedia requiras,
Locupletis lateq^e possidentis.
sed ista fortuita,
Et a minus prudentibus solum laudata,
Virtutem ille et sapientiam excoluit.
Munia Amicitiae privatus dilexit

[1] *Ante*, p. 535.

Publicorum neq^e Oblitus, neque Cupiens,
Pro Patria, pro Legibus Strenuus
Ambitu Procul,
Nec aliud ob praemium,
Quam ut nequid Detrimenti Respub. caperet.
Doctrina, Religione,
Quales Civem, Sapientem, et Christianum decerent
penitus imbutus
Familiae fovens, Amicis charus,
Amore Civium et pauperum felix.
Talem Virum
Quamvis aetate jam provectum,
Mors nimis cita
abripuit.
permanebunt utcunque, propinquis, et apud familiares,
Virtutis Recordatio et Solamen,
Omnibus Contemplatio Morum.

I am not able to give the exact date when Sarah, Dacre's widow, died, but a recital in a deed dated June 1738 speaks of her as being then long since dead. In the book of accounts of the administration suit referred to more particularly in the following chapter, Sarah's name does not appear as one of the defendants later than June 1729, so it would seem that her death took place soon after that date.

J Barrett

Jane, Dacre's eldest daughter, was unmarried at the time of her father's death; and I think from the terms of his will that he considered it was not improbable she would never marry, which, as she was forty years of age when he executed it, was likely enough. She did, in fact, marry within about a year of his death a Mr. Richard Nicholls, of Aveley, 'gentleman.' Lord Dacre does not mention this marriage nor the separation, which we shall see took place between Jane and her second husband, but I have discovered these facts from the perusal of some old title-deeds.

I have not succeeded in finding out where or when she married this Richard, nor much about him. The marriage is not recorded in the Aveley Register, but a post-nuptial settlement of her property, which is dated February 19th, 172⅝, speaks of it as having lately taken place. This document described Nicholls as having 'no estate nor fortune in the world to make a suitable provision for his wife,' and goes on to settle Jane's charge for 2,000*l.* on the settled estates, and all her personal property, as well as the reversion to which she was entitled under her father's will, upon her absolutely.

As Mr. Nicholls is described in the deed in question as 'gentleman' and not 'esquier,' and had no means, and as Lord Dacre does not mention this marriage of his aunt, I imagine it was a very unsatisfactory alliance. It must be remembered that Jane was born in 1684, and it is more than likely that Richard Nicholls was some common young fellow out of the village, who courted this elderly spinster for the sake of her fortune.

There is another point connected with this marriage worth noting, and which looks as if it were one Jane was ashamed of, and desirous of keeping as far as possible secret, which is that, until after her marriage with Mr. Ranby, she is described in the book of accounts of the administration suit not as Jane, the wife of Richard Nicholls, but as 'Jane Barrett, spinster.'

It was probably her step-mother who persuaded Jane to have her fortune settled upon herself. Dacre's widow had had two husbands, and no doubt had outlived any sentiment she might have had earlier in life, and fully realised how greatly the middle-aged bride stood in need of protection against herself, as she had elected to mate with such a husband. That the widow had some hand in arranging for this settlement is pretty evident from the fact that one of the trustees was the then recently created Viscount Grimston, the head of her father's family.

The union between Jane and her first husband did not last

long,[1] as we have a deed, dated November 10th, 1729, between 'Jane Nicholls of Aveley widow, & John Ranby of the parish of St. Giles London Esquier.' This deed recited that a marriage had been arranged and was shortly to take place between the parties. John Ranby, then a rising young surgeon, aged twenty-six, was nearly twenty years younger than his bride, and it seems obvious that in this case, as in that of her previous marriage, Jane's birth and fortune, rather than her own personality, were the attractions that induced this young man to link himself to a woman so much older than himself.

John Ranby was the son of an innkeeper—young, clever, ambitious, and aware of his capabilities, but probably in those days possessed of little or no money. Jane was a well-bred woman, the daughter of a country gentleman of good position, and on her mother's side the granddaughter of a peer, and possessed of what, in the first quarter of the eighteenth century, would have been considered a good fortune. What wonder, then, that the young man who had yet his way to make in the world may have considered that he was greatly advancing his prospects in life by marrying a woman so superior to him in social rank, and who had also a fortune of her own; and that he was willing for these advantages to overlook the great disparity in years which lay between them. Such a marriage was foredoomed to failure; he young, common, clever, and of humble origin; she elderly, well bred, probably narrow-minded and not clever, and brought up a gentlewoman. It was not on these lines that in earlier days parents arranged for the marriages of their children; it is true that they had a care to see that the young people's means were adequate, but in well-arranged marriages money was by no means the only object; it was considered equally necessary to see that their respective social positions, and also their ages, bore a proper relation to each other.

[1] The death of Richard Nicholls is not to be found in the Aveley Register, and as there is a long gap in that register previous to 1717 I have no means of ascertaining his age, assuming him to have been born there.

One of the witnesses to the marriage settlement was Sir Hans Sloane, the famous physician, who was intimately acquainted with Dacre Barrett, and it is not unlikely that he it was who introduced the young surgeon to his old friend's daughter. If he were the author of the match, he probably regretted afterwards his share in the matter, as it was an unhappy one; and at last the quarrels between husband and wife became so acute that in June 1738 they executed a deed of separation.

The wife of George II. died in 1737 from the effects of an operation for hernia. When Ranby, who by this time had attained to great eminence in his profession, was dressing the Queen's wound and causing her considerable pain, her Majesty asked him 'if he would not be glad to be officiating in the same manner to his own old cross wife that he hated so much?'

John Ranby became principal sergeant-surgeon to George II., and was the leading spirit in obtaining official recognition of surgeons as distinct from the company of barber-surgeons. He had a natural son of considerable ability, who was born in 1743. Whether Ranby's intimacy with this boy's mother was one of the causes of his disputes with his wife which led to their separation, or whether she appeared on the scene after the husband and wife had parted, is a point upon which I can throw no light.

Some seven years after their separation, Jane and her husband agreed to sell for 4,700*l.* the property in the neighbourhood of Belhus which her father had left her. Some of this purchase-money went to Mr. Ranby under the provisions of the marriage settlement, as modified by the deed of separation, but 1,040*l.* was paid to Jane, and 1,400*l.* was to be held by the purchaser in order to secure for her an annuity of 100*l.*

It seems not to have been a good arrangement for Jane, as she was then sixty-one, and with the high rate for money, and the shorter expectation of life then prevailing, it would seem that she ought to have been able to secure the desired annuity upon better terms.

It is difficult to identify all the lands she sold, as the

description of the parcels in the conveyance of sale are by no means adequate. From a memorandum in my possession the amount of the land appears to have been about 360 acres, and by another undated memorandum to have been let for 219*l*. 10*s*. The estate comprised the two farms known respectively as Damyns and Smoak Hall, some fields and a tenement called the Cockhide in Upminster and North Ockendon, and other lands in Wennington and Rainham. A considerable portion of this land is now again part of the Belhus property; Lord Dacre bought some of Cockhide, my great-grandfather and grandfather jointly bought Damyns Hall and other lands adjoining the Romford Road, and my father some of the land in Wennington.

Mrs. Ranby died in 1760, aged seventy-six, and her husband some thirteen years later. I have no letters from Jane to Lord Dacre, nor from him to her except when a boy; and he makes no special reference to her in his family history, except the somewhat querulous criticism he passed upon the monument she had erected to her father's memory. I therefore know nothing as to their relations with one another after he had come of age, and no longer under her guardianship. Had he loved her he would probably have said how much he owed to her for her care of him when young; and as we know the Queen spoke of her as being 'cross,' I think it not unlikely she proved an unsympathetic guardian, and that in after life there was no love lost between them.

CHAPTER VIII

THOMAS BARRETT-LENNARD, LORD DACRE, AND HIS DESCENDANTS

As I have stated, Thomas Barrett was a posthumous child born on April 20th, 1717, four months after the death of his father; and his birth was registered at St. Martin's in the Fields, London. He appears early in life to have been styled 'Lennard Barrett,'[1] taking the former name from his mother's family; and it was not until 1755 that he transposed the order of these names into Barrett Lennard. I have found no reference to this change; it may have been merely for the sake of euphony, but I think it is more probable that, upon succeeding to the title of Dacre, he preferred to be the sixth Lennard bearing that title, instead of the first Barrett to do so. As his great-grandfather

Thos Lennard Barrett

Richard (on his father's side) had changed his name from Lennard to Barrett he may well have considered himself entitled to revert to the old patronymic so long as he at the same time retained the name of Barrett in conjunction with it.

He does not appear at any time to have been strong; his great aunt, Lady Katherine Taylor, writing to his aunt Jane Barrett, says, 'he is still a little child for his age, he is very paile and has still that looke about his eyes.' On the other hand, in a letter already quoted from, his mother says, 'as to my little boy he is uery well & thriues finely.' Our portraits of him show that he grew up to be a very good-looking man.

[1] Letter from Harrow, 1732, *post*, p. 582.

Some years after his death his widow's nephew, George Hardinge, thus wrote of him :—

Few noblemen had a more antient or more noble descent, a very elegant scholar and the best company in the world when in tolerable health and spirits ; but he was peevish at times from bad health ; he was a remarkably good Herald and Antiquary. He had a pleasing countenance & a very gallant manner ; he was very like Charles the First in the face.'[1]

Lord Dacre[2] was said to have been of small stature, and this is borne out by a letter from the Hon. George Montagu to Horace Walpole, dated August, 1761, where he writes that he has had ' a very kind letter from my little Lord Dacre.'[3]

Delicate as he may have been as a boy, he managed to attain nearly to the age of sixty-nine, although during many of those years he must have been a very considerable sufferer, as he was a martyr to rheumatic gout, and in 1745 he had so bad an attack of rheumatic fever as to be partially deprived of the use of his limbs. How great an invalid he was may be seen by frequent references to his health in letters from his wife and his friends, and his handwriting in his later life was unsteady and scrawling, and gives the reader the impression of being executed under circumstances of very considerable difficulty.

Mr. Adam Nixon, writing to him from Monaghan, November 22nd, 1752, says :—

I had not heard from you of a long time since I left you at Spaw, wch truly was pain & concern to me—I am rejoiced to find you have been in better health last summer, and am well assur'd you will receave great benefit from bathing in the sea, many persons here who have been afflicted with the same kind of disorder you complain of have recouvered ; gain'd perfect health & strength by bathing in sea.

And Horace Walpole, in one of his published letters to Sir H. Mann, writes in May 1775, ' Lord and Lady Dacre dined

---

[1] *Mis. G. H.*

[2] Throughout this chapter I allude to him as Lord Dacre and to his wife as Lady Dacre, although he did not succeed to the title until 1755.

[3] *Hist. Com.* viii. Part II. p. 114.

with me to-day, poor Lord Dacre was carried about though not worse than he has been these twenty years.'

At the time of the Coronation of George III. in 1760, Lord Dacre was only about forty-three years old, and that he was even then incapable of walking to any great extent is shown by some correspondence between him and the Earl of Bath.'[1] The latter peer, like Lord Dacre, seems to have been physically incapacitated from walking, and so was the Lord President.[2] Lord Bath wrote the following letter to the latter:—

> My Lord
> I take the liberty to send your Lord[p] a Letter I rec[d] late last night from Lord Dacres, complaining of the Injury done to all of us, who are refused Tickets for the Coronation, unless we walk at it. As you are involved in the same injurious Circumstances, we hope you will joyn with us, in endeavouring to obtain redress, and we are ready to do whatever you shall direct us in this Case. We hope it may be considered, that we are to be punished; not, for want of inclination to do our Duty, but *solely* for want of Capacity, and if *Incapacity* in all Cases was to be urged as a reason for depriving Persons, from sharing of his Majesty's favours, God alone knows how far, or how high, that may go. I fear it might make a dreadful destruction amongst a multitude of *Place Men* and Courtiers.

It is satisfactory to know that these crippled peers were allowed, after all, to take part in the ceremony of the Coronation.

In his bringing up Lord Dacre did not have any of those advantages which may be derived from the care of parents. We have seen that his father died before his birth, and that, when he was still very young, his grandfather brought an action against his mother to have himself declared the boy's guardian in her stead on the grounds that she being a Roman Catholic was likely 'to breed him a papist'; and the House of Lords having declared against Lady Anne, the boy was brought up chiefly under the care of his aunt, Mrs. Ranby. He was

---

[1] Thomas Thynn, third Earl of Bath.   [2] Lord Granville.

educated first at Greenwich and then at Harrow, from whence we have the following letter from him to her:—

Dear Aunt
March ye 29, 1732.

As you have been always exceeding good to me; & for which I shall never be able to make you a Return; I beg you'd now please to grant me this Request viz: to Leave off Learning Mathematicks, this Dear Madam may att first seem an unreasonable thing; but I hope ye Reasons which I am now going to give you will make you, according to your usual goodness, Grant me this Request.

You very well know Dear Madam that I have been an old Border, & therefore ought not to be slighted by Weston which I have been very much. For this Morning I heard that Mr Weston was going out with some off[1] ye Gentlemen to teach them to measure Ground; upon this Report I took my hat & stood among ye Rest off those who were going. When to my Great Surprise Mr Weston came down Stairs & bid me begon for I only wanted to be Idle & told me I shou'd not go with him. This has netled me very much because the Boys he took out with him were no farther advanc'd in Mathematick's than I. As for his saying I only wanted to be Idle, I hope you will believe me, when I tell you upon my Honour that ye Chief & only end of my Desire to go out a measuring; was to be instructed in that Art. Neither do I think that I ever gave him half so much Reason to think me prone to Idleness as Barnet & Philips who went with him. If you will be so good then Dear Madam to grant me my earnest Request of Leaving off Mathematicks I shall be exceedingly oblig'd to you.

You may Rember [*sic*] Dear Aunt that I have often told you that Mr Evans taught me Mathematicks in private. I shall still continue to Learn Mathematicks of Mr Evans who is more able to teach me than Weston. For I can assure you I have Learnt more from Mr Evans than I ever did from Weston.

I hope I have now given you Sufficient Reasons for my Desireing to Leave Learning Mathematicks from Mr Weston; I therefore beg you'd be so good to me (Dear Madam) as to grant my Desire. There is an old Saying one Story is good till another is told; but I can asure you on my Honour that what I have told you is true; I beg therefore that if you grant

[1] At a period earlier than when this letter was written 'of' and 'off' were not differentiated.—*C. D.*

me my Request, that you will not be mov'd by Westons fawning & funning, who cares no more for you nor I, than what money he can make off us, else he wou'd not have us'd you in the manner he did when you Came from Lady Lennards[1] to give you old heartychoaks[2] for Supper & to Lay you in Bed with frowsy Bet Rosam to be devour'd by Buggs. The Quarter is now beginning, therefore tis a very fit time to Leave off Mathematicks; I beg you'd Let me have a Letter from you as soon as possible, in which I hope to receive Orders to tell Mr Weston that I Don't Learn Mathematicks any Longer off him, which will be an inexpressible pleasure to, Dear Aunt,

Your most Dutifull Nephew,
T. LENNARD BARRETT.

P.S. I shall take Double pains in Latin & evrything else. I shall be so far from losing the Mathematicks I have already got that I don't doubt to make great improvements in them under Mr Evans's care. Pray don't tell Weston I Learn of Mr Evans.

When Lord Dacre was about seventeen years of age he was entered at Lincoln's Inn. His guardians could never have thought that he would be likely to pursue the law as a profession, but he was probably sent there with the idea that mixing with the students would assist in his education. It has been said that at one time 'The Inns of Court were looked upon as finishing schools in which the sons of the nobility and gentry might learn good manners and accomplishments.'[3] I am unable to say how far he pursued his legal studies, but in the books of the members of the Inn there is the following entry: '21 February 173¾ Hon. Thomas Lennard Barrett of Aveley Essex grandson & heir of Hon. Dacre Lennard Barrett dec^d.'

A Chancery suit was instituted in order that Lord Dacre's estates might be administered under the direction of the Court during his minority, and the Receiver's accounts in this suit show that, in 1733, Mr Ranby was allowed 200*l.* for Lord Dacre's maintenance, when he would have been sixteen years

---

[1] The only person then living properly described as 'Lady Lennard' was Elizabeth, the widow of Sir Stephen Lennard (second Baronet), of West Wickham; she died in June 1732.

[2] Obsolete form of 'artichoke.'—*C. D.*   [3] *S. Arch.* xlvii. footnote, p. 130.

old. The next year 250*l.*, and in 1735 400*l.*, and an additional sum of 133*l.* in July of that year for 'the Extraordinary expences of Mr Barrett going to the University pursuant to the order dated the 21st day of April last past.'

By these accounts it appears that the Irish property in 1730 produced about 1,000*l.* a year, and the disbursements only came to 70*l.* to 80*l.*; Horsford produced about 300*l.* a year, with disbursements of 50*l.* to 70*l.*; and Essex about 950*l.*, with disbursements of nearly 600*l.*; of the latter item about one-half consisted of estate repairs, and the other half of taxes and management. At one period the park at Belhus was let for 95*l.* a year, and the lessee appears to have had the right to kill deer, as there are items allowed him for 'venison for Mr Barrett'; this came on one occasion to 23*l.*, and on another to 39*l.* Venison sold very well in those days, as a year or two later, when the park was no longer let, we find occasional sales of bucks credited at the price of four guineas each.

In 1733 the Court of Chancery allowed 45*l.* for the purchase of linen, and in the following year 200*l.* for the furniture. I think it possible that Mrs. Ranby for a time lived at Belhus during her ward's minority, and allowed the furniture that her father had left her to remain there; but that as Lord Dacre approached his majority she moved it away, and that then the Court gradually allowed some of the infant's income to be spent in furnishing the house, so that when he did come of age it would be ready for him to live in.

There is one item in these accounts which is difficult to understand, and that is 'Raspins for Doggs,' from 1734 to 1737. This curious item appears several times, and the 'raspins' were always bought of one man, who was paid various sums; his bill for them on one occasion amounting to as much as 10*l.* 6*s.* 2*d.*; and during the three years that these delicacies for dogs were supplied the Court appears to have passed payments for them amounting in all to nearly 40*l.* Besides 'raspins' there are a few entries of payments made for 'Dog's flesh,' and 'Dog's meat.' There is, of course, nothing here to show whether these 'raspins' were for Lord Dacre's own dogs, or for those of his keepers. He was, all his life, greatly attached to dogs, and, whether indoors or out, almost always had a small one on his knees, and others following the bath chair in which he was driven about the park; this great devotion to dogs has been inherited by nearly all his very numerous descendants, some of whom carry it to the point of eccentricity.

The following undated letter of Lord Dacre's to Mrs Ranby was written, no doubt, in 1735, shortly before he went to Cambridge :—

Dear Aunt,
   I reciev'd a message from the Keeper just now importing that you were much concern'd that my arm was broke; I easily conciev'd the meaning of it, but can asure you that 'twas not thro any neglect or disrespect that I did not write to you, but because I had nothing worth your notice to send in my letter. I yesterday had small fit of my ague, and twas so inconsiderable that tis hardly to be call'd one. The town is now very empty, and Wednesday was ye last time of performing Operas I was tother day at Mr Dicken's where I saw his brother the Doctor, who is to be my tutor at Cambridge, he says my Chambers are ye best in the College, and I am to go down there ye beginning of October;[1] I have rec^d a letter from my sister which I have enclos'd because I thought you might have a mind to see it. I met Mrs. Savil tother day in the park, and she told me that she shoud go for week or ten days to Marks[2] in a short time. Mr. Savil has been very ill all this winter; to say ye truth I was asham'd to meet her, having been so neglectful of waiting on her; she enquir'd very kindly after you, and presented her humble service. I hope you have had no return of y^r feuver, Mr Ranby & I shall have the pleasure of seeing you in day or two, he presents his respects; and please to accept the same from your humble servant, I desire you'll please to give my service to all the family, I am, Madam,
   Your most Dutifull Nephew,
      THO^s LENNARD BARRETT.
Fryday 1 a clock.

[1] Possibly after all Lord Dacre did not go to Cambridge. I have had the Matriculation books from 1730 to 1750 searched, but no entry of Thomas Lennard Barrett is to be found.

[2] No doubt the Mildmay's house, Marks Hall, near Romford.

The 'Gentleman's Magazine' (1786) in referring to Lord Dacre's death, says that he went to the University of Lausanne, but I have found no reference to this in any of our letters or papers.

Shortly before Lord Dacre came of age he went abroad, certainly to Paris if nowhere else, which is proved by me finding a draft for 200l. which he drew in Paris on January 18th, 1738, on Mr. Ben Periam of Fleet Street. This was no doubt the occasion on which he made the acquaintance of his aunt, Lady Barbara Skelton, which, as we shall see, she refers to in a letter to him written a couple of years later.

In 1725, upon the death of Dacre Barrett, Lord Dacre succeeded as a minor to the entailed estates in Essex, Norfolk, and Ireland; but, as I have stated, Dacre, following the example of his own father, left nearly all that he could away from his heir; and tradition says he had for some years previous to his death allowed Belhus to fall into ruins, and lived at the farmhouse known as Bretts, in Aveley. His grandson probably found Belhus in a bad state of repair, and owing to the provisions of Dacre's will it was certainly destitute of furniture beyond that which the Court of Chancery had allowed to be purchased. Such family plate as Dacre may have possessed would also have passed under his will, and all the pictures there except the three which I have said Dacre bequeathed to whomsoever might live to inherit the estates.[1] It is true that Charles Barrett lived at Bretts, but I must say that I have been unable to find any foundation for the tradition that Dacre Barrett lived there instead of at Belhus, and which my cousin, the late Henry Barrett Lennard, mentions in the notice he wrote of Dacre's life in his collection of 'The Lennard Papers.' Not only have I discovered no reference to his living at Bretts in any of the existing letters, but two letters from Todd, his agent in Ireland, written within a few months of Dacre's death, are directed to him at Belhus, and, as has been stated, Lord Dacre in his account of his grandfather asserts that he died there.

[1] There is a reference to Lord Dacre's lack of furniture or objects to decorate his walls in the letter from Watkinson, *post*, p. 593.

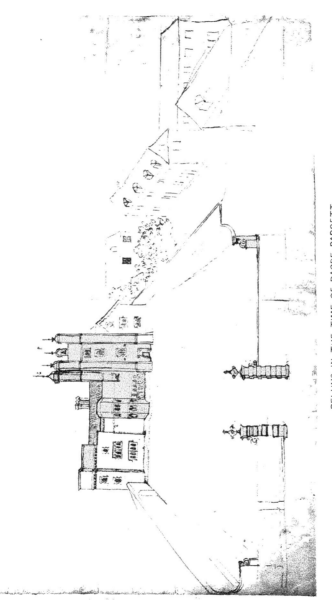

BELHUS IN THE TIME OF DACRE BARRETT

ALTERATIONS TO BELHUS

As my cousin knew his grandfather (Lord Dacre's son) well, he may have good authority for writing, as he did, that when Lord Dacre came into the property ' the house was little better than a ruin, with the roof of the great hall fallen in, and everywhere signs of decay.' My cousin also asserted that the trustees strongly recommended that the mansion should be taken down as not worth repairing, and that Dagenham Hall in a more favoured part of South Essex, should be purchased, but that Lord Dacre indignantly refused to give up the home of his ancestors & determined that the old house should be repaired at all costs.

If the house did need such extensive repairs, it is remarkable that they were not undertaken by the Court of Chancery during Lord Dacre's minority; and although the accounts in the administration suit show that sums of money were from time to time paid to carpenters and other tradesmen, there is nothing in them to suggest that more was spent than would have sufficed to put the farm premises upon the estate in good order. It is rare to find a really old house which has escaped the mischievous hand of the restorer, and in this respect Belhus is no exception to the rule. Instead of complaining at what was done to Belhus with the best intentions and under the best advice available at the period,[1] we ought to think ourselves fortunate that the north side of the house, and the fine old tower that John Barrett built, have been spared to us.

It is difficult to say exactly what alterations Lord Dacre made to Belhus and when he made them, but it was no doubt he who largely remodelled the inside of the house, and is responsible for the front hall, front stairs, the west front, and the three sham turrets.

In a letter Lord Dacre wrote in October, 1747, to Dean Lyttelton of Exeter,[2] he says; ' I am at last got home, & can

---

[1] Tradition says that his friend Horace Walpole advised him largely in this matter.

[2] *B. Mus. Stow. MSS.*, 753; 77; there is another letter from him to the Dean, *ibid.* 754; 102.

assure you that I am not a little pleased to find myself at my poor old habitation & to revisit my Gothic rooms & my young plantations without doors;' and in a letter of the previous month Mr. Nixon of Clones says, 'Rigney was so kind as to give me some time since an Acct of the Improvements you made at Bellhouse, Garden, and Park wch is now a Charming Agreeable Seat.'

These letters make it pretty certain that by that date Lord Dacre had made many of his alterations to the house, and these are not such as would in the present day meet with general approval, as by them Lord Dacre to a great extent transformed an early Tudor manor-house into a sort of 'Strawberry Hill' Gothic castle.

In a published letter to R. Bentley, dated November 1754, Horace Walpole writes :—

I have been at Mr Barrett's at Belhouse; I never saw a place for which one did not wish so totally void of faults. What he has done is in Gothic, and very true, though not up to the perfection of the Committee. The hall is pretty : the great dining room hung with good family pictures : among which is his ancestor, the Lord Dacre who was hanged. I remember when Barrett was first initiated in the College of Arms by the present Dean of Exeter at Cambridge, he was overjoyed at the first ancestor he put up, who was one of the murderers of Thomas Becket.[1] The chimney pieces, except one little miscarriage into total Ionic (he could not resist statuary and Sienna Marble) are all of a good King James the First Gothic. I saw the heronry so fatal to PO Yang,[2] and told him that I was persuaded they were descended from Becket's assassin, and I hoped from my Lord Dacre too.

My cousin, the late Henry Barrett-Lennard, was of opinion that Lord Dacre put a floor across what was then a large hall, and so made what is now called the 'upper drawing-room,' which he thus cut off from what is now the dining-room beneath it; and there is some confirmation for this theory of

[1] *Ante*, p. 177.
[2] H. Walpole had a fishpond which he called Po Yang, and he was annoyed by herons taking goldfish out of it.

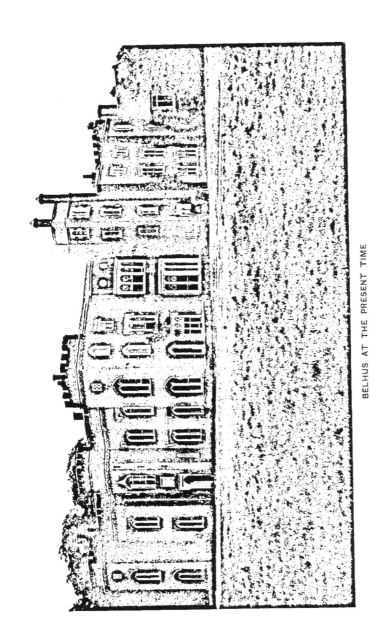

BELHUS AT THE PRESENT TIME

ALTERATIONS TO BELHUS

his in the letter from Nixon quoted from in the course of the next few pages.

Perhaps one of the most regrettable alterations made by Lord Dacre was that of doing away with the walls which surrounded an old-fashioned garden to the south of the house, and making instead the present walled kitchen garden about a quarter of a mile distant from it. This he appears to have done as early as 1744, as we find John Todd, his Irish agent, writing to him on June 19th in that year, and saying, 'as I understand you have been at Considerable expences in & about your Gardens I chose to send this small bill to you (150*l*.) in hopes it will stop some little gaps.'

Lord Dacre says in his MS. Family History[1] that the house which was rebuilt by John Barrett (whose will bears date seventeenth year of Henry VII.)—

But much repaired & improved, still subsists, excepting that the great Gate house which had a large Chamber over it, and several others on each side, was pulled down about sixty years agoe, as it entirely hindered the view of the Park & County. And of later years for the same reason the Old Gardens that surrounded the House were removed which (tho handsome in the Old fashion), with their high Wales entirely shut out the Prospect.

The gate-house, no doubt, was pulled down by Dacre Barrett; we have an inventory of goods at Belhus in June 1696 belonging to Dorothy Lady Dacre,[2] and this mentions bedroom furniture 'In the Gatehouse' and 'In the Room over ye Gatehouse,' so it is clear it was still standing when Richard died in April 1696; and a sketch of the house taken in Dacre Barrett's time shows the garden walls, but no gate-house.

In dry summers some of the lines of the garden walls can still be traced in the grass, and when under-draining the park some forty years ago the workmen dug through the foundations

---

[1] There is no date to this history, which has no frontispiece; his MS. volume of Miscellaneous Extracts of matters concerning the family is dated 1778.
[2] *Ante*, pp. 400, 401.

of these walls.[1] This alteration was evidently considered to be a great improvement at the time it was made, as Mr. Nixon writes from Ireland in November 1752:—

I am much obliged for the acc^t you give me of finishing & furnishing the great room below stairs at Belhus with the pictures of the family which are wthout doubt extremely fine, & beautyful, as you had them from Italy—laying the rising fields to the West open to the house & Park, will be a great improvement to the place. I think you have now finished and left nothing further to be done to make it a Healthy Charming place.

It was not until 1776[2] that Lord Dacre added the outside library and the two floors above it. We have an estimate from a Mr. Watson for building this library and rooms above, the price of which came to 186*l*. 7*s*. 8*d*.; Lord Dacre finding and carting all bricks, tiles, &c., and the builder only to 'compleat the carcasing' of the new work; all plastering of walls, ceilings, laying of floors, painting, &c., to be extras. The new work was solidly built, as the estimate allowed for the foundations being two feet three inches thick, the walls up to three feet three inches high, two feet three inches thick; the rest of that storey was to have walls of twenty inches, and the other two storeys walls of eighteen inches.[3]

Tradition says that Lord Dacre employed the celebrated landscape gardener 'Capability' Brown[4] to assist him in laying out the grounds, and that it is owing to the latter's advice that three rather large mounds were made in the park and planted with lime-trees, in order in some measure to counteract the general flatness of the country; and I have no doubt Brown made that fine sheet of water in the park called the Long Pond, as the estate map of 1739 shows only a stream where the pond now is. The truth of the tradition that Brown

---

[1] They discovered an ancient 'Maidenhead' Spoon, which is now in my possession.

[2] Reference in letter of Lady Dacre.

[3] In the present day fourteen inches is considered a good thickness for a wall, and more than eighteen inches most unusual.

[4] Lancelot Brown, *b.* 1715, *d.* 1783. He began life as a gardener, acquired a large fortune, and became High Sheriff of Hants.

was employed at Belhus is proved by my discovery of some pass-books of Drummond's Bank which show payments to 'Lanc^t Brown' between December 1753 and November 1763 amounting in all to 668*l*. 14*s*. It was in 1771 that a bridge, now long since entirely gone, but which my father remembers as a boy, was constructed over that portion of the pond which flows through a wood at the back of the kitchen garden. The entry referring to it is ' Building & painting bridge in ye Park 42*l*.'

A great judge [1] once said, 'Mistakes are the inevitable lot of mankind;' and in judging of a man's achievements in respect of building and laying out of grounds you should consider what was the state of knowledge and taste at the period in which he lived. If Lord Dacre had these two great experts, Horace Walpole [2] and Lancelot Brown, to help him, he had the advice of men whose taste in those days was considered particularly valuable, and it would be unreasonable to blame him for following the opinions of the best experts then available.

Lord Dacre, who had great taste for art, literature, and genealogies, formed a fine library, largely composed of county histories and heraldic works, furnished the house afresh, and got together an extremely fine collection of family portraits.

These pictures, as regards the Lennards, from the time of Samson who died 1615, form an uninterrupted line of portraits of the elder branch who bore the title of Dacre, and of their respective wives, down to himself. The continuity of those of the younger branch who assumed the name of Barrett, and from whom he descended on his paternal side, is broken only by the absence of a portrait of his own father, who did not live to succeed to the property and was probably never painted.

Besides these pictures of the Lennards, he obtained also portraits of Margaret Fynes, wife of Samson, and of her parents, several Barrett portraits, and those of many collaterals.

[1] Sir G. Jessel, M.R.
[2] Many of the alterations were made by the advice of Sanderson Miller, an intimate friend of Lord Dacre, and who, next to Walpole, was considered the greatest authority on 'the true Gothick.'

The pictures of the Barretts,[1] and those of the younger branch of the Lennards, were probably given him by his aunt, Jane Ranby. He may have obtained some of those of the Lords Dacre from his mother, but she appears to have taken most of the family pictures which she inherited into the two families of Ropers and Moores, into which she successively married. That this was so is shown by the following memorandum in Lord Dacre's handwriting endorsed—

Memorandum about my Brother Moores Pictures, Oct. 30, 1784.

I purchased soon after my mothers death of my Father in Law[2] Mr. Moore for Forty-pounds (which they were valued at by Mr Pond[3] a noted painter) the Picture of Henry Lennard Lord Dacre a whole length and the picture of Mary wife of Thomas Fynes Lord Dacre a quarter length by Lucas de Heer.[4]

My Brother Moore also afterwards gave me my Mothers picture by Murray, a half length, which, with the rest of my Mothers pictures his father, then alive, had given him possession of: And my Brother gave me the said Picture by Murray as he knew I much wished for it; and in gratitude for my having sometime before given him money to pay his debts, which I did freely & unasked, and besides helped him when in Germany. The above three pictures being therefore my own I sent them to Belhouse imediately on my becoming possessed of them in order to compleat the series of original pictures of my Ancestors there.

Hereafter follows the List of my mothers pictures belonging to my Brother Moore which he desired me to keep for him and sent to my house in Bruton Street where they now are.

---

[1] As has been stated, Dacre Barrett left to his successor the portrait of E. Barrett Lord Newburgh.

[2] Meaning stepfather.   [3] Arthur Pond died 1758.

[4] 'At Lord Dacre's at Belhus in Essex is one of the best works of this master. It always passed for a Holbein, but Virtue discovered it to be De Heere, whose mark is discernible.'—*W. His. P.* 'There is at Belhus by a painter of the name of De Hire a portrait of her (Mary, wife of Thomas Fynes Lord Dacre) that is absolutely alive. There is also a masterly portrait of him by Holbein, and a miniature of that very picture is part of the furniture of the room in which his widow is described as sitting in her portrait.'—*Mis. G. H.*

FAMILY PORTRAITS

The list which follows is a somewhat long one, and it is not necessary to give it in full, as many of the pictures it refers to I am unable to trace. Among other portraits it mentions a half-length of the 'Duchess of Cleveland in brown,'[1] at the end of this list of pictures there is the following note :—

Memorandum, that since the writing the notices on the other side all the parties concerned in the reversion of my Brother Moores Pictures after his Death did near two years agoe give me up their right to the Picture of Lord Bayning, Ld Grandison, Mr Walters, K— Chas ye Ist, K: James ye 2^{d}, and Major Henry Roper Mr Trever Roper, his Brother, answered for his consent in his absence, and I therefore hung them up at Belhouse. Dacre. Belhouse Octr 30th 1784.

While on the subject of the portraits at Belhus, it may be mentioned here that in December 1739 a Mr. Watkinson, who was staying in Paris with Lady Barbara Skelton, writes that he is commissioned by her to bring over to Lord Dacre the following portraits to which he ascribes these names and painters, viz. :—

Thos. Fynes Lord Dacre by Holbein, Henry Lennard Lord Dacre by Van Dyke,[2] Samson Lennard and Margaret Fynes, two pictures on boards by Corn^s Johnson [*sic*] or at least I believe so.[3] Francis Lennard & his wife in one picture, a capital picture by Sir Peter Lilly [*sic*], and a large picture of Vendome [*sic*] [Philip de Vendome].

---

[1] It may be of this picture, but more likely, I think, of another portrait of the Duchess at Belhus, that G. Hardinge writes : 'Amongst the family portraits which are heirlooms at Belhus there is a portrait of this Beauty [the Duchess of Cleveland]; the loveliest picture ever painted by Sir P. Lely, half-length. She has a serious and melancholy countenance. *Modest!* and bewitching it corresponds exactly to the lines in Pope,
"Lely on animated canvas stole
The sleepy eye that spoke the melting soul."'
—*Mis. G. H.*

[2] Besides the full-length picture of Henry Lord Dacre previously mentioned there is also at Belhus a half-length portrait of him, which is probably the one referred to above.

[3] Mr. Watkinson must have been misinformed as to the painter of these two portraits, as C. Jansen did not come to England until 1618.

It was no doubt from his aunt that he also obtained, but perhaps on some subsequent occasion, pictures of herself, and her husband the General, both by De Troy.

At the early age of twenty-two, on May 15th, 1739, Lord Dacre married, at St. George's Chapel, Hyde Park, Anne Maria Pratt,[1] daughter of Sir John Pratt, Lord Chief Justice, of the Wilderness, Kent,[2] by his second wife, a daughter of the Rev. — Wilson, Canon of Bangor. Our portraits of her represent her to be a good-looking woman, and Mr. Stephen Norris, of Norwich, writing to Lord Dacre in the year of their marriage, speaks of her as the 'Beauteous M{rs} Barrett.' He may have written in a flattering strain, but he could hardly have used that epithet if she had not been at least good-looking, while a nephew of hers in a letter published after her death says, 'My Aunt was the handsomest creature you ever saw but rather short.'[3] She was of an old Devonshire family, but had only a fortune of 4,000*l*., so it cannot be looked upon as by any means a brilliant marriage from a worldly point of view. It will be seen that Anne Pratt made Lord Dacre a most admirable wife, and was a woman of no ordinary character; she appears to have combined great forbearance with equally great powers of affection, coupled with the possession of an unusual amount of common sense and a great aptitude for business.

In the following year Lady Dacre gave birth to a girl, who was christened Barbara after her great-grandmother, the celebrated Duchess of Cleveland. That the child should be a girl was no doubt a great disappointment to the parents, and I think it is likely that they took medical advice in the hopes that some treatment might render Lady Dacre capable of bearing more children, and so possibly a male heir. The following extract from a letter from Mr. Nixon, dated September 1747, in which he says he should be greatly pleased to hear 'if the

---

[1] *Har. So. R.* xv.

[2] When Sir John bought this house in the parish of Seal it was known as 'The Manor of Stidfule's Place,' and he renamed it the 'Wilderness.'—*S. Arch.* xlvii. p. 102.

[3] *Mis. G. H.*

cold Bath at Marylebone, & Bellhouse, or warm waters at Bath have had the desired effect, if there are signs, or Appearances of any thing that way,' can, I think, bear no other construction.

There was until recently a large fixed bath at Belhus, which from its old-fashioned appearance evidently had been there many years, and which was only fitted for cold water, and is probably the bath alluded to above. From the way Mr. Nixon refers to this bath, fixed baths were evidently in those days quite unusual even in large country houses.

There is something pathetic in the idea of this poor lady shivering, perhaps for hours, in a succession of cold baths both in London and in the country; and she put up with all this discomfort in vain, as she never had another child.

In 1741 Lady Barbara Skelton died in France at the age of sixty-five. She was greatly attached to her nephew, Lord Dacre, as is shown by the following letter which she wrote to him about the time that she was sending him over the family portraits :—

Paris Jany ye 12th 1740.

Dearest nephew.

Tho I writ to you very lately I cant forbear doeing it againe by our friend Mr Watkinson who js yn such baiste to return to you he sets out jn such miserable weather a dog would not goe out of doors unlesse whiped out of the house, tis not Watkinsons caise for I should be uery glaad he would stay longer with me, but I see his heart js with you much more then with me, & that you haue drawn to your self all his loue: I cant say I am not jealous, but at the same time thinke he has placed his affections on those who deserues them best, & on that account forgiue him his jmpatience to be gone. I am desireous he should bring you new assurances of my tender loue, and affections, as allsoe of my gratitude for the sentiments you haue for me, by being so much yn your fauour, & loued by you, js so great a satisfaction, & comfort to me: no words can expresse the joy euery kind expression of yours giues me: it was a hapy sky for me brought you into this country with out which I should neuer haue known the best, & kindest of re-laitions, & that I uallue, & loue as I ought, & you desarue, all that uexes me js not hauing it yn my power to giue you such essentiall markes of my good will as I had formerly, but what I can doe for you depend on it I will, & shall be whilst I haue life Dearest nephew,

Your most affectionet aunt & humble seruant
B. SKELTON.

Since the death of the Earl of Sussex the barony of Dacre had been in abeyance between his two daughters, but on Lady Barbara's death that title passed to her sister, Lady Anne.

In July 1746 Lord Dacre received a letter from a Mr. W. Andrews, of Barnes Hall, Worcester, which redounds so much to the credit of the former, and shows a sense of honour so much higher than that of any ordinary modern standard, that it appears worthy of insertion as throwing light upon his character :—

Your kind letter of the 15th Instant came safe to my hands last Saturday. The parsonage of Aveley in Essex I sold to you, and the purchase money agreed for it, was honestly paid me; It lying at so great a distance from me was the Occasion of my parting with it. Your Letter did not a Little surprise me, when I saw your kind and good natured intention of makeing me a present of Three hundred and thirty pounds, the halfe of what you hinted you had found out the Estate to be worth more than the purchase money you gave for it. It is such a generous Act in you, that I verily beleive no one in England besides your self would have done such a thing, :tbeing an unparrellel'd Act, and for which I return you my Sincere thanks.

Until about fifty years ago there was no vicarage at Aveley, and there never was an incumbent of that place named Andrews. I have no doubt but that this purchase referred to some house in the village which Lord Dacre had bought, and which had commonly been rented by the vicar for the time being.

In the spring of 1749 a terrible misfortune befell Lord and Lady Dacre, as a sudden illness bereft them of Barbara, their only child. This loss must have been an especially crushing one to Lord Dacre; he was proud, and perhaps even vain, of the family he represented; he had spared no pains to get the house and estates into good order, and, as far as possible, restore the fortunes of the family so wrecked by the extravagances both of his mother and of her father. His wife had only had this one child, and they, no doubt, were aware by now that she was unlikely ever to have another, so that her death meant to him not merely the loss of a greatly beloved child, but also the annihilation of all his plans for the future of his descendants. If Lord Dacre had had no other child, and Barbara had survived him, she, like her ancestress Maud de Vaux, and other heiresses of her family, would have inherited the barony of Dacre upon her father's death. If she had lived to marry, Lord Dacre would doubtless have contrived that whoever married her should assume the names of Barrett and Lennard; as it was, Barbara's death caused the offspring of his mother's second marriage to come next to him in succession to the title.

In his Family History Lord Dacre, in an appendix, writes in what at the present day we might perhaps think rather stilted language, the following note on Barbara's death:—

This Anne Barbara (Ah bitter day) was snatched away by a violent feaver on the 14th of March 1749, just as she was entering into the 10th year of her age. Her person was such as gained her favour at first sight, and was an earnest of her mind. It was not possible to find a fault in her shape; her shoulders fell from her neck with a peculiar grace, her hair was of the darkest brown, her complexion the finest white and red, and her skin so delicate that every vein was perfectly discovered through it, the form of her face was round tho' inclining to an oval; her mouth of a middle size, and her nose rather small than large; her eyebrows were narrow and most exactly arched; her eyes were of the finest bleu and had a mixture of softness and Liveliness in them—inexpressible, and (which gave them a particular Beauty) her Eyelashes were most remarkably long: and as dark as her hair. The picture that remains of her when eight years old by no means does her justice. As to the perfections of her mind, they are not so easy to be described, let it suffice then to say that she was all sweetness and goodness, at the same time that she was most remarkably sprightly, and of an understanding and quickness of apprehension, so superior and uncommon, that she surprised and delighted everyone that talked with her—This may be thought a flattering representation of her, But in truth it is not, and therefore (though at the hazard of being thought partial by those who have not known her) I could not resist the desire I had to pay this tribute, and this justice, to her memory.

Shortly after the poor child's death Lord and Lady Dacre, accompanied by her sister Caroline,[1] went for a prolonged tour for over a year on the Continent, partly for health, but more especially to divert their minds from the great loss which they had sustained. They travelled by Paris, Dijon, and Lyons, whence Lord Dacre, writing on 'May y{e} 22 N.S. 1749' to Philip Yorke[2] to thank him for the civilities his party had received while in Paris from a Colonel Yorke, says 'ye more I see of the French the more I like my own countrymen & my own country.' From Lyons the travellers went by water down the Rhone to Avignon, then on to Marseilles and Antibes, whence they took boat and coasted along to Genoa. They spent a considerable time in Florence, Rome, and Naples, and in May 1750 were at Venice as appears from a published letter to Lord Dacre from his wife's brother-in-law, Nicholas Hardinge.[3] While in Italy they formed a friendship with Mr. (afterwards Sir) Horace Mann, who was an English Minister there, and in the letter above referred to Mr. Hardinge writes:—

Mr. Mann says in his letter he hopes you will be induced to make a second trial of the baths of Pisa, and pass another season in Tuscany. This, he says, he is greatly interested to desire, as he never passed any time so happily as with you and your family.

[1] She married afterwards General Count Munster, Attaché to the Bavarian army.
[2] *Add.* 35605, fol. 339. No doubt Lord Hardwicke's eldest son.
[3] *Poems by N. Hardinge.* His son George, a distinguished member of the Bar, became Senior Justice of the Welsh Circuit.

During his absence in France and Italy, Lord Dacre wrote a series of letters to Mr. Hardinge describing their tour, and copies of these were given to my great-grandfather by one of the Hardinges, but unfortunately many of these letters have been lost.

Mr. Richard Dawson[1] wrote to Lord Dacre on April 18th, 1749:—

I am most sincerely concerned for your loss, God comfort you and Mrs Barrett under your afflictions for they are great. I have had my share of trouble in the same way and there is no living in this world without them. I am much pleased you and Mrs Barrett are determined to spend some time abroad as I am convinced it will conduce greatly to the benefit of your health: new objects and moving from place to place will in a great measure remove your melancholy thoughts; your good sense will enable you to bear up and support Mrs Barrett in her present misfortune; let me request the favour of you to spend as much of your time in Company as you can.

How little was the success which for a time attended this plan of travelling abroad may be judged of by the following extract from a letter written by Lord Dacre to N. Hardinge:—

As to my mind ye loss I have had has made an impression on it not to be got out, and I may justly apply to my own case with a small alteration in them, these verses of Waller:—

> 'Who in ye Spring from ye new sun
>   Already has a feavor got
> In vain attempts those shafts to shun
>   Which Phoebus through his veins has shot.
> In vain he would his pain assuage
>   And to thick shadows does retire,
> About with him he bears the rage
>   And in his tainted blood the fire.'[2]

And he goes on to say, 'Mrs Barrett is perfectly well in health, ye state of her mind is I believe pretty much like mine.'

---

[1] His son Thomas was created Baron Cremorne.
[2] 'The Self-Banished,' by Edward Waller.

I know of no other references in our letters as to how the poor mother took her loss, but I have in my possession one touching evidence of the depths of her feelings—a portion of a child's dress that the second wife of Sir Thomas (first Baronet) showed my mother some fifty years ago, saying that Lady Dacre had always kept this dress to the day of her death, being the last one that Barbara had worn.

It was when in Rome that Lord Dacre had a very beautiful portrait painted of him and his wife looking at their lost child. This picture is by Pompeo Battoni, who had a considerable vogue at that date; there is a tradition that Battoni copied Barbara's figure from her portrait by Hudson, which had been sent out on purpose, and, admiring Hudson's painting so much, he insisted on leaving the face blank, so that the latter might insert it after the picture arrived in England.

After their return to England in the spring of 1751[1] Lord Dacre occupied himself in continuing the alterations he was making at Belhus; and it was then too, no doubt, that he began to write the history of his family, which, owing to his bad health, probably occupied him for several years. Far from being better for his foreign tour, his malady seemed to become more aggravated, and at Belhus there is still, or was till recently, the wheel chair in which he guided himself through the rooms on the ground floor, and the low pony chaise given to him by Lord Derby, into which he was lifted in order to drive in the gardens and park.

Although so great an invalid, Lord Dacre probably did a good deal of entertaining while in London, as he had a very considerable service of silver plates, dishes, &c., which he seems to have bought in 1753, as Mr. Thomas Dawson writes to him

---

[1] I am not able to give the date of Lord Dacre's return to England with certainty. In a letter of September 1750, from Florence, Lord Dacre speaks of his intention of returning to England in the following year. His Norfolk agent, Aldham, writing to his Essex agent, Rigney, on April 1st, 1751, says, 'I hope soon to hear of Mr. Barretts safe return to Bellhouse.'

I know of no other references in our letters as to how the poor mother took her loss, but I have in my possession one touching evidence of the depths of her feelings—a portion of a child's dress that the second wife of Sir Thomas (first Baronet) showed my mother some fifty years ago, saying that Lady Dacre had always kept this dress to the day of her death, being the last one that Barbara had worn.

It was when in Rome that Lord Dacre had a very beautiful portrait painted of him and his wife looking at their lost child. This picture is by Pompeo Battoni, who had a considerable vogue at that date; there is a tradition that Battoni copied Barbara's figure from her portrait by Hudson, which had been sent out on purpose, and, admiring Hudson's painting so much, he insisted on leaving the face blank, so that the latter might insert it after the picture arrived in England.

After their return to England in the spring of 1751 [1] Lord Dacre occupied himself in continuing the alterations he was making at Belhus; and it was then too, no doubt, that he began to write the history of his family, which, owing to his bad health, probably occupied him for several years. Far from being better for his foreign tour, his malady seemed to become more aggravated, and at Belhus there is still, or was till recently, the wheel chair in which he guided himself through the rooms on the ground floor, and the low pony chaise given to him by Lord Derby, into which he was lifted in order to drive in the gardens and park.

Although so great an invalid, Lord Dacre probably did a good deal of entertaining while in London, as he had a very considerable service of silver plates, dishes, &c., which he seems to have bought in 1753, as Mr. Thomas Dawson writes to him

---

[1] I am not able to give the date of Lord Dacre's return to England with certainty. In a letter of September 1750, from Florence, Lord Dacre speaks of his intention of returning to England in the following year. His Norfolk agent, Aldham, writing to his Essex agent, Rigney, on April 1st, 1751, says, 'I hope soon to hear of Mr. Barretts safe return to Bellhouse.'

from Dublin on October 6th of that year, and in the course of that letter he says :—

When I was in London Mrs. Barrett was about buying plate, ours is come over, and was made by Archambo & Coy[1] in Coventry Street, Haymarket it has been admired by every one, & indeed I never saw any so finished ; I mention it that if you have any more to buy the man is to be depended upon.

Lord Dacre inherited no house in London; the Earl of Sussex had sold his house there, and Dacre Barrett left the leasehold interest in his Great Russell Street house away from his grandson, so the latter, after lodging for a while in Sackville Street, obtained one in Bruton Street.[2] After his return from his prolonged trip on the Continent, Lord Dacre passed almost all the rest of his life between Belhus and Bruton Street, and for many years after his death his widow went to the former place in May with the regularity of clockwork, and left it for London early in January.

From entries in an account book kept by Lady Dacre, which begins in 1768, of such payment as poor and church rates, window tax, builders' and carpenters' repairs, &c., &c., at Sevenoaks, it appears that at that period, and for the next four or five years, Lord Dacre had a house there, and mention is made of payments of '£27..10 ; half-year's rent' in 1768, '69, and '70, to a Mr. Fermor. This may have been for the hire of the house at Sevenoaks, it was certainly not the ground rent for Bruton Street, which was 17*l.* 11*s.* There is no mention of this rent after 1770, but there is of payments at Sevenoaks until March 1773. I can find no letters addressed to Lord Dacre at Sevenoaks, and I imagine, from the account book, that even when staying there he kept up some establishment at Belhus. There is an entry in November 1772, ' 30,000 tyles at 16/—£24.,' which suggests that at this period Lord Dacre was still altering

[1] Peter Archambo, a celebrated silver-worker.
[2] From the address on a letter to his son the number in the street appears to have been ' 22.' In Lord Dacre's time I imagine the street was not numbered, as letters were addressed to him ' at his house in Bruton Street.'

Belhus, and, if that were the case, it would account for his living at Sevenoaks for a few years while these alterations were in progress; on the other hand, the tiles may have been bought for some of the farms.

In any case he went to Belhus for the summer on May 20th, 1773, and continued for many years to go there every May, except when occasionally illness caused him to delay his departure from London for a few weeks.

Besides going backwards and forwards every year between London and Belhus, he made it a rule to go for a trip for several weeks in the latter half of every year, usually in August or September. The places he went to were either such health resorts as Cheltenham, Bath, Tunbridge, or Buxton, where he could drink the waters; or else places where he could undergo a course of sea-bathing, such as Weymouth, Brighthelmstone (Brighton), or Margate. On these trips he took with him several servants and horses, usually about six of the former and six to eight of the latter; some of the horses are described as coach and some as saddle horses, which, as he certainly was not well enough to ride, were presumably to carry some of his servants. The expenses of these trips naturally varied considerably, according to the distance travelled; but, as a rule, they seem to have cost about 20*l.* to 30*l.* a week, including all travelling and doctors' fees at the different baths.

In 1769 Lord and Lady Dacre went to Paris, and this cost about 25*l.* a week, besides 100*l.* for the journey there and back. In one of Horace Walpole's published letters to his great friend John Chute, dated Paris, August 30th, 1769, he says:—

Judge of my surprise at hearing four days ago that my Lord Dacre and my lady were arrived here. They are lodged within a few doors of me. He has come to consult a Dr. Pomme[1] who has prescribed wine, and Lord Dacre already complains of the violence of his appetite. If you and I had *pommed* him to eternity, he would not have believed us. A man across the sea tells him the plainest thing in the world; that man happens to be called a Doctor; and happening for novelty to talk common

[1] The then fashionable physician of Paris.

sense, is believed, as if he had talked nonsense! and what is more extraordinary, Lord Dacre thinks himself better, *though* he is so.

I doubt whether Lord Dacre derived even temporary benefit from his treatment in Paris, but he seems to have been addicted to trying all sorts of medical and quack treatments, as was perhaps only natural in a person afflicted, as he was, with a lameness which ordinary medical treatment was unable to cure. In Lady Dacre's account book there is a mention of payment of 10*l.* 10*s.* in February 1775 to 'Mr Wyat for electrifying my Lord'; and three years later, in June 1778, he paid nearly 100*l.* to a Dr. Dominiceti and 3*l.* 3*s.* to the doctor's servants for a course of treatment which extended over nine weeks. Dominiceti was an Italian physician, or rather charlatan (his name is not to be found in the register of physicians), of very considerable notoriety and talents. His baths were in Chelsea, and between 1764 and 1780 he is said to have had over 16,000 persons under his care. Sir John Fielding, the well-known London magistrate, was a great believer in this Italian, and wrote 'A Vindication of Dr. Dominiceti's Practice of removing afflicting diseases by medicated baths, stoves, fumigators, and frictions founded upon facts.' On the other hand, Dr. Johnson, the lexicographer, said, 'There is nothing in all his boasted system. No Sir, medicated baths can be no better than warm water, their only effect can be that of tepid moisture.' In spite of his large practice Dominiceti became bankrupt in 1782.[1]

They seem at Belhus to have been very fond of taking medicines, as is shown by many payments on that behalf in Lady Dacre's account book, among which may be mentioned, as showing a childlike belief in the power of drugs to cure, 'a paper of powders for the bite of a mad dog £1. .1.' 'Medicine to cure the Ague £2. .2,' and 'a quart of Daffy's[2] Elixir 10/6.'

[1] Faul.
[2] The Rev. Thomas Daffy, the inventor of this once fashionable medicine, died 1680.

As I have said, Anne Lady Dacre died in 1755, and her son Thomas, succeeding to the title, took his seat in the House of Lords on November 13th in that year. I have no direct evidence as to the relations which existed between Lord Dacre and his mother, but from many letters it is evident that those between him and his half-brothers and sister were of a most cordial and affectionate nature.

We have seen that Lord Dacre was withdrawn from the care of his mother at a very early age, and brought up by relations who were most bitter against her. Moreover, he was no doubt educated in the most extreme school of Protestant thought, at a period when Protestantism was associated in the minds of the majority of Englishmen with the supremacy of the House of Hanover, and when all Catholics were more or less suspected of being disloyal to the throne. No wonder, then, if there should be but little sympathy between a mother and son so circumstanced. The spendthrift, if not absolutely dishonest, career of his mother's third husband, already referred to, was also calculated to cause the mother and son to drift further and further apart. How far this was the case I am not able to say, as, beyond the letter from Lady Anne,[1] written soon after her first husband's death, and the little scrap of letter from her to Lord Dacre,[2] both already referred to, I have found none of her correspondence, nor have I found any reference in anyone else's letters to the relations existing between her and her son, while Lord Dacre, in his Family History, merely records the bald fact of the date of her death. All this, although it only amounts to evidence of a negative character, inclines me to the belief that there existed no great amount of sympathy or affection between the mother and her son.

Among our papers the many letters to Lord Dacre from various authors who were poets, or who wrote on antiquarian subjects, indicate in what direction his tastes lay. He joined the Society of Antiquaries on May 12th, 1743, and in a letter from him,[3] speaking of a great collection then for sale, which

---

[1] *Ante*, pp. 558, 559. [2] *Ante*, p. 564. [3] *B. Mus., Stow MSS.* 753, f. 79.

consisted of miniatures and what he termed 'curiositys,' that had once belonged to the Duchess of Monmouth, he says, 'Which to us Antiquaries & Historians are a great Entertainment & Feast only to look over tho' they are not our own,' which shows in what light Lord Dacre regarded himself.

In connection with his antiquarian tastes, the following letter from George Hardinge is perhaps worth quoting :—

Dear Brother Antiquary

Lord Dacre one day visiting us in Kent recieved information of a curious monument at Chevening Church which had escaped his notice, though his ancestors had resided there, and he had visited the church once before. It called itself, in his report, a monument to a Harman, with whom some of his ancestors the Lennards had intermarried, and who himself was nobly descended.

He was not then quite a cripple, and rode on horseback a little poney. I accompanied him three or four miles towards Chevening. His eye sparkled with joy and family pride. Within half a mile of the church he met a farmer. He entered into a chat with him, and found him a Chevening man—a Churchman too, so much the better. By degrees he insinuated the monument, and confessed he had come on purpose to feast his eyes upon it. 'I am so glad' (said the man) 'that a gentleman of your appearance comes to see it, but indeed gentlefolks do come far and near to see it.'—'What? it is famous then!' said the Peer.—'Oh quite famous—poor Harman!' (think of the Peer's face!)—'What have you heard of him then?' said Lord Dacre; 'you have seen his pedigree?' 'Lord! his pedigree Sir! No not I, but I *knew the man*—as good a creature as ever lived—Harman the butcher killed by the bite of a mad dog!'

Yours ever

G. HARDINGE.[1]

Among the literary persons from whom I have letters to Lord Dacre are R. Gough, the Rev. P. Morant,[2] Sir David Dalrymple, Jacob Bryant, Dean Lyttleton, E. Capell, Horace Walpole, Rev. John Collins, Sir W. Hamilton, W. Barrett of Bristol, Rev. W. Coxe, Dr. Akenside, Rev. Dr. Pegge, Dr.

[1] *Mis. G. H.* iii.
[2] He dedicated the first volume of his *History of Essex* to Lord Dacre.

Campbell, and others. The names of many of these writers will probably be unfamiliar to most persons who read these pages, but they were all well known characters in the literary world of those days.[1]

The letters to Lord Dacre on political matters which remain to us are few in number, and of no special importance. He took no very active part in politics, his bad health, no doubt, having a tendency to prevent his so doing. In one of Horace Walpole's published letters he says:—

Yesterday there was a flurry in the House of Lords when Lord Dacre, who seldom interferes in politics, vehemently attacked the government for its proposal to enlist foreigners amongst our troops, which he was determined to oppose with such influence as he had.

And in November 1763 Lord Dacre was one of the Lords to sign a very long protest to a motion which had been carried in connection with a breach of privilege.[2]

It is said in 'The People's History of Essex'[3] that the county 'beheld with gloomy dissatisfaction the progress and result of the American War,' and that a powerful confederacy was formed to demand financial and Parliamentary reform, and in January 1780 a public meeting was held in Chelmsford at the instance of Luther, one of the members of the county, for the purpose of assisting this movement. Among the names mentioned as supporting the meeting was that of Lord Dacre; he may probably have lent his name to the movement, but it is, I think, nearly certain that his bad health would have prevented him from attending in person.

The obituary notice of Lord Dacre in the 'Gentleman's Magazine,' May 1786, says: 'In politicks he was, to use his own words, a true & zealous friend of liberty & the protestant religion.'

---

[1] There are several instances of Lord Dacre's interest in literary matters recorded in *N. Lit. Ill.* and *N. Lit. An.*

[2] *Rog.* ii. p. 75.

[3] P. 170; also quoted in the *Victoria History of Essex*.

If this description of Lord Dacre's political views was accurate, the following extract from the letter of an Irish agent to him shows how great is the difference between what in the eighteenth century was considered 'liberty' and our ideas on that subject. There had been an election in county Monaghan, and apparently Lord Dacre had not wished his tenants to vote for a Mr. Corry, who was one of the candidates, and nevertheless some of them had done so. The agent, Noble, writes on September 6th, 1768 :—

As to the Moorheads, and some others of your Tenantry, who I think did not behave well towards you on the last Election, I shall show a proper resentment as you desire for such their behaviour, and shall call on them for a year's Rent against Novem^r to distinguish between them and your other Tenants, who showed a proper regard to your recommendation ; in short a most extraordinary Spirit, or I may say Infatuation, prevailed on the late Elections throughout most parts of the Kingdom among the lower sort of freeholders, and which I believe was in order to show the Power, and Strength of the Non Conformists, without any regard to the least Subordination and where these things may end it is hard to say.

John Todd, who was Lord Dacre's agent in Ireland previously to Noble, wrote in 1748 :—

I acquainted Alderman Dawson of the directions you had given me for all your ffreehold Tennt^s to vote for his son to represent our County in the Room of Collon[1] Willoughby dead, for which he told me he would write you a letter of thanks.

It was so common a thing, until a very much later period, for landowners to consider that they had a right to direct their tenants how they should vote, that I should not have printed these extracts had not the above obituary notice laid so much stress on his being so 'true and zealous friend of liberty.' Had he been a strong Tory, and his political views inimical to liberty, it is difficult to see what more he could have done to coerce his tenants into voting as he wished them to do.

Lord Dacre also appears, from the following extract of a letter, written by his Irish agent, E. Mayne, in July 1778, to have viewed with great dislike any form of Protestant religion except that of the Established Church, for Mayne asks, 'By what your Lordship mentioned of Mr. Westly the Preacher am I to understand that a meeting house must not be built by them in the Town?'

That Lord Dacre took a great interest in the management of his estates is shown by the very considerable number of letters which remain from both his Norfolk and his Irish agents, giving him full accounts of all the details of their management. In 1740 he paid a visit to Ireland for the purpose of looking after his property. I do not know when Lord Dacre arrived in Ireland, but from a letter written to him by Todd, his agent, towards the end of 1739, he appears to have intended to go there about May 1740.

Only twenty-three years of age, and recently married, he was greatly interested in his intended visit, and anxious to show to his bride his town of Clones and the considerable estates which he owned surrounding it, for whose improvement he was no doubt enthusiastic, and full of that hope which is so especially an attribute of youth.

Todd did not give him an encouraging account of his house at Clones, called, like so many Irish mansion-houses, 'the Castle.' Surely, even in that country of exaggeration, the title of 'Castle' can never have been more inaptly bestowed than in the case of 'The Castle of Clones.' Todd says that it contained only 'one Parlour and three bed rooms with fire places, and three other little rooms without fire places or any furniture.' The best thing in the place seems to have been 'in the cellar a hogshead of old french Clarett, very good, if not spoiled with this long frost.'

It may have only been Todd's pleasant way of putting things, but if he spoke truth when he said, 'I am sure all the people of Clones will rejoyce to see you and your Consort,' it shows that a very different feeling existed in 1740 towards the landlord of an Irish property from what would be found there in these days.

I cannot say how long Lord Dacre remained in Ireland on this occasion, but if he did accomplish his intention of arriving about May, his stay there appears to have been a somewhat prolonged one.

Mr. Norris, in a letter dated December 29th of that year from Norwich, says :—

Four leases were put into a box, and delivered at Yarmouth to Mr. Thomas Price, master of the sloop called the Elizabeth belonging to Milford in Wales, which will shortly sail for Dublin, and then deliver the box as directed for you at Mr Todd's.

There are other examples afforded by these family letters of the much greater use of water as a means of communication in former days when the so-called roads, passable in summer, were absolutely founderous during a large portion of the year; as, for instance, when Lord Dacre travelled to Italy he used the Rhone as a means of getting to the seaboard, and then took water to the coast of Italy.

The following letter to Lord Dacre from Todd shows that, in spite of the difficulty of travel, he was again in Clones some four years later :—

Dublin Octr 11th 1744

Sir

Yesterday brought me the favour of Yours of the 2^d instant, which gave me the greatest pleasure imaginable to find you gott safe home, and in such high spiritts ever Since you left this, for as Your Letter to me from Dublin mentiond your design of Sailing the Sunday following, And as that Sunday with us was very windy, which continued till Wednesday when it blew a rank Storm, we were all in the Utmost fright about You, and Especially as I gott noe Account of Your Safe Landing during my Stay in the Country, altho' I sent often to Monaghon [sic] hoping to find a letter there, because yours from Dublin was directed for me at Clones in the County of Monaghon, & Soe by mistake lay in Monaghon Post office near

10 days before I heard of it, whereas had it been directed to Clones only it would have come directly to me. I am more particular in mentioning the want of an English Letter because all the Town as well as the people round about it, were every post enquiring for you, both High, and low, Rich, and poor; And as every post Still left us in the dark, Wee assembled in the Evening, drank a good health to you, your Lady, & Miss Barrett, Wishing that Wee or our posterity may never want you, or Some of your Successors, to Rule over us, And praying for your Safe Journey; I don't wonder at all this, As you have made All your Tenn^{ts} happy and Easy, by which, You have daily not only the praises of the Rich, but the prayers, and praises of the poor; Sir, Your most Obed^t humble Servant,

JOHN TODD.

I dont wonder the Flux, and fatigue, you had whilst in Ireland should give you the Spleen for noe One ever took more pains to despatch business, And tho' I had a good deal, it was I must own, very much lightend by your assistance, as I afterwards found for want of it after you left me; As to ye Entertainment you are pleasd to take Notice off whilst wth me, the pleasure I had in seeing you daily, far Outballanced it.

I find no further references to Lord Dacre going to Clones, and I think that after his illness in 1745 he probably felt unequal to the fatigues of such a journey; but he was kept constantly posted up by his agent in all that went on there.

Lord Dacre had two natural children by a person whose name was Elizabeth FitzThomas. The elder, christened Thomas, was born on January 6th, 1762, and the younger, christened Barbara, on July 2nd, 1766.

Both these children were brought up at Belhus by Lord and Lady Dacre, and were treated by them in all respects as if they had been the legitimate offspring of their marriage.

The family tradition of what led to the adoption of young Thomas by Lady Dacre is as follows: One morning the boy was brought into the room at Belhus, now called the south drawing-room, at breakfast time, and being either singularly precocious or previously well coached up, he exclaimed, 'Oh, what a pretty Lady!' whereat Lady Dacre said, 'Come to me, you dear little boy, and I will be a second mother to you.'

This sounds more like fable than fact, but, however that may be, Lady Dacre did act as a mother to the boy, and as an exceptionally good mother too. There was also a tradition that Lady Dacre, knowing she would bear no more children, connived at this intrigue for her husband's sake, as he was so extremely anxious to have a son to whom he might leave the properties he had taken such pains to nurse up. Even if this were the case, it does not explain why after the boy's birth she should raise no objection to a continuance of the intimacy between Lord Dacre and the boy's mother, and also adopt his sister born some four years after he was. It may be that the intimacy having commenced, she was powerless to prevent it, but it would seem improbable that the girl should have been christened *Barbara*, the name of her own dead child, unless with her consent.

We have no grounds for supposing human nature to be any more moral now than in the eighteenth century, but we look at such matters in a different light from what our ancestors did. George II.'s Queen made no objection to the King having any number of mistresses that he chose, provided that she herself held the chief influence over him, and in this respect Lady Dacre may have copied the example of Queen Caroline, who was not then long dead.

In spite of Lord Dacre's lapses from the path of conjugal fidelity, he appears always to have been on the best of terms with his brother-in-law the Lord Chancellor Camden and the rest of his wife's family; which is shown by the fact that he appointed Lord Camden, his son John Pratt, and another member of the Pratt family, to be executors of his will. The following story is told of himself and the Chancellor:—

During a visit of the latter's at Belhus they went together for a stroll, and in the course of their walk passed a pair of village stocks. The Lord Chancellor expressed a wish to see what it was like to be in them. He managed to get in but, when he had satisfied his curiosity, Lord Dacre found he was unable without assistance to extricate his brother-in-law, and so had to go for help, leaving the Lord Chancellor in this highly undignified position. Some time after, when a case arose before the court as to the nature of the punishment by stocks, Lord Camden said, with evident feeling : ' I have tried them, brother, and they are not pleasant.' [1]

Yet another story of Lord Camden : At a family dinner at Bruton Street, when Lord Camden, then Lord Chancellor, and George Hardinge, Judge on the Welsh circuit, were present, Lord Dacre said that he 'wondered, seeing the Law's delays, uncertainties and vexations were so notorious, why so many people went to law?' 'Aye,' said Judge Hardinge, 'if some fellow stole my coat, I'd let him keep it ; egad! rather than sue him ! Wouldn't you, Camden, rather tell him that he was welcome to it ?' 'Yes, brother,' said the Chancellor, ' and to my breeches, too ! '

The following story as to how Lord Camden obtained the supporters which his successor now bears is perhaps worth repeating. These supporters are a griffin and a lion : the former was an ancient supporter of the Lords Dacre, and the latter of Edward Barrett, Lord Newburgh. When Lord Camden was created a peer he asked Lord Dacre in jest, as being an authority on heraldic matters, to suggest supporters for him. Lord Dacre took the matter seriously and offered as supporters two of those which had been borne by his own predecessors 'as a memorial of their alliance and friendship,' which Lord Camden readily accepted and obtained a grant of from the Heralds.[2]

I have obtained a considerable amount of information about the way in which Lord Dacre's two natural children were brought up and educated from Lady Dacre's account book, and also from the perusal of a very long series of letters [3] which she wrote to George Tyler while he was in India. As has been stated, George Tyler was a son of the Hon. Mrs. Anne Tyler, Lord Dacre's half-sister ; he went to India in 1775, and Lady

[1] There is in print a slightly different version of this story.—*Pal.*
[2] *Ld. D. Mis.*, written in a more recent handwriting than the rest of the MS.
[3] Kindly lent to me by Miss Mary Tyler, of Bath.

Dacre wrote to him at least once a year, and frequently more often, until 1804, which was within two years of her death.

Thomas was sent to be brought up at the Rev. Mr. Shepherd's, near Newbury, but even then he was occasionally with Lord Dacre, as we find in June 1769 this entry: 'Jones's expences to & fro' London with Master Thomas 16^s.. 0$\frac{1}{2}^d$.'

In a memorandum written by 'Master Thomas' long after he had married, he says that he went to Cheam School under Dr. Gilpin in 1772. I have found an entry of five guineas being paid to the doctor for Thomas's entrance in June 1770, but the first amount of any importance which appears to have been paid to him by Lord Dacre is 28l. on January 2nd, 1772. In March 1771 a 'Mr. Southgate' was paid seven guineas 'for teaching Master Thomas to read.' Dr. Gilpin was a very celebrated schoolmaster, and an educational reformer in advance of his time.[1] I think it is probable that a boy's name had to be put down for his school, and a fee paid some time before he could be admitted, and that before going there he had to be able to read fluently. After being at Cheam something over three years in 1775 Thomas went to Harrow, where he boarded at the Headmaster's, whose name was Thackeray.[2]

Judging from Lady Dacre's account book, 'Master Thomas' was treated in a very indulgent manner while at school, allowing for the different manner in which children were usually treated in those times compared with to-day. In April 1776 he was given 10s. 6d., probably on going to Harrow, and in the following April he had a 'tip' of double that amount; while during the Christmas holidays of 1776 he was sent 'to the play' three times at a cost of 22s. 6d., and then went back to Harrow with another 'tip' of a guinea. Next Christmas he was again sent to the play at a cost of 18s., and he was given 2l. 12s. 6d. on returning to school. Thomas seems to have been at Harrow until the end of 1778, during which period Lord Dacre's pass book shows that he paid about 90l. a year for the boy's schooling,

[1] *D. N. B.*
[2] The name of 'Thomas' occurs in the school lists of 1775.

a sum which fathers of boys now at Harrow would probably not find sufficient to cover the expenses of one term.

In 1777 Lady Dacre writes: 'Little Thomas has often wished to be of your party at sea, or indeed of any other rather than drudge at Latin, but he is intended for a scholar, & you for a merchant in which I hope you will both succeed'; again from Weymouth, 'Master Thomas is with us it being holiday time & he enjoys swimming in a high degree & would live in the water all day.' In November 1777 Lady Dacre says:—

Your friend Master Thomas is still at Harrow, I won't say how much Latin or Greek he is possessed of, but upon the whole we think he improves and flatter ourselves that if he is not a great scholar, he will not be ignorant, and promises to be as well informed as is common.

A few months later Lord Dacre appears to have been less satisfied with the teaching at Harrow, as Lady Dacre writes: 'Little Thomas is well & improves, we are going to remove him from Harrow & put him under a private Tutor as at publick Schools very little is to be learned'; and no doubt many parents would say the same thing to-day. In November 1778 Lady Dacre says: 'Your friend young Thomas has left Harrow School, & we have placed him with a clergyman in this County where he improves apace.' This gentleman's name was Dr. Bree, and the date of Thomas going to him is fixed by this entry: 'Sept 29th 1778 Gave Thomas in his pocket when he went to Mr. Brees £2..5..6.' In the previous April Mr. Bree was sent 25*l*., which is stated to be 'as a present.' It may be that this was done with some understanding that he should take Thomas later on, and in January 1779 he was paid a draft on Drummond for 32*l*. 16*s*. 6*d*. for Thomas's tuition. In December 1779 Lady Dacre writes: 'We about a month agoe carried Thomas and placed him at Oxford as a student. He seems to be very happy in this situation and I have good hopes he will improve himself and turn out to my Lord's satisfaction.'

In November 1779 there occur these entries: 'Expended on a journey to Oxford to carry Thomas £21..3..10'; and

'Gave Mr Thomas in his pocket at Oxford £10..10.' Thomas matriculated at Brasenose on November 5th, 1779, and was under the Rev. R. Churton, a well-known tutor of that college. In those days it was customary for students to pay their 'battels' to their tutor, and during Thomas's stay at Brasenose Lord Dacre paid 215*l.* 8*s.* 6*d.* to the Rev. Mr. Churton on his son's behalf.

All this recapitulation of the details of money expended on 'Mr. Thomas' may appear trivial and tiresome, but I think there is nothing which shows more clearly the kind and generous manner in which Lord and Lady Dacre treated his illegitimate son ; no parents could have done more for their legitimate heir, and many do much less.

In December 1780 Lady Dacre writes :—

Your brother Harry, & Thomas are now with us ; the latter in a manner has become a man ; he, I am sorry to say it, is very low in stature and I fear he will not be much taller,[1] his person in general however is much improved, and though he is no great scholar I hope he will not be deficient in what a gentleman should know ; I flatter myself too that he has a good heart and will in time become a rational and useful member of society.

In connection with Lady Dacre's description of her adopted son's appearance when a young man, the following mention by a recent writer of his appearance some sixty to seventy years later than the date of Lady Dacre's letter is not without interest : 'A handsome old gentleman of the courtly old school, somewhat short in stature, but with the gracious dignity of one with royal blood in his veins ; the proverbial Stuart beauty had descended to him in its fullness.' And then, speaking of the contrast between him and the writer's grandfather, who was, she says, a very fine, handsome man, she goes on to say that the latter was 'lacking the peculiar distinction, the exquisite refinement, the courtly grace of the little old baronet.'[2]

[1] From a physiological point of view the prepotency of Thomas is remarkable, as nearly all his descendants were, or are, like himself, 'low in stature' and thickset.
[2] Diehl.

Unfortunately Thomas did not make the best use of his time at Oxford, and his name was removed from the books of Brasenose on March 12, 1782. In May Lady Dacre writes:

Thomas has lately been in disgrace from having misspent his time, and been rather extravagant at Oxford, so my Lord has taken him from thence and has placed him at one of the Universities in Scotland where he seems to be improving, and I hope will in time get into favour again, and become a rational and honest man.

It should be remarked how lightly Lady Dacre touches on the shortcomings of her husband's son, and how anxious she shows herself—no mother could be more so—that he might by his future conduct reinstate himself in his father's good graces.

On February 29th, 1782, 'Mr. Thomas' matriculated at St. Andrews University, while his name was still on the books of Brasenose. One is glad to see that the change had a good effect on him, as in January 1783, Lady Dacre says that he 'goes on much to our approbation.' Lord and Lady Dacre were not slow to mark their approbation of 'Mr. Thomas's' improved conduct; in the month of May following Lady Dacre's letter, they sent him a gold watch-chain for which they paid five guineas, and they allowed him to come to Belhus to spend the vacation. So expensive was travelling then that his journey down cost nine guineas besides 1*l.* 16*s.* 6*d.* for post-chaises, and when he left again for St. Andrews, which he did on August 11th, he was given 20*l.* 7*s.* 6*d.* to pay for his return journey. In March 1784 Lady Dacre wrote, 'Mr. Thomas goes on giving us much satisfaction, and is to finish his education in about six weeks when he is to spend the summer with us at Belhus.'

In this month 'Mr. Thomas' received a cheque for 30*l.*, no doubt to pay for his return journey, but his heavy luggage and dogs came later at a cost of 3*l.* 0*s.* 10*d.*; and in September he had 61*l.* 5*s.* 6*d.*, to close his expenses at St. Andrews. During the period 'Mr. Thomas' was at St. Andrews, from January 1782 to March 1784, Lord Dacre paid to Professor John Cook and the Rev. Dr. Berkley on his behalf 558*l.*, so that it would appear to have been more expensive in those days to have had a son at St. Andrews than at Oxford. While at St. Andrews Thomas made the acquaintance of the Earl of Buchan,[1] who wrote to his father about him in these flattering terms:—

Kirkhill, by Ed. 7, September 1784.

My Lord,
    Mr. Thomas appeared to me, from every opportunity I had of conversing with him, & from every account I received from my acquaintance, and correspondents in Scotland, to be worthy of your Lordships affection, and patronage, and I thought it my duty to entrust so amiable a stranger with credentials from my Country that might do him good in his own. I shall be much disappointed, & very much mistaken indeed, if he does not make a very good member of society, and give pleasure to his Friends, & Beneficent Patron. Allow me to add my Lord that well timed praise has often a considerable effect upon the character of a Young Man, & like the purchase of an estate beyond one's capital, creates a greater attention to the means of *making it good* and getting out of debt.

On the crop of young Men that is on our political ground depends the existence of our fallen Empire,[2] and I look at it often with anxiety, & endeavour to promote its growth.

In the following month Lady Dacre, writing to Mr. Tyler, says:—

Your friend Mr. Thomas has at length finished his education and is now come to reside with us, and I think I may say that as young men are now-a-days he may pass muster reasonably well. He is seemingly much improved by his residence in the University of St. Andrews in Scotland. His manner is polite & civil, & he is good humoured and tractable. Next winter we shall endeavour to give the finishing polish by letting him learn to dance & fence, and learning French grammatically, for hitherto he has only picked it up by wrote.

---

[1] David Stewart, eleventh Earl.
[2] Probably alluding to the loss of the American Colonies.

The 'finishing polish,' as far as fencing and dancing were concerned, was put on by a Mr. Gallini, who in January 1785 was paid three guineas 'for entrance of Mr Thomas,' and 18*l*. 2*s*. in the following May, when presumably the 'polishing' process was completed. There occur also entries of payments to a French master, and to 'The Riding House,' so that Thomas had masters in all the accomplishments considered necessary for a young man of position, and it was apparently in order that he might mix in fashionable society that he was given that February a concert ticket costing six guineas; so high priced a ticket must obviously have been for a series of concerts.

It was probably about this period that 'Mr. Thomas' made his entrance into unpaid county work. The banks of the Thames below London are walled in, in order to keep the high tides from overflowing the marshes adjoining the river, and these walls are under the care of an unpaid body of persons called 'Commissioners of Sewers.' The Commissioners are chiefly composed of owners and occupiers of land in the neighbourhood of the river. Some person who only signs himself 'G. B.' wrote a chaffing letter to Thomas, whom he styles 'Dear Mr Commissioner,' to congratulate him on his entrance 'on the public life of a country gentleman,' and from the context of the letter it is clear that it was written before Lord Dacre's death.

If the following story [1] is a specimen of the treatment Thomas often had to put up with from his father, whose temper was no doubt soured by his sufferings, he must have needed all 'the good humour and tractability' Lady Dacre ascribed to him in order to make it possible for father and son to live in the same house. One morning young Thomas, who had taken leave of his father before going to a meet of staghounds at some miles distant, when far advanced on his way, was overtaken by a groom on a galloping horse, who told him his father wished to speak to him. He hurried back, and on entering the Library, Lord Dacre simply said, 'Shut the door which you forgot to close when you went hence.'

[1] *Ex relatione* the late H. B.-L.

In February 1785 Lady Dacre writes :—

Thomas now makes one of our family, and we have the satisfaction to find him rational and well informed, and indeed his society is a great comfort to us, more especially to my Lord, who is always confined to his chimney corner, except when he goes out in his coach for exercise which he does as often as the weather permits.

While nothing was neglected that a liberal education could do in order to fit Lord Dacre's son for the position to which he destined him, his sister Barbara was also well educated. In 1772, at the age of six, she was sent to a school kept by Mrs. Eckley at Hammersmith. The first payment I have found to Mrs. Eckley was in July of that year, and the last in the same month twelve years later, so I imagine, as she had then attained the age of eighteen, her education was considered to be completed, and that she also went to live at Belhus.

In Lady Dacre's letters to George Tyler she constantly refers to his uncle's state of health, and year by year it evidently got gradually worse and worse, although, being always with him, she hardly seems to have appreciated its steady downward progress. In December 1780[1] she writes :—

My Lord's state of health is no worse than when you left us last . . . he is very lame but the vital parts are all good to appearance . . . his disorder in his limbs is often painful, which lowers his spirits at times, but when he is in company & forgets his pains, nobody is more cheerful nor can enjoy the society of his friends in a higher degree than he does himself ;

and again, in January 1783 :—

I now come to your first of friends & Uncle, Lord Dacre ; he is thank God no worse in health than when I wrote last to you ; he suffers a good deal from the disorder in his limbs, and of course his nerves are affected ; but for one so many years afflicted with such a disorder he bears up amazingly well ; and at times

[1] This letter to India, written December 30th, 1780, is endorsed 'Recd. the 20th June, 1782,' so slow was then the communication between England and the East.

enjoys himself & has very cheerful spirits. He is blessed with a great love for books and all sorts of polite learning ; so that he feels less this heavy disorder than many others would do. His eyes too hold out surprisingly which is most fortunate.

In October 1784 Lady Dacre mentions that Lord Dacre 'had a severe fit of illness last spring which lasted a couple of months' ; and in the following spring she makes the reference to him which we have already seen about his always being confined to his chimney corner.

By this time Lord Dacre was, to use the words that his wife many years later applied to herself, 'going down hill apace' ; and on January 6th, 1786, at Bruton Street, his life of suffering— one more distressing than fortunately falls to the lot of most persons—came to an end. The 'Gentleman's Magazine,' speaking of his funeral at Aveley, says that, 'although the Church is not a small one, it was not nearly large enough to contain the crowds who attended to show their respect to his memory.'[1]

Lord Dacre does not seem to have inherited the careless, extravagant disposition of his mother and her father, but by means of assiduously superintending the management of his estates, and being careful to confine his expenditure well within the limits of his income, he was enabled at his death to leave his successor in a very much better financial position than he himself was in when he succeeded his grandfather, Dacre Barrett.

How greatly Lady Dacre felt her loss may be judged by the following extract of a letter to George Tyler (April 7th, 1786) :—

Anyone less esteemed by me than yrself would scarcely have drawn a letter from me at this period. Since the heavy and ever to be lamented loss in the death of my dear Lord, which happened about three months ago, must make me a gloomy correspondent, and which very melancholy event I hope has reached you in due time, so that I shall not dwell on the subject now, as I persuade myself it would be painful to you, and as my tears alas! flow faster than my pen ; Suffice it to say that I

[1] Lady Dacre erected a handsome monument to his memory in Aveley Church.

have lost him that was by far most dear to me in this world, my friend, my constant and beloved companion from my early youth, whose valuable qualities endeared him to all that knew him intimately. His death was a release from a long and painful illness, which indeed he struggled with, and supported with great fortitude. . . . My Lord has left me the receipt of his estates during my life to deal out as I shall judge prudent to Mr Lennard, late Thomas, who is to succeed me. He has also a sister who he has provided handsomely for, and they both now make part of my family, and I please myself with the expectation of their turning out well, and behaving with affection as well as duty to me.

Lord Dacre made his will in February 1784, about two years before his death. It was an extremely long and complicated will, with no less than ten codicils, and it provided for a large number of contingencies. He appointed Lady Dacre, Lord Camden, the Honourable John Pratt (Lord Camden's son), and John Pratt, of the Wilderness (whom he described as his 'nephew,' meaning obviously his wife's nephew), executors of his will.

Among several bequests of legacies were some of books to his literary friends, Lord Camelford, Lord de Ferrers, and Dr. George Aldrich; and among other persons to whom he left legacies of money were the children of his half-brother and sisters, and to Lord Camden, and both the John Pratts, and to one of these he also left 200*l.* 'for purposes well known to him.' This sounds as if it were intended for the mother of his children, and if that were the object of this legacy it affords an additional proof, if any more were needed, of with what a lenient eye the Pratt family regarded Lord Dacre's connection with Elizabeth FitzThomas.

He requested Lady Dacre to take upon herself the care and guardianship of his two children, who he directed were to assume the names of Barrett and Lennard, and the arms and crests belonging to those families. He, however, especially directed that the armorial bearings which they were to take should be distinguished from those worn by their predecessors by a *brisure*, or mark of cadency, which *brisure* Lord Dacre stipulated should be an 'eschallop shell nebulé, argent, and sable'; and he gave particular directions on what portion of the arms and of the crest it should be charged. So interested was he about this matter that he devoted two codicils to giving fresh directions about the charging of this *brisure* on the arms, and he also inserted a clause in the will providing that, as often as either of his children neglected to bear this *brisure*, they should be liable to pay the sum of 20*l.* 'to any person interested in my arms who shall convict them of the same by the oaths of two credible witnesses sworn before a Commissioner of the Peace.'

His son did not obtain a grant of arms from the Heralds' College until 1801, and then he was granted the Barrett and Lennard arms, within a bordure wavy sable, as a mark of cadency, instead of the escalop shell to which Lord Dacre appeared to attach so great an importance. Such is the vanity of human wishes, my great-grandfather and my grandfather, as far as may be judged by their book plates, always used the Barrett and Lennard arms without any mark of cadency; and so disregarded not only Lord Dacre's express wishes, but also the grant from the Heralds' College, while but for this grant we should have legally no right to any arms at all.

Lord Dacre's intention was that, subject to certain legacies, all his property should go to his wife for her life, and after her death be entailed on his son; and a sum of 6,000*l.* paid as a marriage portion for his daughter; and that until Lady Dacre's death his son should have an annuity of 500*l.* and his daughter one of 100*l.* All these dispositions, except the annuities, were to fail should Lady Dacre choose to veto them, and in that case the property was to go to the descendants of Lord Dacre's mother. The chief reason for the great length of his will was that he wished to provide for the contingencies of either his son or his daughter displeasing Lady Dacre.

The will really amounted to little more than a devise to Lady Dacre for her life, with remainders to his mother's descendants, unless the conduct of his children should be such as to make his widow desirous that they, and not his nephews, should inherit her husband's property. In the course of the will Lord Dacre thus alludes to his children :—

Whereas I have by this my will taken special notice of my said son, and daughter, Thomas Fitz Thomas, and Barbara Fitz Thomas, commonly called and stiling themselves Thomas Thomas, and Barbara Thomas, nevertheless I think fit hereby to declare that I am far from justifying such connection as gave them birth, yet as I have no tie or obligatory motive to prefer others to them, natural affection prevails.

The will itself, and the results which followed it, reflect great credit on all the persons concerned. Lord Dacre, by leaving his children dependent on Lady Dacre's bounty, showed he felt confident that she, having practically adopted them and having proved so good a mother to them for many years, would not fail to treat them with the same kindness and consideration when he was gone ; at the same time, with a delicate consideration for his wife, he protected her from any danger of their conduct to her not being all that it should be.

That the two children did behave with propriety and affection towards Lady Dacre is shown by the fact that she consented to Barbara's marriage, and to her portion of 6,000*l.* being raised. While as regards Thomas, she not only allowed him to inherit the estates, but increased his annuity to 1,000*l.*, then to 1,500*l.*, and finally to 2,000*l.*, and also actually gave Belhus to him a few years before her death ; and by her will, after giving legacies to several persons, Barbara among the number, she left all the residue of her fortune to Sir Thomas and his younger children.

Besides these very practical proofs of Lady Dacre's affection for her husband's children, we find frequent references to them in her letters to George Tyler, and all these are couched in terms showing great attachment to them. Among several of such references the following may be cited :—

Feb. 2nd, 1788, Miss Lennard lives constantly with me, & is a pleasant companion, she is mild & gentle, and has the best of tempers, with a great desire to please, and I must in justice to both brother & sister say, that they ever appear to have the truest affection for me, which has endeared them both to me.

Jan. 24th 1791, Miss Lennard is my constant companion, and she is every day more endeared to me by her affectionate attentions.

May 23, 1793, Mr Lennard & his family reside a few miles from me, and we meet most days, in the summer at least, so that we are as one family, without intrenching too much on each other.

Nov 1798, Miss Lennard is my constant companion, and she is a great comfort to me, and as much attached to me and all my concerns as possible. She has never had it in her power to change her condition, but for her advantage I would part from her, tho' it would be a sad loss to me.

In many of her letters Lady Dacre speaks of the very retired, quiet life she is leading, so it may be supposed that Barbara did not obtain many chances of finding a husband; and, moreover, judging from the following extract of a letter from F. H. Tyler, she was not prepossessing in appearance:—

Jan 12th 1789. I passed my Christmas with Lady Dacre and Miss Lennard at Belhus very pleasantly. Miss Lennard is by no means handsome, and has the misfortune of having the jaundice which has changed a very fine skin to a deep yellow at times, yet she has every accomplishment and goodness of heart to make a rational man happy.

Although for the first few months that ensued on the death of his father Thomas continued to live at Belhus with Lady Dacre, it was not for long; and in July 1786 she writes:—

Mr Lennard and his sister now make part of my family. I fancy I shall not keep the former with me many months as he seems to have set his affections on a young lady, a very proper match and may have a reasonable prospect of happiness.

And in the following January F. H. Tyler writes to his brother:—

Thomas has changed his name to Thomas Barrett Lennard Esq. he is going to be married to a Miss St. Aubyn the third daughter of a Sir John St Aubyns with £10,000 fortune, but

Jan. 24th 1791, Miss Lennard is my constant companion, and she is every day more endeared to me by her affectionate attentions.

May 23, 1793, Mr Lennard & his family reside a few miles from me, and we meet most days, in the summer at least, so that we are as one family, without intrenching too much on each other.

Nov 1798, Miss Lennard is my constant companion, and she is a great comfort to me, and as much attached to me and all my concerns as possible. She has never had it in her power to change her condition, but for her advantage I would part from her, tho' it would be a sad loss to me.

In many of her letters Lady Dacre speaks of the very retired, quiet life she is leading, so it may be supposed that Barbara did not obtain many chances of finding a husband; and, moreover, judging from the following extract of a letter from F. H. Tyler, she was not prepossessing in appearance :—

Jan 12th 1789. I passed my Christmas with Lady Dacre and Miss Lennard at Belhus very pleasantly. Miss Lennard is by no means handsome, and has the misfortune of having the jaundice which has changed a very fine skin to a deep yellow at times, yet she has every accomplishment and goodness of heart to make a rational man happy.

Although for the first few months that ensued on the death of his father Thomas continued to live at Belhus with Lady Dacre, it was not for long ; and in July 1786 she writes :—

Mr Lennard and his sister now make part of my family. I fancy I shall not keep the former with me many months as he seems to have set his affections on a young lady, a very proper match and may have a reasonable prospect of happiness.

And in the following January F. H. Tyler writes to his brother :—

Thomas has changed his name to Thomas Barrett Lennard Esq. he is going to be married to a Miss St. Aubyn the third daughter of a Sir John St Aubyns with £10,000 fortune, but

she is to have £1000 a year settled on her which is double the produce of her fortune.

It was not long after this letter that Thomas's wedding to Dorothy took place, as they were married at Bobbingworth Church, Essex, on February 15th, 1787. I have found a formal proof that this marriage was approved of by Lady Dacre in the following writing on a sheet of note-paper, sealed at the bottom with Lady Dacre's seal in a lozenge impaling her arms with those of her husband, and surmounted with a baron's coronet :—

I hereby certify and give it under my hand & seal that the Marriage between Thos Barrett Lennard and Dorothy St Aubyns is entirely with my approbation and consent. ANNE DACRE.

In a letter, dated September 1786, to Lady Dacre from Mr. Thomas B. Bramstone, of Skreens, he says that he will be very pleased to be one of the trustees of the marriage settlement.

Dorothy's mother had some years previously married, as her second husband, Mr. Richard Baker, of Orsett Hall, Essex, and I believe at the time of this wedding they were living at Blake Hall, in the parish of Bobbingworth.

I do not know where the newly married pair lived at first; but in 1788 Lady Dacre writes: 'They being about changing their habitation from a very small house to one far better, and at the same distance from me, we being not above three miles distant from each other.' This change of house no doubt referred to their going to live at Hactons, in the parish of Upminster. After living there for about twelve years, they moved to Harwood Hall, in the same parish, for which Thomas appears to have paid rent of 180*l.*, and at which place I have letters directed to him in 1801. He did not stay there very long, as in a draft letter from him to one of the Norfolk tenants, written from there, and dated December 13th, 1804, he says: 'I leave this place on Monday next for good.' It was then that, owing to Lady Dacre's great generosity, Thomas moved into Belhus, and she rented a smaller house at Beckenham, Kent.

S S

This act of Lady Dacre in giving up Belhus to her adopted son was in keeping with the whole course of her conduct towards him from his earliest youth. Her account books show that she frequently made him presents of such sums as 100*l.* more than once in a year. His eldest child, christened Thomas after his grandfather and father, was born in Sackville Street, on October 4th, 1788, and in Lady Dacre's account book for that period there are these entries:—

	£	s.	d.
Trimming for Baby things	1	5	0
Ditto	1	17	6
Christening suit	3	1	0
Crib &c.	8	16	0
Gave Mr Lennard to defray his lodging in London	30	12	0
Paid for Dr Denman	20	0	0
Paid at Christening standing God Mother	10	10	0
Expences of Child bed linen	61	9	6
The expences of the whole amounting to	129	10	6 [1]

In the following year 'Thomas' was put into the Commission of the Peace, and her account book shows that, as usual, Lady Dacre came to his aid, as is shown by this entry in July 1789: 'Gave Mr Lennard his expences for taking office as Justice of the Peace 30*l.* 12*s.* 6*d.*'

In November 1798 Lady Dacre wrote: 'Mr Lennard is become quite a man of business, acts as Justice of the Peace, and has raised a corps of cavalry[2] which he is training, and Mrs Lennard is working colours to present to the corps.' In taking an active part in the local defences when England was threatened with invasion by France, Thomas was only following the example set him by his ancestor Samson, who, as we have seen, took a like part in the defences of Kent, when the descent of the Spanish Armada seemed imminent, some two hundred and

---

[1] It is, of course, not possible to say what Lady Dacre reckoned as '*the whole*'; the total of above entries is 137*l.* 11*s.*

[2] The official title of this corps was 'The Barstaple and Chafford Volunteer Troop of Yeomanry Cavalry.'

more years previously. The colours worked by Mrs. Lennard are now in the front hall at Belhus; they were presented to the corps by Lady Dacre in August 1799, and she wrote the following vivid account of that function to Barbara:—

Belhouse Augt 21st 1799

My Dearest Mrs Hichens

I feel that I have so much to tell you that a folio sheet is necessary, tho I won't answer for filling half of it. I cannot describe how much I was mortified in Your absence, on a day which I persuade myself You would have been highly gratified with, especially as all completed our wishes, without the smallest accident. The Day was sufficiently good for the purpose, every one seemed pleased, and Your humble servant was highly honoured. To begin with the Breakfast. The Tables in the Dining parlour were plentifully filled with everything good, such as Beef, Veal, Lamb, Hams, Tongues, and Fowls, potted Meat, Tarts, Sallets,[1] &c &c, Chiefly served upon Plate; Swan and the Cook had exerted their Skill, in turning the various sorts of Meat into gimcracks, for instance, one Ham appeared to be a Swan, another an Old Woman resting herself on a Lawn; Boys getting over Stiles; A goose swimming, & fish in the Water; in short, I cannot give You a perfect description, but it was all excessively pretty, and by what appeared it gave much satisfaction to those it was prepared for: They did not know whether all was to be eaten, as many of the Dishes were covered with Lard, but when the Discovery was made, they sliced away and were delighted. The Table was prepared for fourscore, and it was completely filled, With Barvis's Troop, & Lennard's: In the Bow window, There was Coffee, & Chocolate, & in the Breakfast Parlour a long table with Tea, and all sorts of Eatables such as Roles, hot Cakes, &c. The Communication between the two rooms clear, so there was free intercourse between them; The Men not only stuffed off what is above described, in the eating way; but would have Tea & Coffee brought them, tho there was as much red, & white Wine as they chose, set on the Table with the Meat. In short the stuffage continued for at least an hour. Then the Coaches were Called; Mine with four Horses, containing Mrs Lennard, & myself, Mr. Russell, & Tyler, with the Colours, which were consigned to them: We were escorted by Barvis's Troop, up to the Windmill, & so to

[1] Obsolete form of 'Salad.'—*C. D.*

Aveley, followed by Lennard's Troop, and thirteen Carriages of our Company following. The Church Doors were kept shut till we came, & the Church Yard was lined with the Troops, & I was handed by Captn: Barvis, & the Colours carried, by Russell, & Tyler: They were carried up to the Alter, and there Consecrated, by some Prayers suitable. When this was done, we had the Coronation Anthem sung by the Hornchurch Band; Then Morning Prayer by Neucatre, and Mr Wilson gave an excellent Sermon on the occasion. As soon as we in the first Coach with the Colours were seated, The Doors were opened, and The Church so crowded that no room remained, and dreadfully hot it was. When Church was over, I was as before conveyed to the Coach, with the Colours, and the procession went back the same way, & we went to a spot in the Park where two Tents were pitched, just by the gravel pit; Then when both Troops were placed, Your Brother's in front, I moved forward, and presented the Colours, with a short Speech, which I redde;[1] Your Brother on horseback returned me a Compliment, which he spoke off from memory, short but much to the purpose, with which every one seemed pleased, and I not a little so; It was respectfull, but not fulsome. When this was over the two Troops did the Exercise which was well performed, as the Yeomanry had met every day for some time past. I then took leave of the Company upon the Ground, and was escorted home in the same manner by the Troops, who after I was on my feet, gave three Hurzahs, and so ended my part; I had like to have said farce; of the Day. I won't pretend to tell You who were present, it would be too tedious, but in short every Neighbour within a great distance, The Wives of all ye Yeomen, and we reckon that at least 150 breakfasted in the above named two rooms. Lennard, Tyler, Zack^y, & Bartlet dined at Aveley with the two Troops; I presented a very fat Buck, and excepting your Brother, there was not a sober man of the party. I exclude however our two Stewards. You must know the evening of that memorable Day, was destined to Celebrate Your Nuptials, and we had a grand Ball in the evening in the Dining Parlour, a very good set indeed. Your Brother & Sister[2] danced, ye 2 Boys, Tyler, Miss Bartlet, & Miss Wilder; mad^m: Bartlet, & Swan exhibited, The Matchets, Hudson, Nurse Stone, Pickering, Dod, Bromfield, and all our Servants of every denomination. And so ended the Day. But the merri-

---

[1] Obsolete form of 'read.'—*C. D.*   [2] Sister-in-law.

ment was not concluded till last night ; when I treated with Punch on the above mentioned Celebration. And Songs & Corus's . . . among the servants till Bed time. To day all is sober, and quiet : The Hardinges left us at 12 this Day, got safe over, and I persuade myself they were all well pleased. F: Hardinge is much improved, she is much thinner than she was, is now a pretty figure, Dances with great life & spirits, She, Miss Bartlet & a Pupil of Mr Wilsons danced several Reels very prettily indeed : Bartlet was in raptures with his girl, and they out of good nature asked leave to bring J. Wilder home with their own girl, wch I most chearfully agreed to. She danced a little, & is improved : she was decently Cloathed, otherwise I should have made her so ; Mrs Bartlet kept her with Anne, And Yesterday the two girls came & walked all over the grounds with our Maids. I have You see my Dear Bab endeavoured to give You some Idea of this great Fete, I'm sure You will be pleased to hear how it went off, tho you could not partake. I shall hope to hear Mr Hichens had found great Benefit from Bathing, and that he now is able, to exhibit in Country Dances &c. Nothing is Yet settled in regard to my Tunbridge expedition ; after my return I shall look for the pleasure of the visit You owe me here ; But should it be Your plan to pass thro' London when You leave Brighton, I should like to catch a glimpse of You en passant. It is very material that I should inform You of my Dress : The Cambrick Muslin tacked up all round that I might do my honors without impediment. The broad laced Cloak White Chip Hat, with Your Veil ; & over all, a scarlet & black Rose in honor of the Troop. So ends my history ; The particulars will keep cool till we meet, for we had a great deal of fun, and I should have been no worse had I not tossed off last night three glasses of Punch ; small ones however, to Yours & Mr Hichens's Health. Munster has been in high glee, in the thick of everything ; The Hardinges as usual very pleasant & agreeable. And I have been truly gratified. The Lennards & Tyler slept here the Ball night.

We are now in the midst of Harvest Mr Zachary has been so much out of his Wits about this Feast that he has thought of little else, and to-day at Market he says all Romford was in an uproar about it. They were so pleased. I think I told you L^y. Charles Fitzroy had been here with her little Boy.

We are all impatience for the news of the secret expedition : The first Embarkation having happily Landed safely at Embden. The rest seem impatient to follow. God grant us success : It seems well concerted. And as the Combined Fleet are safe in Brest, I hope we shall keep them there. I see the Warrior is come home with our Fleet. I'm sure You will join with me in lamenting L^d: S^t: Vincents ill Health : His poor Wife is to be pitied. Well my Dear it is high Time to release you ; A shocking scrawl this, but You know I never shine in the writing way, so burn this when You have satisfied Your Curiosity. The House for the 3 last days has been a Pigs Sty but we are brushing up, And the place in general is decent : The fruit drops off before 'tis ripe, but we have not wanted of the common sorts. Mrs Munster sends You her Love, & our best Comp^{ts}: attend Mr Hichens

Your ever affec^{ly}:
A. DACRE.

It was probably as a reward for his patriotic exertions in respect of this Yeomanry Cavalry that in June 1801 Thomas was created a Baronet. The patent of creation described him as 'a man emminent for Family Inheritance, Estate, and Integrity of Manners.' I have no means of knowing whose influence it was that obtained him this honour, but inasmuch as Lady Dacre was then alive, and owner of the estates, I do not think it could have been bestowed on him as reward for any influence he could have exerted in Ireland in favour of the establishment of the Union, as I have heard suggested was the case. This honour cost Sir Thomas 366*l*. 9*s*. 6*d*., for fees to the Attorney-General, the Heralds' College, and other public offices.

On July 16th, 1799, his sister Barbara, at the age of thirty-three, married at St. George's, Hanover Square, John Henry Hichens, of Woolley Hall, Berks, eldest son of Richard Hichens, of Poltair, Cornwall. Mr. Hichens, aged only thirty, was already a widower when he married Barbara, having previously married, in 1794, Sarah Emma Rebow, a daughter of Isaac Martin Rebow Martin, of Otley Hall, Suffolk. She died without issue in 1798, and by her he was entitled to over 1,000*l*. a year, derived partly from properties in Somerset, Surrey, Middlesex, Essex, and Suffolk, and partly from a share in the Harwich Lighthouse dues.

Lady Dacre approved of this marriage, and gave her formal consent to it, and was a party to the marriage settlement. One of the principal interests in the accounts of expenditure in bygone days are the sidelights that they throw on the customs of the times at which they were written. Lady Dacre was very greatly attached to her adopted daughter, but her account book makes no mention of any wedding present which she gave her; the only entry which appears to refer to the wedding is, 'July, a large plumb[1] cake £2..2.' In my recollection, wedding presents, now expected from the merest acquaintances, were confined to relations or intimate friends, and I have no doubt but that a hundred years ago they were very uncommon, if not absolutely unknown.

The negotiations for Mr. Hichens' second marriage occupied a considerable time, as Barbara's brother, in an undated letter to Mr. Tyler, speaks of 'This long pending marriage'; and that they had been in progress for some time previous to March 1799 is shown by a letter from the latter.

As Mr. Hichens' first wife only died in the previous year, he does not seem to have lost much time in transferring his affections to Barbara, or to her fortune. At the time of his second marriage he was greatly embarrassed financially, and shortly after that event he was arrested for debt; having obtained release, he and his wife went to the Isle of Wight, and, finding that another arrest was impending, they hired a small boat to take them over to Guernsey, where they appear to have spent the rest of his life.

Such correspondence as I have found points to Barbara being very greatly devoted to her husband. It was arranged by the terms of their marriage settlement that over 4,000*l.* of her fortune should be expended in paying her future husband's debts; and when, after their marriage, his financial difficulties became still more acute, she was anxious that the rest of her fortune should be devoted to relieving his embarrassments. This was a course the trustees naturally could not consent to, but,

---

[1] Obsolete form of 'plum.'—*C. D.*

with much difficulty, they at last arranged a scheme with his creditors by which he was to be allowed 400*l*. a year, and the residue of his income was to be devoted to liquidating his debts. Mr. Hichens died on April 4th, 1804, and Barbara appears to have written to her brother in an angry and excited strain, as Tyler writes to him—

great allowances ought to be made for Mrs Hichens' state of mind at the time she wrote to you; I hope however she is now more resigned. I fear my letter to her which was dictated by Friendship, must, according to the Temper of her Letter to you, have completely disgusted her . . . That part of Mrs Hichens' letter where she states her wishes to imbibe the same disease her Husband died of; to sink part of her Fortune for I know not what, and to reside with his Mother whom she never saw; I must confess rather astonished me.

I do not know whether Barbara carried out her idea of living with Mr. Hichens' mother, but if she did it could only have been for a comparatively short period, as on December 26th, 1806, she married the Rev. Dr. James Thomas Hurlock, a prebend of Salisbury, and rector from 1829 of Langham, Essex. Barbara had no children by either of her husbands, and died October 20th, 1837. Her husband survived her nearly ten years, as he died on February 8th, 1847, and a monument to their memory is on the south wall of Langham Church. Judging from the following inscription on a cast-iron tablet which he caused to be placed at the foot of the steep 'Gun Hill' in the neighbouring parish of Dedham, he must have been in advance of his time in respect of his interest for the sufferings of animals :—

> THE DUMB ANIMAL'S HUMBLE PETITION.
> Rest, driver, rest, on this steep hill,
> Dumb beasts pray use with all good will,
> Goad not, scourge not with thonged whips,
> Let not one curse escape your lips.
> God sees and hears.[1]

Anne Lady Dacre died at her house at Beckenham on

[1] *E. R.* xvii. p. 56.

August 12th, 1806. I have not been able to ascertain the date of her birth, which is not recorded in the parish register of Seal, where I had expected to find it; her nephew, George Hardinge, asserted that she was more than eighty years of age at the time of her death.

Lady Dacre was in many respects a very remarkable woman; I have already referred to the loving care, like that of a mother, which she bestowed upon her husband's two illegitimate children. She also voluntarily continued the annuity which Lord Dacre had paid to their mother, but this did not arise from her being a woman of a feeble, affectionate nature; on the contrary, she seems to have possessed the mind and judgment of a strong-minded man.

I come to this conclusion after the perusal of several memoranda in her handwriting which relate to the management of the estates during her period of widowhood. On one occasion she wrote to Mr. Kent, the then Norfolk agent, who had evidently suggested granting from the same date two leases of equal length, pointing out to him the inconvenience which might be caused to the future owner by the two farms both having to be relet at one time. These memoranda show that she possessed a more intimate knowledge of what timber was being cut, and how each farm was being managed in Norfolk, far away from where she lived, than many men know of the management of their estates upon which they reside.

A paper written by Lady Dacre, headed 'A few remarks, &c.,' which was intended as a reply to the following application from a tenant to Mr. Kent for a reduction of rent, is characteristic of the woman, and shows what considerable knowledge she possessed of agricultural matters —:

After these Heavy Expences we had three or four very Dry Summers which hurt the Crops very much; Barley not more than 4 Comb p^r Acre one year, & the Next 5. My Wheat Mildewd three year together—in the year 1781 I stated these things to my Lord—but Could get no redress; the Year 1782 —& 83—my Crops was better, & the price better, & I Began to hope I should be able to keep my Lease out—but I now finde it Impossible, unless her Ladyship will take it into Consideration, and Make me some Abatement.

I have paid £80 in part of rent due at Mickelmas last and £5..12.. s Land Tax—& I am now £114..8. s in Arrears, if her Ladyship will be so kind as to forgive me that, & to Abate me £20 a Year for the time to Come, I will hold it the Lease out—if not, I hope her Ladyship will give me leave to quit it Mickelmas twelve Month—If Otherwise I and my Family must be Ruind—

J^{no} GRAINGER.

An Account of Money Disbursted at Horsford the Year Before I Entered the Farm

	£	s
For Cleaning 40 Acres of Very foul Land for Turnips	40	0
p^d for Malt Combs for D°	25	0
p^d for 240 lode muck from Norwich at 5^s p^r Load	60	0
for Howing[1] D°	12	0
p^d for Small seeds & Sowing	11	0
Grass Bought of Mr Nash	12	0
For Marling 100 Acre of Land, Brought the Marle a Mile & a half, and paid for d° Clearing & Plowing the Land	400	0
p^d for 600 Rod of Deeking[2] at 1/- p^r Rod	30	0
p^d for Spring & Fuz[3] for D°	7	0
For Making the Road on D°	5	0
P^d for Trenching the Garden, Trees, Bushes, Marle, Gravel, &c.	10	0
p^d Towards the Repairs of the House	46	0
	£658	0

A Few remarks relative to Mr Grangers Bill of Disbursements. Feby ye 24th 1787.

The Clearing the Ground & preparing it for Turnips, the Norwich Muck, the Haughing[4] the Turnips, Grass Seeds &c. Were all for his own benefit, and no doubt he reaped the Advantage the ensuing Year.

[1] Hoeing.   [2] Making banks.
[3] Whitethorn and furze for forming hedge.
[4] Obsolete form of 'hoeing.'—*C. D.*

The Money expended for Marl to the best of my recollection was at his own option. The poor Land was Let at 3^s per Acre, and it was left to himself to improve it or not, as he thought best. By what has appeared since, that expence did not answer, but if a Tenant defrays his money improperly, his Landlord is not obliged to make it good.

The Money expended in Repairing the House was by no means necessary, since I have ever heard the Farm when finished by Ld Dacre was most complete; but if Mr Granger chose to make it fit for the residence of a gentleman, he has no one to blame but himself.

The best Land is only rated at 12^s per Acre, ye 2^d sort at 8^s 6^d The poorest at 3^s The farm lying at 3 miles from Norwich. The Sheep Walk is over Six hundred and 15 Acres of half Year Lands. Let only at £20: a Year. I have been told that the Common Composition is one shilling per Acre, nay in some instances I have heard more is given. Surely such a farm as this cannot want a Tenant, nor can it in the nature of things be dear. If Mr Granger has beggared himself, he will I fear beggar his farm, therefore that should be well looked to during the rest of his Lease. Perhaps it may be the best way to take him at his word, and let him give up his Lease at Mich^s: Twelvemonth, for I can by no means consent to lower the Rent, or excuse him the Arrear now due. I am determined to be steady, and not suffer the Estate to be made worse by my possessing it, for probably the short space of my life.

The Neighbourhood to St. Faiths Fair [1] is certainly a great advantage to that Estate, as indeed the Tenants took care to inform my Lord at the time of the Distemper among the Cattle, and no Fair of any consequence was held; When they pleaded that they gained 5 shill: per acre for all their grass Land by the Scotch Drovers: A pretty good gain in this one instance, where the pastures are Coarse, & the prices low.

I have thought expedient to say thus much.

ANNE DACRE.

Sir Thomas proved a dutiful and affectionate step-son to his father's widow, and appears always to have studied to please her and render the last years of her life less lonely than they

---

[1] The cattle fair which took place formerly at Horsham St. Faith's, a parish adjacent to Horsford, was of very great importance, many beasts coming there all the way from Scotland.

would otherwise have been. In a memorandum in his own handwriting recording some of the chief events of his life, he writes, 'My beloved Lady Dacre died the 12th August'; and he caused a monument to her memory to be erected in Aveley Church,[1] the inscription on which begins, 'Near to this tomb which gratitude has reared.'

It is no part of my plan to carry this family history further, but in conclusion I shall in briefest manner touch on the rest of the career of Sir Thomas and his eldest son.

Sir Thomas followed the politics of his father, who, as we have seen, was a Whig, and he was elected a member of Brooks's Club by the Special Committee on May 11th, 1816. He did not take any very active part in politics, although he represented South Essex in the Whig interest in 1832.

His first wife, Dorothy, was a sister of Sir John St. Aubyn, of St. Michael's Mount, the last baronet of the creation of 1671. She was much devoted to gardening, botany, and painting flowers on china, and we have several pieces of china decorated by her. She died in London, and was buried at Aveley on November 1st, 1830. As illustrating the difference between the elaborate funerals of those days and the more simple ones of the present time, it may be mentioned that the undertakers' bill for Lady Barrett-Lennard's funeral came to a little over 230*l*.

They had the following children :—
Thomas, born October 4th, 1788.
John, born December 30th, 1789.
Dorothy, born May 29th, died May 31st, 1791.
Anne Dorothy, born October 20th, 1794.
George, born June 26th, 1796.
Henry, born January 18th, 1798.
Edward Pomeroy, born June 19th, 1799.
Dacre, born January 30th, 1801.
Charles, born May 24th, 1802.
Julia Elizabeth, born January 18th, 1804.

[1] A receipt I have found shows that this monument cost 74*l*.

Charlotte Maria, born July 5th, 1805.

Frances, born May 30th, 1809.

On June 20th, 1833, at St. George's, Hanover Square, Sir Thomas married, as his second wife, Matilda Georgiana, the widow of Henry Milligen, and daughter of Sir Walter Stirling, Bart., by whom he had one son, Walter James, born April 1st, 1835. Sir Thomas died in June 1857, in the ninety-sixth year of his age, and is buried at Aveley, in the chancel of which church there is a monument to his memory. His widow, who survived him for several years, was on the 13th of May 1873, also buried in the family vault at Aveley, aged 75 years.

Sir Thomas's eldest son, Thomas, was educated at Charterhouse and Jesus College, Cambridge, where he took a Wrangler's degree. He devoted the chief part of his life to politics as an advanced but independent Whig. As early as 1813, when only twenty-five years of age, he went over to Ireland in order to contest county Monaghan.

On December 15th, 1819, Thomas was elected to Brooks's Club, which in those days was more an indication of a man's political views than it is now. He was proposed by Lord William Russell, and seconded by Mr. Western,[1] who was chief among the Whig leaders in Essex.

In April 1820 he was elected member for Ipswich, after a very hard contest, as the result of a petition which he presented against Mr. Crickitt. The contest, one of the most remarkable that ever took place in that borough, he stated in a letter cost him 12,000*l*. Voters were brought at great cost from all parts, one even from Paris; and all sorts of ingenious electioneering tricks were played. A full account of this election is given in Glyde's 'New Suffolk Garland,' which reminds one of the borough election which 'Mr. Pickwick' attended.

After this most costly entry into the world of politics, Thomas transferred his attentions to the borough of Malden, in Essex, with which he remained connected for the rest of his life. He was elected for Malden in 1826, 1830, 1831, 1833,

[1] Afterwards created Baron Western.

1835, and 1847; and was defeated there in 1837, 1841, and 1853.

Thomas married, in 1815, Margaret, daughter of J. Wharton, of Skelton Castle, Yorkshire. She was a very delicate woman, and was taken by her husband to Nice for the benefit of her health. The change of air, however, was not productive of any good results, and she died at the Hôtel des Etrangers there on May 18th, 1818, without having borne him any children.

In 1825 Thomas married, as his second wife, Mary, only child of Bartlett Bridger Sheddon, of Aldham Hall, Suffolk, who had a considerable fortune. By her he had five sons. She died at Naples during the summer of 1844, and is buried at Aveley churchyard in a mausoleum which her husband had erected.

Thomas died at his house at Brighton on June 6th, 1856, about a year before his father, and is buried by the side of his wife in the mausoleum at Aveley.

À propos of the fact that Sir Thomas survived his eldest son, Dean Stephens, in his 'Memoir of Lord Hatherley,'[1] quotes a letter from the latter to Dean Hook. The Chancellor, speaking of a feeling he had noticed in younger people that those of seventy years of age are ready to be put aside to make room for them, says that he has never felt this himself; and goes on, 'So far, however, from thinking them wrong, I really rather sympathise with them, and feel rather like the late Sir Thomas Lennard, who, at ninety-three, used to say to his son, aged seventy (who did not live to succeed him), "Really, Tom, it is too bad of me to live so long!" to which Tom would dutifully reply, "I beg, sir, you will not mention it." They were polite men of the old school.'

Sir Thomas was succeeded in the title and estates by his grandson Thomas, the present Baronet. He was born December 29th, 1826, educated at Peterhouse College, Cambridge, and married in January, 1853, Emma, daughter of the late Rev. Sir John Page Wood, Bart.

[1] Vol. ii. p. 243.

SIR THOMAS BARRETT-LENNARD, 2ND BT. 639

There has been issue of this marriage three sons and five daughters, but of these Charles Dacre and Dorothy died as infants; the surviving children are all married.

Any reader of this book will have noticed the somewhat remarkable fact that since Dacre Barrett, born in the time of Cromwell, there have been only two owners of Belhus between him and its present owner, viz. Thomas Barrett-Lennard, Lord Dacre, and his son Sir Thomas.

ADDENDA

SINCE this book has been in the press I have been lent a bundle of over seventy letters, written between 1744 and 1761 by Thomas Barrett-Lennard, Lord Dacre, to his intimate friend, Mr. Sanderson Miller,[1] of Radway, near Edge Hill. If I had had them sooner I should have made several additions to my chapter on this Lord Dacre; but as it is I must content myself with giving here, in a more or less disjointed form, some of the information about him which I have derived from their perusal. I must first say a few words about Mr. Miller. He was an amateur architect, and considered to be a very first-rate exponent of that form of building and decoration then so popular among many influential leaders of taste which they called 'Pure Gothick.' Miller built, among other places, Hagley Hall for Lord Lyttelton, and he also designed the interior decoration of Kilkenny Cathedral. It is remarkable that a man so well known in his day is now almost quite forgotten, so much so that his name does not appear in the 'Dictionary of National Biography.'

In one letter to him Lord Dacre says —:

Your fame as an architect growes greater and greater ev'ry day, & I hear of nothing else; if you have a mind to set up you'l soon Eclipse Mr. Kent,[2] especially in ye Gothick way, in which in my mind he succeeds very ill.

Although these letters show how greatly Lord Dacre was guided by Miller's advice in the alterations he made to Belhus,

---
[1] How intimate he was is shown by the fact that Lord Dacre signed himself 'your affect & obed^t Servant.'
[2] Wm. Kent, *D.N.B.*

he asked, and obtained, his counsel in more personal matters also.

I think it is clear from the following two letters, from which I give extracts, that Lord Dacre had at about the age of sixteen promised some one, most probably his mother, that when he attained his majority he would become a Roman Catholic:—

April ye 14th, 1744.

What you have said to me in your letters have had a very great effect upon my mind in easing it of those clouds which hung upon it and wch by ye blessing of God I hope soon to entirely get rid of; and indeed it is time for during ye last two years of my life I have been so tormented with a continual succession of scruples that I have a hundred times almost wished to die & indeed I have very often been so ill with ye uneasiness I have undergone that I think it a miracle I am not now in my grave, or what is worse in Bedlam.

April ye 19th, 1744.

Your letter comforted me extreemly for some time, but my uneasinesses are again returned especially with regard to my resolution or vow when between 15 & 16 years old; since I find that in Roman Catholick countries they there permit people at 16 years of age to make their monastick vows which shows that casuists think that people are bound by their vows at that age; for tho' ye Roman Church err in many & very fundamental points yet they have amongst them many very great and learned men who must be as good judges as any of our Divines when and at what age a vow binds. Now I must confess ye thing that most weighed with me to remove my scruples was that as you told me in your letter I conceiv'd that I was too young at ye time I made y^e *resolution or vow* to be bound thereby as not being of an age ripe enough to determine upon such a great matter; but if in other countries people are suffer'd (as at age of sufficient discretion) to shut themselves up for ever in Convents then surely I was likewise of an age to be bound by any *Resolve* I made: This I confess dwells upon my mind night & day; that I confess such ruin; such confusion to myself & family [1] wou'd attend ye Litteral performance of my *Resolution* that tis almost beyond ye power of humanity to sup-

---

[1] It must be remembered that at this period Roman Catholics laboured under very great civil disabilities.

port itself under, and yet at yᵉ same time yᵉ life I lead in yᵒ state of perplexity I am in must be fatal to my constitution if it continues much longer. For God sake then my dear friend write to me & see if you can give me any comfort again & excuse my troublesomness; Tis impossible to express to you what I feel in my mind; even now when I am writing to you I think I am prevaricating with Heaven & endeavouring to quibble off what I ought to do; and yet when I reflect upon yᵉ misery yᵉ execution of my promise will bring upon my family, I can not but think there may be some excuse for my weakness as to this point; but then Jeptha, Annanias & Saphir [*sic*] and such terrible instances when vows & resolutions have been rigorously exacted come into my mind & distract me. . . . I have but one thing to say more to you & tremble to say it that I am sometimes ready to go into despair, and have very wicked thoughts come into my mind; But as you advised me I pray heartily and never suffer them to dwell upon my mind; and I beg you do so for me; I hope to God still to be restored to peace of mind again; and do not despair but that you may be yᵉ instrument of it: Adieu & believe me yours sincerely & affectionately.

Pray write to me as soon as possible.

At the time he wrote this letter Lord Dacre was of an impressionable age, being only twenty-seven years old; but the great mental distress he then laboured under gives an insight into his character, which was one of great sensitiveness, and very highly wrought and nervous.

I have not unfortunately Miller's letter in reply to his friend's appeal; but one can judge of the nature of it from the following passage in a letter Lord Dacre wrote on April 25th, where, after thanking Miller for his advice, he promises to 'throw away all my uneasy thoughts and doubts.'

These letters give abundant proof of the very bad health and frequent fits of depression from which Lord Dacre suffered most of his life:—

Nov. yᵉ 18ᵗʰ 1744.

Tis with much pleasure I tell you that I have almost quite got rid of my Low Spirits, and am now very seldom troubled with them, for which I heartily thank God for tis impossible to paint or describe what I suffered from them for near two years altogether.

May 1725.

The cold bath wch I have gone into these 3 weeks past has quite recovered my weak nerves & restored me to good Spirits & ye Blew Devils are quite gone away, not I suppose very well relishing ye cold water.

In August 1747 he writes from Buxton, whither he had gone for treatment, and he says: 'You know that I was last winter much plagued with ye Rheumatism which by y^e by I believe I contracted by staying too much with my plaisterers and Stucco men in ye damp rooms ye latter end of ye year.'

July ye 8th 1752.

I am in a very Grum mood, and consequently unfit for writing, the Damp changeable weather we have at present disagreeing with me extreemly as it must certainly do with all Nervous people.

In July, 1752, Lord Dacre, by his doctor's advice, went away for sea-bathing, when he stayed with his friend Mr. Stanley, at Paultons, not far from Southampton.

About two years later, in June 1754, after apologising for not replying sooner, he continues :—

As to me the Truth is being as I am a valetudinarian I realy merit some indulgence being not so frequently in a capacity of writing letters as people in good health, for tho' all people have their good & bad hours ; yet we nervous people have five times as many of the last as of the first; and this has been my case for some time and whether it is that such as I are worse in Spring & Autumn than at other times or from what cause it proceeds I know not but of late I have been but very so and so and have had a double portion of my complaints & *Blew Devils* (tho now thank God I begin to mend) which has in good measure disabled me from writing, at least (which is ye same thing) has Deprived me of all inclination to do so.

These letters contain many other references to the bad health to which poor Lord Dacre was such a martyr, but one will perhaps suffice :—

ADDENDA

Bruton St. May ye 31, 1758.

All the time ye late severe East Winds lasted I was half dead. . . . Within this hour ye Rheumatism or ye Devil that plagues me came so into my middle finger that as you see I can hardly write, an hour hence perhaps it will be gone again. . . . Altogether I think I never had so bad a winter, thank God summer & warm weather are come from which I hope I shall get on my legs again, I may use this phrase in ye litteral sense for my legs have been more and more spasmed than ordinary; three times told.

Although he rode a great deal for the sake of his health, as long as it was possible for him to do so, he was a poor horseman, as is shown by the following extract :—

Sept. ye 4th, 1745.

I am in very great want of a horse I wish you cou'd get me one, & I beg you'l try, & I leave it entirely to you. *Si tu me deseris perimus*; that is to say I shall die for want of exercize for my horse has slipt his shoulder & is spoilt; & neither I, nor none of my people understand any thing of horses to get another in his place. You know I am a great coward o' horseback & a very bad rider, ye first ye result of ye last. So ye horse must absolutely be perfectly sure footed & very quiet, and I care for no more; but he must not start nor stumble that poz: as to shape Beauty etc. they are indifferent to me, tho to be sure I wou'd rather have a good looking horse than a bad one; but pray don't get me a prancing horse which is such a one as I know you Love.

One of the chief pleasures in Lord Dacre's life seems to have been altering and, as he considered, improving Belhus, and however much we may regret many of the alterations he made, one cannot help sympathising with him in the great interest he took in all his works there, and in his intense love of the place.

In June 1753 he writes :—' Belhouse has (till the late burning heats) been in greater Beauty than ever it was, we have been very happy.'

And in September 1756 he says:—

Belhouse looks in full Beauty (I mean for Belhouse) and yet, in troth, tho' I can not equal it with the very fine places, I see more that I like worse than it, than I do that I like better, take it and all the conveniences that it has together.

To those who know Belhus all the alterations which he made there are of great interest, and therefore I do not apologise for giving a considerable quantity of extracts from his letters to Miller which bear on this subject.

July 1745.

I have resolved to fit up my new Hall & staircase & make that end of ye house habitable forthwith; ye Stucco men being to come down for that purpose next week; indeed both Mrs. Barrett & myself are quite weary of living in ye way we have done, it being extremely inconvenient to us to have half our house shut up, so that we have but 3 spare beds at present to put our friends in. The two great rooms however we shall leave till ye next year.

October 1746.

I have quite in a manner finished my Vestibule [1] and my great room above stairs [2] will be so before Xmas, and that without pulling off ye roof; I have found out a way and have actually heightened ye ceiling of that room so much that it is now 14 foot high.[3]

January 1748-9.

As to Belhouse I have made my River [4] as wide as Ld North's, and have opened ye springs there is so much that even before ye Rains ye waste water wou'd have turned an overshot Mill. Besides this I have planted above 200 elms, ye least of them above 20 foot high, & many of them 30.[5] These I have put in ye Grove behind my house, where there were any spots thin of trees, and on ye South lawn skirting along ye west side

[1] Now called the 'Front Hall.'
[2] Now the upper drawing-room, which proves the accuracy of the opinion of the late H. B.-L. (*ante* p. 588).
[3] This ceiling is coved so as to get additional height.
[4] What is now the 'Long Pond.'
[5] It is a remarkable feat to have moved such trees, and this before the day of planting machines.

ADDENDA

of it, which will have a very good effect. Another thing I have done (& a great piece of work it is) I have ploughed up all ye ground round about my house (above 60 acres) which I do in order to clean it throughly, and to lay it down quite smooth & fine;[1] In order to which I am preparing a Dunghill of Chalk marsh earth & Dung as Big as my House to spread all over it.

July 1748.

Lord Dacre speaks of a pond at the back of the house which he has found a way of supplying with spring water and so keeping full. This pond, he says, 'will be a great ornament to ye Grove behind my house, and extreemely embelish ye prospect from my North drawing room window.'[2]

December 1751.

After his return from abroad Lord Dacre writes:—

I would have fitted up my great eating room formerly ye Hall if my Architect had not made me too dear an estimate; in Spring however I am determined to do something in this business, and hope before I begin upon anything to have ye benefit of your advice & directions.

March 1752.

The carpenter has come up from Belhouse and says his men are getting on apace with the floor. He asks Miller about having twenty oak shields made on which to paint arms to decorate the ceiling.

June 1752.

Having heard nothing about the shields he has finished the ceiling without them, and says

I am very well contented with the manner in which I have done it. The Room is now almost quite compleated and will look extreemly well; and as I intend to paint it only for y^e

---

[1] This was, no doubt, in connection with Lord Dacre's destruction of the old walled-in garden which lay to the South of the house.
[2] There is no trace of this pond.

present in size, hope it will not be long before we shall Dine in it together. The chimney is according to your plan.[1]

July 1752.

The chimney is finished and put up & has upon the whole a very good effect. My eating room now comes very near being compleated. I have finished the ceiling plain with only a kind of ribban running along the Beams which lightens them a good deal.

September 1752.

He writes asking for suggestions for alterations for a chimney-piece in 'The Parlour we used to eat in.' Lord Dacre says the chimney-piece is all in stone and suggests various Gothic mouldings.

October 1752.

Brown[2] has been here & while he stayed here slaved at setting out the road and the rest of the Shrubbery all day, and drew plans all evening.

January 1754, Bruton St.

I am going with out loss of time to fit up my North Drawing room at Belhouse in order to have it ready to live in when we go there to stay for good which will be about the middle of April.

Lord Dacre then goes on to ask advice about the dado and cornice he proposes to put in the room, on which he writes at great detail. He goes on: 'Pardon this trouble I give you but I pique myself upon fitting up this room in good taste as tis ye pleasantest room I have in summer and ye only cool one.' He says the recesses are to have settees in them in blue damask, 'and there is to be a very large glass and handsome Sienna or Verd Antique table (but narrow) under it opposite to ye chimney to break that long side of ye room.' He goes on:

'the chimney I am resolved not to have a Gothick one. For as tis to be of marble no good one can be made in that stile. The

---

[1] Lord Dacre says in a subsequent letter that the chimney[-piece], exclusive of coving stones, slabs, &c., cost 26*l*.

[2] 'Capability' Brown, *ante*, p. 390.

pillasters are to be of Sienna marble as also the freize, the rest Statuary marble, tho' Lovel advises the ground to be veined marble. The block in the middle we are in doubt whether it should be Sienna, Statuary, or Black & Gold marble.'

February 1754.

Letter thanking Miller for advice as to the North Drawing-room, which Lord Dacre says shall be followed except that relating to the doorway, which he considers should have an arched architrave, as a square one would look too bald without some other member upon it to crown it, and for this he remarks the room is too small.

Bruton St., November 1754.

I have this summer finished my Drawing room at Belhouse and have, and am doing a great deal out of doors particularly in ye fields coming to my house.[1] I am just now carrying on my Shrubbery to ye Shaw [2] which fronts my house: Brown has laid it out and I think well enough.

September 1757.

Asking for advice how to decorate with stucco ornaments the beams, 'cornish' and chimney-piece of a room now called the 'Crest Room.'

I am fitting up my wife's dressing room [3] quite new as also the Bed Chamber within it which is now made a large room by throwing ye maids room into it to lengthen it and carrying out ye wall 10 foot further into ye Court to 'breadthen' it. . . . I intend to fit up ye Chimney with a slip of Black Marble & then lay on Gothick jambs & cornish of wood.

This letter is followed by several others, all relating to the decoration of the ceiling and cornice, which is discussed with greatest minuteness. It was finally, after much correspondence, decided to have shields of coats of arms on the

---

[1] Alluding no doubt to what is now the approach from the Rainham Lodge.
[2] The word 'Shaw,' meaning a small wood, has now become a provincialism.
[3] There is no doubt that 'my wife's dressing room' is the 'Crest Room,' but it is not so clear about which is the 'Bed Chamber.' It is *not* the bedroom now next door, which was not built until 1776-7 (*ante*, p. 590). It may be a bedroom across a passage now sometimes called 'The Book room.'

cornice, a Gothic canopy opposite fireplace, and a ribbon-pattern of stucco on the ceiling, which are there to this day. The total cost of these decorations appears to have come to about 50*l*.

January 1759.

After speaking of his bad health, Lord Dacre writes :—

In the state I am in you will perhaps think me a bold man to begin such a great Work as I am going to mention to you : and yet shou'd I not live to enjoy it perfected it will so far as I go on with it be an ammusement to my mind and a temptation to me to use exercise. In a word then I have had Brown down with me at Belhouse and am going to make a pool where now ye run of Water is, in ye lower part of my Park ; its size will be a^{bt} ten acres ; its form very irregular and twill be a quarter of a mile long. Brown and indeed my own little judgment tells me it will be a very great ornament to that side of the Park and quite change the Face of it ; By what I have said you will immediatly concieve that the rushy part of Bumpstead mead will be converted into Water and that the Black moory soil will be taken away till we come to ye parts of the Meadow that rise and where ye soil is gravel.

There seems to have been considerable delay in beginning the work of making what is now 'The Long Pond,' as the following extract shows that two years had elapsed before the scheme was definitely decided upon :—

19 February 1761.

You will find the place a good deal improved by the Turff being got older and consequently smoother and greener and by the Shrubbery being now in good measure come to perfection. My Breakfast room too has been entirely new fitted up and somewhat enlarged. I have a number of expences upon me this year which are somewhat heavy[1] and yet I doubt if I shall have prudence enough to abstain from meddling with my Water in ye Lower part of my Park. The truth is I never Ride that way but I long to do something there, as I know that that course meadow and moorey sided canal which is now an eye sore might be converted into a very pleasing scene and Brown is of the same opinion ; We have now another scheme for it of

---

[1] This is the year before his son was born.

much less (tho still a good deal) of Expense : It is to make it in ye River stile instead of the Lake.

I regret I have not found a record of what it cost to make the Long Pond and how long it took to accomplish. Lady Dacre, in a letter to George Tyler, dated 1777, said : 'We had a delightful fishing in the piece of Water in the Park to the great delight of the boy [1] and both my Lord and I were in the midst of that affair.'

Lord Dacre appears to have had the greatest objection to write letters; almost all of this collection begin with an apology for not having written sooner. In one he says he has not written more often sometimes from ' Business, sometimes from Low Spirits ; too often from indolence & procrastination.' In another : ' I had for ye most part rather ride Fifty miles to serve a Friend than write him a Letter ; all people have their failings & this is one of mine.' And again : ' I am no news-writer being of all mortals ye most Averse to setting pen to paper.'

This correspondence shows that among Lord Dacre's very intimate friends were Lords Derby, Deerhurst, and Guernsey.

From it we learn also a little about his half-brother, Richard Henry Roper (*ante*, p. 599), who seems to have been in the Army before taking Orders.

June 1754.

. . . My living in Ireland is become Vacant & my brother Henry Roper is going to take orders to qualify himself for it. He has for this year & a half been studying very hard under a clergyman with this view (tho' the Incumbent was then in perfect health). The living will as I hear produce £700 a year if not £800. This is a great thing for poor Harry. The death of the Incumbent was quite unexpected as until a month before he died no one was more likely to live ten years than he. But my Brother being weary of the Army upon many accounts had resolved to Recover ye learning he had lost & to acquire what more was necessary to fit him for the gown in case a favourable occasion offered.

[1] Lord Dacre's son Thomas.

We also see that he was executor to the will of Hugh Smith, his aunt Dorothy's husband (*ante*, p. 599), as in May 1745 he writes:—

When I had hardly any business at all I was so abominably Lazy as never to be able to find time to write, how much less shall I now do it when I am encumbered & loaded with ye care of my Uncle Smiths affairs who is dead & has left me his executor; . . . he has left his two daughters I believe ye greatest fortunes in England.

I will conclude with the following extract from one of Horace Walpole's published letters referring to Lord Dacre's death.

1785.
'I have lost a very old friend, one of my oldest; and a most worthy man, Lord Dacre; but after 40 years of miserable sufferings his death was charming, and not two hours in duration from his seizure. We who are dead in equity though not in law, should hope for such conclusions and have former preludes discounted.'

INDEX

WIVES are indexed under their maiden names; when several persons of one family have similar Christian names and no distinguishing title they are distinguished by Roman numerals after their Christian names, *e.g.*, Lennard, John (I). As a rule those peers who are treated of *fully* are indexed under their family names, but where indexed under title a cross-reference is given.

This Index does not pretend to give a reference to every proper name occurring in the text, but I hope there will be found a reference to all those which the reader requires.

ABDY, Sir Anthony, 542
Abergavenny, Lord, 78; 96: *also see* Nevill, Edward (II)
— George, Lord, 193
Account book, household, of Herstmonceux, 284
Acts, private, of Parliament, obtained by different members of our family, 89, 205-6, 208-9, 304, 330, 396 *n.*
Ague, former prevalence of, in Essex, 543-4
Akenside, Dr., 605
Alceati, A., 347
Aldermaston, Berks, 260; 358
Aldrich, Dr., 621
Alexander, Sir William, 382
Aleyn, Sir C., 32; 40-1; 123; 136
Allen: *see* Aleyn, Sir C.
Alvethley, Alvethlie, Alvythlee: *see* Aveley
America, emigration to, from Ireland, 468
— Leonards of, 1; 2
Andrews, W., grateful letter to Lord Dacre from, 596
Anglesea, Marquis of, 277. 306
— Lady: *see* Bayning, Mary
Anne, Princess, afterwards Queen, 314
Anonymous letter by robber at Chepsted, 32, 33
Apuldrefield, Apurfield, or Apulderfield, 149; 240; 241; 278; held of the King as of his Castle of Dover, 298. 308; sale of, 329-30
Ardingmoare, 83

Arundel, Philip, Earl of, 269; 273 *n.*; 274
— Thomas, Earl of, 273-5
Assington, Suffolk, 359
Assize, judges of, formerly went same circuit year after year, 22
Assizes in 1567, provisions provided for, 22-25
— cooking utensils, &c., lent for, 26, 27
— silver lent for, 'unto my brother Cromer,' 27-9
Astlee, Thos., 201
Audley, Lord Chancellor, 6; Lord Campbell's opinion of, 39. 197; 199; 202
— Philip, 187
Aungier Street, Dublin, 460 *n.*
Aveley, Vicar of, v
— John Barrett settles in, 342. 344; the first de Belhus to settle in, 344; a tomb in Church of, 344; a brass stolen from Church of, now restored, 362-3
Aylet, family of, 369 *n.*
Ayloff, family of, 369; 390 *n.* 3
— T., 211

BABOROUGHAM, 150
Bacon, E., 359 *n.*
— Sir N., 32 *n.*; letter from, 40-1. 123; 359 *n.*
Bailey, Bayley, or Baylee Park, 226; 259: *see also* Leonards of

U U

INDEX

Baker, Chrysogona, 214; her marriage, 242-3; her death, 247. 340; 354
— Elizabeth: *see* Dineley
— Sir John, 243; 340; 354
— Richard (I), 'a ryper,' 30-3
— Sir Richard (II), 242; 340
— Richard (III), 625
Balsham, 150
Baltinglass, Viscount, 285; 290
— Anne, Lady: *see* Temple, Anne (II)
Barnham, Sir F., vii
— Sir Francis, 216; 226; 227; executor to Thomas (VI) Lennard, 242. 257; 259; guardian to sons of R. Lord Dacre, 261
— Martin, 226
— Sir R., 291; 295
Barrett, origin of name, 342; occurs in Roll of Battle Abbey, *ib.*
— *v.* Loftus, great lawsuit of, 437-52
— Anne (I), 349; 352
— Anne (II), 359
— Anne (III), 361; 365
— Anne (IV), 265; letter from, about Lady Sussex, 322. 393; 394; date of birth, 412; letters from, to her brother Richard (II), 429; character and accomplishments, 433; nearly married a Mr. Coote, *ib.*; unhappy life at Belhus, 434-5; brought up by Dorothy Lady D., 435; account of, and her life at Belhus, by R. North, 435-7; letter from, 438; correspondence about future sister-in-law, Lady Jane, 454-5. 468; allegations against, by brother, 469, 471; her version, *ib.*; letters by, to him, 472; her care for her brother's interests, *ib.*; said to oppose his visit to Belhus, 475-6; her intrigues, 476; letter from Lord North defending, *ib.*; disputes with Dacre, 488-9; turned out of Belhus by father and goes to grandmother, 489; marriage of, at Chevening, 490-1. 492; takes large share under father's will, 517-19; letter to Dacre, 522-5; her death, 527; disputes about furniture, 537-8
— Arthur, 340; 354
— Bartholomew, 348, *n.* 3
— Bridget, 349
— Catherine (I), 368
— Catherine (II), 530
— Charles, 340; 358; marriage and death, 360; his children, 361; Bretts settled on him, and he lived there, *ib.*; history of brass on his tomb, 362-3
Barrett, Cicely, 349; 352
— Dacre, letter to, from W. Dawson, proposing marriage between their children, 63; letter to, from his Irish agent, E. Kaine, about marriage of W. Dawson's son to a Miss Dawson, and her character, 64. 214; 361; 393-4; date of birth, 412; goes abroad for education, 414; letter from, in Latin, to his father, 415-17; returns home, 417; employed by father in Ireland, 426; there to prosecute family lawsuit, 437; presents petition, 449; makes a last effort, 450; letters about, by G. Moore, 451-2; pays court to Lady Jane, 452; was not a gambler, 453; negotiations for marriage, 453-5; date of marriage, 455; marriage settlements, 453-6; children by Lady Jane, 456-60; trouble about her dowry, 461-2; freeman of two Irish towns, 463; lived in Ireland till 1687 and then in Liverpool, *ib.*; letters to, and from Lady Jane, *ib.*; father irritated with, goes to England to arrange matters, 464-7; letters from, to Lady Jane, *ib.*; his house in Dublin, 467; letters to, from Clones, 467-8; allegations by, against sister, 469; his description of Owen, 469-70; origin of his dispute with sisters about Dunsink, 471-2; moves from Clones to Liverpool, 472-3; details of journey, *ib.*; birth of son Edward, 474; his stay at Liverpool, fondness for pet birds, and visits to Knowsley, 474-5; cause of friendship with Lord Derby, 475; an ancestor of present Earl of Derby, *ib.*; invitation from father to Belhus, 476; sister's opposition to his visit to Belhus, *ib.*; letter to, from Pigott, *ib.*; letter to, from Lord North, 477; journey of, to Belhus, *ib.*; correspondence between, and Lady Jane, while latter at Liverpool, 478-82; in favour with father, 484; difficulties arise owing to Seacome, 484-5; receives only little rent from Ireland, 485-8; relations with sister, 488-91; induces father to resettle Dunsink,

492 ; attempts to obtain post under Government, 493-4 ; losses at Clones, 494-9 ; his address to King William III., 500 ; death of first wife, 501 ; bad treatment of his children at Belhus, and disputes with father, whom he attempts to have put under restraint as *non compos*, 501-9 ; letters to father begging forgiveness, 509-10 ; returns to Clones, 511 ; an M.P., *ib.* ; marries second wife, *ib.* ; letter from, to her, 512 ; owes money, 515 ; eldest son at Eton, other children left at Clones, 515-16 ; legacy to, from father, 517 ; letter to, from W. Moore, about reconciliation, 518-19 ; letters to, announcing death of father, 519-21 ; brings action to upset will, 521 ; letter to, from his sister Anne, 522-5 ; brings action concerning Dunsink, 525-7 ; third marriage, 528 ; marriage settlement, 529 ; child by third wife, 530 ; congratulation on this marriage, *ib.* ; education of children left at Clones, 531-2 ; letter to, about hunting, 532-3 ; wolves at Clones, and Dacre kept wolf-dogs, 534 ; account of, by Lord Dacre, 534-5 ; date of death, 535-6 ; High Sheriff, 536 ; letter to, announcing death of grandmother, 536-7 ; disputes with his sister about furniture at Belhus, 537-8 ; interested in gardening, 538-9 ; fond of sport and horses, 539 ; interested in politics, 541-3 ; suffered from ague, 543 ; fond of books, 544 ; friendship with Dr. Derham, 544-5 ; member of Royal Society, 545 ; step-son's illness and death, 545-6 ; appointed a D.L. and Colonel of Militia regiment, 546-9 ; his Militia troop in Ireland, 549 ; buys land round Belhus, 550 ; petitions King to grant him title of 'Dacre,' *ib.* ; on affectionate terms with son, 551 ; until his marriage, which he will not forgive, 551-6 ; his detestation of Roman Catholics, 552 ; marriage of daughter Elizabeth, 564-5 ; of daughter Sarah, 566 ; of daughter Dorothy, 567-9 ; had house in Great Russell Street, London, 567, 572 ; litigation about guardianship of grandson, 570-2 ; his lawsuits, *ib.* ; his burial, 572 ; notice of death in newspaper, *ib.* ; his will, 572-3 ; monument to memory of, 573-4 ; death of widow, 574 ; his daughter Jane, 574-8

Barrett, Dorothy (I), 264 ; 393-4 ; date of birth, 412 ; little known of, her bad health, 433, 437. 517 ; 519 ; 527
— Dorothy (II), birth of, 456, 460. marriage, 567 ; correspondence about, 568 ; children, 569 ; monument to, *ib.* ; ancestress of Earls of Derby and Lords Barrymore, 569 *n.*; bequest to, by father, 572
— Edward (I), 340 ; devises to, 351-3. 354 ; High Sheriff, *ib.* ; a book dedicated to, 354-5 ; his rent-rolls, 355-6; his wives and children, 358-9 ; his death, 359 ; his will, 359-60 ; grant of land in Wennington, 360 ; settlement by, on eldest son's marriage, 360-1
— Edward (II), 340 ; 358
— Sir Edward (III), Lord Newburgh, 340 ; 341 ; 359 ; his birth, 361 ; references to, by contemporary writers, 364 ; education, 365 ; wardship, *ib.*; goes to Spain and Italy, 366-7 ; knighted, 367 ; first marriage, 367-8 ; issue by, 368 ; an M.P., *ib.* ; collected a 'Benevolence' in aid of the Palatinate, *ib.* ; increased his estate at Belhus, 369 ; conditions of cultivation in those days, 369-70 ; obtained grant of free-warren and license to make a park, 370 ; connection with the Duke of Buckingham, 372 ; letter to the Duke, 373 ; appointed ambassador to France, *ib.*; settles his affairs preparatory to taking up post, 374 ; correspondence in connection with that post, 374-6 ; does not go, *ib.* ; appointed to Denmark, *ib.* ; again disappointed, *ib.* ; appointed a second time to France, 377-9 ; again disappointed, 379 ; raised to peerage, *ib.* ; appointed Chancellor of Exchequer, *ib.* ; his account of being sworn in, 379-81 ; Chancellor of Duchy of Lancaster, 381 ; other posts filled by, *ib.*; one of the organisers for colonisation of Nova Scotia, 381-2 ; created a baronet, 382 ; death of first wife, *ib.*; his panegyric on her, 383 ; his contest with the Earl of Strafford, *ib.*; second marriage, 384 ; wife's step-children, *ib.* ; panegyric on,

385; letter from, to Sir J. Coke, 385-6; references by, to public affairs, 386; attacks on, by parliamentary party, 387-8; death, 388; will, 388-91; entry about, in Aveley register, 391; leaves Belhus to Richard Lennard, 394-6; tradition as to being in love with Dorothy North, 395; made several wills, *ib.*; evidence as to making his last will, 396; bequest of portrait of, 573

Barrett, Edward (IV), 458; where born, 473-4
— Elizabeth (I), 348
— Elizabeth (II), 350
— Elizabeth (III), 359
— Elizabeth (IV): *see* Moore, Elizabeth
— Elizabeth (V), 63; 511; marriage, 564-5; her trousseau, 565; death, 566
— Frydswid, 350
— George, 243; 340; 348; 351; 352; marriage, 353; will, 353-4; widow's second marriage, 354; his children, *ib.*
— Henrietta, birth of, 456-60, 501. burial of, 566
— Iva, Sarah, 530; marriage, 566; children, 566-7. bequest to, by father, 572
— Lady Jane: *see* Chichester, Lady Jane
— Jane, birth of, 456 and 460. 550; affectionate letter by, to brother, 553-4. 558; letter to father, 571; benefits under father's will, 572; appointed guardian of nephew, 573; first marriage, 574-5; settlements, 575; death of first husband and marriage with Ranby, 576, separation from him, 577; death of, 578. 581; letters to, from Lord Dacre, 582-3, 585. probably lived at Belhus, 584
— John (I), 341
— John (II), 340; 342; 345-6
— John (III), 340; eminent practitioner in civil law courts, 347; Latin epigram to, *ib.*; founder of family, *ib.*; rebuilt Belhus, 348; acquired land there, *ib.*; marriages and children, 348-50; death, 350; will, 350-3; a registrar, 350 *n.*
— Joyce, 349; 352
— Katherine, 354
— Margaret (I), 349; 352
— Margaret (II), 358; 374
— Muriel, 349; 352

Barrett, Richard (I), 214; birth of, 257; settlement on, of Horsford, 257-8; visitor at Herstmonceux, 285; legacy from half-brother, 292. 340; 341; 354; account of, by Lord Dacre, 392; High Sheriff, Essex, *ib.*; health and character, 393-4; Belhus left to him, 394; assumes name of Barrett, 394-5; cousinship between Barretts and Lennards, 395; traditional reason for Lord Newburgh leaving him Belhus, *ib.*; Lord Newburgh's devise to, and the terms of same, 395-7; litigation about Belhus, 397-8; offers loan of Belhus to mother, who accepts offer and furnishes it, 398-401; inventory of her furniture there, 400-1; she leaves it to, 400; more litigation concerning Belhus, 401-2; pays off last incumbrance on Belhus, 403; his estate there, its annual value, *ib.*; marriage, *ib.*; wife's ancestors and estates, 404-9; date of marriage, 409; wife's character, 410; a good-looking pair, 411; house in London, *ib.*; births of children, 412; correspondence with wife, 412-13; death of his wife, 413; an M.P., *ib.*; living in Ireland, 414; sends children to his mother, *ib.*; sends sons abroad for education, 414-17; letter to, in Latin, from eldest son, 415-17; boys return to England, 417; bill for their expenses while abroad, 417-25; made freeman of Lancaster, 426; in Ireland, *ib.*; living at Belhus, *ib.*; his sons in Ireland, 426-7; angry with son Richard, 428-30; becomes reconciled to him and is witness of his fatal accident, 431-2; daughters Annie and Dorothy, 433-7; lawsuit by eldest son concerning property in Ireland to which Anne, wife of, was entitled, 437-52; part taken by, in this litigation, 449; negotiations by eldest son for marriage and settlements made by, upon same, 452-6; difficulty in obtaining payment of Lady Jane's dowry, 461; angry with son Dacre, 464; forgives him, 466; letter from Lady Donegal referring to, *ib.*; his temper gets worse, 469; employs Owen, 469-71; his promise and settlement of Dunsink, 471;

INDEX

gets into arrear with payment of annuity and fells timber at Belhus, 472; invites Dacre to Belhus, 476; his kind reception of Dacre, 479 and 484; makes will in favour, 484; employs Seacome and puts great confidence in him, 484-5; disputes with daughters and sends them away, 489-91; his replies to questions about repeal of Penal Laws, 491-2; resettles Dunsink, 492; dangerously ill, 493-4; strained relations with son, who attempts to prove him insane, 502-9, *passim*; humble letters to, from son, 509-10; will, 517; attempts by D. Lady Dacre to reconcile, with son, 518-19; death, 519-21; evidence as to his state of mind, 522

Barrett, Richard (II), 214; 393; date of birth, 412; goes abroad for education, 414; returns home, 417; attorney in Ireland for father, 426; has appointment at Dublin Castle, 427; letter from, to brother about giving up same, *ib.*; father's anger with, 428-31; action against, in Dublin, 428-9; writes despondent letters to sister and brother, 429-31; kindness of Lady Sheppey to, 430; death from fall off a horse, 431-2; his affectionate character, 432; letters to brother, 432-3; letters about Lady Jane, his future sister-in-law, *ib.* and 454-5; letter from, to brother, 461; Dunsink had been settled on, 471

— Richard (III), 214; 312; birth of, 456-60; good-looking and delicate child, 460; at Eton, 514-5. 517; writes from Eton, 526. 545; 550; on good terms with father until in love with Lady Anne, 551; previous love affair in Ireland, *ib.*; had been attracted to his step-mother's daughter, 552-3; allowance to, by father, 553; letter to, from sister Jane, 553-4; marriage, 554; marriage settlement, 555; goes to Chevening, *ib.*; anxious to avoid sale of, 556; stays at, 557; death, *ib.*; burial, 558; has posthumous son, *ib.*

— Robt. (I), 340; 341; *ib. nn.* 1, 3
— Robt. (II), 340; 346-7
— Robert (III), 340; 352-4
— Robert Valentyne, 341 *n.*
— Thomas (I), 341

Barrett, Thomas (II), 340; 346
— Thomas (III), not of the family, 346
— Thomas (IV), 348; 352
— Walter, 340; 359; 361; death, 364. 366
— Water, 359
— William, of Bristol, 605
Barrett-Lennard, Anne Dorothy, 636
— Barbara (I), 214; birth, 594; death, 596-7; account of, by father, 597-8
— Barbara (II), 214; birth, 610; adopted by Lady Dacre, 611; education, 619; bequest to, by father, 623; Lady Dacre's affection for, 623-4; personal appearance, 624; letter to, from Lady Dacre, 627-30; first marriage, 630-1; second marriage, 632; death, *ib.*
— Charles, 636
— Charlotte Maria, 637
— Dacre, 636
— Dorothy, 636
— Edward Pomeroy, 636
— Frances, 637
— George, 636
— Henry (I), 636
— Henry (II), compiled 'Lennard Papers,' v: *quoted*, 361, 586, 588
— John, 636
— Julia Elizabeth, 636
— Thomas (I), Lord Dacre, 29th Baron, v; wrote family history, *ib.*, vi; friendly with Leonards of America, 2; does not mention Lennards of Heathfield, 4. 214; 339; posthumous birth of, 558; mother writes about, *ib.*; letter by, about step-father and step-sister, 560; litigation about his bringing-up, 570-1; taken to school at Greenwich, 571; his aunt Jane appointed guardian, 573; some land and pictures left him by grandfather, but Belhus bare of furniture, *ib.*; probably did not greatly love guardian, 578; birth, 579; sirname used by, *ib.*; appearance and health, 579-81; letter to, from Earl of Bath, 581; letter from, to aunt when at Harrow, 582-3; at Lincoln's Inn, 583; during minority of, estates administered by Court of Chancery, *ib.*; allowances ordered by Court, 583-4; fond of dogs, 585; letter from, to aunt about going to Cambridge, *ib.*; said to have been educated at Lausanne, 586; goes to

Paris, *ib.*; Belhus unfurnished and in bad repair when, succeeded to it, 586-7; alterations to Belhus made by, 587-91; collected family portraits, 591-4; marriage, 594; birth of daughter, *ib.*; letter to, from Lady Barbara, 595-6; generous treatment by, of Mr. Andrews, 596; death of daughter, 596-7; description by, of daughter, 597-8; foreign tour, 598-600; picture painted in Rome of wife, daughter, and self, 600; increased bad health, *ib.*; house in London, 601; at one time had house at Sevenoaks, *ib.*; annual trips of, 602; trip by, to Paris for treatment, 602-3; treated by Dominiceti, 603; death of mother and succession of, to title, 604; an antiquary, *ib.*; anecdote of visit by, to Chevening— the farmer's mistake, 605; literary friends of, 605-6; his politics, 606-8; visit to Clones, 608-10; natural children, 610; Lady Dacre's adoption of them, 610-11; on good terms with wife's family, 611-12; treatment by, of his children and their education, 612-19; health declines, and death, 619-20; will, 621-3; special stipulations as to arms to be borne by natural children, 621-2; reference to them, 623; his idea of becoming a Roman Catholic; bad health, bad spirits, alterations to Belhus, dislikes letter writing, reference to death of, 641-52

Barrett-Lennard, Sir Thomas (II), 214; birth and parentage, 610; adopted by Lady Dacre, 610-11; education, 613-18; personal appearance, 615; chief beneficiary under father's will, 621-3; obtains grant of arms, 622; affectionate relations with Lady Dacre, 623-9, 635-6, *passim*; first marriage, 625; children, 636; raised a troop of horse, 626-30; created baronet, 630; was M.P., 636; second marriage, 637; death, *ib.*; anecdote of, by Lord Hatherley, 638. 651
— Thomas (III), birth, 636; education, 637; M.P., *ib.*; marriages and children, 638; death, *ib.*
— Sir Thomas (IV), 638
— Walter James, 637
— Lady, *see* St. Aubyn, Dorothy; Wood, Emma

Barrington, Earl of, 569

Barrington, Sir Charles, 242
Barrymore, Lord, descended from Dorothy (II) Barrett, 569 *n.*
Barton, 274
— Martindaile, 274
Barton, William, 511; invitation from, to hawk, 513
Bateman, Mr., 453-4
Bath, Earl of, letter from, 581
Batsford, 164 *n.* 6
Battersey, 188
Battle Abbey, Roll of, errors in, referred to by Dugdale, 343
Bayning, Andrew, 276
— Anne, the Hon., 277; married Henry Murray, *ib.*; created Viscountess Bayning, *ib.*
— Cicely, the Hon., 277
— Elizabeth, the Hon., 214; marries Francis Lord Dacre, 276; marriage settlement, 278; her second marriage, 295; property acquired from second husband, *ib.*; legacy to, from sister, 295-6; litigation with first husband's executors, 296-8; lived in Covent Garden, 298; her estate and household accounts, 298-9; created Countess of Sheppey, 299; death and will, 300, 303-4; dislike to son Henry's wife, 303. 306; 430
— Mary, the Hon., married firstly Viscount Grandison, secondly Marquis of Anglesea, 277, 285; death and will, 295-6; sold interest in Gosfield, 297. 306
— Alderman Paul (I), 276; disagreements with wife, *ib.*
— Paul (II), created, successively baronet; baron; viscount, 277; large fortune, 277. 306; his wife, 277
— Paul (III), viscount, 277; acquisition of portrait of, 593
— Viscountess (I): *see* Glenham, Anne
— Viscountess (II): *see* Bayning, Hon. Anne

Beawflory, 83
Beckenham, 625; A. Lady Dacre dies at, 632
Becket, Thos. à, one of his murderers an ancestor of ours, 175, 177, 588
Bedgbury, Kent, 357
Beighton, 83; Sale of, 91, 210
Belhus, Family Pictures at, vii
Belhus, 264; 279; 308; glass from Herstmonceux at, 170, *n.*; certain pictures at, 300; formerly called Nortons, 345; partition of manor

INDEX

of, 345; once called Barrett's Hall, 351. 355; when rebuilt, 348, 351; did Queen Elizabeth visit? 356-7; coloured glass at, 360; Schedule of that estate, 365-6; grant of free-warren and license to empark, 370; hiding-place at, 392 *n.* 3; deer killed and trees cut in park at, 397-8; being unfurnished, lent to D. Lady Dacre, 398-400; furnished by her and inventory of same, 400-1; a 'Particular' of, in 1651, 403; Lady Dacre enjoys being at, 414; Dacre visits his father at, 477 *et seq.*; needed repairs, 532; rental of, in 1730. 584; park at, let, *ib.*; bad state of repair of, 586-7; alterations to, by T. Lord Dacre, 587-91, 645-650; gatehouse pulled down, 589; again bare of furniture, 586; portraits at, collected chiefly by T. Lord D., 591-4; given over to Sir T. B. L., 1st Bt., by A. Lady Dacre, 625

Belhus, de, this name still attaches to manors in Norfolk, Essex, and Kent, 343-4
— de, family of, estates owned by, 343
— Alice de, 340; 342; 345
— Isolda de, 345
— Sir John de (I), 344
— John de (II), 345
— Nicholas de, 344
— Richard de (I), 343
— Richard de (II), Sir, 343
— Thomas de (I), 340; 344-5
— Sir Thomas de (II), 343-4
— Thomas de (III), 344
Bellerby, 83; 91
Bempton, 83
Benacre, 83
Benevolences, collection of, 368
Berkley, Countess of, 557
Berkshire, T. Howard, Earl of, 413
Berners, John Lord, 185
Bexley, 349
Bickworth, 3
Bilney, 343
Bindloss, Sir Robert, 388; 396
Binge, R., 32
Bird, Ann, xviii; 3
— John, xviii; 3
Birling, 9
Blackall, Rev. Dr., 545
Blackhall, Carlisle, 274
Blackmore, Essex, D. Barrett's third marriage takes place at, 528
Blague, Robert, 349 *n.* 352

Blague, Mary, 349; bequest to, 352
Blake Hall, 625
Blaney, Eliza, 539
— Lord, letter from, 515; 549
Board and lodging, system of providing, for newly married couples by their parents, iii, 227, 241, 439, 442, 453, 455, 460
Bobbingworth Church, marriage at, 625
Bodney, 343
Boleyn, Ann, Queen, trial of, 194
Bond, Sir Thos., 322
Booth, Sir Robert, 465
Bosewell, Raufe, 32; 41 *n.*
Bossevyle, 32 *n.*; 40
Bosville, Ralph, 216
Boswell, Mr., 55
— Ralph, 32 *n.*; 41; 123
— William, letter from, 374-6
Bothinstall, 83
Bouchier, Anne, 152; 185
— Margaret, 189
— Sir Humphrey, 152; 185
Boulogne, C. de Fiennes, Earl of, 154
Bouskail, 274
Bowes, Martin, 349
Bowet, Elizabeth, 60; 61 *n.*; 175; 181
— Sir William, 175; 181
Brabazon: *see* Meath, Earl of
— Edward, Lord, 404
— Elizabeth, 404, 433 *n.*
Brackenthwaite, 274-5
Bradley, 83
Braintree, 364
Bramstone, Thomas B., 625
Brand, Thomas, 559
Brasted, 12-13; 148-9; 243; 257
Brausburton, 83
Bray, 358-9
Braytoft, Elizabeth, 340; 348; 350
— Richard, 340; 348
Bree, The Rev. Dr., 614
Brentford, Brainford, or Braynesford, 386
Brerethwaite, 274
Bretts, manor of, purchase of, 355; settlement of, 361; Chas. Barrett lived at, *ib.*; tradition that Dacre Barrett lived at, refuted, 586
Bribery, instances of, 12, 18, 96, 99-100, 494; some very quaint, 155-6
Brickmaking, art of, lost, 333
Brinckley Borough, 150
Brittains, Hornchurch, 211
Broadmarston, 148; 150
Bromley, Sir Thos., letter to, from J. (IV) Lennard, 11-12
Brook, Sir William, 243; 258-61, *passim*

660 INDEX

Brook, Lady: *see* Lennard, Pembroke
Brown ('Capability'), Launcelot, 390-1; 648-50
— Sir William, letters by, 245
Bruncker, William, 406
Bruton Street; T. Lord Dacre's house in, 601
Bryan, Sir Thos., 189
Bryant, Jacob, 605
Bryttys, Brytys, and Bryttes: *see* Bretts
Buchan, Earl of, letter from, 617
Buckholte, or Buckhold, 84; 104; 196; 296
Buckhurst, Lord, 41; 96; 120-5; 207; 226
Buckingham, Duke of, 372; letter to, 372-3. 373; 377; 379-80
— Second Duke of, 397 *n.*
Bude, or Budaeus, 347 *n.*
Bulleyn, William, *quoted*, 354-5
Bullock, Mr., 542
Bumpsted, manor of, 345; purchase of, 355
— Sir William (I), 345
— William (II), 345
Burgh, 83
— Hubert de, 154
Burghley, Sir William Cecil, Lord, 12; 15; 19; letters to, from J. (IV) Lennard, 19-21; 68; letters by to same, 69-70; letter to, by same, 70-3; letter to, by Archbishop Parker, 75-6, 88 *n.*; letter to, from J. L., 90; from R. Fynes to, 97; Lord Treasurer, 97 *n*; letter to, from R. Fynes, 99; letter to, from Margaret Lennard, 101-2; letter from J. L., 129. 211; devise to, by Anne, Lady Dacre, 223. 225; 234-5; 271; letter to, from Sir H. Duke, 404
Burham, 83; 104; 251
Burials took place formerly soon after death: *see* Funerals
Busbrig, John, 199; 203-4
Bute, Marquis of, his claim to title of FitzHugh, 184 *n.*
Butlers of Hertfordshire, 6
Butler, Lady Eliz.: *see* Derby, Countess of
— Sir John, 8
— Margaret, 8

CADIZ, Siege of: *see* Lennard, Henry (I) Lord Dacre
Cadogan, Charles, afterwards Lord Cadogan, 565

'Calisto,' 313
— the cast of, 313-14
Calthorp, Alderman, 13
Cambridge University, Thos. Lord Dacre at, 584-5
Camden, Lord: *see* Pratt, Charles
— Wm., *quoted*, 80; 162; 211; 215; 238
Camelford, Lord, 621
Campbell, Dr., 606
— Lord, *quoted*, 39, 40
Canterbury, entry among archives of, referring to Joh Lenard, 2
Capell, E., 605
Carey, Sir Edward, 367
— Sir Henry: *see* Falkland, Earl of
— Jane, 367; 372; her death, 382-3
Carleton, 148; 150
— Bacon, 83
— Kingston, 83; 91
Carrick Fergus, 463
Carrick-on-Shannon, R. (I) Barrett M.P. for, 413
Carrow Abbey, 246
Carshalton (Kersauton), 158
Carye, Sir George, 113-15
Castle Jordan, 404 *n.*; 438; 447
Castlemaine, Barbara Lady: *see* Cleveland, Duchess of
— Earl of, 308-9; 329
Cecil: *see* Burghley, Lord
— Sir Robert, 221-3, *passim*; 365
Cely, family of, 362
Chafford and Barstable Militia, 547
Chamberlain, John, letter from, 237; 247; 256
Champneis, Sir John, 349; 353
Champneys: *see* Champneis
Chapuys, letter from, 201
Charles, The Archduke, 188
— I., King, orders by, in Loftus lawsuit, 440, 446; acquisition of portrait of, 593
— II., King, 289; 306; 308; acknowledges Lady Sussex as daughter, 309; gives her away at marriage, 310; gives dowry to her, 311. present to, *ib.*; present to her eldest child, 319; attempts reconciliation between Lord and Lady Sussex, 321, 325; his anger with latter, 324; sponsor at christening of Charles Lennard, 325; neglects to pay Lord Sussex annuity, 327
— V., Emperor, 189
Charlton, R., 397
Chaworth, Lady, letters from, 314-15, 318

INDEX

Cheam School, 613
Cheek, E., 543 *n.*
— Robt., 543
Chelsea, Lord Dacre's house at, 210; petition by Marquis of Winchester concerning sale of same, 211; once the home of Sir Thos. More, 210 *n.*
— Church, tomb at, 211-12
Chelsfield, 149; 246
Chepsted, xviii; 1; 3; 4; 11; robbery at, 30-33. Manor of, 149
Chesterfield, Earl of, 309
Chevening, John (IV) Lennard lived there till 1570, 14; died there, 121; earliest records of Lennards settled there, 1. 148-9; wife of S. Lennard died there, 238; tombs to him and wife, 239; contract for building Chapel to, Church, 38. 148-9; inventory of goods at, 247-9; house rebuilt by Inigo Jones, 254; settlement of, 255; D. Lady Dacre's second marriage at, 263-5; she lives at, 264-5; A. (IV) Barrett married at, 265. 279, 286, 305; 307; 308; 313; E. of Sussex attempts to let, 319; cuts timber at, 320; dies at, 338; his widow and daughters live there, 338; Richard (III) Barrett and bride spend honeymoon at, 555; preparations for sale of, 556; sale accomplished, 558
Chevington, 83
Chichester, Thos. Lennard (VII) lived at, 261
— Lady Jane, 214; D. Barrett pays court to, 452 *et seq.*; character and personal appearance, 454-5; marriage and settlement, 455-6; births of children, 456-9; letter from, 460; difficulty about paying her dowry, 461-2; letter from, her bad spelling, 463; letter from, to husband, confined at Liverpool, 473-4; correspondence with husband while at Liverpool, 477-82; journey from Liverpool to Belhus, 482-3. 489; 490; goes to London to obtain post for husband, 493-4. probable date of death, 501
— Hon. John, 455 *n.*
— Lady Mary, her marriage, 433 *n.*; 460
Chichley, Margery, 346
— John, 346

Chigwell, Essex, 240; M., widow of Gregory Lennard, buried at, 241
Christchurch, Hants, 218
Churton, the Rev. R., 615
Chute, Chaloner (I), 257; 263-4; 390; legacy to, 390; letter to, offering to lend Belhus, 399; accepts offer, 400. 449
— Chaloner (II), 257; his children, 264
— Chaloner (III), lawsuit with grandmother, 'Villainous Viper,' 264. 470
— Edmund, or Edward, 264
— Elizabeth, 264; her marriage, 265
— John, 602
— Thomas, 264; D. Lady Dacre's favourite grandson, 265; his children christened at Chevening, *ib.*; bequest to, of portrait by Lady Dacre, 331; letter from, to D. Barrett, 532-3; his marriage, 533 *n.*; letter from, announcing death of Lady Dacre, 537-8
— Thomas Lennard, 265
Circuits: *see* Assize
Clapham (Cheph'm), 158
Clare, Viscount, 278
Clarendon, Lord Chancellor, 402; *quoted*, 441
Clarke, Mr., letters from, 541-2
Claybury, Essex, 529
Cleveland, Duchess of, 277; 300; 306; letter from, to Charles II., 309. quarrel with her daughter, the Countess, 322-5; letters by, to King, 323-4; bequests by her will, 325. 326. letter from, about extravagance of E. of Sussex, 332; portrait of, acquired, 593
Cleves, Queen Anne of, Lord and Lady Dacre attend her, 196
Clinton, Lord, 152; 181
— Lady: *see* Fynes, Elizabeth
Clogher, Bishop of, Dacre Barrett has litigation with, 572
Clones, 404; discovery and conquest of, 404-5; Crown lease of, 405-6; Crown grant of, 406; description of antiquities at, 406-8; Abbey at, and by whom founded, 406; settlement of, and rental of, in 1680, 455; emigration from, 467-8; terrible state of, 485-8 and 494-9; address to King Wm. III. from, 500; state of the Castle of, in 1739, 608; visits to, by T. Lord Dacre, 608-10

INDEX

Clover, early mention of, 76 *n.*
Cobham, Sir H., diplomatist, 45 *n.*; letter from, to J. (IV) Lennard, 45; curious inquiry as to chastity of, by same, 45-6
— J. Brook, Lord, 349 *n.*
— Lord, 196-7; 199 *n.*
Coke, Sir John, 374; letters to, 377, 385, 445
Cole, Sir Arthur. *See* Ranelagh, Lord
— Eli, letter from, 464
— Sir John, 455; 463
Colley, Sir William, 438; 440
Collins, A., *quoted*, 62; 115; 154; 160
— Rev. John, 605
Coloony, Lord, 433
Common field, the, at Wintringham, 85
Compton Monseux, 82; price sold for, 91
Condé, Jacques, Lord of, 152; 159
Conflans, Abbess of, 322
Congham in Norfolk: *see* Thursby, F.
Conies, curious covenants as to, 13-14
Conway, Lord, 465
— Lord, 441
Coote, Hon. Mr., 433-4
— Sir Charles, 408; 433 *n.*
— Charles, 433 *n.*
— Eli, 302
— Sir Philips, 433 *n.*
Corbet, Sir John, 387
— Sir Thomas, 359; 374
Cordell, Sir William, 8; his intimacy with J. (IV) Lennard, 42; letters by, to same, 42-44; death of, 45. 116; letter by, about Knole, 122-3; his advice, 147
Cotterell, Sir Charles, 265 *n.*
— Sir Charles L., 265; executor to Lady Sheppey's will, 300. 527
Courtney, *quoted*, 244
Courts, 369
Covehithe, 83
Coventry, Sir Thos., afterwards Lord Coventry, 380
Covert, Sir Walter, 9; 112
Cowdrey, Wm., disputes with J. (IV) Lennard, 131; letter by, to same, 132-4; reply to, from same, 134-5; date of death, 134 *n.*
Cowling Castle, Kent, 243
Coxe, Rev. W., 605
Crane, J., letter from, about death of R. (I) Barrett, 520
Cranewell, E., disputes and correspondence with J. (IV) Lennard, about Whitely Wood, 136-9

Cranewell, Giles, 139
Cranwell, Robert, 11
Crayford, 231
Cremorne, Lord: *see* Dawson, Thomas
Cricket, early mention of, 317
Cromer, Mr., High Sheriff, Kent, 22: *see also* Assizes
— Sir William, 22 *n.*
Crompe, Thos., 291-5, *passim*, 319
Crompton, Walter, 349
Cromwell, Gregory, 194
— Thomas, 194; letter to, 195
Cronin, Major, 560
Cudham, or Cowdham, 13; 83; 104; 149; 240; 257; 278; 308; sale of, 330
Culpepper, Alexander, 358
— Katherine, 358
— Walter, 349
— William, 349
Cumberford, Thos., 348
Custos Brevium: *see* Lennard, John (IV); and Teynham, John Lord
Cuxton, Kent, 361

Dacre, Anne, 268; 270; 273 *n.*
— Edward, 271
— Elinor, 272 *n.*
— Elizabeth (I), 268; 270; 274 *n.*
— Elizabeth (II), 272 *n.*
— Francis (I), 269 *n.*; 270 *n.*; 271; letter from, 272; his death, 273
— Francis (II), 273
— George, Lord, 268; death, 269. 273; 274
— Hugh de, Baron of Gilsland, 175; 179
— Sir Humphrey, 171-4; 175; 181; 182 *n.* 2; 188; 268
— Joan, or Johane, Lady, first engaged to John Filol, 57-60; then to R. Fynes, 61-2; marriage contracts of, 59-62, 61 *nn.* 1 and 3. 152; 175; 170; 170 *n.* 6; 181; her will, 185. 268
— Leonard, 269; 270; his death, 271; 274
— Mary (I), 268; 270
— Mary (II), 272 *n.*
— Phillippa, 61-2; 170; 175; 181
— Randall: *see* Ranulph
— Ranulph (I) de, Baron of Gilsland, 175; 178-9
— Ranulph (II) de, Baron of Gilsland, 175; 179
— Ranulph (III) de, 175; 181

INDEX 663

Dacre, Ranulph, or Randolf, last Dacre of the North, 268 ; birth, 272 ; death, 273. 274
— Reginald, 260; query Ranulph Dacre, 260 n.
— Thomas (I) de, Baron of Gilsland, 179
— Thomas (II), 170 ; 175 ; styles himself Lord Dacre and drops prefix of 'de,' 180. 181 n. 1
— Sir Thomas (III), arranges for marriage of daughter Jobane, 57-62 ; for marriage of daughter Phillippa, 61-2. 152 ; 175 ; 181
— Thomas, Lord of the North, 268 ; 273 n.
— William, Lord, 270 n., 273
Dacre, Barony of, held by Lennards from 1612 to 1786. 5
— Castle of, 274 ; 304. 305. repaired, small size of, 320. 328 ; sold, 339
— de, when prefix of de was dropped, 180
— House, 223
— Lady : see Dacre, Joan ; Bouchier, Anne ; Nevill, Mary ; Sackville, Anne ; Fynes, Margaret ; Baker, Chrysogona ; Throgmorton, Elizabeth ; North, Dorothy ; Bayning, Elizabeth ; Lennard, Lady Anne ; Pratt, Anna Maria : see also Dacre of the North
— Lord : see also Fynes ; Lennard ; and Barrett-Lennard
— Lords, of the North, 174 ; latter history of, 268
— Lords, of the South, 174
Daffy, Rev. Thos. 603 n.
Dahl, M., portrait by, 308
Dalrymple, Sir D., 605
Danny Park, 82 ; 194 ; sale of, 210 ; builder of, 210 n.
Dansell, Sir Wm., 21
Danvers, John, 142
Darcy, Lord, trial of, 195
Darrell, Sir Marmaduke, 9
— Mary, of Scotney, courted by Samson Lennard and by Barnaby Goge, 65 et seq. ; letter by, 74 ; marries Goge, 76
— Sir Samson, 259
— Thomas, of Scotney, 67
Dartmouth, Earl of, 328
Dawson, Miss, of Roscommon, 'the worst woman that ever was known,' 64
— Richard, 599

Dawson, Thomas, 599 n. ; 600 ; 601
— Walter, letter from, to D. Barrett about his son's marriage, 63 ; his death, 64, 495 ; 497 ; 501 ; letter from, to D. Barrett, 530
de Batsford, Elizabeth, 152 ; 164
— William, 152 ; 164
de Dammartin, Agnes, 152 ; 157
de Ferrers, Lord, 621
de Gournay, G., 163
— Hugh, 157
de Grey, Lady Henrietta, 557
de Heere, portrait by, 592 n.
de Nevill, 156
de Pageham, 160-1
de Peplesham, Margery, 164
— Simon, 164
de Tingrie, Sibyl, 152 ; 155-7
de Tourval, letter from, 253
De Troy, portraits by, 594
Deane, J., letter from, about death of R. (I) Barrett, 519-20
Deerhurst, Lord, 651
Deerstealers, 126-8 ; 195 et seq. ; 288
Dent, 83
Derby, Earls of, descended from Dorothy (II) Barrett, 569 n.
— Edward, 11th Earl of, 651
— Edward, 12th Earl of, 476
— Edward Stanley, Earl of, 569
— Elizabeth, Countess of, 475 ; 493
— William, Earl of, 474-5
Derham, Rev. Dr. William, 522 ; 544-5
Desborough, 253 n.
Desminers, John, 428
Detton, Mrs., an Eton 'Dame' ; 514-16, passim
Diehl, quoted, 615
Dineley, Elizabeth, 243 ; 340 ; 348, 353 ; bequests to, 351-2. 354
— Phillipa : see Harpsfield
— Thomas, 340 ; 348
Dobson, Rev. J., praise of Lord Newburgh by, 384-5
Dodingsells, Sir Edward, 348
— Elizabeth, 348
Dominiceti, Dr., 603
Donegall, Arthur, 2nd Earl of, 452 461
— Arthur, 3rd Earl, letter from, 516
— Jane, Lady, wanted D. Barrett as son-in-law, 452-3. 455 ; 460 ; her house in Dublin, 460. 461-2 ; letter from, to Dacre, 466 ; sends grandson to Eton, 514. 517
Dorchester, Anne, Viscountess of : see Glenham, Anne

664 INDEX

Dorchester, D. Carlton, Viscount, 306
Dormans Well, 222 ; 224-5
Dorset, Earl of, 237 : *see* Buckhurst, Lord
— Earl of, 277
Douglas, Jas., Earl of, 175 ; 180
— Johanne, 175 ; 180
Dover Castle, 154 ; rent paid to Governor of, 298
Down, 149
Downham, Mrs. Avis, 272
Doyly, Edward, letter from, 246
Drogheda, Viscount, letter from, 410
— Henry, 1st Earl of, 278 *n.*
— Henry, 3rd Earl of, 560 ; 561 *n.*
Druery, Sir Drewe, 223 ; 246
— House, 380 *n.*
Duchesne, *quoted*, 154
Duke, Sir Henry, 404 ; discovered Clones, *ib.* ; letter from, to Lord Burghley, *ib.* ; has long lease of Clones, 405 ; death of, *ib.* ; where buried, 413
— Mary, 404 ; first husband and child by, *ib. n.* ; third husband, *ib.* ; letter to, about her grandchild, Anne, 410, 447-8
Dudley, Edward, Lord, 152 ; 186
— John, Lord, 186
— Joan, 152 ; 186-7
— or Duddeley, John, 117 ; letter from, about Knole, 118-19
Dugdale, Sir William, *quoted*, 343
Dunsink, 404 ; 409 ; 413 ; 455 ; 472 ; 492 ; 501 ; 517 ; 525 ; 527
Dyer, Sir E., 90 *n.*
— Sir Jas., 17 *n.*
Dyke, Sir Thomas, 321 ; 332

EAST Mersea, 161
Ecclesiastical Courts, action in, 55
Eccleston, manor of, 188
Edling, John, accused of murder, 34-36
Edward IV., award by, 173 ; 268
Edward, Prince, christening of, 196
Edwardby, 83 ; 91
Edwards, John, 346
Eirenarcha, the, 234 *n.*
Elizabeth, Queen, Supplication to, by Anne Lady Dacre, 91 *et seq.* ; grant to, by G. Lord Dacre, 98 *n.* ; was acquainted with J. Lennard, 114 ; G. Lord Dacre and wife in attendance on, 208 ; presents to, and from, 210 ; bequests to, 222 ; query, did she visit Belhus? 356-7 ; grant by, of lease of Clones, 405
Elde, F., 536 *n.*

Ellerbye, 83
Ellingstring, 83
Elwill, Sir John, 562
Ely, Viscount Loftus of : *see* Loftus, Adam ; *also* Edward
— Sarah, Lady, her first husband and date of her death, 444 *n.* 445-6
Emigration : *see* America
Emmanuel Hospital, Westminster, 223
Engayn, Ada, 175
— W., 175
Essex, Arthur Capel, Earl of, 450
— R. Devereux, Earl of, letter from, 236-7
Essex Manors, Some, vii
Eton, Richard (III) Barrett at, 514, 516
Eure, Sir Francis, 9 ; 111-12
— William, Lord, 9 ; 112
Evelyn, *quoted*, 313, 326
Everest, 9 *n.*
Evesham, Battle of, 159
Evershott, 83
Ewers with scented water before use of forks general, 27 *n.*
Ewherst, 84 ; 104 ; Sale of, 229
Exeter, Dean of : *see* Lyttelton
— Marquis of, trial of, 195

FALKLAND, Earl of, 367 ; 383
Fanshaw, Sir Richard, 508 *n.*
— Sir Thomas, 508
Faramus : *see* Pharamus
Farmer, Judith, xviii ; 3
— Nicholas, xviii ; 3
Felix Hall, 160 *n.*
Fenn, Hugh, 384
— Katherine, marries Lord Newburgh, 384 ; her bad education and large fortune, *ib.* ; children by first husband, *ib.* ; beneficiary under second husband's will, 389-90 ; third marriage, 397 ; restrained from killing off deer and committing other waste at Belhus, 397-8 ; conveys Belhus to R. (I) Barrett as a result of litigation, 398 ; her death, 402
— Richard, 384 *n.*
Fenner, Mr. Justice, 223
Fermor, Sir William, 384
ffitch, or Fytch, William, 542
Field, Mr., letter to, 252. 284 ; 287 ; 290
Fienes, Enguérrand de : *see* Fynes, Ingelram de
— *See also* Fynes, and 154 *n.* 1
Fienles, John de, 161 *n.* 6

INDEX

Fiennes, Conon de, Earl of Boulogne, 154
— John de, 154; Constable of Dover Castle, *ib.*; this denied by Round, *ib. n.* 5
Fifield, Mr., 427-8
Filiol, or Filoll, Sibyl, her marriage and abduction, 160
— An Essex family, 160 *n.*
Filol, Filoll, and Fyloll, John, 57-61, *passim*
Finche, Heneage, legal opinion by, 267
Fish-ponds, 10; 14; 484 *n.*; robbing same, 485
Fishing: *see* Sporting right
Fishwick, manor of, 188; *ib. n.* 7
FitzHerbert, family of, 353
FitzHugh, the title of, in abeyance, 184 *n.*
— Alice, 152; 183
— Lord, 152; 183; 184 *n.*
FitzRoy, Lady Anne, 214; 306; her beauty, 308; her birth and education, 309; doubts as to paternity, *ib.*; extreme youth of, at marriage, *ib.*; her trousseau, 310; present to, from King, 311; profligate character, 311-12; Rochester's verses about, 312 and 326; a mother whilst still a child, 312; plays in a masque at Court, 313-14; intimacy of, with Duchess of Mazarin, 314-15 and 318; goes to Herstmonceux and hunts, 315-16; tires of the country and goes to France, 318; in Paris with her mother, 321; quarrel with mother about the Ambassador, 322-5; became reconciled, 325; corresponded with her husband while in France, *ib.*; they live together again, *ib.*; in favour with the King, 326; mentioned unfavourably by Evelyn, *ib.*; money paid to, at Newmarket, 327; leaves husband and follows Jas. II. to St. Germains, 328; well received there, 329; occasional visits to England and joins in selling Apuldrefield, *ib.*; returns to England, 338; joins in selling Dacre Castle and Hever, 339; lives with her daughter, Lady Anne, *ib.*; death, *ib.*; notice of, *ib.*; will, *ib.* 551; very defective education, 563
— Lady Charlotte, 310-26
FitzThomas, Elizabeth, 214; 610; 621
FitzWalter, Lord: *see* Cheek, Robert
Fleete, Thomas (II) Lord Dacre a prisoner in the, 189

Fletcher, Mr., Irish agent, 458, 467-8; 485-8, *passim*
Florence, 366
Forrester, Joan, daughter of J. le, 161
Forster, Sir Humphrey (I), 358; 374; 395; 402
— Sir Humphrey (II), 402
— William, 306 *n.*
Fortibus, de, family of, 353
Foster: *see* Forster
Fox, Sir Stephen, 540
Foxcote, Hants, 353-4; 356
Frankeleyn, John, letters from, to J. (IV) Lennard, 30-1, 34, 119-21
Frankelin: *see* Frankeleyn
Franklyn, John, 31 *n.*
— Robert, 142
Freeman, Mr., 550
Freewarren, grant of, over Belhus, 370
Frome, Quyntyne, 83
Frowds, J., 198-9
Fuller, Thomas, *quoted*, 346; 365
Fulmer, 9
Fulmerston, Sir Richard, 269
Funerals: of Mrs. J. Lennard, 46-50; formerly took place soon after death, 145; 212 *n.* 2, 239 *n.*, 259; ex penses of, 360
Fynes, various forms of spelling this name, 154 *n.*
Fynes, Anna, 185 *n.* 3
— Anne, 152; 187; 192; 206
— Catherine, 186
— Edward, 152; 185
— Elizabeth, 152; 181; 184-5
— Sir Giles de, 152; 159-61
— Gregory, Lord Dacre, letter from, 78-9; said to be of 'cracked brain,' 80; disputes with sister and J. Lennard, 80-105; his estates, 82-4, 89 *n.* 152; date of birth, 193; marriage of, 207; only child of, 78 *n.*, 207, 209; in attendance on Queen, 208; attainder of, reversed, 208-9; petition by, for rectification of terms of great-grandfather's will, 209; sells Beighton and Danny, 210; goes with an embassy, *ib.*; ordered to attend Queen, 210; house at Chelsea, 210-11; connection with tradition of Michaelmas goose, 210; character, 211; death and will, *ib.*, 221; tomb, 211-12
— Ingelram de (I), 152; 155
— Ingelram de (II), 152; 159-60
— James, 152; ancestor of Lords Say and Sele, 164-5. 165 *n.* 4

INDEX

Fynes, John de, 160
— John (I) de, 152; 161
— Sir John (II) de, 152; 161-3
— John (III), 152; 162
— John, Sir (IV), 152; 181; 183-5
— John (V), 152; 186; 192
— John (VI), 207
— Margaret, xviii; arrangement for marriage of, 62, 77; her age at marriage, *ib.*, 95 *n.*; attractive as a match, 78; brother's promise as to giving portion to, 78-9; the 'Greyfes of,' 80-100; reversion to large possessions, 85-6; date of birth of, 95 *n.*; allegations against, by Lady Dacre, 95-100; letter by, to Lord Burghley, 101-2; lands settled on, by quadripartite indenture, 104; probable date of the 'Greyfes,' 90. 152; her descent, 154. 193; 214; assumed title of Dacre before it was acknowledged by the Crown, 228 *n.* 2; claim to title allowed by commissioners, 235-8; death, 238; inscription on tomb at Chevening, 239. portrait of, acquired, 593
— Mary, 152; 186
— Philip, 93; 186
— Sir Richard (I) Lord Dacre, 58; contract for marriage, 61. 152; 158; 170-5; 181-5; 268
— Richard (II), 152; 181; 184
— Robert, 58; 61-2; 170; 175
— Sir Roger (I), arranges marriages of sons, 58; marriage contract, 61-2. 152; 164; contract with King to serve in French wars, 165-8; license to build Herstmonceux Castle, 169. marriage and death, 170; cost of building Herstmonceux, 333
— Roger (II), 152; 181; 184
— R., letters by, to Lord Burghley, 96-7, 99
— Thomas (I), 152; 181; 184-5
— Thos. (II) Lord Dacre, 80; 152; 183-5; 186-92; tomb of, 192
— Sir Thos. (III), 152; 185 *n.*; 186-7; 191-2
— Thos. (IV), 152; 185 *nn.* 3, 6; 186; 191
— Thos. (V) Lord Dacre, 152; 185 *n.* 6; 187; 192-6; his trial, 197-203; warrant for execution of, 204; his estates, 205-6. 209; provision for widow of, *ib.*; portrait acquired of, 592 *n.* 4, 593

Fynes, Thos. (VI), 152; 193; 205; 07; 209
— William (I) de, 152; 154; 156-9, *passim*
— William (II) de, 152; 159-60
— William (III) de, 152; 162
— Sir William (IV), 152; 162-4
— William (V), 152; 181; 184-5
Fynes, manor of, 82

GARTH, Sir Samuel, 557
Gavelkind, action based on custom of, 337
Gelsdaile, 274
George III., coronation of, 581
Gepp, Mr., 530
Gernet, Benedict, 175; 178; *ib. n.* 3
— Joan, 175; 178
Gifford, family, 242 *n.*
— Chrysogona, 242 *n.*
— Sir John, 404 *n.*; commences the great lawsuit, 437 and 440-3; besieged in Castle Jordan, 447-8
— Richard, 404 *n.*
Gilbert at Lee, 345
Gilpin, Dr., 613
Gilsland, Barony of: *see* Vaux, Moulton, and Dacre
Glasshouse, 139-41; 228
Glassonby, 274-5
Glenham, Anne, 277; purchased Gosfield, 297. 306
— Sir H., 277
Glynde Place, early owners of, 216 *n.* 1
Goff, General, letter from, 291. 294
Goge, Googe, or Goche, Barnaby, rival with Samson Lennard for hand of Mary Darrell, 68-76; letter from, 77
Goodere, John (I), 529
— John (II), 529; letter from, 529-30
Gore, Mrs., *quoted*, 203
Goring, George, 210; letter from, 221. 224 *n.*
— George (the younger), 210 *n.*
Gosfield, 277; purchase and sale of, 296-7. 344
Gotchmer, or Gotham, 84; 104; 259
Gough, R., 605
Gournay: *see* de Gournay
Gowran, Earl of, 475
Grafton, Duke of, 571
Grandison, Lady: *see* Bayning, Mary
— Viscount, 277; 306; portrait of, acquired, 593
Gray (*sic*), Lord, 543
Gray's Inn, 242; 251; 392

INDEX

Great Russell Street; D. Barrett had house in, 567, 572, 601
'Greenhues,' 275
Greenwich, Thos. Lord Dacre at school at, 571-2
Greenwood, 313; E. of Sussex's debt to, and how settled, 327-8
Gresham, Sir Thos., 9; 110
Grey, Lord, of Werke, letter to, from F. Lord Dacre, 281
Greystock, 273
— Castle, 270
Grimston, Viscount, 575
Grocer's, a, bill in Tudor times, 51-2
Groves, S. Ockendon, 529; 532
Guernsey, Lord, 651
Gurdon, Brampton, 359; 374

HACTONS, 400 n.; 625
Haddock, Josiah, 304
— Mary (widow Usher), married Henry (III) Lennard, 304
Hagley Hall, 641
Haighway, Mr., 567
Hailes, Lord, *quoted*, 180 n. 1
Hale, Sir Matt., *quoted*, 204; arbitration by, 274
Haley, Mr., *quoted*, 202
Hall, Sir Philip, 566; his children, 566-7
— Philip, his career, 566-7; action by, to obtain Belhus estates, 566
— Sarah, 567
Halstead, Kent, 10; 148
Halywell, 83
Hamilton, Sir William, 605
Hampden, Viscount, his claim to title of FitzHugh, 184 n.
Handwriting: *see* Spelling
Hansard, Mrs. Anne, 561-2
Harcourt, Sir S., letter from, 338
Hardinge, Geo., letter from, about Lord Dacre's appearance, 580; letter about visit to Chevening, 605; anecdote about Lord Camden, 612
— Nicholas, 598
Hare, Francis Naylor, 333
— Rev. Robert, 333-4
Harley, Sir E., 361
— Robt., letter to, 338
Harman, Elizabeth, xviii: *see* Lennard, John (IV)
— Henry, 8
— William, xviii, 7-8
Harpsfield, John, 340; 348-9
— Lewes, 350; 351; 353
— Phillipa, 340; 348-51

Harrington, Sir James, 283
Harrison, P., letter by, to J. (IV) Lennard, hopes to 'gett a wyfe to pay my detts,' 144
Harrow School, members of family educated at, 582, 613
Harwood Hall, 625
Hatherley, Lord, anecdote by, concerning Sir Thos. Barrett-Lennard and his eldest son, 638
Hatton, Sir C., Lord Chancellor, 128-30
Haughton, Mr., 399
Havingdon, 83
Hawkhurst, Kent, 341-2
Hawking partridges and woodcock, 512-13
Hawkins, Lady, 240; bequest by, 241
Hawtboyes, or Hautbois, 84; 104; 181; 185 n.; 186 n.; 223 n.; 229; 246; sold, 253
Hayleshmere, or Haylsham, 84; 104
Haywoods, Hants, 356-8
Heathfield: *see* Lennard of Bayly
— Church, tombstone to Lennards at, 3
Hellingly, 198 n.; 204
Henry VII., 188
Henry VIII., 189; 190
Henstead, 83
Herbert, Rev. Edward, 548
Herbert, Hon. John, 277
Heriz: *see* Smith, Erasmus (I)
Heron, W., 164
Herst, Walleran de, 162-3
— Ydonea de, 163
— Manor of, 162
Herstmonceux, Castle of, 169; 174; 203; bad repair of, 225. 226. hospitality at, 228. inventory of goods at, 249-50. Field, steward at, 252; R. Lord Dacre, living at, 253; household account book of, 284-91; visitors at, 285-7. 305. 308. coloured glass from, at Belhus, 170 n.; sale of, 330, 332; destruction of, 333-4; description of, 334-6
— Church, tombs in, 164, 183, 192; bequests to, 190-1
— Estate, rental of, 231-2
— Manor of, 84; 104; 162; 164; 259
Herstmonceux Castle, Household Account Book of, vii
Herstperpoint, 82; 181
Hever, 13; 148-9; sale of, 339
Hichens: *see* Barrett-Lennard, Barbara (II)

Hichens, John Henry, 214 ; second marriage, 630 ; first wife, *ib.* ; financial position, 631 ; death, 632
— Richard, 630
Hicks, Sir Beach, 220 *n.*
— Michael, letter to, 220
Hiding-place at Belhus, 392 *n.*
High Sheriffs, J. (IV) Lennard, of Kent, 7 ; 20-1 ; R. (I) Barrett, of Essex, 392 ; D. Barrett, of Essex, 536
Historical Manuscripts Commission, Reports by, on our family papers, v
Hobart, Sir Henry, 246
Hockering, 343
Holbeach, 84 ; 104
Holbein, portrait by, 592 *n.*
Holland family, 170
— Elizabeth, 152 ; 170
— Sir John, 152
Holman, W., the Rev., *quoted*, 362
Hornchurch, 355 ; 356
Horselunges, 199 *n.*
Horsford, Account of Manor of, vii
Horsford, 84 ; 91 ; 104 ; bare of timber, 105. 181 ; 185-6 ; 223 *n.* ; 229 ; nearly sold, 246, 253 ; settlements of, 257-8, 286, 456, 523
Horton, 148 ; 150
Hough, Rev. Dr., 552
House of Commons, 446
House of Lords, 446-7 ; 450
Howard, Lord, of Effingham, 234-5 ; 366 *n.* : *see* Nottingham, C,. Earl of
Howard, Charles, 274-5
— Sir Philip, 274 *n.*
— Lord William, 270 ; 274 *n.*
— Sir William, 274 *n.*
Humber, fishery in river, 83
Hunsdon, Lord, letters to, from J. (IV) Lennard, 113-15 ; in error said to have assigned lease of Knole to same, 116. 271
Hurlock : *see* Barrett-Lennard, Barbara (II)
— Rev. Dr. J. T., 214 ; marriage and death, 632 ; love of animals, *ib.*
Hurlston, Mr., of the Temple, 88 ; 90 ; 98

INGRAMES, 84 ; 104
Inigo Jones, architect of Chevening, 254
Ireland, state of, in 1674, 426 ; in 1684, 468
Islay : *see* Isley
Isley, Henry, 33-4
— Sir Henry, 11-12
— William, 11-13

JAMES II., King, 328 ; 329 ; portrait acquired, 593
Jenkins, Barking, 508 *n.*
Jephson, Sir John, 404 *n.*
— Lady : *see* Duke, Mary
Jessel, Sir George, *quoted*, 591
John, King, bribes paid to, 155-6
Johnson, Mr., 187
Jones : *see* Inigo
— John, 305
— Oliver, 452 *n.*
— Ri. : *see* Ranelagh, Earl of
Judges : *see* Assize

KAINE, E. (an Irish agent), letter about marriage of Captain Dawson's son, 64 ; anxious to raise troop of horse at Clones, 549 ; letter to R. (III) Barrett, 551 ; letter from, to D. Barrett about marriage of R. (III), 554-5
Keating, Mr. Justice, 461-2
Kelway, 354
Kemp, Mary, 506-7
Kenningtons, 369
Kent, W., 641
Kerck, Captain, 382
Kilkenny Cathedral, 642
Kirkoswald, 274. 305
Kirtling, 263 ; 265
Knebworth, Herts, 358
Knockballymore, 460 ; 511
Knole, 41 ; 116 ; 123-5 ; 231 : *see also* Lennard, John (IV)
Knoles, 253
Knolles, Margaret, 340 ; 346
— Robert, of Mims, 340 ; 346
— Sir Thomas, 346
Knowsley, Dacre's visits to, 474
Knyvett, Sir Henry, of Charlton, 372
— Sir Henry, of Buckenham, 372

LAMBARDE, Wm., *quoted*, 234
Lambert, General, 448
Lamerton, Mr., letters from, 541
Lancaster, R. (I) Barrett, freeman of, 426
Lanercost, Priory of, founded by R. de
— Vaux, 175-6
Langford, Sir Hercules, wanted son to marry Lady J. Chichester, 453
Langham, 632
Langherst, 83
Lanoye, Colonel, 305
La Warr, Lord, 194
Law reform by John (IV) Lennard, 38-9
Lazonby, 274 ; 275

INDEX

Lee, R., a wine merchant, letter from, in 1588, 141
Le Forrester, Joan, 152; 161
— Jordan, 152; 161
— Reginald, 161
Leicester, Earl of, accessible to bribes, 12, 88 *n.*; 96-7, 99; lease by, of Knole to Rolf, 116-17; legacy to, 211
Leighlin, Bishop of, 444 *n.*
Leland, John, Latin epigrams by, to John (III) Barrett, 347
— Thomas, *quoted*, 441
Lely, Sir Peter, 593
Lenard, Joh., 2
Lennard: *see also* Barrett-Lennard
— Alexander, 286
— Anne (I), 8; 9; 111; 148-9
— Anne (II), birth, marriage, death, place of burial, 216
— Anne (III), 304; marriage of, 305
— Anne (IV), Lady, 214. 266; birth of, 312. 325; 329; becomes a Roman Catholic, 330. 338-9; 550; returns to England, 551; very beautiful, *ib.* 552-3; marries R. (III) Barrett, 554; marriage settlement, 555. 556-7; birth of son, 558; letter from, 558-9; second marriage, 559; children by this marriage, *ib.*; third marriage, 560; third husband's career, 560-3; child by third husband, 563; bad education, 563-4; did not assume title of Dacre on sister's death, 564; death and burial, *ib.*; litigation about guardianship of eldest son, 570-1; succeeds to title of Dacre upon death of Lady Barbara, 596
— Barbara (I), 243-4; 259-60
— Lady Barbara (II), 214; birth and marriage, 312. 319. marriage, 329-30. 338-9; 550-1; 555-7; 564; sends portraits to Belhus, 593; portrait of, acquired, 594; death of, 595; letter from, *ib.*
— Benjamin, xviii; 6 *n.*; 8
— Catherine (I.), 4
— Catherine (II), 257; her children, 264. 285
— Catherine (III), 304-5
— Charles, 214; 312; 325
— Dacre: *see* Barrett, Dacre
— Edward (I), 214; 243; 251-2
— Edward (II), 214
— Elizabeth (I), 8; 9; 111-12; 148-9
— Elizabeth (II), 101 *n.*; 216

Lennard, Elizabeth (III), 216; monument to, 227; was very handsome, *ib.*
— Elizabeth (IV), the Hon., her two marriages, 278; legacy to, from father, 294. 302; 493 *n.*
— Elizabeth (V), 583 *n.*
— Frances, 216
— Francis (I), xviii; 3
— Francis (II), xviii; 3; 4
— Francis (II), widow of, 286
— Francis (III), Lord Dacre, lease by, reserving sporting rights, 84. 214; 252; birth of, 255. 258-61, *passim*; probably on bad terms with stepmother, 261, 286; age at father's death, 267; goes to Oxford, *ib.*; inheritance from the Throckmortons, *ib.*; entitled to properties of Dacres of the North, 267-76; marries, 276; marriage settlements, 278; children, *ib.*; house in London, 279; political career, 279-84; query, did he hire Chevening? 279; Herstmonceux account book, 284-5; letter by, about deer-stealers, 288; fond of sport, *ib.*; one of earliest yachtsmen, 289-90; defeated in election for Master of Trinity House, 289; borrows money, 290; wife's allowance, 291; 'discontent betwixt him and his lady,' 291-2; his will, executors, and guardians to eldest son, *ib.*; wife not mentioned in will, 291; legacies given by, 292; retirement into the country, *ib.*; obtains a pardon, 293; wife dull in the country, *ib.*; their discontent patched up, 294; financial position of, at death, *ib.*; sudden death, *ib.*; buried at Chevening, *ib.* 300; 306; portrait of, acquired, 593
— Francis (IV), 214; 278; 294; 297-8; 300; education, *ib.*; lived in France, 301; fought for James II. in Irish campaign, *ib.*; became R.C., 302. 303
— Fynes, 214; 243; 251-2; his children, 252; letter from, 252-3
— George (I), xviii; 1-3
— George (II), xviii; 3
— Gregory, 214; birth of, 216; marriage, 240; settlement on, *ib.*; his son died an infant, 241; his own death, *ib.*
— Henry (I), Lord Dacre, 214; birth of, 216; father security for debts

X X

of, 230; his claim to title of Dacre, 237; father transferred estates to, during former's life, 239; member of Lincoln's Inn, 242; marriage, *ib.*; children, 243; knighted at taking of Cadiz, 244; M.P., *ib.*; his appearance, *ib.*; public offices filled by, 245; friend of Earl of Pembroke and Sir P. Sydney, *ib.*; debts, 246; sells estates, *ib.*; contemplates selling Horsford and Hautbois, *ib.*; letters upon subject, *ib.*; death, 247; that of wife, *ib.*; inventories of goods, 247-50; portrait of, acquired, 592-3

Lennard, Henry (II), 214; 255
— Henry (III), 214; 279; 297; 300; 302; first marriage, 303; mother's displeasure at, 303-4; second marriage; children; death; entitled to snare of mother's estates, 304
— Henry (IV), 214; 312
— Henry (V) a servant? 286-7
— John (I), 1; 3
— John (II), xviii; 3
— John (III), xviii; 3; 4
— John (IV), xviii; 4.; founder of Lennard family, 5; known to Queen Elizabeth, 6; life of, by son, 6-7; date of marriage, 7; wife's family, 8; children, *ib.*; marriages of daughters, 9; prothonotary, 10; made loan to Henry VIII., *ib.*; prothonotary of Common Pleas, *ib.*; J.P. for Kent, *ib*; obtains lease of Chevening and other lands in Kent, *ib.*; bought Chevening, 11; obtains Chepsted, *ib.*; litigation concerning, 11-12; letter from, to Sir T. Bromley, 11-13; acquires Brasted, *ib.*; acquires Cudham and advowson of Hever, and long lease of that manor and park, 13; gets on in profession, 14; profits of one session, *ib.*; buys expensive hangings at Archbishop Parker's sale, 14-15; Custos Brevium, how he obtained post, 15-16; arrangement with Sir Wm. Cecil concerning, 16; value of post, *ib.*; its duties, 17; letter from, to Lord Burghley concerning fees, *ib.*; offers bribe to Lord B., 18; complaint against, by Lord Oxford, *ib.*; letter by, to Lord B. in his defence, 19-20; reluctant to become High Sheriff, 20; letter from, to Lord B. on subject, 20-1; Sheriff in 1571, 21; active magistrate, 29; instructions by, to apprehend certain persons, 30; letters to, by J. Frankeleyn about a robbery, 30-4; letter to, by Robson on same matter, 31; request that, should be one appointed to investigate the same and other misdeeds, 32; anonymous letter concerning this robbery, 32-3; T. Wendy's letter to, about servant accused of murder, 35-6; letter from, to J. Peckham on same subject, 36; J. Peckham's reply to, *ib.*; application by, for freedom of the City of London, 37; builds chapel to Chevening Church, and contract with builder for same, 38; attempt at law reform, 38-9; a friend of Lord Audley, 39; of Sir N. Bacon, 40; letter from Sir N.B. to, 41; will 'settled' by Sir Wm. Cordell, 42; letter to, from Sir W. C., 42-3; sends Sir W. C. 'two potts of sylver,' 43; letter to, from same thanking him, 44-5; letter to, from Sir H. Cobham, 45; difference between them, *ib.*; his notes concerning this difference, 45-6; death of wife, 46; 'blacks' for her funeral, 46-50; accounts delivered to, by servant, 50-1; grocer's bill, 51-2; more accounts of, 52-4; action brought by, in Ecclesiastical Courts, 55; letter to, concerning same, 55-6; letter to, accusing Brydger, 56; memorandum by, concerning accusation of Brydger, 57; arranges for marriages of children Mary and Samson, 62; his spelling and handwriting, 66; said to be 'proud and hasty' by reason of his riches, 67; correspondence with Lord Burghley concerning Samson's engagement to M. Darrell, 68-75; lends money to B. Googe, 77; negotiates for marriage of son Samson to M. Fynes, and his disputes about the settlements, *ib. et seq.*; his income, 87; letter by, to Lord Burghley about these disputes, 90; letter to same on same subject in handwriting of, 101-2; letters to, concerning same matter from F. Walsingham, 103; borrows money, 105; his negotiations for marriage of daughter Mary, 105 *et seq.*; letter by, to Lady Walsing-

ham, 106; letters to, from Sir T. Walsingham, 107-8; letter to, from Lady W., 108-9; his negotiations for marriage of daughter Rachael, 110; negotiates for marriage of daughter Elizabeth, 111-12; owned manor of Romford, 112; purchased manor of Sevenoak, 113; letters by, to Lord Hunsdon 'for his rehavyng of Sevenock,' 113-15; spoken to by the Queen, 114; negotiations by, to obtain Knole, 116-23; said, in error, to have obtained Knole from Lord Hunsdon, 115; lets Knole to his son Samson, 121; lived at Knole, 1570-90, but died at Chevening, *ib.*; compleins possession of Knole kept from him by Lord Buckhurst, 121-2; letter by, as to claims to deer in Knole, 125; letter to, by R. Puleston about deer-stealing at Knole, 126-7; anonymous letter to, on same subject, 128; his troubles about repairs to Knole, *ib.*; letter by, to Lord Burghley on this subject, 129-31; suffering from gout, 129; buys land of W. Cowdrey, 131; his disputes with same, *ib.*; letter to, from same, 132-4; reply by, to same, 134-5; 'sylke for a gowne' promised to wife of, 136; his character, 135-6; correspondence between, and Cranewell about Whitely Wood, 136-9; his glass works, 139; letter to, from R. Puleston about same, 140-1; letter to, offering wine, 141; his use of 'y' where we now use 'i,' *ib.*; letter to, from Mrs. Mason about her daughter's age, 141-2; letter to, from Bishop of Salisbury about presentation to a living, 142; letter to, from P. Harrison asking for financial assistance, 143-5; letter to, from E. Woodgate on same subject, 145-6; date of will and burial, 146; his will, 147-9; list of his manors and lands, 149-50; settlement by, on grandson's marriage, 243

Lennard, John (V), xviii; 3
— John (VI), 214; 217; 242
— John (VII), 241
— Margaret (I), 216; devise to, by Lady Dacre, 224
— Margaret (II) Lady Wildgoose, her monument and death, 243. 285

Lennard, Margarett (III), the Hon., 278; 297
— Margaret (IV), 304; marriage of, 305
— Maria, 4; 5
— Mary (I), 8; 9; 62; 106 *et seq.*; 110
— Mary (II), 32. *n.*; birth and marriage, 216
— Mary (III), 252
— Matilda? wife of George, xviii; 3
— Pembroke, Lady Brook, 243
— Philadelphia (I), 4
— Philadelphia (II), Lady Parker, 243; 253; 285
— Philadelphia (III), the Hon., 278; legacy to, from her father, 294
— Rachael, 8; 9; 110
— Richard (query who was he?), 217
— Richard: *see* Barrett, Richard (I); (II); (III)
— Richard (I), xviii; 3
— Richard (II), 214; 255
— Richard (III) Lord Dacre, 214; 217; disposes by will of 'Baylee,' 226; birth of, 243; age at father's death, 250; sells Hautbois, 253; Horsford reconveyed to him, *ib.*; rebuilt Chevening, 254; first wife, 254-5; settlement on her, 255; her death, *ib.*; his children by her, *ib.*; references to, in State Calendars, 256; his iron works, *ib.*; second marriage, *ib.* Settlement on second wife, 256-7; his children by her, 257; settles Horsford on Richard, 257-8; sudden death of, 259; buried at Herstmonceux, *ib.*; will and nuncupative codicil, 259-61; guardianship of sons F. and T., 261; acquisition of portrait of, 573
— Robert, 214; 251-2; 292; 317
— Sampson, xviii; 5; dedication of book by, to E. of Pembroke, 245
— Samson, life of his father by, 6-7; date of birth, 8 and 215; marriage of, arranged by his father, 62; overtures for marriage of, from his future wife's relations, *ib.*; his courtship of M. Darrell, 65; 67-77; his handwriting and mode of spelling, 67; his good looks, *ib.*; his father negotiates for marriage of, with M. Fynes, and controversies as to her fortune, 77-105; age when married, 77; 95 *n.* and 215 *n.*; money borrowed for, by father, 105; witness

to sisters' settlements, 109 and 112; devise to, by father, 148; bequests to sons of, by J. Lennard, 149. 187; 214; Camden's account of, 215; children, 216–17; member of Lincoln's Inn, 218; M.P., *ib.*; takes part in defence of the country, 218–19; active magistrate, 219–20; letter from, to M. Hicks, 220; inherits property by death of wife's brother, 221; intimate with Sir R. Cecil, 222; devise to, by A. Lady Dacre, 224–5; had to make many repairs to Herstmonceux, 225; makes park at Heathfield, 225–6; panegyric on, 226–7; hospitality of, 227–8; his extravagance, 228–9; sells properties, 229; liable for debts of eldest son, 230; his rent-rolls, 230–1; rents in kind, *ib.*; parts with Knole, 232; has no London house, *ib.*; his visit to London and expenses there, 232–4; claim to title of Dacre *jure uxoris*, 234–8; letter to, from E. of Essex, 236; at death of his wife obtains patent of precedence, 238; death of wife, *ib.*; his own death, *ib.*; transferred estates to eldest son during his lifetime, 239; tomb at Chevening, and inscription on, *ib.*; settlement by, on son's marriage, 243; portrait of, acquired, 593

Lennard, Samuel, xviii; 8; 9; 67; 105; 109; 147–8; letter from, 246
— Sir Stephen (I), of West Wickham, 285
— Sir Stephen (II), of West Wickham, 583 *n.*
— Timothea, 8; 9
— Thomas (I), xviii; 3; 4 and *n.*; 5; 68; 242
— Thomas (II), xviii; 3; 4 *n.*; 253 *n.*
— Thomas (III), xviii; 5
— Thomas (IV), xviii; 3
— Thomas (V), xviii; 3; 4
— Thomas (VI), 214; 216; admitted to Gray's Inn, 242; his will and death, *ib.*
— Thomas, the Hon. (VII), 214; 242; 255; 257–9, *passim*; 261; his death, 262; letter from, 262–3. 285; 287; 291; 292
— Thomas (VIII), 287; 288
— Thomas (IX) Lord Dacre, Earl of Sussex, destroyed documents, vi, 564. 214; 242; 252; paid rent for Chevening, 263, 307; birth of, 278; bequest of portraits to, 300; letter by, to Wm. III., about brother's property, 302. 304. account of, by Lord Dacre, 305; at Oxford, *ib.* 306. goes early to the Court, 307; his income, 307–8; his marriage, 309–10; dowry granted by King, but still unpaid, 311; children, 312; created E. of Sussex, *ib.*; made a Gentleman of the Bedchamber, 312–13; objects to wife's intimacy with Duchess of Mazarin, 314–15; takes her to Herstmonceux, *ib.*; his household accounts there, 316–17; his Countess goes to France and leaves child with him, 318–19; gives up rooms at Whitehall and tries to let Chevening, 319–20; repaired and stayed at Dacre Castle, 320; exceeding his income and borrowing, 321; some evidence as to his gambling, *ib.*; the King attempts reconciliation between, and his Countess, 321–2; letter from, about her, 324–5; reconciled to her, 325; fond of horse racing and gives Newmarket Challenge Whip, 326; his gambling and losses, *ib.*; his efforts to obtain payment from King of wife's dowry, *ib.*; becoming more embarrassed for money, *ib.*; considerable debt due to Greenwood, and how settled, 327–8; cause of final separation of, from wife, 328; a supporter of William of Orange, *ib.*; increasing debts, 330; sale of various estates, *ib.*; improved financial position by death of D. Lady Dacre, 331; misunderstanding with her, *ib.*; sale by him of manorial rights at Carlisle, *ib.*; petition to William III. for payment of wife's dowry, 332; letter about his extravagance by Duchess of Cleveland, *ib.*; sale of Herstmonceux, *ib.*; description of that Castle, 333–6; his litigations, 336–7; letter about borrowing money to D. Barrett, 337; acted as Earl Marshal, 338; death, *ib.*, 541; 550; debts, 555
Lennard, William (I), xviii; 3
— William (II), xviii; 4; 5; 49; 148
— William (III), xviii; 3; 4
— William (IV), law reporter, 5 *n.*
Lennard, William (V), Mayor of Dover, 5 *n.*

INDEX

Lennard, William VI), 214; 251-2; 292
— William (VII), 214; 252
Lennards of Bailey, 4; 225-6; 259; 285; 287-8
Leonard, Ebenezer, 1
— George, 1
— Jhon : *see* Lennard, John (VII)
Lenox, Duke of, 237
Leveson-Gowers, 364 *n.*
— Sir John, 364-5
— Sir Richard, 366; letter to, 386; bequest to, 390. 397
Lewkenor, R., letter from, 124
Leyburne, Elizabeth, Lady Dacre of the North, 269
— Sir Francis, 269
Lichfield, Geo. Henry, Earl of, 571
— Sir H. E. Lee, Earl of, 310
Lincoln, Lord, 210
Lincoln's Inn, 4; 6; 8; 218; 242; 364-5; 583
Linstead, 339
Liskeard, 218
Little, Elizabeth : *see* Litton
— Helen, 358. *n.* 6
— Thomas, 359
Littleton, Sir Adam, 548 *n.*
— Sir Thos., of North Ockendon, 548
Litton, Elizabeth, 358 ; 365
— Sir Robert, 358
Liverpool, D. Barrett at, 473 ; son of, born at, 474 ; he leaves, 477 ; his wife's journey from, 478-82
Llewellyn, Maude, 214 ; first marriage, 240; Second marriage, 241 ; her death, *ib.* ; query, referred to 260 *n.*
— Richard, 240
Loftus, Adam, Archbishop, 438
— Adam, Viscount of Ely, 409 ; promised to make certain settlements on his son Robert and refused to carry out same, 438-44; in prison in Dublin Castle, 444-5. 446-7; his death, *ib.*
— Alice, 410 *n.*
— Anne, 214 ; 393 ; 403 ; when born, 404 ; wrong date assigned to her marriage, 409 *n.* ; probable correct date, 409 ; her claim to Monesterevan, *ib.* ; her attainments, 410 ; said to have lived as one of the family of Earl of Strafford, *ib.* ; her guardians, *ib.*; her appearance, 411 ; reference to portrait of, *ib. n.*; her husband's frequent absences, 412 ; continually child-bearing, *ib.* ; on affectionate terms with her mother-in-law, 413 ; date of her death, *ib.*. 438 ; 446-9
Loftus, Arthur (3rd Viscount), letter to, 451-2
— Sir Edward (2nd Viscount), 439 ; 443 ; 446-7 ; fortified and held Middleham Castle, 448-9 ; letter to, 451
— Henry, his death, 404 ; 446
— Nicholas, 410 *n.*
— Sir Robert, 403 ; 409-10 ; 438 ; agreement made upon his marriage, and date of same, 438 *et seq.* ; of weak intellect, 442-3. 444 ; 447
Londenoys, Richard, 186
London, lands in City of, 83
Londonderry, 463
Longford, Lady, 458
Loughton Hall, Essex, 241
Lovelace, Lord, 532
— Serjeant, 119 ; 120 ; 123 ; letter to, 123-4; 125
Lower, Mr., *quoted*, 203-4
Luckyn, Sir Capel, 528 ; 542 *n.*
— Muriel, 528 *n.*
— Sir William (I), 528 *n.* ; 542 *n.*
— Sir William (II), 542
Lutton, 83; price sold for, 91
Lyttelton, Dean of Exeter, letter to, 587-8. 605
— Lord, *quoted*, 467

McCOLLIN, John, teaches Dacre Barrett's children at Clones, 531 ; letter from, *ib.*
Magdalen College, 305
Malden, borough of, 637
Manchester, Earl of, 380 *n.*
— Lord, 543
Mann, Sir H., 580 ; 598-9
Mantell, W., 152 ; 187 ; 198-200
Mapleton, 84 ; 104
Marillac, C. de, letter from, 200
Marks Hall, Romford, 491
Marmion, barony of, 184 *n.*
Marriages of children at early age, instances of, 58 ; 216 ; 243 ; 309 ; 360-1 ; 368
Marriages, system of arranging, formerly, 57 ; 64-5 ; 226
Married women, former position of, in law, 143
Marsham, Sir Francis, 542
Martock, manor of, 155 ; 157-8
Marvel, Andrew, *quoted*, 311

INDEX

Mary, Princess, afterwards Queen with Wm. III., 313
— *See* Queen
Mason, Mrs., letter by, to J. Lennard. Curious calculation as to her daughter's age, 142
Masque, a, played at Court, 313
Massarene, Viscount, 455; 461
Matilda, xviii; 3
Maud : *see* Queen
Maximilian, Emperor, 188
Maxwell, Ela, 175; 179
Maynard, Lord, 542
Mazarin, Duchess of, 312; 314-15; 318
Meath, Earl of, 278
— Countess of: *see* Lennard, Elizabeth (IV)
Mellefont, 410
Meredyth, Richard, Dean and Bishop, 444 *n*.
Merton College, Oxford, 267
Michaelmas goose, tradition as to, 210
Milbourne, Richard, Bishop of St. Davids, 246
Mildmay, Carew (I), his marriage, 490; 517; letter from, 519. death of, 528. 537; letter to, 538
— Carew (II), 528
— Christian, 340; 361 ; her second marriage, 364-5. 373
— Henry, 476; 485
— Sir Walter, 340; 361; 365
Miller, Sanderson, 591 *n.*; letters to, 641-52
Milligen, Henry, 214; 636
Mills, John, lets Chevening, 10; sells same, 11
Molineux, Lady, 557
Monceux, Drogo de, 163
— Ingelram de, 163
— John (I) de, 163
— Sir John (II) de, 163
— Sir John (III) de, 163
— Maud de, 152; 161-3
— Sir Waleran de, 163
— Walleran de Herst, *alias* de, 163
— William de, 163
Monesterevan, 409; 439; 444
Money, relative value of, compared with former times, 87, 159-60, 205, 360
Montague, A. Brown, Viscount, 53 *n*.
— Hon. George, letter from, referring to Lord Dacre, 580
— Lord, 286
— Lord, trial of, 195
— Hon. R., 322-4
Montgomery, Colonel, 549

Moore, Brent, 511 *n.*
— E., 221 ; letter from, 222; an executor of Lady Dacre's will, 224
— Sir Edward, 511 *n.*
— Elizabeth, 460 *n.* ; marries D. Barrett, 511; children by, *ib.*; marriage settlement, *ib.*; letter to, from Dacre, 512 ; letter from, to Dacre, 512-13 ; her death, 513-14
— Garett, letters from, 451-2
— Henry, an officer in army, and becomes insane, 563; gives portraits to Lord Dacre, 592-3
— Hon. Robert marries Lady Teynham, 560 ; spends step-daughter's fortune, *ib.* and *n.*; date of death, 561; letters about death of, 562 ; record of burial of, *ib.* ; his son, 563 ; sale by, to Lord Dacre, of portraits, 592
— Sir Robert, 217
— Thomas, 511
— William, 508-9
— Hon. William, 278 ; letters from, 493. *ib. n.*; 518
Moorewicke, 83
Morant, Rev. P., 605 ; dedicated his 'History of Essex' to Lord Dacre, *ib. n.*
Morgan, William, 397-8; 524
Morley, Herbert, 216
— William, 216 *n*.
Morville, Ada de, 175; 177
— Hugh de, 175, 177
Mosedail, 274
Moulton, Margaret de, 175; 178
— Thos. (I) de, 175-6
— Thos. (II) de, Baron of Gilsland, 175-7
— Thos. (III) de, Baron of Gilsland, 175; 177
— Thos. (IV) de, Baron of Gilsland, 175; 177
— Thos. (V) de, Baron of Gilsland, 175, 177-8
Mount Coote, 433 *n*.
Mountrath, Earl of: *see* Coote, Sir Chas.
Muilman, Richard, *quoted*, 361
Munster, Count, 598 *n*.
Murray, Henry, 277
Murray, portrait by, 592
Musgrave, Sir C., 339
— Family, their good bargain in buying Dacre Castle, 339 *n*.
— Family of, 274 *n*.

NASHE Hall, 84; 104; 231
Naworth Castle, 270-1

INDEX

Naylor, 'Counsellor,' purchaser of Herstmonceux, 330, 332-3
Nether Calcotts, 84; 104
Nevell, Mr., 96
Nevill, Edward (I), 111
— Edward (II), 9; 96 n. 111
— Margaret, 349 n.
— Mary, Lady Dacre, reference to funeral of, 50; Settlement on, 83; 86. 152; 193; Second and third marriages, 196. 205-6; 206-7; portrait of, acquired, 592
Newark, Viscount, 277
Newbiggin, 274-5
Newburgh, Lady: see Carey, Jane; Fenn, Katherine
— Lord: see Barrett, Sir Edward (III)
Newcomen, Katherine, 433 n.
— Lady Mary: see Chichester, Lady Mary
— Sir Robert, 433 n.
Newington, Kent, 344
Newmarket, 326-7; 367
Newport, 368
Newport Street, St. Martin's Lane, R. (I) Barrett's house in, 411
Newycke, 82
New Year's presents, former custom of giving, 44; 210
Nicholls, Richard, married Jane Barrett, 574-5; his death, 576
Nixon, Adam, of Monaghan, letters from, 580, 588, 590, 594-5
Nockholt, 10; 148
Noke, manor of, 348; 370
Nooington, 82
Norcott, 224
Norden, John, *quoted*, 543
Norfolk, Thomas, Duke of, 269-73
Norris, Sir Edward, 349
— Sir Henry, 152; 185; 349
— Sir Henry: see Norris, Lord
— Lord, 81-3; 86; 88-9; 91; 95; 152
— Margaret, 349-50
— Mary, Lady: see Fynes, Mary
— Stephen, of Norwich, 594
Norryce, Lord: see Norris
North, Dorothy, Lady Dacre, 214; marries R. Lord Dacre, 256; strained relations with step-son, F. Lord Dacre, 261, 286; where she resided, 263-6; her second marriage, 263-4; grandchildren lived with, 265; her death, *ib.*; her character, 266; had life interest in Chevening, 263-5; 307-8; revokes legacy of her portrait to E. of Sussex, 331; legacy to, 390; tradition Lord Newburgh was in love with, 395; letter offering to lend Belhus to, and to Mr. Chute, 399; offer accepted and house furnished by, 400; leaves this furniture by will, *ib.*; inventory of, 400-1; affection for R. (I) Barrett's wife, 413; takes care of grandchildren, 414; enjoys being at Belhus, *ib.*; there on long visit to son, 430; urges on lawsuit, 438, 449; her relations with Owen, 470; her grandchildren Anne and Dorothy take refuge with, at Chevening, 489; goes to see her son Richard about his will, 517; attempts to bring about family reconciliation, 518-19; writes about her pictures, &c., at Belhus, 521; portrait of, acquired, 573
North, Dudley, Lord, 256-8; 263; guardian to R. (I) Barrett, 397
— Sir Dudley, 257-8
— Francis, Lord Chief Justice of Common Pleas, Baron Guilford, 429-30
— Roger, 265; his account of Belhus and his cousins there, 435-7; letter from, 526
— & Grey, Lord, letter from, to Dacre, 477
Northampton, Earl of, 237
Northamptonshire, Lennards settle there, 3; 4
Northhales, 83
Northsted, 149; sold, 246
North Tuddenham, 207; 343
Norton, Elizabeth de, 340; 344-5
— Margaret de, 344
— Richard de, 340, 344-5
Nortons, Manor of, 345
Norwich, Earl of: see Goring, George (the younger)
Nottingham, Chas., 1st Earl of, 237; 366
— Lord, 286
Nova Scotia, Lord Newburgh created Baronet of, and receives grant of land in, 382

O'BRIAN: see Clare, Viscount
— Mary, 300
Odingsel, 344
Olde Court, 84; 104; 160; 259
Onslow, Thos., 216
Otford, Earl of: see Walpole, Horace

INDEX

Ormond, Duke of, 392; 427; 475
Orsett Hall, 625
Otelands, the Court at, 103
Otford, 148-9; Sale of, 229. 231
Owen, Richard, 402 *n.*; his career, 469-71,502-10; executor to Ri. (I) Barrett, 517, 519. action against, to upset will, 521
Oxenbridge, Sir J., 185 *n.* 190
— Thos., 185
Oxenford, Earl of, complaint against John (IV) Lennard, 18, 20
Oxford, Earl of, 277

PAGET, W., letter by, 197
Palin, Rev. Wm., *quoted*, 391
Palmer, Wm., of Grays, 521
Pannesworth, 150
Panthurst Park, 116; 121
Parker, George, 243
— Lady: *see* Lennard, Philadelphia (II)
— M., Archbishop, 14-15; interferes about marriage of Mary Darrell, 68 ; letter by, 75-6
— Sir Thomas, 243; 253; 258-9; 285; 290-1
Parravicinni, Sir Peter, 402
Partridges, live, to be turned out, 288
Patterdaile, 274
Pattrick, Rev. G., Vicar of Aveley, v; copied Lord Dacre's MS., *ib.*
Paulerspurie, 254; 267
Peckham, James, letter to, 36; letter from, 36-7
Pedigree, ancient, at Belhus, 234
Peerages, early custom as to titles of, 174
Pegge, Rev. Dr., 605
Pelham, Sir John, 93-4
— Nicholas, 198; 203
— Sir Thomas, 288
Pembroke, Earl of; friend of Henry Lennard, Lord Dacre, 243 *n.* 3, 245
Penal Laws and Test Act, 491-2
Pennington, Mr., 397 *n.*; 401; his death, 402
Penshurst, 227-8
Pepys, Mr., 262; letter from, 328
Peñam, Benjamin, 586
Perkins, J., xviii; 5
Perry, Edward, 390
— Hugh, 384
— Mary, 384
— Rebecca, 388 *n.* 3
Perry Court, Kent, 341
Peshall, Sir John, action by, to obtain Belhus estates, 567

Pharamus of Boulogne, 155
Pheasants, tame, 288
Pierpoint, Sibil, 181
Piers, John : *see* Salisbury, Bishop of
Pigott, R., 476; letter from, *ib.*, 484; 523
Pointz, John, 340; 346
— Matilda, 340; 346
Pomme, Dr., of Paris, 602-3
Pond, Arthur, 592
Poor, bequests to the, 148, 300, 360, 390
Porkrich, M., letter from, 426
Porte Royal, Abbey of, 324-5
Portland, Earl of, 380 *n.*
Portraits at Belhus: *see* Belhus
Portsmouth, Duchess of, 300; 326
Potatoes, early mention of, 52
Pratt, Anne Maria, 214; marriage, 594; good looks, *ib.*; birth of her only child, *ib.*; its death, 596. 598-603; her adoption of Thomas, 610-11, 613-22 *passim*; executrix of Lord Dacre's will, 621; her kindness to both Thomas and Barbara, 623-6; letter from, to Barbara, 627-30; her death, 632; character, 633-5
— Caroline, 598
— Charles, Lord Camden, 611; in the stocks, 611-12; another anecdote of, 612; his supporters, *ib.*; an executor and legatee under Lord Dacre's will, 621
— Sir John (I), 594
— Hon. John (II), 611; executor of Lord Dacre's will, 621
— John (III), executor of Lord Dacre's will, 621
Prices of various things in former times, 38, 47-54, 230-1, 316-18, 325, *see also* Rental values and Wages
Priest's hole : *see* Hiding-place
Private Act : *see* Acts, private, of Parliament
Prude, Mary, 214; 252
Puleston, R., letter by, to J. (IV) Lennard, about deer-stealing, 126-7; letter by, to same, about glass-making, 139-41. 225; *ib. n.*
Puttenheth, 188

QUADRIPARTITE Indenture, the, settlement of lands by, 82-4; 87
Quarrendon, Viscount, 555: *see also* Lichfield, G. H, Earl of
Queen Mary, grant by, to J. (IV) Lennard, 11

Queen Maud, great-aunt to wife of Ingelram (I) Fynes, 155

RADCLIFFE, Dorothy, 272
— John, of Derwentwater, 272
Radnor, Earl of, 396 *n.*
Raffeley, 83
Raleigh, Sir Walter, 244; a trustee for Throgmorton family, 254
Ramsden, 343
— Bell House, 344
— Crays, 344
Ranby, John, 456; 575; marriage and origin, 576; Queen's remark to, about wife, 577; separation from his wife, *ib.*; Successful career, *ib.*; death, 578; allowance to, by Court for bringing up Lord Dacre, 583-4
— Mrs.: *see* Barrett, Jane
Ranelagh, Earl of, 455; 461
— Selina, Lady, 561
— Lord, 561 *n.*
Ratcliffe, Dr., 545-6
Ratton, Sussex, 243
Rayleigh, 343
Rebow, Serjeant, 475
— Isaac Martin, 630
— Sarah Emma, 630
Records, public, careless custody of, 19
Reddyn: *see* Roidon
Rental values in former days, 84-5, 205, 230-1, 355-6, 369
Revett, Elizabeth, wife of T. Chute, 533 *n.*
Ricot, Berks, 349
Rider, Sir Thomas, 226; letter from, 227, 261 *n.*
Rivers, Earl of, 543
— Sir J., gives 'peece of sylke' to J. (IV) Lennard's wife, 136
Roads, bad state of, 473, 477, 482, 609
Robarts, Susanna, treated D. Barrett's children badly, 503; Seacome offers marriage, 506; evidence by, as to R. (I) Barrett's capacity to make a will, 522
Robson, E., letter from, to J. (IV) Lennard, 31. 32; 34
Rocheford, Lord, trial of, 194
Rochester, Duke of, *quoted*, 312; letter to, 323; lines by, 326
Roe, Sir Thomas, letter from, 376
Roidon, or Roydon, 198-200
Rolf, T., obtained Knole, 116-17; letter from, to J. (IV) Lennard, 117-18
Romford, 112; 148

Romford, manor of, purchased by J. (IV) Lennard, 112
Rooth, Admiral Sir Richard, 517 *n.*
Roper, Hon. Anne, legacy to, 339; her marriage, 559; her children, 560; her fortune dissipated by step-father, *ib.*
— Hon. Charles, 559
— Gertrude, 559
— Henry, Major, 593
— Henry, Rector of Clones, 559
— Hon. Richard Henry, Rector of Clones, 559; once in army, 651
— Trevor, 593
— Trevor Charles, 559
Round, J. H., *quoted*, 2; 154 *nn.* 5, 7
Royal Society, The, 535; 545
Rushe, Anne, 404; 409
— Eleanor, date of death, 403. 408; where buried, 413. 438; Scandal concerning, 441. 443-4
— Sir Francis, 403; descent and marriage, 404; obtains lease of Clones from Jas. I., 405; conditions of same, 406; obtains fee-simple of Clones, *ib.* 409; where buried, 413. 438; 439-40; 444
— Mary, 404; 408; 433 *n.*
— Thomas, 404; 440
Rushes for covering floors, 25
Russell, C. B., 548 *n.*
— Lord William, 637
— Sir William, of Stubbers, North Ockendon, 548
Rye, Sussex, 218
Rye, Mr. Walter, v; vii
Ryper, robbery of a, 30-3

SACKVILLE, Anne Lady Dacre, governed her husband, 80; had disputes with Margaret, her sister-in-law, and with J. (IV) Lennard, 80-102; her answer to Margaret's 'Greyfes,' 91, *et seq.*; she and husband very young when married, 92; was very kind to Margaret and tried to marry her to Sir J. Pelham, 93; gave Margaret money for her trousseau, 95; date of marriage, 95 *n.*; says Margaret and J. Lennard attempted to sow dissension between her and brother, 96; lady of honour to Queen, 208; gifts from and to Queen, 210; executrix to husband's will, 211; death, 212; her will, 221-5. hospital founded by, 223

678 INDEX

Sackville, Sir Richard, 78-9; 207
— Street, 626
St. Albans, Duchess of, 300
St. Andrews, University of, 616-7
St. Aubyn, Dorothy, 214; 624; marriage, 625; death, 636
— Sir John, 624; 636
St. Audoens Church, Dublin, a family burying place, 413
St. David's, Bishop of, 249
St. Faith's, 246
St. Germans, 218
St. John Hope, *quoted*, 360 n.
St. Maws, 218
St. Michael's, Mustowe, 181
— At Plea, 181
St. Michans, 458
St. Sepulchre's Church, 199; 200
St. Stephen's, Westminster: *see* Records
St. Thomas Wateringe, a place of execution, 198
Salaries: *see* Wages
Salehurst, 349
Salisbury, Bishop of, letter by, 143
Saltonstall, Gylbert, 529 n.
— Philip (I), 529 n.
— Philip (II), 529; *ib. n.*; 547
— Philippa, her marriage to J. Goodere, 529; Richard (III) Barrett attracted by, 552-3
— Sir Richard (I), 547
— Richard (II), 547
— Richard (III), 529; his illness and death, 545-6
— Sarah, marries D. Barrett, 528; date of birth, *ib. n.*; parentage, *ib.*; reported character, *ib. n.*; first husband, 529; marriage settlement on, *ib.*; children by first husband, *ib.*; by D. Barrett, 530; bequest to, by Same, 572; date of death, 574. 575
Sandwich, 10
Sandwich, Earl of, 289
Savile, H., letter from, about Countess of Sussex, 323
Say, Geoffrey, Lord, 152; 162
— Joan, 152; 162
Say and Sele, Lord, James Fynes ancestor of, 165
Scorton, 84; 104; Sale of, 229. 231
Scribblestown: *see* Dunsink
Scrivener, John, 110
Seacome, J., 484-5; 501-7, *passim*; 520-3, *passim*
Sedbergh, 83; 91
Serfdom, transfer of serfs, 156-7; 157 n.
Sergeant, Walter (I), 345; 347

Sergeant, Walter (II), 347
Settled property, ingenious method of alienating, 99
Sevenoaks, 113; 148-9; T. Lord Dacre hired house there, 601
Seymour, Jane, Queen, funeral of, 196
Sheddon, Bartlett Bridger, 638
— Mary, 638; her death, *ib.*
Shepherd, the Rev., 613
Sheppey, Countess of: *see* Bayning, Elizabeth
Sherley, or Shirley, Sir T., letter by, 222
Shoreham, 148-9; 231
Shrubland, 358
Sidney, Robt. E., of Leicester, 228
Silvester, manor of, 267
Sissenhurst, Kent, 242
Skelton, Lady Barbara: *see* Lennard
— Col. Bevill, 329 n.
— Lt.-Gen. Charles, 214; 312; 329; 338; 556-7; portrait of, acquired, 594
— Sir John, 329 n.
Skipwith, Susan, 322 n.
— Sir Thomas, 322 n.
Skreens, Essex, 380 n.
Slaney, Lady, mother-in-law to Samuel Lennard, 9
Slaugham, 9
Sloane, Jas., letter from, 541
— Dr. Sir Hans, 545-6; 557; 565; 577
— William (I), 564-5
— William (II), marries Elizabeth (V) Barrett, 63, 564-5
Smith Barry, John, 569
— Dorothy, 569
— Erasmus (I), 568
— Erasmus (II), 568
— Hugh, 456; 459; courts Dorothy (II) Barrett, 567-8; letters from, 568; estates and death, 569; children, *ib.*; tomb of, *ib.*; makes Lord Dacre his executor, 652
— John, letters from, 511, 513-14
— Lucy, 569
— Samuel, 568
Smithfield, Dublin, 458; 467
Smyth, Thomas, 528 n.
Smythwicke, 82
Snowball, Miss, xviii; 3
Somerset, Anne, 340; marriage and death, 358
— the Hon. Sir George, 340; 358
Soulby, 274
Southall, 224
Southampton, letter to Mayor of, 218.
Southcote, Mr. Justice, 21, *ib. n.*; 22

INDEX 679

South Cove, 83
South Sea Company Stock, 339
South Weald, Essex, 568-9
Spelling, former system of, 66-7, 141-2; erratic, 463-4
Sporting rights, early reservation of, by lease, 84; lease of fishing, *ib.*
Sports, mention of:
— Coursing, 288
— Cricket, 317
— Fishing, 84
— Hawking, 84; 317? 514
— Hunting, 84; 252-3; 288; 317; 532-3; 534; 540; 618
— Shooting, 288; 317?
— Yachting, 289-90
Sprowston, 359
Staffol, 274-5
Stamford, Henry Grey, 1st Earl of, 286; 387
Stanford, 354; otherwise Stanford Dinely, 356
Stanford, Mr. Justice, 129
Stanhope, Charles, 3rd Earl, 254
— Earl: *see* Mr. Secretary
— Mr. Secretary, 254; 548; comes to see Chevening, 555-6; conveyance to, of Chevening, 558
Stanway, 343
Stapleton, Lady: *see* Lennard, Barbara (I)
— Sir Philip, 244
Stapleton, Cumberland, 274
Staunton Gumton: *see* Staunton Quinton
Staunton Quinton, 83; price sold for, 91. 100; 142; 148; 150; 231
Staveley, 84; 104
Stirling, Matilda G., 214; 636
— Sir Walter, 636
Stock, Essex, 304
Strafford, Earl of, Lord Newburgh's contest with, 383. 385-6; 409 *n.*; his conduct respecting family lawsuit one of the grounds for his impeachment, 438. 440; Scandal about, and E. Lady Loftus, 441; letter from, concerning her death, 442. 443-5; 447; 449; 523
Strange, Viscount, 569
Stratford Langthorn, Abbey of, 345
Streete, 82
Strickland, Miss, *quoted*, 329; 459
Strype, J., *quoted*, 67, 68, 70, 87
Suffolk, Thomas, Earl of, 270
— Earl of, 237
— Earl of, 546; letter from, 548-9
— Lord, 279
Sunderland, Lord, 325 *n.*

Sundridge, 131; 148-9; 242
Sussex, Earl of: *see* Lennard, Thomas (IX)
— Countess of: *see* FitzRoy, Lady Anne
— S. Lennard, M.P. for county of, 218
Sutton Court, Chiswick, 257; 263-5; 413
Sutton, Essex, 350; 353
Swann, Mr., Irish agent, 426
Swans, covenants as to, 10
Sydney, Sir Philip, friend of Henry Lennard, Lord Dacre, 245

TALBOT, J., 5
Taylor, Lady K., letters from, 558, 579
Teinham: *see* Teynham
Temple, Anne (I), Lady: *see* Throckmorton
— Anne (II), 285 *n.*
— Peter, Sir, 285 *n.*
Temple Church, Chapel of: *see* Records
Tenham: *see* Teynham
Teynham, Henry, 8th Lord, 329; executor to Lady Sussex, 339; married Lady A. Barrett, *ib.*, 559; their children, *ib.*; death, 560; became a Protestant, 570
— Henry, 11th Lord, two daughters married F. H. Tyler, 560 *n.*
— John, 1st Lord, Custos Brevium, 17 *n.*
— Lady, death of, recorded, 557: *see also* Lennard, Anne, Lady
Thackeray, Dr., Head Master at Harrow, 613
Thetford, 269
Thirkylby, 83; 91
Thomastown, 511
Thorisbye, or Thursbye: *see* Thursby
Thornton, the Rev., 567
Three Nuns, Whitechapel, 417 *n.*
Throckmorton, Anne, 285 *n.*
— Arthur, Sir, 254; 267
— Elizabeth, 214; 254; settlement on, 254-5; good looks, 255; death, *ib.*
— Sir Nicholas, 254
Thume, or Thirne, or Thyme, 84; 104; 231
Thursby, F., 86; 98; 152; his notes, 186-7. 207
Tingrie: *see* de Tingrie
Titles: *see* Peerages
Titsey, 9
Todd, John, Irish agent, letters from, 607-10

680   INDEX

Tombs or monuments to members of family at :
  Aveley, 344, 359, 362, 574, 620 *n.*, 636
  Bexley, Kent, 349
  Birling, Kent, 9 *n.*
  Boughton, Kent, 227
  Chelsea, 211-12
  Chevening, 4, 38, 239
  Cuxton, Kent, 361
  Fulmer, Bucks, 9
  Heathfield, 3
  Herstmonceux, 164, 192
  Linstead, Kent, 339
  Plymouth, 329 *n.*
  Romford, 528
  South Weald, Essex, 599
  Sprowston, 359
  Willingdon, Sussex, 243
  Wolvercote, Oxon, 295
Tothill Fields, Lady Dacre builds hospital in, 223
Trevor, family of, 216 *n.*
— John, 216 *n.*
Tudor, H.R.H. the Lady Mary, 188
Tully, J., 305
Twychin, 82
Tyler, Admiral Sir Charles, 560
— Sir Edmund, 181
— Fanny, 560
— Francis Henry, 560 ; married his deceased wife's sister, 560 *n.*, 624
— George, 560 ; 612 ; letters to, 619-21
— Mary, 612 *n.*
— Molly, 560
— Capt. Peter, his marriage, 559-60

UFFORD, Joan, 181
— Sir Robt. de, 181
Usher, M., 214 : *see* Haddock, Mary

VALLADOLID, 366
Vallibus, de : *see* Vaux
— Robert de, 156
Value, comparative, of money now and in Tudor times, 360, *ib. n.*
Van Bobbart, tutor to Dacre and Richard (II) Barrett, letter from, 414-15 ; his accounts while abroad with them, 417-25
Vaux, Hubert (I) de, 174-5
— Hubert (II) de, 175-6 ; 176 *n.* 2
— Maud de, 175-6
— Ranulph de, 175-6
— Robert (I) de, 175, 174-6 ; founder of Lanercost, 176

Vaux, Robert (II) de, 175-6
Venables, Mr., *quoted*, 162
Vendome, Philip de, portrait of, acquired, 593
Venice, 366-7
Venison, price of, in time of George II., 584
Vernon, Sir George, 380 *n.*
Verulam, Earl of, 528 *n.* ; 542 *n.*
Villiers, Barbara : *see* Cleveland, Duchess of
— (or Villars), Colonel, 322
— Francis, Lord, 372 ; legacy left to, by Lord Newburgh, 397, 402
— Vyne, the, 257 ; 264-5 ; 279
— Vyner, Sir Robert, 319 *n.*
— William : *see* Grandison, Viscount

WAAD, Sir William, 220 ; *ib. n.* 3
Wade, Mr.: *see* Waad, Sir William
Wages and salaries, instances of amounts paid for, at various periods, 16, 38, 50, 53-4, 207 *n.*, 316, 510
Wakeman, W. F.: *quoted*, 407-8
Waldegrave, C., 13
Walden, Lord, 543
Walgrave, Sir E., 13
— Frauncyse, Dame, 13
Walker, R., letter from, 124
Waller, Anne, Lady, 286
— Edward, *quoted*, 599
— Thomas, 216
— Sir William, 216 *n.* 279 ; 286
Walpole, Horace, description by, of Herstmonceux, 335-6. 580; letter from, 581 ; said to have advised Lord Dacre about alterations at Belhus, 587 *n.* ; letters from, 588, 602, 606 ; 652
Walsh, Mr. Justice: *see* Welche
Walsingham, Dorothy (I) Lady, 106 ; 108-10
— Dorothy (II), 110.
— Elizabeth, 110
— Sir Francis, two letters from, to J. (IV) Lennard, 102-3
— Guildford, 9 ; 62 ; 106-10
— Mr., lends goods for the Assizes, 27
— Sir Thomas, 106-9
Walter, David, marriage and death, 295. 301 *n.* ; portrait of, acquired, 593
— John, Sir, 295
Wandsworth, manor of, 188
Warren, Earl of, 163
— Edith, daughter of Earl of, 163
Warwick, Countess of, 542 *n.*

INDEX

Watkinson, Mr., brings portraits to Lord Dacre, 593. 595
Weever, John, *quoted*, 346, 364
Welche, Mr., 120; 122 *n*.
Wendover, manor of, 154-8
Wendy, T., letter from, to J. (IV) Lennard, 35
Wennington, 360
Wentworth, Sir George, 409; 441; 447-8; 523
— *See* Strafford, Earl of
West Looe, 244
West Wickham, Lennards of, 8
— *See* Lennard Samuel, and Stephen
Western, Lord, 637
Westgarth, William, 485-6; letter from, describing perils of journey to Clones, 487-8; letter from, describing terrible state of Clones, 496-9. 501-2; 530
Westmeaston, 82
Westmorland, Philippa, daughter of R. Earl of, 175; 180
— Lord, 286
Weston, Catherine, xviii; 4
— Sir Richard, created Baron Weston, 380 *n.*
— Thomas, xviii; 4
Weston Colville, 148; 150; 261
Wharton, J., 638
— Lord, 279; 281
— Margaret, 638; her death, *ib.*
Whitchurch, 368
White, Roland, letter from, 227
Whitely Wood (probably same as Whitney Wood), 136-9
Whitney Wood, 121
Wickham, 150
Wickhurst, manor of, 149; 229
Widdington, Sir T., 274
Wilder, Mr., 560
Wildgoose, Sir A., 243
— Lady: *see* Lennard, Margaret (II)
Wilford, Sir J., 349
William (III.), King, petition to, 332
Williams, Sir J., 322
Willingdon Church, monument in, 243
Willingham, 150
Willoughby, Lord, 279
Willoughbye, C., 32 *n.*; 40
Willowbie, T., 32
Wills, ancient form of, 146, 388-9
Wilson, the Rev. Canon, 594
— Sir T., 381
Winchelsea and Nottingham, Earl of, 286
Winchester, Marquis of, petition against sale of house at Chelsea to Lord Dacre, 211
— Dowager Marchioness of, 211
Windebank, Sir F., 385
Windsor Castle, 312
Wine merchant's letter dated 1588, 141
Wintringham, 83; lease of fishing in 1518 at, 84; farm rents at, 85
Wollefynes, 82; 91
Wolrich, Lady, 246
Wolverton, 354; 356; 367
Wolves at Clones, 533-4
Wood, Emma, 638
— The Rev. Sir J. Page, 638
Woodgate, E., letters from, 77, 145-6
Woodhall, 83; 91
Wootton, Esq., of N. Tuddenham, 152; 207
Worcester, C., Earl of, 358
— E., Earl of, 237
Wotton, Sir E., 254; letter from, 255
— Sir H., letter by, 367
Wray, Queen's Serjeant, 21
Wrenningham, 343
Wrentham Cove, 83
Wriothesley, Sir T., 197
Writing, ancient: *see* Spelling
Wroth, J., 241; 260 *n*. 2
Wyatt, the architect, 334
Wymbledon, 188
Wymples, 83

YACHTING, early instances of: *see* F. Lord Dacre
York, Sir P., counsel for D. Barrett, 571
Young, Arthur, *quoted*, 543

CPSIA information can be obtained
at www.ICGtesting.com
Printed in the USA
BVHW04s1321060918
526699BV00012B/84/P